Public Value

Over the last ten years, the concept of value has emerged in both business and public life as part of an important process of measuring, benchmarking, and assuring the resources we invest and the outcomes we generate from our activities. In the context of public life, value is an important measure on the contribution to business and social good of activities for which strict financial measures are either inappropriate or fundamentally unsound.

A systematic, interdisciplinary examination of public value is necessary to establish an essential definition and up-to-date picture of the field. In reflecting on the 'public value project', this book points to how the field has broadened well beyond its original focus on public sector management; has deepened in terms of the development of the analytical concepts and frameworks that linked the concepts together; and has been applied increasingly in concrete circumstances by academics, consultants, and practitioners.

This book covers three main topics; deepening and enriching the theory of creating public value, broadening the theory and practice of creating public value to voluntary and commercial organisations and collaborative networks, and the challenge and opportunity that the concept of public value poses to social science and universities. Collectively, it offers new ways of looking at public and social assets against a backdrop of increasing financial pressure; new insights into changing social attitudes and perceptions of value; and new models for increasingly complicated collaborative forms of service delivery, involving public, private, and not-for-profit players.

Dr. Adam Lindgreen is Professor of Marketing at Copenhagen Business School where he heads the Department of Marketing. He also is Extraordinary Professor with the University of Pretoria's Gordon Institute of Business Science.

Dr. Nicole Koenig-Lewis is Associate Professor of Marketing at Cardiff Business School, Cardiff University, UK.

Dr. Martin Kitchener FCIPD FLSW FAcSS is Professor of Management at Cardiff Business School and is during 2018–19, Visiting Fellow at Said Business School and Harris Manchester College, Oxford University.

Dr. John D. Brewer, HDSSc, MRIA, FRSE, FAcSS, FRSA, is Professor of Post Conflict Studies in the Senator George J Mitchell Institute at Queen's University.

Dr. Mark H. Moore is Professor of Public Policy and Strategic Management at Harvard's Kennedy School of Government.

Dr. Timo Meynhardt is Professor of Business Psychology and Leadership at HHL Leipzig Graduate School of Management, Germany, and managing director of the Center for Leadership and Values in Society at the University of St. Gallen, Switzerland.

The 'public value project', as the authors called it, spoke to practitioners in the public and voluntary sectors long before it started to generate sustained scholarly attention. In what must be another gratifying move for its key pioneer, Harvard professor Mark Moore, this volume demonstrates amply that nearly three decades on, public value scholarship is thriving. It combines multidisciplinary theoretical contributions with 'hands-on' empirical studies, knowledge-expanding scholarship with improvement-seeking action research and covers local to international domains of application. As a cherry on the cake, it offers apt self-reflection on the public value of the academic enterprise itself. This is a must-read collection for anyone interested in how the common good can be conceptualised, assessed and pursued in practice.

Professor Paul 't Hart, Utrecht School of Governance &
Netherlands School of Public Administration

I have found the notion of Public Value has been one of the most helpful organizing principles when approaching public policy decisions. It provides a sophisticated, yet pragmatic framework for making high quality enduring decisions. There is a tendency in government decision making to start with the solution without adequately exploring the problem. This framework provides a systematic way in which the problem can be interrogated, support for it can be explored, and the capacity to implement any prospective solutions can be analysed. In my view the Public Value framework is an essential guide for public policy makers. This book explores in depth various issues around public value through the eyes of a range of leading authors on the topic.

Jay Weatherill, Former Premier of South Australia

The most important development in the study of public management and administration in the last twenty-five years has been the introduction of the concept of public value. This volume explains, reviews and refines the concept and extends its application into many new areas.

Professor Allan Fels AO, Former Dean, Australia and
New Zealand School of Government

Adam Lindgreen and his fellow editors have brought together a timely collection of papers on the idea of public value in commercial, voluntary, and other organisations. The neo-liberal framework that has dominated social and economic thought for so long stresses individual benefit and advantage above all. The contributors to this collection take up older debates on social responsibility and collective welfare together with renewed debates on social value and communitarian concerns to sow the importance of reinstating ideas of public value and collective welfare in economic and social activities of all kinds. Of particular value is an emphasis on the public value of social science and the universities, moving us away for the overly narrow 'relevance' and 'impact' concerns that have dominated us for so long. These are crucial matters for all of us today and the book will help to establish a new agenda for both social science and public policy.

Professor John Scott CBE

This international volume on the importance of business and other institutions in delivering public value is so very timely. Organizations, society and political leaders are now concerned about what impact our businesses and public institutions are making for the common good. As an academic in a global business school, one of the important questions we ask of our research is whether it will produce impact in policy or practice for the public good. The chapters in this extremely significant volume are of a very high order and answer most of the philosophical and other questions we all have in this arena – a must-buy for anyone interested in public values from our institutions.

Professor Sir Cary Cooper, CBE, 50th Anniversary Professor of Organizational
Psychology & Health, ALLIANCE Manchester Business
School, University of Manchester, UK

Public value for stakeholders is the natural partner to long-term value for shareholders, united through a corporation's purpose. Arguably, there can be no long-term value without public value since a corporation's social function is the basis for earnings and hence the right/responsibility to perform. By merging theory and practice, *Public Value: Deepening, Enriching, and Broadening the Theory and Practice* demonstrates the need to further develop and implement public value as a key strategic element in the private sector, which has never been more important than now – in a time of radical transformation.

Julie Linn Teigland, Regional Managing Partner, Ernst & Young

Public Value: Deepening, Enriching, and Broadening the Theory and Practice brings together some of the world's foremost researchers and practitioners in the field of public value. With the public value project still embryonic, this anthology takes stock of the public value project and considers its value and future direction. The anthology's impressive collection of twenty-four chapters provide thoughtful discussions on why the public value project is so important. I heartily recommend this anthology as a timely, comprehensive, and insightful go-to public value anthology for both researchers and practitioners. Congratulations!

Per Holten-Andersen, Rector of Copenhagen Business School

After decades of neoliberal efforts around the globe to *privatize* and diminish the idea of what is and ought to be public, there is now a strong cross-national effort to *publicize* what is and ought to be public. What a welcome change that is for all of us who care about democracy, equity, justice, education, accountability, caring for our fellow humans, and other important *public* values! This wonderful new book shows just how important this burgeoning public value conversation is to the quality and resilience of our relationships to one another, our communities, our societies, and the world.

John M. Bryson, McKnight Presidential Professor of Planning and
Public Affairs, Hubert H. Humphrey School of Public Affairs,
University of Minnesota, USA

Public Value

Deepening, Enriching, and Broadening
the Theory and Practice

Edited by Adam Lindgreen,
Nicole Koenig-Lewis, Martin Kitchener,
John D. Brewer, Mark H. Moore, and
Timo Meynhardt

Routledge
Taylor & Francis Group

LONDON AND NEW YORK

First published 2019
by Routledge
2 Park Square, Milton Park, Abingdon, Oxon OX14 4RN

and by Routledge
52 Vanderbilt Avenue, New York, NY 10017

Routledge is an imprint of the Taylor & Francis Group, an informa business

British Library Cataloguing-in-Publication Data
A catalogue record for this book is available from the British Library

Library of Congress Cataloging-in-Publication Data
A catalog record has been requested for this book

ISBN: 978-1-138-05966-5 (hbk)
ISBN: 978-1-315-16343-7 (ebk)

Typeset in Sabon
by Servis Filmsetting Ltd, Stockport, Cheshire

Contents

List of figures

List of tables

About the editors

Adam Lindgreen, after studies in chemistry (Copenhagen University), engineering (the Engineering Academy of Denmark), and physics (Copenhagen University), completed an MSc in food science and technology at the Technical University of Denmark. He also finished an MBA at the University of Leicester. He received his Ph.D. in marketing from Cranfield University. His first appointments were with the Catholique University of Louvain (2000–2001) and Eindhoven University of Technology (2002–2007). Subsequently, he served as Professor of Marketing at Hull University's Business School (2007–2010); University of Birmingham's Business School (2010), where he also was the research director in the Department of Marketing; and University of Cardiff's Business School (2011–2016). Under his leadership, the Department of Marketing and Strategy at Cardiff Business School ranked first among all marketing departments in Australia, Canada, New Zealand, the United Kingdom, and the United States, based upon the hg indices of senior faculty. Since 2016, he has been Professor of Marketing at Copenhagen Business School, where he also heads the Department of Marketing. Since 2018, he also is Extraordinary Professor with University of Pretoria's Gordon Institute of Business Science and a Visiting Professor with Northumbria University's Newcastle Business School.

Adam Lindgreen has been a visiting professor with various institutions, including Georgia State University, Groupe HEC, and Melbourne University. His publications have appeared in *Business Horizons, California Management Review, Entrepreneurship and Regional Development, Industrial Marketing Management, International Journal of Management Reviews, Journal of Advertising, Journal of Business Ethics, European Journal of Marketing, Journal of Business and Industrial Marketing, Journal of Marketing Management, Journal of the Academy of Marketing Science, Journal of Product Innovation Management, Journal of World Business, Psychology & Marketing,* and *Supply Chain Management: An International Journal,* among others.

Adam Lindgreen's books include *A Stakeholder Approach to Corporate Social Responsibility* (with Kotler, Vanhamme, and Maon), *Managing Market Relationships, Memorable Customer Experiences* (with Vanhamme and Beverland), *Not All Claps and Cheers* (with Maon, Vanhamme, Angell, and Memery), and *Sustainable Value Chain Management* (with Maon, Vanhamme, and Sen).

The recipient of the "Outstanding Article 2005" award from *Industrial Marketing Management* and the runner-up for the same award in 2016, he serves on the board of several scientific journals; he is Co-Editor-in-Chief of *Industrial Marketing Management* and previously was the joint editor of the *Journal of Business Ethics'* section on corporate responsibility. His research interests include business and industrial marketing management, corporate social responsibility, and sustainability. He has been awarded the Dean's Award for Excellence in Executive Teaching. Furthermore, he has served as an examiner (for dissertations, modules, and programs) at a wide variety of institutions.

Adam Lindgreen is a member of the International Scientific Advisory Panel of the New Zealand Food Safety Science and Research Centre (a partnership between government, industry organizations, and research institutions), as well as of the Chartered Association of Business Schools' Academic Journal Guide (AJG) Scientific Committee in the field of marketing.

Beyond these academic contributions to marketing, Adam Lindgreen has discovered and excavated settlements from the Stone Age in Denmark, including the only major kitchen midden – Sparregård – in the south-east of Denmark; because of its importance, the kitchen midden was later excavated by the National Museum and then protected as a historical monument for future generations. He is also an avid genealogist, having traced his family back to 1390 and published widely in scientific journals (*Personalhistorisk Tidsskrift*, *The Genealogist*, and *Slægt & Data*) related to methodological issues in genealogy, accounts of population development, and particular family lineages.

Nicole Koenig-Lewis is associate professor of Marketing at University of Cardiff's Business School. She is a senior fellow of the Higher Education Academy and a certified member of the Market Research Society. She received her Ph.D. in Business Management from Swansea University in 2004. Prior to Cardiff University, she was an associate professor at Swansea University's School of Management and an assistant lecturer at Technische Universität Dresden, Germany, a Visiting Scholar with ESC Rennes, France and gained experience working as a market researcher. Bridging the gap between academia and business communities, she works closely with various external business partners. She is a founding member of the interdisciplinary Cardiff University Festival Research Group, and she has organized many public value workshops through University of Cardiff's Business School, while obtaining funding to foster international academic collaborations to investigate public value. Her key research themes centre on visitor/consumer experiences and sustainability to understand changing consumer behaviour from multiple interdisciplinary angles aiming to inspire truly sustainable approaches to business. Her current projects are highly interdisciplinary, and tackle the theoretical debate about drivers and barriers to sustainable consumer behaviours in contexts such as sustainable consumption, environmentally-friendly packaging, the sharing economy, and festivals as agents of change. Her research has appeared in *Annals of Tourism Research*, *European Sport Management Quarterly*, *Higher Education Quarterly*, *International Journal of Tourism Research*, *Journal of Business Research*, *Journal of Environmental Psychology*, *Journal of Marketing Management*, *Journal of Services Marketing*, *Tourism Management*, and *Service Industries Journal*, among others.

Martin Kitchener has served as Dean and Head of University of Cardiff's Business School since October 2012. His leadership is defined by his design and implementation of a unique public value strategy, which directs the School to "promote economic and social improvement through interdisciplinary scholarship that addresses grand challenges, while operating a progressive approach to our own governance." In promoting social improvement within its public value strategy, he has introduced significant changes across the School's core activities of research, teaching, and engagement. Cardiff's alternative to the standard business school curriculum encourages students to develop moral sentiment toward the promotion of social and economic improvement, while also developing the skills they need to become responsible leaders, with the confidence and critical capacity to work differently and think holistically.

As a distinctive element of Martin Kitchener's public value strategy, his pursuit of strong and progressive governance increasingly is being embedded into the strategic and operational management of the School. Reflecting his strategic commitment to equality and diversity, the School is one of the first two UK business schools to be recognized by *Athena SWAN* for supporting women's careers; it is the first to operate a shadow management board; it introduced a novel recognition scheme for administrative colleagues; and it has incorporated public value criteria (interdisciplinary and challenge-led work) into its academic hiring processes. In 2017, for the first time, the School entered the *Times Higher Education* Top 100 world subject rankings, as well as the *QS* and *Shanghai World University* subject rankings.

For more than two decades, Martin Kitchener's research has been characterized by collaborations with colleagues from diverse disciplines including nursing, economics, public administration, medicine, and sociology, to address the grand challenges of innovation, organization, performance, and policy in health and social care. In the United Kingdom, he has led studies of various settings, including hospitals, residential children's care providers, and mental health facilities. He recently completed a major, NHS-funded study of the organizational features associated with the successful implementation of hospital patient safety initiatives. Between 1999 and 2007, he worked at the University of California (Berkeley and San Francisco), where he studied the organization of long-term care, academic health centers, and dentistry. His research has attracted substantial external funding, produced outputs that are published widely, and had considerable impact on practice and policy, such as U.S. nursing home reimbursement legislation.

John D. Brewer is Professor of Post Conflict Studies in the Institute for the Study of Conflict Transformation and Social Justice at Queen's University, Belfast, having formerly been Sixth-Century Professor of Sociology at Aberdeen University. He was awarded an honorary DSocSci from Brunel University in 2013 for his services to social science and the sociology of peace processes. He is a member of the Royal Irish Academy (2004), a Fellow of the Royal Society of Edinburgh (2008), a Fellow in the Academy of Social Sciences (2003), and a Fellow of the Royal Society of Arts (1998). He has held visiting appointments at Yale University (1989), St John's College Oxford (1991), Corpus Christi College Cambridge (2002), and the Australia National University (2003). In 2007–2008 he was a Leverhulme Trust Research Fellow. He has been President of the British Sociological Association (2009–2012) and is now Honorary Life Vice President, and has also been a member of the Governing Council of the Irish Research Council and of the Council of the Academy of Social Science. In 2010, he was appointed to the United Nations Roster of Global Experts for his expertise in peace processes and in 2017 he was appointed Professor Extraordinary at Stellenbosch University. He is the author or co-author of 16 books and editor or co-editor of a further five books, and he has published more than 100 peer-reviewed articles. His books include *C. Wright Mills and the Ending of Violence* (Palgrave 2003), *Peace Processes: A Sociological Approach* (Polity Press, 2010), *Religion, Civil Society and Peace in Northern Ireland* (Oxford University Press, 2011, 2013), *Ex-Combatants, Religion and Peace in Northern Ireland* (Palgrave, 2013), and *The Public Value of Social Sciences* (Bloomsbury, 2013). He is General Editor of the book series *Palgrave Studies in Compromise after Conflict* and Co-Editor of the policy press book series *Public Sociology*. He has earned over £6.4 million in grants and was Principal Investigator on a £1.26 million, cross-national, five-year project on compromise among victims of conflict, funded by The Leverhulme Trust, focusing on Northern Ireland, South Africa, and Sri Lanka. Two books are appearing shortly, written on the basis of evidence gathered from this research program: *The Sociology of Compromise after Conflict* and *The Sociology of Everyday Life Peacebuilding*, both in the *Palgrave Studies in Compromise after Conflict* Series. He regularly teaches peace and reconciliation workshops in Sri Lanka and was active in the Northern Irish peace process, facilitating the Faith in a Brighter Future Group of leading ecumenical churchmen and women. He also has been involved as a policy advisor for policing reform in South Africa and Northern Ireland. In 2013, he gave the Academy of Social Science Annual Lecture; in March 2014, the Annual Lord Dunleath Lecture; in April 2014, the Annual Lord Patten Lecture; and in June 2014, the Annual David Stevens Memorial Lecture. In May 2014, he spoke at the Westminster Faith Debate on the motion that religion is a positive force in peace building, and then in 2016, at the British Academy Faith Debate on whether true religion is always extremist.

Mark H. Moore has been on the faculty of Harvard's Kennedy School of Government since 1974. He was appointed the Guggenheim Professor of Criminal Justice Policy and Management in 1979 and created the School's program in that domain, an appointment that focused his attention on the crucial role that the authority of the state plays in distinguishing public from private sector management. He was appointed the Hauser Professor of Non-Profit Organizations in 2005 to lead the Kennedy School's efforts to understand better how the role of government was changing in a world that sought to make greater use of the "public spirit" that was expressed in both the service delivery and policy advocacy parts of the voluntary sector. To further broaden his perspective on leadership and management, he was appointed a Visiting Professor at the Harvard Business School in 2007. In 2008, he was appointed (half time) to be the Simon Professor of Organizations and Management at Harvard's Graduate School of Education, where he helped design and establish a program that awarded qualified students a new professional doctoral-level degree, the Doctorate in Educational Leadership (EdLD). Throughout, he has worked to develop ideas, concepts, and frameworks that could help practicing public leaders and managers diagnose their immediate environments, as well as imagine and test ways in which they could use their particular positions in a particular context to "create public value." His books include *Creating Public Value* (Harvard University Press, 1995), *Recognizing Public Value* (Harvard University Press, 2013), and (with John Benington, eds) *Public Value: Theory and Practice* (London, Palgrave, Macmillan, 2010).

Timo Meynhardt is Professor and Chair of the Dr. Arend Oetker Chair of Business Psychology and Leadership at HHL Leipzig Graduate School of Management and Managing Director of the Center for Leadership and Values in Society at the

University of St. Gallen. He studied psychology in Jena, Oxford, and Beijing and obtained his doctorate and habilitation in business administration at the University of St. Gallen. Before rejoining academia, he worked for five years as a practice expert at McKinsey & Company, Inc., in Berlin. From 2013 to 2015, he held a professorship in management at the Institute of Corporate Development (ICD) at Leuphana University Lüneburg.

In his research, Timo Meynhardt links psychological and business management topics, especially in the fields of public value management, leadership, and competency diagnostics (www.mycompetencyprofile.com). He is committed strongly to research in the field of public value, as well as to the application of the concept in business and administration. He was the first researcher to apply the public value concept to the private sector. He developed a unique public value theory, which conceptualizes public value as "a necessary fiction" for individuals and groups. He publishes the Public Value Atlas for Switzerland and Germany (www.gemeinwohlatlas.de, www. gemeinwohl.ch), which aims to rank and make transparent the public value of companies and organizations. He also developed a Public Value Scorecard, a management tool that helps companies measure public value creation along five basic dimensions. He co-authored the HHL Leipzig Leadership Model (2016). He also developed and runs the competency coaching program "New Leipzig Talents" for outstanding HHL students. Together with Ernst & Young Ltd., he launched a public value award for start-ups. He chairs the public value award for public baths in Germany as well. His articles have appeared in various journals, such as *Business & Society, International Public Management Journal, Journal of Business Research, International Journal of Public Administration, Journal of Public Administration Research and Theory,* and *Journal of Management Development.* He is eager to engage the general public in public value discourses and thus publishes in *Frankfurter Allgemeine Zeitung, Harvard Business Manager, Neue Zürcher Zeitung,* and *Wirtschaftswoche.*

About the contributors

Rebecca Abushena is a senior lecturer in the marketing department at Manchester Metropolitan University, following a return to academia after five years working in management consultancy. She previously worked as a researcher at University of Manchester's Business School, where she completed her Ph.D. in international business. Her research interests include qualitative methodology techniques, such as CAQDAS, and multinational firm internationalization and interfirm linkages.

Rhys Andrews is Professor of Public Management in Cardiff University's Business School. His research interests focus on the management and performance of public organizations. He is co-author of *Strategic Management and Public Service Performance* and *Public Service Efficiency: Reframing the Debate*.

Anne Bäro is a research associate and doctoral candidate at the Dr. Arend Oetker Chair of Business Psychology and Leadership at HHL Leipzig Graduate School of Management. Her dissertation studies focus on public value, entrepreneurial value creation, and value creation in the sharing economy. She completed her Master's degree with a focus on work, organizational, and business psychology at the Free University of Berlin and York University in Toronto. She gained practical experience in her work as a scientific research assistant at Max Planck Institute for Human Development in Berlin and the Canadian Centre for German and European Studies in Toronto. Previously, she worked as a psychological consultant, dedicated to personnel selection and executive development. Her current research interests reflect the culmination of these experiences. While continuing to expand her field experience as a psychologist, she strives to understand and explain the drivers of public value creation in private organizations; she currently is developing a public value reporting framework that will be applicable in practice. Her doctoral research is being conducted under the supervision of Timo Meynhardt, in partnership with the Center for Leadership and Values in Society at the University of St. Gallen.

John Benington is Emeritus Professor of Public Policy and Management at Warwick University, where for more than 20 years he led a large, interdisciplinary team of researchers in the Institute of Governance and Public Management (IGPM), as well as pioneering the development of the Warwick MPA and other post-experience Masters and diploma programs for public policymakers and managers. Prior to his university career, he had 20 years' management experience in public and voluntary services, community development, and economic development, leading to a role as Director of Economic and Employment Development on the Sheffield City Council and membership on the chief officers' management team for the local authority, from 1981 to 1985. Since his retirement, he has remained actively involved as Chair of Trustees for a small voluntary organization that is building and developing a girls' school in Ibba South Sudan. He continues to write and teach about public leadership and public value.

John Byrom is a lecturer in marketing at the University of Manchester. His research interests include retail marketing, marketing management, and consumer behavior. He has published in *Cities, European Journal of Marketing, Journal of Business Research, Journal of Marketing Management*, and *Marketing Theory*, and he is co-editor of *Case Studies in Food Retailing and Distribution* (Elsevier, 2018).

Kate Clark is an archaeologist whose career includes senior roles in museums and heritage in Australia and the United Kingdom. She has a long-standing interest in the values that people place on heritage, developed through working with a wide range of community groups and international heritage organizations. Her research into the industrial archaeology of the Ironbridge Gorge shaped her later work on the importance of understanding the conservation of buildings and landscapes. Since then, she has championed the role of public value in heritage and written about planning, heritage management, evaluation and research, house museums, and heritage leadership. She is Visiting Professor of Heritage Valuation at the University of Suffolk.

Claire Dewhirst is Head of the Centre for Educational Development at Queen's University, Belfast. She has been actively involved in compulsory and post-compulsory education for over 25 years, having taught in secondary schools in Fife before moving into higher education teaching. Her interests lie in partnership working and communities of practice. In particular, she is interested in how changing practices affect stakeholders and end users. She has been a member of the KESS partnership for five years. In addition, she held the post of Research Impact Manager during REF 2014.

Alpa Dhanani is a reader in accounting and finance at Cardiff University's Business School. One of her research interests includes not-for-profit accountability, and she has published a number of articles in this field in journals such as the *Accounting, Auditing and Accountability Journal* and *Journal of Business Ethics*, as well as two monographs for the Association of Chartered Certified Accountants.

Scott Douglas is Assistant Professor of Public Management at Utrecht University's School of Governance. His research focuses on the intersection of performance management and collaborative governance, examining how management control systems can support successful public value creation by multiple partners. He frequently collaborates with practitioners to evaluate the success of public action in challenging domains such as counterterrorism, public health, and education. He completed his Ph.D. at Oxford University and has published in journals such as *Evaluation, International Journal of Public Administration*, and *Public Management Review*.

Tom Entwistle is Professor of Public Policy and Management in Cardiff University's Business School. His research interests lie in the areas of partnership, governance, and intergovernmental relations. His work has been published in *Journal of Public*

Administration Research and Theory, *Public Administration*, and *Urban Studies*. He is the Co-Editor of *Public Service Improvement: Theories and Evidence* (Oxford University Press, 2010) and co-author of *Public Service Efficiency: Reframing the Debate* (Routledge, 2013).

Andreas Fröhlich is a doctoral candidate at the Dr. Arend Oetker Chair of Business Psychology and Leadership at HHL Leipzig Graduate School of Management. His research focuses on the combination of psychological and business-related topics, and in particular public value (*Gemeinwohl*), value awareness, value creation, and the relations among these concepts. He holds an MA in Strategy and International Management from University of St. Gallen, a BSc in Physics from Vienna University of Technology, and a BSc in Business Administration from Vienna University of Economics and Business. Since 2014, he has been a management consultant with McKinsey & Company, attempting to synthesize and leverage insights from academia and practice.

Leon Gooberman is a lecturer in Employment Relations at Cardiff University's Business School. His research interests include the evolving nature of employer collective action in the United Kingdom, as well as the processes and impacts of regional deindustrialization. His journal articles have appeared in *Business History* and *Economic and Industrial Democracy*.

Martin Grimmer is Dean and Professor of Marketing at University of Tasmania's School of Business and Economics. Professor Grimmer received his Ph.D. from University of Tasmania, and his undergraduate, honour's, and master's degrees in psychology from University of Queensland. His research and teaching focus is on consumer behavior, with a specialization in pro-environmental/sustainable consumption. He conducts research into the effect of corporate reputation on purchase behavior, the factors that affect consumer attitudes toward and purchases of green products, ways to bridge the intention–behaviour gap in pro-environmental consumer behavior, and attitudes toward ethical food. Professor Grimmer is a Fellow of the Australian Marketing Institute, a Life Fellow of the Australian and New Zealand Academy of Management, and a Companion of the British Academy of Management.

Valeria Guarneros-Meza is a reader in public policy and politics at De Montfort University. She has a Ph.D. in public policy from the same university. Her research focuses on the relationship between public management processes and citizen participation. Her research has been published in journals such as *Public Management Review* and *Urban Studies*.

Christine Harland is Professor and holder of the Gianluca Spina Chair in Supply Strategy in the School of Management at Politecnico di Milano. Her research interests focus on public procurement, supply strategy in complex interorganizational networks, and humanitarian aid supply chains. She is Associate Editor of *Journal of Supply Chain Management* and was previously Editor of *Journal of Purchasing and Supply Management*. One of the co-founders of the International Research Study of Public Procurement (IRSPP) in 2003, she continues to help organize this research network that performs biannual international research studies among more than 50 nations.

Jean Hartley is Professor of Public Leadership at The Open University Business School, leading a program of research on public leadership through the Citizenship and Governance@OU initiative, as well as the Academic Director of The Open University Centre for Policing Research and Learning, which works closely with 18 UK police forces to create and use knowledge to improve policing and thus create public value. She researches and writes on leadership with political astuteness for public managers and recently co-edited *The Routledge Companion to Leadership* (2017). Her numerous published articles pertain to leadership by elected politicians, public managers, and professionals in policing, health, and local government. She also researches innovation, knowledge sharing, and improvement in public service organizations. She has undertaken both theoretical and empirical research on public value.

Marco Hauptmeier is Professor of International Human Resource Management at Cardiff University's Business School. He holds a Ph.D. from Cornell University; he won the Thomas A. Kochan & Stephen R. Sleigh Best Ph.D. Award in the USA. He has worked at the Max Planck Institute for the Study of Societies and was a visiting scholar at the Juan March Institute in Madrid and at Boston University. He has published in *British Journal of Industrial Relations*, *European Journal of Industrial Relations*, and *Work Employment and Society*, among others.

Bernadette C. Hayes is Professor of Sociology and Director of the Institute for Conflict, Transition, and Peace Research (ICTPR) in the School of Social Sciences at the University of Aberdeen. She has published extensively in the areas of gender, social stratification, religious and ethnonational identity, politics, and victims' issues. Some of these publications have been specifically cross-national in focus; others have been devoted exclusively to empirical examinations of these issues within Irish society, North and South.

Jo Hicks is Director of Academi Wales and Deputy Director for the Welsh Government. She has more than 15 years' experience in leadership and organizational development. As part of her all-Wales role, she leads a team of internal and external leadership practitioners and consultants, focusing on and supporting chief executives, boards, executive teams, senior professionals, and public-appointed officials. She has represented her country at the Young Leaders Forum in Sydney, at the G20Y Summit in Montreux, and at the Behavioral Exchange Harvard University. She is an experienced trainer and facilitator for ILM Level 7, accredited 360°, mental toughness, and emotional intelligence feedback coach. She also is a contributing co-author to *Changing Times for the Public Sector in Developing Resilient Organizations* (Kogan Page, 2014).

Joona Keränen is an associate professor at Lappeenranta University of Technology's School of Business and Management. His research focuses on customer value management in business-to-business markets, developing sustainable value propositions, and the marketing of complex projects and solutions. His work appears in *Journal of Business Research*, *Industrial Marketing Management*, *Journal of Product & Brand Management*, and *Management Decision*, among others. He obtained his Doctor of Science from Lappeenranta University of Technology in 2014.

Rob Lennox is a research associate at the University of York, where he received his Ph.D. from the Department of Archaeology in 2016. He works for the Chartered Institute for Archaeologists as policy advisor, responsible for its advocacy work, and is involved in a range of historic environment sector policy development and advocacy forums. He is widely published in archaeological media. His political interests include examining new and emerging government policy agendas and trends, such as planning reform, Brexit, and governments' cultural, environmental, and foreign policies. Other interests include cosmopolitanism, Heidegger, and heritage. He is actively exploring research collaborations in these and other areas.

Jane Lynch is a senior lecturer at Cardiff University's Business School. She is a research leader for the International Research Study on Public Procurement. Her research interests include social procurement, community benefits of local sourcing, supplier consortia, and effective collaboration. She regularly presents papers at international supply chain and logistics conferences and has published in *International Journal of Production Economics*. Additional roles include being senior associate of the Institute for Collaborative Working, Wales; facilitator for ISO 44001 Collaborative Relationships; Co-Chair of Joint-bidding Steering Group with Welsh Government; and sitting on the judging panel for the GOAwards (Wales).

Dominic Medway is Professor of Marketing in the Institute of Place Management at Manchester Metropolitan University. His work pertains primarily to the complex interactions among places, spaces, and those who manage and consume them, reflecting his academic training as a geographer. He has published extensively in a variety of journals, including *Environment & Planning A*, *European Journal of Marketing*, *Industrial Marketing Management*, *Journal of Environmental Psychology*, *Marketing Theory*, and *Tourism Management*.

Chris Nailer is a senior lecturer in management at the Australian National University's Research School of Management. His research interests include entrepreneurship, innovation, and the growth dynamics of companies, particularly international growth. His work appears in *European Business Review* and *International Journal of Market Research*, as well as in many government and industry reports. He obtained his Ph.D. from the Australian National University in 2015.

Gerwin Nijeboer works as a consultant at EY. After an inquiry undertaken for the municipality of Barreiro, he started to specialize in public value and the public value scorecard methodology. In cooperation with, among others, Timo Meynhardt, he currently is working on developing public value further by creating awareness of public value theory and the public value scorecard, as well as developing their wider, more practical uses, by combining scientific theories with practical approaches.

Mirko Noordegraaf is Professor of Public Management at Utrecht University's School of Governance. He focuses on public management, with a particular emphasis on public managers, performance management, professionalism, and professionals. In 2015, he published *Public Management: Performance, Professionalism and Politics* (Palgrave). He is an associate editor for *Journal of Professions and Organizations*.

Mark Olssen is Emeritus Professor of Political Theory and Education Policy in the Department of Politics at the University of Surrey and Professor of Higher Education in the School of Education at Auckland University of Technology. His most recent books are *Liberalism, Neoliberalism, Social Democracy: Thin Communitarian Perspectives on Political Philosophy and education* (Routledge, 2010) and *Toward a Global Thin Community: Nietzsche, Foucault, and the Cosmopolitan Commitment* (Paradigm Press, 2009). He is also co-author (with John Codd and Anne-Marie O'Neill) of *Education Policy: Globalisation, Citizenship, Democracy* (Sage, 2004) and author of *Michel Foucault: Materialism and Education* (Greenwood Press, 1999/Paradigm Press, 2006). He has published many book chapters and articles in academic journals in Britain, America, and Australasia.

Daniel Prior is Professor of Strategic Sales Management and Director of the Executive MBA Strategic Marketing & Sales at Cranfield University. Previously, he was a senior lecturer in management at the University of New South Wales, Australia. His main research interests focus on the economic impacts of buyer–supplier relationships. His work appears in *Industrial Marketing Management, Journal of Business & Industrial Marketing, Journal of Business Research*, and *Journal of General Management*, among others. He obtained his Ph.D. from Macquarie University in 2008.

Eileen Regan has been based in the Research and Information Service (RaISe) of the Northern Ireland Assembly since 2000. As a member of RaISe's Board of Management, her responsibilities include managing the Finance and Economics Research Team, which delivers a range of services to Assembly committees, as well as serving as an elected Member and Senior Secretariat. She also is responsible for academic engagement, which includes managing the development of success-ful knowledge exchanges and transfers between legislatures and academia. She co-founded the Assembly's Knowledge Exchange Seminar Series, which seeks to promote evidence-led policy and law-making, which has successfully partnered with local universities since 2012. In addition, she has spoken on related topics at various inter-parliamentary conferences and served on various relevant boards and panels.

Mark R. Rutgers is Professor of Social Philosophy and Dean of the Faculty of Humanities at Leiden University. He received his Ph.D. from Leiden University in 1993 and worked previously at the Department of Public Administration at Leiden University and Political Sciences at University of Amsterdam. He has pub-lished in, among others, *Administration & Society, Administrative Theory & Praxis, American Review of Public Administration, International Review of Public Administration, Journal of Banking Regulation, Journal of Public Administration Research & Theory, Public Management Review*, and *Review of Social Economy*. He serves on the boards of many journals. His research interests include public values, the history of (the study of) public administration, oaths of office, and administrative ethics.

Carol Ann Scott is an international consultant with expertise in measuring museum value and building the capacity of museums to create public value. She is the author of "Museum Measurement: Questions of Value" in *International Handbook of Museum Studies, Volume 2, Museum Practice*; co-author (with Jocelyn Dodd and Richard Sandell) of *Cultural Value of Engaging with Museums and Galleries: A Critical Review of the Literature* for the AHRC Cultural Value Project; author of *Museums and Public Value: Creating Sustainable Futures* (Ashgate 2013); and Editor of a volume of *Cultural Trends* dedicated to *Emerging Paradigms: National Approaches to Measuring Cultural Value* (June 2014). She is a member of the Executive Board of the International Council of Museums (ICOM), Immediate Past President of the UK branch of ICOM, and a former President of Museums and Galleries Australia.

Shandana Sheikh is a doctoral researcher at Cardiff University's Business School. Her research particularly focuses on female entrepreneurship, their challenges, and public value amidst an entrepreneurial ecosystem. Prior to her doctoral studies, she received her MBA in marketing from Lahore School of Economics and an MSc in marketing and strategy from University of Warwick's Business School. She also has worked as a teaching fellow at Lahore School of Economics, where she taught undergraduate- and graduate-level courses.

Sally Shortall is a sociologist based in the Centre for Rural Economy in Newcastle University. She received her Ph.D. from the National University of Ireland. She has published in *Gender, International Journal of Sociology and Social Policy, Journal of Rural Studies, Place & Culture, Politics and Policy, Public Administration, Social Policy and Administration, Sociologia Ruralis, Sociology*, and *Social Sciences*, among others. Her research interests pertain to agriculture and rural development, particularly the role of women in agriculture, farm families, women on farms, rural development theory and practice, food, governance, community, and stakeholder engagement in policy processes, as well as how knowledge gains legitimacy and how evidence can be used to inform policy. She has carried out policy research for the Scottish Government, FAO, European Commission, OECD, European Parliament, and, most recently, the Scottish Government. First Minister Nicola Sturgeon established a Task Force to implement the recommendations of the research led by Shortall for women in agriculture in Scotland. She currently is finalizing her report on rural proofing and the Rural Needs Act for Northern Ireland.

Zoe Sweet is Director of Organisational Development at Academi Wales, responsible for the delivery of its programs in leadership, management, and organizational development. She is currently pursuing a Ph.D. in mental toughness and resilience in public service leadership and has published and presented papers at the British Academy of Management: The Social Construction of Mental Toughness (2012) and Organisational Development Network Europe: Managing Change Successfully: A Cultural Case Study (2013) conferences. She is a qualified mental toughness, emotional intelligence, and leadership psychometrics assessor. She is a contributing co-author to *Changing Times for the Public Sector in Developing Resilient Organizations* (Kogan Page, 2014), a contributing author to *Developing Mental Toughness* (Kogan Page, 2015), and author of *Understanding Mental Toughness: Sustain, Support and Stretch Your Resilience* (Academi Wales, 2016).

Francis Teeney is a chartered psychologist with the British Psychological Society. He has been a research fellow at the University of Aberdeen and at Queen's University, Belfast, where laterally he was attached to the Senator George J. Mitchell Institute for Global Peace, Security and Justice. He participated actively in the Northern

Ireland Peace Process, frequently commenting on radio, television, and other media outlets. He was a founding member of the hugely successful Queen's University blog "Compromise after Conflict," which attracted 1.5 million hits and had a truly global following, frequently being used by the BBC and covered in the *Times Higher*. His other interests include the study of emotions and health, especially their impacts on societies emerging from conflict, and the use of social media in a highly politicized world.

Gwen Thomas is a senior lecturer in accounting at Cardiff University's Business School. She is a qualified chartered accountant who worked at KPMG for many years in its auditing, tax, and financial planning departments, prior to joining Cardiff University. She is currently Program Director for the undergraduate accounting and finance schemes at Cardiff University, and she teaches a range of accounting and taxation modules.

Helen Walker is Professor of Operations and Supply Management at Cardiff University's Business School. She just has completed her three-year term as President of IPSERA, the leading and largest international association in the purchasing and supply field with 350 members. She has published in journals such as *Decision Sciences*, *Human Relations*, and *International Journal of Operations and Production Management*. She and her co-authors have been the recipients of 10 best paper awards, twice winning the Louis Brownlow Award in *Public Administration Review*. She is on the editorial board of several journals including *Journal of Operations Management* and *Public Administration Review*. She has led organized special issues on sustainable procurement issues. Other research interests include supply strategy, corporate social responsibility, and sustainable supply chain management, in a variety of contexts including the public sector (NHS, local government, United Nations), and the private sector (PepsiCo, Boots).

Gary Warnaby is Professor of Retailing and Marketing, based in the Institute of Place Management at Manchester Metropolitan University. His research interests focus on the marketing of places (particularly in urban contexts) and retailing. The results of this research have been published in, among others, *Area*, *Cities*, *Consumption Markets & Culture*, *Environment and Planning A*, *European Journal of Marketing*, *International Journal of Management Reviews*, *Journal of Business Research*, *Local Economy*, *Marketing Theory*, and *Tourism Management*. He is co-author of *Relationship Marketing: A Consumer Experience Approach* (Sage, 2010), co-editor of *Rethinking Place Branding: Comprehensive Brand Development for Cities and Regions* (Springer, 2015), and *Designing with Smell: Practices, Techniques and Challenges* (Routledge 2017).

Richard Watermeyer is a reader in education at the University of Bath. He is a sociologist of education (knowledge, science, and expertise), with general interests in education policy, practice, and pedagogy. He is specifically engaged with critical sociologies/pedagogies of higher education, with a focus on new conceptualizations of academic praxis and the current and future role of the (public) university as it intersects with the forces of change due to marketization, globalization, and neoliberalization. He was the first social scientist to be seconded to the Office of the Chief Scientific Adviser for Wales and has held previous academic appointments at the universities of Cardiff, Surrey, and Warwick.

Iain Wilkinson is Professor of Sociology in the School of Social Policy, Sociology and Social Research at the University of Kent. Much of his research is engaged with issues relating to problems of social suffering, including explorations of how individuals are socially and culturally disposed to interpret and respond to problems of suffering. His research also involves inquiries into the social and cultural conditions that give rise to humanitarian moral feelings, as well as the role played by the politics of compassion in public life. His publications include *Anxiety in a Risk Society* (Routledge, 2001), *Suffering: A Sociological Introduction* (Polity, 2005), *Risk Vulnerability and Everyday Life* (Routledge, 2010), and (co-authored with Arthur Kleinman) *A Passion for Society: How We Think about Human Suffering* (University of California Press, 2016).

Shumaila Yousafzai is a reader at Cardiff University's Business School, where she teaches entrepreneurship, marketing, and consumer behavior. After her undergraduate studies in physics and mathematics (University of Balochistan) and an MSc in electronic commerce (Coventry University), she finished her PG Diploma in research methods from Cardiff University. She received her Ph.D. in 2005 from Cardiff University. In her research, she focuses mainly on topics linked to the contextual embeddedness of entrepreneurship, firm performance, institutional theory, and entrepreneurial orientation. She has published articles in *Computers in Human Behavior, Entrepreneurship Theory and Practice, Industrial Marketing Management, Journal of Applied Social Psychology, Journal of Business Ethics, Journal of Small Business Management, Psychology & Marketing,* and *Technovation.* She also has co-edited a special issue on women's entrepreneurship for *Entrepreneurship & Regional Development.*

Foreword and acknowledgements

A systematic and interdisciplinary examination of public value is necessary to establish an essential definition and current view of the field. In reflecting on the "public value project," we consider not only how the field has broadened beyond its original focus on public sector management, but also how it has deepened through the development of analytical concepts and frameworks linking its constitutive concepts. Furthermore, it has been applied increasingly to concrete circumstances by diverse academics, consultants, and practitioners. We use the term "public value project" strategically, because though public value has an academic basis, producing various important theoretical and research questions, it also has a profoundly practical purpose. The connection between conceptualization and practice is what gives public value its vitality and richness.

Yet, its common appearance in academic journals may have led public value to lose some of the energy that comes from constant contact with practice. In response, we frame this anthology not solely according to an academic research tradition but in relation to practice. We include case studies herein but avoid making any clear distinction between theory and cases. Sometimes cases challenge theory in useful ways, particularly when they move beyond standard ideas for improving the welfare of the disadvantaged and begin focusing on issues of right-based relations, social justice, or eliminating bigotry and repression. These ideas about equity in social and political settings complement studies of economic standing, rights, and entitlements, together with concepts of right-based relationships, which include both duties and privileges.

In this anthology, the included cases provide two important functions. First, they establish the (paradoxically) theoretical contribution that because the concept of public value is inherently a practical idea, used to evaluate and change conditions in the world, public value only can acquire a useful, concrete meaning when it is applied to concrete circumstances. Second, the institutional domain in which the public value concept might be useful is wider than often assumed, but caution is necessary in using this concept, once it leaves the domain of politics and government and takes up residence in the voluntary sector (where it fits pretty comfortably) or the commercial sector (where it can fit, but more awkwardly and, in a way, that is vulnerable to abuse, such as when public value gets used to justify commercial enterprises that generate profits without recognizing the interests and rights of employees, suppliers, consumers, or citizens in society as a whole).

With this line of thought, we sought to discuss ways to deepen and enrich theories of public value, as well as broaden both the theory and practice of creating public value, to include voluntary and commercial organizations and collaborative networks. We also remained very aware of previous work (principally by John Brewer) describing the ways in which public value ideas can make claims on and transform the conduct of social science, in addition to how universities might contribute more valuably to public discourse – what has been called the "humanitarian project" of social science and universities. Accordingly, we designed this anthology to discuss the challenge that the concept of public value poses to social sciences and universities.

Among the theoretical articles, we also sought contributions that could address three main questions:

- Who is an appropriate arbiter of public value: individuals who hold more or less similar ideas about a good and just society or collectives that act through voluntary associations and political activities to produce a more collectively shared idea of desired individual and social conditions?
- What sorts of individual and social conditions are, or should be, the focus of public value theory and practice (e.g., overall material well-being, material welfare of the least advantaged, social discrimination and oppression of those in low status social positions who cannot defend their rights, suppression of political rights that would allow people to protect themselves from government oppression and use government resources to advance their individual and collective social conditions)?
- How can the practice of acting in society help society define and create public value (politics and government, spreading to include actions launched from other institutional platforms)? This topic pertains to the spread of the ideas of public value creation to organizations in the voluntary sector (service delivery and political advocacy) and even the corporate sector.

In summary, the 24 chapters in this anthology reflect three main topic sections:

- Deepening and enriching the theory of creating public value. This section consists of three subsections:
    - Different arbiters of public value: individuals and collectives.
    - Different concepts of public value: material welfare and right-based relationships.
    - Actions to define and create public value.
- Broadening the theory and practice of creating public value to voluntary and commercial organizations and collaborative networks.
- The challenge and the opportunity that the concept of public value poses to social science and universities.

The anthology's epilogue offers further reflections on the public value project.

Deepening the theory of creating public value

In the first part of this section – Different arbiters of public value: individuals and collectives – Timo Meynhardt begins by describing "Public Value: Value Creation in the Eyes of Society". This expert contributor notes current challenges to the corporate world that question its very value to society at large. Companies have various opportunities to leverage societal trends, such as sustainability, which might imply, inaccurately, their alignment with the broader public. But when companies fail to manage their public value explicitly, they risk losing their license to operate. Furthermore, companies fail to exploit opportunities to contribute to the common good (public value) fully. With the author's public value scorecard, companies can systematically integrate diverse perspectives on the different interpretations and meanings attached to their value creation, as well as understand the drivers of their performance from a societal perspective. This chapter thus introduces basic ideas of public value thinking and its consequences for leadership.

Timo Meynhardt and Andreas Fröhlich continue this discussion by arguing that public value might be minimized or destroyed if individuals and organizations become overwhelmed by the mental demands of (post)modern society and thus do not recognize how and for whom value might be created. In "More value awareness for more (public) value: recognizing how and for whom value is truly created", the authors elaborate a micro-foundation of value, in which value gets created through subjective psychological evaluations, measured relative to humans' basic values (how value is created) and personal frames of reference (for whom). These two dimensions establish a (public) value matrix of value categories that represents the psychological basis of evaluations. People may differ in the emphasis they assign to each category, as well as in their competence in recognizing certain value categories as relevant. Such "value awareness" in turn should influence (public) value creation.

Next, in "The rationalities of public values: conflicting values and conflicting rationalities", Mark R. Rutgers addresses how public values provide distinct directions and forms of legitimation. He proposes a typology of six relations among values, reflecting their contextual nature and the complexity with which values interact, including their potential incommensurability for public administration. Combining Rescher's view of values as rational legitimizations of action with Weber's distinction between purpose and value rationality, the author also shows that values function fundamentally differently, depending on their use in value-rational or purpose-rational arguments. Both lines of inquiry converge though: Empirical research on public values must recognize that values have different meanings, depending on their relations to other values and their argumentative functions. Thus, the meaning of public values can never be taken at face value.

Scott Douglas and Mirko Noordegraaf agree that different stakeholders prioritize different value dimensions yet expect public organizations to deliver on all of them, so in "Designing spaces for public value creation: consolidating conflicting dimensions of public value in the design of public organizations", they propose ways that organizations might design internal structures to match their context and serve all the value dimensions. In four types of organizational spaces, different values can meet and interact effectively. That is, designers might (1) separate organizational units with different value propositions, (2) spread the responsibility for different dimensions of value across different units, (3) contrast different dimensions within the same unit, or (4) integrate all dimensions in singular units. The most suitable design achieves an instrumental match with the task environment and an institutional match with the authorizing environment, producing both efficiency and legitimacy. However, managers still must work constantly to nurture appropriate organizational dynamics.

In the second part of this section – Different concepts of public value: material welfare and right relationships – John D. Brewer, Bernadette C. Hayes, and Francis

Teeney, with their short case study, apply public value social science to the difficult issue of organized violence and its victims. "Compromise after conflict: a case study in public value social science" thus describes the public value of peace research, as illustrated by a six-year research program, funded by the Leverhulme Trust, on compromise by victims of conflict in Sri Lanka, South Africa, and Northern Ireland. This version of public value social science in practice addresses all three dimensions of the field, namely, research, teaching, and civic engagement.

By reviewing contemporary research on social suffering, Iain Wilkinson reveals contemporary intellectual and political developments that have inspired social scientists to address suffering as a key concern, which seemingly constitutes a return to the "social question" of the nineteenth century. With "Social suffering and public value: a spur to new projects of social inquiry and social care", the author argues that current social research reflects "classical" examples of critical pragmatism, as championed by Jane Addams, W.E.B du Bois, or Albion Small. In this view, social science must commit to projects of ameliorative social reform, and a caregiving pedagogy is necessary to any effort to understand the meaning and value of human life, in social terms.

With the sense that public value also can broaden current knowledge of organizational value creation, Timo Meynhardt and Anne Bäro argue that an organization's value to society depends on its contributions to the common good, as perceived by the public. The chapter "Public value reporting: adding value to (non-)financial reporting" recommends that organizations should engage in public value reporting, which enables them to get a better grasp of their dynamic environments, respond to societal needs, and legitimize their actions. The authors discuss three concrete approaches that can enhance existing reporting measures: the Public Value Scorecard, the extension of the materiality matrix, and definitions of key performance indicators relevant for public value creation.

The municipality of Barreiro, located next to Lisbon in Portugal, offers the setting for "Putting the system in a room: the public value scorecard as a connection framework". This municipality has long struggled, and Gerwin Nijeboer argues that for the local economy to survive, its public and private sectors must cooperate as they have not done in decades. Applying the Public Value Scorecard could open the pathways to this collaboration and help them take the first steps toward renewed cooperation.

When managed strategically, public procurement also can facilitate broader government objectives related to public value. Therefore, in "Leveraging social public procurement to deliver public value through community benefits clauses: an international study", Jane Lynch, Christine Harland, and Helen Walker present an international analysis of six public procurement case studies to show how public spending can be leveraged strategically to ensure greater social, economic, and environmental value. Applying agency theory to cases from three economically developed and three less developed nations, they consider how social procurement and the use of community benefits clauses in public contracts provide public value. This review reveals which factors are key for managing public spending to benefit local communities, including gaps in the policy, implementation, and evidence of impact.

The third and final part of this section – Actions to define and create public value – starts with a chapter that argues that public value is the key concept related to creating, using, and sustaining a democratic public sphere. John Benington and Jean Hartley therefore use "Action research to develop the theory and practice of public value as a contested democratic practice" and explore how public value relates to similar concepts, as well as why it constitutes a "game-changer" for leadership and public management. Action research provides an appealing methodology, because it engages actively with processes of change in real time, is sensitive to pluralist and contested interpretations by different stakeholders, and exposes lived material to dialectical challenge from theory. Key elements of public value thus emerge as a contested democratic practices, according to three action research case studies. In turn, the authors identify six theoretical public value dimensions that would benefit from further research.

By offering "A dynamic process theory of public value", Christopher Nailer, Daniel D. Prior, and Joona Keränen propose that public administrators undertaking multi-stakeholder public projects must address three main considerations. First, they need to understand the process by which they can achieve socially valued outcomes. Second, they must comprehend ways to attain consensus among competing, legitimate interests. Third, a common vocabulary must span economic and socio-political rationales for public value. The process theory of value can explain the anticipation and realization of public value by individual stakeholders, because it encompasses anticipated value, activity–resource interactions, realized value, and mediating consensus. To illustrate the proposed framework, this chapter presents case studies of the Collins Class submarine project, the Canberra Light Rail project, and heat transfer management projects by TPI Control.

Jo Hicks and Zoe Sweet focus on leaders in the Welsh public sector, to understand their "Purpose, passion, and perseverance: creating public value through public sector leadership". Questions of public value at individual and organizational levels in times of constant change, challenge, and complexity are difficult for leaders and may depend on leadership development processes. The authors thus present a case study that details what public value really means to public service leaders in a variety of senior positions and how they function as members of society, both provider and user, to create value through leadership.

For Tom Entwistle, Rhys Andrews, and Valeria Guarneros-Meza, local strategies should prioritize public value by engaging with citizens and stakeholders. Noting that conventional democratic theory suggests that people served by smaller local governments feel empowered, these authors also recognize how altered engagement forms, associated with public value, may shift this prediction. Therefore, in "Towards public value local government: size, engagement and stakeholder efficacy", they analyze whether the size of the jurisdiction influences stakeholders' sense of efficacy in the Welsh local government, potentially moderated by the presence of a citizen panel. According to their findings, size is negatively associated with stakeholder efficacy, but to compensate, larger local governments can develop citizen panels.

Broadening the theory and practice of creating public value to voluntary and commercial organizations and collaborative networks

Moving into the next section, Alpa Dhanani and Gwen Thomas evaluate "Development NGOs and public value", by describing the activities of Northern development non-governmental organizations (NGOs) through a public value lens. These NGOs serve two distinct publics: Southern communities from poorer, less developed, and less industrialized nations that the NGOs serve, and Northern counterparts from richer, more developed, and more industrialized countries that support the NGOs' activities. Two paradigms have informed NGOs' development approaches: a traditional welfare-based model and more recent rights-based models. This chapter provides a critical evaluation of how NGOs seek to create value for the Southern public, as well as their practices to shape the perceptions and values of the Northern publics.

Proposing "The public value of the sociology of religion", John D. Brewer applies a public value social science model to the sociology of religion, to illustrate its wide potential applicability across disciplines and intellectual fields. Using the return of religion to the public sphere, the author suggests new opportunities for sociologists to gain a publicly recognized voice and articulate the public value of the sociology of religion, leading to the potential intellectual renewal of this field for mainstream twenty-first century social science.

In their contribution to the discussion of public value, "Employers' organizations and public value", Leon Gooberman and Marco Hauptmeier explore its application to employers' organizations, defined as bodies formed of public- or private-sector employers. Two types of these organizations can contribute to public value creation. First, some of them promote equality, diversity, and corporate social responsibility through voluntary self-regulation, so they create public value in the workplace. They also influence governments, thereby creating public value for society. Second, other employers' organizations participate in collective bargaining with unions and thus deliver public value by establishing regulated, equally available pay and employment conditions. The concept of public value creation can be meaningfully extended to include hybrid organizations that focus on employment relations.

Another new direction for defining public value might result from pursuing avenues of value creation beyond public management, such as entrepreneurship. Describing "Public value creation through the lens of women's entrepreneurship", Shandana Sheikh and Shumaila Yousafzai argue that entrepreneurial individuals and firms create public value; female entrepreneurs in particular create multiple forms of public value that accumulate to produce public value at the societal level. With these arguments, the authors also propose ways to move the debate about public value forward, namely, by facilitating and legitimizing women as entrepreneurs and value creators in the public sphere.

With a particular focus on public value in UK museums, Carol Ann Scott realizes that the use of the term "public value" has declined in this sector, but museum discourse increasingly describes ways to effect social change, generate social benefits, and evoke social impacts. The term "social" thus appears to describe most activities that encompass the principles and practices of public value. "Museums and public value: taking the pulse" also addresses possible reasons for the disappearance of "public value" terminology, as well as the related issues for professional practice and public expectations of museums.

Kate Clark and Rob Lennox also propose that values get used in cultural heritage practices, and understanding which public values matter and why can inform decisions about what heritage resources to protect. As they write in "Public value and cultural heritage", heritage practitioners struggle to define the significance and importance of historic buildings, places, and things, yet they also need to understand how caring for heritage can deliver wider economic, social, and environmental benefits. To do so, they should define how their heritage organizations create value, not only just with what they do but in how they do it.

The challenge and the opportunity that the concept of public value poses to social science and universities

The final section consists of four chapters, starting with "The public value of social science: from manifesto to organizational strategy", by Martin Kitchener, who integrates sociology and management research into public value to outline a strategy for universities to deliver public social science concepts. The contemporary setting of social science features growing challenges that demand strategic responses, so this chapter introduces Brewer's conception of the new public social science, to specify the required outputs within Moore's implementation triangle. Drawing from higher education management literature, he also identifies which environmental and capacity elements will influence the development of this public social science for higher education, leading to his appraisal of the prospects for this development.

Also focused in the education sector, the case study reported in "Knowledge exchange seminar series: an effective partnership to increase the public value of academic research findings" describes a knowledge exchange seminar series in Northern Ireland, between the Assembly and universities in the region, reflecting Brewer's ideas of new public social science. In this collaboration between government and academics, the focus is on problems rather than disciplines. Sally Shortall, Eileen Regan, and Claire Dewhirst describe how the seminar series prompted participants to apply their skills to analyze fundamental problems related to culture, the market, and the state, such that they produced questions and provided research evidence that informed potential solutions. These efforts produced a list of "hot topics" or government priorities, circulated to all university staff. Researchers also presented their findings in Parliament Buildings, the devolved government. Together, they developed a policy brief, written in plain English, responding to Brewer's call for academics to focus on communicating to make themselves understood.

Similarly concerned about "The dissipating value of public service in UK higher education", Richard Watermeyer and Mark Olssen highlight the needs of academic researchers working in UK universities to demonstrate scientific transparency and public accountability so that they can acquire public research funds and support their occupational livelihood. Adding public citizenship into the criteria for research excellence produces new assessments of scholarly worth, as well as changes in the behaviors and self-rationalizations of academic researchers. They seek to engineer and profit from public interactions, in ways that tend to be selfishly rather than altruistically motivated. The authors thus contest the myth of a new agenda for higher education, which wrongly assumes that academics avoid public life and also tries to impose an ideal of academics' public responsibility that conflicts with historical views of public intellectuals and even paradoxically separates academics from the agora and meaningful contributions to public life.

Finally, Dominic Medway, Gary Warnaby, John Byrom, Martin Grimmer, and Rebecca Abushena argue that universities actively seek to achieve carbon neutrality. To assist them, the authors propose addressing research activities associated with gathering and disseminating data, which are responsible for emitting large quantities of carbon. In their chapter, "How far would you go? Assessing the carbon footprint of business travel in the context of academic research activity", they consider the challenges academics face if they attempt to calculate their carbon footprint. Various policy issues accordingly arise at the macro-, meso-, and micro-levels. In support of practical management efforts, this chapter presents the results of applying various official carbon calculators to a small-scale research project.

Epilogue

In the epilogue, Mark H. Moore, in "Reflections on the public value project", reflects on how the public value project has developed over time. He first discusses the challenge facing public managers as one of "creating public value." The chapter then traces the development of the ideas through the processes of both simultaneous invention and diverse development, as it has been grasped by scholars with both broader and deeper perspectives than Moore's own. In particular, this chapter considers the future of the public value project against the neo-liberal tide.

Closing remarks

We extend a special thanks to Routledge and its staff, who have been most helpful throughout this entire process. Equally, we warmly thank all of the authors who submitted their manuscripts for consideration for this book. They have exhibited the desire to share their knowledge and experience with the book's readers – and a willingness to put forward their views for possible challenge by their peers. We also thank the reviewers, who provided excellent, independent, and incisive considerations of the anonymous submissions.

We hope that this compendium of chapters and themes stimulates and contributes to the ongoing debate surrounding public value. The chapters in this book can help fill some knowledge gaps, while also stimulating further thought and action pertaining to the multiple aspects surrounding public value.

Adam Lindgreen, Ph.D.
Copenhagen, Denmark and Pretoria, South Africa

Nicole Koenig-Lewis, Ph.D.
Cardiff, Wales, UK

Martin Kitchener, Ph.D.
Cardiff, Wales, UK

John D. Brewer, HDSSci
Belfast, Northern Ireland, UK

Mark H. Moore, Ph.D.
Cambridge, Massachusetts, USA

Timo Meynhardt, Dr
Leipzig, Germany and St. Gallen, Switzerland

1 February 2019

Part 1

Deepening and enriching the theory of creating public value

Part 1.1

Different arbiters of public value: individuals and collectives

1 Public value

Value creation in the eyes of society

Timo Meynhardt

Introduction

Businesses form and transform social conditions. Like all other institutions, corporations are both drivers and results of the environment in which they operate. Therefore, leaders are highly instrumental not only in making markets, but in doing so also building societies. In modern times, such value creation for society has had an indispensable impact, improving the quality of life on our planet in many respects. It has clearly been a success story, even though not all contributions are necessarily positive. In any case, business activities require societal acceptance, which is not a given. In fact, we now enter an era in which top executives are under pressure to defend or revise the notion of *value creation* itself to remain in sync with customers' needs, citizens' expectations, and societal changes at large. We return to Peter Drucker's reminder that "free enterprise cannot be justified as being good for business. It can be justified only as being good for society" (1973, 41).

Only recently, BlackRock CEO Larry Fink echoed this statement in his annual letter to CEOs of public companies. His call is quite powerful, considering that BlackRock manages more than $6 trillion in investment around the world. Fink argued: "To prosper over time, every company must not only deliver financial performance, but also show how it makes a positive contribution to society" (Fink, 2018).

Take Nestlé, the Switzerland-based giant in nutrition, health and wellness. For decades, this corporation has pursued an approach of simultaneously addressing societal challenges and generating profits - the so-called shared value approach (Porter & Kramer, 2011). However, our research shows time and again that in the Swiss population's judgement, this corporation still ranks low in terms of its public value, i.e. in its contribution to the common good (www.gemeinwohl.ch). Although it is a multinational firm operating in diverse cultures, not to be respected in their home country, is embarrassing. What's wrong here? As complex as it may be, it boils down to one basic factor: Nestlé has not succeeded in touching people's hearts and minds in a positive way.

Nestlé is a case in point, but it represents many companies who are realizing that their actual "good" behaviour does not automatically translate into societal acceptance and a renewed license to operate. To be clear, we are not suggesting that the public simply "does not get it" or that citizens are not interested in properly grasping the business facts. A far more complex bundle of causes is at work.

Obviously, a further, bigger step than just doing good is required to cross the divide between what companies do and what society at large recognizes as truly valuable.

The *public value* concept attempts to bridge this divide: Public value reflects a contribution to the common good as experienced by society. In our era of transparency, any business behavior and any traditional "value" must be challenged to check whether it reflects such a contribution. This goes far beyond political marketing, reputation or brand management. It is about a deeper *why*, which is positively linked to the functioning and betterment of society.

For many leaders, thinking in public value terms comes naturally; for others, seeing themselves as creating or destroying public value requires considerably more effort. In the following section, the notion of *public value*[1] will be introduced and outlined. It is meant as an invitation to reflect further on fundamental questions about means and ends in corporate life that do not have easy answers. In the process, readers should remain prepared to develop a positive mindset on leading for public value.

Taking society seriously

Former Nestlé CEO Paul Bulcke (2014) clearly addressed the new challenge, saying that those who fail to create public value "will end up alienating themselves from society, and that is a risk we should not take. It's important not to forget that it is society that grants us the permission to be in business and allows us to succeed" (*own translation*).

Managing a corporation's public value is a big challenge, since it is not simply delivered but needs to be perceived in order to be realized. Actually, the noun *value* disguises that value comes into being only as a result of relationship. Therefore, the only viable solution to assuring public value development is credible dialogue, and discerning short-term public opinion as well as long-term value change. Since profit *per se* has become a contested idea, Pandora's box has been opened. Consider the ripples following former General Electric CEO Jack Welch's statement that pursuing shareholder value as a strategy was "the dumbest idea in the world" (2009). The idea of shareholder value now requires much broader justification that is deeply grounded in society.

We have to acknowledge that in a world of distributed power, volatility, co-creation and disruptive changes there can be no single, uncontested management paradigm. More than ever, value is in the eye of the beholder as a web of meaning, purpose and emotion. Paradoxical as it may sound, in a world of hard-nosed material conflict, more than ever we need to come to terms with soft issues. Thereby, we might even need to move from a chief *executive* officer to a chief *experience* officer, who is primarily concerned with managing value as a matter of interpretation and sense making. In other words, real value is what the beholder considers to be truly valuable. We are reminded that the world we live in is one of perceived reality.

We need to accept in a fundamentally new way that the rise of subjectivity is not a temporary phenomenon, but a profound top management challenge. The reason is simple: The more complex business activities in a global marketplace become, the less you can fight complexity with complexity. The contrary is true, namely that the less customers, citizens and politicians understand value chains and economic facts, the more they need to simplify their perceptions and rely on their emotional responses. As natural response, humans feel positive about something if there is a direct personal gain or a positive impact on the community or society they live in. This is what *public value* refers to. It is a measure for assessing how, in a bigger picture, value is created to the benefit of society. It points to an organization's contributions to both social stability and progress as perceived by the people. Although this perception should be fact-driven, it is primarily a matter of attitude. "Facts" need to be interpreted and made sense of based on concrete experience.

In its original definition, public value creation "is situated in relationships between the individual and 'society', founded in individuals, constituted by subjective evaluations against basic needs, activated by and realized in emotional-motivational states, and produced and reproduced in experience-intense practices" (Meynhardt 2009, 212).

It is not only at the level of corporate action but also at the products and services level where we see this challenge of creating a sense of belonging, identity, and of avoiding social conflict. Take a seemingly simple example. The pervasive WhatsApp messenger service has provided people with a most convenient communication platform. Adults and youngsters alike often send more than a hundred messages a day. Its global success story is one of superior functionality, comfort and ease in low-cost communication. At the same time, WhatsApp provides a social infrastructure with its own set of rules and codes of conduct. The most important qualifier here is whether to be in or out. Even primary school children have set up class communities, which have an in-group and an out-group. As with any developing trend, the social pressure on parents to allow their children to join – socially, educationally and in considering their monthly internet budget – can become significant. Besides the question whether or not to join such a community, a number of possible side effects such as constant availability, chain letters or mobbing, need to be taken into account. WhatsApp enables new forms of social interaction, creates new 'publics' with their own behavioural rules. This illustrates how technology can drive social relationships. Here, value creation is not limited to individual customer value or shareholder value, but gains a public dimension. Appealing to customers' choices, market forces or regulation procedures would provide too easy an explanation for how WhatsApp has changed communication and societal structure. Importantly, we have to acknowledge the role businesses play in the making of society. The WhatsApp example points to a fundamental mechanism available to businesses in creating or destroying public value, often even unknowingly.

The quest to open Pandora's Box

The notion of *public value* foregrounds the societal dimension of value creation. Other attempts at focusing on societal values, such as in responses to the sustainability challenge, corporate social responsibility, and shared value point in the same direction. Although we acknowledge the merit of the latter kinds of ideas, they can only serve as door openers – but not more than that! Further, they could soon be outdated if other critical issues come knocking at the door, as history has shown often happens.

For instance, who would have predicted 20 years ago how digitization would enter our lives and profoundly change our daily infrastructures? Customers are currently more informed than ever. And even though there is mixed evidence on the *ethical customer*, there is a clear power shift towards the customer as having significant influence on a corporation's public value via the social media.

As companies need to stay agile in turbulent times, we need to confront the complexity of the much-cited notion of *value*. It is not enough for top management to discuss whether sustainability programs should be better managed or corporate social responsibility (CSR) should be better integrated into business strategies. The larger task at hand is one of coming to terms with current business realities, to manage *public value*, i.e. value in a much broader sense (Meynhardt & Gomez, 2016). The appeal of *public value* stems from its plurality of perspectives, since it also helps us address the widening gap between the "facts of business life" and the public perception of what the economy is good for.

A classic example of this, is the launch of New Coke in 1985 when Coca-Cola changed its tried and trusted formula. The company experienced a disaster even after marketing attempted to re-energise the brand. Customers and the wider public complained, so that the new product was eventually withdrawn. It was not because the product did not taste good; nor was it because of pricing or placement. In fact, market research in the laboratory revealed broad acceptance. A couple of months after release, at the height of criticism, the Cuban leader Fidel Castro who had been a long-time Coke drinker, in an ironic comment interpreted the change as a "sign of American capitalist decadence". The rest is history: Coca-Cola went back to the "real thing", and they exceeded all previous sales. One plausible explanation for the 1985 disaster is that the company did not anticipate the strong emotional attachment to its product, based also on cultural sentiments, like the American way of life and liberty. In 2014, Coca-Cola again offended certain societal groups when its Super Bowl commercial using "America the Beautiful" as theme song provoked angry protest. This time, Coca-Cola had explicit good intentions of relating its product to the societal value of diversity in the many US identities. Even if "only" a specific section in the political spectrum reacted negatively, it led to heated public debate.

Stories such as this one, demonstrate a new quality symptomatic of how businesses not only touch on and exploit societal norms, but also actively shape society in ways that make businesses more vulnerable than ever to public debate and media coverage. The interaction of media, politics, customers, citizens, NGOs and so on, provides a melting pot in which public opinion is constructed. Of course, such negative press ("shit-storms") always comes to an end. However, the fundamental challenge of finding customers' "sweet spots" without being drawn into moral or political conflict, remains and, if achieved, is likely to last longer. The Coke examples indicate the tricky relationship between customer value and public value in an ecosystem of co-creation (Meynhardt, Chandler & Strathoff, 2016). Obviously, there is no sustained customer value without public value, but without the former, the latter would not be attractive for business.

The scale and scope of (geo)political conflict, technological progress and cultural conflict requires that capitalism in its different shapes around the globe will learn a new set of skills. Like it or not, in responding to financial crises, political upheavals or simply the brutal transparency in the internet world, corporations cannot bypass societal expectations and argue that profit *per se* is social. Ignoring social expectations can be valid in some places, but not in others. Society is no longer a stable boundary condition for markets, which business respects by obeying the law. Actions can be legal, but still not necessarily legitimate. To address this gap, we suggest viewing corporations as public value-producing institutions and rediscovering their social function.

As powerful actors, corporations can infuse their environments with value which goes far beyond their technical task at hand. Willingly or not, they feed back systemic properties, such as social peace, ideas of justice or trust in capitalism. These effects can be factually limited to a specific social context, but are almost immediately amplified owing to media and social media coverage. The images and symbols corporations produce are accessible in almost every customer's living room, far beyond the place of initial action. For instance, although the nuclear power plant disaster of 2011 in Fukushima was limited to a specific geographic area, it had global societal consequences. Similarly, the number of suicides at the Chinese company Foxconn since 2009 has sparked debate worldwide.

The bad news is that, given current circumstances, a corporation's license to operate can come under attack more swiftly than ever. In the foreseeable future shareholders are likely to ask for their companies' public value to avoid the risk of economic underperformance. At the same time, concerning broader ideas of societal progress and stability, some corporations can be prepared to reinterpret and reconfigure their value chain more easily than others. The good news then is that corporations necessarily develop awareness of how they create public value and, in doing so, how they contribute to the common good. The concept of *public value* provides a solution to the difficulty of systematically absorbing and managing expectations in society. It also helps to establish a perspective that views corporations as positive forces in society.

Interestingly, boardroom executives rediscover a basic truth, namely that corporations depend on society for their business performance as much as society depends on corporations. Frankly, society has always been a virtual board member and part of the so-called C-suite. CEOs now have to find a new and explicit language and new ways of addressing "society". For whichever reason, the general public does not study balance sheets before acting, buying elsewhere or voting for tighter regulations. The challenge to CEOs is not as much to better explain strategy, to share profits or to consider stakeholders' claims and needs, as it is to cope with the unpredictability of how society attributes meaning and purpose to business.

While a number of narratives has been developed to explain the purpose of business, none of the management paradigms given in Table 1.1 is completely uncontested. Each one of these paradigms has a justified focus and has found societal acceptance. For instance, only recently, CSR and sustainability were introduced into societal discourse about corporations. These themes articulate both a value change and increased sensitivity concerning corporations' social impact. In the 1970s, when Milton Friedman's famous argument that a corporation's first social responsibility is to increase its profit was coined, it found far greater acceptance than it does today. While *value for owners* is a legitimate and even legally enforced claim in capitalist society, it can easily promote financial performance at the cost of other goals. Similarly, *value for customers* is an obvious corporate goal, but one that, given undue emphasis, can easily underrepresent its potential detrimental impacts on society. As with every other paradigm, it is dangerous to claim its supremacy, because it can soon be overtaken by a new one.

The idea of public value

The concept of *public value* enables us to answer the question whether a company adds value to society and, relatedly, what makes an organization valuable to society – not just in economic-financial terms. It takes a society's viewpoint by looking at corporations from the outside and giving voice to the general public. This means that

Table 1.1 Different management paradigms

	Shareholder value	Stake-holder value	Corporate social responsibility	Customer value	Sustainability	Shared value
Justified focus	Value for owners	Claims of interest	Side effects	Customer orientation	Long-term perspective	Societal needs as growth opportunities
Risk	Dominance of financial performance	Unmanageable integration of heterogeneous expectations	No relevance to core business	Too much focus on *satisfaction*	*Green washing*	Short-sighted economic view
Consequences	Single-minded quantitative approach	Paralysis by conflicting expectations	Loss of credibility: *alibi*	Unbalanced view of societal consequences	Lack of societal acceptance	Lack of cultural sensitivity

public value breaks with the existing notion of value creation as one that functions purely in financial terms. It includes understanding and harnessing moral, political or aesthetic value. Such an influence on values that contributes to the functioning of society is termed *public value creation.*

The creation of public value relies on an idea of the broader public, and represents mental images of community and society. This concept constructs what is *public* as the collectively shared valuation of the social collective. In this view, *the public* is not a social aggregation, but a state of mind that is influenced by organizations and their activities. This broader perspective is based on state-of-the-art ideas in psychology on basic human needs.

In this sense, value creation is based on more than a cost-benefit ratio. While seeing shareholder value as a valid measure of how efficiently capital is allocated, the new understanding of value creation assumes that every measure, of which most are essentially social, needs legitimation. As noted above, public value is "produced and reproduced in experience-intense practices" (Meynhardt, 2009, 212), and it needs some degree of affective approval to come into existence. To be clear, it does not suspend any fact-based or material properties of value creation. However, it shifts the ground towards a systematic consideration of psychological realities. In some cases it could be sufficient to develop a firm's marketing strategy, needing merely the right type of public value propositions and thereby connecting to the emotions and values of the public. In other cases, it might not be about communication only, but on a much deeper level, it could be about a need to reconfigure the product or value chain to make a more credible public value case. In either case it is perception that matters.

The idea that perception-is-reality is familiar to marketing executives, who know that value is not delivered, but only perceived. In contrast to customer value creation, public value creation focuses on contributions to what people view as "society" and its wellbeing. It relies on images and relationships which have a strong impact on corporations. In the words of the second century philosopher, Epictetus: "People are not disturbed by things, but by the view they take of them".

Even if corporations do not view responsibility for, say, social peace in a country or any political context as their core business, they evidently contribute to it. Large corporations most likely have a bigger public value footprint than small ones, but the latter play such a role as well. A societal perspective is not a nice-to-have for good times; it can be sensed and felt as an essential component. How sure are you that your customers are primarily price sensitive? How do you know which new stakeholders will emerge and claim some stake in the near future? A business needs to know this, before others force it to such awareness. In today's corporate world, there is still a long way to go before we will fully understand how management contributes as "an organ of society" (Drucker, 1973). Public value is about enquiring, anticipating and evaluating how businesses impact on attitudes people have of society. Consumers have the power to vote by keeping their wallets closed, and companies do not need to give in to customers' every whim. Also, sensitivity to the general public does not give that public primacy, but at least it shows consideration of the environment which ultimately grants the license to operate.

Public value calls for a robust value proposition that builds on a societal contribution that is boisterous even if new stakeholders appear or state regulations change. A public value proposition can be compelling enough to help a company attract and retain employees, which increasingly seek purpose and meaning in the workplace. Consider, for example, Bayer's public value proposition "Science for a better life", Whole Food's "Feed your better nature", or Nestlé's "Good food. Good life", which all go well beyond a narrow customer value perspective in actually providing public value propositions. The question is whether companies can turn their intended public value into realized public value.

Public value starts with the human condition. It is not abstract society, but concrete individuals and groups who decide what is or is not legitimate. Therefore, human needs stipulate benchmarks for corporate action. Like individuals, societies develop needs which have to be addressed if we are to survive and prosper as a social collective. However, addressing societal needs is one thing, and achieving societal impact another. Figure 1.1 represents this challenge, which holds true for every management paradigm.

Any of the paradigms mentioned above can provide a frame of reference, which could – legitimate as it may be – become an end in itself. Public value helps in overcoming the tendency to look at society through only one lens. It always involves an amalgam of utilitarian, financial, moral, political and hedonistic aspects. Whether the corporate world becomes too alienated from the main stream is a question of public value. Testing a new product or service against public value means listening to people's views on how this product or service is likely to affect social conditions and the broader society, not only the customer. A CEO addressing public value is one that actively begins to take responsibility for avoiding harm to society, and earnestly tries to build legitimacy for seeking profit. In capitalism, it is not a good idea to simply damn a shareholder value orientation, nor is it a good idea to stick to a purely financial bottom line with some sort of CSR add-on. Also not suitable would be to package value creation in some sustainability chic, or to rely only on the shared value idea of win-win situations.

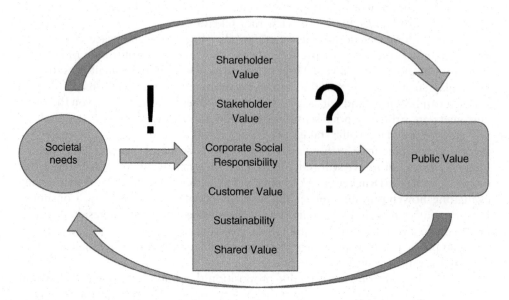

Figure 1.1 Management paradigms as the means of creating public value

At first glance, public value thinking introduces "society" as another stakeholder. It is true that for companies engaged in stakeholder dialogue, it sounds easy to extend the list of stakeholders. Public value, however concerns more; it involves all features that either affect all existing stakeholders or that cannot be deduced from a specific stakeholder interest, but concern the societal context as a whole and the external effects. The latter cannot fully be captured within a stakeholders' perspective, because it concerns the whole system.

To illustrate such a system perspective, consider a corporation intending to build new headquarters. They have to focus on the building's function and architectural structure as well as how it is embedded in a certain street and district. Attention to the neighbours' claims requires a perspective that will look at the wider impact, to answer questions such as: How will this project affect the traffic, including public transport, in the area? What are the implications for the quality of living in the neighbourhood and its attractiveness? What does this investment signal to citizens and how does it influence their trust in the business? This public dimension is complex, and almost always entails compromise and trade-offs. However, without a public value perspective, it would be almost impossible to articulate the impact of the project on society at large. Public value addresses this by calling for explicit consideration of impact that can form and transform a societal context. Such sensitivity is necessary to remain in dialogue with society, since otherwise large projects would risk being rejection despite the corporation's best intentions.

The example of building a new headquarters is similar to other significant company investments such as changing technology, or just relocating the business from one place to another. One finds simple win-win situations only very rarely. Public value helps us uncover potential pitfalls but also important societal gains.

This becomes of particular importance in today's less homogenous and more conflict-ridden societies. Public value inquiries, more than ever, concern the common ground people feel they share or accept as a matter of what they call "society at large".

You see what you measure: introducing the public value scorecard (PVSC)

Public value is what the public values. Critics often fear a "tyranny of the majority", also because the majority can change its mind from one moment to the next. The main point is that whether or not corporations listen to society, they actively build and change it. The challenge to management is one requiring awareness, measurement, and managing value in the eye of the beholder.

Recently, a range of different new measures have been developed to better understand and manage a corporation's value to society. There is no doubt about a new quest for a broader notion of *performance* in a complex world; however, how best to measure value and performance is less obvious. Whether sustainability indicators, corporate responsibility rankings, or shared value measures are the right instruments, remains unclear. All reveal an increased need to legitimate doing business in a capitalist system. Every instrument offers some narrative for doing things differently. While all these measures have good intentions, their normative premises are questionable and they share the risk of underestimating the role of the general public or "society".

Public value encompasses a complex bundle of different cultural expectations. Take banks that must adjust their credit policies or tax behaviour, to avoid heavy penalties. This could be constructed as a naïve call for banks to adhere to Western values, such as human rights. However, we call for a tailored approach that takes the cultural context seriously, by accepting that public value can be different in different parts of the world, where there is also variation in common good ideas.

How should we sustain and innovate businesses in an increasingly complex world of shared power where the voice of public opinion is becoming louder? Given current volatility, with a number of "unknown unknowns", it is not enough to rely on stakeholder dialogue to find out how best to satisfy society. There are simply too many very divergent interests at work. Besides, business needs to take risks to innovate, which naturally requires trade-off decisions from stakeholders. There is a simple and yet most challenging answer, namely: Improve how you manage your public value; listen to society and build your public value proposition.

Corporations have an impact on public value by influencing the collectively shared values related to society, the public or the community. Therefore, corporations can and should look for broader and other measures than the limited set used before. Current measures do not capture the decline of trust in corporations, nor the growing awareness that corporations create value. Where these are covered, reference is mainly to negative social and environmental impacts or externalities, or to job creation or tax payments. The public value principle allows us to analyse holistically where a corporation has added value to society and where it has destroyed it.

Following here, before describing the public value scorecard (PVSC) we briefly look at the conceptual background which guides the measurement methodology. It rests on the assumption of public value theory that public value is created if people see corporations contributing to basic need fulfilment and thereby co-creating society with its societal orders, its social cohesion and individual autonomy. This micro-macro link guides the measurement approach: *Public value* describes the value created from a societal viewpoint, while *human needs* address the fundamental psychological level in which all evaluation is rooted.

Public value reflects basic needs, and basic needs provide the psychological basis for public value. From individuals' viewpoint, corporations impact their lives in many ways, thus influencing their basic needs fulfilment. Following needs theory, four equally important dimensions can be distinguished: First, the basic need for a stable and coherent conceptual system, and for the predictability of cause and effect relationships in one's environment translate into an instrumental–utilitarian value dimension which focuses on efficiency, and on balancing effort and use. Within the PVSC logic this use value will be subdivided according to technical and financial aspects, resulting in two instrumental–utilitarian sub-dimensions. Second, the basic need for a positive self-evaluation translates into a moral–ethical value dimension, which focuses on personhood, dignity and respect. Third, the basic need for positive relationships with significant others forms the individual-level basis of a political–social value dimension which focuses on group identity, belonging and attachment. Fourth, the basic need to avoid pain and experience pleasure is reflected in a hedonistic–aesthetical value dimension which focuses on flow, fun and positive emotion (Meynhardt, 2009; 2015).

Against this background, public value has five primary drivers that make up a public value profile. Public value takes shape within the borders defined by basic needs which provide the building blocks for whatever actual public value. The following five leading questions are formulated to guide any public value inquiry regarding products or services:

1. *Is it useful? (Instrumental-utilitarian)* If a product or service really solves a problem or fulfils a customer's need, *use value* is generated in that a basic utilitarian human need is addressed. More than ever, it is a challenge to identify whether a solution solves a relevant problem from a societal perspective. The very idea of what is or is not useful has become a theme in public discourse. While products and services might efficiently solve a "problem", society could view this as decadent or a waste of resources. Even worse, imagine the consequences if society does not accept what technological progress could have discovered or engineers have developed.

2. *Is it profitable? (Instrumental-utilitarian)*: A critical contribution to society has been efficiently allocating capital. Without minimal profitability to cover future costs, a major reason for corporate survival is lost. Even so, this basic insight is not given; it needs solid legitimization from society. General mistrust of shareholder value concerns not only the amplitude of shareholder value or the balance between the short term and long term, but the very notion of shareholder value. Although a profit motif is socially constructed, people are motivated to achieve efficient cost-benefit ratios, with money to some extent signalling this.

3. *Is it decent? (Moral-ethical)*: Ethical leadership has become a critical challenge to managers. The moral dimension of management has been addressed by the CSR movement, fostering activities in line with moral standards of doing business. The decency dimension is deeply rooted in a basic human need for respect and dignity. From a public value perspective, a corporation's behaviour is decent if the general public morally accepts and appreciates such a behaviour. A sense of justice, fairness or equity is prone to be at the centre of public debate. The challenge is not only to find a balance between local requirements and global standards, but also to develop a credible and robust proposition that is aligned with society.

4. *Is it politically acceptable? (Political-social)*: Corporations know that moral standards can conflict with political boundary conditions or group interests. Power relations could favour indecent behaviour. The basic need for belonging to a social group can be even stronger than the need to adhere to moral values of justice or fairness. In a globalized economy with very different cultures and values it is increasingly important to balance own moral standards with political and social issues. Take the Swiss commodity trader GlencoreXstrata, which operates globally to efficiently meet the basic material demand for their manufacturing. The corporation is constantly challenged to interact efficiently with very different national cultures, while adhering to values and norms of its headquarter country, Switzerland.

5. *Is it a positive experience? (Hedonistic-aesthetical)*: Finding a customer's sweet spot, to know how to please him or her, to make him or her buy one's product and return, is daily business. Addressing the basic need for pleasure and fun is always a good idea to attract customers. However, to recognise the consequences and impact on values in society which relate more generally to societal values of joy, hedonism and aesthetics is a new and explicit public value challenge. Consider how Apple products can create a positive experience in terms of design, elegant simplicity and comfort. Again, it is not just an individual experience, but an active contribution to social relations in a given society, since it enables a set of collectively shared values.

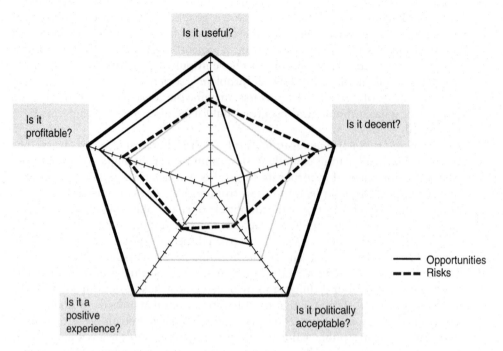

Figure 1.2 The public value scorecard

Taken together, a specific public value profile is plotted into a scorecard (Figure 1.3): The higher the opportunities compared to the risks, the higher the public value.

Figure 1.2 shows a real example of a leadership team's application of a specific scorecard version to self-assess the public value of its divestment decision (cf. Meynhardt, 2015). From a business perspective (usefulness and profitability), the opportunities (the solid line) clearly outweighed the risks (the dotted line). However, a conflict emerged between the moral-ethical dimension and the political-social one. Whereas the project was seen as bearing a moral risk, the political dimension appeared to be less risky.

There are a number of ways for coming up with a specific profile (e.g. interviews, surveys or social media listening techniques).[2] In each corporation the profile, and measures to deliver it, have to be tailored to time and circumstances. For example, the PVSC unit of analysis can be other than just a new project; it can also be a product, practice or service, or even an organization. Almost any object of evaluation can be analysed using this method. As a management tool, it supplements existing feedback mechanisms such as customer satisfaction or stakeholder dialogue. The new management information should give the public (or selected publics, or groups representing a public) an explicit voice to articulate how a corporation infuses society with value beyond its products and services.

A growing number of corporations explicitly embark on a public value proposition, and hence are exposed to society in a way that requires management attention. For instance, Google's claim "Do no evil" or Samsung's "Making a better world" signal impact well beyond an isolated customer value. Such strategic propositions require systematic measurement to prove whether or not (or to what extent) a company fulfils its commitments.

The PVSC can be used to organize societal feedback for the very first time. We do not pretend that corporations are uninformed about their stakeholders. However, time and again, we see that corporations do not explicitly engage in dialogue about their social function, unaware of their public value, and thus often surprised by it. Companies are even often unsure whether they overestimate or underestimate their public value, and try to legitimize their actions with add-on activities of CSR projects or social investments. Instead, they should first fathom their societal value and critically reflect on their business model.

If one were trying to set up a public value measure in a company, as with every new measure, one would need to ask who benefits from it (Meynhardt & Bäro, 2019). Similar to the emergence of customer satisfaction, public value measures require internal partners who use the results to improve their own daily operations. In practice, we see a number of different rationales companies offer for wanting to increase their public value.

Prevent – what we should stop doing

If a corporation performs legal practices that are widely perceived as illegitimate, it should stop these. Consider the recent vigorous public debate in the chemical industry about the ingredient bisphenol-A (BPA). In some parts of the world, it has been banned for use in baby bottles, but not in others. While scientific studies suggest it is innocuous, consumer rights activists propose that BPA is a dangerous carcinogenic substance. This has led to decreasing sales of BPA-containing plastics for food packaging. Calls from the chemical industry to stick to scientific findings have gone unheeded. In the long run, public value cannot be sustained or developed against societal norms or a stable public opinion.

Identify – what we should keep doing

It is often easier to say what is wrong and to stop bad practices than to come to terms with what characterises a company positively. To understand oneself as an "organ of society" (Drucker, 1973) is a rewarding exercise. Currently, many corporations are unaware of their public value. In this respect, they undervalue their societal contribution. For example, FC Bayern Munich, Germany's most successful football club, engaged in a project to determine its public value (Meynhardt, Strathoff, Beringer & Bernard, 2015). Winning the Champions League and two other national titles in 2013 clearly marked the beginning of a new era for the club. The management team's aspiration became to establish this club as a global player in the football industry. Research made it clear that the club could not sustainably grow against its public value. The management had to unite the seemingly paradoxical goals of strengthening the club's Bavarian roots and achieving global growth.

Explore – what we should start doing

In public value measurement exploration is the area of innovation and growth. A new business model built on a public value proposition would be most attractive. At least from an economic perspective, the shared value approach gives some hints. However, public value orientation is far more than seeking economic growth by combining business interests and societal needs. Exploring public value opportunities also involves dialogue with relevant groups, evaluation of other than economic opportunities, and – above all – it is about carefully managing trade-offs.

Consumer industries obviously gain advantage as they can combine customer value with public value, e.g. in terms of morally conscientious products. However, bearing different moralities in different places in mind, it isn't easy. The best way is to generate profit by solving a social problem, for instance providing low-cost housing or access to medicine in developing countries. However, for established industries to re-design the value chain in complex ecosystems of myriads of interactions and interdependencies, is often much more challenging. Notably, young entrepreneurs now, from the start, are founding their business models on a public value proposition which goes much further than traditional social entrepreneurship approaches. They do not necessarily start with a social challenge, but are dedicated to finding new ways of actively shaping society, e.g. by directing technological advancement directly to public value. Such start-ups intend to make a difference in providing goods and services which change our way of living together. Recently, together with the consultancy arm of Ernst & Young Ltd., we started to evaluate and award those business models by using the PVSC.[3]

In sum, in each area of approaching public value creation, a PVSC could be used to chart the risks and opportunities ahead. This methodology can then be customized to a particular management challenge. Very similar to a balanced scorecard approach, each corporation develops its own specific PVSC. Such value relativism is the only normative element of public value as it both enables and limits public value measurement.

Public value leadership

Public value does not exist automatically; it has to be created jointly, since it is a collective experience. This is an opportunity to lead.

The Leipzig Leadership Model (Kirchgeorg, Meynhardt, Pinkwart, Suchanek & Zülch, 2017) provides a major example of how public value thinking can be integrated into leadership practice. This new model makes the case that companies are better off if they build their strategy explicitly and justify activities according to a logic of value contribution which consistently connects different levels of impact from helping individuals to develop and grow, companies to perform, through to creating public value (Figure 1.3).

Given the extent of ever-changing challenges, the model puts the quest for purpose at the core of leadership. This is not an idealistic or naïve response to disruption nor an esoteric exercise to fight complexity. Rather, it calls for deeper reflection on means-ends-relationships, justifying causes and compelling ideas. In this way, it is an answer to overwhelming uncertainty, volatility or ambiguity. The model states: If complexity is the challenge, purpose is the answer. Consequently, it is a primary order leadership task to credibly attach meaning to products and services which are regarded as ones that contribute in a broader sense.

Without an attractive and compelling *why* it becomes ever more difficult to attract and retain talent. However, leaders have to answer by consistently justifying and

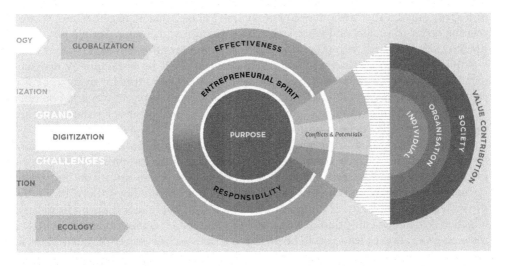

Figure 1.3 The Leipzig Leadership Model

connecting the *how* (entrepreneurial spirit, responsibility) and the *what* (effectivity) to a higher cause. In particular, in times of disruption and change systematic reflection on why we do what we do requires awareness of the multitude of values and mindsets.

It includes a profound value proposition directed at a purpose which transcends individual gain and makes itself a means to the common good. This new type of value creation is called *public value creation*. There are other sources of common good experience, but public value is defined as the one source fuelled by organizations.

Within the Leipzig Leadership Model, the notion of *public value* is used as a mechanism to legitimize what organizations do and how they do it. Public value thinking is attractive to leaders, because it provides a guiding principle, a kind of polar star, in times of increasing complexity and desperate need for orientation. This very function of providing a deeper "why", going beyond individual gains, helps people to (re)connect with their world, whether in small communities or on a global scale.

This is not merely a new version of enlightened self-interest; rather it is a call to face the complex trade-offs as well as the potential of seeing the bigger picture. On the one hand, this type of meaning is often a scarce resource, because it implies making an organization's activities instrumental to the common good. On the other hand, any public value-driven purpose comes at the price of taking responsibility and accepting limited direct influence on actual outcomes, as public value is perceived and not simply delivered.

Public value – where it takes us

Public value redefines the notion of *value creation* by taking moral, political, utilitarian and hedonistic aspects into account as equally valid components of value creation. It does not suspend the profit motive, but enquires about its legitimate cause in society and how it interacts with other values. If a corporation complains that the broader public might not be able to recognise the "real value" a business brings to the table, it should be aware that "you can only see what you know". Often a business can create or destroy public value without even knowing it. Public value management is a way of relating better to society and being open to adaptation and change. Simply put: In an open society, we need open organizations to keep the promise of liberty.

Public value is more than reputation management, CSR or sustainability management. It is also not a zeitgeist-driven management paradigm. It helps us to recognise precisely the existing social functions of a business with all its paradoxes and potential contradictions. Public value is about common good contributions or failures that are rightly or wrongly associated with a company.

Further, public value orientation is not a choice. The more the idea of purpose in the workplace enters a company's discourse, the more the public value principle becomes a lens for recognizing a corporation not just as a tradable bundle of resources, but also as a productive social system that is nurtured by society. Primarily, the increasing complexity of doing business without it being moralization in society, which makes public value thinking attractive to leaders. It remains to be seen whether the next generation of leaders will be prepared to harness the power of public value in an entrepreneurial and responsible way. We now also have first evidence that higher public value leads to higher financial performance (Bilolo, 2018). The other way around, not leading for public value, can in turn harm shareholders' interests.

Interestingly, the general public is already prepared to provide feedback. In Switzerland, for instance, we established the abovementioned orientation via a public value atlas which ranks 106 corporations, NGOs and public institutions based on responses from 14,500 people (www.gemeinwohl.ch).[4] This public value information is a new feedback currency that signals a company's standing in society, as described in the Nestlé example elaborated above.

The important question is whether a company's business model is robust enough to withstand a public value assessment. Is there a defence line for a deeper *why*? Public value is an investment in a joint future that contrasts with simply looking for interest on investment. It represents a kind of true value, while a stock price represents only a part of it. However, such "truth" is established only through people appreciating it. At least in the long run, every corporate action will have to gain legitimacy based on public value. The PVSC helps us to determine and fulfil a corporation's creative social function.

Ultimately, public value provides deeper answers to *why* questions. It allows one to operationalize the gap between what companies do and what they are actually valued for from a societal perspective. Applying the public value principle to strategy is a starting point to benefit from well-intended activities or to readjust where necessary. Opening the strategic focus to a broader understanding of value creation provides not only a bigger picture of what a company contributes to a functioning society, it also taps into personal potential to realize an individual's contribution to the common good and to grow and find purpose and meaning as an executive.

It is imperative that leaders multiply their capacity to respond to the external world they deal with, not because they want to become management philosophers, but because they want either to reduce the pain of negative public opinion or to improve their company's market position in a multi-stakeholder world with a massive gap between formal power and actual authority.

Public value challenges leaders to engage in processes of weighting, balancing or trading off different public values and inherent conflicts. In that public value is grounded in interpretation, purpose and meaning, it takes a leadership mindset to address this challenge. It transforms a leader's role towards a broader engagement in anticipating, formulating and managing their company's societal license to operate. This is not a mechanistic process; rather it is a journey in which leaders need to be aware of opportunities and limits. Although there are property rights of shareholders, we have to realize that, like a country, a social system cannot be owned. Therefore, public value leadership requires vision and passion, but also humility.

Such a public value awareness (Meynhardt & Fröhlich, 2019) probably seems obvious to many, even if odd or unfamiliar to others. Listening to society involves mindfulness, among other things, first listening to oneself and one's personal values. Sensing attractive possible futures while acknowledging actual or potential value conflicts is bound to become a critical competence for responsible leaders. It approximates the idea of an "idealistic pragmatist" (Nonaka & Takeuchi, 2011). Or, in Scott Fitzgerald's words: "The test of a first-rate intelligence is the ability to hold two opposing ideas in mind at the same time and still retain the ability to function" (1956, 69).

Notes

1 The term *public value* was coined by Mark Moore (1995) to be relevant in public administration. In my work I started to define it more widely and to transfer the concept to any type of organization (cf. Meynhardt, 2009; 2015; Meynhardt et al. 2017) and even to individuals (Meynhardt, Brieger & Hermann, 2018; Meynhardt & Fröhlich, 2019).
2 The methodological background as well the more technical part of the PVSC is outlined in Meynhardt, 2015.
3 See www.eypva.com
4 The public value atlas follows the same theoretical considerations like the PVSC. It is also available for Germany (www.gemeinwohlatlas.de).

References

Bilolo, C. (2018). *Legitimacy, Public Value, & Capital Allocation*, London: Routledge.

Bulcke, P. (2014). Wir müssen uns vom Streben nach kurzfristigem Gewinn verabschieden, *Neue Zürcher Zeitung*, 2, 3 October.

Drucker, P.F. (1973). *Management: Tasks, Responsibilities, Practices*. New York, NY: HarperBusiness Edition.

Fink, L. (2018). *A Sense of Purpose, Larry Fink's annual letter to CEO*. Available online at www.blackrock.com/corporate/en-no/investor-relations/larry-fink-ceo-letter

Fitzgerald, F.S. (1956). *The Crack-Up*. New York: New Directions.

Friedman, M. (1970). The Social Responsibility of Business is to make profit. *New York Times Magazine*, 13.

Kirchgeorg, M., Meynhardt, T., Pinkwart, A., Suchanek, A., & Zülch, H. (2017). *Das Leipziger Führungsmodell: The Leipzig Leadership Model*, 2nd edition. BoD – Books on Demand.

Meynhardt, T. (2009). Public value inside: What is public value creation? *International Journal of Public Administration*, 32(3), 192–219.

Meynhardt, T. (2015). Public Value: Turning a Conceptual Framework into a Scorecard. In Bryson, J.M., Crosby, B., & Bloomberg, L. (Eds), *Public Value and Public Administration*. Washington, DC: Georgetown University Press, 147–169.

Meynhardt, T., & Bäro, A. (2019). Public Value Reporting: Adding value to (non-) financial reporting, In Lindgreen, A., Koenig-Lewis, N. Kitchener, M., Brewer, J., Moore, M.,

& Meynhardt, T. (Eds), *Public Value – Deepening, Enriching, and Broadening the Theory and Practice* (pp. 87–108). London: Routledge.

Meynhardt, T., & Fröhlich, A. (2019). More Value Awareness for More (Public) Value: Recognizing how and for whom value is truly created. In Lindgreen, A., Koenig-Lewis, N. Kitchener, M., Brewer, J., Moore, M., & Meynhardt, T. (Eds), *Public Value – Deepening, Enriching, and Broadening the Theory and Practice* (pp. 23–39). London: Routledge.

Meynhardt, T., & Gomez, P. (2016). Building Blocks for Alternative Four-Dimensional Pyramids of Corporate Social Responsibilities. *Business & Society*, 0007650316650444.

Meynhardt, T., Brieger, St. A., & Hermann, C. (2018). Organizational public value and employee life satisfaction: the mediating roles of work engagement and organizational citizenship behavior. *The International Journal of Human Resource Management*. doi 10.1080/09585192.2017.1416653

Meynhardt, T., Chandler, J.D., & Strathoff, P. (2016). Systemic principles of value co-creation: Synergetics of value and service ecosystems. *Journal of Business Research*, 69(8), 2981–2989.

Meynhardt, T., Strathoff, P., Beringer, L., & Bernard, S. (2015). *FC Bayern Munich: Creating Public Value Between Local Embeddedness and Global Growth*. The Case Centre.

Meynhardt, T., Brieger, S.A., Strathoff, P., Anderer, S., Bäro, A., Hermann, C., Kollat, J., Neumann, P., Bartholomes, S., & Gomez, P. (2017). Public value performance: What does it mean to create value in the public sector? In R. Andessner, D. Greiling, and R. Vogel (Eds), *Public Sector Management in a Globalized World*, 135–160. Wiesbaden, Germany: Springer Gabler.

Moore, M.H. (1995). *Creating Public Value: Strategic Management in Government*. Cambridge, MA: Harvard University Press.

Nonaka, I., & Takeuchi, H. (2011). The wise leader. *Harvard Business Review*, 89(5), 58–67.

Porter, M.E., & Kramer, M.R. (2011). Creating shared value. *Harvard Business Review*, 89 (1–2), 62–77.

Welch, J. (2009). Interview, *Financial Times*, 12 March.

2 More value awareness for more (public) value

Recognizing *how* and *for whom* value is truly created

Timo Meynhardt and Andreas Fröhlich

Introduction

How individuals and organizations experience the world and interact in it has changed in (post)modern society (Habermas, 1988; Selznick, 1994) in a way that challenges our mental abilities. Due to a range of matters, such as information overload (van Knippenberg, Dahlander, Haas & George, 2015), excessive "freedom, autonomy, and self-determination" (Schwartz, 2000, 79), a multi-directional and enlarged dependency on an interconnected society and how we influence it (e.g. Scholte, 2005; Coleman, 1999), we face the increasing risk of making evaluations and using value concepts and facts detached from *how* and *for whom* value is truly created. This leads to sub-optimal decisions, lack of orientation and perhaps even to (public) value destruction.

As a solution, we ought to reconsider *how* and *for whom* value is truly created on a fundamental, psychological level and thereby acknowledge humans as the ultimate arbiters of value. This requires revisiting existing concepts of (public) value from a psychological perspective, but also exploring the role of these value concepts in actual evaluation processes. In particular, the competence to recognize how and for whom value is truly created (termed "value awareness") needs to be defined and investigated. This endeavour could help deal with the challenges of (post)modern society, lead to improved evaluations, and ultimately, to decisions that create more value for those making decisions, those impacted by decisions and society at large.

A psychological perspective on (public) value and value awareness would also address calls for investigating micro-foundations in management, and strategy in general (Barney & Felin, 2013), as well as micro-foundations of value in particular (Aguinis & Glavas, 2012). Whereas a macro-foundation relates to collective properties of value, we focus on the individuals enacting it while they perceive and evaluate, interpret and reason in order to make sense and construct their psychological reality.

Such a perspective would also follow the idea of offering a modern, "co-productive view" on value, "alternative to the views on value which we have inherited from the industrial era" (Ramirez, 1999, 61). Further, it would address a need for defining and applying awareness constructs more broadly than is commonly done (Gomez & Meynhardt, 2012; Tenbrunsel & Smith-Crowe, 2008) and contribute to the understanding of competences (Boyatzis, 2008) linked to (public) value creation.

Our objective therefore is to elaborate on a micro-foundation of (public) value that is rooted in human psychology and to explore value awareness as a competence linked to (public) value creation. Firstly, we use public value theory to define *value* as the result of human subjective psychological evaluation against basic values and to explain how value is truly created. Secondly, we use social cognition and human development theory to introduce the concept of *personal frames of reference* that serve to explain for whom value is truly created. We combine these dimensions to form a (public) value matrix that structures the value categories that form the basis of any evaluation. Analogies to moral sensitivity research help us understand the role these categories play in evaluation processes through defining the constructs *value emphasis* and *value awareness* and their links to (public) value creation. Finally, implications for research and practice are discussed and the limitations of the study are explicated.

Theory development

How *is value truly created? Value as the result of subjective psychological evaluation against basic values*

If one accepts a humanistic worldview, humans have to be acknowledged as the final arbiters of value creation. "True value" is then created only through direct human appreciation. Following this idea, Meynhardt (2009; 2015), in his theory of public value, and referring to Heyde (1926), analysed the concept of *value* from a philosophical and psychological perspective. In this endeavour, *value* is defined as the result of a psychological evaluation of an object by a subject against a basis of evaluation. In this line of thinking, *value* defines and expresses the quality of the relationship between subject and object.

The basis of evaluation is composed of the emotional-motivational forces that initiate an evaluation in a subject's mind. This basis, Meynhardt (2009) proposes, is structured by the four non-hierarchical basic needs of humans identified by Seymour Epstein (2003) in his cognitive-experiential self-theory which resulted from a comprehensive synthesis of research and theory on human needs. Basic needs thus constitute the basis of evaluation and form basic value categories, namely the moral-ethical, the hedonistic-aesthetical, the utilitarian-instrumental and the political-social categories.

Any object "has value" for a subject if it impacts directly or indirectly on these basic value categories. The more stable the value of an object is, the more it relates to "values" in the traditional sense of stable preferences (Graumann & Willig, 1983). Importantly, all emotional-motivational forces, and the basic value categories themselves, can be seen as valued objects and thus, provided there is some stability as order parameter (Meynhardt, 2015), they translate into values in this traditional sense. According to this logic, basic value categories can be regarded as the "basic values" of a subject. Going forward, we will adhere to this terminology and assume that basic values (BVs) constitute the basis of evaluation. Table 2.1 provides an overview of the relation between basic needs and BVs.

As mentioned, in theory the BVs are non-hierarchical (Meynhardt, 2009). Humans differ regarding the emphasis they put on different BVs, and even in individuals the levels of importance assigned to different BVs can vary depending on the object being evaluated and the situational context of space and time in which the evaluating individual finds him/herself. In Epstein's own words, "[w]hich function, if any, is dominant varies among individuals and within individuals over time" (Epstein, 1989, 8).

Table 2.1 Relation between basic needs and basic values

Basic need for . . .	Translation into a motivation for . . . (Examples)	Basic value
positive self-evaluation	positive self-concept and self-worth consistent relationship between self and environment feeling of high self-esteem (in social comparison)	moral-ethical
maximizing pleasure and avoiding pain	positive emotions and avoidance of negative feelings flow experience experience of self-efficacy due to action	hedonistic-aesthetical
gaining control and coherence over one's conceptual system	understanding and controlling environment predictability of cause and effect relationships ability to control expectations to cause desired outcomes	utilitarian-instrumental
positive relationships	relatedness and belongingness attachment, group identity optimal balance between intimacy and distance	political-social

Adapted from Meynhardt, 2009, 203

The existence of these BVs has already been put to an empirical test. An examination of public organizations suggests that at least three of the four basic values can be distinguished (Meynhardt & Bartholomes, 2011).

Moreover, according to this view, value is primarily subjective; objectivity of a value arises only when multiple individuals share similar valuations. Objectivity is thus still "bound to subjects" (Meynhardt, 2009, 199). This is in line with a "co-productive view" of value, according to which value creation is "synchronic and interactive, not linear and transitive" and "[v]alue is not simply 'added,' but is mutually 'created' and 're-created' among actors with different values" (Ramirez, 1999, 50).

Importantly, Meynhardt (2009) originally derived his definition of value in the context of public value theory, with a rather narrow definition of "the public" as referring to a larger society. However, we believe that Meynhardt's idea of recognizing humans and their BVs as the ultimate arbiters of value creation is relevant beyond a holistic societal context. As Meynhardt and Bartholomes (2011, 288) stated, value "is created or destroyed in all spheres of life". Especially in a world that is facing high availability of information and options, also confronted with multiple proxies of value reflected in numbers or other concepts, a focus on what is truly valuable may help any agent (be it an individual or an organization) make better evaluations and create true value through impacting on our BVs. Meynhardt (2009, 209) himself argued that "delivering 'facts' is not an undisputable value per se" and in a world where there are too many (potentially false) facts, focusing on the actual, psychological value could provide the orientation that many individuals and organizations are lacking.

Based on these considerations, we argue for extending Meynhardt's (2009; 2015) public value theory to all spheres and contexts within society, including the individual, private surroundings, organization and community. By building on Meynhardt's first two propositions (2009, 199, 202) we arrive at the following first proposition of a more generalized theory of value as rooted in basic values:

Proposition 1: Value is the result of an evaluation of an object by a subject against four non-hierarchical, interrelated, but not substitutable basic values (BVs), namely the moral-ethical, the hedonistic-aesthetical, the utilitarian-instrumental and the political-social values. Value is created for a subject if the subject's BVs are positively impacted (i.e. its basic needs are fulfilled) and value is destroyed for a subject, if its BVs are negatively impacted (i.e. the fulfilment of basic needs is reduced or inhibited) by the evaluated object. Value is bound to subjects and can be "objectified" by being shared across multiple subjects.

For whom *is value truly created? Personal frames of reference as a fundamental second dimension of the basis of evaluation*

Research in social cognition and human development (e.g., Fiske, 1995; Fiske & Taylor, 1991; Kegan, 1982, 1995; Kohlberg, 1984) suggests that humans do not merely evaluate objects *for themselves*. In fact, other "[p]eople are the single most important parts of our worlds" and "[b]ecause so much of our lives depends on other people, we have developed many strategies for thinking about them" (Fiske, 1995, 152). As Schutz and Luckmann (1973, 74) put it: "My experiences of things and events [. . .] contain references to the social world – to the world of my contemporaries and my forefathers. I can always interpret them as proofs of the conscious life of other beings". In other words, assuming the perspective of others in making sense of the world, is a critical human characteristic (Kegan, 1982).

Most explicitly in our professional lives, value is often seen as something one should maximize *for others*. It is represented in constructs like *customer value, stakeholder value* or *shareholder value*. Beyond that, humans do think of and take into account the perspective of others, even in situations where there is no imperative to do so. Even through the eyes of a single subject, *value* cannot exist without defining "*for whom?*"

But how are ideas of ourselves, other individuals or groups exactly involved in our evaluations? Research suggests that any individual or group involved in the evaluation of a subject functions like a *personal "frame of reference"* (Schutz & Luckmann, 1973). This personal frame of reference is a "concept" (Fiske & Taylor, 1991, 98) in the subject's mind that can, for example, refer purely to the subject's self, i.e. the subject's "self-concept" (Baumeister, 1995, 53), the subject's family, the subject's organization, the subject's community, or society as a whole.

In this sense, value is created by an object in the mind of a subject, if the object is positively evaluated against the personal frame of reference (PF) and the associated values involved in the evaluation of the subject. Technically speaking, as the basis of evaluation *values* are then not directly bound to subjects, but are bound to PFs that represent concepts that the subject has of itself and others. One example for this way of thinking is the idea to define an individual's self-concept as a frame of reference of social cognition (Orlik, 1979). Obviously, a subject can have multiple PFs and more than one can be involved in the evaluation of an object at the same time.

In the previous section we identified BVs as a structural dimension of the basis of evaluation. PFs now can be understood as a second dimension in structuring this basis. BVs are used to structure *how* value is created, while PFs structure *for whom* it is created. Based on this, we articulate our second proposal as:

Proposition 2: Value is also the result of an evaluation of an object by a subject against the subject's personal frames of reference (PFs), which represent the subject's concepts of itself or any other concrete or abstract individual or group "for whom" an object is evaluated. Each personal frame of reference represents a part of the basis of evaluation. Therefore, besides the four BVs, the PFs serve as a second dimension to structure this basis.

Categorizing personal frames of reference

How many PFs are there and how can they be categorized? Schutz & Luckmann provided a structure for the social world as experienced by a subject, which can serve as a basis for categorizing the PFs. They make an important distinction between a subject's immediate experiences, i.e. with other people in the here and now, and mediated experiences based on "derived typifications", i.e. on mental concepts of others based on the subject's prior experience and "stock of knowledge" (Schutz & Luckmann, 1973, 74). Thus, evaluations can rely on both experiences and concepts, and PFs as concepts can be actualized through immediate experiences of a subject. We will therefore treat each PF as a concept, a "type" or a "representation" (Schutz & Luckmann, 1973, 76) that is composed of invariable attributes ascribed by the subject, but that can be constantly actualized through immediate experiences that can also be a part of the evaluation.

The second important distinction Schutz and Luckmann (1973) make refers to the PF's level of anonymity which is determined by the generality of the subject's knowledge of the PF attributes, or in our words, the PF's *degree of publicness*. A PF directly inferred from a former (or actual) experience of a concrete individual or group represents low anonymity, or low publicness. PFs derived from "generalizations of social reality", e.g. PFs representing social collectives such as "the state" that cannot be experienced immediately, represent high anonymity, or high publicness. One can see that PFs "are not in themselves secluded, isolated schemata of meaning but are rather bound to and built upon one another" (Schutz & Luckmann, 1973, 81). This means that more public (or anonymous) PFs can contain less public (or less anonymous) PFs. For example, "the state" can contain certain other PFs representing individuals or groups that belong to "the state".

From the above a structure for PFs can be extracted, starting with the least anonymous or least public frame (the self) through to the most anonymous or most public frame (society). Between these two frames there are more or less public others, representing individuals or groups of humans, such as a person's spouse, family or organization.

Human development psychology suggests that PFs are involved in all experiences and evaluations, often on an unconscious level. It also suggests that people often differ in terms of which PFs they apply and can recognize (Kegan, 1982; 1995; Kohlberg, 1984). Consequently, in an evaluation, subjects can end up maximizing value for one PF, while destroying value for others, often without even knowing it. This becomes even more relevant in an interconnected society when individuals and organizations increasingly influence and depend on other individuals and groups of humans and on society as whole.

Combining the insights of Schutz and Luckmann (1973), Kohlberg (1984) and Kegan (1982; 1995) we suggest the following categorization of PFs:

- *The self*, representing a self-concept separate from other humans, and composed of (constantly actualized) concepts of one's own needs, ideologies and other attributes.

- *Others*, representing concepts of individuals or groups of humans with whom the subject has a relationship, to which he/she may or may not belong, and that vary according to degrees of publicness or anonymity. This PF is obviously a composite of many different PFs, so that any meaningful evaluation analysis probably requires further differentiation or selection depending on the context of the evaluation. As a starting point, we can differentiate the most typical relationships in which an individual finds him/herself, as in

  - *private surroundings*, representing *others* in a private context,
  - *an organization*, representing *others* in a professional context,
  - *a community*, representing *others* in a public context.

- *Society*, representing a concept of the most *generalized other*, which is an "operational fiction of society" (Meynhardt, 2009: 212) and a universal community of distinct "value-originating, system-generating, history-making" identities (Kegan, 1982, 104–105).

We suggest using the above-mentioned PFs as five categories to structure the second dimension of the basis of evaluation. As indicated above, within each PF one can differentiate more fine-grained PFs. For example, one could identify various frames within an organization, such as an individual's work group, the department to which he/she is assigned and the organization as a whole. Also, depending on the context and, e.g. the purpose of the empirical inquiry, certain PFs can be added or removed. For our purposes, the delineation into five PFs seems to be a sufficient starting point.

Importantly, while human development theory would associate different PFs with different stages in development, we need to emphasize that human development is seen as a dynamic process in which people do not systematically proceed from one stage to another, but regularly face a struggle between conflicting contexts associated with different stages (Kegan, 1982). In view of this argument, it is important to add that we consider the fact *that* humans *differ* in terms of which PFs they apply or can recognize to be more important than *how* these differences are linked to the development of humans. Based on these deliberations, we articulate our third proposition:

> Proposition 3: Building on social cognition and human development theory, five major personal frames of reference can be distinguished, namely the self, the private surroundings, the organization, the community, and society. Humans differ regarding the personal frames of reference they emphasize in their evaluations and their competence to recognize them.

Combining basic values and personal frames of reference: value categories and the public value matrix

We have elaborated on the idea of recognizing humans as the highest arbiters of value creation to identify *how* and *for whom* an object is truly of value. We therefore attempted to answer both questions in a manner that reflects human nature in the best possible way, drawing on multiple streams of research. We attempted to answer the *how* question by anchoring value in BVs of humans, and the *for whom* question by introducing PFs as concepts that humans apply to make sense of the social world. These two dimensions structure the basis of evaluation into different *value categories*, each of which can be more or less *relevant* in evaluation processes.

Schutz (1974, 350) considered the problem of relevance to be of central importance in the social sciences, i.e. the question as to why the human mind selects or regards as *relevant*, certain elements of human experience rather than others. Through consciously inquiring into our "relevance systems" or "relevance structures" we determine "whether something 'really matters' to us" (Schutz & Luckmann, 1973, 182). The *value categories* can therefore also be seen as components of the relevance system that people apply in evaluation.

The value categories can be best illustrated by combining PFs and BVs in a matrix, as illustrated in Figure 2.1, which we call the *(public) value matrix*.

The (public) value matrix' fields illustrate the *value categories* representing a structure, or an aggregate of the basis of evaluation of humans. According to the theory presented above, any psychological evaluation process will involve one or more of these value categories. When more than one category is involved, there will be some weighting and negotiation to arrive at a final evaluation result. For example, a moral-ethical evaluation related to the self may conflict with a utilitarian-instrumental evaluation related to society and result in different evaluations depending on the particular emphasis the subject puts on the respective fields. Even within a given value category, micro-evaluations between different emotional-motivational forces or values can take place. For example, within the utilitarian-instrumental dimension of the self, a person can value "pleasure" and "health" that could lead to conflicting evaluations of certain objects.

In constructing this matrix, we deliberately combined the two dimensions in an orthogonal way, assuming independence for analytical purposes, and to serve a theoretical derivation of constructs as set out in the following section. We are aware that the exact relationship (and potential dependences) between the two dimensions still needs to be empirically tested and verified.

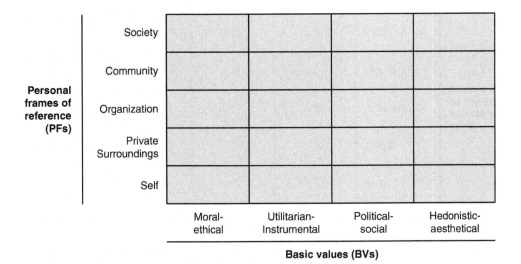

Figure 2.1 The (public) value matrix

The role of value categories in evaluations: value emphasis

Our conceptual considerations have already suggested that humans differ in terms of which value categories they apply in evaluation and also how they apply them. This means that any evaluation can involve negotiation of various sub-evaluations between and within the value categories. As a part of this evaluation, every emotional-motivational force, every BV, every PF and consequently every value category, will have a different relative weighting or level of importance between 0 and 100 per cent, while the sum of all weightings adds up to 100%. This is what we have termed a value category's *value emphasis*. In the language of Schutz and Luckmann (1973), value emphasis describes the composition of the relevance system that a person applies in an evaluation and the extent to which certain components (or sub-systems) are more or less relevant in the overall evaluation (or in an aggregated relevance system).

One can imagine extreme cases where a single value category is given a 100% emphasis and all the other categories get 0%, but in most cases there will be some disbursement. A (public) value matrix with an indication of each value category's emphasis illustrates, in our terms, a person's *value emphasis profile*. Figure 2.2 illustrates a possible value emphasis profile. Of course, as mentioned earlier, the profile could vary not only between different persons, but also within a single person. However, our consideration of human development suggests that within a given time-frame a particular person can show some stability. Also, some typical profiles could be evident, depending on demographics or other variables. Based on this, we suggest a fourth proposition:

> Proposition 4: Value emphasis refers to the relative importance (between 0 and 100%) a subject consciously or unconsciously places on a certain value category in the (public) value matrix as part of an evaluation. The illustrated (public) value matrix with an indication of the emphasis a subject puts on each value category is called the subject's value emphasis profile.

Personal frames of reference (PFs)		Moral-ethical	Utilitarian-Instrumental	Political-social	Hedonistic-aesthetical
	Public	5%	10%	0%	5%
	Community	5%	5%	5%	5%
	Organization	2%	3%	0%	2%
	Family	3%	2%	10%	3%
	Self	10%	5%	15%	5%

Basic values (BVs)

Figure 2.2 Illustrative value emphasis profile

Value awareness

The considerations so far have suggested that humans not only differ in terms of which value category they emphasize, but also in terms of the category of which they are aware during evaluation. We suggest this competence be termed *value awareness*.

In an attempt to define *value awareness* more clearly, established research in the moral awareness domain (Miller, Rodgers, & Bingham, 2014; Rest, 1986; Tenbrunsel & Smith-Crowe, 2008) serves as an anchor point.

Analogic to Butterfield, Trevin, and Weaver's (2000) definition of "[c]ognitive perspective taking" (Miller, Rodgers, & Bingham, 2014), *value awareness* can be defined as a subject's competence to recognize that an object could impact certain value categories, or alternatively, as a subject's competence to recognize that a value category is relevant in an evaluation. In this sense, the level of value awareness reflects the configuration of a *higher-order* relevance system, integrating multiple value categories.

Importantly, research on moral reasoning processes suggests that intuitive, unconscious processes also play a role in our evaluations, even if they are only consciously recognized in processes of "post hoc reasoning" (Haidt, 2001, 818). Therefore, value awareness does not necessarily require conscious recognition of a value category at the moment of evaluation; recognition could also occur afterwards.

Notably, our definition of *value awareness* is closer to James Rest's (1986) original, rather broad definition of *moral awareness*, than any more recent definitions. This observation agrees with Tenbrunsel and Smith-Crowe's (2008, 555) conclusion that "Rest assumed a much broader interpretation of moral awareness than do the studies that have followed". According to them, "[t]hese studies assume that for decision makers to be morally aware, they must perceive the decision as a moral one". Nowadays, "[m]oral awareness is most often measured by directly asking participants whether an issue presents an ethical dilemma, thus introducing the possibility of a moral dimension that might not have been perceived had the question not been asked" (Tenbrunsel & Smith-Crowe, 2008, 556), which seems not to be what Rest intended. Consequently, Tenbrunsel and Smith-Crowe (2008, 584) call for a broader understanding of the perspective of the decision maker, arguing that the "decision frame" through which a subject perceives a situation, is not necessarily an ethical one, but can also be, e.g., a business frame or a legal frame. Our definition of value awareness can therefore be seen as a way of involving different "decision frames" through which a subject can perceive a situation. Thus our definition is a response to the claim of Tenbrunsel and Smith-Crowe (2008) to broaden the definition of moral awareness and get closer to Rest's original definition. Nevertheless, our construct also goes beyond their claim, as it allows for involving multiple "frames" in an evaluation at the same time, and deals with categorizing and recognizing these frames. Additionally, value awareness is not restricted to ethical or general decision situations, but plays a role in any evaluation of any object.

Further, our consideration of awareness also agrees with Gomez and Meynhardt's (2012) argument in their study of cognitive styles in top management, where they identified a lack of breadth in moral awareness research. They argued that "research should move from a focus on moral awareness to value awareness in a very broad sense" (Gomez & Meynhardt, 2012, 83). "If one accepts that, besides moral values,

Personal frames of reference (PFs)	Moral-ethical	Utilitarian-Instrumental	Political-social	Hedonistic-aesthetical
Public	36%	0%	44%	86%
Community	69%	50%	70%	22%
Organization	83%	10%	0%	86%
Family	33%	50%	47%	46%
Self	57%	30%	67%	61%

Basic values (BVs)

Figure 2.3 Illustrative value awareness profile

there are others such as political, utilitarian or hedonistic values, one must drastically enlarge the scope of enquiry" (Gomez & Meynhardt, 2012, 88). Furthermore, their analysis of self-reported data from Germany and Switzerland empirically supports the idea that individuals differ in their awareness levels (expressed in terms of cognitive styles), in the sense that certain individuals can hold multiple perspectives (or consider multiple value categories) at the same time, while others can't.

While a measure for value emphasis was described in relative terms, value awareness is better defined in absolute terms, as it is not restricted by a maximum total. Therefore, one can imagine a subject being "fully unaware" of a value category as never considering this category during evaluation (awareness thus 0%), and a subject being "fully aware" as always considering this category (awareness thus 100%), with the various awareness levels being independent of those for other categories. The illustrated matrix with all value awareness levels of a subject added to the fields, can be referred to as the subject's value awareness profile. This brings us to our fifth proposition:

> Proposition 5: Value awareness refers to a subject's competence to recognize (during or after evaluation) that a value category, i.e. a field in the (public) value matrix, could be (or was) relevant in the evaluation of an object. It can be described on an absolute scale for each value category, ranging from 0% (fully unaware) to 100% (fully aware). The illustrated (public) value matrix with an indication of the value awareness level of a subject in each value category is termed the subject's value awareness profile.

More value awareness for more (public) value: linking it all together

So how does this all come together? A subject's partially conscious, partially unconscious value emphasis per definition directly influences the result of his/her evaluation, as the value categories count toward the total value based on their emphasis. This means that categories which are not emphasized do not count to the total value, regardless of whether they would increase or decrease it. Categories that are emphasized do count toward the total value, again, regardless of whether they would increase or decrease it. Since our theory does not prescribe certain emphasis profiles, the subject, in principle, completely determines which categories are emphasized and which not.

However, what if a subject doesn't even recognize that an object could impact a value category? In other words, what if a subject has no awareness of a value category? Then the subject either emphasizes the category without being aware of it, or does not emphasize the category, also without being aware of it. In both cases, value is created or destroyed beyond the subject's control (i.e. as an unconscious choice). Unaware subjects can thus be seen as *slaves to their own unawareness*, dominated by their own unconscious evaluation processes. Subjects are free to emphasize what matters to them, and consequently to maximize value, only through developing their awareness.

Moreover, maximizing value goes beyond creating value for subjects themselves, due to the involvement of PFs. Being unaware of any *other* or *society* as a PF potentially eliminates possible sources of value for other individuals and for the larger society as well, i.e. it eliminates sources of public value creation. Of course, awareness may not necessarily lead to more emphasis, as a subject could still, for certain reasons or affections, or due to trade-offs, emphasize other value categories. Moreover, true value creation for others would have many more prerequisites, such as that others have to share the evaluation of the subject who performs an action or decision.

Nevertheless, awareness at least *gives us the right choice*. Assuming that humans have an interest in maximizing value, we can assume that they would be inclined specifically to emphasize a value category if, ceteris paribus, it increases value.

Value awareness essentially means being able to assume a meta-perspective on one's value categories and as such to recognize the relevance systems one applies, or could apply. The more relevance systems humans can recognize, the more they can consciously emphasize. So, value awareness provides a new degree of freedom in human evaluation, by broadening our horizon, or expanding our aggregated relevance system by more BVs and more PFs. With more value awareness, humans could be better equipped to meet the demands of (post)modern society as they increase their cognitive complexity to find, emphasize and consequently create true value for themselves, others and society as whole. This leads to the following, final, proposition:

> Proposition 6: Increased value awareness increases the chance of (public) value creation for active subjects (those making a decision or performing an action) and passive subjects (those impacted by the decision or the action). Thus, it is worthwhile to examine the levels of value awareness humans have, how they relate to (public) value creation and how we can influence them.

Discussion

Theoretical considerations

As this paper shows, a micro-foundation of (public) value provides a basis for understanding the processes, antecedents and consequences of (public) value creation.

Obviously, there is much to be learnt from established research in psychology (e.g., Baumeister, 1995; Fiske & Taylor, 1991; Kegan, 1982, 1995; Kohlberg, 1984; Schutz & Luckmann, 1973). This concerns especially which mental constructs are involved in evaluation processes related to public value, and how they are involved.

This work contributes to providing a micro-foundation of public value in two main ways: First, with the (public) value matrix, it provides a structured, comprehensive framework of mental (public) value categories by distinguishing not only basic values, but also personal frames of reference as fundamental dimensions of the basis of evaluation. Through the (public) value matrix, all traditional value concepts related to individuals or groups of humans, as well as public value concepts in particular, can and have to be seen in a new light. If one accepts that humans are the highest arbiters of value creation, one cannot but consider how "true value" is created. Comparatively, all other value concepts seem shallow and empty. The exact categories, as well as the dimensions of a psychological basis of evaluation can vary and need to be refined using empirical methods. Even so, before empirical confirmation, we believe it likely that they will address the questions of "how" and "for whom" true value is created on a psychological level.

Second, through defining value awareness and value emphasis, this chapter not only sheds light on the role of value categories in the evaluation process, but also introduces critical antecedents for public value creation, related to motives and competences of individuals. Public value now is something a subject is "able to think about" and that it can "desire". In that, this contribution sheds a new light on how public value as the operationalized common good can function as a regulative idea for individuals (Meynhardt, 2009). This opens up new research areas related to psychological processes (such as decisions or actions) involved in public value creation. Beyond that, the existence of different levels of value awareness and value emphasis could also have implications for public value measurement. A more accurate assessment of public value is possible if we consider the levels of emphasis and awareness of subjects.

On a more general level, these contributions help address calls for developing and refining concepts and typologies as a basis for finding common ground in the "new approach" to public administration (Bryson, Crosby, & Bloomberg, 2014, 445).

Apart from these contributions in the public value domain, there are also implications for other research areas. Firstly, through relating human development theory to public value and social cognition theory, we are able to substantiate the notion that different PFs are applied depending on a person's stage of development. Especially, the establishment of *society* as the highest, most generalized PF serves to connect the research areas of human development, social cognition and public value. Secondly, as indicated earlier, by addressing claims for a more generalized, comprehensive definition of awareness than the ones commonly in use (Gomez & Meynhardt, 2012; Tenbrunsel & Smith-Crowe, 2008), we have affected the moral awareness and moral decision making domains.

Practical implications

Our consideration of value as rooted in human psychology offers a new, broader perspective on value concepts not only in theory, but also in practice. Traditional, predominantly financial value concepts can be challenged regarding the extent to which they help create true psychological value for individuals, groups, organizations, and society as a whole. Potentially, new, non-financial concepts can emerge. The (public) value matrix could serve to explore how and for whom individuals and organizations truly create or destroy (public) value, which would have important implications for individuals and organizations.

For individuals, the public value matrix and methods based on it, could serve to facilitate decision making, self-reflection and personal development. Individuals could discover new sources of value and/or change their priorities regarding what to focus on. For instance, self-centred individuals can realize what the effects of their actions are in wider contexts and in society as a whole, whereas individuals identified with a certain context could realize how dependent they are and focus more on other contexts and on needs that are purely their own. Individuals with an instrumental focus, who live their lives as means to an end, could discover the moral dimension of their actions or the hedonistic value of the present moment, whereas hedonists might recognize the value of goal-orientation. Generally speaking, they could find more meaning and purpose, and achieve more happiness in their lives.

Organizations could realize similar benefits. For example, employees and managers could find more meaning in their work and create more value for their organizations and society, or customers could be better equipped to make meaningful buying decisions. An increased focus on how and for whom value is truly created could lead to faster decision making, better performance, higher stakeholder satisfaction, or an increased contribution to social welfare or public value in general. If relations like these were validated, the concept could find its way into organizational practice – e.g. through scorecards (Meynhardt, 2015) or other decision making tools – and complement existing instruments.

Further, if just a few of the relations above could be validated, new approaches in e.g. training, development, recruiting, communications or marketing can emerge to help individuals and organizations achieve higher levels of value awareness, and consequently create more (public) value. For instance, one could think of public value awareness training where people learn how to become more aware and to apply different value categories in evaluation. Communications and marketing departments can address certain value categories to make their products and services even more valuable to stakeholders and to their own employees. Of course, companies could also reflect seriously on what awareness and emphasis profiles they would want in new recruits, especially for top positions both in the private and the public sector. In a world where individuals and organizations face increased mental demands, the competence to deal with such demands and to focus on true value creation could prove to be one of the most critical success factors of our time.

Limitations and further research

As with any work, this study has a number of limitations that can point to areas for further research. Firstly, as with other conceptual work, our contribution here remains to be tested empirically. Our theory contains several constructs and relationships that still need to be validated. As a first step, the *value categories* as well as the constructs *value emphasis* and *value awareness* have to be validated. Here one could start with simple self-reports of subjects and traditional questionnaire techniques. To address the limits of these techniques, situational judgment tests, implicit association tests and other more creative approaches can provide further insight. The second step would be to validate the link between value awareness/emphasis and (public) value creation. One could think of assessing (public) value creation as such through techniques similar to the ones applied in measuring awareness. However, value creation (or certain elements of it) can also be approximated by other established constructs, such as individual or collective performance, individual or collective happiness, social welfare, public value, etc. A correlation analysis could allow one to derive the most desirable value awareness profiles in the sense that they are antecedent to (public) value creation. Such profiles are likely to trigger the search for ways to increase value awareness of individuals and organizations.

Further, even though we attempted to consider established criteria of good theory (e.g. Bacharach, 1989) and especially, construct clarity (Suddaby, 2010), our theory is subject to certain other limitations beyond the need for empirical validation.

Firstly, combining various research areas carries the risk of too much breadth and too little depth in dealing with each area separately. We selected established theories and constructs within each area and attempted to combine them meaningfully, but did not consider a number of other potentially relevant theories in each area. This calls for a more thorough review of other available theories and constructs to substantiate, add to, or challenge the theory presented above.

Second, we focused primarily on the positive effects of value awareness. While we are confident that these effects will dominate on an aggregate level, we have to acknowledge that psychology also suggests negative effects of value awareness. Value awareness is strongly connected to fundamental processes concerning and constituting an individual's self and identity. These processes are complex and cannot be reduced to purely rational and predictable optimization processes (Baumeister, 1995). As such, depending on the state and context in which an individual finds him/herself, it is easy to visualize potentially negative effects of value awareness. On an individual level, for instance, humans naturally attempt to sustain their self-conceptions (Baumeister, 1995; Swann, 1987). An individual's increased understanding of these conceptions can reveal inconsistencies or deficits that constitute additional mental demands for the individual, potentially resulting in biased evaluations, sub-optimal decisions, procrastination, lowered self-esteem, identity crises and related outcomes. Alongside the need for empirical validation of these potentially negative effects, one would require any practical application of awareness concepts to consider possible drawbacks and apply suitable mitigation strategies.

On a contextual level, potential trade-offs between different PFs and, associated with that, trade-offs between value creation on the individual and the collective level, remain to be addressed. We argued that, from an individual perspective, more value awareness is likely to lead to more value creation. However, the "net value creation" most likely involves trade-offs between PFs, in which some PFs will be less emphasized than others. This, in turn, could prompt an individual into actions that reduce or even destroy value for certain PFs. For example, increasing individuals' value awareness could prompt them to prioritize their own needs over those of others. We still need to explore what scenarios like this one mean for the factual, i.e. inter-subjectively shared, evaluation of (and for) the humans represented in a PF. In this regard, challenging questions can arise, such as whether it is better to focus more on the value for the individuals constituting a group as opposed to the value for the group as an entity.[1]

As a final limitation, we focused on establishing the constructs *value awareness* and *value emphasis* and their role in the process of evaluation, while only broadly touching on the entire process as such. A theory of value rooted in human psychology offers room for much more detailed treatment of the value creation process and the introduction of other, potentially equally relevant, constructs that could serve as components of and antecedents to (public) value creation.

Conclusion

In this conceptual contribution we have elaborated on a micro-foundation of (public) value based on the idea that humans are the final arbiters of value creation. Arguing that basic values and personal frames of reference define "how" and "for whom" value is truly created on a psychological level, we arrived at a (public) value matrix as a systematic framework of fundamental value categories involved in any evaluation. Building on this framework we define value awareness as a cognitive competence that helps individuals and organizations to recognize *how* and *for whom* value is truly created or destroyed, which should allow them to make better evaluations, create more value, and find more value in a world of abundant information and options, and blurred standards and boundaries.

Note

1 Paradoxically, this question cannot be answered without considering the value emphasis of the subjects who are trying to answer it.

References

Aguinis, H., & Glavas, A. 2012. What we know and don't know about corporate social responsibility: A review and research agenda. *Journal of Management*, 38(4): 932–968.

Bacharach, S.B. 1989. Organizational theories: Some criteria for evaluation. *Academy of Management Review*, 14(4): 496–515.

Barney, J., & Felin, T. 2013. What are microfoundations? *The Academy of Management Perspectives*, 27(2): 138–155.

Baumeister, R.F. 1995. Self and identity: An introduction. In A. Tesser (Ed.), *Advanced Social Psychology*: 51–97. New York: McGraw-Hill.

Boyatzis, R.E. 2008. Competencies in the 21st century. *Journal of Management Development*, 27(1): 5–12.

Bryson, J.M., Crosby, B.C., & Bloomberg, L. 2014. Public value governance: Moving beyond traditional public administration and the new public management. *Public Administration Review*, 74(4): 445–456.

Butterfield, K.D., Trevin, L.K., & Weaver, G.R. 2000. Moral awareness in business organizations: Influences of issue-related and social context factors. *Human Relations*, 53(7): 981–1018.

Coleman, Jr, H.J. 1999. What enables self-organizing behavior in businesses. *Emergence*, 1(1): 33–48.

Epstein, S. 1989. Values from the perspective of cognitive-experiential self-theory. In N.E. Eisenberg, J.E. Reykowski, & E.E. Staub (Eds), *Social and Moral Values: Individual and Societal Perspectives*: 3–22 (8th ed.). Erlbaum: Hillsdale.

Epstein, S. 2003. Cognitive-experiential self-theory of personality. In T. Millon, M.J. Lerner, & I.B. Weiner (Eds), *Handbook of Psychology: Personality and Social Psychology*: 159–184. New York: Wiley.

Fiske, S.T. 1995. Social Cognition. In A. Tesser (Ed.), *Advanced Social Psychology*: 149–193. New York: McGraw-Hill.

Fiske, S.T., & Taylor, S.E. 1991. *Social Cognition* (2nd ed.). New York: McGraw-Hill.

Gomez, P., & Meynhardt, T. 2012. More foxes in the boardroom: Systems thinking in action. In S.N. Grösser, & R. Zeier (Eds), *Systemic Management for Intelligent Organizations. Concepts, Models-Based Approaches and Applications*: 83–98. Berlin, Heidelberg: Springer.

Graumann, C.F., & Willig, R. 1983. Wert, Wertung, Werthaltung. In H. Thomae (Ed.), *Enzyklopädie der Psychologie, Bd. I: Theorien und Formen der Motivation*: 312–396. Göttingen: Hogrefe.

Habermas, J. 1988. *Der philosophische Diskurs der Moderne: Zwölf Vorlesungen*. Frankfurt am Main: Suhrkamp.

Haidt, J. 2001. The emotional dog and its rational tail: A social intuitionist approach to moral judgment. *Psychological Review*, 108(4): 814.

Heyde, J.E. 1926. *Wert: Eine philosophische Grundlegung*. Erfurt: K. Stenger.

Kegan, R. 1982. *The Evolving Self: Problem and Process in Human Development*. Harvard: Harvard University Press.

Kegan, R. 1995. *In Over our Heads: The Mental Demands of Modern Life*. Harvard: Harvard University Press.

Kohlberg, L. 1984. *The Psychology of Moral Development: The Nature and Validity of Moral Stages*. San Francisco, London: Harper & Row.

Meynhardt, T. 2009. Public value inside: What is public value creation? *Intl Journal of Public Administration*, 32(3–4): 192–219.

Meynhardt, T. 2015. Public value: Turning a conceptual framework into a scorecard. In L. Bloomberg, B.C. Crosby, & J.M. Bryson (Eds), *Public Value and Public Administration*. Washington, DC: Georgetown University Press.

Meynhardt, T., & Bartholomes, S. 2011. (De) Composing public value: In search of basic dimensions and common ground. *International Public Management Journal*, 14(3): 284–308.

Miller, J.A., Rodgers, Z.J., & Bingham, J. 2014. Moral awareness. In B.R. Agle, D.W. Hart, J.A. Thompson, & H.M. Hendricks (Eds.), *Research Companion to Ethical Behavior in Organizations. Constructs and Measures*. Cheltenham, UK, Northampton, MA: Edward Elgar.

Orlik, P. 1979. Self-concept as a frame of reference of social cognition. *Zeitschrift für Sozialpsychologie*, 10(2), 270, 167–182.

Ramirez, R. 1999. Value co-production: Intellectual origins and implications for practice and research. *Strategic Management Journal*: 49–65.

Rest, J.R. 1986. *Moral Development: Advances in Research and Theory*. New York, London: Praeger.

Scholte, J.A. 2005. *Globalization: A Critical Introduction* (2nd ed.). Basingstoke: Palgrave.

Schutz, A. 1974. *Der sinnhafte Aufbau der sozialen Welt: Eine Einleitung in die verstehende Soziologie*. Frankfurt am Main: Suhrkamp.

Schutz, A., & Luckmann, T. 1973. *The Structures of the Life-World*. Evanston, IL: Northwestern University Press.

Schwartz, B. 2000. Self-determination: The tyranny of freedom. *American Psychologist*, 55(1): 79.

Selznick, P. 1994. *The Moral Commonwealth: Social Theory and the Promise of Community*. Berkeley, Los Angeles, London: University of California Press.

Suddaby, R. 2010. Editor's comments: Construct clarity in theories of management and organization. *Academy of Management Review*, 35(3): 346–357.

Swann, W.B. 1987. Identity negotiation: Where two roads meet. *Journal of Personality and Social Psychology*, 53(6): 1038–1051.

Tenbrunsel, A.E., & Smith-Crowe, K. 2008. Ethical decision making: Where we've been and where we're going. *The Academy of Management Annals*, 2(1): 545–607.

van Knippenberg, D., Dahlander, L., Haas, M.R., & George, G. 2015. Information, attention, and decision making. *Academy of Management Journal*, 58(3): 649–657.

3 The rationalities of public values
Conflicting values and conflicting rationalities

Mark R. Rutgers

The never-ending story

Core concepts (power, society, state, gender) are usually troublesome, and this also applies to public values. What are values? What specifically are public values? How do values combine (or not)? Can we rationally decide on values? These questions remain open to debate in the ongoing discourse on the nature of values in the social sciences, and on public values in the political sciences and the study of public administration. This chapter is not intended to repeat these discussions, but focusses on two specific issues: how do values relate to each other, and how do they relate to rationality? These general issues concerning values do have a bearing on the subcategory of public values. The aim is to better understand why it is so difficult to establish how public values are used and relate to each other, both in research and in practice.

In the discourse on public values, an avalanche of different values can be found. Either in attempts to identify what are relevant values for citizens, public managers, civil servants, NGO's, private organizations, or whichever actor is or should be participating in the public sphere. The possible sources and means to identify public values are a core concern, and approaches may vary considerably. Bryson, Crosby and Bloomberg (2014) present an overview, and in line with for instance Stoker (2006) regard the public values discourse as the successor of a 'traditional' and a 'new public management' approaches in the field. Within the approaches to public values different schools, too, can be distinguished (Beck Jørgensen & Rutgers, 2015): the study of administrative ethics, 'public value management' (inspired by Mark Moore's idea of creating public value), and a more eclectic 'public value perspective'. This chapter reflects the last school and does not focus on ethics or management of public values, but on the more conceptual question how public values (justice, freedom, equality, and health) may be related to each other.

Resolving value conflicts and dilemmas is a serious and problematic issue in public administration. In ethics and in value theory it is common to distinguish between two general philosophical positions on this matter: value 'monists', who argue that value conflicts can be rationally resolved, and value 'pluralists', who argue that they cannot because we sometimes lack a measure for comparison. These abstract debates do surface in the study of public administration, as shown by the debate raised by Overeem and Verhoef's (2010) rejection of the claim by some authors that value pluralism has normative consequences for the field.

Although much has already been published on the nature of public values, some preliminary observations should be made. Public values research is confronted with the difficulty of focusing on a complex concept, uniting two concepts that themselves are contested: value and public. Both are notoriously tricky and widely discussed.

To start with: there are many definitions of values, such as Kluckhohn's "a conception, explicit or implicit, distinctive of an individual or characteristic of a group, of the desirable which influences the selection from available modes, means, and ends of action" (1962, 395). The crux of Kluckhohn's and many other definitions is that values express something desirable, or as Rokeach (1973) states, something "personally or socially preferable" (1973). More broadly, as I myself phrased it before: "Values are concepts we use to give meaning and significance to reality: We judge or qualify something as (amongst others) beautiful, courageous, honest, or holy, or on the contrary as ugly, cowardly, deceitful, or devilish" (Rutgers, 2015).[1] Thus, values are a specific kind of concepts, not used to capture or describe (conceptualize) 'what is', but to prescribe or evaluate, i.e. to give a qualitative assessment. Values share the notorious difficulty of all concepts in that there is an uncertain relationship between terms and values: the same term can be used for different values (ranging from slightly different characteristics to completely different concepts). Sometimes this is obvious, sometimes it remains unclear and unnoticed. Just as we may regard some terms as denoting the same concepts ('human being' and 'homo sapiens'), we may also regard them as essentially different when they apply to very different contexts. Sometimes we do not realize that we are using the same term, but not the same concepts. For instance, 'an efficient procedure' and 'an efficient person' do not seem to fit the definition of 'efficient' (cf. Rutgers & Van der Meer 2010). It implies that we have to take into consideration in what context a term is used: something has a value and so acquires a positive or negative meaning in a specific perspective.

Another concern is whether or not values are to be regarded as subjective or objective. They are subjective in the common understanding that individuals vary in their attribution and ranking of values. The values at our disposal are social constructs and not individuals' choices as such. In this sense they are no private values, and are objectively given to an individual within a socio-cultural setting: one cannot value something as *gezellig* if the concept does not have a meaning for the people to whom this (subjective) evaluation is conveyed. This brings us to another aspect of the social nature of values. Most authors distinguish between, on the one hand, 'liking, preferring, or desiring' and, on the other, 'valuing' as a human phenomenon: valuing then refers to an explicit judgment about something being good (beautiful, important, abject, and so on). Thus, values are concepts used in an argument; animals do have 'desires', 'wants', or 'preferences', but do not make arguments. According to Nicholas Rescher, values are to be understood as used in the rational legitimization of action: "a value represents a slogan capable of providing for the rationalization of action" (Rescher, 1982, 9). This shows why values are so important: they can be regarded as "any concept that expresses a positive or negative qualitative (or evaluative) statement and has a 'motivating force, that is, it gives direction to people's thoughts and actions" (Rutgers, 2014). They function as rational legitimations and explanations: "To have a value is to be able to give reasons for motivating goal-oriented behaviour in terms of benefits and costs, bringing to bear explicitly a *conception* of what is in a man's interest and what goes against his interest: to operate within reason-giving contexts with reference to a 'vision of the good life'" (Rescher, 1982,10). For Rescher this implies that values are always "a part in a long story" (26). When focussing on *public* values, this 'long story' becomes even longer if public values are not just regarded as an individual's values *about* what is public (i.e. in the general interest or so), but when we look for values held *by* a public. In the latter case we do find authors struggling to construct such a public foundation of public values in terms of some legitimizing mechanism (consensus, majority, elite, etc.) for a relevant group or constituency (citizens, taxpayers, local community, policy recipients, or the like) (cf. Bryson, Crosby & Bloomberg, 2014). Definitions of public values therefore tend to be either minimalist ('what the public desires') or complex, such as Bozeman's (2007) often cited definition. In either case the very construction of 'the public' is an issue: "Is it a matter of majority preference, consensus, or does it not have an empirical grounding, but rather a philosophical one?" (Beck Jørgensen & Rutgers, 2015, 3).

Without going into the empirical (or practical) matter of constructing a public with shared values, a few conceptual observations can be made. The meaning of 'public' is primarily established in opposition to what is private – what Weintraub (1997) calls the "grand dichotomy". Arendt, for instance, points to five distinct oppositions implied in the public/private dichotomy (1958, 50–52 and 72–73). Geuss, while rejecting the identifications with collective versus individual, and altruistic versus egoistic, concludes that no single substantive distinction can be found (2001, 106). Finally, Weintraub sees at least two fundamental and analytically distinct criteria: visibility and collectivity in play. On the basis of the interpretations selected, authors may arrive at different theories that result in different meanings of 'public'. Weintraub, for instance, discusses four broad 'models', such as the 'liberal-economic model' and the 'republican virtue model'. There are shared starting points, but also substantial internal diversity and even disagreement. The variety is so overwhelming that Geuss regards the public/private distinction not as a starting point but rather as a distinction attributed *post hoc*. He argues we should not look for the implication of the distinction, but "Rather, first we must ask what this purported distinction is for, that is, why we want to make it at all" (Geuss, 2001, 107). This indeterminate nature is reflected in the attempts to identify what is public in public administration by looking at legal statutes, 'what people value', etc. It should be noted that almost without exception the public value discourse focusses on establishing how 'a public' endorses specific 'public values' and not just agrees on private values. This is the ongoing discussion in the discourse on public values among authors such as Moore, Bozeman, Benington, Meynhardt, Beck Jørgensen, and more (cf. Bryson, Crosby & Bloomberg, 2014). This bring us to a possible distinction between an approach in terms of 'public value' versus one on 'public values'.

Following Mark Moore (2003) public value as a core concept in public value management has been as "the analogue of the desire to maximise shareholder value in the private sector" (Coats & Passmore, 2008). The core concern is link specific actions by means of a reference to the common good. Creating public value focuses on producing both concrete products (libraries, houses), as well as, ways of being (safety, justice). Some authors actually stress a difference between public value and public values (cf. Van der Wal, Nabatchi & De Graaf, 2015). The distinction concerns a more 'managerial' and empirical approach to public values versus a more pluralistic and normative approach. The difference is at best conceptual, as thus perceived public value concerns public values. It is confusing (if not silly) to regard a singular and a plural as referring to very different concepts. If 'creating a flourishing public library' constitutes a public value in a more empirical sense, and, as Nabatchi puts it, this "refers to an appraisal of what is created by government on behalf of the public," then clearly such an appraisal has to be grounded in some normative understanding of what the relevant public values in a normative perspective are, such as Bozeman's elaborate definition (2007, 13; cf. Rutgers, 2015).

In the following I will focus on the relation between public values as providing different directions and legitimations for actions. More in particular, values are regarded as (normative) arguments for rational legitimization. Distinctions such as between instrumental and fundamental values, as well between performance and procedural values will be challenged. To begin with, it will be stressed that the relations between values are complex; also, the proposed typology of relations is still simplifying reality. It continues with discussing the specific relevance of incommensurability of values for public administration. The second part deals with the question how public values can be part of rational argumentation, and it is here that the link between values and actions is analyzed. In the conclusion I argue that the combination of these two puzzles highlights the complexity of the concept for empirical research on public values, because the meaning of public values (and hence their interaction) is very contextual.

The complex story

According to De Graaf and Van der Wal, "[m]anaging tensions between public values" (2010, 625) is a core topic in our field. This reflects an ongoing interest in value conflicts, albeit in terms of values that are regarded as opposing, incompatible, dilemmatic, incomparable, or incommensurable. Clearly, different values can be equally important, and their realizations may conflict. Especially in ethics, the issue of an 'ethical dilemma' can be an unresolvable opposition whereby both values pose a moral demand on what to do, but cannot both be achieved because realizing one makes realizing the other impossible. The well-known ultimate consequence is perhaps the problem of the dirty hands: to do right, one has to do wrong (Walzer 1973). The dilemma is that no overarching moral argument can be found that can provide a way out. It is often assumed that this is because there are fundamentally different moral systems involved (cf. Berlin, 1998; Hampshire, 1989). The traditional moral dilemmas in literature concern the dilemma of the police officer on whether or not to use torture in order to establish where a terrorist hid a bomb. A suggested way out is that the police officer should do the morally wrong thing (i.e., torture) in order to do the morally right thing (i.e. save innocent people), yet should feel absolutely tormented about having done so. Put differently, in everyday reality we need to act. Not acting is usually wrong, i.e. part of the dilemma – making it actually a trilemma.

There is much interest in the way value conflicts are resolved in administrative practice. Oldenhof, Postma and Putters (2014) studied how conflicting values such as efficiency and equity, efficiency and democratic legitimacy, and equity and liberty (52) are dealt with in administrative practice. However, the interest in clashing values too easily obstructs interest in the equally important matter of values as mutually reinforcing or supporting the realization of other values. This can perhaps be constructed in terms of an instrumental relation between values, i.e. the one presupposing the other ('heroism requires bravery'; 'integrity presupposes honesty'), but also in terms of an 'added value' or juxtaposition of values ('a good and honest citizen', 'a loyal and dutiful servant'). The focus is often limited to incompatible or conflicting values; in everyday life and administration we have to deal with more intricate interactions and trade-offs.

To gain insight it can be helpful to analytically distinguish the possible relations between values. In practice, however, identifying the actual relations, let alone their strengths, is a different matter. The list of six relations outlined here should primarily be understood as a heuristic device to highlight the complexity of the matter at hand:

a. Complementary: values point in the same direction and go together; they support and/or strengthen each other. 'Equality' and 'justice' are possible examples here.

b. Instrumental: a value presupposes some other value(s): so-called 'ultimate values' are the clearest examples: 'justice', 'the good life' etc. all require a vast number of other values if they are to be achieved or realized, or to achieve freedom other values have to be realized.

c. Diverting: values points in different directions for action, and as a result influencing the options for achieving them. For instance, in order to achieve equality, we have to limit freedom; efficiency and legality can support or hamper each other. Thus, the effect can be positive or negative. A basic negative effect is that the energy and time spent on realizing one particular value will diminish the possibility of realizing another. Strengthening democracy can, for instance, also promote social equity. In other words, a host of intermediate positions is possible, ranging from a value that only slightly points in a different direction but still strengthens or reinforces the other value, to working against it and distracting, diverting, or disturbing the realization of a value.

d. Opposing: a value is in opposition to another value, i.e. they are in outright conflict, the one negating the possibility of the other. The simplest examples are the opposites of 'good' and 'bad', 'beautiful' and 'ugly', but also 'loyalty' in as far as it negates 'honesty' and/or 'fairness'. In case of a dilemma we are faced with an unresolvable opposition (unless another value is used to sidestep the opposition).

e. Unrelated: there may be no immediate or obvious relation between values: 'an honest and eloquent person'; 'an efficient and aesthetically pleasing solution'. If the co-existence of values adds to a more positive (or negative) appreciation it concerns one of the previous relations. 'Unrelated' seems likely to apply when values from very different contexts or value systems are in play but simply have no bearing upon each other.

f. Incommensurable: whereas the previous types are generally accepted, the possibility of this nonrelation, which precludes co-existence, is contested. Its supporters stipulate that some values are rationally incomparable and untranslatable because they are part of completely different 'worldviews' or 'ethical spheres'. Interestingly, they can have a profound impact on each other, because they provide arguments for different kinds of action, i.e., they relate to the same object or part of reality, even though they construct (i.e., value) it utterly differently. For instance, we may have to weigh 'the sanctity of human life' versus 'the running costs of a hospital'. The values indicate different courses of action, but incommensurability points to a situation where a rational comparison, and hence a choice between alternatives, is impossible. In the next section the relevance of this relation will be further discussed.

This abstract presentation of six relations obviously defies everyday complexity: the relative strengths or weights of values may differ, and undoubtedly many more values interact simultaneously. The overview stresses that the nature of the relations between public values (as between public and private values) can be highly contextual. Thus it is likely that in some cases (conceptual interpretations and empirical contexts) 'democracy' and 'equality' support, in others hinder each other. The perspectives of different persons and groups on what public values mean, and what is actually valued, demand careful attention. The complexities increase in the case of cross-cultural debates and comparisons. In other words, we have to realize that the meaning of a specific value depends on its relations with other values, and that what at first sight seem similar or dissimilar terms may be hiding similarities and differences in for instance empirical studies on values in the public sector.

The Gordian knot

Of the possible relations, incommensurability is the trickiest and most disputed; it is a concept linked to philosophical and theoretical concerns. Yet it seems to become more and more popular in 'everyday' studies in public administration, as if it was an everyday phenomenon. It suggests that we are or should be able to distinguish clearly between 'merely' conflicting values (however difficult to deal with), and others that defy any rational resolution. Is it really an important concept, dealing with a phenomenon fundamental to the study of public administration? I will argue that it is when we reflect on the very foundations of public values, but hardly when we deal with value conflicts in practice. In the latter case decisions have to be made. Just as in ethics, there are different ethical systems that at a fundamental level oppose each other, but all can also inform a practical ethical decision (Svara, 2007, 68). It should be noted in advance that this topic is closely intertwined with discussions on value pluralism and conceptual relativism. Value pluralism posits a specific ontological theory on the nature of values. It amounts to conceptual relativism, i.e. a theory that regards specific systems of concepts (and values) as totally incomparable: "not inter-translatable" (Davidson, 1974/2001, 190).[2]

The theory of incommensurability originates from Thomas Kuhn's theory on the rationality of the sciences (Kuhn, 1970): only in the context of a scientific paradigm with its accepted ontology and epistemology are rational arguments possible. The choice between paradigms is not rational, because it lacks a shared context of assumptions. Paradigms can be fundamentally different and incomparable: incommensurable. Paul Feyerabend even made incommensurability a core concept in his 'radical methodology', but he explicitly regards it as a theoretical phenomenon: rare, and not relevant to the everyday scientist (Feyerabend, 1975, 114). Others have argued that it is a more common concern, possibly even *within* a conceptual framework (cf. Hintikka, 1988), and also relevant outside academia, such as in debates on public values. Translated to public values, such fundamental differences can for instance result from values embedded in specific ideological and/or religious word views, in particular in relation to topics concerning life and death (abortion, euthanasia).

Opponents often rely on Donald Davidson's broadly accepted rejection of the very notion of a conceptual framework, because it is based on a duality between language or conceptual scheme and reality to begin with. The argument results in the conclusion that "we could not be in a position to judge that others had concepts or beliefs radically different from our own" (Davidson, 1974/2001, 197). Putnam (2004), on the other hand, defends conceptual relativism (39). He points to the *possibility* of languages that are not just contradictory, but incompatible.

We are dealing with an ongoing, highly philosophical debate (cf. Wang, 2007), but nevertheless incommensurability is posed in the discourse on public values in our own field. De Graaf and Paanakker (2014), for instance, state: "Incommensurability, particularly between procedural and performance values, seems inherent to value conflict in public governance" (4). This implies that we should at least be able to attribute a specific value to either kind, before establishing whether or not they are also incommensurable. But can we? Roughly speaking, process or procedural values concern 'the rule of the game', i.e. how we are supposed to act; performance values concern 'what is achieved'. But are values such as honesty, integrity, lawfulness always to be regarded as procedural, or are effectiveness, justice, and efficiency always performance values, as authors claim? Take 'efficiency'. This value is particularly interesting: Waldo (1984), for instance, has argued that efficiency is always a 'second-order value': one can only be efficient while striving to achieve some other value. What is more, the term 'efficiency' seems to be used in two very different contexts (cf. Rutgers & Van der Meer). From an Aristotelian perspective it refers to 'efficient cause', indicating an ability: the efficient administrator is a capable person, irrespective of specific achievements. From the (relatively recent) economic perspective, efficiency refers to a relation between input and output, giving the expression 'an efficient administrator' a rather different, silly meaning. The point here is that efficiency can be *both* a performance and a procedural value. This brings us to the question how values are used in different ways as arguments, a topic we will discuss in the next section.

The earlier example of comparing the value ('sanctity') of human life to the economic value or costs of providing medical treatment seems a likely candidate for the label 'incommensurable': 'sanctity' is not a value fitting economic discourse, nor do 'costs' seem to fit the discourse on human dignity. There can be no clash in the ordinary sense between incommensurable values, as we lack a context in which both values can be adequately compared. Yet, striving for the one value will exclude or hinder realization of the other; otherwise the values would be simply unrelated. Perhaps the clearest illustrations are values arising from different religions, such as miracles, sacrifices, rituals, which are meaningless to others. However, in a meta-perspective we may regard them both as meaningful in terms of their function in society. Yet this meta-perspective does not provide a yardstick to choose between the two values as such, even though it is possible to argue that one ritual is functionally better than the other at providing social stability, cohesion, or the like. Neither does invoking the notion of 'the general or common interest' provide an easy way out, because this relies on a particular world view to begin with. The main question becomes: what is a valid comparison? We are told not to compare apples and pears, but both are fruit and can be compared as such – perhaps not regarding their taste (as either apples or pears), but their sweetness, nutritious value etc. can without doubt be objectively compared once these aspects have been accepted as a yardstick. It suggests that incommensurability is a 'level' issue: on their own terms or within their own systems, values may defy comparison, but not from another perspective. The question thus becomes whether we can validly agree on a useful other approach, or meta-approach, if we are to compare and decide? In the example of 'human dignity' versus 'economics' in health care, selecting 'fairness' or 'equality' as a pivot may help to balance the two 'incommensurable' values. The most common way out in public administration is probably to apply a *procedural approach* to making a choice: i.e. not comparing the values in question as such, but by using 'neutral' or different means to choose a course of action. Here we enter the discussions on 'how to arrive at public value?' as mentioned before: the study of public administration exists on the interstices of creating and managing public values in society as a core political and administrative topic.

To conclude this brief outline of the viability of the concept of incommensurability for the study of public values: it is a theoretical issue. Without delving into the debate between value monists and pluralists mentioned earlier (of which this is part), we should note that even if 'unification' is theoretically possible, it is by no means evident that in administrative practice this will be helpful in resolving clashes between posed public values. As Overeem and Verhoef (2010, 1105) indicate, value pluralism does not help to solve dilemmas we are faced with. In practice we do have to deal with conflicting values, and it is usually unlikely that we have the time or expertise to make a thorough philosophical and/or empirical study. For instance, Dworkin argues for monism in terms of 'human dignity' as a touchstone for resolving value conflicts. This implies that there are no real conflicts between citizens' claims (cf. Van Donselaar, 2011), but it can be doubted whether this is very helpful in administrative practice (although then it should be noted that this empirical argument is irrelevant in a conceptual discussion). Thus, Wagenaar's research indicates that in everyday administrative practices value conflict is indeed "dealt with" rather than resolved (1999, 447; cf. Wright, 2010, 312). Wagenaar, although referring to the term, does not need it, nor provides any useful interpretation of the concept of incommensurability (or value pluralism). This seems to be the case for most authors in the studies of public administration. Talisse also argues that value pluralism "entails nothing about what one should do." (2010, 71). Most authors seem to agree on this issue, albeit for different reasons (i.e., theoretical versus empirical). However, Spicer (2010) may still have a point when he says that there is a normative argument to be derived from the incommensurability of values: it is a waste of time to try to rationally resolve conflicting values if they are incommensurable.

Whether or not values are merely extremely difficult to reconcile or are outright incommensurable, in practice we are sometimes simply unable to resolve a problem involving such values quickly enough. Nevertheless, a decision can be rationally agreed upon in either case by sidestepping this issue: we can take either another value to balance or decide, or take a formal or procedural approach, i.e. agree upon 'flipping a coin' to decide fairly, or construct a legitimate political and legal system in which decisions can be made authoritatively. Thus, history tells us about the Gordian knot that the Phrygians had in their city and was impossible to untie. Alexander the Great, however, "when he could not find the end to the knot to unbind it, he sliced it in half with a stroke of his sword, producing the required ends".[3] So, it seems that if different values are irreconcilable, we may need to 'cut the knot': whether or not one or the other is better, not acting is often not an option even though we may regret or even feel remorse about choosing the one value over the other. Neither value pluralism nor incommensurability change this reality.

This brings us to the second main topic of consideration we touched upon earlier: the way public values are part of an argument.

Values in rational argumentation

Values are at the heart of public administration, and so is rationality. Hodgkinson regarded public administration as "philosophy in action" and a matter of 'value-awareness' (1982, 3), and Robbins (1980, 26) argues that administrators and philosophers engage in similar endeavours: the evaluation and interpretation of what is important in life. Nevertheless, in public administration the focus is often not so much on values as on instrumental rationality, and in its wake efficiency – something that has been criticized particularly in post-modern theory. It is Weber that not only provided our field with the concept of bureaucracy, but also with its prime theory of rationality (Schreurs, 2000, 76). Central to Weber's theory is the distinction between purpose and value rationality (*Wertrational* and *Zweckrational*).[4] The issue in the previous section was that value pluralism and the theory of incommensurability argue that in some cases rationality breaks down. Here the focus is on the very nature of rational argumentation in relation to values. It will be argued that there are two different kinds of argumentation in which values are used, and that this also applies to the use of public values.

Weber distinguished between purpose rationality and value rationality as two fundamentally different ways people relate to action. People act in a value-rational way when they are guided by their convictions, i.e. on the basis of duty, dignity, beauty, religious instruction, reverence, or whatever the importance of a 'case' appears to demand. The action is based on precepts or demands, and its consequences are not relevant. Examples would be public values, such as 'justice', ''freedom,' and 'democracy'. Weber limits value rationality to 'value spheres' that are associated with ultimate values such as religion, politics, erotic love, science and the like (Friedland, 2014, 222): "A value-rational action is characterized by the conscious belief in the ethical, esthetical, religious or however else to identify unconditional intrinsic value (*Eigenwert*) of a specific way of acting (*Sichverhaltens*) purely as such independent of the effects." (Weber, 1972, 13; translation author). The opposite applies to a purpose-rational action, which is concerned with the most favourable, efficient means to attain a given end (cf. Denhardt, 1981, 630). For Weber purpose or instrumental rational orientation is the ideal-typical kind of social action (Schöllgen, 1984, 91), as it "involves an orientation toward the constraints of an external objective world that conditions one's success in obtaining an actor's own [pursued ends]" (Friedland, 2014, 221). Here we can point to public values such as 'efficiency', 'safe roads', 'drinking water,' or 'housing,' i.e. what 'creating public value' is about.

Petra Scheurs's close reading of Weber (2000) has revealed several specific differences between value and purpose rationality. The difference most acknowledged, as we have seen, is whether the meaning of an action is located in either the consequences or results (i.e. purpose-rational), or in the intrinsic value of acting (i.e. value-rational). Thus it is either the outcome (*Erfolg*) or the acting as such (irrespective of what it may further achieve) that constitutes the meaning of a social action, and may figure in a description or explanation of this action. 'Values' appear as internally, 'purposes' as externally binding. Both value and purpose are values in a more generic sense. In other words, in case of an intrinsic value Weber uses the term *values*, and in case of extrinsic value, the term *purposes* (cf. Rutgers & Schreurs, 2003). But how do the two interact or are they related? Authors have wrestled with the questions whether or not it is possible to rationally assess opposing values, and how values and goals or purposes are related. Can values (in Weber's sense), for instance, become purposes, or are purposes or goals simply values in the end?

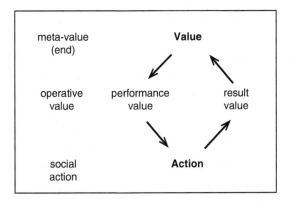

Figure 3.1 The relation of value and action
Based on Rutgers & Schreurs, 2003

To avoid confusion, I will use the term Values (with a capital) as the more encompassing and transcending concept. What is more – and here we deviate from Weber's scheme – Values or ends denote the more 'ultimate' aims, objects, goals or ends to which social action is oriented: other values (and purposes) relate to them as supportive, instrumental, possibly necessary, or sufficient preconditions. This is in line with Friedland's observation that purpose rationality "always contains and conceals a value rationality" (2014, 249), and Diekmann's remark that for Weber the orientation on values is a means to arrive at rational knowledge (1961, 18). Therefore, we have to pose the 'ultimate' Value as preceding value and purpose rationality (see Figure 3.1).

All action is Value (or end) oriented, but in two distinct ways, as we have seen: an action can be understood as trying to realize an end either in terms of the acting (or performing) itself, 'irrespective of the outcome', or in reference to the result or outcome of that action, 'irrespective of the process'. What we have arrived at is a result or outcome value, as well as the possibility of a performance or action value; both can be the legitimation or basis for evaluation of an action in relation to the end to be achieved. As a result, value, an end (Value) applies to the outcome of the action only, such as 'winning the game." However, an action can also be valued in the light of the desired action or desired as such, whereby: "The end result has no bearing on the meaning of the action" (Rutgers & Schreurs, 2003). In the latter case it is 'taking part in the game' that is the value, not winning.

The core question is how a Value relates to an action as a performance and/or the result of that action. For instance, acting efficiently, justly, or democratically does not automatically result in efficient, just, or democratic results. Conversely, acting democratically, efficiently, or justly may result in undemocratic, inefficient, or unjust outcomes. It can make sense to 'efficiently carry water to the ocean', if understood as a performance value. This may be what is perceived as 'wrong' in cases where 'performance indicators' take preference over an orientation on results.[5]

In case a Value is understood or operationalized as a performance value (i.e., *acting*), it concerns a *value-rational* argumentation. If interpreted in terms of a result

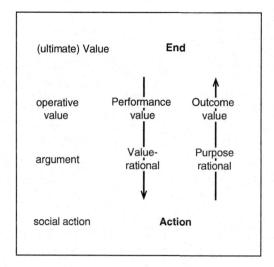

Figure 3.2 The end/action model

As adapted from Rutgers & Schreurs, 2003

or outcome it is *purpose-rational*. Thus, argumentation or reasoning can take two directions: reasoning from an end to decide what action is to be undertaken: rational deliberations what to do. Or looking at the result of an action in *rational evaluation* (what has been achieved, see Figure 3.2).

There is no longer anything special or mysterious about trying to realize 'honor' or 'beauty' as a result value, and trying to evaluate the actions in question as purpose-rational. It fits the criticism of this approach as having a focus on instrumental rationality: "This is what the criticism of the dominance of purpose- or technical rationality amounts to, whilst the fixation on the outcome makes us unaware of the way we are acting and what this implies", and what is more, the danger of a limited perspective, "not only applies to purpose rationality, but can also be directed to value rationality" (Rutgers & Schreurs, 2003).

In the discussions in public administration this implies that references to public values can also concern their use as either performance or outcome values. The difficulty noted earlier, of pinpointing a specific public value as either a procedural or performance value, in a sense evaporates; it can be both, depending on the argument in which that value figures.

Some concluding observations

The debates about the importance of concepts such as incommensurability, value pluralism, or conceptual relativism should be assessed for what they are: important philosophical and conceptual matters of dispute that may help us to better grasp the very nature of values, and hence public values. It seems unlikely they will have any direct practical consequences in public administration, especially because we lack the very means to establish empirically when or if for instance incommensurability occurs. The practical problem of having to resolve the tension between values remains. What is more, in empirical reality the relations between values are intricate and contextual. The previous discussion implies that for empirical research we can in any case bracket 'incommensurability' and/or equate it with (factual) opposition or deviation, as far as it concerns the desired course of action from the perspective of another value. This does not result in a solution, but neither does adhering to incommensurability.

The complexity of understanding what kind of value we are dealing with increases: values are to be understood as part of a 'long story', in this case of a particular argument. This is all the more so in case a value is, or is stipulated to be, a *public* value – maybe simply because its 'public' status requires further argumentation, but also because it suggests a higher status than 'merely' a private value. It can for instance help to understand why a distinction between procedural and performance values is so unclear. What category it might fit is not inherent in a value as such, but in the use of a public value in argumentation. That is, a specific value may itself provide different directions for action, depending on the context in which it is used: democracy can be interpreted as posing demands for performances as well as results, and these can in principle be at odds. Again, this implies that research on public values should include a multitude of aspects and not take a posed public value at face value, so to speak. The problem with studying public values doubles if we confound the two lines of study: all too easily values are regarded as fitting one possible kind of rational argumentation and provide just one direction for action, and may therefore have different relations to other values depending on their specific use in argumentation. This all adds to the well-known difficulty in empirical research to establish whether all individuals concerned are using the same terms and values to begin with. As in everyday practice, it is not to be expected that everyone is aware of how they are actually interpreting or using a value in a specific context; it is *not* safe to rely on respondents' own observations in such cases. Simply having respondents fill in a questionnaire as if the terms denoting values that are used are similar is more problematic in this context, and even more so in cross-cultural research (cf. Yang, 2016). There, we not only have to wrestle with the relations between public values, and between values and terms, but what is more, we have to actually translate and decide to what extent it makes sense to regard terms and concepts as cognitively equivalent across times and places.

Notes

1 Cf. "The term ['value'] can be limited to what might be said to be on the plus side of the zero line; then what is on the minus side (bad, wrong, and so forth) is called disvalue." Or, "what is on the plus side is then called positive value and what on the minus side, negative value." (Macquarrie, 1972, 229)
2 In a similar way it has long been popular to use the term 'paradigm', often suggesting a link with Thomas Kuhn's theory, but usually simply meaning 'example' and including observation that are not in line with Kuhn's theory.
3 http://en.wikipedia.org/wiki/Gordian_Knot (accessed 11/05/2014).
4 In this context *Wert* and *Zweck* are often translated by *value* and *instrumental*, or *value* and *means-ends*. However, Schreurs calls this translation 'puzzling' as *Zweck* refers to a purpose rather than an instrument or means (2000, 51).
5 Although we should be aware that performance indicators may actually not constitute performance values at all, but refer to results to be achieved.

References

Arendt, H. (1958). *The Human Condition*. Chicago/London: University of Chicago Press.

Beck Jørgensen, T. and Rutgers, M.R. (2015). Public Values: Core or Confusion? Introduction to the Centrality and Puzzlement of Public Values Research. *The American Review of Public Administration*, 45(1), 1–9.

Berlin, I. (1998). The originality of Machiavelli. In I. Berlin, *The Proper Study of Mankind. An Anthology of Essays* (pp. 269–325). New York: Farra, Straus and Giroux.

Bryson, J.M., Crosby, B. and Bloomberg, L. (2014). Public Value Governance: Moving beyond Traditional Public Administration and the New Public Management. *Public Administration Review*, 74(4), 445–456.

Bozeman, B. (2007). *Public Values and public interest. Counterbalancing economic individualism*. Washington: Georgetown University Press.

Coats, D. and Passmore, E. (2008). *Public Value: The Next Steps in Public Service Reform*. London: The Work Foundation.

Davidson, D. (1974/2001). On the very Idea of a Conceptual Scheme. In D. Davidson, *Inquiries into Truth and Interpretation* (pp. 183–198). Oxford: The Clarendon Press.

De Graaf, G. and Paanakker, H. (2014). Good Governance: Performance Values and Procedural Values in Conflict. *The American Review of Public Administration* published online 16 April 2014. doi: 10.1177/0275074014529361

De Graaf, G. and Van der Wal, Z. (2010). Managing Conflicting Public Values: Governing With Integrity and Effectiveness. *The American Review of Public Administration*, 40(6), 623–630.

Denhardt, R.B. (1981). Toward a critical theory of public organization. *Public Administration Review*, 41, 628–635.

Diekmann, J. (1961). *Max Webers Begriff des "modernen okzidentalen Rationalismus"*. Düsseldorf: Zentral-Verlag für Dissertationen Triltsch.

Feyerabend, P.K. (1975). *Against Method: Outline for an Anarchistic Theory of Knowledge*. London: NLB.

Friedland, R. (2014). Divine institution: Max Weber's value spheres and institutional theory. *Religion and Organization Theory*, 41, 217–258.

Geuss, R. (2001). *Public Goods, Private Goods*. Princeton: Princeton University Press.

Hampshire, S. (1989). *Innocence and Experience*. Cambridge, MA: Harvard University Press.

Hintikka, J. (1988). On the Incommensurability of Theories. *Philosophy of Science*, 55, 25–3.8.

Hodgkinson, C. (1982), *Towards a Philosophy of Administration*, 2nd ed. Oxford: Basil Blackwell.

Kelly, C. (2008). The Impossibility of Incommensurable Values. *Philosophical Studies: An International Journal for Philosophy in the Analytic Tradition*, 137(3), 369–382.

Kluckhohn, C. (1962). Values and value-orientations in the theory of action: An exploration in definition and classification. In T. Parsons and E.A. Shils (eds), *Toward a General Theory of Action* (pp. 388–433). Cambridge, MA: Harvard University Press.

Kuhn, Th.S. (1972). Scientific Paradigms. In B. Barnes (ed.), *Sociology of Science* (pp. 80–104). Harmondsworth: Penguin.

Macquarrie, J. (1972). Value and valuation. In P. Edwards (ed.), *The Encyclopedia of Philosophy* (Book 8) (pp. 229–234). Reprint Edition. London: Collier MacMillan.

Moore, M.H. (2003). *Creating Public Value. Strategic Management in Government*, 8th ed. Cambridge MA: Harvard University Press.

Nabatchi, T. (2012). Putting the "Public" Back in Public Values Research: Designing Participation to Identify and Respond to Values, *Public Administration Review*, 72(5), 699–708.

Oldenhof, L., Postma, J. and Putters, K. (2014). On Justification Work: How Compromising Enables Public Managers to Deal with Conflicting Values. *Public Administration Review*, 74(1), 52–63.

Overeem, P. and Verhoef, J. (2015). Value Pluralism and the Usefulness of Philosophical Theory for Public Administration. *Administration & Society*, 47(9), 1103–1109.

Putnam, H. (2004). *Ethics without Ontology*. Cambridge MA: Harvard University Press.

Rescher, N. (1982). *Introduction to Value Theory*. Washington: University Press of America.

Robbins, S.P. (1980). *The Administrative Process*, 2nd ed. Englewood Cliffs: Prentice-Hall.

Rokeach, M. (1973). *The Nature of Human Values*. New York, NY: Free Press.

Rutgers, M.R. (2003). *De Verlicht Bestuurskundige. Over de raakvlakken van filosofie en bestuurskunde*. Leiden: Universiteit Leiden.

Rutgers, M.R. (2015). As Good as It Gets? On the Meaning of Public Value in the Study of Policy and Management. *The American Review of Public Administration*. 45(1), 29–45.

Rutgers, M.R. and Schreurs, P. (2003). Reassessing Purpose and Value. Towards an End/Action model of values in public administration. In M.R. Rutgers (ed.), *Retracing Public Administration* (pp. 257–290). JAI press/Elseviers International.

Rutgers, M.R. and Van der Meer, H. (2010). The Origins and Restriction of Efficiency in Public Administration: Regaining Efficiency as the Core Value of Public Administration, *Administration & Society*, 42(7), 755–779.

Schöllgen, G. (1984). *Handlungsfreiheit und Zweckrationalität. Max Weber und die Tradition praktischer Philosophie*. Tübingen: J.C.B. Mohr.

Schreurs, P. (2000). *Enchanting Rationality: An Analysis of Rationality in the Anglo-American Discourse on Public Organization*. Delft: Eburon.

Spicer, M. (2010). On Value Pluralism, Its Implications and the Nature of Philosophy. *Administration & Society*, 47(9), 1077–1086.

Stoker, G. (2006). Public value management: A new narrative for network governance? *The American Review of Public Administration*, 36(1), 41–57.

Svara, J. (2007). *The Ethics Primer for Public Administrators in Government and Nonprofit Organizations*. Boston etc.: Jones and Bartlett.

Talisse, R.B. (2010). Value Pluralism: a philosophical clarification. *Administration & Society*, 47(9), 1064–1076.

Van der Wal, Z., Nabatchi, T. and De Graaf, G. 2015. From galaxies to universe: A cross-disciplinary review and analysis of public values publications from 1969 to 2012. *The American Review of Public Administration*, 45(1), 13–28.

Van Donselaar, I. (2011). Ronald Dworkin, justice for hedgehogs. *Rechtsfilosofie & Rechtstheorie*, 40(2), 177–181.

Wagenaar, H. (1999). Value Pluralism in Public Administration. *Administrative Theory & Praxis*, 21(4), 441–449.

Waldo, D. (1984). *The Administrative State: A Study of the Political Theory of American Public Administration*, 2nd ed. New York: Holmes & Meier.

Walzer, M. (1973). Political action: The problem of dirty hands. *Philosophy and Public Affairs*, 2(2), 160–180.

Wang, X. (2007). *Incommensurability and Cross-Language Communication*. Aldershot: Ashgate.

Weber, M. (1972). *Wirtschaft und Gesellschaft: Grundrisse der verstehende Soziologie*, [Economy and Society: An Outline of Interpretive Sociology] 5th ed. Tübingen: Mohr.

Weintraub, J. (1997). The Theory and Politics of the Public/Private Distinction. In J. Weintraub and Krishan Kumar (eds), *Public and Private in Thought and Practice. Perspectives on a Grand Dichotomy* (pp. 1–42). Chicago & London: The University of Chicago Press.

Wright, B.E. (2010). Public Administration in 2020: Balancing Values as a Journey, Not a Destination. *Public Administration Review*, 70, 312–313.

Yang, L. (2016). Worlds Apart? Worlds Aligned? The Perceptions and Prioritizations of Civil Servant Values among Civil Servants from China and the Netherlands. *International Journal of Public Administration*, 39(1), 74–86.

4 Designing spaces for public value creation

Consolidating conflicting dimensions of public value in the design of public organizations

Scott Douglas and Mirko Noordegraaf

Introduction

The concept of public value has expanded the ambition of public organizations, encouraging them to create desirable societal outcomes together with stakeholders (Moore, 1995; Williams and Shearer, 2011). However, different tasks and different stakeholders prioritize different dimensions of value. Public organizations have to satisfy competing demands for optimal efficiency, maximum legitimacy, and utmost quality from diverse stakeholders such as tax payers, politicians, professionals, and clients (Hood, 1991; Noordegraaf, 2015).

This poses organizations with tough dilemmas. How can the public prosecution service combine a rapid response to injustice with careful legal proceedings? How can universities support the development of academic quality while maintaining outstanding facilities? How can a hospital combine the highest quality care with the lowest possible costs? How can elderly people be provided with customized care in the face of limited public means?

Public organizations do not have the luxury of cherry-picking dimensions of value; they have to fulfil all dimensions at the same time to satisfy all their stakeholders (Talbot, 2008; Moore, 2013). Yet serving all dimensions of public value leads to constant choices and challenges for frontline staff, managers, and stakeholders, potentially leading to never-ending confusion and conflict. Public organizations so risk chasing all dimensions of value, but attaining none of them.

We here approach the tension between the different dimensions of public value as an organizational design problem. How should the responsibilities for the different dimensions of value be allocated across the organizational structure? Where in the organization should the different dimensions be brought together? What management work is required to deal with the remaining conflict between the different dimensions? We suggest that organizations should design different types of organizational *spaces* where value is created, differing in the extent to which the different dimensions of value are separated or integrated.

We identify four different design options, representing highly stylised ideal types:

1. Separate different value propositions across different organizational units
2. Spread the responsibility for different dimensions of value across different units
3. Contrast different dimensions within the same unit
4. Integrate all dimensions in singular units

The choice between these four ideal types depends on both the task and authorizing environment. The organizational design should suit the task at hand, allowing for the maximum creation of value given the complexity and dynamics of the task at hand (Mintzberg, 1991). However, the organizational design also needs to be legitimate in the eyes of the stakeholders to ensure their support and collaboration (Moore, 1995). This balance between task and authorizing environments could result in organizational designs which are not necessarily the most effective, but deemed right from a stakeholder perspective. Organizational design is therefore both an instrumental and institutional choice.

For example, the prosecution service may choose to create separate divisions for different value propositions – e.g. bulk traffic violations versus long-term organized crime cases – as each proposition requires a different balance between efficiency, quality, and legitimacy from both a task and authorizing perspective. Hospital may contrast the demands for efficiency, quality, and legitimacy by distinguishing between budgeting, medical, and legal roles in a management team. This contrast between financial or medical considerations is deemed right by external stakeholders, requiring ongoing deliberation between the different officers in the organization of patient care.

We will explore these different design options and their implications for management below. We first draw on the public management literature to analyse the different dimensions of public value. We then build on the organizational design literature to sketch four different design options. We illustrate these designs with our own empirical observations of public organizations. All examples are drawn from the professional service domain, covering prosecutors, universities, and healthcare providers, to show how even similar organizations have to make different design choices.

Our exploration highlights that even careful organizational design cannot eliminate all the tensions between the different value dimensions. Trade-offs will continue to manifest themselves through choices and conflicts for frontline employees, managers, and stakeholders. Each design option requires constant management work to stimulate the right dynamics and adapt to changes in the task and authorizing environment (Moore, 2013). However, we do contend that by creating appropriate organizational spaces, public organizations will be better able to navigate and combine the different dimensions of value.

Dissecting dimensions of value and components of organizations

Different dimensions of value

The concept of public value encourages public organizations to strive for desirable societal outcomes, working with private and public stakeholders to fight injustice, boost education, encourage public health, etc. (Moore, 1995; Moore, 2014). In achieving these grand goals, however, different stakeholders attach different priority to the different dimensions of value; stressing diverse elements such as cost-effectiveness, quality, or legitimacy.

The diversity in value dimensions stems from the different logics feeding the public debate about what is valuable (Noordegraaf, 2015). A *performance* logic prioritizes cost-effectiveness and strict standardization; a *professional* logic favours service quality and staff discretionary space; and a *political* logic focuses on legitimacy and accountability mechanisms. Different actors, such as taxpayers, politicians, managers, and professionals will favour different combinations of these logics and their respective value dimensions.

The ongoing debate between the different stakeholders and logics translate into a conflicting set of expectations for public organizations, asking them to be cost-effective, high-quality, and legitimate at the same time. While these dimensions can reinforce each other in theory, it requires great skill to navigate between these conflicting demands in practice (Reay and Hinings, 2009). If organizations fail on one of the dimensions, they risk losing support of key stakeholders in their authorizing environment (Moore, 1995; Talbot, 2008). For example, a hospital achieving excellent medical results but poor financial results, pleases the patients but alienates financial backers, and runs the risk of being shut down.

Combining different dimensions of value

The observation that public value embodies conflicting dimensions is not new. The multiplicity of expectations is perhaps the most important feature of organizations in the public domain (Selznick, 1957). Much attention has therefore been given to the clash of the different logics within an organization (see also e.g. Hood, 1991). The different logics are often described as separate worlds in constant competition with each other. Besharov and Smith (2014) detail, for example, the collision between doctors who observe medical logics versus controllers who observe financial logics.

Researchers suggest different options for bringing these dimensions together. Pache and Santos (2013) describe how organizations can select elements from the different logics to build a new logic. Thacher and Rhein (2004) explore how different logics are used by the same people at different times. Besharov and Smith (2014) detail the circumstances under which logics can live separately alongside each other.

The problem with these approaches is that they all assume that the dimensions cannot truly coexist with each other in the same time and place. In this view, managing public organizations is not about satisfying all dimensions at the same time, but about figuring out which dimension of value should take precedence in which circumstance. At best, the different dimensions and logics are laid out neatly alongside each other, but never really meet.

However, outcomes on the different dimensions of value are usually intrinsically intertwined in both the task and authorizing environment. A singular treatment decision for a patient has an effect on the quality, cost-effectiveness, and legitimacy of the care provided. Compartmentalizing decisions risks alienating stakeholders vital to the organization. The challenge is not to determine which dimension of value should take precedence, but to discover how all dimensions can find an equal place within the organizational design.

Different components of an organization

The design of an organization specifies the arrangement of its key components. In a narrow sense, the organizational design defines the separation and connection between different units, including the operating core of frontline staff, line management, strategic leadership, technical experts, and support staff (Mintzberg,

1979). In a broader sense, the organizational design also encompasses the mechanisms for communication, coordination, and decision-making between these units, making culture, values, and symbols part of the organizational design (Schein, 2010).

Organizational design is traditionally focused on the internal arrangement of the organization to best suit the complexity of the task (Mintzberg, 1991), yet Public Value Management challenges organizations to cooperate intensively with external partners in the execution of tasks (Moore, 1995). Public organizations are now encouraged to collaborate with their partners in co-creating value. Organizations therefore need to be designed to be able to actively cooperate with external partners (Alford and O'Flynn, 2012).

The design of organizations, is not only shaped by demands of the task environment, but also needs to take account of the wishes of the authorizing environment (Moore, 1995). The preferences of stakeholders may require the separation or integration of certain functions. For example, business-minded governments may require universities to outsource 'non-core' tasks such a catering and IT. In an opposite movement, home care nursing teams could be made responsible for their own finance functions because politicians want financial considerations to be an integral part of the considerations of professionals. Organizational design is therefore both an *instrumental* choice for what works given the task at hand, and an *institutional* choice for what is supported by stakeholders.

Different options for integrating dimensions of value

Given the need to address multiple dimensions of value to comply with the task and authorizing environment, organizations can design their internal structure in several different ways. In all of these options, the different dimensions of value still have a place, but the manner in which they come together differs. We propose four ways in which the different dimensions can be embedded in the organizational design (Table 4.1). Naturally, these four options represent highly stylised ideal types, with more nuanced manifestations in practice:

1. *Separate* responsibilities within the organization so that distinct organizational units focus on separate value propositions and their separate task/authorizing environments.
2. *Spread* responsibilities within the organization so that different units focus on their own dimension of value but bring these together within the same value proposition.
3. *Contrast* different perspectives on value within a unit so that multidimensional value is created by a collision between the different perspectives.
4. *Integrate* responsibilities for all dimensions of value within singular units, so that these components work towards serving all value dimensions simultaneously.

From a task perspective, these different organizational designs represent the *possibility* of separating or combining the different dimensions of value If it is possible for one part of the organization to maximize cost-effectiveness in the treatment of clients, while another part of the organization maximizes quality for those same clients, these responsibilities can be spread across different departments. However, if costs and

Table 4.1 Overview of different organizational design options

Demands from task and authorizing environment	Weak links between dimensions		Strong links between dimensions	
Options	Separate	Spread	Contrast	Integrate
Structure	Separate units service separate value propositions and their distinct groups of stakeholders	Different units work on their own dimensions of value, but jointly deliver value to the same stakeholders	Different staff have contrasting roles, but deliberate as one unit to deliver value together to the same stakeholders	All staff focus on all dimensions of value delivered to the same stakeholders
Culture	*Living apart together* Independence allows for customized value production	*Constant orchestration* Coordination creates integrated value production	*Productive conflict* Collision between different perspectives creates balanced value	*Reflective synthesis* Constant reflection on different dimensions creates balanced value
Management activities	*Proposition management* Political work to set environments for each proposition, managerial work to evaluate portfolio composition	*Coordination management* Managerial and technical work on coordination, philosophical work to find value which appeals to all units	*Deliberation management* Political, philosophical, and managerial work to balance the interplay between roles and specialities	*Reflection management* Managerial and philosophical work to stimulate and control reflection processes

quality are intimately linked, the organizational design must intertwine the different dimensions within the same units.

From an authorizing perspective, these different organizational designs represent the *desirability* of separating or combining the different dimensions of value. Fencing-off the responsibility for finance in a distinct department within a hospital, for example, signals that the question of costs-effectiveness is important, but requires specialized consideration within the organization. Integrating this responsibility in the medical team would signal that the dimensions of quality and costs are equal and should be balanced by the units themselves.

Different activities of management

We do not suggest that the tensions between cost-effectiveness, quality, and legitimacy can be solved through the static fiction of an organizational blueprint.

Public value management is all about the *dynamics* beyond the structure. We therefore also consider the cultural interaction required by the design, highlighting the different management interventions required to make these designs work in practice.

In line with the work of Moore, we distinguish between four types of management interventions in the internal and external environment of the organization (Moore, 2013; Douglas and Noordegraaf, 2016). Making the organizational design work requires *philosophical* work 'naming and justifying the important public values to be achieved by a public agency', *political* work 'building a broad, stable agreement about the important dimensions of value that those who can call the organization to account will use to evaluate agency performance', *managerial* work 'linking a performance measurement system to a performance management that can drive public efforts toward improved performance', and *technical* work 'finding or developing empirical measures that can reliably capture the degree to which the nominated values are being realized' (Moore, 2013: 90–91). When these interventions are combined in different ways, a specific management approach is generated, which will be shown beneath – varying from proposition management and coordination management to deliberation and reflection management.

Again, we do not suggest that the design of static structures can eliminate all conflict between the different dimensions of value. We do believe that the design of appropriate organizational spaces can clarify and explicate the interaction between the different dimensions, nurturing a more productive form of conflict. The four different design options create different types of operational spaces for value to come together, as appropriate to the task and authorizing environment. Keeping these spaces productive does require constant management interventions, but the reward could be the simultaneous production of value across all dimensions.

Exploring different design options

Separate different value propositions into distinct units

A single organization may be faced with multiple task and authorizing environments. For example, a Prosecution Service is typically responsible for processing thousands of appeals to traffic fines, interventions against petty crime such as shoplifting or burglary, prosecution of serious crimes such a murder, and long-term investigations into organized crime and corruption (Ridderbos, 2013).

These five different activities come with five different task and authorizing environments. The task of processing 10.000s traffic violation appeals a month requires standardized procedures and large-scale automation. Citizens making an appeal expect quick decisions, with no errors, while the Ministry of Justice wants to minimize the costs. By contrast, the task of investigating organized crime requires professional expertise and long-term investments. The same Ministry would demand results but also extreme care in this politically sensitive domain.

In this fractured environment, an organization may opt to create separate divisions with separate value propositions. In the Netherlands, the Prosecution Service decided to create five separate 'working environments' (Ridderbos, 2013). Each unit focused on a separate value proposition. The Central Processing Unit is responsible for dealing with the traffic violations, the Serious Crime Unit investigates organized crime and corruptions, et cetera. Each of these organizational units have their own configuration of cost-effectiveness, legitimacy, and quality, striking a balance as appropriate to their environment. Although they are all engaging in the same fundamental activity – prosecution – these different divisions are effectively living apart together in the same organization.

Having separate organizational units does require active *proposition management* from the organizational leadership, specifically demanding political and managerial work. The leadership needs to build the appropriate authorizing environment for each proposition to support the respective balance of value dimensions. In the case of the Central Processing Unit, the stakeholders will demands efficiency first, but legitimacy and quality have their place in as well. For the Serious Crime Unit, the organizational leadership has to enshrine the values of quality and legitimacy within the authorizing environment. The stakeholders will here rightly demands cost-effectiveness as well, but the leadership needs to make sure that the stakeholders appreciate that efficiency here does not come through standardization but through specialization.

Having separate value propositions also requires regular managerial consideration of the activity portfolio. Separate divisions with distinct tasks and stakeholder environment could be made into separate organizations. Some hospitals, for example, spin-off specialized clinics for cost-effective hip surgeries to achieve a lean and focused processing centres (see Noordegraaf and Burns, 2016). In the case of a prosecution service, however, the divisions are tied together by their shared constitutional mandate to act as the sole organization for prosecution on behalf of the state.

Spreading different value dimensions across connected units

Organizations may be asked to work on distinct tasks, but have to offer these tasks in a joint proposition to their stakeholders. In a university, for example, there is often a distinction between the core processes of teaching versus auxiliary processes such as IT-support, maintenance, and catering. The auxiliary processes thought to benefit from a continuous drive for efficiency, whereas the core processes require a more subtle balance between quality and efficiency (Girth et al., 2012). The organization can then opt to spread the different tasks of value production across the organizational structure (see Weick's description of organizations as 'loosely coupled' systems (1976)).

When spreading tasks, distinct units will get specific responsibilities. In a university, for example, the IT unit takes care of the digital services, the catering contractor provides the food, the real estate unit manages the property portfolio, while the teaching staff take care of education. However, these activities do not create value as such by themselves. A classroom cannot generate value without a teacher, but also not without IT-support (Santiago and Carvalho, 2008). Although different units have specific roles and processes, they ultimately work towards the same value proposition.

Combining the distinct activities into unified value creation requires constant *coordination management*. Spreading tasks across different teams demands extra time from the professionals and managers to coordinate between the different units. The different parts of the organization cannot perform their tasks without each other, but they are not sufficiently interconnected for their interactions to occur organically (Mintzberg, 1991). The organizational leadership has to spend much managerial work on facilitating the required communication between the different units and their processes.

The organizational leadership should also regularly explore whether auxiliary teams could not play a greater role in the public value production. For example, IT could be a key partner in an innovative teaching environment, rather than simply a support function. Integrating this unit more closely with the rest of the organization could generate more value. The authorizing environment, however, may not always support the integration of auxiliary activities. In the name of economy and marketization, for example, many universities, schools, and hospitals are obliged to outsource catering and maintenance services to private contractors (e.g. Girth et al., 2012).

Contrasting different dimensions of value within the same units

Organizations can face a task environment where the dimensions of cost, quality, and legitimacy are more intimately intertwined, but still cannot be fully integrated. The treatment decisions made in a hospital department, for example, simultaneously impact the quality, price, and societal desirability of the healthcare provided. However, the authorizing environment is often fractured, with Medical Associations, health financiers, and patient groups pushing for different dimensions of value. In addition, managing the medical, financial, or legal dimensions of care requires different skill sets (e.g. Frank and Danoff, 2007).

In this environment, organizations can opt to contrast different roles within the same unit. Unit members have their own value focus but are jointly responsible for delivering multidimensional value. For example, a hospital department might consist of medical, legal and financial members, with the different roles equally represented in the management team. While the medical professionals monitor quality, the legal specialists monitor the legitimacy of the treatment, and the controllers monitor the costs. In their joint decisions, the team members have to bridge the different value dimensions through a productive form of conflict.

Nurturing this productive clash of perspectives requires *deliberation management* from the leadership of the organization. They have to nurture and streamline the deliberation between the different perspectives, without smothering productive conflict through excessive regulation (Noordegraaf and Burns, 2016). The aim is to make sure that the experts are able to represent their specific perspectives, but also feel sufficiently responsible for the other dimensions of value to seek consensus (cf. 'pragmatic collaboration' by Reay and Hinings, 2009).

The leadership also has to make sure through political work that no perspective dominates the deliberation (e.g. Reay and Hinings, 2009). Controllers who put up financial barriers or doctors who insist that good patient care has no price can frustrate the balancing of the different dimensions, especially if these arguments are aggressively supported by external stakeholders such as healthcare insurers or medical associations. The leadership will have to give voice to oppressed perspectives in order to safeguard a balanced production of value.

Integrating different dimensions of value into single units

In a final ideal type, organizations may also be faced with task and authorizing environments where the value dimensions are so intimately linked that value creation should be an integral responsibility of the entire unit. In home care for the elderly, for example, neighbourhood teams of social workers and nurses regularly visit the elderly patients at home to perform low to medium complex care tasks. The proper fulfilment of these tasks requires customization towards the abilities and wishes of each patient, while also being able to work with the family, friends and other care professionals in each of the individual patient's environment. Separating the different tasks and dimensions of value could create overly complex organizations and unnecessary standardization, but it is still important to work efficiently.

In this type of environment, an organization could opt to design none-differentiated units with an integral responsibility for quality, costs-effectiveness, and legitimacy. A home care organization in the Netherlands made all neighbourhood teams fully responsible for their own budgets, procedures, and care plans (Leichsenring, 2012). The central management only provided minimal checks and balances. The idea is that the professionals delivering the care should get the tools and space to balance the different dimensions of value.

Integrating the different dimensions within the same unites requires active *reflection management* from the leadership in the organization. Integration depends on a constant and conscious balancing of the different dimensions of value by the professionals. In this case, it means that classic nursing professionals have to expand their initial focus on medical quality to include considerations of cost-effectiveness and legitimacy in their day-to-day decisions (Noordegraaf, 2007). The leadership has to provide the professionals with the motivation and the tools to integrate these various dimensions.

The organizational leadership also has to massage the authorizing environment to accept this integrated arrangement. External quality or cost monitors might be uncomfortable with the lack of managerial control, while patients' groups might disagree with the differing levels of care as a consequence of differing team decisions (Douglas and Noordegraaf, 2016). The leadership therefore has to spend much political work to nurture a consensus on this integrated approach to public value creation.

Conclusion

The four different design options offer different organizational spaces to match diverse task and authorizing environments. These options are stylised ideal types and will not eradicate tensions, but do offer space for more productive conflict. We illustrated our argument with examples from different professional organizations and linked these organizations to specific organizational designs. But at the same time, we argue that there might be diversity *within* these organizations, such as specialized centres for hip surgery within hospitals. This means that within more generic designs, more specific designs should be created.

First, appropriate organizational design is not all about structure, but also about culture. The structure creates the spaces where the different dimensions of public value can come together, but frontline staff, support staff, and stakeholders need to use this space effectively. In each type of structure, the effective dynamic depends on a constant and balanced interaction between the parties involved. The organizational leaders will have to support and exemplify the values and behaviour required to make the organizational design work.

Second, although most of our design options give units specific responsibilities for specific dimensions of value, each member of the organizations should have an overall concern for public value creation in general. All members of the organizations must continually assess how much public value is being created, both on their specific dimensions and across the board. The leadership has to remind members of the bigger picture and be attentive to opportunities to improve the overall creation of value.

Finally, the appropriate design may change with shifts in the task and authorizing environment. The role of different parts of the organization could evolve with the changing nature of the job and shifting expectations of society. The leadership of the organization therefore has to constantly monitor the task and authorizing environment to determine when and where to redesign the current organizational structure.

On the whole, public value management transforms the relatively static phenomenon of organizational design into a dynamic and lively affair. Organizational design is about designing *multiple* spaces for public value, where different stakeholders *interactively* intertwine the different dimensions of value, while constantly *adapting* to changes in the environment.

References

Alford, J. and O'Flynn, J. (2012). *Rethinking Public Service Delivery: Managing with External Providers*. London: Palgrave Macmillan.

Ansell, C. and Gash, A. (2008). Collaborative governance in theory and practice. *Journal of Public Administration Research and Theory*, 18(4), 543–571.

Besharov, M.L. and Smith, W.K. (2014). Multiple institutional logics in organizations: Explaining their varied nature and implications. *Academy of Management Review*, 39(3), 364–381.

Douglas, S. and Noordegraaf, M. (2016). Public managers as architects of performance: The construction of performance management systems and the impact on organizational performance. In revision with journal.

Fisher, E.S. (2008). Building a medical neighborhood for the medical home. *New England Journal of Medicine*, 359(12), 1202–1205.

Frank, J.R. and Danoff, D. (2007). The CanMEDS initiative: implementing an outcomes-based framework of physician competencies. *Medical Teacher*, 29(7), 642–647.

Girth, A.M., Hefetz, A., Johnston, J.M. and Warner, M.E. (2012). Outsourcing public service delivery: Management responses in noncompetitive markets. *Public Administration Review*, 72(6), 887–900.

Hood, C. (1991). A public management for all seasons. *Public Administration*, 69(1), 3–19.

Leichsenring, K. (2012). Integrated care for older people in Europe-latest trends and perceptions. *International Journal of Integrated Care*, 12(1).

March, J.G. and Olsen, J.P. (1976). *Ambiguity and Choice in Organisations*. Bergen: Universitetsforlaget.

Mintzberg, H. (1979). *The Structuring of Organization: A Synthesis of the Research*. Upper Saddle River: Prentice-Hall.

Mintzberg, H. (1991). The effective organization: forces and forms. *Sloan Management Review*, 32(2), 54–67.

Moore, M.H. (1995). *Creating Public Value: Strategic Management in Government*. Boston: Harvard University Press.

Moore, M.H. (2013). *Recognizing Public Value*. Boston: Harvard University Press.

Moore, M.H. (2014). Public value accounting: Establishing the philosophical basis. *Public Administration Review*, 74(4), 465–477.

Noordegraaf, M. (2015). *Public Management: Performance, Professionalism and Politics*. London: Palgrave Macmillan.

Noordegraaf, M. and Burns, L. (2016) in Hoff et al. (eds) *The Healthcare Professional Workforce*. Oxford: Oxford University Press.

Pache, A.C. and Santos, F. (2013). Inside the hybrid organization: Selective coupling as a response to competing institutional logics. *Academy of Management Journal*, 56(4), 972–1001.

Reay, T. and Hinings, C.R. (2009). Managing the rivalry of competing institutional logics. *Organization Studies*, 30(6), 629–652.

Ridderbos, M. (2013). Financial Management. In M. Noordegraaf, K. Geuijen and A. Meijer, *Handboek Publiek Management* (pp. 285–313). Den Haag: Boom Lemma.

Santiago, R. and Carvalho, T. (2008). Academics in a new work environment: The impact of new public management on work conditions. *Higher Education Quarterly*, 62(3), 204–223.

Schein, E.H. (2010). *Organizational Culture and Leadership*. San Francisco: Jossey-Bass.

Selznick, P. (1957). *Leadership in Administration: A Sociological Interpretation*. Berkeley, CA: University of California Press.

Skelcher, C. and Smith, S.R. (2015). Theorizing hybridity: Institutional logics, complex organizations, and actor identities: The case of nonprofits. *Public Administration*, 93(2), 433–448.

Stoker, G. (2006). Public value management a new narrative for networked governance? *The American Review of Public Administration*, 36(1), 41–57.

Talbot, C. (2008). Performance regimes – The institutional context of performance policies. *International Journal of Public Administration*, 31(14), 1569–1591.

Thacher, D. and Rein, M. (2004). Managing value conflict in public policy. *Governance*, 17(4), 457–486.

Williams, I. and Shearer, H. (2011). Appraising Public Value: Past, Present and Futures. *Public Administration* 89(4), 1367–1384.

Part 1.2

Different concepts of public value: material welfare and right relationships

5 Compromise after conflict

A case study in public value social science[1]

John D. Brewer, Bernadette C. Hayes and Francis Teeney

Introduction

There are two strains of public value addressed in this volume. Mark Moore's approach to public value (see Moore, 1997; 2013), which sees public value as a core concern in management and organization studies in order to ensure public practices and resources generate value, is different to Brewer's approach (2013; 2014), which defines it as a new type of social science suitable for the new millennium that is capable of addressing issues that enable social science to respond to the threats engulfing our humanitarian future. In Brewer's view, public value social science is about creating global citizens with a responsibility to our shared humanitarian future, and we see the research described in this case study as very much the sort of public value social science advocated in parts of this volume.

In the case of public value research on peace processes, this intellectual project plays out as the ambition to be better capable of understanding the nature of peace processes and the sorts of issues they throw up for analysis and amelioration. Public value research on peace processes helps societies emerging out of conflict to make sense of themselves, helps them respond to rapid social changes provoked by peace, and to understand the structural factors that privilege some groups and disadvantage others in peace processes. However, it does not concern only research, but has implications for the way we teach about peace processes and our civic engagements to assist in delivering peace, as this case study will emphasise. However, before we outline the case study, it is worth painting the broader backcloth.

The public value of peace research

Peace processes are normally approached from the standpoint of political science, International Relations, and human rights law. The principal emphasis is upon the introduction of good governance structures and thus on institutional reform. Peacebuilding in effect turns into statebuilding. The assumption is that once problematic politics is sorted out through new governance structures, everything else falls into place and the society naturally over time becomes reconciled to itself and its past.

This approach is naïve. It is necessary to distinguish between the political peace process, which concerns itself with institutional reform to introduce new governance structures, and the social peace process, which is about reconciliation between erstwhile protagonists, social relationship-building across a communal divide, civil society repair, and the replacement of brokenness by the development (or restoration) of tolerance and compromise. These concerns are either ignored by negotiators in the political peace process or assumed to follow naturally from the signing of the agreement itself. The sorts of actions that focus the social peace process include truth and reconciliation procedures, forgiveness and atonement strategies, policies that facilitate and encourage public tolerance and compromise, new forms of memory work, memorialisation and remembering, public apologies, new cultural symbols, such as national flags, anthems and the like, and the reassessment and re-evaluation of identity (this approach is expanded in Brewer, 2010; Brewer, Higgins and Teeney, 2011; Brewer, 2015).

If we focus attention on the political peace process, the domain for its operation and implementation is naturally political. Peace processes become the responsibility of governments, and the political actors that make up or aspire to be governments. However, once we recognise there is also a social peace process, peace processes become everyone's responsibility and the domain in which they function and are consolidated widens to include civil society. The social peace process thus depends for its progress on the empowerment of civil society rather than statebuilding.

The aftermath of organised violence and civil war and the difficult demands of post-conflict reconciliation and healing are examples of just the sorts of issues that threaten our humanitarian future in the twenty-first century and which form the remit of the new public value social science as we describe it (see Brewer, 2013). One of the marks of this new form of public social science is its emphasis on post-disciplinarity (on post-disciplinarity see Brewer, 2013; Jessop and Sum, 2001; Sawyer, 1999), where the nature of the problem determines the perspective not approaches from within closed disciplinary boundaries, and where collaborations should extend across large subject areas rather than narrow cognate fields in order that all its technical features can be addressed in the one piece of research (for an interesting application of a post-disciplinary research agenda to 'dark tourism', which includes visits to sites of conflict, violence and death, see Stone, 2011).

Public value research on peace processes as we envisage it is inherently post-disciplinary. Public value research on peace processes needs to link with mental health specialists when dealing with post-trauma growth, say, or with computer scientists and electrical engineers when exploring cybercrime and it role in organised violence, or, with public health specialists when considering the medical health issues of children born of rape or HIV-AIDs, which are legacies of conflict, or with drama and creative art experts when exploring the role of performance art in helping people manage the problems of dealing with the past. The social peace process brings together theologians when reflecting on the meaning of political forgiveness, planners and architects when redesigning for shared space, or geographers when conflict transformation impinges on territory and borders, and so on. The social peace process is inherently post-disciplinary.

The public value of this research is that it helps create global citizens with a responsibility to our shared humanitarian future. This affects the teaching of peace processes, the kind of research topics we address, and the sorts of civic engagements we undertake. Co-produced knowledge is well suited in the study of the social peace process and it requires that the engagements go upwards to governments and international agencies as well as downwards to victims and survivors; and this civic engagement must include the uncivil parts of civil society, such as ex-combatants, dissidents, spoilers and opponents of peace.

The capacity of public value research on peace processes, as part of the new public value social science, to garner moral sentiment and sympathetic imagination is essential when it comes to emotionally empathising as researchers with the categories of people affected by violence and who have the difficult task of learning to live together after it. Garnering these qualities in students on courses dealing with peace processes is also an essential task of our teaching, so students empathise with the marginalised and distant other suffering the consequences of violence and living in fear or anger as they try to develop a shared future with former enemies. By so doing we help to create global civic awareness about people living in societies emerging out of conflict. The ethical responsibility of our science is to try to make a difference to their lives.

It is worth briefly focusing on a module one of the authors (Brewer) taught on the sociology of peace processes at Aberdeen University as an example of the teaching strategy of public value social science that tries to achieve these ambitions in the classroom. Public value teaching is part of public value social science and this example grew out of the Leverhulme-project to illustrate the principle of research led teaching.

Public value social science teaching of peace processes

The module concerned was a fourth year, 12-week elective course open to all students in the School of Social Science (sociology, politics and international relations, and social anthropology) but was also popular amongst European Studies students. It was capped at 25 as an elective but was very popular, and normally has a reserve list. It was taught between 2004 and 2011. Its subject matter and curriculum reflected post-disciplinary public social science, drawing on all the above disciplines, as well as economics and social psychology, in order to better understand the process of societal healing after communal conflict, dealing with issues like civil society, memory, truth recovery, victimhood, religion, gender, emotions and citizenship education. It covered cases like Northern Ireland, South Africa, the Balkans, Rwanda, Sudan, Israel-Palestine, Bougainville and Poland. It was designed to educate students into global citizenship with an awareness of the impact of new forms of organized violence on societies that were emerging out of conflict. Students were told at the beginning that the course would make more demands of them than the standard lecture-seminar format, because they will be co-participants in the course, leading small groups, setting their own assignments, undertaking role plays and having to confront the real world of other people's suffering. One or two normally left at that point, and were replaced by reserves.

The course was conducted as a two-hour seminar. Full lecture notes were placed on the web for the whole course in advance, as were power point slides. This was done to emphasize the lack of importance of the lectures and note taking and, as a corollary, the importance of reading. Each session started with a short reminder of the lecture theme, after which the class broke into seminar mode. This was not a format students were used to and it took some weeks before the class gelled.

We do not want in this chapter to put stress on the curriculum content as a form of public issue social science but rather to stress the performative strategies adopted as teaching methods in order to reduce the gulf between the classroom and the real world outside. Seminars took different forms, and rotated frequently so students had a variety in the learning experience and outcomes. One format was a role play in which volunteers took the role of victim/survivor or ex-combatant in order to play out in class the conflicting demands each category has in a peace process. Other seminars involved peace activists coming into the classroom to recount their first-hand experiences. In some we played DVDs or videos in which participants in a conflict share their experiences, which could occasionally be harrowing and emotionally demanding. On some occasions, local representatives of INGOs were invited to talk to the class about what it is like in Aberdeen to think globally but act locally. Student presentations were organized in a particular way to encourage co-production. A seminar topic was set – perhaps on retributive versus restorative justice, the righteousness or not of victims displaying anger, or sport as a peace strategy – on which opposed positions could be taken. The class was split up into smaller break-out groups within the seminar room and students who did the reading lead the discussion; sometimes they were required to report back, sometimes not. It was responsibility for leading and managing the group discussion that was the learning outcome, not the communication skills in reporting back. In this way students were taking some responsibility for their own learning. They also get to choose their assignment topic in order to pursue their individual interests.

The course was assessed on each occasion through comments sent to the class representative and through an anonymous web-based questionnaire that permits more in-depth comments. The following is a selection of comments from the 2011–2012 class on the effectiveness of the format in realizing what here we have called public value social science. 'It was so much better than it looked on the course list. It appealed to me because I've always been interested in the idea of being a global citizen.' 'As a sociologist I cannot help but be concerned about people, and harm to them from conflict. Peace processes was a magnet to me.' 'Interesting and relevant to today.' 'Peace processes is a subject of importance today.' 'Peace processes, conflict, are a personal area of interest and I have been looking forward to taking this course for two years.'

What follows now are comments from the same cohort on whether the teaching format helped in the performance of personal and social transformation. 'He effectively integrated the entire class to the extent that at the end of the semester the majority were on speaking terms. He changed the dynamics of a lecture. Every week he changed how the class was taught, different, effective teaching methods that involved you.' 'The course was very innovative in the range of assignments, for example the role play, this turned out to be very interesting, very clear and easy to understand while also showing the complexities.' 'Its form[at] allows for more informal, more personal study atmosphere, moreover, the relation of course content with examples from around the world made for a good mix of theory and practice often lacking in other courses.' 'It gave me new friends and a confidence in my own abilities.' 'It has inspired me to explore future options as a citizenship educator.' 'Going global, being up-to-date, that's what I liked about it.' 'The course opens your eyes to what is happening in the world.' 'It was very nice to be able to engage with the material by myself and gauge my own responses. I enjoyed the flexibility of the course and the different teaching methods.' 'The seminar style of teaching was a refreshing change and made the class more interactive.'

The teaching dimensions of public value social science have been stressed in order to emphasise that it is not solely a research strategy. It is necessary now, however, to outline the case study on research amongst victims of conflict.

The compromise after conflict research programme

The new public social science of peace processes, in teaching and research, has a normative public value that can be summarised as follows: to try to make a difference to the lives of ordinary people who are struggling with the aftermath of conflict by empowering them to realise fairness, justice and tolerance. Societies emerging out of conflict need public social science more than most, and public value research on peace processes helps them come to terms with their violent pasts and assists them in inheriting a more peaceful future. We would like to illustrate these claims by addressing the example of the Compromise after Conflict research programme. The award of £1,267,093 was made in July 2009 for six years, with the research programme beginning 1 September 2009. The award was made to the Principal Investigator, John Brewer, and two Co-Investigators, Bernadette Hayes and Francis Teeney, all then at the University of Aberdeen. It employed three Research Fellows – Katrin Dudgeon (4 years), Natascha Mueller-Hirth (4 years) and Corinne Caumartin (2 years) – and funded four PhD students for three years – Laura Fowler, Sandra Rios, Rachel Anderson and Clare Magill. We established an International Advisory Board, chaired by Professor Ian McAllister from Australia National University, to which was submitted an Annual Report for their critical evaluation. In April 2013, Brewer and Teeney moved to Queen's University, from where the grant was then administered, leaving some staff – Hayes and Mueller-Hirth – and PhD students in Aberdeen. The award came to an end on 4 September 2015.

We had two main objectives – one conceptual, the other empirical – enabling us to theorise the nature of compromise after conflict, and to study it empirically in post-conflict societies. Empirically, our research programme addressed the processes and resources that develop and sustain feelings of compromise amongst victims of communal conflict in Northern Ireland, Sri Lanka and South Africa. These countries were deliberately chosen because they represented what Weber called a 'naturally occurring experiment', in that they had different kinds of peace process and conflict transformation had occurred in different time periods. This allowed us to introduce a longitudinal element in our research to establish whether time really does heal, and to establish whether different forms of peace process assist in the development of compromise amongst victims.

Conceptually, we sought to establish the different emotions wrapped up with feelings of compromise, as well as the kinds of social relationships on which it was premised and which it entailed. We also wanted to understand the range of factors that inhibited the development and practice of compromise and which factors promoted it. Our aim therefore was to deconstruct the emotions and behaviours embedded in compromise and to locate them within a repertoire of affective-relational responses to stress. We hypothesised that these responses were hope-anticipation, forgiveness-redemption and memory-remembrance. We set out an operational starting point that compromise amongst victims-perpetrators should be understood as a process that involves hope-anticipation of the future, forgiveness-redemption for perpetrators and forms of memory-remembrance of the conflict that transcend divided memories. This repertoire of stress responses was at one and the same time the process by which compromise works and the resources for garnering and sustaining it.

Our research design was purposely cross-national and mixed in methods. Our over-arching research ambition was to engage in an empirical investigation of what is a slippery concept in order to get a firm hold over its conceptual meaning and actual practice by victims of communal conflict. We conducted in-depth interviews with a cross-section of victims in all three arenas of contemporary conflict, garnered through victim support groups, personal contacts and the snowball technique, and conducted social surveys of the general population in Northern Ireland and Sri Lanka. The survey in Northern Ireland was a nationally representative sample of the adult population, with sample size of 1,500; the survey in Sri Lanka was not nationally representative and had a sample size of 500.

The findings are not important in the context of the chapter (for some of the results however, see Brewer and Hayes, 2011; 2013; 2015a; 2015b; Rios, 2015; Graham, 2016), but we highlight instead four particular achievements which evidence public value social science as forms of civic and public engagement.

Online interactive data archive. The programme has established a public facing online interactive data archive for use by members of the public and civil society groups (churches, schools, youth groups, ex-combatant groups, victims' groups, etc.), as a resource to help them work through the issues of conflict transformation. It has its own web domain and can be accessed at http://compromiseafterconflict. org. The archive addresses twelve themes from the data (forgiveness, religion, survival, fear, anxiety, inequality, etc.) and is enriched with drawings made by a Colombian victim, and has photographs, web links and YouTube clips to assist the text. It was only launched on 4 September 2015 and as at 23 October 2015 it had received 904 visitors. We recognise the importance, however, of continually publicising it as a resource for open access use.

Palgrave Book Series. The programme has its own book series *Palgrave Studies in Compromise after Conflict* (www.palgrave.com/series/Palgrave-Studies-in-Compromise-after-Conflict/PSCAC/). This is designed as the publication outlet for our own books deriving from the research but also for other appropriate work. Three books have appeared, two are in press, and a further six are under contract. The Series publishes senior authors and early career researchers. Two of the books are revised versions of PhDs funded under the programme (Fowler and Rios). It has an International Advisory Board: John Braithwaite (Australian National University); Hastings Donnan (Queen's University Belfast, UK); Brandon Hamber (University of Ulster, UK); Ian McAllister (Australian National University); William Mishler (University of Arizona, USA); Barbara Misztal (University of Leicester, UK); Orla Muldoon (University of Limerick, Ireland); Clifford Shearing (University of Cape Town, South Africa). It acts as an important outlet for the new approach to peace processes that emphasises social peace.

Social media penetration. We made very effective use of social media to publicise the research, disseminate news and works-in-progress, and to engage with users. At 7 April 2017, our Twitter following @Compromisestudy stood at 7976, while the individual accounts of Brewer (4476 followers) and Teeney (1259 followers) increased the reach of the programme dramatically. Large numbers of our followers are global figures, international governments, religious leaders, and mainstream media. They range from the White House to the EU, Downing Street, the UN, Ghandi Foundation, the Mandela Foundation, the Vatican, NATO, BBC, and all manner of political parties and pressure groups. Our Facebook page (www.facebook.com/pages/Compromise-After-Conflict/397300973637278) has 722 'likes' and has a total reach of many thousands each week due to the high profile of our followers. We ran a very successful blog during the tenure of the programme at http://blogs.qub.ac.uk/compromiseafterconflict/, which was highly effective in terms of message dissemination and public engagement. We ran simultaneous articles with local press and even had a two page spread in the *Times Higher Education* (see http://bit.ly/GHW4OL). Over its length the blog received in excess of 1,500,000 hits. Twitter and Facebook accounts will continue beyond the life of the programme but the blog has terminated.

Sri Lankan widows and orphans initiative. Following on from the Principal Investigator's visit to Sri Lanka in February 2012 as part of the programme, it was agreed with members of the Asian Institute of Missiology, the programme's local research partner, to engage in a small scale but active civil society peacebuilding project. The first contact was made in a village in the Northern Province, where John Brewer met some of the widows and their children. The inaugural meeting took place in March 2012 to bring together Sinhalese and Tamil widows and their children as part of grassroots peace building and reconciliation work. The intention was to enable them to see that they shared a victimhood experience and that their pain, grief and loss were the same. The second meeting took place in December 2012. The first two meetings were funded from within Sri Lanka. At the first meeting held in Anuradhapura, participated in by both Sinhalese and Tamil widows and their children, one of the Tamil participants said of this inaugural meeting: 'it was marvellous and really touched all in this vulnerable stage of life. It is appreciated by all.' Regretfully the initiative proved to be short lived because of the deteriorating security situation in Sri Lanka and the inability to generate interest amongst Western donors.

Conclusion

In this case study we have tried to show that public value social science is capable of being practised, both in terms of teaching and research. It has high ambitions but these can be realised. The case study described here was purposely conceived within the model of public value social research and designed to implement it. Public value social science research, however, can also be realised after the fact by the way in which its findings are used and the public engaged. It can be written in a way that encourages emotional empathy in others and which tries to make a difference to the lives of ordinary people.

Note

1 We gratefully acknowledge the support of the Leverhulme Trust in funding the research on which this paper is based under grant number F/00 152/AK

References

Brewer, John D. (2010) *Peace Processes: A Sociological Approach.* Cambridge: Polity Press.
Brewer, John D. (2013) *The Public Value of the Social Sciences: An Interpretative Essay.* London: Bloomsbury Academic.

Brewer, John D. (2014) Society as a Vocation: Renewing Social Science for Social Renewal. *Irish Journal of Sociology* 22(2), 127–137.

Brewer, John D. (2015) Peace Processes. In J. Wright (ed.), *International Encyclopedia of Social and Behavioral Sciences*, 2nd edn (pp. 648–653). Oxford: Elseviers.

Brewer, John D. and Hayes, Bernadette C. (2011) Victims as Moral Beacons: Victims and Perpetrators in Northern Ireland. *Contemporary Social Science: Journal of Academy of Social Science* 6(1), 73–88.

Brewer, John D. and Hayes, Bernadette C. (2013) Victimhood Status and Public Attitudes toward Post-Conflict Agreements: Northern Ireland as a Case Study. *Political Studies* 61, 442–461.

Brewer, John D. and Hayes, Bernadette C. (2015a) Victimhood and Attitudes Towards Dealing with the Legacy of a Violent Past: Northern Ireland as a Case Study. *British Journal of Politics and International Relations* 17(3), 512–530.

Brewer, John D. and Hayes, Bernadette C. (2015b) Victimisation and Attitudes Towards Former Political Prisoners in Northern Ireland. *Terrorism and Political Violence* 27(4), 741–761.

Brewer, John D., Higgins, Gareth I. and Teeney, F. (2011) *Religion, Civil Society and Peace in Northern Ireland*. Oxford: Oxford University Press.

Graham, Laura (2016) *Beyond Social Capital: The Role of Leadership, Trust, and Government Policy in Northern Ireland's Victim Support Groups*. London: Palgrave.

Jessop, Bob and Sum, Ngai-Ling (2001) Pre-Disciplinary and Post-Disciplinary Perspectives. *New Political Economy* 6(1), 89–101.

Moore, Mark (1997) *Creating Public Value*. Cambridge, MA: Harvard University Press.

Moore, Mark (2013) *Recognizing Public Value*. Cambridge, MA: Harvard University Press.

Rios, Sandra (2015) *Religion, Social Memory and Conflict: The Massacre of Bojayá in Colombia*. London: Palgrave.

Sayer, Andrew (1999) *Long Live Postdisciplinary Studies! Sociology and the Curse of Disciplinary Parochialism/Imperialism*. Department of Sociology, Lancaster University, Lancaster. Available online at www.comp.lancs.ac.uk/sociology/papers/Sayer-Long-Live-postdisciplinaryStudies.pdf

Stone, P.R. (2011) Dark Tourism: Towards a New Post-Disciplinary Research Agenda. *International Journal of Tourism Anthropology*, 1 (3/4), 318–332.

6 Social suffering and public value

A spur to new projects of social inquiry and social care

Iain Wilkinson

Introduction

One of the distinguishing features of social science in the twenty-first century lies in a new-found concern with problems of 'social suffering'. Over the past thirty years or so this has featured as a headline interest in some important works of critical sociology and anthropology (Bourdieu et al., 1999; Kleinman et al., 1997; Das et al., 2001; Renault, 2008). With reference to 'social suffering' researchers declare a commitment to understand how human suffering is caused by society, but with a focus brought to how this is encountered and manifested in people's experiences of day-to-day life. Forms of social organization and uneven distributions of socio-economic resources are made subject to critical debate with attention placed on lived experiences of pain and misery. More directly, this involves researchers documenting the ways individuals give voice to their distress and how suffering is manifested in their physical and mental health conditions. The incidence of social suffering is understood to expose how society operates to damage people's human dignity and personhood. Here social life is taken as a distinctly moral experience that greatly matters for people (Kleinman, 1998; 2006). Readers are invited to feel for the plight of individuals caught up in situations of adversity. A deliberate attempt is made to stir up emotions of sympathy and compassion on the understanding that these hold the potential to operate as a means to forge bonds of social solidarity and a political concern for social justice (Farmer, 2006). In this regard, research and writing on social suffering is directly concerned with advancing the public value of social science (Brewer, 2013). Here the conduct of social research is informed by an earlier 'classical' example of critical pragmatism championed by figures such as Jane Addams, W.E.B du Bois and Albion Small (Addams, 1998 [1910]; Becker, 1971; Deegan, 1988; Morris, 2015). It is directed by the understanding that social science should be committed to projects of ameliorative social reform. The pedagogy of caregiving is deemed a necessary part of the processes through which we might apprehend the meaning and value of human life in social terms (Wilkinson and Kleinman, 2016).

Arguably this approach is connected to a wider movement within contemporary social science that seeks to better understand the roles played by human emotions in the conduct of social life (Forgas, 2001; Lvon and Barbalet ,2004; Williams, 2001). Research and writing on social suffering can be portrayed as part of an 'affective turn' where scholars attend to how human thoughts and behaviors are directed by moral feelings, and further take note of how these are set to shape our politics (Ahmed, 2014). Here a connection might also be drawn to critical movements operating within medical sociology that aim to expose the damage done to people through the 'medicalization' of health. It is notably the case that social suffering features as a concern among those intent on questioning the values governing the conduct of modern rationality as applied to health care and the practice of medicine, and more often than not this is accompanied by a protest against the ways these are set opposed to humanitarian principle and the appeal of moral sentiment (Abramowitz et al., 2015; Farmer et al., 2013).

The attention that is brought to problems of social suffering can also be related to the fact that over the last fifty years or so, new communication media, and especially through the forms of cultural experience made possible by television and the internet, have transformed the ways we relate to our moral situation and the needs of others (Wilkinson 2005; 2013). The daily routine of watching television news or trawling viral video sites brings us into contact with dramatic scenes of war, famine, atrocity and abuse that were unknown to previous generations (Thompson, 1995, 226–227). Insofar as it is now commonplace for us to gaze upon human suffering at a safe distance far removed from actual contexts of violence and harm, it is argued that we need to re-think our ethical situation and reappraise the bounds of moral responsibility (Boltanski, 1999; Chouliaraki, 2006; 2013; Cohen, 2001). It is argued that the dramatic scale of the world problems now made visible for us, and especially through graphic depictions of human suffering, is operating to transform social subjectivity in ways we scarcely recognize or understand (Biehl, Good and Kleinman, 2007). Some of those involved with problems of social suffering share in an attempt to make better sense of our existential condition in a cultural context where it is commonplace for human misery to be commercialized as news 'infotainment' (Kleinman, 1995; Kleinman and Kleinman, 1997). On this view, by documenting expressions of moral feeling that take place in response to the suffering of others, and by attending to how these appear to influence the dynamics of social action, we are seeking to understand distinctly new possibilities for human consciousness and behaviour (Rifkin, 2009).

At another level of understanding, however, the twenty first century interest in social suffering marks a return to traditions of social inquiry that place a high value on the cultivation of our potential for 'fellow feeling' (Mullan 1988). 'Social suffering' is a concept that originates in the eighteenth century enlightenment of sympathy (Frazer, 2010; Wilkinson and Kleinman, 2016, 25–29). It belongs to an earlier cultural and political movement that welcomed the eighteenth century flowering of humanitarian sensibility as a means to further the bounds of social recognition and social understanding. In this context 'the social question' was first posed along with the understanding that it involved us in a political debate over how to respond to the moral feelings we experience when we are made to observe the suffering of others (Himmelfarb, 1991). It was commonly the case, moreover, that those such as William Wordsworth, who was among the first draw a focus to 'social suffering' as such, were of the opinion that compassion had a vital role to play in making it possible for us to grasp how conditions of social life directly matter for people (Wilkinson and Kleinman, 2016, 25–29).

Throughout the nineteenth century this was an issue of great controversy. Among educated elites, humanitarian sentiment tended to be portrayed as an irrational force that, if left unchecked, was set to become a moral corruption. Social sympathy was variously cast as a feminine weakness, an encouragement to indiscriminate charity and as a lust for sensationalism that led people to indulge in acts of promiscuous voyeurism (Barker-Benfield, 1992; Halttunen, 1995; Reddy, 2000). As Hannah Arendt reminds us, there were also occasions where 'the passion of compassion' was understood to operate as an encouragement to revolutionary insurrection, for it was widely assumed that a morally outraged and sentiment fired response to human suffering could be used to justify violence as the means to make right the world (Arendt, 1963, 59–114). For these reasons, moreover, among most early practitioners of social science, and especially those concerned with the status of sociology and anthropology as 'science', the 'rebellion of sentiment' tended to be cast as an anathema to sound reason and principled judgement (Bannister, 1991; Haskell, 2000; Lepenies, 1988; Poovey, 1995; 1998; Roberts, 2002, 258–295).

In this chapter I offer a brief review of contemporary research and writing on social suffering. This is designed as an invitation to further dialogue and debate. The first section offers a more detailed overview of the range of interests and concerns that characterize the ways in which problems of social suffering are addressed in current sociology and anthropology. The second section further outlines how these developments are set to court moral and political controversy. I conclude by arguing that the renewed gathering of interest around problems of social suffering is set to make the public value of social science a pressing matter for debate. More directly, this draws a focus to many longstanding tensions and hostilities in the relationship between social science and modern humanitarianism. I suggest that here we are challenged to reformulate and revise the ways we assess the role of moral sentiment in the production of social understanding. I also hold that the conduct of social research is drawn into debate in terms of how it operates a moral practice, and at this point it stands to be judged not so much in terms of the production of critique, but rather in its contribution to the practice of human care.

The field of social suffering

The concept of 'social suffering' is used to refer us to the lived experience of pain, damage, injury, deprivation and loss. Here it is generally understood that human afflictions are encountered in multiple forms and that their deleterious effects are manifold, but a particular emphasis is brought to bear upon the extent to which particular social conditions and distinct forms of culture both constitute and moderate the ways in which suffering is experienced and expressed. With reference to 'social suffering' researchers attend to the ways in which the subjective components of distress are rooted in social situations and conditioned by cultural circumstance. It is held that social worlds are inscribed upon the embodied experience of pain and that there are many occasions where an individual's suffering should be taken as a manifestation of wider processes of social structural oppression and/or collective experiences of cultural trauma (Wilkinson, 2005; Kleinman et al., 1997; Kleinman and Wilkinson, 2016).

In the sociology of health, social medicine and medical anthropology, 'social suffering' is associated with efforts to broaden the biomedical conceptualization of pain so that recognition is brought to the ways in which both the experience of pain and a person's responsiveness to its 'treatment' are moderated by cultural conditions and social contexts (Bendelow, 2006; Delvecchio Good et al., 1992). And here it also features as part of a critical engagement with conventions of health care practice that aims to make these more attuned to the lived experience of illness and the involvement of people's social biographies within the generation of debilitating forms of mental anguish and distress. With a focus brought to problems of social suffering, a person's health condition is cast as a cumulative product of social processes and critical life events. It is argued that in the quality of a person's physical and mental health we are presented with a moral barometer of their social experience (Kleinman, 1988; 1999; 2006).

In the contexts of French sociology and psychology, research and writing on 'social suffering' has been taken up as a means to bring public attention to the cumulative miseries of ordinary life, and here such work tends to be overtly political in its intentions and design (Renault, 2008). It operates as part of a movement to expose the negative social effects of neo-liberal economic policies. It works to expose the harms that are done to people trapped living in poor housing conditions in areas mired in social deprivation. It documents the many humiliations and agonizing frustrations borne by the unemployed as well as those struggling to survive on the low wages they receive for the exhausting hours spent performing menial work tasks (Dejours, 1998; Bourdieu et al., 1999). Practitioners argue that where government ministers and policy makers are often inclined to 'explain away' such suffering as an unfortunate and unavoidable 'side-effect' of social life in capitalist societies, by contrast, we should regard this as morally and politically unacceptable and as a pressing matter for critical concern. Accordingly, 'social suffering' is addressed as a problem that issues a humanitarian challenge to the moral conventions of our political culture, and further, aims to provoke us into a critical questioning of the cultural and political processes whereby 'we' are acclimatised to regard the suffering of 'others' as a 'normal' or 'necessary' condition of social life.

The concern to 'bear witness' to the experience of 'marginality', and especially the plight of the poorest sections of society, has also drawn many to place problems of 'social suffering' at the centre of the attempt to draw public attention to the experience of people living in developing societies, and in this respect, many of those concerned with problems of social suffering are also engaged in an attempt to re-align the polarities of global social understanding. The documentation of experiences of people suffering from diseases of poverty is taken up as a means to engage in global public debate over the structural conditions that systematically reproduce the material and social deprivation of the so-called 'Third World' (Farmer, 1997; 1999; 2005; Farmer et al., 2013). Indeed, the advocacy of human rights and humanitarian social reform is made explicit in many instances where 'social suffering' is deployed as a descriptive tool and/or analytical device for conveying the human consequences of the physical violence, emotional distress and social deprivation experienced in contexts of war, civil conflict and totalitarian abuse (Das, 1995; 2007; Scheper-Hughes, 1992; 1997; 1998).

It is possible to characterise a great deal of research and writing on 'social suffering' as a critical praxis that seeks to establish the right of people to have rights (Arendt, 1973). Some label what takes place here as a 'politics of recognition'. Axel Honneth argues that it is often the case that contexts of social suffering are discussed as part of a 'disclosing critique' that aims to make known the 'pathologies of the social' in which 'the other of justice' is denied moral recognition and respect for their rights (Honneth, 1995). For example, Paul Farmer contends that 'a failure of imagination is one of the greatest failures in contemplating the fate of the world's poorest', and aims to use ethnographic texts and photography as a means to shock his readers into questioning the human values and responsibilities that bind them to the victims of suffering (Farmer, 2006: 145). He uses whatever 'rhetorical tools' are available to him to convey the experience of individuals dying from AIDS and seeks to offend readers' sensibilities with images of the physical torment suffered by people living in circumstances of extreme material deprivation. Farmer uses such methods to advocate an expanded notion of human rights that gives as much importance to the right to 'freedom from want' as to civil and political rights.

Similarly, Veena Das explains her work as an attempt to devise 'languages of pain' by which social sciences might be crafted as a textual body on which 'pain is written' (Das, 1997, 67). Her ethnographic practice is designed to fashion a re-entry to 'scenes of devastation' and worlds 'made strange though the desolating experience of violence and loss (ibid.). Here the efforts made to convey the standpoint of women who have been subjected to brutal acts of violence in the internecine conflicts of India's civil wars are intended as a means to 'convert' such experience into a script that can be used to establish ties of empathy and communal self-understanding. Das presents this as part of a 'work of healing' that creates a social space for the recognition of human rights and possibilities for a retrieval of human dignity (Das, 1994; 1995; 2007; Das et al., 2001).

Whilst engaging with such struggles for recognition, writers such as Farmer and Das tend to present this as merely a point of beginning. The foregrounding of people's experiences social suffering is intended not only as a plea for recognition but also as a means to initiate a wider set of inquiries into the institutional foundations of civil society and the grounds upon which it may be possible to realise people's social and economic rights. For example, Farmer writes:

> [R]ecognition is not enough. ...We need another modern movement, a glo-balized movement that will use whatever stories and images it can to promote respect for human rights, especially the rights of the poor. For such a movement to come about, we need to rehabilitate a series of sentiments long out of fashion in academic and policy circles: indignation on behalf not of oneself but of the less fortunate; solidarity; empathy; and even pity, compassion, mercy, and remorse. . . . Stories and images need to be linked to the historically deeper and geographically wider analyses that can allow the listener or the observer to understand the ways in which AIDS, a new disease, is rooted in the historically defined conditions that promote its spread and deny its treatment; the ways in which genocide, like slavery before it, is a fundamentally 'transnational' event; the reasons why breast cancer is inevitably fatal for the most affected women in who live in poverty; the meaning of rights in an interconnected world riven by poverty and inequality. In short, serious social ills require in-depth analyses.
>
> (Farmer, 2006, 185)

In many instances, documents of social suffering are committed to humanitarian projects of social reform. Humanitarian care for people is identified with care for human society as such, and further, by our participation in acts of caregiving, it is argued that it is made possible to work at understanding how human social life is made possible, and in particular the forms of social life which make possible pro-social human relationships (Wilkinson and Kleinman, 2016: 161–187). This is the approach that sustained Jane Addams' approach to 'doing sociology' in the context of the activities of the progressive era Chicago settlement community of Hull-House (Addams 1965 [1892]; 1998 [1910]; 2002 [1902]). Addams not only set caregiving as the practical aim of her sociology, but further, she understood acts of care to hold the potential to expose how social life takes place in enactments of substantive human values. The experience of caregiving was taken as the grounds for critical thinking about human social conditions and the potential for sociology to be applied to their amelioration. These commitments and terms of understanding are once again being advanced as a prime concern in the humanitarian medical anthropology of Philip Bourgois, Paul Farmer, Arthur Kleinman and Nancy Scheper-Hughes (Bourgois, 2002; Bourgois and Schonberg, 2009; Farmer, 1992; 1999; 2006; 2013; Kleinman, 1980; 2006; Scheper-Hughes, 1992; 1998; 2005; 2011). In this context, research and writing on social suffering represents a call for social scientists to move beyond the politics of recognition so as to directly involve themselves in actions to deliver humanitarian social change. The work of critique is merely taken as a means to clear a space in which to advance projects of practical care.

Re-awakening controversy

As mentioned at the outset of this chapter, the earliest references to 'social suffering' were connected to initiatives to promote humanitarian social concern and these attracted a great deal of public controversy, intellectual dispute and political contest. This was partly linked to the political fallout from a radical break in received traditions of moral understanding whereby accounts of human affliction in terms of religious theodicy were being replaced with explanations that drew man-made conditions of society into debate (Vidich and Lyman, 1985; Morgan and Wilkinson, 2001). Where for most of human history, the experience of suffering had been invested with religious meaning, here for the first time it was addressed in largely secular terms as a matter that sounded a distinctly *social* alarm, and which further pointed to the fact that something was seriously wrong with the conditions of society in which people were made to live. Many of the early controversies attached to 'social suffering' were also connected to disputes surrounding the moral status of 'the social' as a category of human understanding, and further, to how this should be formulated as a matter of study and debate.

For many, these became most heated in contexts where it was claimed that critical thought about social life and movements to secure progressive social change should be open to the influence of moral feeling. Where on the one hand, some, and especially those identified as 'humanitarian', took the view that the moral feelings aroused in face of the brute facts of human suffering were a vital and necessary part of the cultivation of social consciousness and conscience, others, and especially those set on a mission to 'scientize' the study of society, held that these should play no part in rational processes investigation and debate (Wilkinson and Kleinman, 2016: 148). Critics of social sensibility were worried by the possibility that moral sentiment was open to corruption to a point where it became more a vice than a virtue (Halttunen, 1995). They also worried over the extent to which it could be appropriated in the service of projects of ideological manipulation (Ellis, 1996, 190–221). Humanitarian moral feelings, and especially those connected to the 'the social question', were portrayed as wild and unruly, and as opposed to reason and principled debate (Arendt, 1963). By contrast, those prepared to take social sympathy as a guide to critical thought and action tended to see a greater danger lying in the propensity for cultures of rationalization to operate, as Max Weber famously put it, 'without regard for persons' (Weber, 1948, 215). In this context, the 'rebellion of sentiment' tended to be directed towards laissez-faire economics and utilitarian forms of thinking in social policy that, by advancing the rule of calculation above all other considerations, operated to draw a dispassionate veil over many desperate human situations and personal miseries (Roberts, 2002, 258–331).

It might be argued that in more recent debates connected to problems of 'social suffering', sociologists and anthropologists are revisiting these earlier controversies and are occupying similar value positions. For example, critics such as Craig Calhoun and Lilie Chouliaraki are overwhelmingly preoccupied with exposing the ways in which 'the humanitarian imperative to reduce suffering' and 'the humanitarian imaginary' are used to constrain critical thought and to promote self-serving strains of sentimentality (Calhoun, 2004; 2008; Chouliaraki, 2013). Similarly, and with more direct concern with the involvement of research and writing on social suffering in contemporary humanitarian politics, Didier Fassin portrays 'humanitarian reason' as a delusional ideology that more often than not operates to institute relations of domination across society. He further argues that here social scientists tend to be fooled into thinking that simply by listening to the misfortunes of others that they are engaged in some form of emancipatory social practice (Fassin, 2012). Although very much concerned with the culture and politics of their times, in these instances once again an overwhelming emphasis is placed on the potential for humanitarian culture and moral sentiment to operate to occlude clear sighted critical rationality, and often this is coupled with further worries relating to its potential to promote ideologies of discriminatory social control above any serious attempt to address the real causes and scale of human suffering.

Taking an opposing view, those associated with research and writing on social suffering prefer to place a greater emphasis on the propensity for technocratic discourse to explain away people's hardships so that that these are reduced to a meaningless triviality. For example, Pierre Bourdieu argues that we should be more worried by the moral position occupied by critical social scientists when they operate from an 'objectivising distance that reduces the individual to a specimen in a display case' (Bourdieu, 1999a, 2). He urges us to attend to the 'symbolic violence' perpetrated by rationalising conventions of academic writing that work to clear and cut a way through the many hermeneutic confusions and epistemological frustrations borne by people under common sense conditions of everyday life. As he puts it, the greater danger here is that in our social science 'we do nothing but gloss one another' (Bourdieu, 1999b, 607).

By no means is this to deny that there are many risks inherent in forms of writing that seek to cultivate a sympathetic approach to social understanding, rather the key point here is that every symbolic portrayal of social life risks being used in harmful ways that diminish people's humanity. Practitioners of social science cannot operate above the fray of morality and politics. In all their research, and all the more so because it directly concerns what matters for people, they are engaged in enactments of human value. Accordingly, those with a commitment to expose conditions of social suffering do not shy away from courting 'unstable emotions' or from having their work associated with the many controversies are readily attached to modern humanitarianism, for these are taken to be a condition of human social life as such (Farmer, 2006). It is suggested if we are serious in our efforts to understand how social life matters for people we must be prepared to broker with the difficulty of making adequate sense of human suffering, and further that this requires us to deal with many painful and morally provocative feelings.

Moreover, it is suggested that this must involve more than critique, for there is a danger here that, within social science at least, critique has a potential to operate as an evasion of social life. While occupying the critical 'high ground', it is argued that social scientists often fail to critically question the values enacted through their own practices within the academy and research field. In this regard, the pedagogy of care that is advocated in some accounts of social suffering is taken not only as part of a moral commitment to people's wellbeing, but also as an essential part of the attempt to understand how social life is made humanly possible and humane. Here research and writing on social suffering is informed by classical traditions of critical pragmatism where researchers hold themselves up to be judged in terms of the practical actions and lived possibilities that result from their work (Wilkinson and Kleinman, 2016).

For discussion

With a focus brought to problems of social suffering researchers tend to operate with the understanding that they are involved in reconfiguring the value orientations of social science and its practice. We are called to attend to the ways in which individuals and societies experience suffering as well as the historical and cultural conditions under which this is ascribed with moral meaning. The problem of human suffering is identified as a decisive element within the formation of individual personalities and within the overall character of societies. The social practices by which individuals struggle to endure this experience, along the institutional arrangements that are set in place under the effort to minimise its deleterious effects on human life, are held to exert a major influence over the formation of political cultures and the dynamics of social change. Here there is also an overt concern to expose the connections between modern humanitarianism and our capacity to relate to one another as social beings in need of social care. Social science is conducted with the understanding that caregiving makes a vital contribution to the development of social understanding, and that our capacity for social understanding is advanced through caregiving.

Writing at the turn of the twentieth century some of early pioneers of sociology such as Lester Frank Ward, Albion Small and Jane Addams promoted the view that sociology should be allied with humanitarianism. While many of the social scientists of their day stood opposed to do-gooder confusion and openly disparaged its sentimentalism, these three held out the hope that sociology might still operate as the handmaid to humanitarian social reform. On this view, it was still possible for rational social science to collaborate with sentiment-fired social inquiry, and it was still possible for critical reason to be informed by humanitarian feeling. However, with the advance of academic sociology and the cementing of the links between scientific accreditation and the pursuit of career, such vision was lost (Becker, 1971; Mazlish, 1989). Largely speaking, at its origins social science within the academy was set antagonistically opposed to humanitarianism.

Research and writing on social suffering courts dispute. This not only relates to the struggle to diagnose the causes of human suffering and to identify what can be done to help people in situations of adversity. It also draws traditions of social inquiry into debate on account of their moral value and human purpose. In the historical record of human suffering, we repeatedly come across the extreme paradox that through experiences that entail the most terrible uprooting of life, people are brought under the compulsion to reach out for what really matters in their lives. This appears to be engrained in the character of the work that takes place here, and social science is also made to account for itself on these terms. Social science is continually set to confront its limits, but also with a commitment to making these more suited to what social life matters *for people*. The hope here is that there are still better ways to relate to our modern human condition, and that it is yet possible for us to realise more humane forms of society.

References

Abramowitz, S., Marten, M. and Panter-Brick, C. (2015) 'Medical Humanitarianism: Anthropologists Speak Out on Policy and Practice'. *Medical Anthropology Quarterly*, 29(1): 1–23.

Addams, J. (1965 [1892]) 'The Subjective Necessity for the Social Settlements'. In Lasch, C. (ed.) *The Social Thought of Jane Addams*. Indianapolis: The Bobbs-Merrill Company.

Addams, J. (1998 [1910]) *Twenty Years at Hull House*. New York: Penguin.

Addams, J. (2002 [1902]) *Democracy and Social Ethics*. Urbana and Chicago: University of Illinois.

Ahmed, S. (2014) *The Cultural Politics of Emotion*. Edinburgh: Edinburgh University Press.

Arendt, H. (1963) *On Revolution*. Harmondsworth: Penguin.

Arendt, H. (1973) *The Origins of Totalitarianism*. New York: Harcourt Brace Janovich.

Bannister, R.C. (1991) *Sociology and Scientism: The American Quest for Objectivity, 1880–1940*. Chapel Hill: UNC Press.

Barker-Benfield, G.J. (1992) *The Culture of Sensibility: Sex and Society in Eighteenth Century Britain*. Chicago: University of Chicago Press.

Becker, E. (1971) *The Lost Science of Man*. New York: George Braziller.

Bendelow, G. (2006) 'Pain, Suffering and Risk'. *Health, Risk & Society*, 8(1): 59–70.

Biehl, J., Good, B. and Kleinman, A. (2007) 'Introduction: Rethinking Subjectivity'. In Biehl, J., Good, B. and Kleinman, A. (eds), *Subjectivity: Ethnographic Investigations*. Berkeley: University of California Press.

Boltanski, L. (1999) *Distant Suffering: Morality, Media and Politics*. Cambridge: Cambridge University Press.

Bourdieu, P. et al. (1999) *The Weight of the World: Social Suffering in Contemporary Life*. Cambridge: Polity Press.

Bourdieu, P. (1999a) 'The Space of Points of View'. In Bourdieu, P. et al., *The Weight of the World: Social Suffering in Contemporary Society*. Cambridge: Cambridge University Press.

Bourdieu, P. (1999b) 'Understanding'. In Bourdieu, P. et al., *The Weight of the World: Social Suffering in Contemporary Society*. Cambridge: Polity Press.

Bourgois, P.I. (2002) *In Search of Respect: Selling Crack in El Barrio*. Cambridge: Cambridge University Press.

Bourgois, P.I. and Schonberg, J. (2009) *Righteous Dopefiend*. Berkeley: University of California Press.

Brewer, J.D. (2013) *The Public Value of the Social Sciences: An Interpretive Essay*. London: Bloomsbury.

Calhoun, C. (2004) 'A World of Emergencies: Fear, Intervention, and the Limits of Cosmopolitan Order'. *Canadian Review of Sociology*, 41(4): 373–395.

Calhoun, C. (2008) 'The Imperative to Reduce Suffering: Charity, Progress and Emergencies in the Field of Humanitarian Action'. In Barnett, M. and Weiss, T.G. (eds), *Humanitarianism in Question*. Ithaca: Cornell University Press.

Chouliaraki, L. (2006) *The Spectatorship of Suffering*. London: Sage Publications.

Chouliaraki, L. (2013) *The Ironic Spectator: Solidarity in the Age of Post-Humanism*. Cambridge: Polity.

Cohen, S. (2001) *States of Denial: Knowing About Atrocities and Suffering*. Cambridge: Polity Press.

Das, V. (1994) 'Moral Orientations to Suffering: Legitimation, Power and Healing'. In Chen, L.C., Kleinman, A. and Ware, N.C. (eds), *Health and Social Change in International Perspective*. Boston: Harvard School of Public Health.

Das, V. (1995) *Critical Events: An Anthropological Perspective on Contemporary India*. Delhi: Oxford University Press.

Das, V. (1997a) 'Language and Body: Transactions in the Construction of Pain'. In Kleinman, A., Das., V. and Lock, M., *Social Suffering*. Berkeley: University of California Press.

Das, V., Kleinman, A., Ramphele, M., Lock, M. and Reynolds, P. (eds) (2001) *Remaking a World: Violence, Social Suffering and Recovery*. Berkeley: University of California Press.

Deegan, M.J. (1988) 'WEB Du Bois and the Women of Hull-House, 1895–1899'. *The American Sociologist*, 19(4): 301–311.

Dejours, C. (1998) *Souffrances en France: La banalization de l'injustice sociale*. Paris: Seuil.

Delvecchio Good, M., Brodwin, P.E., Good, B.J., and Kleinman, A. (eds) (1992) *Pain as Human Experience: An Anthropological Perspective*. Berkeley: University of California Press.

Ellis, M. (1996) *The Politics of Sensibility: Race, Gender and Commerce in the Sentimental Novel*. Cambridge: Cambridge University Press.

Farmer, P. (1992) *Aids and Accusation: Haiti and the Geography of Blame*. Berkeley: University of California Press.

Farmer, P. (1997) 'On Suffering and Structural Violence: A View from Below'. In Kleinman, A., Das, V. and Lock, M. (eds), *Social Suffering*. Berkeley: University of California Press.

Farmer, P. (1999) *Infections and Inequalities: The Modern Plagues*. Berkeley: University of California Press.

Farmer, P. (2005) *Pathologies of Power: Health, Human Rights and the New War on the Poor*. Berkeley: University of California Press.

Farmer, P. (2006) 'Never Again? Reflections on Human Values and Human Rights'. In Peterson, G.B. (ed), *The Tanner Lectures on Human Values*. Salt Lake City: University of Utah Press.

Farmer, P., Kleinman, A., Kim, J. and Basilico, M. (eds) (2013) *Reimagining Global Health: An Introduction*. Berkeley: University of California Press.

Fassin, D. (2012) *Humanitarian Reason: A Moral History of the Present*. Berkeley: University of California Press.

Forgas, J.P. (2001) *Feeling and Thinking: The Role of Affect in Social Cognition*. Cambridge: Cambridge University Press.

Frazer, M.L. (2010). *The Enlightenment of Sympathy: Justice and the Moral Sentiments in the Eighteenth Century and Today*. Oxford: Oxford University Press.

Halttunen, K. (1995) 'Humanitarianism and the Pornography of Pain in Anglo-American Culture'. *The American Historical Review*, 100(2): 303–334.

Haskell, T.L. (2000) *The Emergence of Professional Social Science: The American Social Science Association and the Nineteenth-Century Crisis of Authority*. Baltimore: JHU Press.

Himmelfarb, G. (1991) *Poverty and Compassion: The Moral Imagination of the Late Victorians*. New York: Alfred a Knopf Inc.

Honneth, A. (1995) *The Struggle for Recognition: The Moral Grammar of Social Conflicts*. Cambridge: Polity Press.

Kleinman, A. (1980) *Patients and Healers in the Context of Culture: An Exploration of the Borderland Between Anthropology, Medicine, and Psychiatry*. Berkeley: University of California Press.

Kleinman, A. (1988) *The Illness Narratives: Suffering, Healing and the Human Condition.* New York: Basic Books.

Kleinman, A. (1995) 'Pitch, Picture, Power: The Globalization of Local Suffering and the Transformation of Social Experience'. *Ethnos*, 60(3–4): 181–191.

Kleinman, A. (1999) 'Experience and Its Moral Modes: Culture, Human Conditions and Disorder'. In Peterson, G.B. (ed) *The Tanner Lectures on Human Values*, Salt Lake City: University of Utah Press.

Kleinman, A. (2006) *What Really Matters: Living a Moral Life Amidst Uncertainty and Danger.* Oxford: Oxford University Press.

Kleinman A. and Kleinman, J. (1997) 'The Appeal of Experience; The Dismay of Images: Cultural Appropriations of Suffering in Our Times'. In Kleinman, A., Das, V. and Lock, M. (eds), *Social Suffering*. Berkeley: University of California Press.

Kleinman, A. Das, V. and Lock, M. (eds) (1997) *Social Suffering*. Berkeley: University of California Press.

Lepenies, W. (1988) *Between Literature and Science: The Rise of Sociology*. Cambridge: Cambridge University Press.

Lvon, M.L. and Barbalet, J.M. (2004) 'Emotion and the "Somatization" of Social Theory'. In Blaikie, A. et al. (eds) *The Body: Critical Concepts in Sociology, Vol. 2 Sociology Nature and the Body* (pp. 175–192). London: Routledge.

Mazlish, B. (1989) *A New Science: The Breakdown of Connections and the Birth of Sociology.* Pennsylvania: The Pennsylvania State University Press.

Morgan, D.G. and Wilkinson I. (2001) 'The Problem of Suffering and the Sociological Task of Theodicy'. *European Journal of Social Theory*, 4(2): 199–214.

Morris, A. (2015) *The Scholar Denied: WEB Du Bois and the Birth of Modern Sociology.* Berkeley: University of California Press.

Mullan, J. (1988) *Sentiment and Sociability the Language of Feeling in the Eighteenth Century.* Oxford: Clarendon.

Poovey, M. (1995). *Making a Social Body: British Cultural Formation, 1830–1864.* Chicago: University of Chicago Press.

Poovey, M. (1998) *A History of the Modern Fact: Problems of Knowledge in the Sciences of Wealth and Society.* Chicago: University of Chicago Press.

Reddy, W.M. (2000) 'Sentimentalism and its Erasure: The Role of Emotions in the Era of the French Revolution'. *The Journal of Modern History*, 72(1): 109–152.

Renault, E. (2008) *Souffrances Sociales: Philosophie, Psychologie et Politique.* Paris: Editions La Découverte.

Rifkin, J. (2009) *The Empathic Civilisation: The Race to Global Consciousness in a World in Crisis.* Cambridge: Polity Press.

Roberts, F.D. (2002). *The Social Conscience of the Early Victorians.* Palo Alto: Stanford University Press.

Scheper-Hughes, N. (1992) *Death Without Weeping: The Violence of Everyday Life in Brazil.* Berkeley: University of California Press.

Scheper-Hughes, N. (1997) 'Peace Time Crimes'. *Social Identities* 3: 471–497.

Scheper-Hughes, N. (1998) 'Undoing: Social Suffering and the Politics of Remorse in the New South Africa'. *Social Justice*, 25(4): 114–142.

Scheper-Hughes, N. (2011) 'Mr Tati's Holiday and João's Safari – Seeing the World through Transplant Tourism'. *Body & Society*, 17(2–3): 55–92.

Thompson, J.B. (1995) *The Media and Modernity: A Social Theory of the Media.* Cambridge: Polity Press.

Vidich, A.J. and Lyman, S.J. (1985) *American Sociology: Worldly Rejections of Religions and their Directions.* New Haven: Yale University Press.

Weber, M. (1948) 'Bureaucracy'. In Gerth, H.H. and Mills, C.W. (eds) *From Max Weber* (pp. 196–240), London: Routledge.

Wilkinson, I. (2005) *Suffering: A Sociological Introduction*. Cambridge: Polity Press.

Wilkinson, I. (2013) 'The Provocation of the Humanitarian Social Imaginary'. *Visual Communication*, 12(3): 261–276.

Wilkinson, I. and Kleinman, A. (2016) *A Passion for Society: How We Think About Human Suffering*. Berkeley: University of California Press.

Williams, S.J. (2001) *Emotion and Social Theory: Corporeal Reflections on the (Ir)Rational*. London: Sage.

7 Public value reporting

Adding value to (non-)financial reporting

Timo Meynhardt and Anne Bäro

Introduction

Organizations are starting to understand themselves as part of society, acknowledging that their actions affect communities and society at large. The notion of *public value* articulates what makes an organization valuable to society by operationalizing a firm's contribution to the common good as perceived by the public (Meynhardt, 2009; 2019). In this chapter, the authors present an approach to Public Value Reporting which is relevant to organizations, non-governmental institutions, and public administrations. This approach enables these organizations and institutions to gain a better grasp of the dynamics of events in their environment, to be more responsive to societal needs, and to legitimize their actions. In order to translate theoretical reasoning into measures of corporate performance, we identify and discuss three concrete approaches to enhance existing reporting measures, (1) the Public Value Scorecard, (2) the extension of the materiality matrix, and (3) the definition of key performance indicators relevant for public value creation. Finally, we explore ways in which a public value perspective can broaden the current understanding of organizational value creation and, thus, advance (non-)financial reporting.

In their last annual report, the pharmaceutical company Bayer stated: "[In line with our mission], we aim to improve people's quality of life" (Bayer Annual Report, 2016, 44). This official statement exemplifies how organizations increasingly aim to put social improvement at the heart of their business activities (e.g. Schwartz & Carroll, 2007). Moreover, it particularly emphasizes that reporting today is about more than merely economic growth (EY, 2017). Organizations are rediscovering their societal purpose as social entities, not only affecting individuals' welfare but also society's growth. At the same time, new statutory provisions and regulatory trends, like the EU directive 2013/34 on disclosure of non-financial and diversity information, force organizations not only to consider non-financial information in management activities, but also to align their business activities to societal needs when adding value (Porter & Kramer, 2011; Meynhardt & Gomez, 2016).

A problem with a number of approaches in use is that they neglect listening to those they aim to address, namely the public. How, for example, does Bayer know whether acquiring Monsanto, and with it the provision of genetically engineered seeds, contributes to people's quality of life, or not? Maybe it is not as much about the access to seeds and pesticides, but rather about ensuring human health, food safety, and consumer protection. Clearly, the external perspective is missing here. The affected public's opinion is necessary to decide whether this type of "joint value creation" actually is in the interests of the public. The 50,000 emails and more than 5,000 letters, postcards, and Twitter posts, that expressed concern about the Bayer-Monsanto transaction, cast doubt on society's approval (*New York Times*, 2017).

This example underlines that corporations' contribution to public value is not only recognized, but often more visible than expected (Meynhardt, 2019). Moreover, it exemplifies that organizations cannot simply "create" value, as value has to be appreciated by the public; it is only perceived, never just delivered (Meynhardt, 2009). The authors go even further, proposing that public value creation is an organization's source of societal legitimacy. But how can public value creation be captured? A few attempts have already been made by the Global Reporting Initiative (GRI), the International Integrated Reporting Council (IIRC), or the Sustainability Accounting Standards Board (SASB). Even though these institutions' approaches have fundamentally contributed to a more holistic perspective of corporations' social impact, they have one important deficit: by normatively specifying their own assumptions on what comprises public value, they neglect public opinion (Bilolo, 2018). Consequently, researchers and practitioners now agree on the necessity of developing instruments for measuring how society evaluates the contribution an organization makes based on public perception.

The notion of public value currently in use, is derived from the public value theory which investigates what makes an organization valuable to society (Meynhardt, 2015; 2019). It analyses a firm's contribution to the common good, because "free enterprise cannot be justified as being good for business. It can be justified only as being good for society" (Drucker, 1973, 41).

This chapter is structured as follows. First, we provide a short overview of two public value approaches relevant to defining measures of corporate value creation. Second, is the main section, which is devoted to discussing how corporate reporting can use public value by presenting concrete approaches to enhance existing reporting measures, introducing the Public Value Scorecard, extending the materiality matrix, and theoretically and practically deriving key performance indicators relevant to public value creation. Our aim is to show how organizations can make use of the notion of public value in order to shift from an "inside-out" to an "outside-in" perspective. Finally, managerial and practical implications are discussed.

Theoretical background

The Public Value Account according to Mark H. Moore

The research field of public value evolved from Mark Moore's seminal book *Creating Public Value: Strategic Management in Government* in 1995. Analogous to a shareholder value orientation in the private sector, he developed a normative theory of administrative management practice by emphasizing that "the aim of managerial work in the public sector is to create public value just as the aim of managerial work in the private sector is to create private value" (Moore, 1995, 28). He conceptualizes *public value* as making the net benefit of government actions transparent, and thus showing the extent to which equity, liberty, responsiveness, transparency, participation, and citizenship have been realized (Moore, 2013). Moreover, he poses the *strategic triangle*, an operational framework that guides public managers towards creating public value. Hence, in his public value approach, Moore articulates concrete guidelines for action civil servants ought to follow in order to create value for the public (Meynhardt et al., 2017b).

In his follow-up book, *Recognizing Public Value*, Moore (2013) addresses the question as to how public managers can account for the public value they created, and he illustrates how they can translate the concept of public value into a tangible scheme for managers to create useful performance measurement and management systems. Based on his *strategic triangle*, Moore develops the *Public Value Account* as a practically useful basis for measuring public value performance. With this instrument, government actions and results are evaluated according to the material consequences those actions have for individual and societal welfare. Thus, the Public Value Account is aimed at capturing the particular perspective associated with the "public value" circle of the strategic triangle (Moore, 2013).

Comparable to a ledger account recording private business transactions, Moore (2013) postulates a public value "income statement" contrasting incurred expenses ("financial costs") on the one hand, with valuable results created ("gross public value") on the other hand. Hence, the Public Value Account depicts costs and revenues, i.e. what is given and gained to achieve results reflecting what citizens value and expect agency operations to produce (Moore, 2015). Such value-creating results include the achievement of collectively defined outcomes, unintended positive externalities, fairness and justice in which agency operations are carried out, or the extent of client satisfaction (Moore, 2013). See Table 7.1 for the general form of the Public Value Account.

Thus, Moore (2013) suggests that public-sector managers act like private-sector managers when it comes to committing themselves to a "bottom line" which defines the organization's objectives and the associated value they intend to create. Concretely, Moore's accounting scheme encompasses two parts: a utilitarian framework and two deontological elements, namely fairness and justice. Utilitarianism attributes the value proposition to tangible assets. Deontological assumptions, related to a question of legal legitimacy, locate value in the extent to which individuals fulfill their moral obligations and responsibilities to one another, and the extent to which organizations adhere to those inherent moral norms.

Table 7.1 The Public Value Account

Financial costs	Gross public value
Use of collectively owned assets and associated costs	Achievement of collectively valued social outcomes
Financial costs	Mission achievement
Unintended negative consequences	Unintended positive consequences

	Client satisfaction
	    Service recipients
	    Obligatees

Social costs of using state authority	Justice and fairness
	    At individual level in operations
	    At aggregate level in results

Adapted from Moore, 2013, 50, 56

While financial costs, incurred by raw materials, salaries, buildings and facilities are relatively easy to estimate, Moore (2013) admits the challenge of filling in the revenue side of the Public Value Account with concrete dimensions as well as numeric values. The performance and success of private-sector organizations is relatively easy to determine using monetizing and financial measurement possibilities, such as financial returns. However, defining public value and specifying when it was created, appears to be much more difficult (Moore, 2013). He, therefore, proposes an assumption that public value has been created when citizens and elected representatives consider the achieved social outcomes as valuable (Moore, 2013). A sound basis for estimating the intended public value is the agency's mission. For example, if the mission is to enhance the quality of life in a particular city, that marks the baseline for value creation and for developing a solid strategy to increase public value (Moore, 2015). To operationalize the postulated dimensions, Moore (2013) suggests the created public value should be determined using surveys, feedback mechanisms, expert judgments, or policy analysts (Moore, 2013). Either way, public managers should engage in "value-oriented" management (Moore, 2013, 47) to define and recognize the value they created in the public sector.

What makes Moore's approach noteworthy, is his favorable attitude toward public institutions. Instead of considering them "a necessary evil" (Moore, 1995, 28), he considered public organizations as value-creating entities that operate to satisfy the public's needs. Objectives and values public managers realize, are commonly derived with public administrations acting in the best interest of the community (Moore & Khagram, 2004). Hence, the public becomes the "arbiter" of public value (Moore, 2014, 466). Moore also faced the methodological challenge of translating his philosophical concept of *public value* into a tangible system and practically usable tool for public managers. With his postulated Public Value Account, he intended to support public managers not only to recognize, define, and calculate the value they created, but also to preserve or even further increase public value in the future. Notable here, is Moore's ambition to reach a "reasonably satisfying conceptual definition of public value" (Moore, 2015, 126), which considers not only citizens, taxpayers, and clients, but also criminals, polluters, and tax defrauders for whom public managers are responsible. He seems satisfied with an imagined public, "more or less appropriately constructed" (Moore, 2012, 22).

However, Moore's accounting scheme falls short as a public value reporting framework for several reasons. First, in many ways his accounting concept remains vague, as for example when he states that "schools, police departments or social service agencies may develop [normative] concepts of value and systems of measurement specific to their particular kind of work" (Moore, 2015, 126). He also includes unintended spillover effects, which are hard to measure. Besides, it remains unclear whether these unintended consequences should be considered by-products or part of the core value dimensions.

Second, Moore (2012) postulates that "there is very little difference between private and public sector cost accounting" (6). Knowing the (financial) revenue a firm has generated, he states, already captures how much public value has been created. However, one cannot assume that having a financial system which keeps track of costs paid out, and revenues collected from paying customers, implies public value creation. Such a shortcut falls short of uncovering the different institutional logics. For example, a recent study[1] has shown that utterly profitable organizations such as Google, Nestlé, or Facebook can be evaluated as rather poor public value contributors.

Last, the main weakness of Moore's approach seems to lie in his aim to "call a public into existence" (Moore, 2013, 270). When public managers themselves are obliged to estimate the value they aim to create, and to fill the accounting frame with self-imposed indicators and measures, collectively valued outcomes are only partly acknowledged. Moreover, views on what is valuable and vital often vary greatly between administrators and society, especially when it comes to costs. For Moore, "the people" cannot know what they want or what their public agencies can actually produce (Moore, 2013, 70). That is why he finds that public value is determined by public managers. As they decide about what is valuable and what is not, Moore constructs them as the actual arbiters of public value.

Apart from these shortcomings, Moore's (2013) Public Value Account is very plausible and endorsed by experience. Thus, it can be regarded as a cornerstone in the field of public administration. Particularly, he indicated "the importance of thinking multi-dimensionally when both creating and recognizing public value" (Bilolo, 2018, 100). However, Moore's approach is not well suited as a material starting point for private-sector firms to report on their public value contribution.

Extending the notion of value creation – public value

The postulated Public Value Reporting framework is based on the public value concept coined by Meynhardt (2009), which according to Bryson et al. (2015), is "an important though less widely cited approach" (10). The concept and its underlying assumptions are explained in more detail in the box below.

PUBLIC VALUE – IDEA IN BRIEF

In his psychology-based approach Meynhardt (2009) describes public value as a subjective emotional-motivational assessment related to a concept of the public that is grounded in individuals' representations and interpretations. Notably, public value is subjective in nature and always lies in the eye of the beholder, which makes it a non-normative paradigm.

Meynhardt's approach is based on the cognitive-experiential self-theory by Epstein (2003) who identified four basic human needs: the need for maximizing pleasure and minimizing pain, the need for self-enhancement, the need for maintaining control and coherence, and the need for relatedness. Accordingly, human beings aim to satisfy their basic needs in order to ensure personal well-being (e.g. Deci & Ryan, 2000). Consequently, "an evaluation of any object against basic needs is called a value" (Meynhardt, 2015, p. 321). Hence, if on the basis of basic human needs, an individual's evaluation of the relationship between an object (e.g. an organization or product) and a group in public, is positive, those needs are fulfilled and public value is created (Meynhardt, 2015). Altogether, Meynhardt's (2015) public value concept is based on four theoretical assumptions: (1) value exists in relationships, (2) the public is inside, (3) public value is grounded in basic needs, and (4) public value creation is perceived, not delivered, and thus relative.

According to Meynhardt (2009), public value is created when organizations fulfill basic human needs. Guided by the principle "public value is what the public values" (Talbot, 2006, 7), his concept articulates clearly what society counts as valuable in an organization. That public value creation is embedded in public perception, enables an organization to direct specific efforts toward a mutually valued purpose, which is crucial for society to appraise the organization as legitimate.

Yet, for contemporary society there is a crisis of confidence in the market economy. In the current climate of political and economic uncertainty, society's trust in capitalism and its externalities has reached an all-time low. The market economy's "deep-seated hostility to profit" (Drucker, 2001, 19) has brought increasing resistance to private sector organizations and the capitalistic system (Bhattacharjee et al., 2017). For example, in 2017, only half of the general population in the United States trusted private sector organizations. The overall trust of U.S. citizens in their institutions, i.e. businesses, NGOs, government, and the media reached a record low of only 43 percent (Edelman, 2018). Similarly, data from Germany reveals that 85% of the respondents are fairly to very concerned that the common good is not sufficiently attended to (CLVS, 2015). This indicates that organizations are failing in making their social contributions transparent. For organizational existence, what an organization does, and also how it reaches certain societal groups or the general public with its products and services, is pivotal (Meynhardt et al., 2017a).

Despite low confidence, considerable growth has been observed in the last couple of years of sustainable, responsible, and impactful (SRI) investments. In fact, people prefer to invest in business ideas or products which they believe support the progress towards a viable and just society (Bilolo, 2018). Especially the Millennials (the generation born between 1982 and 2000), who represent the future investment generation, indicate a particular preference for SRI investments (Morgan Stanley, 2016). These so-called "sustainability natives" form a new generation characterized by the natural belief that sustainable action is indispensable and, thus, non-negotiable, also when it comes to investment decisions (Bilolo, 2018). These examples demonstrate that organizational legitimacy emerges not only from financial support, i.e. from customers buying products, but also from the public permitting corporations to continue operating (Moore & Khagram, 2004).

However, today's economy still plays by its own set of rules. Organizations often put self-interest at the center of their business activities. Corporations like Bayer adopt an "inside-out" perspective when they pretend to know what is good for the general public, instead of properly surveying those they aim to reach.

From this perspective, it is high time that organizations gain a better understanding of the current dynamics in their surroundings, and discursively engage with them to increase trust and to meet societal needs, instead of considering themselves isolated from their environment. As Drucker (2001) put it: "The purpose of business must lie in society since business enterprise is an organ of society" (20).

Recently, an empirical study[2] analyzed the relevance of a public value reporting approach from the perspective of relevant stakeholder groups. Specifically, the authors wanted to know, first, whether current corporate reporting approaches provide a sufficient picture regarding organizations' societal value creation and, second, whether Public Value Reporting would provide a useful additional information base for stakeholders. In order to answer these questions, an online questionnaire was circulated to be completed by practitioners, mainly from the fields of Finance, Strategy and Business Development, Sustainability, as well as Investor Relations in Austria, Switzerland, and Germany.[3] The data obtained in this way indicated the following:

First, corporate reporting insufficiently portrays societal value creation. More than 80% of the respondents evaluated existing reporting approaches, such as CSR Reports or Sustainability Reports, to be insufficient regarding the presentation of an organization's societal value creation.

Second, respondents widely agreed that financial value is relevant, but not sufficient for determining a firm's value creation. Thus, financial measurement alone cannot provide sufficient insight into corporate performance, because good decisions can only be made on the basis of holistic information that includes the full costs and benefits of a firm's value creation.

Third, Public Value Reporting would be practically relevant. In sum, the surveyed stakeholders were actually highly interested in holistically evaluating corporate performance that includes societal perspectives.

Specifically, stakeholders perceive the degree to which a company fulfills its core tasks to be the most important value dimension by far. Morality and quality of life come next. Nonetheless, the relatively strong interest in morality indicators shows that "soft" performance indicators are becoming increasingly important to stakeholders. It is not only corporate scandals that cause higher sensitivity, but also changed demands of employees, customers, investors, political circumstances, or even the general public (Meynhardt et al., 2017a).

The previously outlined study findings may only give a snapshot, but they explicitly indicate a mandate for innovation that reporting experts perceive. Moreover, they show, that it is no longer acceptable to legitimize free enterprise based on its capacity to create jobs or pay taxes. In a world where profit maximization is no longer an uncontested capitalist idea, "an explicit public value proposition becomes a driver for resilience, innovation, and [. . .] the purpose the public and employees are looking for" (Meynhardt et al., 2014, 81).

By incorporating implications for individual welfare as well as society's development, the public value lens extends the scope from sole financial and material performance indicators to a multi-dimensional framework of value creation. This is a much more fine-grained approach to value creation which does not supersede financial-economic value creation, but rather aims to integrate it into a coherent whole, "where hard and soft factors have to stand the test of society" (Meynhardt et al., 2014, 82). Similarly, public value theory discloses organizational value creation as a significant entity impacting society, and not as an externality or nice-to-have. Thus, new opportunities arise if organizations not only become aware, but deliberately start to manage their public value.

Notably, the public value approach does not postulate a new paradigm; rather, it emphasizes that an organization's value creation results from the interaction of various criteria and valuation dimensions (Meynhardt, 2015). Creating public value means not only maintaining but also enhancing individuals' chances of positive experiences in society, creating optimal conditions for personal growth and development. Consequently, public value is not solely customer satisfaction, and shareholder value does not become obsolete when public value diminishes (Meynhardt, 2013; 2019). Further, public value offers a comprehensive approach that does not favor one perspective over the other, but integrates multiple aspects of valuation within one theoretical framework (Meynhardt, 2015). On these grounds, public value can be considered a holistic concept integrating multidimensional value orientations, and thus enabling more value-centered management of the organization (Meynhardt et al., 2014). Moreover, by applying an anthropocentric understanding, the pubic value concept reinforces the relationship between the organization and the public and, thus, shifts the way of thinking from "inside-out" to "outside-in" (Bilolo, 2018; Meynhardt & Gomez, 2016).

Public Value Reporting

The public value concept theoretically contributes to the debate on organizational legitimacy by providing new insight into how individual and societal well-being are affected by organizational action. As mentioned previously, public value creation cannot simply be delivered, but has to be recognized. Thus, to make valid predictions on their societal value contribution as perceived by their different public(s), as well as on areas of improvement, organizations need qualified measurement tools (Meynhardt et al., 2017b).

In order to translate theoretical reasoning into measures of corporate performance, we identify and discuss three alternative approaches to enhance existing reporting measures, namely the Public Value Scorecard, the extension of the materiality matrix, and the definition of key performance indicators relevant to public value creation.

The Public Value Scorecard

To estimate the intended or realized public value creation of organizational initiatives or projects, the Public Value Scorecard (PVSC) has been developed (cf. Meynhardt, 2015). The PVSC is a managerial instrument that can be combined with other management systems in order to assess various value dimensions, as well as associated areas of tension and trade-offs. Moreover, the tool captures subjective evaluations regarding the perceived impact certain projects, initiatives, products, or services have on an organization's public value (Meynhardt, 2013). Due to the importance of financial-economic implications for management decisions, a fifth dimension has been incorporated as part of the instrumental-utilitarian dimension (Meynhardt, 2015). Thus, the instrumental-utilitarian dimension comprises of a utility indicator and a financial-economic indicator.

Against this background, participants have to answer several questions along the public value dimensions. One general version for framing the questions is the following:

- Utilitarian-instrumental values (1): Is it useful?
- Utilitarian-instrumental values (2): Is it profitable?
- Moral-ethical values: Is it decent?
- Political-social values: Is it politically acceptable?
- Hedonistic-aesthetic values: Is it a positive experience?

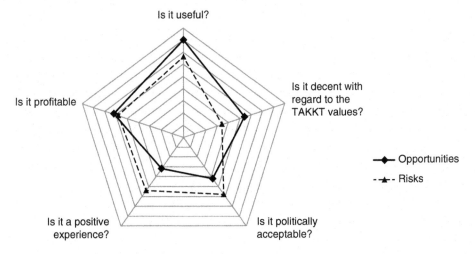

Figure 7.1 The Public Value Scorecard
Adapted from Meynhardt, 2015, 147–169

The PVSC enables managers (or institutions) to address the trade-offs between financial and non-financial objectives, as well as to do a thorough analysis of societal needs and concerns (Meynhardt, 2015).

In contrast to the Balanced Scorecard approach by Kaplan and Norton (1996), the PVSC does neither aim at causal relationships nor is it intended to serve as strategic control model. On the contrary, it is not only aware of the human appraisal's subjectivity in scorecard approaches (Nørreklit, 2000; 2003), but the PVSC is explicitly designed to foster articulation of (collective) subjectivity as expressed by the answers in five evaluation dimensions.

Data can be gathered using surveys, specific interview techniques, workshop methods as well as by applying social media analysis (Meynhardt, 2015). Results are schematically represented in a pentagonal profile, directing management attention to perceived opportunities and risks with regard to the five dimensions given above.

Figure 7.1 depicts the pentagonal profile arising from an intended direct sourcing in Asia at the organization *TAKKT*, a Business-to-Business direct marketing specialist for office equipment (cf. Meynhardt & Bäro, in press).

Whereas tools based on the concept of corporate social responsibility consider moral-ethical aspects only, the PVSC broadens the scope to include a number of other collectively shared values (cf. Meynhardt, 2015). Additionally, by applying a holistic viewpoint, the PVSC allows for an integration of internal and external perspectives. Also, this methodology enables organizations to detect fields of activity with regard to potential opportunities and risks. Hence, solutions that respond to the public's needs, are encouraged.

The Public Value Matrix

Materiality refers to the principle of defining critical economic, environmental, and social topics, which can be relevant to an organization, due to them having a significant impact on its business performance, or substantially influencing the assessment and decisions of its stakeholders. Nearly all materiality matrices follow the same structure by joining topics relevant to the organization with topics relevant to pertinent interest groups, i.e. connecting all groups who contribute to and are affected by corporate action aimed at fulfilling stakeholders' interests.

"Material" topics are those highly important to both the organization and the stakeholders, which are, thus, marked by points in the coordinate system and will guide the subsequent reporting process. Specifically, materiality serves three concrete functions: external communication, stakeholder involvement, and efficient resource management (Eccles & Krzus, 2014). However, the approach gives rise to questions, such as ones regarding which topics deserve consideration and which do not. Moreover, it bears a number of methodological challenges, such as ones on how to obtain the necessary data, how to set weightings and relative priorities, and, eventually, who will be taking these decisions (Eccles et al., 2015; Freeman et al., 2010).

Opponents of the materiality matrix criticize it as a "vague concept," of a "highly subjective" nature (Edgley et al., 2015, 5, 14), or they call it a mere buzz word, "because dots plotted on creatively designed squares are not material at all" (Cohen, 2014). Indeed, the definition of materiality varies in the literature, or is even "non-existent" (Eccles et al., 2015). Whereas some organizations define present topics, others concentrate on topics that could become relevant in the future. Moreover, in many cases its operationalization is non-transparent, imprecise (if not inaccurate), and precludes comparability (Edgley et al., 2015). Thus, if the organization itself eventually determines what it takes as material (Eccles et al., 2015), it becomes its own final arbiter in deciding what is important to the user audience, and what not. This casts doubt on the organization's reputation and could lead to experts' reluctance to accept the materiality concept. However, materiality is an important and practically relevant tool.

The conventional materiality approach does not necessarily account for topics relevant to the public, which is important when bearing in mind that every organization is "an organ of society" (Drucker, 2001, 20) that acts in a public space. Hence, merely concentrating on maximizing stakeholder value neglects the multi-dimensionality of organizational value creation (or destruction). Thus, in order to foster a broader perspective of topics pertinent to the organization, the process of materiality analysis can be enhanced in a way that reflects the added value from a public value perspective. The process can also direct the organization's efforts in a direction more closely related to the initial idea. One such possible approach is depicted in Figure 7.2.

Again, critics could argue that a modification of the materiality matrix toward public value criteria cannot eliminate the previously outlined methodological shortcomings. However, materiality's objective is to be highly relevant for decision-making processes in private organizations, driving strategies, and reporting in a profound way. Despite its methodological challenges, and not being theoretically embedded, its practical advantages outweigh the theoretical shortcomings. Executed properly, the materiality matrix can function as a convincing reporting tool, visualizing topics considered material by different interest groups, as well as the public. Thus, when a societal perspective is added, materiality matrices are capable of guiding the corporate strategy, tightening reporting efforts to improve communication with stakeholders and the relevant public(s), which can help to turn merely notable features into ones with impact.

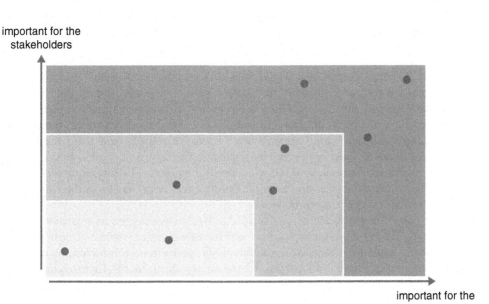

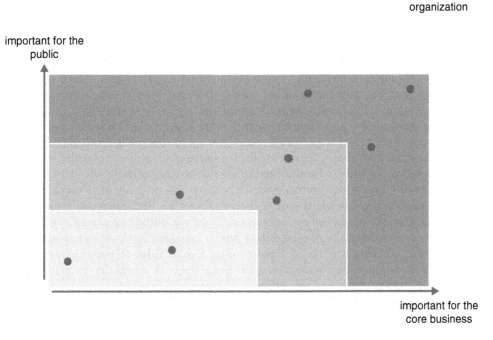

Figure 7.2 The graphics illustrate the proposed modification of the materiality matrix

Source: own illustration

Defining public value performance indicators

A third possible approach to enhance existing Public Value Reporting, is to look at key performance indicators on which organizations already report, and that therefore are broadly accepted. Key performance indicators (KPIs) are quantifiable values that organizations gauge to evaluate their success in reaching key business objectives. KPIs are not only highly important for planning, controlling, and organizing firm processes, they also create transparency, and support organizational decision-making (Meier et al., 2013). Existing databases, providing corporate responsibility indices, i.e. single ESG (Environmental, Social, and Governance) data points, are suitable as a starting point for generating relevant public value key performance indicators. To determine which of these data points are relevant for public value, a rating project was undertaken in which independent raters were asked to allocate ESG data points to the identified public value dimensions. To ensure reliable and valid results, the researchers imposed rigid requirements regarding the selection of the obtained database, the rating instructions, and the selection of the raters. The following section will outline the process of generating tangible public value data that form the foundation of a Public Value Reporting framework.

In this case, Thomson Reuters' Asset4 database was selected as a proxy for this rating study. Asset4 enjoys a reputation as a leading global provider of non-financial information, providing objective, reliable ESG performance information to both investment professionals and corporate executives (Sustainable Investment, 2017). With its easy access to a wide range of individual data points and performance indicators (about 1,300), and its well documented rating methodology, Asset4 is well-known in both research and practice. It is the resource of choice for generating tangible public value data (cf. Bilolo, 2018).

Asset4 data points were obtained from Thomson Reuters in February 2016. The final sample consisted of 1,094[4] Asset4 data points which were originally classified into four pillars, each covering Corporate Governance, Economic, Environmental, and Social features. For every pillar, Asset4 provided brief descriptions which are shown in Table 7.2. The descriptions reveal that creating shareholder value is the prevailing principle for providing this type of data. The description of the social pillar, for example, indicates that performance indicators in this pillar apply to more than one public value dimension. This provides an initial explanation as to why the given ESG data points should not be allocated solely on the basis of their macro level pillars.

In order to identify key performance indicators and to generate a reliable Public Value Reporting framework, it is important to detect the data points on which raters agree regarding the public value dimensions. Thus, the outlined research is guided by the question: Which of the obtained data points provided by Asset4 are relevant for public value, and thus are reliable sources for a Public Value Reporting framework? To provide coherent rating instructions, the researchers took a theory-based approach (cf. Bilolo, 2018). All rating instructions are shown in Table 7.3.

The provided instructions are derived from the four-dimensional public value framework and the emerging public value landscape (cf. Meynhardt, 2009), as well as the findings of the exploratory factor analysis undertaken by Meynhardt and Bartholomes (2011). The entire rating process was organized and facilitated by the authors and a third researcher with profound knowledge of public value research.[5] The actual rating process started in February 2016 with the initial precoding conducted by the two doctoral researchers. The first cohort (n=10 raters) proceeded in August 2016 and coding terminated with the last rating in January 2017 undertaken by the second cohort (n=10 raters).

All raters were instructed to evaluate and assign all Asset4 data point to one of the four public value dimensions: utilitarian-instrumental (UI), hedonistic-aesthetical

Table 7.2 Asset4 pillar description

Pillar	Total	Original description (Asset4)
Corporate governance	240	The corporate governance pillar measures a company's systems and processes, which ensure that its board members and executives act in the best interests of its long-term shareholders. It reflects a company's capacity, through its use of best management practices, to direct and control its rights and responsibilities through the creation of incentives, as well as checks and balances, eventually to generate long-term shareholder value.
Economic	130	The economic pillar measures a company's capacity to generate sustainable growth and a high return on investment through the efficient use of all its resources. It reflects a company's overall financial health and its ability to generate long-term shareholder value through its use of best management practices.
Environmental	212	The environmental pillar measures a company's impact on living and non-living natural systems, including the air, land and water, as well as complete ecosystems. It reflects how well a company uses best management practices to avoid environmental risks and to capitalize on environmental opportunities in order to generate long-term shareholder value.
Social	512	The social pillar measures a company's capacity to generate trust and loyalty with its workforce, customers and society, through its use of best management practices. It reflects the company's reputation and the health of its license to operate, which are key factors in determining its ability to generate long-term shareholder value.
Total data points	1,094	

Note: Original pillar descriptions provided by Asset4 which were directly requested from Thomson Reuters.
Source: Own illustration adapted from Bilolo (2018, 135).

(HA), moral-ethical (ME), and political-social (PS). As depicted in Table 7.3, every public value dimension was guided by a leading public value question (LQ) and substantiated with concrete examples, providing a firm foundation for coding all 1,094 Asset4 data points.

To further reduce uncertainty and complexity of the rating procedure, general guidelines, specific rules, and several exceptions were explicitly formulated *a priori* to the individual rating. For example, uncertainty emerged among raters when data points could relate to more than one public value dimension. This is in keeping with theoretical considerations outlined in the public value landscape (cf. Meynhardt, 2009, 208). One could argue that the performance indicator "research and development for diseases in the developing world" is related to product quality and profitability (UI), but also contributes to the quality of life of certain individuals (HA), has moral implications (ME), and contributes to social cohesion (PS), since the organization acts as a good corporate citizen. Hence, there can be first-order and second-order organizational implications regarding basic human needs. Thus, during the precoding process, the authors agreed that for reasons of simplicity only the primary effect of the performance indicator would be evaluated and assigned to one of the four public value dimensions. To achieve this, they defined four analysis levels, one for each public value dimension, labelled as "focus" in the instructions, *a priori*: (1) products

Table 7.3 Rating instructions

UI	Utility and profitability, cost-benefit ratio
LQ	Is the organization useful? Are the organization's products and services useful?

Dimension	Indicator
Focus	Products & Services
Sustainability	Products, Internal Processes P&S

- Profitability
- Product quality, product innovation
- Resource efficiency
- Product and service quality responsibility, e.g. product labeling

HA	Quality of life
LQ	Does the organization contribute to the quality of life of an individual?

Dimension	Indicator
Focus	The Individual / Individual Groups
Sustainability	Public spaces/the environment (nature)

- Is there an identifiable group other than the public?
Customers, employees, low income groups, disabled, elderly, indigenous people, whistleblowers, …
- Does the organization contribute to the identifiable group's …
… well-being, security, fun, joy, happiness, pleasure, or satisfaction?
- How does the organization contribute to the beauty of public spaces/the environment? Does it protect cultural heritage?

ME	Moral Implications, Fairness
LQ	Negative Check: Does the organization act illegally or immorally?
	Positive Check: Does the organization have processes to counter unethical / immoral behavior?

Dimension	Indicator
Focus	Immoral actions, controversies
Sustainability	Immoral actions, controversies

- Protection of Diversity and Equal Opportunities
- Negative Screenings (no relation to "sin" industries)
- Lawsuits, penalties, violations of the law
- Controversies in the media

PS	Political Chances and Risks
LQ	Does the organization contribute to social cohesion?

Dimension	Indicator
Focus	The community, the public
Sustainability	Issues neither related to nature nor P&S

- Corporate governance codex regulation that is not directly related to groups
- Community focus
- Good corporate citizen – policies for that purpose, global signatories, initiatives, public commitments, CSR committees
- Comply with regulations (local)?

Note: The table depicts the coding instructions the authors generated after the precoding round. The coding guide was given to the raters in both rounds and remained unchanged across all coding rounds.

and services (utilitarian-instrumental dimension), (2) individuals or specific groups (hedonistic-aesthetic dimension), (3) immoral actions and controversies (moral-ethical dimension), and (4) communities and the public (political-social dimension).

Further, preliminary research on distinguishing the four public value dimensions has shown that the utilitarian-instrumental and the hedonistic-aesthetical dimensions are not quite distinct, and are not perceived as separate dimensions (Meynhardt & Bartholomes, 2011; Strathoff & Bilolo, 2014). To some extent, this thwarted the assignment of data points to these two dimensions. Therefore, raters were advised to categorize performance indicators that focus on product quality and organizations' profitability to the utilitarian-instrumental dimension, and performance indicators that affect individuals' experiences or well-being, as well as data points that refer to the beauty of public spaces, to the hedonistic-aesthetical dimension.

Regarding the moral-ethical dimension, note that it originally relates to the appreciation of an organization's moral and political functions, and whether or not these lead to individual feelings of equality, justice, and fairness (Meynhardt, 2009). Examples include controversies in the media resulting from publicly perceived inappropriate behavior of the organization. However, a group discussion underscored the considerable difficulty raters had in identifying 'what moral behavior is' rather than 'what it is not'. Consequently, raters were advised not only to categorize moral behavior, but also immoral organizational behavior. Examples researchers gave, included legal transgression, discrimination against certain minorities, or child labor.

Finally, regarding the political-social dimension, raters were instructed to assign performance indicators that describe the organization's endeavors to foster social cohesion within society and to be a good corporate citizen (cf. Meynhardt & Bartholomes, 2011). Examples include being engaged as global signatories, in sustainability initiatives or CSR committees, as well as complying with regulations that confirm commitment to apply a community focus and show public concern.

Additional rating instructions included that participants leave a blank space if they perceived the performance indicator as unrelated to public value creation. Moreover, the raters had the option to fill in a second public value dimension if they were not sure about the focus of the respective performance indicator. Further, if the performance indicator was only related to certain industries or countries, e.g. code vs. case law countries, one vs. two board structures, the financial sector vs. chemical processing sectors, or if the data point was a non-comparable number, e.g. amounts given in euros as opposed to US-dollars, raters were asked to state that explicitly in the comment column. Raters further had the opportunity to leave general remarks or to name performance indicators that they would like to discuss in the joint follow up session.

Every rater had to attend a joint two-hour online kick-off meeting where the spreadsheets for processing the data, as well as the underlying public value theory, were explained in great detail.[6] Ultimately, both rating rounds concluded with a joint two-hour online follow up meeting in which raters gave detailed feedback (oral and written). Altogether, the standardized procedure, i.e. providing elaborate coding instructions during mandatory online sessions, ensured that raters – especially those not familiar with the topic of public value – were familiarized with the concept. Providing the same instruction material in all rating rounds, and scheduling time for questions and feedback on the coding instructions, resulted in a high degree of standardization.

Regarding group composition, 50% of the raters had no experience of public value research and 50% had up to three years of public value related research experience. Consequently, there was a reasonable 50% split between public value experts and novices. Individual characteristics should be taken into account when interpreting the final results. Regarding age and educational level, the rater group can be described as largely homogeneous, as raters' age ranged between 25 and 35 years old, and all raters hold a university degree. However, this was not considered a disadvantage in this study, since prior research suggests that similar characteristics among raters enhance reliability (e.g. Peter & Lauf, 2002).

Additionally, in order to prevent group work, raters were explicitly instructed to work independently. Geographic dispersion of raters across four countries (Germany, Austria, Great Britain and Kenya) and not knowing each other, ensured an independent rating process. To ensure that dominant group members did not influence other group members' outcomes, raters of both rating rounds were instructed to forward their spreadsheet and individual feedback to the joint follow up meetings in advance.

By utilizing the previously outlined standardized procedure, the researchers accomplished rating of each of the presented 1,094 data points by a minimum of two raters. Taken together, these results suggest that agreement among raters regarding the allocation of the key performance indicators to the public value dimensions, is good to moderate. The results further indicate that the developed classification scheme was effective across different rater cohorts: the reliability study conveyed agreement rates of 85% for the two rating groups. Hence, results are reliable and valid.[7]

In summary, the guiding question of whether Asset4 data points are suitable to generate both reliable and valid data relevant to public value, can be confirmed. All Asset4 performance indicators that the independent raters considered irrelevant for public value (creation), were excluded from the framework. Moreover, the final distribution of the Asset4 data points to the four public value dimensions shows that performance indicators are not directly transferable.

In order to reach the final set of indicators for the Public Value Reporting framework, the 1,094 data points had to be further reduced to a set of key performance indicators that is both feasible and closely related to public value. In order to achieve that, only indicators categorized by at least nine out of ten raters, were considered. Thus, 251 indicators were initially excluded. In order to assure that each performance indicator adequately represents the majority opinion and is representative regarding its public value relevance, only indicators with an agreement rate of 90% (valid for both rating rounds) remained in the final framework. Thus, a further 581 performance indicators were excluded in the second step. Since Asset4 provides alternative operationalization of certain data points, duplicate entries were also excluded. Eventually, another 59 data points were removed.

The reduction of the indicator set from 1,094 to 203 performance indicators seems fairly conservative, but guarantees that the framework is not only feasible for theory and practice, but also ensures that it only includes indicators with a high agreement rate regarding being representative of the four public value dimensions.[8] Table 7.4 illustrates the distribution of the remaining 203 performance indicators across both public value dimensions and ASSET4 pillars.

Table 7.4 Allocation of Asset4 ESG data points to the public value dimensions

	Total	*Utilitarian-instrumental*	*Hedonistic-aesthetical*	*Moral-ethical*	*Political-social*
Corporate governance	15	0	0	1	14
Economic	34	20	11	3	0
Environmental	5	0	3	2	0
Social	149	5	87	33	24
	203	25	101	39	38

Note: The table shows the translation of the four Asset4 pillars (Corporate Governance, Economic, Environmental, Social) into the four public value dimensions (utilitarian-instrumental, hedonistic-aesthetical, moral-ethical, and political-social) and the final distribution of data points.

The generated outcome is a theoretically derived framework, utilizable in organizations that not only want information on their public value, but also want to strategically manage their contribution to the common good with the help of public value. The final framework includes 203 of the Asset4 key performance indicators: 38 political-social, 101 hedonistic-aesthetical, 39 moral-ethical, and 25 utilitarian-instrumental. A minimum of 25 key performance indicators were identified for each public value dimension, having been found both reliable and valid (cf. Bilolo, 2018). Further, as presumed, the results show that the Asset4 ESG rationale cannot be directly transferred to the four public value dimensions, utilitarian-instrumental, hedonistic-aesthetical, moral-ethical, and political-social.

Notably, the concept of defining key performance indicators has been strongly contested by several researchers. Especially, the challenges associated with gathering data on moral-ethical indicators and measuring their outcomes, was criticized. A particularly devastating critique came from Boiral (2016, 755), who argues that reporting key performance indicators is only "symbolic management" not intended to ensure higher levels of transparency, but rather aimed at positively influencing the organizations' target groups, such as stakeholders or the general public. Similarly, Merkl-Davies and Brennan (2011) characterize corporate reporting as a form of impression management, intended to neutralize negative externalities and to increase organizational legitimacy.

However, we believe that the developed Public Value Reporting framework is a solid instrument capable of delivering valuable insight on the quality of the relationship between the organization and society. Utilizing this Public Value Reporting framework could give organizations an indication of whether their reporting on certain indicators is influential in the creation of public value. Moreover, managing an organization's public value creation using underlying key performance indicators, could help managers relate to the wider community and society in which their organization is embedded. It can also support "organizations identify the potential for (re) gaining and sustaining legitimate action" (Meynhardt, 2015, 155). As a result, firms are enabled to find levers not only to gain a detailed understanding of the different public value dimensions and their associated key performance indicators, but also to improve their public value (Meynhardt et al., 2017c). Further, it can prevent organizations from reflecting only their own interests, and facilitate distributing information relevant to the stakeholders, as well as the general public.

Conclusions

In times when "the economic way of thinking knows the price of everything, but the value of nothing" (Ackerman & Heizerling, 2005 as cited by Wang & Christensen, 2015, 7), organizations are forced to legitimize their actions time and again by reconciling with the values cherished in the public domain. Assessing organizational actions on the basis of basic human needs and public perceptions, enables a new and broader understanding of value creation, and directs the organization toward a collectively valued purpose. This way, public value becomes a useful compass in search of purpose and meaning in doing business (Meynhardt et al., 2014).

In this chapter we have outlined several approaches to help guide the organization from applying an "inside-out" perspective toward an "outside-in" perspective. Moving the focus from what is internally expected to create value to what is actually perceived and appreciated as value contribution, empowers organizations to engage in discourse with their surroundings and, thus, renders it more responsive to societal needs.

Specifically, the previously outlined Public Value Reporting holds several strategic opportunities, including effective risk management, an enhanced ability to recognize the organizational purpose, as well as a much more multifaceted view regarding entrepreneurial opportunities. Organizations have indeed learnt to make use of public value to better legitimize their reason of being and their license to operate. Additionally, these new measures exceed prevalent instruments that merely concentrate on revenue streams. Instead they reflect a comprehensive cost-benefit analysis that includes accomplishments and failures of organizational action.

We are aware that the outlined approaches are only small steps – building blocks – on the way to enrich corporate reporting and, concomitantly, business communication in general. Our aim is to illustrate that corporate reporting is a two-way transactional process, not just the distribution of information (Macnamara, 2016). Hence, a reporting framework that provides an opportunity to reduce information asymmetries between the external and internal view on an organization, seems vital. However, this is not yet another accounting initiative trying to integrate financial and non-financial reporting. Rather, Public Value Reporting intends to portray an organization's value creating activities that are not yet captured in corporate reporting. Thus, it is an attempt to make such activities tangible strategic assets that benefit society. In times of growing mistrust in organizations as the nation's wealth-creating engines, Public Value Reporting becomes a business imperative.

The Bayer-Monsanto deal exemplifies that traditional corporate reporting provides a diminished picture of the company's value, leaving out relevant business information: the view and verification of the public. Public value positions an organization in a broader context of societal stability and progress, recognizing the people who buy products, vote for initiatives, and decide whom to work for. Thus, it makes sense to gain improved understanding of the public's concerns that go beyond stakeholder approaches (Meynhardt et al., 2017c), because "public value is what the public values" (Talbot, 2006, 7). Consequently, in order to contribute to the common good and to "improve people's quality of life," Bayer would have to ask people outside for their opinions, whether its public value proposition is backed in society.

However, not only the public needs to be convinced. Prior studies suggest that corporations who are highly valuable to society, attract and retain investors, while low valued corporations are mostly abandoned (Bilolo et al., 2016). Previous research indicates that value creation across various dimensions will lead to better firm performance in the long run (Donaldson & Preston 1995; Meyer & Rowan, 1977). Further, research building on the identified performance indicators, presents significant evidence for the positive relationship between public value and market-based financial performance, i.e. dividend-yield and yearly return, and negatively associated with accounting profitability measures, i.e. volatility of stock returns and systematic risk (cf. Bilolo, 2018). Hence, it is not an exaggeration to say "public value potentials are growth potentials" (Meynhardt et al., 2014, 84). Today, asking the right questions can be as important, if not more so, as providing answers.

Acknowledgements

The authors would like to thank Céline Bilolo and the large number of raters who gave of their time and effort to our data collection. The completion of this undertaking would not have been possible without their support. Further, we thank Christine Anthonissen and Sebastian Ottow for their helpful feedback and suggestions in developing the chapter. We are also grateful to two anonymous reviewers for their invaluable comments and suggestions for improving the chapter and strengthening our ideas.

Notes

1 In 2017, the Center for Leadership and Values in Society at the University of St. Gallen in cooperation with HHL Leipzig Graduate School of Management published the third Public Value Atlas for Switzerland. This Atlas is aimed at making transparent the public value of important firms, non-governmental organizations (NGOs), and public administrations, ranking them based on their public value. The study is based on responses from more than 14,500 people between 18 and 92 years. Detailed results and a thorough description of the study design are available at www.gemeinwohl.ch.
2 The empirical study was conducted by HHL Leipzig Graduate School of Management, in collaboration with the Center for Leadership and Values in Society (University of St. Gallen) and the Center for Corporate Reporting (CCR) in Zürich.
3 The entire study and its results can be obtained from the authors.
4 The initially collected number of 1,301 data points was reduced by 207 due to doublings (summaries and sub-summaries calculated by Asset4), as well as restrictions resulting from simultaneously conducted research endeavors (cf. Bilolo, 2018). Since the rule for key performance indicators is "the less, the better" (e.g. Badawy et al., 2016), the authors accepted this consequence.
5 The process was coordinated by the authors and Céline Bilolo, a doctoral candidate at the Institute for Public Finance, Fiscal Law, and Law & Economics at the University of St. Gallen, Switzerland.
6 The material used in the online meetings, as well as the full coding instructions, are available upon request.
7 For a detailed calculation of the reliability coefficients, refer to Bilolo, 2018.
8 For the list of the final Asset4 performance indicators relevant to public value, contact the authors.

References

Ackerman, F. and Heizerling, L. (2005). *Priceless: On Knowing the Price of Everything and the Value of Nothing.* New York, NY: New Press.

Bayer Annual Report (2016). Available online at www.annualreport2016.bayer.com/down loads.html (accessed January 11, 2018).

Bhattacharjee, A., Dana, J. and Baron, J. (2017). Anti-profit beliefs: How people neglect the societal benefits of profit. *Journal of Personality and Social Psychology*, 113(5), 671.

Bilolo, C. (2018). *Legitimacy, Public Value, & Capital Allocation*. London: Routledge.

Bilolo, C., Berndt, T. and Meynhardt, T. (2016). *Decision Usefulness of Corporate Legitimacy: Does Public Value Matter for Investors?* (Working Paper). Paper presented at the 20th Financial Reporting and Business Communication Conference. June 30–July 1, 2016. Bristol, United Kingdom.

Boiral, O. (2016). Accounting for the unaccountable: Biodiversity reporting and impression management. *Journal of Business Ethics*, 135(4), 751–768.

Bryson, J.M., Crosby, B.C. and Bloomberg, L. (Eds). (2015). *Public Value and Public Administration*. Georgetown University Press.

CLVS (2017). *Public Value and I: Interesting results in 2017*. Available online at www.gemein wohl.ch/en/gemeinwohl-und-ich (accessed March 1, 2018).

Cohen, E. (2014, December 28). *Why the materiality matrix is useless* [Web log post]. Available online at http://csr-reporting.blogspot.de/2014/12/why-materiality-matrix-is-useless.html (accessed February 11, 2018).

Donaldson, T. and Preston, L.E. (1995). The Stakeholder Theory of the Corporation: Concepts, Evidence, and Implications. *The Academy of Management Review*, 20(65–91).

Drucker, P.F. (1973). *Management: Tasks, Responsibilities, Practices*. New York, NY: HarperBusiness Edition.

Drucker, P.F. (2001). *The Essential Drucker: The Best of Sixty Years of Peter Drucker's Essential Writing on Management*. New York, NY: HarperCollins Publishers.

Eccles, R.G. and Krzus, M.P. (2014). *The Integrated Reporting Movement: Meaning, Momentum, Motives, and Materiality*. Hoboken, NJ: John Wiley & Sons.

Eccles, R.G., Krzus, M.P. and Ribot, S. (2015), Meaning and Momentum in the Integrated Reporting Movement. *Journal of Applied Corporate Finance*, 27(8–17). doi:10.1111/jacf.12113

Edelman (2018). *Edelman Trust Barometer: Global Results*. Available online at http://cms.edelman.com/sites/default/files/2018-02/2018_Edelman_Trust_Barometer_Global_Report_FEB.pdf

Edgley, C., Jones, M.J. and Atkins, J. (2015). The adoption of the materiality concept in social and environmental reporting assurance: A field study approach. *The British Accounting Review*, 47(1), 1–18.

Epstein, S. (2003). Cognitive-experiential self-theory of personality. In T. Millon, M.J. Lerner and I.B. Weiner (Eds), *Handbook of Psychology* (Vol. 5, pp. 159–184). New York: John Wiley & Sons, Inc.

EY (2017). Global business leaders and investors unite to develop framework that measures long-term value creation for all stakeholders. Available online at www.ey.com/gl/en/newsroom/news-releases/news-ey-global-business-leaders-and-investors-unite-to-develop-framework-that-measures-long-term-value-creation-for-all-stakeholders (accessed February 7, 2018).

Freeman, R.E., Harrison, J.S., Wicks, A.C., Parmar, B.L. and De Colle, S. (2010). *Stakeholder Theory: The State of the Art*. Cambridge: Cambridge University Press.

Gomez, P. and Meynhardt, T. (2015, January 11). Gewinnstreben und die Frage der gesellschaftlichen Akzeptanz: Gastkommentar zum Shared-Value-Konzept. *Neue Zürcher Zeitung (NZZ)*. Available online at www.nzz.ch/meinung/debatte/gewinnstreben-und-die-frage-der-gesellschaftlichen-akzeptanz-1.18459041

Kaplan, R.S. and Norton, D.P. (1996). *The Balanced Scorecard: Translating Strategy Into Action*. Harvard Business Press.

Macnamara, J. (2016). Listening: The missing element of public communication – and the secret to success. *The Reporting Times* 8, 7.

Meier, H., Lagemann, H., Morlock, F. and Rathmann, C. (2013). Key performance indicators for assessing the planning and delivery of industrial services. *Procedia Cirp*, 11, 99–104.

Merkl-Davies, D.M. and Brennan, N.M. (2011). A conceptual framework of impression management: new insights from psychology, sociology and critical perspectives. *Accounting and Business Research*, 41(5), 415–437.

Meyer, J.W. and Rowan, B. (1977). Institutionalized Organizations: Formal Structure as Myth and Ceremony. *American Journal of Sociology*, 83(2), 340–363. Available online at www.jstor.org/stable/2778293

Meynhardt, T. (2009). Public Value Inside: What is Public Value Creation? *International Journal of Public Administration*, 32(3–4), 192–219. doi:10.1080/01900690902732632

Meynhardt, T. (2013). Public Value Scorecard (PVSC). In *Organisationsentwicklung – Zeitschrift für Unternehmensentwicklung und Change Management* 4, 79–83.

Meynhardt, T. (2015). Public Value: Turning a conceptual framework into a scorecard. In J.M. Bryson, B.C. Crosby and L. Bloomberg (Eds), *Public Value and Public Administration* (pp. 147–169). Washington, DC: Georgetown University Press.

Meynhardt, T. (2019). Public Value: Value Creation in the Eyes of Society. In A. Lindgreen, N. Koenig-Lewis, M. Kitchener, J. D. Brewer, M. H. Moore, and T. Meynhardt, (Eds), *Public Value: Deepening, Enriching, and Broadening the Theory and Practice* (pp. 5–22). Abingdon: Routledge.

Meynhardt, T. and Bäro, A. (in press). Haniel: Implementing the Corporate Responsibility Strategy.

Meynhardt, T., Bäro, A. and Vieten, N. (2017a). Public Value Reporting – Der Nächste Schritt. *The Reporting Times*, 11.

Meynhardt, T. and Bartholomes, S. (2011). (De)Composing Public Value: In Search of Basic Dimensions and Common Ground. *International Public Management Journal*, 14(3), 284–308.

Meynhardt, T., Brieger, S.A., Strathoff, P., Anderer, S., Bäro, A., Hermann, C., Kollat, J., Neumann, P., Bartholomes, S. and Gomez, P. (2017b). Public value performance: What does it mean to create value in the public sector? In R. Andessner, D. Greiling and R. Vogel (Eds), *Public Sector Management in a Globalized World*, 1st ed. (pp. 135–160). Wiesbaden, Germany: Springer Gabler.

Meynhardt, T. and Gomez, P. (2016). Building Blocks for Alternative Four-Dimensional Pyramids of Corporate Social Responsibilities. *Business & Society*, 58(2), 404–438.

Meynhardt, T., Gomez, P. and Berndt, T. (2017c). How non-financial reporting can make use of Public Value: Getting Serious About Society. *The Reporting Times*, 10.

Meynhardt, T., Gomez, P., Strathoff, P. and Hermann, C. (2014). Public Value: Rethinking Value Creation. *Dialogue Review*, 6 (Dec 2014/Feb 2015), 80–85.

Moore, M.H. (1995). *Creating Public Value. Strategic Management in Government*. Harvard University Press.

Moore, M.H. (2013). *Recognizing Public Value*. Harvard University Press.

Moore, M.H. (2014). Public Value Accounting: Establishing the Philosophical Basis. *Public Administration Review*, 74(4), 465–477.

Moore, M.H. (2015). Creating a Public Value Account and Scorecard. In J.M. Bryson, B.C. Crosby and L. Bloomberg (Eds), *Public Value and Public Administration* (pp. 110–130). Washington, DC: Georgetown University Press.

Moore, M.H. and Khagram, S. (2004). On Creating Public Value: What Business Might Learn from Government about Strategic Management. *Corporate Social Responsibility Initiative*. (Working Paper No. 3). Available online at www.hks.harvard.edu/m-rcbg/CSRI/research/publications/workingpaper_3_moore_khagram.pdf

Morgan Stanley. (2016). Investing in the Future: Sustainable, Responsible and Impact Investing Trends. Available online at www.morganstanley.com/ideas/sustainable-investing-trends (accessed December 17, 2017).

New York Times (2017, August 22). Bayer-Monsanto Deal Faces Deeper Scrutiny in Europe. Available online at www.nytimes.com/2017/08/22/business/dealbook/bayer-monsanto-eu. html (accessed January 18, 2018).

Nørreklit, H. (2000). The balance on the balanced scorecard a critical analysis of some of its assumptions. *Management Accounting Research*, 11(1), 65–88.

Nørreklit H. (2003). The Balanced Scorecard: what is the score? A rhetorical analysis of the Balanced Scorecard. *Accounting, Organizations and Society*, 28(6) 591–619.

Peter, J. and Lauf, E. (2002). Reliability in Cross-National Content Analysis. *Journalism & Mass Communication Quarterly*, 79(4), 815–832.

Porter, M.E. and Kramer, M.R. (2011). Creating shared value. *Harvard Business Review*, 89(1–2), 62–77.

Schwartz, M.S. and Carroll, A.B. (2007). Integrating and unifying competing and complementary frameworks: The search for a common core in the business and society field. *Business & Society*, 47(2), 148–186. doi:10.1177/0007650306297942

Strathoff, P. and Bilolo, C. (2014). Of Hedgehogs and Foxes: The Influence of Individual Cognition on Public Value. Paper presented at the 2nd International OFEL Conference on Governance, Management, and Entrepreneurship. April 4–5. Dubrovnik, Croatia.

Sustainable Investment (2017). Available online at www.nachhaltiges-investment.org/Ratings/ Researchkonzepte/Asset4.aspx?lang=en-GB (accessed March 6, 2018).

Talbot, C. (2006). *Paradoxes and Prospects of 'Public Value'*. Paper presented at Tenth International Research Symposium on Public Management, April 10–12th 2006, Glasgow.

Thomson Reuters (2016). *ESG research data: A rich source of environmental, social and governance (ESG) research data, providing performance information for in-depth, socially responsible investment analysis.* Available online at http://financial.thomsonreuters. com/en/products/data-analytics/company-data/esg-research-data.html (accessed January 25, 2018).

Wang, B. and Christensen, T. (2015). The Open Public Value Account and Comprehensive Social Development: An Assessment of China and the United States. *Administration & Society*, 49(6), 852–881. doi:10.1177/0095399715587522

8 Putting the system in a room

The public value scorecard as a connection framework

Gerwin Nijeboer

Introduction

This chapter is a case study on the Portuguese municipality of Barreiro, a neighbouring town of Lisbon. The 2009 economic crisis hit Portugal, like most European countries, hard, but the Barreiro municipality was experiencing problems even before this economic crisis. Cooperation was required between the public, the public sector and the private sector to boost the local economy. However, for various reasons they had not cooperated for decades. Public value and the practical use of the public value scorecard (further, PVSC) (Meynhardt, 2015) offered a methodology to connect the different stakeholders and support their first steps towards renewed cooperation. More concretely, public value creation occurs in relationships between the individual and 'society', individuals produce it, subjective comparisons with basic needs constitute it, emotional-motivational states activate and realise it and it is produced and reproduced in experience-intense practices (Meynhardt, 2009).

This chapter will examine whether the Barreiro municipality could use the PVSC as a connection framework and a tool to tackle its problems and create commitment. Specifically, we will find answers to the following questions:

1. How will investing in the Barreiro municipality's public value improve its cooperation with the profit sector?
2. Which initiatives could improve the cooperation between the municipality and the private sector?
3. What, according to the PVSC, is the public value of these initiatives?

The rest of the chapter describes the Barreiro municipality's situation, the implications of relevant academic theory as well as the PVSC's practical use as a connection framework.

Barreiro, city with possibilities

Barreiro is one of 308 municipalities in Portugal. It is located on a peninsula between south/southeast Lisbon and the southern shore of the river Tajo's mouth. Barreiro has an enjoyable sea climate.

Barreiro is close to Lisbon, the capital of Portugal, but can only be reached from Lisbon by boat. Located between two bridges, Barreiro is only accessible

Table 8.1 Population of Barreiro (number of people)

	2001	2011	2016
Barreiro	79,012	78,764	75,978

Source: Barreiro, 2017

over land by means of a detour, not directly. It was Portugal's most important industrial centre and an important centre of the European chemical industry for several decades. During the 1980s, the heavy industries were closed and relocated to areas beyond the municipality. In 2016, the municipality had approximately 76,000 permanent inhabitants (Table 8.1). Throughout Barreiro's history, its population was highly skilled and educated, but over the last decade this too has experienced a decline.

Barreiro is not Portugal's only municipality with problems. Nationwide, Portugal suffered significantly from the 2009 economic crisis, as demonstrated by increasing unemployment rates and average unemployment durations between 2009 and 2014 (Instituto Nacional de Estadística, 2017).

According to Benington and Moore (2011, 12)

> the economic crisis and its consequences were a catalyst for a radical review of the government's roles and responsibilities. "Doing more with less" became a strong mantra, because public sector spending needed to decrease sharply in real terms over the next few years.

According to the European Union (EU), World Trade Organization (WTO) and other international treaties' frameworks, Portugal is in the middle of a rapid modernisation process. The central government, for example, is reducing superfluous bureaucracy, which allows companies to build, develop and grow faster. Measures have also been taken to encourage foreign investors (Wanna et al., 2015).

Regardless of nationwide developments, or which political party holds power locally, local governments have to do their share of actively promoting development in sectors that could be a grand factor in the modernising of their cities and towns, therefore adding value to their local communities. The local governments need to develop in more farsighted and reflexive ways, which often require extensive dialogues between them, the public and other stakeholders about the nature of the problems to be addressed and the strategies required to tackle them (Benington and Moore, 2011). Barreiro still suffers from the closing of its heavy industries and their relocation beyond the municipality boundaries during the economic crisis. The population is decreasing, due to the lack of sufficient work and the right kind of work. In addition, tourists tend to skip Barreiro due to its inaccessibility. This same inaccessibility makes it hard to convince investors to invest in the area.

When the different stakeholder groups were interviewed, it became clear that there was little to no communication between the Barreiro municipality, the public and/or the private sector. This lack of communication and connection meant that the different groups had no idea what they could do for one another. The municipality mostly took the initiative to organise meetings between the different stakeholders at various times, after which communication between them ceased. One of the entrepreneurs argued that, "besides taxes and bureaucracy, the public sector does not seem to have anything to offer which can motivate the private sector to participate in any initiatives. This has been the situation for more than 20 years".

It became clear that it was crucial for the Barreiro municipality to initiate cooperation between the private sector, the public and the public sector in order to boost its economy and for it to be more attractive for businesses, employees, investors, tourists and potential inhabitants. From the municipality's point of view, the creation of public value could stimulate cooperation. Moore (1995, 10) defines public value as equating "managerial success in the public sector with initiating and reshaping public sector enterprises in ways that increase their value to the public in both the short and the long run". If the municipality could define and improve its public value in the short and long term as well as realise effective cooperation with other sectors, it could increase the public value. Basically, public value starts and ends with the individual. The PVSC, which Meynhardt (2015) developed, is used as a connection framework to connect individuals and to gain insight into individual perspectives of public value. By means of the PVSC, public value is measured according to individual evaluations (Meynhardt, 2009).

Why is public value relevant?

The pursuit of public value requires the support of key external stakeholders such as any government, partners and stakeholders, users, interest groups and donors (primarily tax-paying citizens). Public sector decision makers must be accountable to these groups and engage them in an ongoing dialogue about the organisational means and ends (Moore, 1995). Moore's arguments included the idea that citizens could debate the role of government in society and contribute to it by deciding which circumstances and social conditions should be a collective public responsibility that the government should manage (Benington and Moore, 2011).

The most important context change was the abovementioned 2009 global economic crisis, which acted as a catalyst to radically review government roles and responsibilities (Benington and Moore, 2011). According to Benington and Moore (2011, 15), public value thinking and action include the capacity to analyse and understand the interconnections, interdependencies and interactions between complex issues and across multiple boundaries; between different sectors, different levels of government, different services and different professions involved in tackling a common problem; between political, managerial and civic leadership and processes; between strategic management, operational and frontline delivery; and between producers and users of services.

As a concept, public value helps to make sense of a complex new pattern and strengthens the capabilities required to think and act effectively – horizontally, vertically and diagonally – along several dimensions and often simultaneously. This is not easy, because it requires a radically different approach to policy development and public management as well as linking policy to implementation and strategy to operations that deliver greater public value (Benington and Moore, 2011).

Why does the PVSC connect?

Moore (2003; 2013) first used the term public value scorecard, but this only applied to the public sector. Meynhardt (2015, 157) states that public value starts and ends within the individual:

> it is delivered, not perceived. Public value is therefore measured against individual evaluations, since people act according to the meaning they attach to their perception. The PVSC does not ask "What's in it for me?" but forces respondents to reflect on the social impacts and the question "What makes X valuable to society?"

The abovementioned perceptions, on which public value is based, can be divided into four basic value dimensions derived from psychology: (1) moral-ethical, (2) hedonistic-aesthetic, (3) utilitarian-instrumental and (4) political-social. Meynhardt (2015) introduced a fifth dimension, (5) economic-financial, because, without a financial measure, practitioners may not accept a PVSC's outcome. Meynhardt (2015) translates these five dimensions into five questions:

1. "Is it useful?" – utilitarian-instrumental values
2. "Is it decent?" – moral-ethical values
3. "Is it politically acceptable?" – political-social values
4. "Does it allow for positive experiences?" – hedonistic-aesthetic values
5. "Is it profitable?" – economic-financial values

Any organisation can adapt these five generic public value dimensions, which are each assessed using a total of 18 statements for any purposes. Nine statements are linked to opportunities. The other nine statements are linked to risks. Within the nine statements for opportunities and risks, there are three statements linked to the actual status, three statements linked to short term development and three statements linked to long term development.

Each of the 18 statements contains five value statements sentences referring to the five dimensions. The inquiry technique encourages respondents to rank each value statement from 1 being the least important value to 5 being the most important value. The scorecard itself may be used to evaluate projects and initiatives formatively or summatively (Meynhardt, 2015). The result always comprises two profiles – one for chances, one for risks – for each of the five dimensions (Figure 8.1).

Due to the forced ranking, the sum of all dimensions is always constant resulting in increased validity due to having to always trade-off different values (Meynhardt, 2015). The methodology also provides a different view of how sustainable public value creation is.

The tool provides transparency regarding PV's potential impacts on the wider public, which were previously not analysed by means of a systematic metric. Such "blind spots" may, for example, comprise discrepancies between moral and political issues. The PVSC therefore provides additional management information (Meynhardt, 2015).

An extended dialogue platform can be established if the group(s) of involved respondents require(s) this. On the whole, this scorecard indicates areas where action

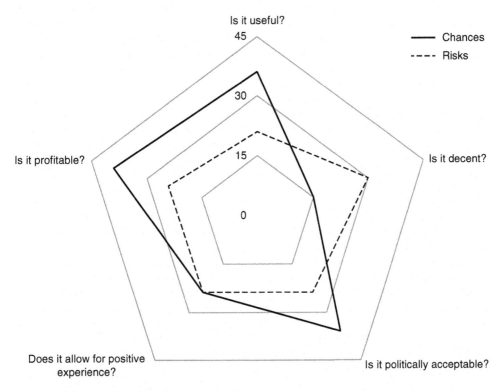

Figure 8.1 Public value scorecard (example)
Source: Adapted from Meynhardt, 2015

could be taken due to discrepancies between the different shareholders. Such a public value case could supplement new projects' classic business case by enlarging the public value consequences' perspective.

Beck Jørgensen and Bozeman (2007, 377) argue that "if there is any single item for a public value research agenda, it is developing approaches to sorting out values and making sense of their relationships". The advantage of this approach is that it focuses on the relationships ("subject-object relations") where the different values emerge. Meynhardt (2009, 207) proposes a complementary public value landscape and states that "Based on the four basic value dimensions developed, we can add to both a non-empirical, deductive method and an empirical, inductive method when discussing how to construct out *talk* about public values. Deductive construction then is understood as a combination of basic dimensions".

Consequently, the PVSC translates theory into a tool. Meynhardt (2015) describes this as:

- Public value is subjective – it therefore enquires about people's perceptions instead of gathering "facts".
- Public value, in keeping with needs theory, can be decomposed into several dimensions – different value perspectives are therefore included.
- Public value is non-normative – the scorecard has no value hierarchy.

On the whole, the PVSC is a great methodology to use as a connection framework within different groups with different values. As stated in the introduction, public value and the practical use of the PVSC offer a methodology to connect different stakeholders and help them with their first steps towards renewed cooperation (Meynhardt, 2015).

Let's connect and create public value!

The intentions were there, the public value theory and the PVSC clear and regarded as a great methodology to counter the problems at the Barreiro municipality. The next step was to take action, work on making connections and create public value. In a nutshell, this was no easy task.

The first step was to organise a structured workshop to introduce public value and the PVSC to the participants and, using the PVSC as a tool, discuss possible initiatives for cooperation. The workshop's design was not a challenge, but finding participants was.

The history of a lack of cooperation between the different stakeholders made the municipality sceptic. Eventually, the municipal employees who would join the discussion were selected by means of purposive sampling. Their expertise and their diversity in terms of the subject under study were the basis for their selection (Sekaran and Bougie, 2013). A total of 20 relevant entrepreneurs, all locals and aligned to Barreiro, who had beforehand indicated their willingness to cooperate for Barreiro's benefit, were asked to attend the meeting well in time. However, only three eventually joined the discussion. There were 20 participants – entrepreneurs, municipal employees, Barreiro citizens and TIAS School for Business and Society students. The latter would facilitate the discussion, giving the participants an opportunity to speak freely about what they considered most important in the change process (Sekaran and Bougie, 2013).

The entrepreneurs, municipal employees and citizens were all involved in the development of the municipality and its economic challenges. The TIAS School for Business and Society students were included to keep the discussions alive and structured. Before the discussion, they had been given a general introduction to the situation in Barreiro and taken on a guided tour through it, which gave them a better understanding of the (economic) situation and the problem statement. This was not only helpful for the discussions afterwards, but also deepened them.

The total duration of the workshop was four hours, which were structured and divided into:

30 minutes – Introduction of the participants and situation
60 minutes – Introduction to public value and the PVSC
90 minutes – For the various discussion groups to discuss and provide answers to the
                 questions
30 minutes – For each group to present their initiative
30 minutes – For filling in the PVSC questionnaire

In more detail, the first connection was made before the discussions were started: All the participants agreed that they had joined the working session because they believed in the need for cooperation in Barreiro's further development. The participants were introduced to the public value concept and the PVSC methodology in a 60-minute workshop. At this point, the second connection was made, because the topic was new to all of them and they were on the same knowledge and expertise level regarding public value and the PVSC.

After the introduction, the participants were divided into three separate groups, each consisting of representatives from the municipality, entrepreneurs and civilians. They were given 90 minutes to discuss three questions and provide an answer for these from their own perspective.

1.   Why should the public and private sector work together?
2.   What would the benefit of cooperation between the public and the private sector be?
3.   Which initiative would have a chance of success?

Based on this discussion, each group chose one of the discussed initiatives that they all thought would have a chance of successfully improving the public value. Subsequently, they presented this initiative to the large group. The presentation was aimed at explaining why this initiative could be successful and to receive feedback from all of the working session participants.

After the presentation, each individual was asked to fill in the existing generic PVSC questionnaire in respect of their chosen initiative. It normally does not take longer than 15 minutes to fill in the questionnaire, which generates quantitative data (Sekaran & Bougie, 2013). The PVSC is thus used as a connection framework, inventorying the different, individual perspectives and merging all the individual perspectives into a general framework – the PVSC.

The discussion is not limited to stakeholders

The discussions clarified that the stakeholders chosen beforehand were also the most important municipal stakeholders. The municipality plays an important role in Barreiro; in turn, the entrepreneurs play an important part in its development, while the civilians live there and make a municipality worth having. The presentation of the initiatives clarified that other shareholders needed to be aligned with the stakeholders' future conversations. For example, there was a discussion on students leaving Barreiro after graduating, which no one seemed to understand. The discussion clarified that the offered education did not match the different companies' needs and they thus hired people from outside Barreiro. By aligning the schools as a stakeholder in a following discussion, Barreiro could work towards a solution for this problem and create public value.

Results obtained with the PVSC

The discussions and questionnaire revealed three different initiatives that the participants in the different groups produced during the session. These initiatives were refined and discussed further without the intervention of anybody or anything outside the groups. The three initiatives on which the groups eventually agreed were:

Group 1: Create a council
Group 2: Put the system in a room
Group 2: Build a platform

The three initiatives would be discussed on this basis of their individual PVSC's. The PVSC indicates areas where action could be taken due to relevant discrepancies between the different shareholders' views. These discrepancies help identify public value opportunities and risks. The former measures public value creation, the latter its destruction. In total, 20 questionnaires were collected, divided over the three groups: (1) Put the system in a room: seven questionnaires, (2) Create a council: six questionnaires, (3) Build a platform: seven questionnaires.

Initiative group 1: Create a council

The first group's initiative was for the municipality to create an independent council for entrepreneurs and civilians that would provide them with information or answers. When the questionnaires' data were processed, the results were as follows: The initiative was regarded as a good opportunity, useful, profitable and politically acceptable (see the assessment profile in Figure 8.2). It is noticeable that consensus on a positive experience is not that important. This dimension is also the one where the risk seems to be least likely. The results regarding the opportunities and risks are almost identical, which tells us that, for the participants, the most important risk dimensions are the same as the most important opportunity dimensions.

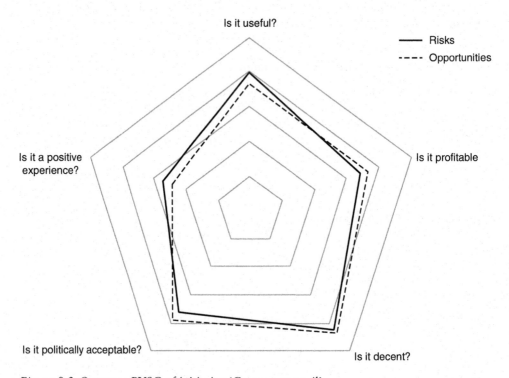

Figure 8.2 Outcome PVSC of initiative 'Create a council'

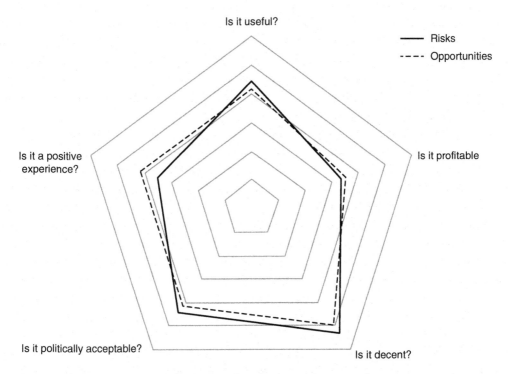

Figure 8.3 Outcome PVSC of initiative 'Put the system in a room'

Initiative group 2: Put the system in a room

The second group's initiative was placing all of the system problems the municipality faced in one room with the entrepreneurs and the public. When processing the questionnaires' data, the results were as follows. The initiative was regarded as a good opportunity that was useful, would provide a positive experience and would be politically acceptable (see the profile assessment in Figure 8.3). The participants doubted the initiative's profitability, or regarded this as least likely and having the least likely risk. Note that the results of the opportunities and the risks are almost identical, which tells us that, for the participants, the most important risks dimensions are also the same as the most important dimensions of opportunity.

Initiative group 3: Build a platform

The third group's initiative was to build a platform, which they explained as creating a platform on which all the municipal stakeholders could meet. Trust and relationship would have to be built physically at first, but after some time this platform could then be built digitally. When processing the questionnaires' data, the following results were generated:

The building a platform initiative was regarded as a good opportunity that was politically acceptable and could be profitable (see the assessment profile in Figure 8.4). The consensus that it was useful and that a positive experience is not important, is

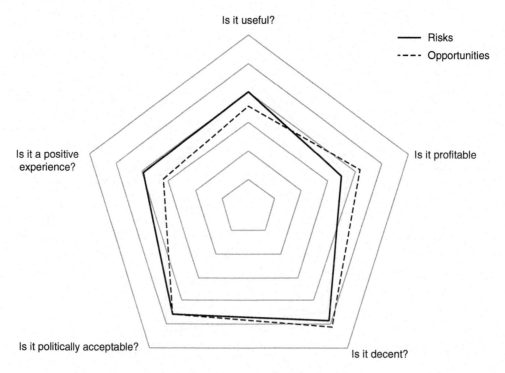

Figure 8.4 Outcome PVSC of initiative 'Build a platform'

noteworthy. In addition, the opportunity and risk results are not as identical as in the first two initiatives, which indicates that the participants regarded the risk dimensions and the opportunity dimensions' importance differently.

Putting the system in a room: future search

All of the working session's participants of the 'put the system in a room' initiative considered the initiative as able to contribute to effective cooperation between the Barreiro municipality and the private sector. Putting the system in a room relates to Weisbord's (2004, 427) theory of future search, which he describes as "an extremely promising method for getting whole systems in one room and focusing on the future". In short, the theory describes how, in the past, only experts were asked to solve problems. Since then, problem solving has evolved to everybody improving whole systems. This is in line with the notation of public value and the use of the PVSC as a connection framework. The basic idea is that public value starts and ends with the individual. To realise connection between individuals and to gain insight into individuals' perspective of public value, the PVSC, as developed by Meynhardt (2015), is used as a connection framework. Consequently, through the PVSC, public value is measured against individuals' evaluation and everybody improves entire systems (Meynhardt, 2009; Weisbord, 2004).

The public value of Barreiro

The municipality of Barreiro took a brave step by investing in and facilitating a working session on public value. The discussions were good, although perhaps more emotional at times than the participants wanted. Coming together, connecting and discussing cooperation are not common in Barreiro. Achieving this is already a positive development. It proved that investing in the municipality's public value could improve cooperation with the private sector to challenge the economic issues.

During the discussions of the PVSC, it became clear that a connection had been made. Instead of criticising one another as at the start of the working session, there was cooperation when thinking about ideas and looking forward to doing so again.

Discussion

The Barreiro municipality's goal is to improve the economic situation. Improving this situation can only be a success if there is better cooperation between the municipality and the most important stakeholders in the area. The PVSC brought stakeholders with different backgrounds and mindsets together. Meynhardt, Hermann and Anderer (2015) describe the different mind-sets as the difference between hedgehogs and foxes. This animal metaphor describes the fundamental differences in human beings' preferences regarding organising and processing information as well as experience. Above all, the animal metaphor teaches us not to blame others for not seeing the world "correctly", but urges us to respect different styles of relating to the world around us. The PVSC allowed these differences to be bridged, created conversation and allowed a respectful discussion.

During the discussions, it became clear that the municipality is seen as a machine and a structure, not as a 'complex adaptive system'. This first step towards the stakeholders is a different municipal approach. Continuing the sessions, looking for cooperation and, therefore, investing in the public value will help the Barreiro municipality analyse, understand and strengthen the interconnections, interdependencies and interactions between complex issues and across multiple boundaries; between different sectors, different services and different professions involved in tackling a common problem.

The municipality needs to decide whether it is willing to involve 'everybody' in improving the entire system, which is crucial for gaining public value and for continued investment in it.

Implications

Based on the visit to the municipality, the view of the situation and the PVSC results, it is clear there is still a lot of work and development to be done before realising more public value, but the first steps have been taken. By helping the municipality of Barreiro on the road towards its goal, the following conclusions, which are most aligned with public value, have been drawn:

1. Keep investing in communication between the public and the private sectors. Employ an independent mediator who can lead these discussions. This will create a better understanding and will improve the conversations' effectiveness.

2. The compositions of the groups are important. The groups must be balanced, have a positive attitude and the intention to set goals for a successful situation.
3. The group composition is also important to build relationships and create an atmosphere of confidence within the group. A confident and open atmosphere is important to make true progress towards the future.
4. Start small and do not create expectations that cannot be met. Keep managing these expectations. The relationship will improve if confidence and positive experience are created upfront.
5. Draw up rules for the discussions and keep an open mind regarding different methods and perspectives. Dare to think outside the box.

Limitations and outlook

In this case study, the PVSC was used as a connection framework to view the risks and opportunities of the initiatives that the three groups produced and discussed. The results were processed in the Netherlands and communicated by means of a visit paper and afterwards sent to the municipality of Barreiro representatives. This is a limitation, because the strength of the PVSC methodology lies in it providing additional management information that can be further discussed. Depending on the group(s) of involved respondents' (e.g. stakeholders, managers, investors) agreement, an extended dialogue platform could be established. On the whole, the PVSC indicates areas where action could be taken due to the relevant discrepancies between the different shareholders' views. This case study lacks further discussions of and extended dialogue on the influence of the PVSC's outcome on the three different initiatives and of the five dimensions' deepening of the risks and opportunities.

Acknowledgements

TIAS School for Business and Society and the Dutch-Portuguese Chamber of Commerce made the trip and the required introductions possible. Erik Vermeulen MSc and Ralph van Breda MSc, who contributed to this chapter, deserve a very special mention.

A special thank you to Stefan Anderer from HHL Leipzig Graduate School of Management, who reviewed the case study and provided insight and expertise during its writing. This truly helped.

I would also like to express my gratitude to Dr Nicole Koenig-Lewis and Prof Dr Timo Meynhardt for sharing their pearls of wisdom during the course of the writing and, of course, thanks to the anonymous reviewers for their insights.

References

Barreiro (2017). In *City Population*. Available online at www.citypopulation.de/php/portugal-admin.php?adm2id=1721504
Beck Jørgensen, T. and Bozeman, B. (2007). Public values. An inventory. *Administration and Society*, 39(3), 354–381.
Benington, J. and Hartley, J. (2009). *Whole Systems Go. Improving Leadership Across the Whole Public Service System. Propositions to Stimulate Discussion and Reform*. London: Sunningdale Institute National School of Government.

Benington, J., and Moore, M.H. (2011). Public Value in Complex and Changing Times. In J. Benington and M.H. Moore (Eds) *Public Value: Theory and Practice* (pp. 1–30). London: Palgrave Macmillan.

Instituto Nacional de Estadística (2017). *Unemployment rate by Sex, Age group and Highest completed level of education; Annual*. Available online at www.ine.pt/xportal/xmain? xpid=INE&xpgid=ine_indicadores&indOcorrCod=0000651&contexto=bd&selTab=tab2

Meynhardt, T. (2009). Public value inside: What is public value creation? *International Journal of Public Administration* 32(3–4), 192–219.

Meynhardt, T. (2015). Public value: turning a conceptual framework into a scorecard. In J.M. Bryson, B.C. Crosby and L. Bloomberg (Eds), *Public Value and Public Administration*. Washington: Georgetown University Press.

Meynhardt, T., Hermann, C. and Anderer, S. (2015). Do you think like a hedgehog or a fox? *Dialogue Review*, (8), 62–65.

Moore, M.H. (1995). *Creating Public Value: Strategic Management in Government*. Cambridge: Harvard University Press.

Moore, M.H. (2013). *Recognizing Public Value*. Harvard University Press.

Moore, M.H. (2003). The PVSC: a rejoinder and an alternative to "Strategic performance measurement and management in non-profit organizations" by Robert Kaplan. Cambridge: Hauser Center for Non-profit Organizations. Working paper #18.

Sekaran, U. and Bougie, R. (2013). *Research Methods for Business: A Skill-Building Approach*. Chichester, West Sussex: Wiley.

Wanna, J., Lindquist, E.A. and De Vries, J. (Eds) (2015). *The Global Financial Crisis and its Budget Impacts in OECD Nations: Fiscal Responses and Future Challenges*. Cheltenham: Edward Elgar Publishing.

Weisbord, M.R. (2004). *Productive Workplaces Revisited: Dignity, Meaning, and Community in the 21st Century*. Hoboken: John Wiley & Sons.

9 Leveraging social public procurement to deliver public value through community benefits clauses

An international study

Jane Lynch, Christine Harland, Helen Walker

Public Procurement is an indispensable socio-economic activity for good governance

(Kashap, 2004, 133)

Introduction

Public administrators face increasing pressures to design policies which improve public value or as Green (2016, 3) terms, provide a "public purpose"; this purpose he defines as "a morale, methodological and intellectual impetus for working in ways that contribute to public life and societal good". Public value is a multi-dimensional construct (O'Flynn, 2007); a major challenge is that perceptions of public value by end users differ across society. When examining public value by country or by government, the value concept becomes difficult to define clearly (Moore, 1995). In the private sector an individual organisation is better positioned to target the consumer and adjust their value propositions accordingly; but in the public sector, Moore (1995, 30) highlights the challenge of managing the "collective consumer" inferring how it becomes more difficult for public administrators to substantiate the collective meaning of value, a view which is further endorsed by O'Flynn (2007). Consequently, a growing field of research evidence explores how value may be achieved by governments in addressing broader sustainable social development goals, the responsibility of which is increasingly being directed towards procurement (Preuss, 2007; Brammer and Walker, 2011). There is growing evidence that sustainable goals such as reducing carbon, tackling poverty, lowering unemployment figures or providing low cost healthcare services to the community may be achieved through strategic use of public procurement (McCrudden, 2004; Lynch et al., 2013).

Here the strategic use of public procurement is explored to improve understanding of how public procurement can provide connections between government policy aspirations to deliver public value and the delivery of value appreciated by communities.

It has been stated that policies based on principal agent theory should be designed to increase the competitiveness of markets and increase efficiency (Boyne et al., 2003). Governments implement these policies through public bodies such as local authorities (or municipalities), education, healthcare and social services which are better positioned to understand value from a regional or local perspective. These public bodies can set out objectives which meet the needs of the local community and this may involve using local suppliers for goods and services (Moore, 1995). However, when favouring local suppliers, procurement managers often fear that they are in breach of directives. Taking a socio-economic approach to procurement is still sometimes perceived as costly and not representing best value (Erridge, 2007). Public buyers are expected to make commercial decisions when sourcing goods and services for achieving maximum public value. Despite these barriers, it is recognised that sourcing locally has the potential to deliver many benefits and values such as tackling environmental concerns, reducing poverty, social inclusion and community development (Erridge, 2007). This sustainable yet commercial approach to public procurement aligns well with the definitions of public value. For example, value is defined by Horner and Hazel (2005, 34) as "created through economic prosperity, social cohesion or cultural development".

Research design

Findings highlighted in this chapter from an international research group: International Research Study of Public Procurement (IRSPP) further confirm that when a sustainable approach is taken for managing public spend, there are multiple ways for achieving a much wider positive impact than just social benefit. The six case studies examined in this chapter evidence that supplier selection has significant impact on the local community and this can be negative or positive. Governments which promote a sustainable, socio-economic approach when managing spend realise greater levels of public value from tax payers' money. This chapter features important insights from six nations, some of which apply policy led initiatives and some which do not. As a basis for comparison, Indonesia, Rwanda and Zambia (COMESA) represent three examples of less developed nations; Wales (UK), Netherlands and Australia (Western) represent three industrialised and economically developed nations. Approaches to policy design, legislation, guidance and policy implementation are explored and compared.

The case study data was collected by the IRSPP (International Research Study in Public Procurement) research group, which in 2015 was on its sixth phase of investigations. The theme of the 2015 study was community benefits. Wales was identified as an example of best practice and this case was used as a sample to inspire and motivate other participants who were each asked to complete a template document. Invites were sent out to over 80 countries and those wanting to or suitably positioned to engage with and showcase examples of community benefits submitted their cases by template and later attended an intense three-day workshop. Academic participants from 15 countries in total partnered with senior procurement practitioners or policy makers from their representative nations and presented their cases, discussing procurement policies, regulation, legislation and guidance documents relating to community benefits. Each nation presented one in-depth case example where community benefits had been evidenced through public spend.

This chapter provides a summary of the literature and theoretical underpinnings for social procurement and community benefits and how this related to public value. Case findings for six nations are provided and used to draw conclusions on how social procurement and community benefits are used to deliver different conceptions of public value.

Literature review

In this section the literature on social procurement and community benefits are explored and links made to the concept of public value.

Social procurement

What is social procurement, how might it deliver benefits to communities and how might this impact on delivering public value? First we consider the various definitions of social procurement (Furneaux and Barraket, 2014). Broader commentaries on social procurement include aspects such as quality of life, sense of well-being, and mental health (Waugh 2004), but a range of different social goals have been pursued in public procurement. A study in Northern Ireland of social and economic policy goals in public procurement states:

> Such goals may include equal opportunities (gender, race, religion, disability), employment rights (part-time workers, transfer of undertakings), development of small and medium-sized enterprises (SMEs) or employment creation (for example, the long-term unemployed).
>
> (Fee 2002,107)

Social procurement is one strand of sustainability and is tasked with meeting a number of different sustainable objectives (Walker, 2015), "such as ensuring a strong, healthy and just society, living within environmental limits, and promoting good governance" (Walker and Brammer 2009). In practice, social objectives are evident in international sustainability strategies – examples are provided below:

The United Nations (2015) Agenda for Sustainable Development by 2030 is based on the three dimensions of sustainable development: economy, society and environment. United Nations (2015) focuses on people, planet, prosperity, peace and partnership.

The European Union has created a Europe 2020 strategy to focus on smart, sustainable and inclusive growth (European Commission, 2010). European Commission (2010) stated that the five main targets of this Europe 2020 strategy are:

- 75 % of the population aged 20–64 should be employed;
- 3% of the EU's GDP should be invested in R&D;
- the "20/20/20" climate/energy targets should be met (including an increase to 30% of emissions reduction if the conditions are right)
- the share of early school leavers should be under 10% and at least 40% of the younger generation should have a tertiary degree
- 20 million less people should be at risk of poverty.

Based on this, 17 sustainable development goals and targets include among others: end poverty, end hunger, healthy lives and well-being, quality education, gender equality, water and sanitation availability, access to energy, economic growth, resilient infrastructure, inequality among countries, safe cities, sustainable consumption and production, climate change, sustainable use of oceans and seas and protect ecosystems (United Nations, 2015).

The African Union (2015) has introduced an even longer-term plan: AGENDA for 2063, which is a framework document outlining 'The Africa We Want' and includes a vision and aspirations for inclusive growth, sustainable development and global strategy to benefit all Africans by optimizing the use of Africa's resources. The document by The African Union (2015) includes:

- a prosperous Africa based on inclusive growth and sustainable development
- an integrated continent, politically united, based on the ideals of Pan Africanism and the vision of Africa's Renaissance
- an Africa of good governance, respect for human rights, justice and the rule of law
- a peaceful and secure Africa
- an Africa with a strong cultural identity, common heritage, values and ethics.

ASEAN (2012) promote the ASEAN 2020: Partnership in Dynamic Development, which includes:

- We reiterate our resolve to enhance ASEAN economic cooperation through economic development strategies, which are in line with the aspiration of our respective peoples, which put emphasis on sustainable and equitable growth, and enhance national as well as regional resilience.
- We pledge to sustain ASEAN's high economic performance by building upon the foundation of our existing cooperation efforts, consolidating our achievements, expanding our collective efforts and enhancing mutual assistance.
- We commit ourselves to moving towards closer cohesion and economic integration, narrowing the gap in the level of development among Member Countries, ensuring that the multilateral trading system remains fair and open, and achieving global competitiveness.
- We will create a stable, prosperous and highly competitive ASEAN Economic Region in which there is a free flow of goods, services and investments, a freer flow of capital, equitable economic development and reduced poverty and socio-economic disparities.

All three strands of sustainability – social, economic and environmental – can be significantly improved by spending public money in local business communities (Walker et al., 2012). The broader concept of sustainable procurement has, in the past, tended to focus more on environmental issues (Miemczyk et al., 2012) and less so on economic and social issues. Calls have been made to include more socio-economic elements in sustainable procurement (Amann et al., 2014; Witjes and Lozano, 2016).

Social procurement in the public sector context is an emerging policy lever and research area. Recently, a literature review considered socially responsible sourcing, which, in supply chain terms, are the upstream social issues, i.e. relating to those organisations and their supply chains that supply governments (Zorzini et al., 2015). They consider issues around human rights, community development and ethical sourcing. Out of 157 articles within this review, only 8% were in the public sector. There are relatively few public procurement studies within the broader social and sustainable procurement literature.

Distinctions may be drawn between social procurement studies in developed nations such as UK, New Zealand and Denmark, nations which have recently developed at a similar rate (e.g. BRIC: Brazil, Russia, India and China); and less developed nations, such as in Africa.

In developed nations there are various interpretations of social procurement internationally, such as buying from minority owned SMEs in the USA, and buying small and local in the UK. (Brammer and Walker, 2011). Social public procurement studies in developed nations have considered job creation in Denmark (Zelenbabic, 2015), utilizing unemployed people in the UK (Erridge and Henningan, 2007, Willis, 2010), buying from small and local businesses in the UK (Walker and Preuss, 2008; Walker and Brammer, 2009; Meehan and Bryde, 2015), labour standards in Australia and New Zealand (Ravenswood and Kaine, 2015), procuring from social enterprises in the EU (Pirvu and Clipici, 2016), promoting equality and human rights in the USA (McCrudden, 2004), and ethical procurement (Hawkins et al., 2011). Some of these studies focus on communities and the places we live in, such as socially sustainable communities in the USA (Clark, 2007), revitalizing historic buildings in Hong Kong (Cheung and Chan, 2014), and the social and cultural values placed on forests affecting wood procurement in the USA (Bull et al., 2001). In these community-oriented studies connections between social procurement and community benefits are quite easy to make. Other studies that focus on a particular product or service, such as fuel poverty in energy procurement in the UK (O'Brien and Hope, 2010), social benefits of food procurement such as those derived from food containing the least amount of additives possible (Tikkanen, 2014), and contributing to education and quality of life, are less clear how they connect to and benefit specific communities. Social food procurement has been examined in school meals provision (Sonnino, 2009; Sumberg and Sabates-Wheeler, 2011; Lehtinen, 2012; Ruge and Mikkelsen, 2013; Galli et al., 2014) and provision of hospital food (Sonnino and McWilliam, 2011); community benefits can be inferred to accrue to those communities where the schools and hospitals are located, but there is little by way of evidence as to whether the public wanted these initiatives and if they were valued.

In BRIC countries, social public procurement has been explored in China (Yin et al., 2015), in India related to the disclosures of central public sector organisations on economic development, philanthropy and community development practices (Mansi, 2015), in Russia related to corruption (Ostrovnaya, 2015), and in Brazil related to the public sector's role in organic food procurement (Blanc and Kledal, 2012) and ethical consumption (Ariztia et al., 2014). However, like those studies in developed nations, none of these studies question what the public wanted and if these initiatives led to accrual of public value.

In less developed countries, the number of social public procurement studies is particularly small. One study examined how agricultural development might be connected to school meals provision in sub-Saharan Africa (Sumberg and Sabates-Wheeler, 2011). Whilst it is not explicit within these studies, school meals provision in sub-Saharan Africa is likely to have a different meaning to schools' meals provision in developed countries. In the former, improved agricultural development may give rise to school meals being provided as opposed to school children not being fed, whereas in developed countries, school meals are readily available, but the concern is about their nutritional value and quality. It seems reasonable to infer that public value of school meals provision in sub-Saharan Africa is highly connected to community benefit and social procurement. In developed countries, it is less clear that the public values nutritional, healthy food. Media stories to the contrary show parents and children protesting at the change from junk, high carbohydrate, highly processed foods that the children enjoy.

It is clear, therefore, that social procurement priorities differ across nations according to their level of economic development. These priorities differ because communities in these varying economic contexts value different things. A starting point for this research, therefore, was that public value might be conceived in different forms of benefits to communities according to their economic status and priorities.

Community benefits

Studies by Lynch et al. (2013) and Wontner et al. (2015) have focused on UK and Welsh community benefits policies which support the sourcing of goods and services locally where possible. In Wales, the government recognises that "Key policies like Community Benefits continue to play an important role in the delivery of wider Government objectives" (WPPS, 2015). Community Benefits Policy in Wales focuses on two areas: encouraging workforce initiatives and optimising the local supply chain. "The Welsh Government will change the way it buys to create more benefits for local communities and open the door to SMEs under the Procurement Policy Statement" (Reynolds, 2012).

However, little is known across governments about the implementation of community benefits policies, measurement tools and the wider impact on society that sourcing locally may have, and importantly, in understanding whether these policies really do change perceptions of public value.

This research sought to explore how public value and community benefits priorities might differ between developed and less developed nations, and how public procurement might be used in different ways to attempt to deliver community benefits. Beyond this, it sought to explore the consideration and evidencing of public value arising from the use of public procurement to deliver community benefits, and whether differences were apparent between developed and less developed nations.

Theoretical underpinnings

A range of theories have been adopted to explore social procurement (Touboulic and Walker, 2015), and here we focus on principal agency theory. Eisenhardt (1989) introduced agency theory and identified that a principal and agent (i.e. buyer and supplier) may have conflicting goals, information asymmetry and different attitudes towards risk. This articulation of agency theory built on previous studies such as Ross (1973) and Mitnick (1973).

Many public procurement studies have adopted agency theory to explore the relationships between a principal (public sector organisation) and an agent (supplier) (Kauppi and van Raaij, 2015; Solino, 2015; Terman, 2015; Viking and Lidelow, 2015). Kaupi and van Raaij (2015) consider maverick buying and non-compliance to centrally negotiated framework agreements, proposing that guidance and training can help non-compliance, and that maverick buying is related to goal incongruence and information asymmetry from both a principal and agent perspective. Solino (2015) applies agency theory to investigate the payment of contractor agents in road management systems, assuming information asymmetry and the risk aversion of agents. Terman (2015) considers two ways that public managers can internally organize agency attention to influence formal bureaucratic policymaking in the context of contracting and procurement. Viking and Lidelow (2015) explore how housebuilding contractors (agents) interpret local public procurement requirements, and how structure and human agency influence the emergence of local requirements.

These previous studies of principals and agents in public procurement have tended to consider the public sector organisation (principal), and the supplier or contractor (agent). By way of contrast, in the context of this study, central governments (principals) delegate procurement responsibilities to local authorities or municipalities (agents). The principal and the agent may appear to work cooperatively but they are likely to have conflicting goals and priorities, and the agents may exhibit more risk aversion. Information asymmetry implies that the local authority may have more knowledge and information about strategic community priorities than central government, or vice versa. This study will explore the relationship between central government (principals) and local government (agents), goal congruence, information asymmetry and risk aversion in the context of pursuing community benefits as part of the social sustainable procurement agenda.

However, the principals (central government) and agents (local governments) aspirations to deliver community benefits represent a very top-down, hierarchical approach, a 'we know best' attitude to deciding what will and will not benefit communities and whether those communities perceive value in those benefits. Therefore, principal agent theory is stretched in the discussion to consider 'principal–agent–client' positions. The case studies are examined for evidence of received value by clients that may be interpreted as public value, rather than governments' perceptions of what is good for communities.

The research was a phase in an ongoing research programme on public procurement – the International Research Study of Public Procurement.

International Research Study of Public Procurement (IRSPP)

Professors Christine Harland and Jan Telgen are founders of IRSPP which, since 2002 has explored contrasting international approaches for the use of public procurement as a lever of broader government reform. Each of the six IRSPP studies to date have focused on six different themes involving 40 participating nations (Table 9.1).

Figure 9.1 provides a maturity framework developed from and then used in IRSPP research studies to establish the stage of maturity and development in public procurement across nations (Harland et al., 2007). This includes understanding the extent of compliance with legislation (if it exists at all), to providing value for money, to delivering broader government policy objectives. Clearly this framework is a government centric perspective and the 'broader government policy objectives' are governments' views of what should be achieved, rather than the public's view. IRSPP6 therefore stretched the application of this to consider evidence, if any, of value received by clients.

In the context of this study we focus on evidence of specific socio-economic sustainability policies, offering value for money through wider community benefits and compliance with any directives, legislation and contract clauses which include elements of attempts to achieve socio-economic impact. The case studies were prepared to a

Table 9.1 Six research themes explored by IRSPP

Year	Theme
IRSPP 1	Explored what is known about public procurement and what are the major issues facing this field.
IRSPP 2	Examined similarities and differences across public procurement in health, defence, education and local government.
IRSPP 3	Examined how to build capacity and capability in public procurement.
IRSPP 4	In the wake of the financial crisis, this study explored the role of public procurement in designing and delivering economic stimulus packages.
IRSPP 5	Focused on the engagement of small and medium enterprises (SMEs) in public procurement contracts and how to improve their involvement.
IRSPP 6	Examined evidence of community benefits policies and implementation of community benefits clauses (social, economic and environmental).

Source: Harland et al., 2012; Lynch et al., 2016

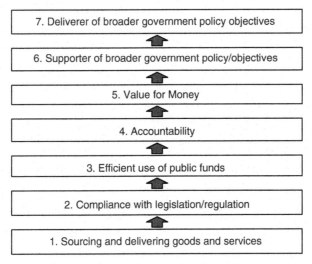

Figure 9.1 Seven stages of public procurement development
Source: Harland et al., 2007

semi-structured case study template over a six-month period by academics who paired with public procurement practitioners, non-government organisations, (NGOs) or consultants, representing 15 nations. Each 'country case study' had to commit to present their cases and have them discussed at a 3-day workshop in The Hague, Netherlands. For the purposes of examining principal–agent–client differences in community benefits and public value, six case studies have been selected to compare between three cases in developed nations and three cases in less developed nations. Below we present the key findings from these six cases presented at IRSPP 6 (2015).

Findings

This section of the chapter highlights some of the key policies for each nation and how they translate into community benefits in developed economies: Australia,

Netherlands and Wales, compared to those in less developed economies: Indonesia, Rwanda and Zambia. Evidence is sought in each of the cases of any received client value that might be conceived as 'public value'. First, highlights of the socio-economic policy landscape impacting on social public procurement are provided.

Australia – The primary focus of relevant socio-economic policies is on creating better regions and communities that are more cohesive. The overarching philosophy of the Western Australian approach to government expenditure is the provision of "community benefit". A set of projects identified provided community benefits in the non-metropolitan area of Western Australia. "Royalties for Regions", underpins the Western Australian Government's long-term commitment to developing Western Australia's regional areas into strong and vibrant communities that are desirable places to live, work and invest. It was reported that it was first perceived by the public as a political game (or stunt), but has since gradually gained community support, respect and involvement. Many of the projects are very minor in terms of overall government procurement spend and community impact while others have effectively changed the landscape and provided political, economic, and behavioural benefits. In most of the projects the outcomes are claimed to lead to positive results.

Netherlands – The primary focus here is on creating employment. The Public Procurement Act (Aanbestedingswet 2012), which took effect from 1 April 2013, provides a general legal framework for public procurement regulations and implements the following European Public Procurement Directives:

- Directive 2004/18 on the co-ordination of procedures for the award of public works contracts, public supply contracts and public service contracts (Consolidated Public Sector Directive).
- Directive 2004/17 coordinating the procurement procedures of entities operating in the water, energy, transport and postal services sectors (Utilities Directive).
- Directive 2007/66/EC amending Directives 89/665/EEC and 92/13/EEC with regards to improving the effectiveness of review procedures concerning the award of public contracts (Public Contracts Review Procedures Directive).

Dutch public procurement law recognises the general principles of public procurement law (non-discrimination, transparency and proportionality). In terms of community benefits the emphasis is on economic regeneration by creating employment opportunities. Since 2014 the organisation PIANOo has been the central contact point for Sustainable Public Procurement for all Dutch public procurers. Central government implements social return on investment (SROI) for 'works' and 'services' contracts valued over 250 euros, but this is not monitored or enforced through local policy.

Wales – The primary focus here is on reducing poverty. Following the Welsh Government Response to Europe Report (2020 Strategy), the Community Benefits Policy (2011–2016) has been a strategy for improving Sustainable Development in Wales. This policy has been underlined by the then Minister of Business and Finance, Jane Hutt (Assembly Member) in the Wales Procurement Policy Statement. The policy states that recognising Community Benefits via the Community Benefits measurement tool needs to be an integral part of planning procurement "irrespective of value" (Community Benefits Guidance, 2014). The Community Benefits Policy focuses on two areas: encouraging workforce initiatives and optimising the local supply chain. "The Welsh Government will change the way it buys to create more benefits for local communities and open the door to SMEs under the Procurement Policy Statement" (Reynolds, 2012).

Indonesia – The primary focus is on improving the health of individuals. The origins of the National Public Procurement Agency (NPPA) were founded on the Center for Public Procurement Policy Development (PPKPBJ in Indonesia). NPPA is a public procurement policy-making agency that focuses on quality, credibility and transparency in procurement practices. With a primary focus on improving health in local communities, the Government of Indonesia emphasises social and environmental factors. An e-Purchasing system was launched in 2012 to enable Ministries and Local Goverments to obtain more easily the products/services they need. Currently, there are around 4000 products avaliable in the e-Catalogue together with the price of each product. Ministries and local governments propose a set of products that they want to buy and then the public procurement organisation, LKPP, upload announcements to invite vendors to offer their products and prices to be listed in the catalogue. At the next step, LKPP invites the vendors to verify the vendor administration requirements, negotiate price, or compete in providing the products or services. The types, specifications and final negotiated prices are then uploaded in LKPP's website (inaproc.lkpp. go.id), where anybody can see the catalogue transparently.

Rwanda – Here the primary focus is on reducing poverty. There is a central government policy which is aimed at reducing poverty and includes emphasis on community benefits. In 2008, the Rwandan Government launched the Vision 2020 Umerenge Programme (VUP). The connection between public procurement and community benefits is embedded in government philosophy: "Procurement law shall be used if it is established that it shall contribute to the economy, create employment and involvement of the beneficiary community". Whilst the role of procurement is to create employment opportunities for local people, there are still challenges to overcome with consistency and standardisation of procurement processes. Procurement policy is managed at the regional (district) level and self-policing is the main mechanism for monitoring compliance.

Zambia – Here the primary focus is on supporting small enterprises. Public procurement of this nation is managed through the Common Market for Eastern and Southern Africa (COMESA) comprising 19 countries. COMESA undertook a diagnostic study and survey on public procurement in 10 Member States. The findings of the study illustrated major shortcomings. Historically, COMESA has identified deficiencies in procurement practices, weak institutional capacity, discriminatory practices, restrictions against fair competition, lack of information on public procurement opportunities, and revenue loss through non-transparent practices. To address these, COMESA embarked on a Public Procurement Reform in 2001 to facilitate more liberalized trade within the 19 member countries. The process was aimed at promoting good governance through public procurement reform that would yield greater efficiency gains from the procurement process leading to enhanced economic development. In 2003, the Member States adopted the COMESA Procurement Directive which urged Member States to: upgrade their procurement systems to international standards, harmonize their procurement policies and procedures, and build capacity for efficient management of public procurement systems. COMESA does not currently have Community Benefits Regulations. However, the COMESA directive encourages countries to identify measures that may be implemented to facilitate participation in public procurement by small enterprises.

Discussion

Data was collected for each of the selected 6 nation case studies covering public procurement policy, directives, laws, rules and guidance, contract clauses and evidence of measurement or tools for measuring performance. Reflecting on Harland et al.'s (2007) seven stages of public procurement development framework (Figure 9.1), a ranking was formed for each case study by one of the IRSPP organisers and checked and verified by another organiser. Table 9.2 provides these rankings where 0 = no evidence of socio-economic sustainability policy and 4 = strong evidence.

In terms of evidencing examples of community benefits through public procurement in Table 9.3, 0 = no evidence of community benefits at all and 6 = very strong evidence with plenty of examples of community benefits which are being measured.

The research findings offer a comparison of the six country cases: Australia, Netherlands, Wales, Indonesia, Rwanda and Zambia and highlight differences between principal and agent priorities and evidence of client value (Table 9.4).

The findings in Table 9.4 suggest that the strategic scope and development of a nation's socio-economic policies does not necessarily guarantee their implementation through public procurement to try to deliver community benefits. For example, in the Netherlands there are strong central government policies, but the weakness lies in the local procurement implementation of those policies. In contrast, in countries that are weak at a national level at forming policies, laws and regulations to make socio-economic improvements, such as Rwanda and Zambia, strong, local government and local public procurement that are close to the needs of the people use community benefits clauses and collect evidence of people's appreciation for each project. Centralist, top-down policy making in the developed countries does not necessarily lead to good

Key to Table 9.2 Analysing socio-economic sustainability policies across the six country cases

0	1	2	3	4
No evidence	Starting to create	Evidence, but no specific socio-economic elements	Evidence and some evidence of socio-economic elements	Strong evidence and strong evidence of socio-economic elements

Table 9.2 Evidence of socio-economic sustainable public procurement policies for six country cases

Nation	Public Procurement Policies	Public Procurement Directives	Public Procurement Laws, rules, guidance	Methods, contract clauses, award criteria	Monitoring/ measurement tools	TOTAL
Australia	4	3	3	3	0	13
Netherlands	4	4	2	4	1	15
Wales	4	4	4	3	4	19
Indonesia	3	0	3	1	2	9
Rwanda	2	0	3	0	1	6
Zambia	1	3	1	0	2	7

Key for Table 9.3 Analysing community benefits clauses across six country cases

0	1	2	3	4	5	6
No evidence	Very slight evidence	Some evidence	Strong evidence	Very strong evidence	Very strong evidence and some measurements	Very strong evidence and lots of measurements

Table 9.3 Case study evidence of community benefits clauses across six country cases

Country case study	*0* No evidence	*1* Very slight evidence	*2* Some evidence	*3* Strong evidence	*4* Very strong evidence	*5* Very strong evidence and some measurements	*6* Very strong evidence and lots of measurements
Australia					X		
Netherlands			X				
Wales						X	
Indonesia		X					
Rwanda						X	
Zambia						X	

Table 9.4 Principal-agent-client summaries of policies, implementation and perceived public value

Country case	Principal (central government) priorities	Agent (local government) action	Evidence of client value in the cases
Australia	Strong policies, to strengthen regional communities	Strong evidence of the use of community benefits clauses for implementing policies through a range of local projects engaged with the community	It is claimed that over time the community started to appreciate these projects and value them despite first thinking they were a political stunt. Western Australia present quite strong evidence of this community engagement and appreciation
Netherlands	Strong policies to deliver social improvement through increasing employment	Weak local implementation of these policies with only some evidence of use of community benefits clauses to increase employment	There is little evidence provided of engagement of the public and local communities in these policies and little evidence of improved social value through increasing employment
Wales	Very strong policies to reduce poverty through economic growth of smaller businesses and procurement from local sources	Very strong implementation of policies through local government letting contracts with community benefits clauses	Very strong evidence of engagement of and improvements for local communities. Strong evidence for each project with measures of value added, testimonials, videos of how local people's lives have been improved

(Continued)

Table 9.4 (Continued)

Country case	Principal (central government) priorities	Agent (local government) action	Evidence of client value in the cases
Indonesia	Fairly weak national policies, laws and regulations to improve the health of individuals	Local procurement keeps contracts as small as possible to minimise corruption but this impacts on spread of policy implementation, using standardisation through E-Procurement for improving efficiencies so costs of providing products and services that improve health are reduced. Aiming for 'value for money' on maturity framework	Very little evidence of any benefits to communities through this value for money initiative. No evidence of any understanding of public value and whether there is a perception of improvement
Rwanda	Aspirational, high level policies for reducing poverty and improving economic growth but very weak on mechanisms to flesh out these policies	Highly decentralised with local control of procurement. Fighting to reduce corruption locally and to engage local communities so they benefit from employment and development of local businesses	Very strong evidence was provided in the workshop of how projects were established and run locally to improve employment. Projects were driven by the needs of the local people
Zambia	Little evidence of national policies, laws and regulations to promote economic growth, deferring to policies of COMESA	Engaged local governments regularly using community benefits clauses for addressing needs of local people. Employment, particularly of women, enables them to feed their families	Projects record value for local communities e.g. a terracing and landscaping project valued at 120, 678 Euros resulted in 89,725 people being employed (49,990 males and 42,735 females).

implementation and evidence of public value. It is only in Wales that strong central policies are well implemented, and measures evidence the impact on communities for each public procurement.

There may be an underlying reason why Wales, Rwanda and Zambia show similarities in success of delivering community benefits that seem to be valued by the public. Whilst Wales has been classified here as a developed nation, rural Wales is in extreme poverty. West Wales is one of the poorest regions in Northern Europe (Eurostat, 2017). In this and in previous phases of IRSPP it has been found that countries in crisis are more likely to recognise and use the power of public procurement to help deliver broader government objectives (Harland et al., 2013).

Lessons learned

Our findings, like those of Kaupi and van Raaij (2015) also imply conflicting objectives; whilst it may be beneficial to government to promote the use of sustainable procurement and community benefits clauses through policies, regulations and guidance; individual local government organisations have their own local objectives and spend their budgets in accordance with their own priorities. Similarly, Solino (2015) found information asymmetry and risk aversion with agents; whilst principals' policies may promote sustainable procurement through community benefits clauses, established relationships between local procurement (agents) and their existing suppliers may not include such practices or aspirations. Implementing such changes may be viewed as a risk in those long-standing relationships.

Conversely, where there is strong belief in local agents of the value of pursuing community benefits in local contracts, but less evidence of principals centrally driving this through policies, regulations and guidance, these bottom up projects can be used to influence formal bureaucratic policy making, as discussed in Terman (2015).

The presence of otherwise of layers of policies, regulations and guidance from principals in central government and their agents on the ground spending public money is not necessarily the effective driving force in using public spending to deliver broader benefits for communities.

Effective use of community benefits clauses in public procurement appears to be needs driven, rather than necessarily principal driven, accentuating information asymmetry and conflicting goals between principals and agents. Principal Agency theory, therefore, has provided a useful theoretical lens through with which to observe and provide possible explanations for why we see a mismatch between principals and agents, policy and practice, but it still takes a government perspective unless the needs of the public as clients are considered. Agency theory has been useful to understanding that information asymmetry may be possible between policy makers as principals and public procurement as agents. This echoes the findings of Kaupi and van Raaij (2015) in that the principal here designed and promoted adherence to centralised procurement practices and framework contracts and the agents did not necessarily conform with these, choosing to do their own 'maverick' buying.

Extending principal agent theory to become principal-agent-client theory here allowed closer examination of the relationship between local government and public procurement's engagement with local communities in projects, and the perceived and evidenced public value of those projects. So, whilst in developing countries such as Rwanda and Zambia the principals either had no community benefits clauses imposed on their agents (Zambia) or only an expressed policy preference for considering community benefits (Rwanda), their agents locally were pursuing them vigorously and evidencing the impact.

In the developed countries where there were significantly more layers of bureaucracy considering and pursuing social procurement and community benefits, it was only in Wales that the agents were effectively implementing these and evidencing tangible community benefits.

Future studies might embrace Public value theory (Geuijen et al., 2017) which links policy and its implementation far more holistically addressing international challenges, something Geuijen et al. refer to as global wicked problems.

References

Amann, M., Roehrich, J., Eßig, M. and Harland, C. (2014). "Driving sustainable supply chain management in the public sector. The importance of public procurement in the European Union". *Supply Chain Management – An International Journal*, 19(3): 351–366.

African Union (2015). Available online at https://au.int/ [accessed 21/09/17].

Ariztia, T., Kleine, D., Maria das Graças, S.L., Agloni, N., Afonso, R. and Bartholo, R. (2014). "Ethical consumption in Brazil and Chile: institutional contexts and development trajectories". *Journal of Cleaner Production*, 63: 84–92.

Asian (2012). SME Development. Government Procurement and Inclusive Growth Report Available online at www.adb.org/sites/default/files/publication/30070/sme-development.pdf [accessed 21/09/17].

Blanc, J. and Kledal, R. (2012). "The Brazilian organic food sector: Prospects and constraints of facilitating the inclusion of smallholders". *Journal of Rural Studies*, 28(1): 142–154.

Boyne, G., Farrell, C., Law, J., Powell, M. and Walker, M. (2003). *Evaluating Public Management Reforms*. Buckingham: Open University Press.

Brammer, S. and Walker, H. (2011). "Sustainable procurement in the public sector: an international comparative study". *International Journal of Operations & Production Management*, 31(4): 452–476.

Bull, G. et al. (2001). "Wood procurement policy: An analysis of critical issues and stakeholders". *Forestry Chronicle*, 77(2): 325–340.

Cheung, E. and Chan, A.C. (2014). "Revitalizing Historic Buildings through a Partnership Scheme: Innovative Form of Social Public-Private Partnership". *Journal of Urban Planning and Development*, 140(1): 9.

Clark, W.W. (2007). "Partnerships in creating agile sustainable development communities". *Journal of Cleaner Production*, 15(3): 294–302.

COMESA Available online at www.comesa.int/ [accessed 12/06/16] .

Community Benefits Guidance (2014): "Delivering value through the welsh pound". Available online at http://gov.wales/topics/improvingservices/bettervfm/publications/community-benefits-2014/?lang=en [accessed 21/08/17].

Eisenhardt, K.M. (1989). "Agency theory: An assessment and review". *Academy of Management Review*, 14(1): 57–74.

Erridge, A. (2007). "Public procurement, public value and the Northern Ireland unemployment pilot project". *Public Administration*, 85(4): 1023–1043.

Erridge, A. and Henningan, S. (2007). Public Procurement and Social Policy in Northern Ireland: The Unemployment Pilot Project. In G. Piga and K.V. Thai, *Advancing Public Procurement: Practices, Innovation and Knowledge-sharing* (pp. 280–303). Boca Raton, FL: PrAcademics Press.

European Commission: Public Procurement (2010). Available online at https://ec.europa.eu/growth/single-market/public-procurement_en [accessed 21/09/17].

Eurostat Regional Yearbook (2017). KS-HA-17-001. Available online at https://ec.europa.eu/eurostat/documents/3217494/8222062/KS-HA-17-001-EN-N.pdf/eaebe7fa-0c80-45af-ab41-0f806c433763 [accessed 17/01/19].

Fee, R. (2002). "Contract compliance: subnational and European influences in Northern Ireland". *Journal of European Social Policy*, 12(2): 107–121.

Furneaux, C. and Barraket, J. (2014). "Purchasing social good(s): a definition and typology of social procurement". *Public Money & Management*, 34(4): 265–272.

Galli, F., Brunori, G., Di Iacovo, F. and Innocenti, S. (2014). "Co-Producing Sustainability: Involving Parents and Civil Society in the Governance of School Meal Services. A Case Study from Pisa, Italy". *Sustainability*, 6 (4): 1643–1666.

Geuijen, K., Moore, M., Cederquist, A., Ronning, R. and van Twist, M. (2017). "Creating public value in global wicked problems". *Public Management Review*, 19 (5): 621–639.

Green, A.R. (2016). *History, Policy and Public Purpose: Historians and Historical Thinking in Government*. New York: Springer.

Harland, C., Nassimbeni, G. and Schneller, E. (eds) (2013). *The SAGE Handbook of Strategic Supply Management*. Los Angeles, London, New Delhi, Singapore, Washington DC: Sage.

Harland, C., Qatami, L. and Warrington, J. (2007). "Concept of evidence-based public procurement". Proceedings of 16th Annual IPSERA Conference, Bath, UK, April 1–4.

Harland, C., Knight, L., Telgen, J., Thai, K., Callendar, G. and McKen, K. (eds) (2012). *Public Procurement: International Cases and Commentary*. Oxon: Routledge.

Hawkins, T.G. et al. (2011). "Public Versus Private Sector Procurement Ethics and Strategy: What Each Sector can Learn from the Other". *Journal of Business Ethics*, 103(4): 567–586.

Horner, L. and Hazel, L. (2005). *Adding Public Value*. London: The Work Foundation.

Kashap, S. (2004). "Public procurement as a social economic and political policy". International Public Procurement Conference, Fort Lauderdale, Florida, USA, 3: 133–147.

Kauppi, K. and van Raaij, E.M. (2015). "Opportunism and Honest Incompetence-Seeking Explanations for Noncompliance in Public Procurement". *Journal of Public Administration Research and Theory*, 25(3): 953–979.

Lehtinen, U. (2012). "Sustainability and local food procurement: a case study of Finnish public catering". *British Food Journal*, 114(8–9): 1053–1071.

Lynch, J., Walker, H. and Harland, C. (2013). "Utilizing a community benefits tool in support of the local multiplier effect for sustainable procurement innovation". Supplement to the 2013 Annual Statistical Report on United Nations Procurement: Procurement and innovation: UNOPS.

Lynch, J., Walker, H., Uenk, N. and Schotanus, F. (2016). "Community benefits of public procurement: a comparison between local governments in Wales (UK) and Netherlands". Conference proceedings for 25th IPSERA, Dortmund.

Mansi, M. (2015). "Sustainable procurement disclosure practices in central public sector enterprises: Evidence from India". *Journal of Purchasing and Supply Management*, 21(2): 125–137.

McCrudden, C. (2004). "Using public procurement to achieve social outcomes". *Natural Resources Forum*, 28(4): 257–267.

Meehan, J. and Bryde, D.J. (2015). "A field-level examination of the adoption of sustainable procurement in the social housing sector". *International Journal of Operations & Production Management*, 35 (7): 982–1004.

Miemczyk, J., Johnsen, T.E. and Macquet, M. (2012). "Sustainable purchasing and supply management: a structured literature review of definitions and measures at the dyad, chain and network levels". *Supply Chain Management*, 17(5): 478–496.

Mitnick, B.M. (1973). Fiduciary rationality and public policy: The theory of agency and some consequences. *Public Choice*, 24(1): 27–42.

Moore, M.H. (1995). *Creating Public Value: Strategic Management in Government*. Cambridge, MA: Harvard University Press.

O'Brien, G. and Hope, A. (2010). "Localism and energy: Negotiating approaches to embedding resilience in energy systems". *Energy Policy*, 38(12): 7550–7558.

O'Flynn, J. (2007). "From new public management to public value: Paradigmatic change and managerial implications". *Australian Journal of Public Administration*, 66(3), 353–366.

Ostrovnaya, M. (2015). "The impact of procurement procedures on rent-seeking of procurers and suppliers: the case of Russia". *Voprosy Gosudarstvennogo I Munitsipalnogo Upravleniya – Public Administration Issues*, (1): 69–91.

Pirvu, D. and Clipici, E. (2016). "Social Enterprises and the EU's Public Procurement Market". *Voluntas*, 27(4): 1611–1637.

Preuss, L. (2007). Buying into our future: sustainability initiatives in local government procurement. *Business Strategy and the Environment*, 16(5): 354–365.

Ravenswood, K. and Kaine, S. (2015). "The role of government in influencing labour conditions through the procurement of services: Some political challenges". *Journal of Industrial Relations*, 57(4): 544–562.

Reynolds, A. (2012). "Wales transforms procurement with policy statement". *Supply Management*, December.

Ross, S.A. (1973). "The economic theory of agency: The principal's problem". *The American Economic Review*, 63(2), 134–139.

Ruge, D. and Mikkelsen, B.E. (2013). "Local public food strategies as a social innovation: early insights from the LOMA-Nymarkskolen case study". *Acta Agriculturae Scandinavica Section B – Soil and Plant Science*, 63: 56–65.

Solino, A.S. (2015). "Optimizing performance-based mechanisms in road management: an agency theory approach". *European Journal of Transport and Infrastructure Research*, 15(4): 465–481.

Sonnino, R. (2009). "Quality food, public procurement, and sustainable development: the school meal revolution in Rome". *Environment and Planning A*, 41(2): 425–440.

Sonnino, R. and McWilliam, S. (2011). "Food waste, catering practices and public procurement: A case study of hospital food systems in Wales". *Food Policy*, 36(6): 823–828

Sumberg, J. and Sabates-Wheeler, R. (2011). "Linking agricultural development to school feeding in sub-Saharan Africa: Theoretical perspectives". *Food Policy*, 36(3): 341–349.

Terman, J. (2015). "A State-Level Examination of Bureaucratic Policymaking: The Internal Organization of Attention". *American Review of Public Administration*, 45(6): 708–727.

Tikkanen, I. (2014). "Procurement and consumption of local and organic food in the catering of a rural town". *British Food Journal*, 116(3): 419–430.

Touboulic, A. and Walker, H. (2015). "Theories in sustainable supply chain management: a structured literature review". *International Journal of Physical Distribution & Logistics Management*, 45(1–2): 16–42.

United Nations: General Assembly 2015. Available online at www.gov.uk/government/topical-events/united-nations-general-assembly-2015 [accessed 21/08/17] .

Viking, A. and Lidelow, S. (2015). "Exploring industrialized housebuilders' interpretations of local requirements using institutional logics". *Construction Management and Economics*, 33(5–6): 484–494.

Walker, H. (2015). New development research at IPSERA: aligning research and practice and future trends. *Public Money & Management*, 35(2): 141–144.

Walker, H. and Brammer, S. (2009). "Sustainable procurement in the United Kingdom public sector". *Supply Chain Management – An International Journal*, 14(2): 128–137.

Walker, H. and Preuss, L. (2008). "Fostering sustainability through sourcing from small businesses: public sector perspectives". *Journal of Cleaner Production*, 16(15): 1600–1609.

Walker, H., Miemczyk, J., Johnsen, T. and Spencer, R. (2012). "Sustainable procurement: Past, present and future". *Journal of Purchasing and Supply Management*, 18(4): 201–206.

Waugh, H. (2004). "Paths to sustainable procurement". *Health estate*, 58(10): 31.

Willis, K.G. (2010). "Is all sustainable development sustainable? A cost-benefit analysis of some procurement projects". *Journal of Environmental Assessment Policy and Management*, 12(3): 311–331.

Witjes, S. and Lozano, R. (2016). "Towards a more Circular Economy: Proposing a framework linking sustainable public procurement and sustainable business models". *Resources Conservation and Recycling*, 112: 37–44.

Wontner, K., Walker, H., Harris, I. and Lynch, J. (2015). "Barriers and Enablers to a 'Living Wage' in Public Sector Contracts". Proceedings for 24th IPSERA Conference, Netherlands.

WPPPS (2015) (Wales Public Procurement Policy Statement). Available online at http://gov.wales/topics/improvingservices/bettervfm/publications/procurement-policy-statement/?lang=en [accessed 21/09/17].

Yin, Y., Zhang, X., and Feng, Y. (2015). "Study on Modes of the Sustainable Public Procurement". *4th International Conference on Energy and Environmental Protection* (ICEEP 2015): 867–887.

Zelenbabic, D. (2015). "Fostering innovation through innovation friendly procurement practices: a case study of Danish local government procurement". *Innovation – The European Journal of Social Science Research*, 28(3): 261–281.

Zorzini, M., Hendry, L.C., Huq, F.A. and Stevenson, M. (2015). "Socially responsible sourcing: reviewing the literature and its use of theory". *International Journal of Operations & Production Management*, 35(1): 60–109.

Part 1.3

Actions to define and create public value

10 Action research to develop the theory and practice of public value as a contested democratic practice

John Benington and Jean Hartley

Introduction

The concept of public value is finding its way into both academic writing and public policy discourse at an increasing pace, since its introduction by Mark Moore (1995) initially as part of the debate about strategic management in the public sector. However, use of "public value" language has since proliferated in a rather fuzzy and slippery way (Hartley et al., 2017). There is now a risk that 'public value' degenerates into a magic concept (Pollitt and Hupe, 2011) which can be used in a variety of superficial ways to describe various disparate phenomena.

However, in this chapter we will argue that public value (when clarified and sharpened to include not only strategic management but also the democratic processes of creating value in the public sphere), is a concept with considerable potential for understanding and improving leadership, management and organization in society. We also argue that action research has considerable potential to advance both the theory and practice of public value.

This chapter first outlines this wider conception of public value as a key part of creating, using and sustaining a democratic public sphere (Benington, 2011). We then explore how public value relates to nearby concepts like 'public goods' and 'public interest', the significance of 'creating the public' in public value, and why it is a "game-changer" (Sørensen, 2016) for the fields of leadership and public management.

We then argue for the value of action research as a key, but not the only, methodology for studying public value. Action research is a rich methodology for the investigation of public value because it engages actively with the processes of change in real time, is sensitive to pluralist contested interpretations of events and processes by different stakeholders, and it exposes this lived material to a dialectical challenge from theory.

Finally, the chapter illustrates some key elements of public value as a contested democratic practice through the presentation of three action or co-research case studies, in which the authors have been involved.

What is the public, what is value and what is public value?

There are widely divergent definitions of public value which can be confusing. However, Hartley et al. (2017) argue that

> different conceptualizations of public value have hampered the development of a cumulative body of empirical research. Yet, their existence should not act as a

brake on empirical research as long as scholars are clear and explicit about their definition of the concepts.

(673)

In this chapter, we work with Benington's (2011) conceptualisation of public value as a contested democratic practice which critically addresses the question of what adds value to the public sphere.

This formulation builds on, but goes beyond, the conceptualisation of public value by Moore (1995) in his seminal book *Creating Public Value: Strategic Management in Government*. Mark Moore was writing in the USA at the time of the Reagan administration which had a relentless focus on shrinking the state because it was seen as 'crowding out' private sector investment (Bacon and Eltis, 1978), with government taxation a burden on the economy and on the freedom of individuals to make their own unfettered choices within a private competitive market. Within this framework, the private sector was seen as more efficient and effective than the public sector and it was therefore hard to evaluate the contribution of government or publicly owned organizations, either in terms of their performance as organizations or of their wider contribution to society, partly because their output and outcomes were not reducible to simple financial measures. Moore developed a framework for the public-services equivalent of private value (the latter measured financially in a competitive market). He created and analysed teaching cases to build up a theory and practice of public value, where value was not only found in organizational performance but also in impact on society (e.g. reduction in crime; safer parks, confident parenting; social justice). He linked the value created by public organizations to the public good, or what is beneficial to society. This drew on economic theories about public goods as "non-rival and non-excludable" (Samuelson, 1954) and also a long line of political philosophy about what constitutes the public or common good (Grange (1996) in relation to Confucius, Dewey and Rorty; Ostrom, 1990).

Crucially, Moore's framework helped public managers, (traditionally thought of as administrators who passively carried out the wishes of elected politicians), to shift their stance to become proactive in not only recognising but also creating public value, through strategic management. Moore was clear that appointed public managers had to respect and defer to the wishes of their elected political masters (Alford, 2008) but that they could shape thinking and action by paying attention also to a wider range of stakeholders (their "authorising" environment), by being crystal clear about what public value outcomes their organization and its partners were aiming to achieve (the public value proposition) and by taking account of what operational resources (finance, expertise, equipment) could be harnessed to achieve this public value purpose. Moore argued that combining these three elements above in a strategic triangle, provides public managers with a clear framework to achieve public value (Benington and Moore, 2011).

Other scholars have argued that public value can be created by a wider range of actors than solely public managers. Elected and appointed politicians, private sector partners, voluntary organizations, civil society associations and other sections of the public can all be harnessed behind the creation of public value outcomes (Benington and Moore 2011; Bryson et al., 2017; 2016). As Alford (2016) notes, it is not that public value necessarily emanates from public actors but that it is received by the public. Moore (2013) also supports the inclusion of this wider set of actors in the processes of creation of public value.

Other scholars have outlined differing approaches to public value, such as Bozeman (2007) with an interest in society's normative value inputs as well as outputs; Meynhardt (2009) with a focus on internal psychological values across all sectors; and Stoker (2006) with public value seen as a new paradigm in public management. However, in this chapter we have chosen to focus in some detail on Benington's (2011) conception of public value as a contested democratic process which critically addresses questions about what adds value to the public sphere. For Benington, public value is based on two inter-linked questions, one focused on inputs from different public(s) ("what does this public most value in this specific context?") and one focused on outcomes for society ("what adds most value to the public sphere?"). These two dimensions can often be in tension with each other.

In addition, differences of ideologies, interests and priorities between different groups within the public may be surfaced when these two public value questions are posed. The process of listening to these competing voices, and trying to negotiate some common purposes, helps to create a public which is conscious of its values, and clear about its goals and priorities. Different stakeholders may hold differing values (inputs) and have differing perceptions of and attitudes towards the public benefits (the outputs). Public value is inherently contested in society and therefore needs to be set within a democratic process if such tensions, differences and divergences are to be heard, recognised, 'held', explored and to some extent resolved or at least addressed for the benefit of the common good.

The values held by individuals, as citizens, consumers or members of diverse communities are an important element of public value, and may be deep-seated beliefs or may be influenced by context. Values are not the same as wants, needs, expectations or aspirations, though these are sometimes confused in the public management literature. At the individual level, values can be discerned in part in the abstract (e.g. someone may have a deep commitment to honesty or transparency); but they can also be discerned in particular contexts through the priorities and choices which people make in practice, or which they wish to have made for them by their representatives. Making one choice over another usually means that one value is more highly prized (in that context) than the other. For example, if sufficient members of the public indicate that they value rehabilitation in prison over punishment, then that may shape penal policy and prison practice.

However, there are problems with discerning public value only from the summation of individual values – a key issue for political philosophers. First, within many European and Eastern cultures, society is not seen simply as the aggregation of individual interests and values, but starts instead from a conception of some common interests or identities (often focused around community, nationhood or history). The word 'individual' itself derives from Latin and means not divisible, which implies a larger unit of analysis (like individual slices of cake or individual members of a species). Instead, there are many philosophical, sociological and psychological theories which argue that the social group and public institutions pre-exist the individual or at least co-exist and shapes thinking and values (Foucault, 1970; Habermas, 1962; Tajfel, 1982).

The second problem is that a simple aggregation of individual values could lead to majoritarian prioritisation which neglects or over-rides minority views. This can be problematic both in terms of social justice and also in terms of innovation in society (newly accepted normative values in society often start as marginalised or minority views). Third, an individualised view of society ignores the fact that knowledge and information are unequally distributed in society. Some individuals have more specialised expertise, understanding or access to knowledge, which can affect their judgement about what constitutes public value outcomes. For example, in a recent study, police officers were found to have greater awareness of the range of policing activities and priorities than did members of the public (Vo et al., 2017). Professionals in a society may espouse particular values that are not necessarily carried by the majority (a doctor or an imam saving the life of a terrorist because of their belief that all human beings are valuable). When a public manager in Melbourne insists on planning for water needs in 50 years' time, in contrast to the politicians' and public's focus only on immediate water shortages, this is addressing the question of what will add value to the public sphere, in the next generation. Professionals can, of course, also use their knowledge in self-interested ways (Le Grand, 2003) so the result is not always public-spirited. Nevertheless, differentiated access to knowledge can help to preserve values which might otherwise be overlooked or suppressed in popular public debate.

These problems with majoritarian values act as an alert that the values expressed by the public are insufficient in aggregate, by themselves, as the expression of public value. Moore (1995; 2013) addresses this through drawing on normative values in society (social justice, transparency, legality and so on) as does Bozeman (2007). However, Benington takes a pluralist rather than a unitarist view of values, and suggests that different publics may hold quite different values. These competing values have to be articulated, tested, refined, changed, debated, explored, and argued out in the public sphere, as part of a "contested democratic practice". Consequently, Benington's (2011) second dimension of public value is what adds value to the public sphere.

The concept of the public sphere means that scholars and practitioners need to pay attention to the construction of the 'public' not just the creation of 'value'. Habermas (1962) conceived of the public sphere as an arena in which people come together to debate and shape public matters, and to challenge values, decisions and activities in the market, the state, and civil society. According to Habermas, the public sphere is open to all citizens, using discussion and critical debate to influence political action. Fraser (1990) and others have argued that Habermas's view of the public sphere is both gender and class biased, and implies white middle-class men involved in civilised conversations in gentlemen's clubs. However, one can see the public sphere in action in more raw, diverse and conflictual terms in the public debates following London's Grenfell Tower major fire, in which over 70 people died in 2017. This high profile national conversation, in various electronic, media, and angry face-to-face meetings caused a radical reassessment of government policies and priorities for social housing, fire security and building standards. An increasingly strong public voice has emerged from among the victims and the diverse local communities involved in this terrible tragedy, which has "called a public into existence" (Dewey, 1927) and created a public sphere in which 'what the public most values' has been made plain to central and local government. Additional examples of the public creating a democratic space and dialogue around contested issues include the growing challenge to the private service sector for its reliance upon zero hours employment contracts, and to the voluntary sector for the practice of "chugging" – aggressively accosting people on the street to give charity donations.

Marquand (2004) develops the related concept of the public domain: "central to it are values of citizenship, equity and service. It is a space . . . where strangers encounter each other as equal partners in the common life of a society" (27). Sennett (2017) (acknowledging his debt to Habermas) discusses another closely related concept, the public realm:

> The most important fact about the public realm is what happens in it. Gathering together strangers, enables certain kinds of activities which cannot happen, or do not happen as well, in the intimate private realm. In public, people can access unfamiliar knowledge, expanding the horizons of their information. Markets depend on these expanding horizons of information. In public, people can discuss and debate with people who may not share the same assumptions or the same interests. Democratic government depends on such exchanges between strangers.

Bryson et al. (2015) and Sennett (1977) note that the public sphere is where public values are held, created or diminished. The public sphere is not co-terminus with the state. It is an arena for democratic contestation of what the public most values, and of what adds most value to the public sphere. This takes the concept of public value away from its original conceptualisation as being primarily concerned with the management of public organizations. The public sphere is therefore much broader than the public sector or public services owned or commissioned by the state. Public value can be created within the state, within the market or within civil society, or by a combination of actors from all three. So, using the concept of the public sphere enlarges the scope of public value thinking beyond its original focus on the work of public managers, and extends it to also include democratic processes and actors from the public, private and third sectors.

Benington's (2011; 2015) two dimensions of public value can be in tension with each other. This can be normal and healthy within a democracy. The scope for dissent and avenues for exploring dissent are widely seen as essential for liberal democracies. Habermas (1962) has been criticised for having an idealised view of the public sphere, underplaying inequalities and with an over-reliance on rationality and consensus (Mouffe, 2000). Mouffe's concept of 'agonistic pluralism' starts by accepting that there are differences of interest and ideology among different stakeholders, that conflicts are inevitable but that democratic spaces and practices are ways to channel conflict constructively. "'Antagonism' implies a bi-polar conflict between friend and enemy, while 'agonism' (derived from the Greek word for contest or games) suggests a struggle between competing ideas and interests, but the possibility of a negotiated settlement.

Benington (2015) also raises important questions about how to create a public, or publics, who are conscious of their interests, values and aims, well-informed and capable of engaging in democratic debate with others of equally strong but different persuasions? So there can be many voices and indeed many publics. Sometimes the role of public leaders is to help to create and/or convene publics which can debate and explore the public value relevant to them and to wider society (including future generations), and to create public spaces (safe but stretching 'holding environments') where different publics can meet to work through difficult and sometimes painful questions and choices Sometimes the work of public leaders is to reach out to connect with publics which are in danger of being antagonistic in a binary way, polarising us and them, friend and foe, and scapegoating 'the other' (e.g. vigilante groups, xenophobic populist movements), and to draw them instead into pluralist 'agonistic' dialogue which aims to acknowledge differences but to negotiate coalitions of common interest. This recalls the work of Dewey (1927) that the most important problem facing the public is discovering itself and identifying its own true interests.

Sørensen (2016) talks about public value in this sense as a 'game-changer' because it focuses on the most fundamental democratic processes whereby individuals and groups in society come together to explore, negotiate and hopefully reconcile differences in their interests and perspectives about what they most value and what is going to add most value to the public sphere.

Action-research and public value

The further development of public value theory and practice will suffer if it continues to lack grounding in empirical research. A recent essay on public value research (Hartley et al., 2017) shows that there are many opportunities to improve the empirical base of the public value framework but that "despite the growing discourse on the theory and practice of public value, there are very few publications which are based on empirical research. Most publications are, instead, theoretical, conceptual, scholarly, synthetic or descriptive" (670).

Empirical research has been hampered in part by the inherent complexity of public value as a theory and as a framework for action, and the fact that the situations in which it is a helpful explanatory (and possibly predictive) asset are dynamic, pluralistic and often volatile. However, Hartley et al. (2017) show that this is only a partial explanation for the relative lack of empirical research and that there are many opportunities to remedy the situation.

Action-research has a long and productive history in both the USA and UK (Elden and Chisholm, 1993; Israel et al., 1992; Lewin, 1951; Eden and Huxham, 1996). It has been described by Reason and Bradbury (2001, 1) as:

> a participatory, democratic process concerned with developing practical knowing in the pursuit of worthwhile human purposes, grounded in a participatory worldview which we believe is emerging at this historical moment. It seeks to bring together action and reflection, theory and practice, in participation with others, in the pursuit of practical solutions to issues of pressing concern to people, and more generally the flourishing of individual persons and their communities.

Action research in the social sciences has strong roots in at least two philosophical and methodological traditions. The work of Kurt Lewin provides a clear rationale for action research, arguing among other things that "there is nothing so practical as a good theory" (1943–44, 169) Lewin pioneered research that started with a practical problem or issue and then used social psychological theory and active field experimentation to understand and change social situations and individual behaviour. Lewin's "field theory" grew into the area now called organization development, with an emphasis on understanding and intervening in organisational and human systems (Cummings and Worley, 2014).

The second strand which underpins much action research derives from the Tavistock Institute of Human Relations and its theories of 'socio-technical' systems (the interaction of thinking feeling human beings with technical and organisational systems, e.g. Miller and Rice, 1967). Intervention in the socio-technical system creates change at many different levels (including unconscious feelings and behaviours) which can be observed or inferred and which enables the engaged researcher to reflect on and develop theories of change.

Why do we argue that action research is an appropriate methodology for the theory and practice of public value? First, action research accepts that social science is embedded in a system of contested values (Brydon-Miller et al., 2003). Action research is essentially pluralist, and is interested in uncovering differing perspectives about any given situation. It recognises that action may sometimes be challenged from a variety of stakeholders with differences of interest, and seeks to understand multiple perspectives. This is highly relevant to public value, where the tensions which can exist between what publics want and what adds value to the public sphere are sometimes partly played out in the beliefs and priorities of different actors in the situation.

Importantly, though, action research can handle complexity and dynamic change. It does not develop research through a priori hypotheses about what needs researching or how research should be conducted, but comes from a pragmatist approach, where the theoretical questions may be revealed through engagement with action and where the action can also be shaped by theory. Action research therefore is interested in how change happens and the unpredictable nature and unintended consequences of change in complex systems. Observation, intervention and reflection in a recursive cycle are key themes in action research. This resonates well with the dynamic complexity which often exists in the discernment and creation of public value, and how this can change through time, space, flow and context.

It is not surprising, then, that to the extent that there exists any empirical research on public value much of it is analysed through case studies (Hartley et al., 2017). Case studies are particularly valuable in examining processes over time (Hartley, 2004) and in assessing and analysing the interconnectedness which can occur in open systems. They are also highly relevant for understanding the changing contexts in which human behaviours and institutional actions take place. Some case studies may draw on action research; others in related methodologies like co-research bring action perspectives from practitioners into the team. These methodologies have a particular philosophical and methodological match with public value seen as a contested democratic practice.

Of course, action research is not the only methodology which is relevant to analysing or creating public value. A host of different research methods and methodologies can be used, depending on the research question being explored. Qualitative and quantitative approaches, those based on understanding patterns or those based on meaning, each can be highly relevant to the theory and practice of public value (Hartley et al., 2017).

Public value as contested democratic practice: three case studies

Having explored our formulation of public value as a contested democratic practice and argued the case for action-research to trace these dynamics in real time, we now turn to exploring these issues through three case studies which test public value theory and develop its practice.

These cases show people and organisations trying to create public value by tackling complex cross-cutting problems in contested and potentially divisive contexts. All three case studies involve leaders and managers from the public service sector working with a range of stakeholders from both the private sector and civil society to try to create a 'holding environment' within which tough questions can be confronted, and painful choices about priorities between competing publics negotiated. All three are based on real-life situations in which one or both of the authors has been involved as an action-researcher or co-researcher. All investigate how to create a public sphere in which divisive issues can be explored through pluralist 'agonistic' dialogue rather than through binary 'antagonistic' conflict.

The three case studies start from three different places along a spectrum ranging from contest to physical conflict. The Coventry case study surfaces underlying differences and tensions between a range of interest groups within the city, but shows how these can be resolved through civilised democratic dialogue in a public forum. The East of England case study starts further along the contest/conflict spectrum, where there has been a recent breakdown of trust between the police and the public in a rural community, but trust is restored and physical conflict prevented through careful listening by the police to various publics and their value priorities, leading to a collaborative initiative to address their fears and frustrations. The Drumcree case study in Northern Ireland starts at the far end of the contest/conflict spectrum, where there is a long and deeply entrenched history of violence between 'tribal' groups within the community, and where public value thinking and action was used to radically reframe the problem and to act as a catalyst for a restoration of public order.

Case Study 1: Creating a coherent public in Coventry

The Coventry case study illustrates the complex processes of trying to "create a public" which is conscious of itself as more than an aggregation of competing individuals and interest groups (Benington, 2015; Dewey 1927; Prebble, 2016), and which is capable of beginning to take responsibility for difficult communal decisions. In preparing its Local Development Plan in 2005, Coventry City Council decided to promote an active process of consultation with a wide range of interest groups (sometimes called stakeholders) within the community. They asked one of the authors to facilitate this process of public participation and involvement. The ball-room of a local hotel was hired for a day and all the major interest groups in the city were invited to send representatives – the employers and the trades unions; the unemployed; the physically and mentally disabled; young people and elderly people's organisations; all the major faith groups (Christian, Jewish, Sikh, Hindu and Muslim); voluntary and grassroots neighbourhood organisations; the various public services (education, heath, police, fire, and social and welfare benefits services).

A three-stage process was designed and used in creating a public which could deliberate on the future of the city. First (seated at separate tables, with conversation facilitated by roving microphone), each of these diverse interest groups was invited in turn to identify the major issues they were grappling with, or concerned about, from their specific separate point of view. They were also invited to identify the 'rubbing points' or conflicts they felt with any of the other interest groups. This highlighted for example tensions between the police and ethnic minorities who felt they were often harassed unfairly; fears by older people of young people whom they found noisy and boisterous on the streets; resentment by some white working-class residents of some of the ethnic minority groups whom they saw as taking their jobs and under-cutting their wages; fears among mentally ill people of stigmatisation by some public agencies; frustration by the police with other public services which only worked office hours instead of 24/7.

In the second stage, the facilitator encouraged frank face-to-face dialogue between each of the conflicting groups in pairs (e.g. ethnic minority groups challenged the police about their sense of being discriminated against; older people confronted young people about their fears). An appreciative enquiry method (Cooperrider and Srivastava, 1987; Hammond, 2013) was used in which the participants were asked to listen carefully to what the other party had to say, and to double-check that they had heard and understood correctly, before responding. This exercise was carried out in a 'gold-fish bowl' format in which the pairs in each of the dialogues sat facing each other in the middle of a circle with everyone else sitting round the outside of the circle, listening in and providing independent and often critical feedback on the dialogue.

The third stage of the process involved each group sharing their hopes and visions for the future of the city, and trying to identify some shared concerns and common goals between the different interest groups, and to negotiate a coalition to work together to achieve these public value outcomes for the city.

In this illustrative case, creating a public capable of grappling with difficult choices between competing interests and perspectives often has to begin by acknowledging and confronting the differences between different groups rather than starting with an abstract or utopian discussion about public value or the common good. The formulation of public value as a contested democratic practice does not assume a common interest but recognises that there may be many publics (Benington, 2015; Prebble, 2016) who each have particular interests, priorities and perspectives about value in the public sphere. This process of the public discovering its own interests as a city depended on first of all clarifying, vocalising and listening to the interests of different parts of the public, or different publics, which made up Coventry before trying to develop a sense of common purpose.

Case Study 2: A rural crime initiative in Cambridgeshire

Cambridgeshire Constabulary, a police force in the east of England, was trying to decide what to do about hare coursing (illegal hunting of hares with dogs) in its rural areas. Illegal hare coursing might sound like a trivial crime, but it was problematic on several levels. First, the number of incidents was high in the winter and spring season (over 800 incidents in one year) but seasonal (less in summer and autumn). As well as the cruel treatment of mammals, hare coursing may result in damage to crops, fields, gates and other property by the coursers driving 4x4 vehicles across fields. There is also a lot of illegal betting and possible money laundering. Second, hare coursing was seen by local communities as a 'signal crime' indicating other crimes taking place on farms, churches and rural businesses. Theft of farm equipment can be very expensive, and damage to crops may mean ruin for the year. So the prevalence of hare coursing was seen by local people as an indicator of the success or not of their local police force. Seeing large numbers of hare coursers carrying out illegal activities without being challenged by the police had a significant impact on the confidence they had in their police force on all matters. Finally, many rural residents reported being intimidated and physically threatened by hare coursers, and as they lived in isolated locations this had created fear and anxiety within the resident rural community.

Cambridgeshire Police therefore faced a dilemma. Hare coursing was initially seen as 'small beer' compared with the demand for policing in dense urban areas, where crimes were more complex and affected more people. There were more people to protect. Additionally, at a time of budget cuts, choices and priorities about value outcomes had to be made. There had previously been a rural crime team, but it had been disbanded to achieve other policing priorities. However, matters came to a head when rural discontent was mobilised and orchestrated by a local voluntary organisation called Country-Watch. A larger, more cohesive, more vociferous and more agitated 'public' was brought into being. The chief constable attended a meeting of more than 300 angry rural residents, from all classes and backgrounds. His key concern was of possible vigilante action by residents, which could constitute a risk to life. The chief took rapid action, and supported by his police and crime commissioner, rapidly set up a new rural crime team.

Unlike the earlier team, this team was selected for their farming and rural knowledge and background, which helped to increase confidence in the police. (Earlier contact where locals felt the police did not know the difference between a rabbit and a hare had not gone down well.) Rather than focusing solely on crime, the police team saw their role as listening and responding to the public's fears and concerns and taking action to circulate information and to prevent as well as catch hare coursers as well as tackle farm and heritage crime. The police rural crime team aimed to consult, inform, involve and provide reassurance to the public, which was re-prioritised by this police force as a key public outcome of their work. A senior police officer stated that although "you can have all sorts of models looking at demand, ultimately you are dealing with human beings and the nature of concern". For their part, rural residents started to accept that the nature of remote countryside meant that a police presence was not always possible, and they started to co-produce solutions with the police, working collaboratively with them to identify and stop hare-coursers. The small police rural crime team was seen as having re-established legitimacy in that they demonstrated to rural residents that they understood rural issues and listened to and addressed the concerns of sometimes isolated families. Through close and continuing dialogue with stakeholders within the rural community the police diverted potential conflict into constructive collaboration, and re-prioritised prevention, the reduction of fear, and restoration of confidence in policing, as successful outcome measures, not just arrests and convictions.

This case study (Parker et al., 2017) was based on the co-research method (Hartley and Benington, 2000) and involved serving police officers and academics working together in the field over several months. Unlike the other two case studies this research was carried out retrospectively as well as in real time. The findings from the co-research highlighted three main themes.

First, the case shows the co-production of public value. The Rural Community Action Team (RCAT) formed by the police in response to local public dissatisfaction provided the community with a dedicated team to talk, listen and communicate with, and who could reassure the community in their isolation and fear. The RCAT was perceived by the local community as legitimate because it understood rural culture, concerns and terminology, and took the public's voice and value priorities seriously. By asking (in effect, though not explicitly) what does the public most value, and what will add most value to the public sphere, the RCAT diminished the risk of vigilantism by the rural community, and restored a sense of public order. It was found that the problem could not be resolved simply through police resources, as different stakeholders had very differing views about what would add most value to the public sphere. Co-production with the RCAT was valued, with the rural community working with the police on some initiatives to prevent or catch hare coursers and to address other crimes committed in rural areas.

Second, the case illustrates reducing and possibly displacing public value. Public confidence and public value had previously been reduced when the police withdrew an earlier RCAT service, and the community felt let down. The public threatened to take action into their own hands and to form vigilante groups. The public's co-operation was withdrawn because of the perceived lack of a meaningful police response to their concerns. The researchers also identified the risk of displacement of public value. This was linked to the success of the RCAT team in driving out hare coursers from Cambridgeshire – but possibly diverting hare coursing to neighbouring counties. This raises the question of public value which might potentially be created through partnership working across boundaries and between neighbouring police services.

Third, the case raises the question of whose is the public value. A third finding from the co-research was the tension within public value thinking and action between short and long term outcomes and between local and national/international priorities. On being asked about prioritising police resources, interviewees showed that they recognised the above tensions but nevertheless argued for their voice and priorities to be heard: "You could never compare rural crime with child abuse, so people understand resources are needed there, but also that as they pay taxes they should have some support." The priority to invest in the RCAT was near unanimous among the rural community interviewed, although one interviewee questioned its ranking as a police priority within the wider context of international crime. This means that decisions will sometimes need to be made to invest resources in matters that the general public (by majority view) do not think are priorities, but which are important for adding value to the public sphere over the longer term. Lastly, perhaps the most contentious issue raised in this research is whether travellers (widely believed to be the group engaged in hare coursing) are to be regarded as one of the publics in this rural community and whether they should be given their own separate voice and viewpoint alongside other residents.

Case Study 3: Reframing Public Value at the Drumcree Demonstrations in Northern Ireland

The Drumcree case study is a more extended and explicit attempt to use public value theory to reframe the strategy for policing the Drumcree demonstrations in Northern Ireland, to try to restore a framework of law and order and contested 'agonistic' dialogue in place of violent conflict. This action research, carried out over three years, is more fully analysed in Benington and Turbitt (2007) and in Benington (2015). It is quoted by Hartley et al. (2017) as a strong example of empirical research into public value, noted for its longitudinal and ethnographic methodology. This case study is much more complex and messy than the previous two. It involves a conscious attempt to use the concept of public value to achieve a radical change in the strategy for the policing of the annual Drumcree demonstrations in Northern Ireland between 2002 and 2004. Chief Superintendent Irwin Turbitt was first given responsibility as Silver Commander for the policing of the Drumcree demonstrations in 2002. He decided that a new strategy was needed to transform the terms of the engagement, which had been extremely violent for almost 20 years. The protagonists were a large phalanx of protestant unionist marchers and a smaller but very vociferous organisation of Catholic republican residents of the Garvachy Road area, with the police sandwiched in the middle between the two conflicting sides, trying to keep them apart but often bearing the brunt of the injuries. Turbitt invited Benington to join him in testing public value theory to reframe the problem and the strategy for policing Drumcree. He asked Benington to shadow him and the police and the army during the annual Drumcree Sunday demonstrations in July 2002, July 2003 and July 2004, and in the preparation and de-briefing for these July events with the police and army. During the Drumcree weekend Turbitt and Benington discussed the events as they unfolded during the day and late into the night, a process helped by sharing a Portakabin at the army barracks where the police were billeted for the weekend of the demonstrations. Their discussion kept moving between theory and practice, in an exploratory way using public value theory to develop and test an innovative new strategy, and action-research to try to understand unfolding events and to predict what might happen.

The events that lie at the heart of the Drumcree conflict are superficially rather simple. One group of citizens (Unionist Orangemen from Loyal Orange Lodge No. 1) have an annual march, or parade, with drums and music, from Portadown to Drumcree Parish Church, where there is a church commemorative service for First World War soldiers, after which they march back to their starting point. Their preferred return route included the Garvaghy Road where another group of citizens (largely Nationalist Republicans represented by the Garvaghy Road Residents Coalition) do not welcome them, see their marching through their area as provocative. They protest and campaign for the Orange Order to use a different route. There are at least three different interests and perspectives in play during the Drumcree parade each July: the Protestant Loyalist Unionist group, the Catholic Republican Nationalist group, and the state (including not only the police, but also the UK government, the British army and local elected councillors).

In preparing for Drumcree 2002, Turbitt had started to think about how to promote positive outcomes for the public sphere, rather than just allowing the police to become a passive referee in the contest, or a wedge keeping two battling sides apart from each other (which was costly in terms of resources and the safety of police officers). After months of discussion (with Benington, with his police commander and other colleagues, with his counterparts in the Army, and with diverse stakeholders and communities involved in the Drumcree demonstrations), Turbitt concluded that public value would be increased if responsibility was pushed back on to the two conflicting parties (Protestants Unionists and Catholic Republicans) for making sure that their democratic right to demonstrate was carried out within the framework of the law. The aim was to de-escalate the conflict by getting each side to take responsibility for ensuring that the demonstration took place within the framework of the law, rather than escalating into violence and criminal disorder. In effect, he was aiming to redefine and redraw the division within the conflict as not between loyalists and republicans but between law-keepers and law-breakers. To symbolise this shift of responsibility on to the demonstrators to keep within the law, Turbitt reduced rather than increased the size of the heavy reinforced police barriers which traditionally had been used to prevent the Orange marchers from proceeding down Garvaghy Road. He also strengthened the capacity of the police to collect video evidence (e.g. from helicopter cameras) in real time, of any criminal offences committed, so that arrests and criminal charges could be made rapidly and decisively.

This new policing strategy did not start well. Over 1,200 Orangemen and women marched from Portadown, initially in a dignified way but within a short space of time each side was hurling insults at each other. Violence escalated after the church service, at Drumcree Bridge. The new (smaller, lighter) police barrier was smashed down, and there were then several minutes of sustained assault, with a crowd of Orange supporters throwing rocks, bottles, branches and other missiles at the police, and the police responding by striking offenders with their truncheons, and firing plastic bullets. The police were dangerously exposed for about half an hour to direct violence from the crowd without any protection from crowd-control obstacles or water cannon, and were forced into more or less hand to hand combat, protected only by their riot gear and shields. Eventually heavy crowd-control equipment and water cannon were brought forward and control was regained. However, 31 police officers had been injured, some requiring hospital treatment.

Turbitt was visibly distressed by this turn of events. It appeared that the new strategy had failed painfully. The attempt to reframe the problem and to re-create a responsible public seemed not to have worked – the Orange Order had failed to contain their followers to demonstrate lawfully. The reduced size barriers had not led to less conflict but to more, and several police officers had suffered from direct assaults from demonstrators.

However, public value creation can be painful, and requires persistence, courage, stamina – and clear thinking. Heifetz's (1994) theory of adaptive leadership suggests that a degree of distress is often necessary for achieving important changes in thinking and behaviour, but that this distress must be carefully regulated.

Turbitt concluded that a disproportionate share of the distress was being experienced by the police. He therefore set about increasing the level of distress experienced by the demonstrators. He organised the rapid arrest of those offenders where there was clear video evidence of criminal behaviour. The video monitoring system had enabled the collection of "the best evidence of the worst offences by the worst offenders". Police started making arrests of marchers s they were leaving the scene, some by bus. Within a few days, 31 people had been arrested and 30 charged (from serious charges including riot to less serious such as disorderly behaviour). Common law riot is a very serious charge and requires strong evidence to secure a conviction. This time the evidence was available on video, and those charged were denied bail and spent time on remand in jail – including some well-known members and supporters of the Orange Order. This had never happened before at Drumcree, and caused considerable discontent within the Orange community.

Turbitt came under pressure from many different quarters to drop or reduce the charges. However, he judged that the law needed to be upheld, and the level of distress needed to be maintained if the adaptive changes in thinking and behaviour necessary to create the public value outcomes, were to be achieved. Later in the year, 15 people pleaded guilty to common-law riot and received suspended prison sentences of 12 to 18 months.

The following year the Orange Order volunteered to help police the Drumcree march with their own marshals wearing orange arm bands, to show that they accepted responsibility for demonstrating within the framework of the law. They wanted to redefine themselves as responsible citizens exercising their right to demonstrate as part of a contested democratic process, rather than as criminals intent on using violence to promote their interests (Benington and Turbitt, 2007).

Conclusions

This chapter including these three case studies highlight six theoretical dimensions of public value which would benefit from further research. First, how to conceptualise and research the plurality of diverse publics, and the competing interests and constructed meanings of public value, where there are multiple stakeholders. Second, how to embrace and test the recognition that creating public value is a dynamic process, often embedded in social contest and political struggle, and not simply a technocratic measurement of public management performance outcomes (as one strand of public value literature appears to assume). Third, there is the question of how, and under what conditions, democratic 'agonistic' dialogue can be used as a constructive and creative way of finding, recognising, creating and sustaining public value – and preventing a breakdown into destructive conflict and violence. Fourth, we highlight the challenges of creating 'holding environments' (Heifetz, 1994) (safe physical or psychological spaces) in which public value dialogue can explore difficult and contentious issues. Fifth, further research could extend analysis further of the ways in which public value can be created not only by the public sector, but by a wide range of stakeholders from the private and third sectors, including political leaders and civil society activists. Sixth, we note that public value tends to focus attention horizontally and outwards towards citizens and communities, not just vertically inwards and upwards towards employers and managers, because a key question concerns outcomes not just processes. These six dimensions clearly raise many tensions and questions about how to theorise, research and practice public value as a contested democratic practice.

References

Alford, J. (2008). The limits to traditional public administration, or rescuing public value from misrepresentation. *Australian Journal of Public Administration*, 67(3), 357–366

Alford, J. (2016). Co-production, interdependence and publicness: Extending public service-dominant logic. *Public Management Review*, 18(5), 673–691.

Bacon, R. and Eltis, W. (1978). *Britain's Economic Problem: Too Few Producers*. London: Macmillan.

Benington, J. (2011). From private choice to public value. In Benington, J. and Moore, M. (eds), *Public Value: Theory and Practice* (pp. 31–49). London: Palgrave Macmillan.

Benington, J. (2015). Public value as a contested democratic practice. In Bryson, J. Crosby, B. and Bloomberg, L. (eds), *Creating Public Value in Practice*. Boca Raton, FL: Taylor and Francis.

Benington, J. and Moore, M. (2011). *Public Value: Theory and Practice*. London: Palgrave Macmillan.

Benington, J. and Turbitt, I. (2007). Policing the Drumcree demonstrations in Northern Ireland: testing leadership theory in practice. *Leadership* 3(4), 371–395.

Bozeman, B. (2007). *Public values and Public Interest: Counterbalancing Economic Individualism*. Washington, DC: Georgetown University Press.

Brydon-Miller, M., Greenwood, D. and Maguire, P. (2003). Why action research? *Action Research*, 1(1), 9–28.

Bryson, J., Crosby, B. and Bloomberg, L. (2015). *Valuing Public Value*. Washington DC: Georgetown University Press.

Bryson, J., Sancino, A., Benington, J. and Sørensen, E. (2017). Towards a multi-actor theory of public value co-creation. *Public Management Review*, 19(5), 640–654.

Cooperrider, D. and Srivastva, S. (1987). Appreciative inquiry in organizational life. *Research in Organizational Change and Development*, 1, 129–169.

Cummings, T. and Worley, C. (2014). *Organization Development and Change*. Stamford CT: Cengage Learning.

Dewey, J. (1927). *The Public and its Problems*. Athens, OH: Ohio University Press.

Eden, C. and Huxham, C. (1996). Action research for management research. *British Journal of Management*, 7, 75–86.

Elden, M. and Chisholm, R. (1993). Emerging varieties of action research. *Human Relations*, 46, 121–142.

Foucault, M. (1970). *The Order of Things: An Archaeology of the Human Sciences*. London: Tavistock.

Fraser, N. (1990). Rethinking the public sphere: A contribution to the critique of actually existing democracy. *Social Text*, 25/26, 56–80.

Grange, J. (1996). The disappearance of the public good: Confucius, Dewey, Rorty. *Philosophy East and West*, 46(3), 351–366

Habermas, J. (1962, trans 1989). *The Structural Transformation of the Public Sphere*. Cambridge: Polity Press.

Hammond, S. (2013). *The Thin Book of Appreciative Inquiry*. Bend, OR: Thin Book Publishing.

Hartley, J. (2004). Case study research. In Cassell, C. and Symon, G. (eds), *Essential Guide to Qualitative Research Methods in Organizations* (pp. 321–333). London: Sage.

Hartley, J., Alford, J., Knies, E. and Scott, D. (2017). Towards an empirical research agenda for public value theory. *Public Management Review*, 19(5), 670–685.

Hartley, J. and Benington, J. (2000) Co-research: a new methodology for new times. *European Journal of Work and Organizational Psychology* 9(4), 463–476.

Heifetz, R. (1994) *Leadership without Easy Answers*. Cambridge, MA: Harvard University Press.

Israel, B., Schurman, S. and Hugentobler, M. (1992). Conducting action research: relationships between organization members and researchers. *Journal of Applied Behavioural Science*, 28, 74–101.

Le Grand, J. (2003) *Motivation, agency and Public Policy: Of Knights and Knaves, Pawns and Queens*. Oxford: Oxford University Press.

Lewin, K. (1943–44). Problems of research in social psychology. In Cartwright, D. (ed.), *Field Theory in Social Science*. London: Social Science Paperbacks.

Lewin, K. (1951). *Field Theory in Social Science*. New York: Harper and Row.

Marquand, D. (2004). *Decline of the Public*. Cambridge: Polity Press.

Meynhardt, T. (2009) Public value inside: What is public value creation? *International Journal of Public Administration*, 32, 192–219.

Miller, E. and Rice, A. (1967) *Systems of Organization*. London: Tavistock.

Moore, M.H. (1995). *Creating Public Value: Strategic Management in Government*. Cambridge, MA: Harvard University Press.

Moore, M.H. (2013). *Recognizing Public Value*. Cambridge, MA: Harvard University Press.

Mouffe, C. (2000). *Deliberative Democracy of Agonistic Pluralism*. Vienna: Institute for Advanced Studies.

Ostrom, E. (1990). *Governing the Commons: The Evolution of Institutions for Collective Action*. Cambridge: Cambridge University Press.

Parker, S., Hartley, J., Beashel, J. and Vo, Q. (2017). Leadership to create public value in complex and contested situations. *Conference paper*. Second International Public and Political Leadership Conference. April, The Open University, Milton Keynes.

Pollitt, C. and Hupe, P. (2011). Talking about government: The role of magic concepts. *Public Management Review*, 13(5), 641–658.

Prebble, M. (2016). Is 'we' singular? The nature of public value. *American Review of Public Administration*. doi: 10.1177/0275074016671427

Reason, P. and Bradbury, H. (2001). *Handbook of Action Research: Participative Inquiry and Practice*. London: Sage.

Samuelson, P. (1954). Pure theory of public expenditure. *Review of Economics and Statistics*. 36(4), 387–389.

Sennett, R. (1977). *The Fall of Public Man*. Harmondsworth: Penguin.

Sennett, R. (2017). The Public Realm, available online at www.richardsennett.com/site/senn/templates/general2.aspx?pageid=16&cc=gb (accessed 23 June 2017).

Sørensen, E. (2016). Public value. *Conference paper*, Public value symposium, Inland Norway University, Norway, December.

Stoker, G. (2006). Public value management: A new narrative for networked governance? *The American Review of Public Administration*, 36(1), 41–57.

Tajfel, H. (1982) *Social Identity and Intergroup Relations*. Cambridge: Cambridge University Press.

Vo, Q., Hartley, J., Khalil, L., Beashel, J. and Parker, S. (2017). Understanding public value through policing priorities. *Report*. Milton Keynes: Centre for Policing Research and Learning, The Open University.

11 A dynamic process theory of public value[1]

Christopher Nailer, Daniel D. Prior and Joona Keränen

Introduction

The realm of public value has broadened and deepened rapidly since the publication of Mark Moore's seminal work (Moore, 1995). According to a recent survey of the field, 'Public Value' covers not only remedies to market failures and externalities, but also the institutions and mechanisms that enable markets and societies to function; it covers not only the *outputs* of public offerings but also *outcomes*; and it is something perceived to be valuable by a collectivity of people – the citizenry – rather than simply an aggregation of individuals (Alford and O'Flynn, 2009, 175–176). More broadly, public value represents a "a reflection of collectively expressed, politically mediated preferences consumed by the citizenry – created not just through 'outcomes' but also through processes which may generate trust or fairness" (O'Flynn, 2007). In contrast to private value, public value has four distinct properties (Moore, 1995). First, it relates to the public as a whole rather than to specific individuals. Second, it depends on resources that the state procures (i.e. through taxes and the authority of the state). Third, it depends on the consensus of bodies associated with legitimizing resource use. Fourth, it is subject to multiple stakeholders, making its assessment complex and often contested. Public value is therefore broader than private value and includes, "first, what the public values; second, what adds to value in the public sphere" (Benington, 2009, 233); public value thus extends beyond market or economic considerations to ecological, political, social and cultural dimensions. And it includes the processes by which these ends are achieved.

In our view, there are two major gaps in the current discussion of public value: First, there are widely differing views of the notion of 'value' itself (Khalifa, 2004; Payne and Holt, 2001). Economists use the terms 'utility' or 'cost-benefit'. Marketing concepts such as 'customer satisfaction' have been incorporated into public value evaluations. Sociologists talk about 'values' in the sense of underlying belief-systems that inform specific value judgments. Hence the lack of a common vocabulary about 'value' reduces clarity. Secondly, despite a broad consensus that public value is "what the public values" (verb), there is an overemphasis on 'value' as a noun, on seeking to understand how this substance 'value' is created, quantified and apportioned, and there is a relative lack of focus on the processes by which the public does its valuing (verb). Recent work by Meynhardt (2009, 198; 2015) points the way towards a deeper understanding of public valuing processes, building on the theory that value is relational and active, arising "between a subject that is valuing an object and the valued object" (note: 'valuing' as verb). A later study of the systemic and dynamic character of value processes, shows how 'value' is the end-result of a dynamic and emergent process: "Through the act of valuation (i.e. evaluation) value *comes into being* as an emergent phenomenon" (Meynhardt et al., 2016, 2983). This systemic approach highlights the important interplay between the individual, the collective and the surrounding environment, making the process dynamic and adaptive to feedback. This approach places a strong focus on people as the subject, liberating the discussion of public value from specific value content: "Public value is anything people put value to with regard to the public." (Meynhardt, 2009, 205). And because the process starts with people as the subject, *the public* is 'inside'; public value is therefore "perceived, not delivered"; and public value for the individual can be destroyed if parts of the system fail to work (Meynhardt, 2015). In summary:

> Public value creation is situated in relationships between the individual and society, founded in individuals, constituted by subjective evaluations against basic needs, activated by and realised in emotional-motivational states, and produced and reproduced in experience-intense practices.
>
> (Meynhardt, 2009, 212).

The purpose of this chapter is, therefore, to address these issues as follows: First, we argue that there is a need for a clearer understanding of the dynamic processes by which the public does its valuing. While the notion of value as emergent and time-dependent is well established, the concept needs further clarification in the public sector context. We argue that a better understanding of value processes in the public sphere helps to bridge the terminological divide between economists and sociologists, between private-sector dominant reasoning and social-sector reasoning. The chapter outlines a process theory of value and applies this to 'public value' so that both the economic cost-benefit rationale and a wider consideration of 'what the public values' can be taken into account. Our specific contribution is to add to the work of Meynhardt and others by showing how public value is anticipated, value (or disvalue) is realised, and those outcomes are reappraised, setting up the next cycle of anticipated value, continuously over time.

Second, we argue that understanding public value as a dynamic process helps to clarify the separate dynamics of a) achieving consensus amongst the competing legitimate interests of society and b) the activities and resource commitments necessary to realise the value that is anticipated by that consensus. There is scope for heterogeneous stakeholders to place different emphases on the various components of public projects (Benington, 2009; Thomas et al., 2015). There is also scope for fundamental agreement on other aspects. Through a description of 'mediating consensus', this chapter outlines a mechanism that underpins the agreements amongst diverse stakeholders.

The chapter begins with an overview of the process theory of value. Next, the chapter illustrates applications of the process theory of value through three case studies. Lastly, the chapter offers a series of reflections on the process theory of value in the public context.

An overview of the process theory of value

Management theory increasingly treats 'value' not simply as the outcome of supply-driven 'value-adding' activities or buyer-supplier exchanges, but rather as an experience that involves multiple parties and has duration over time (Helkkula et al., 2012). Process theories provide new insights into phenomena that emerge and evolve dynamically over time. The creation of value involves processes that occur prior to, during and after actions, interactions and transactions (Payne et al., 2008). The notion of value as an experience involving a series of interactions has become popular within the marketing literature. The foundations of this notion lie in psychological theories of value developed initially in the Austrian School of Philosophy in the nineteenth century (Smith, 1994). The process theory of value builds on this work, as well as later work by two American philosophers, Ralph Barton Perry (1926) and Stephen Pepper (1958). This approach could hold the key to a richer understanding of value in general and of public value in particular.

The Austrian philosopher Alexius Meinong (1853–1920) conceptualised 'value' as a mental process that unfolds over time, an experience that involves: i) the value subject – the individual who has the experience, ii) a 'value emotion' or reaction which is directed at iii) a value object, and, iv) a value judgement (Schuhmann, 2001). His contemporary, Christian von Ehrenfels (1859–1932), the founder of Gestalt psychology, explained how 'value' arises through feelings and desire. In line with von Ehrenfels, Perry (1926) describes value as an expression of bias or interest, resulting from irrational, motor-affective processes: "To like or dislike an object is to create that object's value." He developed a view of value as the result of 'purposive action' towards an 'object of interest', mediated by the 'expected effects' of those actions. Purposive action is taken in pursuit of the goal (or interest) in anticipation that it will be effective. Perry's theory is neutral as to specific value content, allowing different subjects to attribute different 'value' to the same object and for the 'value' to vary in different contexts. He thus introduces the idea that an object can be invested with 'value' in anticipation, and that 'valuing' motivates action, thus allowing the initial valuing process to precede any action, interaction, exchange or transaction process.

Pepper builds further on Perry's foundations, proposing first, that 'interest' is triggered by biophysical tensions (needs), and secondly, that the core of the valuing process lies in a 'mediating judgment' – the judgment that the goal object will, in fact, produce satisfaction. The goal object continues to be invested with value only so long as the 'mediating judgment' is believed to be true. The 'mediating judgment' may, in fact, be false; the goal object, once attained, might not lead to a resolution of the tensions triggering 'interest'. The subject doing the valuing may have to adjust his or her mediating judgment through learning and experience; they may need to adjust their anticipations upwards or downwards or even redirect them to a different goal object. This provides a mechanism for judgments of value to arise in anticipation, for the anticipation to motivate action towards a goal, and for the judgment of value to vary upwards or downwards, in the light of experience, without any change in the properties of the object itself. Meinong and Ehrenfels, Perry and Pepper thus shift the emphasis from 'value' as an abstract noun – a substantive or property of objects – to 'valuing' as a verb, an action or process that takes place over time. This shift of focus, from noun to verb, from substantive to process, is also evident in the current literature on public value (Bennington, 2011; Meynhardt, 2009; 2015).

The theory of value as a process that unfolds over time, starting with an anticipation of value, and varying according to the ongoing experiences of interacting participants, fits well with the realm of public value. Moore notes the relevance of citizens' desires and aspirations as the key determinant of public value (Moore, 1995).

In Perry's theory, 'interest' can be expressed by any actor capable of purposeful action – groups as well as individuals. In process theories generally, 'actors' include individuals, groups, firms, or other organisations. So while our discussion focuses on the 'actor' – singular – it needs to be noted that a social group, a political party, or a public institution, acting with purposeful intention in accordance with a social consensus, a legal mandate or an organisational mission may also constitute an 'actor' in this model (Meynhardt et al., 2016). This process theory of value also fits well with Stoker's arguments as to why public value is superior to New Public Management in delivering social benefits: It incorporates political processes that enable collaboration at the group level; it is flexible, amenable to change, uncertainty and ambiguity, and it focusses on processes that achieve common purposes (Stoker, 2006). We therefore adopt the term 'mediating consensus' in place of Pepper's term 'mediating judgment' to indicate that the 'judgment', in the public context, depends upon a consensus of shared belief across a community that a particular course of action will work as a way of achieving communal desires and aspirations. In the case of pubic value, the formal expression of shared views through the processes of representative government is crucial for legitimising the use of public resources.

The elements and operation of the process theory of value

The process theory of value involves four main elements which interact as a system: i) anticipated value, ii) some activity (actions) involving the use of resources (which are exchanged or recombined through interactions) and iii) realized value, these four elements arranged in a cycle informed by (and, in turn, modifying), iv) mediating consensus. The mediating consensus is itself informed by a sense-making process, which includes, on the one hand, the complex and contested opinions of multiple stakeholders and, on the other, research evidence and reasoned debate directed towards the goal. The structure of this systemic process theory of value appears in Figure 11.1.

Anticipated value

'Anticipated value' is the value each actor (individual or group) hopes or expects to receive from an action or interaction they are about to undertake towards an object of interest. This concept is similar to 'expectations' found in the service quality literature (Parasuraman et al., 1985). Anticipated value involves the actor's hope or desire for the achievement of particular outcomes. Anticipated value applies to all actors who may have a stake in a particular situation. Anticipated value is specific to each actor, and thus varies amongst stakeholders. Since value is an emergent and phenomenological experience, what one actor values is usually invisible to other actors until he or she begins to act; it may then be inferred from their behaviour. 'Value' may be positive or negative ('dis-value'). Positive value is expressed in attraction or motivation towards an object of interest; negative value is expressed in aversion, or motivation away from the object. Positive anticipated value thus motivates actors to engage in actions, interactions and transactions and to commit the use of resources towards the achievement of an object of interest. Anticipated value also shapes subsequent perceptions. By developing a set of expectations about a given experience, this can serve as a basis for later judgements (the mediating consensus).

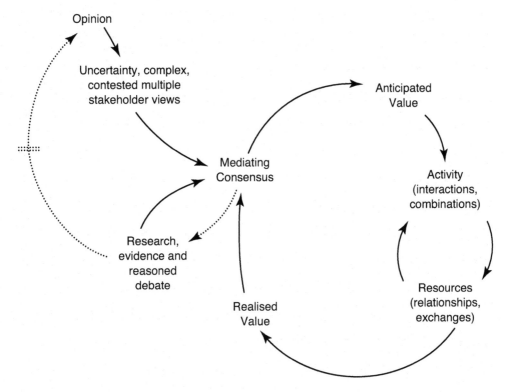

Figure 11.1 The process theory of value applied to public services and programs

Activity, interactions and resource combinations

'Activity' involves any actions, interactions or combinations undertaken by an individual or group in pursuit of the 'object of interest' – the goal of their anticipated value. In the public context, this would include citizens voting taxes, representative passing legislation, service providers designing services, recruiting staff and contractors, delivering services and monitoring outcomes. It would include clients interacting with service provides and integrating publicly funded services into their daily lives. It would also include activists of all persuasions lobbying for or against the expansion of the services in question and journalists and experts commenting on the proceedings. It includes all of the activity and resource usage generated by the provision of services for the community through the medium of public resources, as well as the processes through which those resource uses get to be decided. 'Resources' includes any resource used in the delivery of services – mainly derived from taxation revenue and authorised by the agency of the state.

Realized value

'Realized value' is the value an actor receives during and after an action, interaction or transaction. Value is 'realised' when actors integrate the outcomes of actions, interactions, transactions and resource combinations through usage within their daily lives.

An actor realizes positive value if the outcomes of actions or interactions correspond closely with, or exceed, anticipated value. Realised value can also have serendipitous properties. It may appear as 'value' at a time closely proximate to an action or inter-action. Equally, it may only emerge later, through subsequent usage or experiences, including unexpected events, circumstances or interactions. In the context of Public Value, positive or negative 'unintended consequences' resulting from the actions of public agencies would constitute unexpected positive or negative realised value. The only difference in this model is that 'realised value' is experiential and relative to the actor in question.

Mediating consensus

In his model of the valuing process, Pepper ascribes central importance to the 'mediat-ing judgment' – the judgment that the goal object or 'object of interest' will in fact bring about a resolution of the tensions we usually describe as 'wants' or 'needs'. Since interest arises in anticipation, the mediating judgment involves acts of belief. The hungry Inuit fisherman anticipates the value of fish that he cannot see under the ice. Believing he knows where they are, he judges that cutting a hole in the ice here will enable him to catch some to eat. This anticipation of value motivates him to use his energy and resources to cut the hole. If his mediating judgment is true, he realises positive value (gets fish to eat); if it is false, he realises negative value (time and energy spent for no result); he may have to adjust his mediating judgment about where the best place is to cut holes in the ice (Pepper, 1958). The mediating judgment, in the form of embedded prior beliefs, thus initiates the value activity cycle. At the end of the cycle of activity, the mediating judgment compares the realised value with the anticipated value, and modifies the prior beliefs, resulting in an adjustment in the anticipated value in subsequent cycles, perhaps even resulting in a redirection of the anticipated value to a different object of interest. The process theory of value is thus continuous over time, enabling modifications in the judgments of value by each actor in the light of learning and experience (Woodruff, 1997).

Cases in public value

To illustrate the process theory of public value, we present three case studies. Case 1 focuses on the implementation of the Collins class submarines by the Royal Australian Navy. Case 2 centres on the consultation and initiation of the Canberra light rail project. Case 3 is of Finnish heat transfer management firm, TPI Control, and its rela-tionship with publicly owned buildings and other infrastructure. To compile the case material, we rely primarily on secondary sources in the form of government reports and industry commentary.

Case 1 – Collins class submarines[2]

On 3 June 1987, the Commonwealth of Australia entered into a contract to procure and build six Collins class submarines. These diesel-powered submarines were to pro-vide a key element of Australia's naval capability for the next twenty years. Preceded by the Oberon class, the Collins class submarines were to represent the latest in technological achievement. A submarine provides clandestine naval capabilities to a navy. It gathers intelligence and supports covert activities. Submarines can also act as parts of fleets and deter surface shipping or directly engage opposing submarines in warlike situations. A functional view of public value might focus on the proficiency to which submarines can conduct these operations. However, this approach poses difficulties since it is often unclear whether a given activity is necessary or beneficial. An economic view of public value might centre on the costs and benefits of the specific submarine. Costs relate to the construction and sustainment of the submarine as well as to the personnel required to deploy the submarine. In a broader sense, the Australian people expect a submarine to perform well and to improve the defensive capability of Australia.

The first submarine, the HMAS Collins, began active service in August 1993. Within weeks, however, the HMAS Collins was recalled from active service since the vessel was, in fact, incomplete. Significant combat systems, internal pipes and fittings had not been installed. Some sections of the hull were actually sheets of timber painted black for photographs. In June 1994, HMAS Collins was finally completed. However, the added work intensity resulting from the remediation the HMAS Collins contributed to substantial delays for the remaining five submarines still under construction. Despite these additional efforts, each subsequent submarine was also plagued with problems. Many of these related to the previously unanticipated issues associated with incorporating new computer systems and local content. The series of technical issues and significant delays prompted the Minister for Defence to conduct an independent analysis in 1998. The report found that the Collins class submarines were unable to perform at the desired level for military operations. Many of the problems were attributed to poor design and manufacture, inappropriate design requirements deficiencies in the contract structure, and ineffective working arrangements between a range of contractors. Since the report, significant effort was invested in addressing the problems with the Collins class submarine program albeit at an additional $1 billion cost to the Australian taxpayer.

In terms of the process theory of value, the Collins class submarine program provides some interesting insights. The initial recognition of the need to replace the preceding Oberon class submarines emerged in 1978 on the basis of a report from the Royal Australian Navy. This report highlighted a need for more than six submarines and that the submarines be constructed in Australia. After a series of additional consultations, requests for tenders began in 1983. In this five year period, significant scope existed for personnel to change, for technological capabilities to change, and, for political conditions to change. This suggests that the mediating judgement process was not straightforward, with each change in decision-maker producing a new set of previous experiences and bases for judgement that then influenced how they perceived the requirement for a submarine capability. The intention to build in Australia also raised serious questions as to whether the capability existing to do so in a time and cost effective manner. After the request for tenders, a series of funded studies were conducted to assess the merits of the major bids. This process introduces an additional set of mediating judgements into an already complicated decision-making process. Once the construction process had commenced, the construction-related problems prompted additional government reviews and, ultimately, significant remediation activities.

The Collins class submarine implementation is regarded as one of Australia's poorest examples of government procurement. The process theory of value highlights the importance of mediating judgements. The diversity of stakeholders and the relative sophistication of the requirement suggest considerable confusion as to the procurement and construction process. This ultimately led to low public value by not providing a functional submarine capability in a timely or cost-effective fashion.

Case 2 – Canberra light rail

With a population of about 380,000, the city of Canberra covers some 814 square kilometres, laid out broadly according to a plan devised in 1913 – which included a proposed tramway system that was never built. In 2004, a feasibility study estimated the cost of 54 km of light rail linking the city's major centres at A$890 million, as compared to A$668 million for dedicated busways.[3] However, in 2008, the local Labor government only won power through an alliance with the Greens Party, which pushed strongly for the light rail project to go ahead. By then, the estimated cost had risen to A$2.02 billion. Anticipated value was mainly composed of transport efficiency and environmental savings.[4]

Urban planners and designers argued strongly for Canberra's light rail project based on other kinds of anticipated value. They noted the urgency of addressing the deteriorating urban amenity if the city's high dependence on private cars continued and stressed how light rail represented a once-in-a-generation opportunity to lock in the city's, livable, human character, and create a showcase for a sustainable capital city, 90% powered by renewable energy by 2020.[5]

Community groups had lobbied effectively for improved public transport for many years. Surveys conducted by the ACT Government indicated 55% of Canberra residents supported the light rail project, while 34% were opposed and 11% undecided; a later survey indicated almost 57% of Canberra residents would be more likely to consider public transport if there was an accessible light rail system[6]. However, in early 2014, the opposition began sensing a shift in public opinion and commissioned its own study of the economic and financial case for the project. Leaked government polling that year indicated the light rail project might be a "potential vote-changer", with 40% of voters then saying they would be less likely to vote for a pro-light rail candidate, as against only 32% 'more likely'.[7] However, in February 2016, the ACT Government went ahead, awarding a contract to design and construct, operate and maintain the first 12 km phase of the light rail project in a public-private partnership agreement[8]. Construction was scheduled to commence "in the coming months", with completion scheduled for 2019, with the project consortium having a 20-year contract to operate the project. With local elections due in October 2016, ACT Liberals began promising that they would scrap the light rail project if they were returned to government.[9] As the parties' campaigns unfolded through the year, the light rail project rapidly became the dominant issue. By September 2016, project work was clearly visible at street level. The October election was close; Labor won 39% of the vote, the Liberals 36% and the Greens 11%, giving the Government and its Greens partners a modest electoral endorsement of the light rail project.

The Canberra light rail case illustrates how anticipated value depends on a mediating consensus that varies by stakeholder group and over time. While those individuals able to access the 12km of track anticipate value in the form of improved amenity, other taxpayers without direct access share in the costs but perceive no benefit. And while there are plans to extend the light rail system to cover other arterial roads in Canberra, this is a long-term proposition, and many taxpayers are reluctant to wait. Hence, the Canberra light rail project continues to be subject to divided opinions and the community consensus is likely to show further swings as it unfolds.

Case 3 – TPI Control and heat transfer management[10]

TPI Control is an innovative, small-sized technology firm in Finland focused on a specific industrial niche: heat transfer management. Heat transfer systems are especially important in large, complex, and often densely populated buildings, such as hospitals, schools, shopping centers, and manufacturing plants, where thermal conditions (i.e. heating and cooling) have a major influence on the building's life-cycle, energy consumption, environmental impact, and the safety, comfort, and well-being of occupants. Given that a majority of these buildings are owned by public actors, such as municipalities, cities, and governments, and financed by public funds (via taxes), there is a general expectation (the 'mediating consensus') that such buildings would serve the public and society as well as possible.

While the anticipated value of optimal heat transfer systems in complex buildings has the potential to benefit a broad network of (mostly) public stakeholders – including owners, operators, users, environment, and society more broadly – realization often relies on the property management. The property management is usually a commercial actor, who maintains the building on behalf of the public owner(s), and is driven by economic goals. As such, it tends to favor heat transfer systems that fulfill minimum technical requirements with a low purchasing price and short-term cost savings, and, neglecting the anticipated value that would accrue to public actors more broadly over time. This is a key issue for TPI Control as well, whose competitive advantage is based on improving customers' energy-efficiency, cost savings, eco-friendliness, and usability in the long-term, but with a higher initial price.

To combat this issue, TPI Control has made significant investments into chemical expertise, environmental technology, and remote automation to be able to understand, measure, and monitor broader public value realization beyond operating costs. These include, among the other things, improved indoor air quality and operating conditions, as well as decreased district heating consumption and environmental footprint, which tend to benefit community stakeholders. Armed with this evidence, TPI Control then communicates it to different stakeholders, trying to strengthen the mediating consensus regarding the social, environmental and economic outcomes their systems generate. This often takes a concentrated process; TPI Control feels that systemically quantified evidence may slowly alter stakeholder perceptions.

In terms of process theory of value, the TPI Control case highlights how an individual business actor's focus on short-term economic value may leave a large portion of other forms of anticipated value (particularly environmental and social value) unrealized for other stakeholders. On the other hand, it also illustrates how individual actors can use documented value evidence to influence mediating judgments through a deliberate process based on tangible evidence.

Applications of the process theory of public value

Table 11.1 summarizes the elements of the process theory of public value in terms of the three case studies. While each case is different, common themes are observable. In terms of mediating consensus, it is clear that a committee-based approach to public decision-making is commonplace. From our observations, an inclusive approach towards stakeholders and effective communications help to build a stronger mediating consensus towards a particular project. Given this, it is clear that the anticipated value of diverse stakeholders is a key influence on the process. These earlier phases in the cycle determine the legitimacy (or otherwise) of the associated

Table 11.1 How the cases illustrate the process theory

Observations	Collins Class Submarine	Canberra Light Rail	TPI Control
Mediating consensus	Stakeholders: • Government departments; • Defence industry • Australian public Consensus: • Committee-based decisions • Political trends	Stakeholders: • Government departments; • Light rail industry • Local community Consensus: • Committee-based decisions • Political trends	Stakeholders: • Building owners • Tenants • Government regulators • Maintenance/ construction companies Consensus: • Committee-based decisions: government, body corporate, company
Anticipated value	Expectations: • Defence of Australia • Economic efficiency • Technical supremacy • Timeliness	Expectations: • More efficient public transport • Environmental friendliness • Economic efficiency	Expectations: • Economic efficiency/ profitability (owners) • Comfortable living (tenants) • Social inclusion (community)
Activity/ resource	Significant investments in • Insufficient initial development • Remediation • Project variations • Developing 'custom' solutions	Significant investments in • Planning and consultation • Design • Public debate	Significant investments in • Chemical expertise, • Environmental technology, and • Remote automation
Realized value	Generally perceived as negative Submarines now functional Significant learning by defence procurement agencies	Perceived as positive by residents in close proximity; some negatives during implementation due to significant public works Land sales along the route Still unfolding	Demonstrating the potential for benefits to flow from private actors to other stakeholders Broad-ranging views of public value attributable to different stakeholders

activities and resource uses. The culmination of this process is the value realized by stakeholders.

Reflections on the process theory of value in the public sector

There are two central problems in most questions about public value:

1. How do we determine whether particular activities and resource uses are effective as means of realising socially valued outcomes?
2. How do we obtain a consensus amongst the competing legitimate interests of society, that this is so?

In the process theory shown in Figure 11.1, the mediating consensus is informed by research, evidence and reasoned debate, which aims to address the first problem, and by public opinion, which is complex, ephemeral, based on rarely questioned prior values and beliefs, and usually contested. Research also helps to appraise each cycle of activity by comparing realised value with anticipated value and outlining any implications for the mediating consensus in the next cycle. Gradually, over time, the evidence of research and reasoned debate makes its way into the public domain as an influence on public opinion, but usually only after a substantial period. Public opinion and reasoned debate thus operate on different timescales, which helps to explain why it is so difficult to achieve a durable mediating consensus on the means and ends of public activities.

Another difficulty with building and maintaining the mediating consensus is because some of the things the public values can only be realised after many cycles of activity and yet they require sustained commitments of resources over long timescales. For example, the restoration of damaged natural environments, the design and development new defence equipment, or the redevelopment of slum areas into public housing all require long-term mindsets. Such initiatives often generate short-term disvalue to particular stakeholder groups within a community. One of the biggest debates in public policy circles revolves around the noise created by the high impact and extreme speed of the public opinion-cycle, amplified by means of social media, as matched against the timeframes necessary for the achievement of real public value. By incorporating 'opinion' and 'research evidence' as separate influences on the mediating consensus, the dynamic process theory reflects the tensions that play out between these competing sources of authority.

Conclusion

This chapter offers a unique interpretation of public value as a process that unfolds dynamically over time. Many assessments of public value rely on cost/ benefit assessments or other evaluation methods that collapse all decision variables to a single present moment and do not incorporate notions of perceived value or reflect how this unfolds dynamically over time. Our dynamic process model demonstrates how value arises in anticipation based on prior beliefs which come to be embodied in a mediating consensus. We suggest that the community's perceived value of public activities and resource uses varies over time, in accordance with the unfolding evidence of factual research together with ephemeral and contested opinions; further, our model shows that the community's cyclical reappraisal of what it observes while a public project is unfolding may fracture the mediating consensus, resulting in a shift from anticipating value to anticipating disvalue, resulting in a consequential loss of community endorsement of the project. By formally separating the workings of the value activities and resource uses from the mediating consensus, we show how many of the arguments in public value revolve around the strength (or otherwise) of the consensus, rather than being arguments about whether specific activities and resource uses are, or are not, likely to realise value for the public. The model highlights the importance for those who act in the public interest, of investing time and effort in building and reinforcing the opinions and perceptions side of the mediating consensus in addition to presenting their project justifications in terms of formal quantitative evidence. Our dynamic process model works at the individual, group and community levels, with some individual cycles of value anticipation/activity/realisation/reappraisal operating on very short cycles and other more complex community cycles operating over cycles of multiple years. The interweaving of individual and group value cycles creates added complexity in real cases. By being agnostic as to specific public value content, the process model provides a common language bridging the economic and the socio-political perspectives. In doing so, the workings of the mediating consensus shows how the same set of activities or outcomes may contribute to a combination of positive and negative outcomes simultaneously, across different stakeholder groups or at different times. The case studies provide examples of how this framework applies. Overall, this chapter advances debate as to the nature of public value creation and realization, clarifying the process by which the public does its valuing.

Notes

1 Parts of this chapter are based on the first author's PhD thesis entitled 'Business models evolving to realise value – A process perspective,' submitted to the Australian National University in 2014.
2 The second author wishes to thank Mehdi Rajabu Asadabadi for compiling much of the material for this case.
3 Hughes, D. 2014. "ACT Government chooses 'wrong mode, wrong alignment' for Gungahlin tram." *Canberra Times*, 14 October 2014.
4 ACT Government (2008) *ACT Light Rail Proposal to Infrastructure Australia*, pp. 57–63.
5 "Light rail brings a bold new vision for our city." *Canberra Times*, 24 March 2014.
6 "Canberra Light rail to Deliver $1bn in Community Benefits, Business Case Shows." *Canberra Times*, 1 November 2014.
7 "Barr brushes off leaked union light rail polling." *Canberra Times*, 3 September 2015.
8 "China-linked John Holland wins PPP deal." *Australian Financial Review*, 2 February 2016
9 "Liberal threat to scrap light rail." *Australian Financial Review*, 17 April 2015.
10 The materials for this case were compiled within the BICS (Boosting the Internationalization of Cleantech SMEs) project funded by the Finnish Funding Agency for Technology and Innovation.

References

Alford, John and Janine O'Flynn. 2009. "Making Sense of Public Value: Concepts, Critiques and Emergent Meanings." *International Journal of Public Administration*, 32(3–4): 171–191.

Benington, John. 2009. "Creating the Public in Order to Create Public Value?" *International Journal of Public Administration*, 32(3–4): 232–249.

Benington, John. 2011. "From Private Choice to Public Value." In J. Benington and M. Moore (eds), *Public Value: Theory and Practice* (pp. 31–49). New York: Palgrave Macmillan.

Helkkula, A., C. Kelleher and M. Pihlstrom. 2012. "Characterizing Value as an Experience: Implications for Service Researchers and Managers." *Journal of Service Research* 15(1): 59–75.

Khalifa, Azaddin Salem. 2004. "Customer Value: A Review of Recent Literature and an Integrative Configuration." *Management Decision* 42(5): 645–666.

Meynhardt, Timo. 2009. "Public Value Inside: What is Public Value Creation?" *International Journal of Public Administration*, 32(3–4): 191–219.

Meynhardt, Timo. 2015. "Public Value: Turning a Conceptual Framework into a Scorecard." In J. Bryson, B. Crosby and L. Bloomberg (eds), *Public Value and Public Administration* (pp. 147–169). Washington DC: Georgetown University Press.

Meynhardt, Timo, Jennifer Chandler and Pepe Strathoff. 2016. "Systemic Principles of value co-creation: Synergetics of value and service ecosystems." *Journal of Business Research*, 69: 2981–2989.

Moore, M.H. 1995. *Creating Public Value: Strategic Management in Government*. Cambridge, MA: Harvard University Press.

O'Flynn, Janine. 2007. "From New Public Management to Public Value: Paradigmatic Change and Managerial Implications." *Australian Journal of Public Administration* 66(3): 353–366.

Parasuraman, A., V.A. Zeithaml, and L.L. Berry. 1985. "A Conceptual Model of Service Quality and Its Implications for Future Research." *Journal of Marketing* 49(4): 41–50.

Payne, Adrian and Sue Holt. 2001. "Diagnosing Customer Value: Integrating the Value Process and Relationship Marketing." *British Journal of Management* 12(2): 159–182.

Payne, Adrian, Kaj Storbacka and Pennie Frow. 2008. "Managing the Co-Creation of Value." *Journal of the Academy of Marketing Science* 36(1): 83–96.

Pepper, Stephen Coburn. 1958. *The Sources of Value*. Berkeley, CA: University of California Press.

Perry, Ralph Barton. 1926. *General Theory of Value*. Cambridge, MA: Harvard University Press.

Schuhmann, K. 2001. "Value Theory in Ehrenfels and Meinong." In L. Albertazzi, D. Jacquette and R. Poli (eds), *The School of Alexius Meinong* (pp. 541–569). Aldershot: Ashgate Publishing.

Smith, Barry. 1994. *Austrian Philosophy. The Legacy of Franz Brentano*. Chicago, IL: Open Court.

Stoker, Gerry. 2006. "Public Value Management: A New Narrative for Networked Governance?" *American Review of Public Administration* 36(41): 41–57.

Thomas, John, Theodore Poister and Min Su. 2015. "In the Eye of the Beholder: Learning from Stakeholder Assessments of Public Value." In J. Bryson, B. Crosby and L. Bloomberg (eds), *Public Value and Public Administration* (pp. 170–186). Washington DC: Georgetown University Press.

Woodruff, Robert. 1997. "Customer Value: The next Source for Competitive Advantage." *Journal of the Academy of Marketing Science* 25(2): 139–153.

12 Purpose, passion and perseverance

Creating public value through public sector leadership

Jo Hicks and Zoe Sweet

Introduction

Academi Wales (2017) is the National Centre for Leadership and Management excellence for public services in Wales. Established in September 2012 via the programme for government. Academi Wales seeks to build a future for Wales where leadership of our public services is driving improvement in the lives of people living in Wales. It does this through engagement with over nine hundred public, third and voluntary sector organisations and offers development opportunities in the fields of organisational development, leadership and management development. Individuals may engage with Academi Wales' activities over short, medium or longitudinal periods of time focusing on both professional and personal development.

The contribution is written from a practitioner perspective with links to the academic and research findings on the subject of public value. It seeks to offer both practitioners and academics an insight into the nature of public service leaders and how individuals view public value, contribute to it and access to development support to improve their performance and impact.

Every day public service leaders are tasked with delivering in an environment of increasing public demand, facing diminishing resources and with frequent political intervention. The prevalent environment appears to be one of increased public scrutiny and greater digital mobility, where information is more readily available and 'consumer' expectations are heightened.

Professor Mark H. Moore in his seminal work *Creating Public Value* (1995) recognises the challenge ahead of public leaders where they seek to deliver in the face of public problems, still prevalent in 2015, Moore explains:

> All the real work remains to be done in the thousands of particular circumstances in which public leaders confront public problems and seek to solve them
> (Moore, 2015, 30)

Public service leaders, as individuals he suggests may inhabit both the role of deliverers and recipients, citizen and client, and the duality of this may indeed prove both a tension and a driver to meaningful public value creation.

If we recognise that the individual is at the heart of the delivery chain, existing at the mid-point of a continuum that permeates across actual and perceived structures, we can recognise and support a relationship between them.

Figure 12.1 Suggested delivery chain continuum

Can we enable and influence, through leadership development activity, the individuals' creation and contribution of public value through personal, team and organisational performance potentially reducing the competing commitment as described previously. Moore (2015) in fact suggests that to do this we need to

> diagnose the position of the particular managers in particular situations and help guide them forward to more effective democratic governance and value creating performance.
>
> (Moore, 2015, 30)

Academi Wales is the Welsh Government centre for leadership excellence and has a unique position in its ability to both develop and influence the skills, knowledge and behaviours of those working and leading in the public sector in Wales.

As an organisation it recognises for itself and for the organisations it serves, "if an organization cannot answer why and how its activities contribute to society as a whole, its very licence to operate is at risk" (Meynhardt et al., 2014, 81). Academi Wales must also respond to and influence the cultural context of the public service landscape and through its direct support to public service leaders, provide them with support to ensure they can maximise their own, their teams and their organisations contribution to public value creation.

In recent history, Wales, has seen the introduction of 'The Wellbeing of Future Generations Act 2015' (Welsh Government, 2016) and 'The Social Services and Wellbeing' (Wales) Act 2014 (Welsh Government, 2014), legislation that looks to drive a societal wide agenda for Wales. In Academi Wales, we have researched and worked on the Government-led initiative, *One Welsh Public Service*, which provides congruence for those working across the public service agendas. Public Value, it's meaning across organisational boundaries and the ability for individuals, teams and organisations to use it to deliver for future generations in Wales is important, even if it is in its simplest terms the "framework that can broaden and deepen efforts by strategic individuals and teams" (Moore, 2015, 30).

The case study

Through the form of a narrative case study this chapter focuses on the experiences of six public service leaders. The six participants each hold leadership positions across the spectrum of public services in Wales and were not selected through typical criteria of age, gender, role etc., or indeed hierarchy or organisational position, but on the basis of their involvement in a variety of leadership learning experiences. Three leaders have undergone short-term development interventions and three leaders have received longitudinal development and support. The purpose of this is to gain some insight to the phenomenon of public value creation relative to public service leaders and to examine whether and how they access support to ensure their effectiveness. As identified by Murray (1955) the use of case studies is,

> the only possible way to obtain the granite blocks of data on which to build a science of human nature.
>
> (Murray, 1955, 15)

It is through the exploration of the experience of these public services leaders that we will determine their meaning of public value, how they understand it, influence it and are enabled to deliver it personally or organisationally. It will also provide insight into the leadership development they seek out that enables and shapes the focus of their decisions, interactions and performance across the structures they impact and are impacted by. As highlighted by Clandinin and Connelly (2000, 20) "narrative inquiry is an umbrella term that captures personal and human dimensions of experience over time and takes account of the relationship between individual experience and cultural context" it allows for researchers to understand the experience of its subjects or participants.

In this instance, the case study presented will provide that insight on the relationships between the individuals' experiences and the cultural context with a suggestion for how leadership development has and can impact Public Value in public service leadership.

The participants

All six case study participants are drawn from across the public service in Wales and it can be argued, all deliver what each considers a leadership role within and for their respective organisations. The group are widely representative of sectors considered to deliver public service, and by definition as being able to access leadership development from Academi Wales, they specifically represent, National Government, the National Health Service, a Charity, a Third Sector organisation and the Housing sector in and working for Wales.

All six participants it can also be argued represent the variances in traditional hierarchies of leadership roles, for example they represent the experiences of a first level line manager through to a Chief Executive and a Board member, yet were not selected to purely represent this. All six participants are or have been on leadership development journeys and evidence has been gathered from the participants through a number of methods.

The method

All six case study subjects were asked to complete a questionnaire in order to better understand their personal narrative around their public service role, their view of public value, their development enablers and their expectations as both deliver and recipient. Each participant questionnaire is used in conjunction with other known development material related to the case study participant and Academi Wales. All six case study participants have been participants in the Academi Wales Public Service Summer School and it is this common experience, in an immersive experiential learning environment that provides a reference for the contextual experiences of the participants related to their development.

Case study – creating public value through public sector leadership

1. *Why did you choose a public service career?*

For several of the participants it is clear that there are two key considerations related to this question. The first is that many of them choose, definitively, a career in public service and secondly that this was informed either by a specific experience that prompts that choosing or by knowing what is or isn't important to them individually.

Participant 1 identifies a lifelong passion for issues of social injustice, inequality and discrimination and subsequently a public service role that does "enable me to connect my values and passions with opportunities to facilitate real change in people lives". It is an early experience in a particular circumstance and sector that pre-empts a 20-year career commitment that the participant believes at the core enables "people to live a better life".

Participant 2 talks about applying their skills to public benefit and the fact that they are "not commercially inclined which helped tip the balance towards a public service role", so in essence knowing where they do not want to focus and understand their own preference and implying that they are not driven by a need to be commercially successful.

Participant 3 expresses a similar to Participant 1 having chosen a public service career "because equality and inclusion are very important to me" even though not implicit, suggesting again that a lived experience is informing choice.

Participant 4 was particularly clear in their response to this question "to impact on people's lives, for the better, with a focus on their experience" and again like Participant 2 is able to identify this choice as more important to them than the need to deliver shareholder return.

Experience also influences Participant 6, who had engaged in undergraduate study in health and social care and also mentions a work placement that formed their choice to work in public service where they felt they could work in "supportive cultures . . . concentrating on communities".

It is only Participant 5 that in particular feels and states that they "fell into public service by chance" with this occurring after (like Participants 2 and 4) becoming conscious of a path they didn't want to pursue. However on joining public service and staying "I feel a strong sense of purpose. . . . I enjoy being able to work in partnership . . . to develop and work on policies which aim to improve the lives of the people in Wales".

All six participants identify through the medium of their varied experiences, degrees of understanding self and what matters to them that a role in delivering a public service might fit with their personal values and passions.

2. *What is your definition of public value?*

The participants were not provided with any research or literature to support their knowledge of public value prior to engaging in the questionnaire. All of the case study participants are able to provide what they consider a definition of public value, for some it is stated as personal view, for others an adopted organisational perspective, for several it is clear that it does not exist without the citizen and a few consider in even more detail the link to their own identity.

Participant 1 defines public value as "delivering value, as defined by the public, to the public" and goes on to add that it is the contribution of this value from core services "like health, education and housing that provide the solid foundations for society", they comment that once this value is added citizens are then "enabled to live enriched lives by kinship, connection, art and culture". Implying that providing value goes beyond the fundamentals of what society should morally offer to include what it can.

Participant 2 whilst able to come to a definitive view – "My definition of public value is: What is the patient receiving as a service that (would make it) could be personalised to their context?" – explains that they have given this idea considerable thought because they believe it can be quite different in the public sector (when compared with the private sector). Participant 2 considers that "the distance between the source of pay and the employee is huge. Although the trust/health board pays the wage it is eventually derived from the contributions we make to our national insurance" making a connection between our individual and organisational contribution to supporting value.

The focus for Participant 3 is to define public value from an organisational standpoint "in the simplest terms the actual value of an organisation to the public; the value it contributes to society", suggesting that it only has value if it contributes. Participant 3 explains that value also drives an organisations ability to be efficient and effective i.e. to deliver value for its public.

Participant 4 shares a focus with Participant 1 and expands on both the suggestions and the challenges for organisations and determines public value to be "a focus on what worth/difference/impact etc. we (organisations) have through their service, action, intervention with the general public". They go on to state that "we should view public value through the eyes of the people in our communities in terms of value to them". "If what we do delivers little or no benefit to them we need to think again". Congruent with ideas from Participant 2, Participant 4 summarises by asking "how have we improved their lives".

Participant 5 shares an organisational construct view with Participant 3 providing a definition of public value determined from a strategic organisational perspective "how do we do what we do in the best way possible, which makes sense to ourselves as an organisation, to those we work with and people we serve". "We the public servants work for the common good of the population of Wales" is how Participant 6 defines public value and goes on to state "placing citizens at the forefront of all key decisions we are making, letting the citizen have a role in the social transaction between the state and themselves".

What is apparent across each of the study participants is the intention to provide for the public; however the commonality of viewpoint from which this emerges stretches between organisational intention and personal commitment. There are associations across the question where some study participants are able to articulate the complexity of connections between organisational, personal, community and the citizen.

3. How do you embed value at the heart of delivery – in your role, your team and your organisation?

In this area the responses from the participants varies widely. Participant 1 and 6 both look to apply or work within a methodology, set of guidelines or framework of support that determines measuring and delivering expectations for their public/customer. Participant 3 and 5 focus on organisational principles and their individual role in team encouragement. Participant 4 also appears to look from an organisational perspective yet includes their approach that considers organisational drive along with challenges and issues.

Participant 1 focuses distinctly on the method used organisationally and an explanation of that at team and management level, "a manager's job is to measure the capacity of the system to deliver value and unlock the barriers preventing staff from doing a great job". Participant 1 goes onto to say that identifying the barriers is the work of the director team and this senior team is also responsible for "creating an employment environment that is open to experiments, uses data to measure performance and facilitates a culture this is congruent with organisational values". Whilst participant 1 identifies this team as their team they do not uniquely identify their personal role and responses. Participant 1 also shares the method used to understand public demand within the organisation as "systems thinking – what's important to the people we serve and how well we are delivering to that". Participant 1 states that "we understand most of the things that go wrong for customers are due to the way systems of work are organised and so focusing on designing good systems is paramount". Participant 1 comments that this "focus on systems, instead of people, results in a truly blame free culture and creates an environment open to experimentation and learning from mistakes".

Participant 2 provides a number of personal and professional examples where they believe they as an individual add public value at the heart of delivery. These examples encompass learning activity "constantly learn/teach/train in my interactions with patients and team members", effective use of resources and time "I have redeployed my time to support the team . . . helped me to understand the demands and complexity of the supporting staff roles and helped improve the pathways for patient care" demonstrating personal commitment and a focus on the patient "I make up for cancelled session by using my administrative/learning time to catch up", "I personally address patients in my assessments and letters in order to reduce the feeling that my patients are being referred to in the third person" and by direct community based contact – "I run clinics twice a week in one of the most deprived areas of Wrexham . . . this was motivated by the realisation that a lot of my patients didn't drive, couldn't afford to drive and the public transport was very infrequent." Participant 2 is very clear about the link between public value, personal commitment and delivering for society.

Participant 2 mentioned that since attending the Academi Wales Summer School 2016 is "spending more time with my clinical team . . . role modelling and encouraging learning as members of a multidisciplinary team". Participant 2 suggests the idea that "when resources are being cut it makes sense to pool our resources, this should include joint learning, resources could be physical, psychological or thought for better ways of working." Participant 2 recognises that they "have not yet become involved in any service delivery activity in my organisation" but does not provide any reason for not yet engaging at this level.

Participant 3 offers initially what can be considered a view based around organisational principles and identifies that "our principal is to constantly ask ourselves how our work improves the lived experiences of our customers, how well do we deliver on the guiding principal and how the extreme importance of keeping the overriding mission in mind when seeking to deliver projects". Participant 3 finds it more challenging to express their own contribution but does suggest that their personal approach is to "consider every day, how useful or valuable has this action been" and to encourage their team to "consider value in terms of their work, to take ownership of their work and empower them to evaluate their decisions and output". Participant 3 does not provide specific examples, or the structured methodology suggested by participant 1 but point outs that "we may not always get things right but if our aim is constantly to improve and be the best we can then we can learn from everything that we do".

Participant 4 appears clear and systematic in both their leadership process and personal expectation – that

> you put the patient and the public at the centre of every conversation you have; you ensure that employees and volunteers are very clear about why our organisation exists and who we are here to serve; you demonstrate and role model what you expect to see in everything you do: you recognise those who have public value at the centre of their approach and you celebrate it publicly; you take action and provide support to ensure every team member can practice this way , you measure approach as much as technical skills, you change team members who can't or won't, operate with public value at the heart of what they do and you ensure that member of the team, regardless of role, witness the service we provide and interact with member of public.

It is useful to note that Participant 4 touches on approaches, the importance of reward and celebration and also the challenge of those who are not driven from a public value perspective.

Participant 5 identifies that for them is it about the "relentless pursuit of making life better – to understand what is going on – to seek out and create opportunities for seeing through the eyes of others, understanding the challenges and barriers and exporting how to improve". Participant 5 identified that part of their role as leader is to "encourage my team to do the same and support them in doing so". Participant 5 does not provide any further examples to evidence this.

Participant 6 comments that "it is about keeping decisions ground in every day society and keep at the forefront would I want this to affect my family and the people I care about." Participant 6 identifies that those in non-executive leadership roles "must always be mindful of Nolan's seven principals of public life". Participant 6 references here the 'Nolan Principles' first published in 1995 which are the basis of ethical standards expected for public office holders.

4. How does your expectation of public value differ as a deliver and recipient?

Even though this question asks how expectations differ and therefore might be considered a leading question for some study participants, there is recognition of both sameness and difference across the study participant group as deliverers and recipients. Much of it focuses on expectations with at least two of the participants focusing on specific experiences.

Participant 1 identifies that they "have very high expectations of public value both within delivery as well as being a recipient . . . however as a recipient of many public services I have had mixed experiences". Participant 1 recognises "that when you are 'on the inside' your perspective is more subjective". The participant does not go on to explain this any further. Participant 1 does identify that 'the hardest part is engaging with staff who clearly want to deliver great value but obviously feel powerless in the system they work in, unnecessary bureaucracy, over specialisation and inter-department fragmentation creates an experience of public service that falls short and must be exceptionally frustrating", however Participant 1 does not provide the framing for this, i.e. their experience with this as a deliverer or recipient.

Participant 2 shares their feelings of responsibility and accountability:

> I feel that I have to uphold and have a consistent way of applying standards of expectation of myself at work and as a citizen. I understand the pressure that services (be it the police, councils, health and social care) are under and try to connect with the "human" delivering the service and try to disregard minor inconveniences that may occur in the process of receiving public services.

Participant 2 goes on to share two very specific experiences where they have strongly resisted using their workplace identity to circumvent or speed up receipt of public services in challenging situations and that this was part of their accountability to be consistent where they exist as both deliverer and recipient.

Participant 3 articulates their position as "not a deliverer of public services but in a position to try to better inform and shape services to meet the needs of different communities". And therefore purely frames their experience through observing that "my experience of working with the public sector is of individuals committed to doing their best to achieve this, prepared to listen, learn and develop despite sometimes challenging circumstances". Participant 3 believes that "empowered individuals can transform the organisation that they work for and create sustainable, positive change" and goes on to explain that "as a recipient of public services, I am always conscious . . . that behind the service lies a host of people and process that are well-intentioned and which seek to be informed, developed and adapted." Participant 3 seems the clearest in the demarcation that even though they might work with or be a partner of public service organisations, as well as a recipient, that they do not identify their organisation as a public service deliverer. There is potential here for greater questioning around that demarcation and the individuals experience of that and the challenges presented for collaborative delivery with public service bodies. It might be interesting study to understand the 'story' of the organisation this Participant identifies with.

In some contrast to Participant 3, Participant 4 offers an absolute, that in relation to the experience "it – shouldn't differ at all – as a recipient you should expect to receive a service, advice, support etc. that improves your situation and life experience and life changes which should chime with a deliverer perspective". Participant 6 also comments that "as a recipient you should also contribute yourself by using public services wisely and contributing to the development of solutions/interventions alongside service providers and experts. You should play your part to ensure maximum public value can be generated from public organisations". This explanation might resonate with that of Participant 2 where they describe their personal responsibility.

Participant 5 articulates their thinking succinctly and states in answer "I am not sure it does, I have high expectations". However there is no further expansion or analysis.

Participant 6 comments that being a receiver of public service "can make you a harsher critic of public value when you know how the machinery of government is implemented". Again this viewpoint might present opportunity for further investigation of the experience of the individual which is not shared.

What is apparent in the narrative responses for this question is the difference between those who describe their experiences (in either role as a public value recipient or deliverers or both) through difference, potential aspiration of sameness, or perhaps a viewpoint that puts a sense of personal accountability at the centre of the expectations regardless of each role.

5. What development enables you to add public value though your role? (Please refer to both formal and informal development)

The answers to this question are as you might expect linked in some ways to the public value definition as given by each study participant and therefore cover a range of suggestions and needs. However some participants are able to be holistic in their requirements and relate specific growth in knowledge, skills or behaviour in their leadership development to specific development interactions and interventions. Three of the study participants specifically mention their growth through leadership development with Academi Wales.

Participant 1 identifies that they believe

> the sure fire way to add public value is through listening to what matters to the public we serve. In a leadership role that means role modelling this behaviour as well as ensuring that the method for continuous improvement has the customer views at the heart of any redesign. Good leadership is all about asking better questions and facilitating learning and growth in others.

Participant 1 notes that as an individual

> development opportunities are everywhere; in an informal conversation, in an online blog, at a conference presentation, inside fifteen minutes of meditation as well as a formal training session. It is important to be open to learning and the critical ingredient for that is humility – which is not necessarily a common quality, many of us get promoted into leadership roles because of our accumulation of knowledge and experience and it can be easy to get sucked in to being the person who provides all the answers.

Participant 2 reflects

> Having attended summer school I have become very conscious of the fact that, over the years, my learning activity through conferences and meetings has been

very technically focused. Summer School helped me to experience and develop in the interpersonal and social aspects of learning and change. This has helped me to feel more confident in my interactions at work and outside work in my personal/social life. . . . From these experiences I feel capable to translate/transfer my learning across various area of my work/life contexts. I strongly feel that professional training for doctors CPD (Continuous Professional Development) would greatly benefit from the approach taken by Academi Wales of incorporating social learning and interaction to influence change.

Participant 3 notes, in congruence with comments by Participant 1 that

the most important thing I try to remember is that we are all always learning. . . . Every experience is a development opportunity, positive and negative. More formally I look to engage with professional development programmes as relevant and (try!) to keep up to date with current thinking and development within the field of personal and professional development.

Again participant 3 focuses on a guiding principle or an ethos rather than specific mechanisms or a preferred route to their personal of learning and support.

Participant 4's perspective focuses on a range of development activity

networking with leaders across public and private organisations to broaden perspectives; spending time with the public you serve and the front-line staff and volunteers who serve the public every day; leadership development to keep up to date with latest thinking and practise to inform; mentorship and coaching to enable you to be the best that you can be, to stay true to yourself and your values, and to maintain resilience despite pressures and challenges working at a senior level in public service and with a public profile that you often have no control over.

Participant 5 articulates their development as "always keen to learn from others, be it people I work with, in other organisations, or from listening to members of the public". Participant 5 describes having

taken as many development opportunities as possible. I feel it is important to have a good Understanding of oneself, including strengths and your weaknesses. . . . I like to put myself in other situations: I have spent two months working in Uganda and I volunteer . . . this brings home how difficult it can be to navigate public services and make a difference on the ground.

Participant 6 identifies that

my personal and professional development makes me a more authentic and grounded leader. . . . I stay connected in my public life though helping at community based projects because I personally believe it give me a better understanding of public value.

In conclusion

Moore (1995) outlines that public value exists as part of a strategic triangle for consideration by public managers and leaders and that in determining the work these must be considered. Legitimacy and support, operational capabilities and public value represent these strategic dimensions and Moore (1995) suggests that all must be aligned to enable the creation of public value.

Through the evidence provided by each of the case participants these strategic dimensions exist albeit at varying levels of intensity for each participant. All participants whether through their reasons for joining public services or taking up public service careers believe that there is a legitimacy not only to their role but also to the service they provide. Where the legitimacy element it intensified and potentially broader than Moore's (1995) assertion is when the public role is aligned to personal values and purpose.

Although the theme of organisational support was not addressed as part of this study the offer of development support was addressed through the questioning and each participant recognised the value of support in the acquisition of knowledge, skills and behaviours that enable them to be the best that they can be. Common to the participant's responses is also the recognition of the personal responsibility for putting learning and development into action. As identified by Moore at the start of this chapter the challenge for public service leaders is the thousands of particular circumstances that occur for them to deal with, the responsibility to apply any development and know-how rests with the individual, regardless of possible organisational methods for management of this, such as appraisals and learning pathways. However, this relies on a level of self-awareness from the individuals in accessing development support and stretch that impacts on the successful creation of public value.

Each of the participants responds differently to Moore's dimension of operational capabilities, two respondents see this as orchestrating through strategic direction, two participants through operating and organisational principles and one participant recognises this surfaces when facing challenges and issues. These varying responses maybe in part due to the varying experiences and exposure of the participants and related to their different roles and assumptions about hierarchy. A commonality exists however as each participant recognises that embedding the value in operational capabilities is rooted through people and their behaviour.

As per Moore's recommendation that all must be aligned to enable the creation of public value, there is no evidence through the cases that the individuals purposefully align the three strategic dimensions. However, there is a recognition throughout the responses that three aspects are recognised mediums for the creation of public value.

> Identifying public value is not an easy proposition . . . there will always be compromise and invariably an individual's demand will be subordinate to those of society in general.
>
> (Elias, 2016, 5)

In order to deliver a public value for society, it has to be commonly understood, judged both for fairness and efficiency and effectiveness whilst also being underpinned by legitimacy and support, linked to organisational capacity and the value chain of the organisation. Some of our case study participants touch on the structure of their delivery, from organisations with activities, processes and procedures, that provide outputs, sometimes delivered with partners or co-producers, these in turn deliver the customer or client satisfaction that delivers the outcomes and that this in itself provides public value in society.

Academi Wales therefore can influence to a greater or lesser degree how those it engages with create public value in society and as such seeks to understand how it can enable others positively in this endeavour.

The participants encapsulate the range of development needs that exist in the public service in Wales. Whilst the maturity of each participant on their development journey may be different, key learning can be linked to experiences both personal and community based in nature. The opportunity to move beyond technical/professional competence and develop expertise and confidence beyond one's own role can only enable a capability to deliver in and for society, to deliver for something greater than their own personal attainment or gain. Two of the study participants talk specifically about the importance of experience of delivering in a different community, different to that which they usually work. The breadth that this experience provides gives confidence to the individual that they can indeed make a greater contribution outside their own organisational structure. Yet,

> Not every tiny organisation is a "society maker", but at the same time, many firms, public administrations and non-governmental organisations not only provide good and services, but also shape our experiences of what it means to live within a certain society.
>
> (Meynhardt et al., 2014, 82)

Each organisation that provides service to the public, so therefore all organisations, have the ability to shape the experiences of those that it serves, Academi Wales must do the same within the realms of its leadership development. It must provide blended experiential learning, where individuals are immersed in a community that is constantly learning to lead. What this very short analysis suggests is that more can be done to understand how value creating performance is enabled. The work of Timo Meynhardt (2014) and his four key questions for delivering public value might provide further insight for Academi Wales, even though much of his work to date focuses on the role of private sector organisations and their relationship with delivering public value.

In this short analysis some of the narrative alludes to considerations related to navigating the big questions for public sector work and the significant contribution it makes in society now. If indeed organisations like Academi Wales can impact on and develop the leadership of public sector organisations, it must consider how the development it delivers facilitates how individuals connect their personal purpose with the need to add public value.

Regardless of leadership position or role, the experience of being recipients of services fundamentally impacts on our expectations as leaders and deliverers. As Moore (2015) suggests and is evidenced here, the individual is at the heart of the delivery chain; therefore the focus in creating public value through leadership development must start with the experience of the individual.

References

Academi Wales (2017). Available online at www.gov.wales/academiwales (accessed 22 May 2017).

Clandinin, D.J. and Connelly, F.M (2000). *Narrative Inquiry: Experience and Story in Qualitative Research*. San Francisco, CA: Jossey-Bass.

Elias, S. (2016). *Value Confusion: The Problem of Lean in Public Services*. Lean Competency Service Ltd.

Meynhardt, T. Gomez, P., Strathoff, P. and Hermann, C. (2014). Public Value: rethinking value creation, dialogue. Available online at www.alexandria.unisg.ch/237589/1/20150107155547.pdf (accessed on 19 May 2017).

Moore, H.M. (1995). *Creating Public Value – Strategic Management in Government*. Cambridge, MA: Harvard University Press.

Moore, H.M. (2015). Public Value: A Quick Overview of a Complex Idea. Public Value Lecture, University of Cardiff.

Murray, H. (1995). Introduction. In A. Burton and R. Harris (eds), *Clinical Studies in Personality*, Vol.1. New York: Harper and Row.

Welsh Government (2014). Social Services and Wellbeing (Wales) Act 2014. Available online at http://gov.wales/topics/health/socialcare/act/act-nhs/?lang=en (accessed 22 May 2017).

Welsh Government (2016). Well-being of Future Generations (Wales) Act 2015. Available online at http://gov.wales/topics/people-and-communities/people/future-generations-act/?lang=en (accessed 22 May 2017).

13 Towards public value local government

Size, engagement and stakeholder efficacy

Tom Entwistle, Rhys Andrews and
Valeria Guarneros-Meza

Introduction

Public organizations across the world are increasingly urged to refocus their strategies on the pursuit of public value (Moore, 1995; Brewer, 2013). But understanding what 'the public most value' and 'what adds value to the public', as Benington (2009, 233) puts it, requires first and foremost, engagement with the citizens and stakeholders who benefit from and pay for public services. This chapter revisits the old question of what size of local government is most conducive to the development of engaged and empowered citizens, but we ask this question in the new context provided by public value management.

The old answer to the question was clear: small scale government (in terms of population size) is good for citizen participation. The 'small is beautiful school' (Kelleher and Lowery, 2004) argues that residents served by smaller local governments will feel more engaged by local issues and more empowered by local politicians. But the case for small government presumes that citizens participate though traditional political institutions where decisions are made by politicians and influenced by political processes – like voting and campaigning (Niemi et al., 1991; Morrell, 2003) – that are hierarchical and episodic.

Emerging forms of public value management cause us to question the conventional size-participation formula. First because the issues are different. In place of a very political choice between parties or people, public value requires that deliberation on both very big questions about 'the role of government in society' (Benington and Moore, 2011, 9; Moore, 2014) but also smaller aspirational aspects of service planning, provision and performance which are of little political salience. Second, public value governments need to engage citizens as stakeholders – taxpayers, consumers, clients and co-producers – rather than as card carrying party members (Moore, 2013). Stakeholder engagement, both beyond and between elections, is ongoing and increasingly network-like in character (Moore, 2014, 466). Participation is no longer *just* realised through the traditional institutions of representative democracy but rather less heroically, through hearings, consultations and debates increasingly orchestrated through various forms of electronic and social media.

We argue that changes in the form and focus of stakeholder participation heralded by the new public value management suggest that larger governments may have an engagement advantage over their smaller neighbours. While lacking the close ties of small communities, larger governments have a greater capacity to communicate policy and performance issues to citizens, but also to provide them with better opportunities to engage with the decision-making process through a panoply of sophisticated techniques and technologies (Dunleavy et al., 2006; Welch, 2012).

Our argument is developed over four sections. First, we review the traditional analysis which suggests that small scale government is good for citizen engagement. Second, we point to changes in both the form and focus of engagement which might give larger units of government an advantage. Finally, following a short description of our methods, we test our theory by analysing whether jurisdiction size and form of engagement influences citizen readiness to participate in Welsh local government. The statistical results suggest that size is negatively associated with citizen perceptions of their efficacy as stakeholders in local decisions, but larger local governments can overcome the burden of bigness through the use of citizen panels. Theoretical and practical implications are discussed.

Small is beautiful?

Small scale government has long been seen as central to the cultivation of engaged and empowered citizens. Political efficacy – as political scientists describe it – captures the feeling amongst citizens that they have something to say; they have an opportunity to say it; and that they can make a difference (Dahl and Tufte, 1973; John, 2010; Soul and Dollery, 2000; Newton, 1982). Since Aristotle argued that the civic friendship upon which the common good depended could not be achieved in cities with more than 100,000 citizens, theorists of participatory democracy have continually asserted that small is beautiful for efficacious engagement with politics and policy-making (see Newton, 1982; Sharpe, 1970).

Traditionally theorists distinguish between two dimensions of political efficacy. Internal efficacy asks whether individual citizens feel they have the capacity, or competence, to engage with the sorts of issues considered in public debates. Neimi, Craig and Mattei (1991: 1407) define internal political efficacy as the belief in 'one's own competence to understand and participate effectively in politics'. Researchers treat internal political efficacy rather as a type of human capital – 'a stable psychological resource' as Valentino, Gregorowicz and Groenendyk (2009) put it – that is developed over time and equips those who possess it with the resources to participate in political decision making. Researchers further assume that individual citizens can accurately perceive and report on the component parts of their own efficacy.

External political efficacy recognises that participation reflects not only a citizen's sense of their own political competence but also an assessment of the likely responsiveness of the political environment. Do citizens believe that the political system will listen to and act on their engagement (Craig et al., 1990, 291)? This question can, in turn, be further sub-divided. Because debates are rarely swayed by individual action, the notion of collective political efficacy – 'an emergent group level attribute' (Caprara et al., 2009, 1004; Anderson, 2010) – gauges perceptions of group level capacity to campaign for particular goals. Regime based efficacy captures the perceived responsiveness of political institutions, while incumbent based efficacy refers to the perceived responsiveness of the particular incumbents of those institutions (Craig et al., 1990).

The argument that small-scale government fosters political efficacy stands on four legs. The first is focussed on the relationship between citizens and a geographical place. 'The small-is-beautiful school', as it is dubbed by Kelleher and Lowery (2004), 'suggests that citizens are locally orientated' (Kelleher and Lowery, 2009, 66).

Dahl (1967, 954) argues that the spatial dimensions of a polis need to be 'human, not colossal, the dimensions not of an empire but of a town'. Small scale promises a knowledge of, and connection with, a specific place so that citizens, as Dahl puts it, can know the 'town ... [and] its countryside about' (1967, 954). Hidalgo and Hernandez (2001, 274) describe this as 'place attachment', defining it as 'an affective bond or link between people and specific places'. Advocates of small-scale governance argue that citizens feel more efficacious in relation to the governance of the very local places to which they have an attachment simply by virtue of the greater stake they have in the future of those places. They further suggest that citizens will be more interested by, and knowledgeable of, the 'smaller issues' which are determined at this level of governance (Kelleher and Lowery, 2009, 66; Oliver, 2000; Fischel, 2001).

Closely related to the attachment to a particular place and its issues, is the social attachment to the people associated with that place. Altman and Low (1992, 7) explain that 'places are repositories and contexts within which interpersonal, community and cultural relationships occur'. A small scale of governance promises improved knowledge of and empathy for fellow citizens. 'At its best', as Dahl (1967, 954) puts it, 'citizenship would be close to friendship, close even to a kind of extended family, where human relations are intense rather than bland'. In more theoretical terms, small numbers reduce heterogeneity and the associated 'costs of collective action and cooperation' (Rodriguez-Pose et al., 2009, 2043) by making it easier to communicate, develop shared values, and foster the sense of reciprocity, which underpins political efficacy (Niemi et al., 1991).

Third, small scale governments offer a closer connection between citizens and their decision makers. 'The essential point', again according to Dahl (1967, 957), 'is that nothing can overcome the dismal fact that as the number of citizens increases the proportion who can participate directly in discussions with their top leaders must necessarily grow smaller and smaller'. Importantly, in emphasising access to 'top leaders', Dahl discounts the democratic benefits of increased elected representation; irrespective of the ratio of citizens to representatives, the relational distance between 'top leaders' and citizens increases with population size. Hence, the smaller the scale, the better, according to Lowndes and Sullivan (2008), will be the accessibility, responsiveness and accountability of governments. Kelleher and Lowery (2009, 64) explain that the problem is a collective action one in which: 'Any act of participation by a citizen is less likely to influence outcomes on local public goods as the number of citizens within a city grows'.

Fourth and finally, in the interests of both public service efficiency and equity, small governments will be better able to offer bespoke policies and services to the local population. Assuming there is considerable variance in individual and community preferences, the larger the scale, the greater the divergence between the nature of citizens' demands and the supply of standard or one-size-fits-all government services (Weisbrod, 1997; Wallis and Dollery, 2006). The smaller the population served by any one government, the closer the match between any one service and the preferences of its users/ recipients/ beneficiaries. As Rodriguez-Pose (2009, 2043) explains, smaller governments can provide a more fine-grained 'tailoring of policies to local preferences'. Where services are more closely matched to the preferences of citizens, so the argument goes, they might well be more satisfied with their government's performance and more inclined to feel that they are able to influence decisions (Kelleher and Lowery, 2009).

While it is true, as Kelleher and Lowery (2009) explain, that these arguments can be turned on their head – citizens might feel attachment to larger areas and bigger issues; larger and more diverse populations might provide more opportunities for collective action; larger areas might attract better and more communicative leaders; and scale economies might allow for a better and broader range of services – empirical evidence is largely consistent with the theoretical claims of the small is beautiful school. Within the European context, Denters (2002) finds that trust in elected officials and satisfaction with services is higher in small local governments in Denmark, the Netherlands, Norway and the UK. Mouritzen (1989) reports that citizen satisfaction and political participation is higher in small Danish municipalities, and Rose (2002) uncovers a negative relationship between municipality size and non-electoral political participation in Denmark, the Netherlands and Norway. In Australia, Drew and Dollery (2014), find a negative relationship between council size and citizen satisfaction with advocacy and engagement opportunities. While recognising that national elections prompt more interest than local elections, Morlan (1984) finds that the smaller the local government, the higher the participation rate. Although Kelleher and Lowery (2009) furnish evidence of a positive relationship between size and voter registration and civic organization membership in the United States, a recent quasi-experimental study by Lassen and Serritzlew (2011) indicates that citizens in large Danish municipalities experience a considerable loss of political efficacy.

Public value, engagement and efficacy

While persuasive in its own terms, the small is beautiful case stands on the increasingly dated presumption that citizens participate *only* though traditional political institutions where decisions are made by politicians and influenced by political processes – like voting and campaigning (Niemi et al., 1991; Morrell, 2003) – that are hierarchical and episodic. Public value theorists provide a more citizen centric account of the public sphere. Benington (2009, 234) calls for 'a shift away from producer-led to consumer-led models of government and public service'. Stoker (2006, 47) talks of 'consent beyond the ballot box', in which 'it is necessary to have all stakeholders involved'; Bozeman (2002, 150) calls 'for a framework to promote deliberation about public value'; while Yang (2016, 884) suggests that governments 'pay particular attention to enhancing capacity in involving and empowering disadvantaged citizens'.

But stakeholder engagement is not just desirable for legitimacy reasons. Stoker – and others writing in a similar vein (Whitaker, 1980; Pestoff, 2006; Bovaird, 2007; Needham, 2008; Yang 2016) – see stakeholders as critical to the co-production of public value outcomes. Changes in driving habits or waste recycling require, according to Stoker (2006: 48), 'intensive dialogue and high levels of trust between the public and authorities'. 'Coproduction', as Whitaker (1980, 241) explains, 'is essential in services which seek to change the client'. New developments in the technology of engagement are key to the attempt to reframe the relationship between citizen-stakeholders and the state. As far back as 1979, Margolis argued that traditional approaches to direct and representative democracy were fundamentally ill-suited to the challenge of governing the complex mass societies of the contemporary world, and that alternative approaches to citizen participation may be required. Picking up the baton, Stoker (2006, 48) talks of the way in which ICTs can offer 'opportunities to get people's participation in ways that are flexible, attractive to them, and not too time consuming'.

Driven, as Fung (2006, 67) puts it, by a sense 'that the authorized set of decision makers – typically elected representatives or administrative officials – is somehow deficient', the last few decades have seen a huge growth in the range of engagement techniques which promise participation beyond traditional forms of direct or representative democracy (Michels, 2011). In their survey of public participation in local government, Lowndes, Pratchett and Stoker (2001) describe a range of new participatory techniques – embracing surveys, juries, web sites and focus groups – being developed and applied by UK local governments. Blomgren Bingham, Nabatchi and O'Leary (2005, 552–554) similarly describe a range of 'new governance processes' – including deliberative democracy, e-democracy, public conversations, participatory budgeting, citizen juries, study circles – as used across different levels of government. Sandfort and Quick (2015) report on a series of cases in which deliberative approaches to engagement were used to develop capacity and create public value. Engagement can, as they put it (Sandfort and Quick 2015,: 520) 'influence both how citizens understand substantive issues and how they understand their agency in developing or acting on solutions'.

Citizen panels are one of the most widely adopted of these new forms of engagement. Panels typically take the form of a representative sample (usually of 1000 citizens) of the local population which is maintained to respond to a series of survey and consultation activities over a period of time (Van Ryzin, 2008; Stewart, 1996). During the 1990s and 2000s representative panels of this sort were adopted widely across UK local government (Martin, 2009). Although the evidence on the effectiveness of citizen panels and other tools for promoting public participation is sketchy and largely anecdotal (Carpini et al., 2004), it does suggest that practitioners find the technique valuable for eliciting greater citizen engagement with decision-making (Andrews et al., 2008). In particular, feedback from the participants in citizen panels indicates that they gain a sense of empowerment from being involved in local decision-making. Indeed, Brown (2006, 205) goes so far as to suggest that institutions of this sort may 'hold more promise for realizing radical democratic ideals than the direct democratic procedures idealized by many democratic theorists.'

Changes in the technology of engagement suggest that the relationship between size and efficacy may also be changing. In place of the political efficacy required by campaigning and voting, new forms of engagement require citizens to develop a sense of their efficacy as stakeholders. The internal and external dimensions of political efficacy have been developed to understand traditional – very often state wide – forms of political participation like voting and campaigning (Niemi et al., 1991; Morrell, 2003). There are, however, two reasons to think that the type of efficacy needed to engage citizens as stakeholders in local managerial matters may be somewhat different to the state-wide political variant.

First, public value management extends the scope of citizen engagement to embrace administrative aspects of service planning, provision and performance. Participation in these matters presumes a knowledge of, and interest in, what might be regarded as mundane or technical aspects of public service management. Participation in these administrative matters is not normally realised through the explicitly political acts of voting and campaigning but, rather less heroically, through participating in meetings and consultations of one form or another. Crucially, citizens contribute resources to these processes as stakeholders – users, funders, co-producers – rather than as voters. Without the parties, profile or passion of national issues, 'behavior in local compared to national politics', as Morlan (1984, 459) explains, 'is quite different'.

Second, unlike political participation – which is regarded as available to all – the opportunity to participate in the administrative decision-making process is not uniformly provided to all communities. Without the statutory framework which makes voting in one place very similar to voting in another, different local governments will attach different degrees of priority to citizen engagement at the same time as they adopt different techniques or methods for its realisation. Differences in the participation opportunities offered to stakeholders are compounded by the heady pace of developments in communication technologies. This will inevitably mean that opportunities to participate – and the sense of empowerment which needs to accompany them – will vary significantly across local government boundaries.

Although all governments – whether large or small – can experiment with new forms of engagement, these developments are particularly germane to big governments. Partly because new forms of engagement and stakeholder efficacy heralded by public value management may give them opportunity to redress the participation deficit. By introducing new participatory structures that reach out to citizens, larger governments may lessen the relational distance between citizens and key decision makers (Dahl, 1967) and overcome the social dislocation effects associated with community size (Coffe and Geys, 2006). Citizen panels may therefore represent a civic investment particularly appropriate to larger governments in that they might bring government closer to citizens in a way that can make them feel more informed about, and empowered to influence, decision-making. Furthermore, the new structures for public participation require considerable resources both for their administration in the narrow sense of the word, but also for the locally differentiated services and extended time lines that they are likely to demand (Irvin and Stansbury, 2004). Larger governments may then have both a greater need but also a greater capacity to fund engagement initiatives. Bearing this out, Yang and Callaghan (2005) find that large US municipalities are more committed to citizen involvement efforts than their smaller counterparts. It seems reasonable to hypothesise, therefore, that large governments will have both a greater will and a greater capacity to resource and deliver the kinds of stakeholder engagement envisaged by public value management.

Data and methods

We test three hypotheses drawn from the preceding sections. First – consistent with the orthodox small is beautiful school – we suggest that attempts to engage citizens in managerial matters will be damaged by local government size:

> Hypothesis 1: Local government size will be negatively related to stakeholder efficacy.

Second – to test the engagement benefits of new technology – we propose that the adoption of a citizen panel will lead to improvements in citizens' sense of their stakeholder efficacy:

Hypothesis 2: The use of a citizen panel is positively related to stakeholder efficacy.

And finally, we ask whether the adoption of a panel will compensate or moderate for the negative effects of local government size on stakeholder efficacy:

Hypothesis 3: The use of a citizen panel will moderate the negative relationship between local government size and stakeholder efficacy.

The context for the research is local government in Wales, one of the four constituent nations of the United Kingdom. With 22 local governments with populations ranging from the tiny Merthyr Tydfil (56,000) to the capital City of Cardiff (305,000), Wales provides a particularly suitable setting for testing the size efficacy relationship. Furthermore, while not using the public value tag, the Welsh Government (WG) has promoted a distinctive public service improvement agenda focused on the provision of 'citizen-centred' public services (Martin and Webb, 2009).

Dependent variables

As we have argued, the sense of efficacy underwriting participation in the administrative processes of local governments needs to be assessed rather differently to traditional approaches. In place of the measures of political efficacy, we use measures of stakeholder efficacy focused on gauging whether citizens have the interest, knowledge and confidence to contribute to managerial decisions. We use measures of stakeholder efficacy drawn from the Living in Wales Survey conducted in all local government areas across Wales during 2006. These data were collected by IPSOS-MORI and GfK NOP using a standard questionnaire template independently verified by the WG's Statistical Directorate. The survey data were weighted by age, gender, ethnicity and household size to provide as representative a sample as possible. The survey asks residents about their quality of life, including their attitudes towards participation in the service delivery decisions made by the local government. Two of these survey items are of particular relevance to our study. The first asks respondents to indicate on a four-point scale (ranging from 'nothing at all' – coded 1 to 'a great deal' – coded 4) the amount they 'know about participating in making decisions about the running of your local authority services'. We use answers to this question as a measure of *internal stakeholder efficacy*. A second survey item asks respondents to assess on a five-point scale (from 'strongly disagree' – coded 1 to 'strongly agree' – coded 5) the extent to which they would agree about their actually having 'an opportunity to participate in making decisions about the running of my local authority services'. We use answers to this question as a measure of *external stakeholder efficacy*. The mean level of *internal stakeholder efficacy* for our sample is 1.7, while the mean level *external stakeholder efficacy* is 2.5.

Independent variables

Local government size

To assess scale effects on stakeholder efficacy we measure the size of the population served by a local government using population figures for each Welsh local government area in the 2001 UK national census. This provides a clear and transparent proxy for the size of the political community in question.

Citizen panels

To investigate whether efforts to promote participatory initiatives within the area served by each local government influence the size-efficacy relationship, we use a measure of whether or not a local government was operating a citizen panel in 2006. We constructed our measure of panels through a search of local government cabinet minutes available on each of the council websites in 2012. An initiative as important and costly as a citizen panel is extraordinarily unlikely to be authorised and operated without reports to cabinet. It is therefore reasonable to conclude that where there is no mention in the minutes, there was no active panel. Although a panel, of itself, provides an opportunity to participate, we take the decision to establish and maintain a panel as indicative of the priority and resource attached to citizen engagement within a particular government. Local governments with panels are likely to have made other efforts to extend participation opportunities to their citizens (Andrews et al., 2008).

Individual level control variables

Our regression models also include individual level controls shown to influence political efficacy in previous studies (e.g. Lassen and Serritzlew, 2011). The age, ethnic origin, gender, working status, social class, and levels of neighbourhood trust of respondents to the Living in Wales survey are all measured using dichotomous variables except age, which is measured using the self-reported figure.

Local government level control variables

Political culture

We draw upon two measures to control for the influence of political culture on stakeholder efficacy. First, electoral turnout in the Welsh local government elections during May 2004 – the most recent elections prior to the distribution of the 'Living in Wales' survey of 2006. Second, electoral marginality gauged as the percentage point difference between the vote share of the political party attaining the largest number of votes and that of the party gaining the second largest number of votes in the previous local election.

Community organizational life

In each local government area, we measured the number of community, social and personal services organizations (such as voluntary associations, film societies or sports clubs) per 1000 capita registering for value added (or goods and services) tax in 2005.

Socio-economic disadvantage

The relative socio-economic disadvantage of citizens was measured using the average ward score on the indices of deprivation in 2004. This is the population-weighted measure used by WG to gauge levels of deprivation amongst the population. It is constructed from seven different dimensions of deprivation (income, employment, health, education, housing, crime, living environment).

Demographic diversity

The multiplication of social identities in socially heterogeneous areas may affect levels of stakeholder efficacy. To measure demographic diversity, the proportions of the ethnic and social class sub-groups identified in the 2001 UK national census (such as ages 0–4, Black African and Lower Managerial and Professional Occupations) for each local government area were squared, summed and subtracted from 10,000, with high scores reflecting high diversity. These scores are equivalent to the Hehrfindahl indices used by economists to measure relative market fragmentation.

Population density

Population density figures for 2001 are also included in the statistical models. Descriptive statistics for all the independent variables included in the statistical modelling are shown for the full sample and for those local governments with and without a citizen panel in Table 13.1.

Findings

Three regression models are presented in Table 13.2. To illustrate the effects of local government size and the use of a citizen panel on internal (ISE) and external

Table 13.1 Descriptive statistics for independent variables

	Full sample (22 local governments)		With citizen panel (10 local governments)		Without citizen panel (12 local governments)	
	Mean	*s.d.*	*Mean*	*s.d.*	*Mean*	*s.d.*
Knowledge about participating	1.71	.79	1.67	.77	1.74	.81
Opportunity to participate	2.53	1.21	2.51	1.20	2.54	1.22
Age	52.96	17.35	52.93	17.63	52.98	17.14
Gender	.42	.493	.42	.49	.42	.49
Work status	.48	.499	.48	.50	.47	.50
Social class	.48	.500	.49	.50	.46	.50
Ethnic origin	.99	.119	.98	.15	.99	.09
Trust neighbourhood	.75	.432	.75	.43	.76	.43
Community organizations per 1,000 capita	1.66	.63	1.63	.58	1.68	.67
Deprivation	23.09	8.28	20.61	4.90	25.05	9.75
Social class diversity	8705.88	65.87	8722.09	46.83	8693.17	75.21
Electoral marginality	85.33	12.91	86.28	15.34	84.60	10.57
Voter turnout	44.05	5.10	43.25	5.21	44.69	4.93
Population	130617.87	58350.66	160607.9	59373.39	107089.9	45295.69

Table 13.2 Local government size, use of citizen panel and stakeholder efficacy

	Full sample		With citizen panel		Without citizen panel	
	ISE	ESE	ISE	ESE	ISE	ESE
Population	-4.72**	-7.14**	-.60	-1.55	-4.03**	-3.61**
Citizen panel	.031	5.67**				
Individual level variables						
Age	1.22	-2.28*	.81	-2.84**	.69	-.99
Male	5.37**	1.41	3.78**	1.00	3.87**	1.11
Employed	4.14**	2.20*	2.81**	.51	2.86**	2.32*
Higher social class	9.90**	4.18**	6.33**	3.02**	7.60**	3.20**
White	1.13	-0.02	1.55	.55	-.15	-.75
Neighbour–hood trust	3.01**	3.57**	1.24	1.84+	2.95**	3.36**
Institutional level variables						
Community organizations per 1000 capita	1.42	3.30**	-.02	.15	-.38	2.25*
Deprivation	1.88+	4.77**	1.75+	7.63**	2.79**	3.98**
Social class diversity	3.39**	6.87**	-1.52	.74	4.62**	5.91**
Ethnic diversity	-2.42*	-3.05**	1.75+	2.34*	-.65	-3.34**
Electoral marginality	1.80+	2.65**	-.07	.83	.77	.93
Voter turnout	0.91	1.48	-.50	.79	2.72**	2.18**
Population density	0.44	2.20**	-.88	-.50	1.76+	.40
R squared	.038**	.026**	.038**	.041**	.045**	.049**
N	6227	5601	2727		3500	

Note: ISE = internal stakeholder efficacy; ESE = external stakeholder efficacy. t-scores shown in table: +p<0.10, *p<0.05, **p<0.01

stakeholder efficacy (ESE), the first model incorporates all of the control variables, plus population. Next, the citizen panel variable is added to the models. To analyse the role that citizen panels might play in moderating the size-efficacy relationship, the third model presents estimates of stakeholder efficacy for those Welsh local governments with a citizen panel in 2006. In the final model, estimates for local governments without a citizen panel are presented.

All of the models explain a statistically significant proportion in the variation in respondents' attitudes towards public participation. Four individual level control variables are significant at explaining knowledge of participation (ISE): gender, work status, social class and levels of trust in the neighbourhood. However, for perceived opportunity to participate (ESE), age is an important predictor whereas gender, which played a role in determining ISE, is not. Four local government level control variables explain variations in both ISE and ESE. In particular, (and somewhat unexpectedly) deprivation and social class diversity are positively associated with knowledge of participation opportunities, as, more predictably, is electoral marginality. The negative sign for the statistically significant ethnic diversity coefficient suggests that the more ethnically diverse an area is, the lower the knowledge about participation. In addition, community organizational life, voter turnout and population density are all positively associated with the perceived opportunity to participate.

The findings for the key explanatory variables used to test our hypotheses are displayed at the top of Table 13.2. In the first model, population is negative and statistically significant for both dimensions of stakeholder efficacy. This finding provides strong support for the first 'small is beautiful' hypothesis that the smaller the population size the higher is stakeholder efficacy. When it is added to the models, the dichotomous variable that captures whether or not a local government was operating a citizen panel during the study period exhibits the anticipated positive sign for both ISE and ESE. However, it is only a statistically significant determinant of the perceived opportunity to participate, adding further explanatory power to the model – the R squared increases by almost 1%. Our second hypothesis therefore receives only partial confirmation.

To test our third hypothesis regarding the moderating effects of a citizen panel on the size–efficacy relationship we split the sample of respondents between those living in an area in which the local government operates a citizen panel and those residing in an area in which there is no such panel. The sign for the population size variable in the second model is negative as before, however, it is no longer statistically significant, which implies that large local governments may at least be able to mitigate the disengagement associated with bigness by introducing a citizen panel. Further corroboration of this finding is furnished by the results for the sample of respondents in areas without a citizen panel. Here, the coefficient for population size remains negative and statistically significant. Thus, we can conclude that for internal and external stakeholder efficacy our third hypothesis receives confirmation, giving us some confidence in the theoretical arguments that we have developed. That said, although the findings suggest that large local governments operating panels can potentially mitigate the disempowering effects of size, they may not be able to turn their bigness into an advantage: the sign for population size in the second model is still negative, even if it is no longer statistically significant.

In sum, our first hypothesis on the benefits of smallness for stakeholder efficacy is supported using measures of both internal and external efficacy. Our second hypothesis on the benefits of citizen panels for stakeholder efficacy receives mixed support, being confirmed for the measure of external efficacy but remaining unconfirmed for internal efficacy. Finally, our third hypothesis on the moderating effects of citizen panels on the size-efficacy relationship is supported for measures of both internal and external efficacy. This finding offers important new evidence on the actions that large local governments can take to address the participatory problems posed by their sheer size.

Conclusions

Although exploratory and provisional, this paper has added a new public value dimension to our understanding of the relationship between local government size and citizen efficacy. Unlike the traditional analysis of political efficacy, a public value perspective recognises that increasingly governments engage their stakeholders in different ways and on different issues to conventional political approaches. Analysed in this way we find that governments with large populations *may* have a greater capacity to offer wider and more diverse opportunities for engagement with public service decisions. Indeed, our results show that the use of citizen panels can make a difference to the way citizens perceive their opportunity to participate in the decision-making of large local governments. These findings have important theoretical and practical implications.

Our analysis expands on existing empirical work by establishing a connection between size, citizen panels and citizens' awareness of, and opportunity to, participate in local public service delivery decisions. To date, quantitative research has largely neglected these important and timely dimensions of efficacy, preferring to focus on issues of trust, satisfaction and political activism rather than attitudes towards direct involvement in public policy-making. At the same time, we identify a specific strategy that large units of government can adopt in order to overcome the gap in perceived efficacy caused by scale effects. Citizen panels may have many purposes for local governments, but everything else being equal, our findings highlight the vital role they can play in empowering citizens in large local communities. A finding of particular importance to those that put the citizen at the centre of defining and delivering public value (Yang, 2016).

The analysis does though have a number of limitations. Although the study has affirmed the plausibility of our theoretical arguments on the determinants of efficacy, longitudinal and comparative studies are required to reveal the precise dynamics of public value management in small and large local governments, especially in cases where changes in the size of those governments are observed. Future research in local government systems outside the UK could reveal whether our findings are generalisable to countries with very different institutions and political cultures to those found in Wales. It would also be valuable if subsequent work sought to develop multi-items scale for measuring stakeholder efficacy akin to those deployed for the analysis of political efficacy (see Lassen and Serritzlew, 2011).

Detailed qualitative (and quantitative) investigation in those big councils successfully reaping the benefits of citizen panels for public participation is required to fully explore the ways in which such activity can be best directed to mitigate the negative impact of size. This qualitative approach could be supplemented with the collection of administrative data from local governments and primary survey data to develop rich, context-sensitive profiles of the perceived legitimacy of efforts to promote public participation, especially if the views of all key stakeholders (e.g. local government officers, elected members, central government officials and local citizens) were incorporated. At the same time, in-depth case studies could also be utilised both in this setting and others to examine the effects of size on stakeholder efficacy in more fine-grained detail: How do local governments use panels to engage citizens, and in turn, how do citizens use their new sense of efficacy to engage with the policy and administrative processes of local governments? More challenging still, how can local governments capture the benefits of a more engaged and efficacious citizenry to ensure the delivery of public value?

For the present though, we have provided a piece of the mosaic of evidence which suggests that when it comes to citizen engagement in public value management, small isn't necessarily beautiful. Larger governments may – through their greater capacity to communicate and engage – be able to turn around some of the disadvantages of size. In place of the presumption that economies of scale necessarily come at the price of a government which is more distant and detached from its citizenry, larger governments may have the potential to deliver both efficiency *and* engagement.

References

Altman, I. and Low, S.M. (1992). *Place Attachment*. New York: Plenum Press.

Anderson, M. (2010). Community psychology, political efficacy and trust. *Political Psychology*, 31(1), 59–84.

Andrews, R., Cowell, R., Downe, J., Martin, S. and Turner, D. (2008). Supporting effective citizenship in local government: Engaging, educating and empowering local citizens. *Local Government Studies*, 34(4), 489–507.

Benington, J. (2009). Creating the Public in order to create public value, *International Journal of Public Administration*, 32(3–4), 232–249.

Benington, J. and Moore, M.H., eds. (2011). *Public Value: Theory and Practice*. Basingstoke: Palgrave Macmillan.

Blomgren Bingham, L., Nabatchi, T. and O'Leary, R. (2005). The new governance: Practices and processes for stakeholder and citizen participation in the work of government. *Public Administration Review*, 65(5), 547–558.

Bovaird, T. (2007). Beyond Engagement and Participation: User and Community Coproduction of Public Services. *Public Administration Review*, 67(5), 846–860.

Bozeman, B. (2002). Public-Value Failure: When Efficient Markets May Not Do. *Public Administration Review*, 62(2), 145–161.

Brewer, J.D. (2013). *The Public Value of the Social Sciences*. London: Bloomsbury.

Brown, M.B. (2006). Citizen panels and the concept of representation. *Journal of Political Philosophy*, 14(2), 203–225.

Caprara, G.V., Vecchione, M., Capanna, C. and Mebane, M. (2009) Perceived political self efficacy. *European Journal of Social Psychology*, 39, 1002–1020.

Carpini, M.X.D., Cook, F.L. and Jacobs, L.R. (2004) Public Deliberation, Discursive Participation, and Citizen Engagement: A Review of the Empirical Literature. *Annual Review of Political Science*, 7(1), 315–344.

Coffe, H. and Geys, B. (2006). Community heterogeneity: A burden for social capital? *Social Science Quarterly*, 87(5), 1053–1072.

Craig, S.C., Niemi, R.G. and Silver, G.E. (1990). Political efficacy and trust: A report on the NES pilot study items. *Political Behavior*, 12(3), 289–314.

Dahl, R.A. (1967). The city in the future of local democracy. *American Political Science Review*, 61(4), 953–970.

Dahl, R.A. and Tufte, E.R. (1973). *Size and Democracy.* Stanford, CA: Stanford University Press.

Denters, B. (2002). Size and political trust: Evidence from Denmark, the Netherlands, Norway and the United Kingdom. *Environment and Planning C – Government and Policy,* 20(6), 793–812.

Drew, J. and Dollery, B. (2016). Does size still matter? An empirical analysis of the effectiveness of Victorian local authorities. *Local Government Studies,* 42(1), 15–28.

Dunleavy, P., Margetts, H., Bastow, S. and Tinkler, J. (2006). New Public Management is dead – long live digital-era governance. *Journal of Public Administration Research and Theory,* 16(3), 467–494.

Fischel, W.A. (2001). *The Homevoter Hypothesis: How Home Values Influence Local Government Taxation, School Finance and Land-Use Policies.* Cambridge, MA: Harvard University Press.

Fung, A. (2006). Varieties of participation in complex governance. *Public Administration Review,* 66(1), 66–75.

Hildago, M.C. and Hernandez, B. (2002). Place Attachment: Conceptual and Empirical Questions. *Journal of Environmental Psychology,* 21(3), 273–281.

Irvin, R.A. and Stansbury, J. (2004). Citizen participation in decision making: Is it worth the effort? *Public Administration Review,* 64(1), 55–65.

John, P. (2010). Larger and larger? The endless search for efficiency in the UK. In Baldersheim H. and Rose L.E. (eds), *Territorial Choice: The Politics of Boundaries and Borders.* Houndmills: Palgrave.

Kelleher, C.A. and Lowery, D. (2004). Political participation and metropolitan institutional contexts. *Urban Affairs Review,* 39, 720–757.

Kelleher, C.A. and Lowery, D. (2009). Central city size, metropolitan institutions and political participation. *British Journal of Political Science,* 39(1), 59–92.

Lassen, D.D. and Serritzlew, S. (2011). Jurisdiction size and local democracy: Evidence on internal political efficacy from large-scale municipal reform. *American Political Science Review,* 105(2): 238–258.

Lowndes, V., Pratchett, L. and Stoker, G. (2001). Trends in public participation: Part 1 – local government perspectives. *Public Administration,* 79(1), 205–222.

Lowndes, V. and Sullivan, H. (2008). How low can you go? Rationales and challenges for neighbourhood governance. *Public Administration,* 86(1), 53–74.

Margolis M (1979). *Viable Democracy.* New York: St Martin's Press.

Martin, S. (2009). Engaging with citizens and other stakeholders. In Bovaird T. and Loffler E. (eds), *Public Management and Governance* (pp. 279–296). London: Routledge.

Martin, S. and Webb, A. (2009). Citizen-centred public services: Contestability without consumer-driven competition? *Public Money & Management,* 29(2), 123–130.

Michels, A. (2011). Innovations in democratic governance: How does citizen participation contribute to a better democracy? *International Review of Administrative Sciences,* 77(2), 275–293.

Moore, M.H. (1995). *Creating Public Value.* Cambridge MA: Harvard University Press.

Moore, M.H. (ed) (2013). *Recognising Public Value.* Cambridge MA: Harvard University Press.

Moore, M.H. (2014). Public Value Accounting: Establishing the Philosophical basis, *Public Administration Review,* 74(4), 465–477.

Morlan, R.L. (1984). Municipal vs national election voter turnout: Europe and the United States. *Political Science Quarterly,* 99(3), 457–470.

Morrell, M.E. (2003). Survey and experimental evidence for a reliable and valid measure of internal political efficacy. *Public Opinion Quarterly,* 67(4), 589–602.

Mouritzen, P.E. (1989). City size and citizens' satisfaction: Two competing theories revisited. *European Journal of Political Research,* 17(6), 661–688.

Needham, C. (2008). Realising the Potential of Co-production: Negotiating Improvements in Public Services. *Social Policy and Society*, 7, 221–231.

Newton, K. (1982). Is small really so beautiful. Is big really so ugly? Size, effectiveness and democracy in local government. *Political Studies*, 30(2), 190–206.

Niemi, R.G., Craig, S.C. and Mattei, F. (1991). Measuring internal efficacy in the 1988 National Election Study. *American Political Science Review*, 85(4), 1407–1413.

Oliver, J.E. (2000). City size and civic involvement in metropolitan America. *American Political Science Review*, 94(2), 361–374.

Pestoff, V. (2006). Citizens and coproduction of welfare services. *Public Management Review*, 8(4), 503–519.

Rodriguez-Pose, A, Tijmstra, S.A.R. and Bwire, A. (2009). Fiscal decentralisation, efficiency, and growth. *Environment and Planning A*, 41(9), 2041–2062.

Rose, L.E. (2002). Municipal size and local nonelectoral participation: Findings from Denmark, the Netherlands, and Norway. *Environment and Planning C – Government and Policy*, 20(6), 829–851.

Sandfort, J. and Quick, K.S. (2015). Building Deliberative Capacity to Create Public Value. In Bryson, J.M., Crosby, B.C. and Bloomberg, L. (eds), *Public Value and Public Administration* (pp. 39–52). Washington DC: Georgetown University Press.

Sharpe, L.J. (1970). Theories and values of local government. *Political Studies*, 18(2), 153–174.

Soul, S. and Dollery, B. (2000). The effect of municipal population size on political effectiveness: An empirical note on four local government jurisdictions in New South Wales. *Regional Policy & Practice*, 9(2), 64–66.

Stewart, J. (1996). Innovations in democratic practice in local government. *Policy and Politics*, 24(1), 29–41.

Stoker, G. (2006). Public Value Management, *American Review of Public Administration*, 36(1), 41–57.

Valentino, N.A., Gregorowicz, K. and Groenendyk, E.W. (2009). Efficacy, emotions and the habit of participation. *Political Behaviour*, 31(3), 307–330.

Van Ryzin, G.G. (2008). Validity of an on-line panel approach to citizen surveys. *Public Performance and Management Review*, 32(2), 236–262.

Wallis, J. and Dollery, B. (2006). Revitalizing the contribution non-profit organizations can make to the provision of human services. *International Journal of Social Economics*, 33, 491–511.

Weisbrod, B.A. (1997). The future of the nonprofit sector: Its entwining with private enterprise and government. *Journal of Policy Analysis and Management*, 16, 541–555.

Welch, E.W. (2012). The relationship between transparent and participative government: A study of local governments in the United States. *International Review of Administrative Sciences*, 78(1), 93–115.

Whitaker, G. (1980). Coproduction: Citizen Participation in Service Delivery. *Public Administration Review*, 40(3), 240–246.

Yang, K. (2016) Creating Public Value and Institutional Innovations across Boundaries: An Integrative Process of Participation, Legitimation, and Implementation. *Public Administration Review*, 76(6), 873–885.

Yang, K. and Callaghan, K. (2005). Assessing citizen involvement efforts by local governments. *Public Performance & Management Review*, 29(2), 191–216.

Part 2

Broadening the theory and practice of creating public value to voluntary and commercial organizations and collaborative networks

14 Development NGOs and public value

Alpa Dhanani and Gwen Thomas

Introduction

Drawing on prior research in several divergent fields including development, the voluntary, non-profit sector, management and accounting, the objective of this chapter is to evaluate the ethos, activities and approaches of international NGOs to development through the lens of public value(s). This objective is motivated both by the increasing popularity of Northern NGOs in the development of the global South, and the attractiveness of the concept of public value to nurture and inform practices of public sector entities and beyond. An opportunity is thereby afforded to connect the practices of NGOs with the diverse features of public value. The global North and South are relative terms where the North refers to countries that are richer, more developed and more industrialised than their Southern counterparts who are poorer, less developed and less industrialised. Previous terms used in this context include developed and developing countries and the First World and the Third World. The encounter of NGOs with the distinctive publics in these two global settings makes them a unique context within which to study the notion of public value. At the same time, this concept serves as a valuable framework through which to understand the NGO phenomenon and nurture organisations' efforts to realise their aspirations of a fairer, more equitable and just society.

Development non-governmental organisations (NGOs) have in recent years taken centre stage in the global aid architecture, playing an important role in the transition to a more global civil society (Stoddard, 2003). Alongside their activities of service provision, development NGOs have institutionalised and promoted the ideals of global humanitarianism and in turn instantiated an ethics of global compassion and advanced the normative discourse of universal human rights in society (Beck, 2005). Today, the term NGO has virtually become a household name and humanitarian organisations have become the face of development, helping to interpret and make sense of the many complexities surrounding its advancement, and ultimately shape societal views of development in the North (Kirk, 2012).

The term public value was first coined by Moore (1995) to nurture public sector organisations to create value for their citizenry. Since then, the concept has evolved considerably such that today it has widespread appeal and has attracted much attention from public sector academics and practitioners (see, for example, Kelly et al., 2002; Stoker, 2006; Jorgensen and Bozeman, 2007; Mendel and Brudney, 2014). The divergent dimensions of public value that have emerged over time serve as a useful framework to inform practices of organisations beyond governmental entities, including NGOs. Notwithstanding the role of NGOs in creating public value through their aspirations to advance societal development and build an equitable, fair and just society, the chapter commences with an analysis of the two paradigms that determine NGOs' approaches to development through the public value lens. Moreover, within the context of creating value for the Southern publics, the chapter critically examines the value implications for Northern and Southern governments of their interactions with NGOs as integral players in the development project; highlights NGOs' efforts to continue to do good and deliver public goods without necessarily enhancing public value (Mendel and Brudney, 2014); and draws on Stoker's (2006) application of the public value framework to networked governance to nurture NGOs' efforts. Finally, the chapter considers how the educational and campaigning practices of NGOs shape the perceptions and values of the Northern publics who support the organisations' activities towards their Southern counterparts.

Development NGOs

Attempts to meaningfully label, classify or group the thousands of assorted, disparate bodies loosely linked together under the 'non-governmental organisation' mantle are notoriously fraught with difficulties. Since 1945 when the first formal consultative status was given to such bodies in Article 71 of Chapter 10 to the UN Charter (1945) their scope and power have grown. In the wake of advanced globalisation, there is agreement that there has been nothing short of an explosion in the profile, number and influence of such bodies over the last three decades (Edwards and Hulme, 1995; Ebrahim, 2003).

Whilst almost all aspects of the background, motivation, objectives and method of operation will vary between each and every NGO perhaps the only common feature is the underlying desire to do good and to facilitate change for the betterment of society (Weidenbaum, 2009). Each organisation's story will be different, but origins will typically be rooted to a greater or lesser degree in religion, ethics, morality, decency, possibly outrage and indignation at perceived injustices or suffering (Stoddard, 2003; Fassin, 2009). In their quest for a fairer world, NGOs endorse values such as equality, justice and solidarity (Fassin, 2009), and the moralistic values they espouse are reflected in their care and compassion. The ethical nature and non-profit status of NGOs that free them from the pursuit of financial objectives, have traditionally placed them in a position of trust in society.

Three key areas of NGO activity comprise humanitarian aid in the form of an emergency response to a crisis, longer term anti-poverty developmental work, and campaigning or lobbying pursuits. Most large development organisations participate in all three of these activities. Income to support the international development work of NGOs is derived from a variety of different sources amongst which grants from governments and international institutions, as well as private donations are often instrumental. Direct involvement and engagement of publics from the global North is also critical to the operations of NGOs through their volunteering practices and campaigning activities that lobby government and corporate organisations to advocate change and justice for people living in poverty (Devereux, 2008; Lough and McBride, 2014).

Public value

The study of 'public value' or 'public values' has over the last twenty years become a fertile area of academic debate. In the context of public service reform, Kelly et al. (2002) identified three principal and inter-related features most valued by the public. They comprise the effective provision of services, overall outcomes for society, and trust between citizens and government agencies. Recognising the inter-relationships between the factors however, benefits of service provision would effectively be obliterated in the absence of citizen trust, which also incorporates ideas of legitimacy and public confidence.

The enormous scope of the public value concept has been widely recognised and Jorgensen and Bozeman (2007) attempted to bring some order to the ensuing diverse and vast literature by developing an inventory of public values which usefully categorises the considerable array of interpretations and understandings of the term. Though remaining in the domain of public administration, the values highlighted provide evidence of broader insights and perceptions including references to human dignity, protection of rights, listening and openness, citizen involvement and self-integrity. This resonates with Stoker's (2006) notion of networked governance that is premised on the development of "networks of deliberation and delivery in the pursuit of public value" (Stoker, 2006, 42).

There is general agreement therefore that public value goes beyond but does not exclude financial or economic efficiency. It embraces the unquantifiable, intangible and more elusive but nonetheless fundamentals of civil existence, including ethics, morality, justice and dignity. It involves nothing short of a "change in people's perception of living in a community and society" (Meynhardt et al., 2014, 5). A related feature is its abstract and ever evolving nature. It is a concept which encourages reflection and continuous learning and adapting to new circumstances and situations (Stoker, 2006).

With such a broadening of the concept it has unsurprisingly been recognised as relevant in many and diverse spheres and public value theory "is not the domain of any single discipline" (Meynhardt, 2009, 193). As a consequence a number of public and other organisations have additionally adopted the notion as a useful guide for decision making and accountability. The British Broadcasting Corporation (BBC), for example, founded on the three public principles of universality, fairness and equity, and accountability, identified its role as creating democratic, cultural and creative, educational, social and community and global values for the public, and concluded that "public value is the best yardstick for valuing the BBC's future contribution" (BBC, 2004, 8). The National Trust in turn used a public value approach to stimulate debate regarding its heritage protection activities (National Trust, 2006). The Association of Certified Chartered Accountants (ACCA), a global accountancy organisation, highlighted the role of the accountancy profession in creating public value and similarly indicated its commitment to public value at the core of its strategy (ACCA, 2011).

Given that doing good and societal improvement are essentially at the very core of what NGOs represent and embody the very purposes for which they exist, there is immediately the suggestion of a fundamental relationship between such organisations and the concept of public value. However, it is important to recognise in this context that creating public value goes beyond performing good works. Whilst philanthropy, for example, is intrinsically commendable, encouraging the relevant actors to embrace the notion of creating public value at critical stages of the granting process from preliminary discussions to eventual funding is likely to achieve meaningful societal development (Mendel and Brudney, 2014). Little has been done, however, to formally link some of the aforementioned threads in the general public value debate with the core values, ethos and activities of NGOs and in particular how they address the challenges facing them and the questions being asked of them at the current time. This chapter aims to highlight some of those fruitful areas of discussion.

The brief discussion above revolves around value and values and will be explored further in the chapter, but additionally from a development NGO perspective, consideration of the *public* angle is of particular interest. The Oxford English Dictionary (2016) provides various definitions of the public including "ordinary people in general; the community", "a section of the community having a particular interest or connection", and "the people who watch or are interested in an artist, writer, or performer" (i.e. the idea of *my* public). Aspects of all three definitions are relevant to the current discussion (Figure 14.1). NGOs generally need to address the needs and requirements of at least two distinct publics, in the form of the Southern public which is being served (linking with the first definition) and the Northern public which has to be nurtured to support NGO activities (more akin with the third definition). The second definition can perhaps be seen to link both parties, each connected by the success or otherwise of the applicable project. Providing value, and being accountable to both publics, as well as other pressures both within and outside the organisation can give rise to particular tensions and at times "competing loyalties" (Stoddard, 2003, 34).

The remainder of this chapter examines the NGO phenomenon through a public value lens, drawing specifically on the paradigms that underlie development activities; the actual interventions and processes surrounding them to create societal benefits; and the lobbying and advocacy practices of NGOs to Northern communities to galvanise their support to achieve a more equitable and just society.

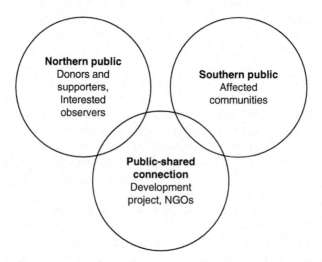

Figure 14.1 NGOs: dichotomy of 'the public'

Publics valued

The qualities of charity and philanthropy have from the outset been instrumental in funding NGO development operations. Gradually and increasingly, however, since the late 1990s the sector has witnessed a paradigmatic shift away from a charity based model to a rights based approach (Offenheiser and Holcombe, 2003). Whilst the traditional charity focused approach to development is premised on the idea that those in poverty need to be rescued by well meaning, more fortunate benefactors, the rights based approach challenges this view and is based on the simple notion that each human life is of equal value (United Nations, 1948) with the resultant emphasis on justice, dignity and empowerment (Offenheiser and Holcombe, 2003; Donaghue, 2010; Kindornay et al., 2012; Kirk, 2012). This idea is not new. Martin Luther King Jr. had famously observed that "Philanthropy is commendable, but it must not cause the philanthropist to overlook the circumstances of economic injustice which make philanthropy necessary" (King, 1963). Nearly half a century later nevertheless another notorious activist, Nelson Mandela, similarly reflected that "overcoming poverty is not a gesture of charity. It is an act of justice. It is the protection of a fundamental human right, the right to dignity and a decent life" (Nelson Mandela, 2005) (BBC, 2005). Presently, a number of leading NGOs have committed to the rights-based approach to development as prominently publicised in their literature.

The charity model of development views poverty as a consequence of adverse circumstances which unfortunate victims are unable to resolve, and considers the role of development to offer solutions that provide for constituents in poverty. Efforts of poverty alleviation are consequently couched in terms of a culture of dependency between beneficiaries and givers and the altruistic efforts of Northern supporters (Offenheiser and Holcombe, 2003; Kirk, 2012). By contrast, the rights based approach views poverty as an inequitable sharing of the earth's resources in which constituent initiatives to exercise their agency and aspirations are hindered by persistent systemic challenges. The approach places a moral responsibility on the duty-bearers (state and non-state actors) not only to recognise these obstacles but critically their complicity in them, and to challenge and correct them to create a fairer world (Donaghue, 2010; Kindornay et al., 2012). Moreover, it endeavours to empower constituents to exercise their rights and in turn their agency and autonomy (Donaghue, 2010). As such, the rights based model recognises the instrumental role of beneficiary communities in the development project and seeks to foster a culture of interdependence and partnership between the different development actors.

The philosophical orientation of NGOs towards development has profound implications for how international development is approached, ranging from how the publics are valued to how organisations engage in their activities. From a public value perspective, the charity model of development values the altruistic instincts of Northern supporters and NGOs, that is, their moral values. At the same time, however, its regard for beneficiary communities as unfortunate victims in need of help and dependency encourages responses of pity which in turn identifies them as objects of charity (Offenheiser and Holcombe, 2003). In so doing, the process dehumanises and devalues Southern communities. In contrast, the rights based approach is founded on principles of humanity and dignity and respect. It places a moral responsibility on members of the global society to act and so recognises and values the rights of Southern constituents, and also places an onus on the Northern public to identify and correct societal inequities and injustices. Furthermore, it values constituent agency and capability through its emphasis on development initiatives that foster community self-determination and action. From a public value perspective, altruism and dignity and humanity are identified as important features of the higher order 'constellation' in Jorgensen and Bozeman's (2007) inventory of public values. The application of these features to the NGO context, however, highlights an important distinction between the values of the two publics of NGOs, a distinction based on the connections of these features with the two paradigmatic approaches to development.

Public value creation

Societal development and improving people's lives is at the heart of the public value debate (see for example Moore, 1995; Kelly et al., 2002; Mendel and Brudney, 2014). This section addresses three distinct aspects of value creation pertinent to NGOs. First, as a consequence of the public sector context in which public value has predominantly been discussed, public value creation is often couched in terms of effective service delivery. However, service delivery is only one dimension of NGO efforts to deliver societal advancement. Second, proponents of public value argue that value is not created or destroyed in itself but rather needs an audience to appreciate it (Kelly et al., 2002; Meynhardt, 2009). For NGOs, this audience necessarily comprises the Southern publics for whom organisations exist. Nevertheless, the relevance and expectations of the Northern public also need to be recognised as the principal funders and implementers of the development project. Finally, in both the global North and the global South, distinguishing between the state and the public, in line with the origins of the public value debate, is pertinent in the value creation discourse of NGOs.

Value creation for Southern publics, as discussed earlier, takes place primarily in terms of humanitarian responses to emergency crises and longer term development, and within this setting, NGOs engage in service delivery and capacity building of which campaigning and advocacy is a part (Donaghue, 2010; Banks et al., 2015). Whilst both strategies subscribe to the rights based approach to development aforementioned, service delivery may be closely connected to the more traditional charity oriented model. Service delivery endeavours to address issues of the basic rights of constituents (rights to health, rights to education etc.) through the provision of facilities such as healthcare and education, albeit the nature of this activity, *to provide*, is also consistent with the charity oriented model of welfare. Capacity building, in contrast, is oriented towards practices of change. It seeks to challenge the inequities and injustices of society through the pursuit of transformative agendas which empower constituents to advance their agency and capabilities and give them the power, capacity and access to further their rights and improve their destinies (Offenheiser and Holcombe, 2003; Donaghue, 2010).

Despite the extensive activities of NGOs and their multimillion pound budgets, in recent years questions have been raised about the ability of NGOs to meet their longer term goals towards development and social justice, that is, to create public value for the betterment of society. While the thesis of aid and international assistance has been considered appropriate in itself, and many recipient communities acknowledge the benefits they have accrued from development interventions, paradoxically, there is a widespread belief amongst the Southern publics that cumulatively, the effects of aid and aid intervention particularly in terms of long term correction have been largely negative (Anderson et al., 2012). Practitioners and academics alike have echoed similar views in a number of best-selling books of recent times (Easterly, 2006; Banerjee and Duflo, 2011; Munk, 2014). Writers highlight not only the lack of effectiveness of aid interventions but also the unintended and unexpected consequences of such interventions. Osserwaarde et al. (2008), Abirafeh (2009), Korf et al. (2010), Banerjee and Duflo (2011) and Anderson et al. (2012), for example, note that many of the dozens of 'common sense' development projects such as food aid and the once hailed concept of microfinance have played a limited role in poverty alleviation, and may even have aggravated it; NGO interventions have contributed to the creation or reinforcement of tensions and divisions amongst different groups of society; and constituents have experienced negative feelings of disrespect and disempowerment as a result of development interventions. Similarly, the sector attracted much criticism for its response to two recent humanitarian crises, the 2004 tsunami and the 2010 Haiti earthquake. Organisations were reproached for the inefficiencies and ineffectiveness with which they operated, including delays in the resettlement of local communities which introduced additional health and safety risks (Smirl, 2015); overprovision and imposition of Western style housing and planning facilities to create new development that was 'right' (Smirl, 2015), and the marginalisation of the communities most in need of assistance (Amarasiri de Silva, 2009; Korf et al., 2010). Overall, the high expectations placed on NGOs have often failed to come to fruition, and their once considered position of advantage to create value for the Southern public has been called into question. The remainder of this section delves into some of the activities, operations and relationships of NGOs with constituents to better understand their value creation processes and the constraints they face within this remit.

Value from Northern governments and other institutional funders

Northern governments, and more recently, big philanthrocapitalists and private foundations are the principal funders of NGO activities. They engage in contractual arrangements with development organisations usually through a competitive tendering process to support the development project. Research suggests that their funding processes have played a significant role in shaping the activities of NGOs from dictating the areas of need that organisations respond to, to their approach to the development project. Some academics go as far as to suggest that NGOs have been coopted by Northern governments (Edwards and Hulme, 1995; Banks et al., 2015).

Institutional donors set the broad agenda for development activities through their tendering processes. Critics explain that their distance from the grassroots level has, however, meant that their agendas are sometimes at variance with those of the communities they work with. Morfit (2011), for example, noted the frustration communities in Malawi felt when donor fashion prioritised HIV/AIDS interventions at the expense of other, more pressing concerns. Similarly Hillier and Dempsey (2012) and Rawlence (2016) noted donor refusal to fund droughts in Africa until such escalated into full scale famine because they sought proof of humanitarian crises before committing funds to the cause. Moreover, Anderson et al. (2012) reported beneficiary frustration at the shifting trends and fads in donor priorities which may mean that projects are not allowed sufficient incubation time to bring benefits to the communities or come to a halt just as they are proving to be valuable.

In addition, donors' funding models favour service delivery based projects over those engaged in capacity building because by their very nature these projects have characteristics of what Mendel and Brudney (2014) refer to as public good in a public value context: a briefer time orientation and within this period often pre-definable, recordable shorter term measurable outcomes that meet the target driven arrangements of funders. In contrast, capacity building projects that seek rights and autonomy for constituents are by their very nature longer term in time orientation and often lack the identification of discrete outcome measures to capture features such as empowerment (the number of people empowered / the extent of empowerment for example), which leads to their exclusion. Such practices are, however, more in tune with public value where the enduring, more holistic consequences of organisational interventions of doing good are felt and societal benefits are achieved (Mendel and Brudney, 2014). Such value, as Mendel and Brudney (2014) add, however, is unavoidably shrouded in uncertainty and unpredictability as consequences may be unintended and unknown, features that target driven processes of funding struggle with. Importantly, target driven service delivery interventions may also in themselves fail to achieve the social benefits desired from development projects, but this aspect of social outcomes and value will unlikely feature in funding processes. A leading Northern NGO, for example, noted in its annual report its achievement in meeting its target to build 'x' many new schools in the Sub-Saharan region, but also highlighted the limited benefit of this facility for the local communities as formal schooling was not part of the indigenous culture.

Attempts to engage in capacity building projects have also, it appears, been modelled along the same lines as service delivery projects with specific performance targets. The proxy outcome variables developed, however, often only bear a vague relationship with the transformative objectives of the projects. Public value creation, as defined by Mendel and Brudney (2014), may consequently fail in such cases (Anderson et al., 2012). For example, examining aid intervention to improve gender relations in Afghanistan in the aftermath of the Taliban invasion, Abirafeh (2009) noted that participating organisations were able to demonstrate their achievements in terms of progressing women's education and economic empowerment as intended, but the organisation-centric approach to the interventions and its Western orientation undermined the indigenous women's agency and made life more difficult for them socially.

Related to their emphasis on targets and outcomes, researchers comment that funding processes are highly proceduralised and prescriptive. They require contenders to offer detailed plans of solutions to development problems upfront, and follow extensive processes and procedures involving comprehensive checklists and paper trails (Anderson et al., 2012). While such processes, critics explain, facilitate close monitoring and control once funding has commenced, they are representative of a top down approach to development that encourages organisations to offer standardised, technical solutions to poverty alleviation (Chahim and Prakash, 2014). Moreover, increased attention to such measures has evolved into an obsession with them and more emphasis is placed on ticking the relevant boxes than determining whether value has been added to the beneficiary communities (Anderson et al., 2012).

Constituent participation and value creation

Writers of public value (Kelly et al., 2002; Stoker, 2006; Jorgensen and Bozeman, 2007) explain that citizen preferences and engagement in directing organisational activities are central to the creation of public value as the public is best placed to determine what is truly of value to it. NGOs also identify the communities they work with as their primary stakeholders to whom they believe they are foremost accountable, followed by other stakeholders including donors and funders, the general public and corporate organisations (Dhanani and Connolly, 2015). However, research suggests that the reality is different from the rhetoric and perhaps the most significant consequence of the bureaucratised funding arrangements and accountability to donors as discussed above is to crowd out the very public which donors and NGOs are seeking to address and the involvement and engagement of this public with the development interventions (Abirafeh, 2009; Anderson et al., 2012; Banks et al., 2015).

Such practices mean that from a public value perspective, the Northern NGO phenomenon has fallen short in its value *of* the public and its value *to* the public, and consequently the achievements of its own missions and aims. In turn, this threatens the relationship of trust that organisations attempt to cultivate with their constituents to enable effective change. Trust is a fundamental feature of public value and the absence of constituent trust and confidence in organisations may obliterate the benefits of effective service delivery (Kelly et al., 2002). In addition, how organisations conduct themselves and interact with their constituents is instrumental to the trust relationship (Kelly et al., 2002) and as detailed below directly influences the extent to which their efforts to deliver value will be effective.

Observing how organisations value the Southern public, current approaches to development often appear to disempower and frustrate affected communities by offering them pre-manufactured solutions that ignore local agency, capabilities, experience and knowledge (Tembo, 2003; Abirafeh, 2009). Indeed, Anderson et al. (2012) report that some constituents voice feelings of disrespect as they interpret NGOs as taking advantage of their circumstances to attract funding. These practices are ultimately an antithesis to the rights based approach to development and the public value agenda. Moreover, as a consequence of disregarding the complex and contextualised positions of the communities, that is, the circumstances, histories and realities facing the Southern publics, organisational solutions to poverty alleviation have unsurprisingly had limited success. Furthermore they have in some instances resulted in unintended consequences as alluded to above. Given the North - South binary, valuing indigenous cultures and showing a sensitivity towards them is an important value consideration. Surprisingly, however, beneficiary culture has attracted cursory attention in the NGO world (Lenneberg, 2010). Abirafeh (2009) in her study that assessed the intervention of NGOs to promote the rights of women in Afghanistan, for example, noted that the Western based drive to push for change was not only critical of the 'Afghan way', but a failure to understand and appreciate the historical and cultural contexts of the communities resulted in the destabilisation of gender relations within them. Similarly, Amutabi (2006), reporting on the NGO factor in Africa, hinted at the negative cultural consequences of gender mainstreaming in Kenya, and more recently Smirl (2015) noted that the rehabilitation efforts in Aceh post-tsunami led to the construction of standardised, small single unit family homes even though it is culturally common for multiple family units to co-habit.

Value from Southern governments

According to academics, the on-going emphasis on service delivery, whether on a large scale or on a small scale in concert with other NGOs has itself been problematic in terms of reducing the pressure on Southern state governments to provide such services for their own citizenry (Donaghue, 2010; Ellis, 2010). This has, in turn, weakened the position of citizens and local social movements in demanding these services from their own governments and holding them to account. As such, while continued service provision has allowed NGOs to provide technical solutions and meet donor targets, "the real contribution [of NGOs]", has been to "defuse political anger and dole out as aid or benevolence what people ought to have by right" (Roy as cited in Ellis, 2010, 68). In fact, as Anderson et al. (2012) note, beneficiary communities almost unanimously voice a preference for NGOs to help them to seek their rights from national governments. Emphasis on service delivery is as such paradoxical to organisations' aspirations towards a more just and equitable society. Concentration on welfare and service delivery over advocacy and democracy has not only prioritised public good over public value as Mendel and Brudney (2014) defined, but has also depoliticised development by contributing towards the creation of what Wood (1997) termed franchise states, where state governments are not accountable to their citizens.

NGOs: implications of professionalisation and managerialism

Whilst the underlying values and ethos of NGOs are their greatest assets, the requirements and pressures of, and uniformity in funding processes, together with their aspirations to grow and lead the sector, have led to the creation of like-minded and increasingly professionalised and managerialist establishments (Kothari, 2005; Srinivas, 2009). This professionalism and managerialism have in turn led to organisational preferences for certified specialists over indigenous knowledge and experience, together with intra-sector development toolkits with pre-made checklists of needs and pre-made solutions over locally informed interventions (Kothari, 2005; Srinivas, 2009). In addition, as discussed above, the emphasis on measurement and targets has distanced organisations from their focus on how to realise their core values and be accountable for them. While some academics express sympathy for the position NGOs have found themselves in, others are less forgiving and believe that organisations have exacerbated the shift towards donor led agendas as they tamper with their missions and activities to fit with donor expectations to attract their funding (Jakimow, 2007). Moreover, Isbister (2010) and O'Dwyer and Unerman (2007) note that NGOs have themselves become comfortable with the notion of doing good and delivering public goods in Mendel and Brudney's (2014) terms, and lack the zeal to work towards genuine attempts to create public value, that is, public benefits, even when appropriate opportunities present themselves. In this light, Dhanani and Connolly (2015) note that organisations appear to rely on the notions of doing good and delivering public goods in their endeavours to legitimise their activities to external audiences and cultivate donor and public trust.

NGO *public value: new opportunities*

Funding arrangements and NGO operations have hallmarks of both traditional public administration and new public management. This position is unsurprising given the role of Northern governments in the development project. Specifically, the funder–NGO model is akin to the purchaser-provider model of new public management (Stoker, 2006) that relies on a range of interventionist organisations and a market oriented approach to management. Moreover, funding arrangements are dominated by the interests of the funding agencies, driven by bureaucratic processes that emphasise checklists and tick box exercises–typical of traditional public administration–and systems of performance targets. The new paradigmatic framework of public value that has swooped through public sector agencies in recent years in recognition of the limitations and failures of its predecessors, offers new opportunities for NGOs. This framework promises a different way to approach the development, measurement and management of organisational objectives. Making references specifically to public sector organisations, Moore as cited in Nixon (2014, 5) described the advancement of the public value framework as being about "the difference between aiming for an arbitrarily defined performance target to give the appearance of accountability and performance and developing a shared understanding of the important values that citizens, taxpayers and clients want to see achieved".

Specific to the context of NGOs, Stoker's application of the public value framework to networked governance offers new opportunities that comply with organisations' aspirations towards a fairer and more just society. While Stoker's notion of networked governance is based in the public sector context and emphasises the role of citizens and taxpayers as legitimate members in the design and implementation of public services, the approach can be applied to NGOs (and their public sector funders) to facilitate the shared, bottom-up decision making process in the development communities. Funding agencies would in this case encourage such practices via their NGO partners.

Stoker's idea of networked governance is premised on the development of alliances to engage members in the search for solutions to the complex and shared problems through deliberation and delivery in pursuit of public value. This model befits the notion of beneficiary participation in international development, in which genuine participation would entail constituent engagement in the identification and prioritisation of areas of need, design and implementation of organisational initiatives and the evaluation and assessment of these interventions. The adoption of Stoker's model in the North may encourage its implementation at the grassroots level in the South. His notion of public right to consultation, for example, may offer a practical means by which to mobilise holistic constituent participation in the funding arrangements between donors and organisations, securing the associated time and resource commitments. Moreover Stoker's idea of networked governance as a system to enable an organised democracy and to develop citizen confidence in the public sector context would translate into a similar system for Southern communities, nurturing constituent agency, empowerment and confidence, in line with earlier discussions. Furthermore, the pursuit of public value means that organisational interventions are assessed not in terms of targets met but in terms of the net benefits to the communities they are intended for as stressed by writers in both the public value and development literatures (Mendel and Brudney, 2014; Banks et al., 2015). Stoker's emphasis on the importance of the virtuous qualities of adaptability and flexibility of service/development interventions to accommodate individualised local contexts, changing circumstances and unexpected consequences, is invaluable in recognition of the un-predictabilities, ambiguities and uncertainties of development interventions aforementioned (Mendel and Brudney, 2014; Duval et al., 2015). Under Stoker's model, development organisations would occupy a facilitative role and be held to account for their achievement of public value and their ability to facilitate responses to the localised individual and changing circumstances. Finally, Stoker's comments on the universality of networked governance have much significance in international development where currently marginalised communities are further distanced through development interventions (Amarasiri de Silva, 2009; Korf et al., 2010). Here, he explains people's individual capacities should be developed so that they can contribute to the process of networked governance by exercising their rights and responsibilities and contributing to ideas of development and design and implementation of projects. How this may be achieved is, however, not detailed by Stoker, and from an international development perspective this is a critical feature and indeed one that the entire development project is itself seeking to address.

Publics valued and publics' values: the North

Northern publics are an instrumental and in turn a valued feature of international development. They perform multiple roles including those of tax payers, private donors, volunteers, and campaigners and lobbyists. Generosity of the British public is apparent from Oxfam GB's £118 million income from private donations (some 65% of its institutional income) in 2014 (Oxfam, 2015), and the Disasters Emergency Committee's (DEC) success in raising £37 million in response to the 2014 North African Ebola crisis that claimed over 11,300 lives and affected close to 29,000 people, and a further £87 million in response to the 2015 Nepalese earthquake that fatally injured 8,000 people and displaced close to 2.8 million (DEC, 2016). Similarly, volunteerism is a popular feature of the British public; Foster (2013) valued voluntary activity in the UK in 2012 at an estimated £23.9 billion, approximately 1.5% of GDP (although the benefits of this activity are not specific to international development but apply to charity and other organisations more generally).

Prior research suggests that the Northern (UK) public's generosity and engagement with the development project is reflective of individuals' personal values and moral codes (Lindstrom and Henson, 2011; Glennie et al., 2012). Individuals' prosocial values, that is, their felt social responsibility, a moral concern for others and altruistic tendencies mediate important relationships such as those between religious affiliation and giving (both religious and secular), and education and giving (Bekkers and Schuyt, 2008; Hardy et al., 2008; Bekkers and Wiepking, 2011). As such, the Northern publics' moral values play an important role in the development project.

From a public value perspective, Meynhardt et al. (2014) recognise that organisations have a moral responsibility to influence society's perceptions and values to enable advancements within it. Today, NGO communications and the strategies of representation employed within them are at the heart of influencing and shaping Northern publics' values and views about the development project and nurturing their involvement and engagement with it. Development organisations have demonstrated an immense credibility as institutions of representation of the South

(Dogra, 2012) and are the face of international development. Within this capacity, however, despite the paradigmatic shift towards the rights based approach to development aforementioned, representational practices, as detailed below, appear to be embedded in the charity based model of development and following on, public attitudes to development also exude attitudes, behaviours and values consistent with this latter model.

Research into communication and representational practices suggests organisational tendency to 'other' Southern public, that is, to differentiate them from the Northern public and create an 'us and them' situation in which cultural and intellectual superiority of the North is signalled. Representations, for example, distance the South from the North through binary depictions such as the passive, dependent South devoid of any agency and the active, generous North; the privileged and the underprivileged; and the rural, poor and vulnerable and the urban, modern and prosperous (Dogra, 2012; Vestergaard, 2013). Moreover, imagery practices sometimes violate the dignity of the very people that they represent and exist for (Plewes and Stuart, 2007; Kennedy, 2009). Furthermore, causes of poverty are often internalised with a focus on overpopulation, corruption and violence, and external factors emphasise natural and medical disasters that negate any connections to or contributions by the North (Dogra, 2012). Solutions to poverty tend also to be shown in terms of simple and easy 'Band-Aid' type of development activities that are justifiable by the extreme helplessness and dependency of Southern communities and exercisable on shoestring budgets courtesy of generous donors (Kennedy, 2009; Dogra, 2012). Even practices that rely on concepts such as justice and rights to support concerns such as hunger, Dogra (2012) notes, fail to express the inequities and injustices in global society and the complicity of the global North in this process.

Research into the perceptions of the public of the development project echoes the findings and deductions of those examining representational practices. Supporters' moral values are polarised in that they emphasise emotions such as pity and compassion and tendencies of paternalism, what Cullity (2010) labels morality of care and concern for the unfortunate others. There appears a general lack of awareness of the morality of respect that takes "proper account of the rights and dignity of others" (Cullity, 2010, 160). In other words, NGO engagement with the Northern public appears to have reinforced stereotypical thinking and a charitable engagement with the Southern public. The Northern public remains relatively passive about issues of global justice and solidarity and its complicit role in sustaining some of the global inequities of the world and perceives its involvement with the project in terms of monetary and time donations (Tallon and McGregor, 2014). Organisations' formal responsibilities to educate Northern publics about the development project, appear to have been overshadowed by their priorities to raise funds and improve market share in an increasingly competitive field (Orgad, 2013). However, while the emotional approach of 'tugging at heart-strings' may be successful to attract donor attention, it may compromise constituent dignity and respect and mislead Northern understanding of the development project and Southern communities, and in turn limit its involvement in the fight for justice. Indeed, the Make Poverty History campaign that was designed specifically to galvanise public support in response to prevailing injustices, whilst successful in communicating the need for change, failed to mobilise the British public in the fight for global justice and instead dwindled to monetary funding assistance (McCloskey, 2011).

Moreover, to add to this debate, more recent NGO representational practices have witnessed a shift in focus from imaginaries of the South to those of the North, that is, an emphasis on the self rather than the 'them' (Jefferess, 2002; Vestergaard, 2013). Not only has donor coverage become a more prominent feature in NGO communication, but the related discourses increasingly rely on an exchange logic in which the giving process takes a transactional characteristic. Communication strategies offer audiences the possibility of instant moral compensation, that is, a sense of self-fulfilment from helping the distant other or an opportunity to assuage their guilt (Jefferess, 2002; Vestergaard, 2013). This approach to attract constituent engagement with the development project shifts the public value dimension from the Southerners and the alleviation of poverty to the Northerners and their sense of gratification and aggrandisation. Organisational attempts to create the feel good factor for Northern publics contradict the rights based approach to development and reflect the hedonistic perspective of Meynhardt's (2009) dimensions of public value that side-line discussions surrounding inequities and injustices in society and the causes of poverty, and promote objectification of the Southern publics.

Conclusions

In recognition of the dichotomy of a Southern–Northern public that is unique to NGOs, this chapter examined the activities of NGOs through a public value lens. In so doing, it operationalised the many and diverse features of public value conceptualised in prior research and applied them to a sample of the many and varied activities and operations of NGOs. Features of public value examined include dignity, respect and humanity; the value creation activities of NGOs; the trust implications between organisations and their diverse constituent groups; and the tensions, conflicts and constraints created by the interaction of the different actors of the NGO project. To this end, the chapter examined the charity and rights based philosophies that underlie NGO activities; evaluated the programmes and projects aimed at the communities served; and assessed the campaigning, fundraising and educational practices of NGOs.

Figure 14.2 summarises the public value considerations of NGOs as studied in this chapter. As public benefit organisations, NGOs have a responsibility to create value for their Southern constituents. Moreover, in accordance with the rights based philosophy of development, organisations also have a responsibility to value their constituents and their abilities and agency, which in itself will encourage value creation by supporting activities that are of most value to constituents; taking consideration of local circumstances, cultures and experiences and knowledge, and empowering constituents and enabling them to exercise agency and autonomy. In turn, these approaches to development will engender constituent trust in the development project and NGOs as facilitators of the project. Moreover, in their aspirations towards a fairer and more equitable society, organisations need to nurture the moral responsibilities of Northern publics and revisit their utilitarian drive for donor monies; and support Southern governments in their efforts to create value for Southern constituents. In turn, the respect that organisations bestow on the Southern communities, that is, how they conduct themselves, and the values they seek to create for constituents, will further cultivate Southern community trust in the development project and NGOs as its expediters. Finally, Northern governments and other institutional funders need to recalibrate their role in the creation of public value for the

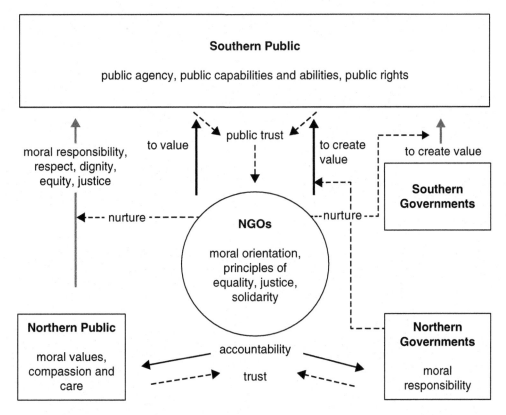

Figure 14.2 Public value considerations of NGOs

Southern communities, shifting away from the new public management style of funding arrangements and embracing a public value orientation. Even though the rights based approach to development and notion of public value are closely synchronised, there is an absence of the manifestation of public value in practice as the rights based approach appears to remain predominantly theoretical and overshadowed by the charity based model of development. Whilst there are multiple explanations for this occurrence, including the co-optation by Northern governments and corporatisation and professionalisation of NGOs, the public value framework that the public sector is familiar with, may serve as the catalyst with which to mobilise a genuine rights based agenda in practice.

Whilst the chapter is informative in its application of the public value lens to NGOs, as an introductory piece it examined only a small subset of NGO attributes and activities. Potential areas that may benefit from a public value framework but are beyond the remit of this chapter include NGO collaborations with corporate organisations, the value offered by volunteers and other supporters of NGOs and the value implications of development of codes of conduct to enhance aid effectiveness and organisational accountability. Going forward, the framework may also be suitable to theorise and inform empirical, data driven, studies of NGOs. Moreover, whilst the critical stance of research to date has been insightful to identify and explain why NGOs may not be fully realising their aspirations, emphasis on the critical may side line studies that demonstrate successful interventions and approaches which may be equally valuable in sharing good practice and offering learning opportunities.

References

Abirafeh, L. (2009). *Gender and International Aid in Afghanistan: The Politics and Effects of Intervention*. Jefferson, NC: McFarland and Company Inc.

ACCA (2011). *The Accounting Profession's Role in Creating Public Value*. London: ACCA, available online at www.accaglobal.com/content/dam/acca/global/pdf/public-value-report.pdf (accessed 22 July 2016).

Amarasiri de Silva M. (2009). Ethnicity, politics and inequality: post-tsunami humanitarian aid delivery in Ampara District, Sri Lanka. *Disasters*, 33(2), 253–273.

Amutabi, M.N. (2006). *The NGO Factor in Africa – The Case of Arrested Development in Kenya*. New York: Routledge.

Anderson, M., Brown, D. and Jean, I. (2012). *Time to Listen: Hearing People on the Receiving End of International Aid*. CDA Collaborative Learning Projects.

Banerjee, A. and Duflo, E. (2011). *Poor Economics: A Radical Rethinking of the Way to Fight Global Poverty*. New York: PublicAffairs.

Banks, N., Hulme, D. and Edwards, M. (2015). NGOs, states and donors revisited: still too close for comfort? *World Development*, 66, 707–718.

BBC (2004). *Building Public Value: Renewing the BBC for a Digital World*. BBC, available online at http://downloads.bbc.co.uk/aboutthebbc/policies/pdf/bpv.pdf (accessed 12 September 2016).

BBC (2005). In full: Mandela's Poverty Speech, Thursday, 3 February 2005, available online at http://news.bbc.co.uk/1/hi/uk_politics/4232603.stm (accessed 22 July 2016).

Beck, Ulrich. (2005). *Power in the Global Age: A New Global Political Economy*. Cambridge: Polity.

Bekkers, R. and Schuyt, T. (2008). And who is your neighbour?: Explaining the effect of religion on charitable giving and volunteering. *Review of Religious Research*, 50(1), 74–96.

Bekkers, R. and Wiepking, P. (2011). A literature review of empirical studies of philanthropy: eight mechanisms that drive charitable giving. *Nonprofit and Voluntary Sector Quarterly*, 40 (5), 924–973.

Chahim, D. and Prakash, A. (2014). NGOisation, foreign funding and the Nicaraguan civil society. *Voluntas*, 25(2), 487–513.

Cullity, G. (2010). Compromised humanitarianism. In K. Horton and C. Roche (eds), *Ethical Questions and International NGOs: An Exchange between Philosophers and NGOs*, Springer Science and Business Media, 157–174.

DEC (2016). Appeals, available online at www.dec.org.uk/appeals (accessed 6 June 2016).

Devereux, P. (2008). International volunteering for development and sustainability: outdated paternalism or a radical response to globalisation? *Development in Practice*, 18(3), 357–373.

Dhanani, A. and Connolly, C. (2015). Non-governmental organizational accountability: talking the talk and walking the walk? *Journal of Business Ethics*, 129, 613–637.

Dogra, N. (2012). *Representations of Global Poverty: Aid, Development and International NGOs*. London: Palgrave.

Donaghue, K. (2010). Human rights, development NGOs and priorities for action. In K. Horton and C. Roche (eds), *Ethical Questions and International NGOs: An Exchange between Philosophers and NGOs*, Springer Science and Business Media, 39–64.

Duval, A., Gendron, Y. and Roux-Dufort, C. (2015). Exhibiting nongovernmental organizations: reifying the performance discourse through framing power. *Critical Perspectives on Accounting*, 29, 31–53.

Easterly, P. (2006). *White Man's Burden: Why the West's Efforts to Aid the Rest Have done so Much Ill and so Little Good*. New York, N.Y: Penguin Books.

Ebrahim, A. (2003). Making sense of accountability: conceptual perspectives for northern and southern nonprofits. *Nonprofit Management and Leadership*, 14, 191–212.

Edwards M. and Hulme, D. (1995). *Non-Governmental Organisations: Performance and Accountability Beyond the Magic Bullet*. Earthscan.

Ellis, P. (2010). The ethics of taking sides. In K. Horton and C. Roche (eds), *Ethical Questions and International NGOs: An Exchange between Philosophers and NGOs*. Springer Science and Business Media, 65–86.

Fassin, Y. (2009). Inconsistencies in activists' behaviours and the ethics of NGOs. *Journal of Business Ethics*, 90, 503–521.

Foster, R. (2013). *Household Satellite Accounts – Valuing Voluntary Activity in the UK*. London: Office for National Statistics, available online at http://webarchive.nationalarchives. gov.uk/20160105160709/ and www.ons.gov.uk/ons/dcp171766_345918pdf (accessed 29 June 2016).

Glennie, A., Straw, W. and Wild, L. (2012). *Understanding Public Attitudes to Aid and Development*. Institute for Public Policy Research and Overseas Development Institute, June.

Hardy, S., Padilla-Walker, L. and Carlo, G. (2008). Parenting dimensions and adolescents' Internalisation of moral values. *Journal of Moral Education*, 37(2), 205–223.

Hillier, D. and Dempsey, B. (2012). *A Dangerous Delay: The Cost of Late Response to Early Warnings in the 2011 Drought in the Horn of Africa*. London: Oxfam and Save the Children, available online at http://policy-practice.oxfam.org.uk/publications/a-dangerous-delay-the-cost-of-late-response-to-early-warnings-in-the-2011-droug-203389 (accessed 25 October 2015).

Isbister, J. (2010). Whose impact, and is it all about impact? In K. Horton and C. Roche (eds), *Ethical Questions and International NGOs: An Exchange between Philosophers and NGOs*. Springer Science and Business Media, 147–156.

Jakimow, T. (2007). The rationale of self-help in development interventions: a case study of a self-help group programme in Tamil Nadu. *Journal of South Asian Development*, 2(1), 107–124.

Jefferess, D. (2002). For sale – Peace of mind: (Neo-) colonial discourse and the commodification of third world poverty in world vision's telethons. *Critical Arts*, 16(1), 1–21.

Jorgensen, T. and Bozeman, B. (2007). Public values: An inventory. *Administration and Society*, 39(3), 354–381.

Kelly, G., Mulgan, G. and Muers, S. (2002). *Creating Public Value: An Analytical Framework for Public Service Reform*. Strategy Unit, Cabinet Office UK, available online at www. sgb.gov.tr/IPA%20Projesi/1.%20Bile%C5%9Fen%20-%20E%C5%9Fle%C5%9Ftirme/E %C4%9Fitim%20Sunumlar%C4%B1%20ve%20E%C4%9Fitime%20%C4%B0li%C5% 9Fkin%20Dok%C3%BCmanlar/5.%20Kamu%20De%C4%9Feri%20-%20Politika%20 Analizi%20ve%20De%C4%9Ferlendirme/%C4%B0ngilizce%20Dok%C3%BCmanlar/ Petrus%20Kautto/%C4%B0lgili%20Dok%C3%BCmanlar/Creating%20Public%20Value. pdf (accessed 19 May 2016).

Kennedy, D. (2009). Selling the distant other: humanitarianism and imagery-ethical dilemmas of humanitarian action. *Journal of Humanitarian Assistance*, February. Available online at www.jha.ac (accessed 22 August 2016).

Kindornay, S., Ron, J. and Carpenter, C. (2012). Rights-Based approaches to development: implications for NGOs. *Human Rights Quarterly*, 34, 472–506.

King, M. (2010). *Strength to Love*. U.S.: Fortress Press, originally published in 1963.

Kirk, M. (2012). Beyond charity: helping NGO lead a transformative new public discourse on global poverty and social justice. *Ethics and International Affairs*, 26, 245–263.

Korf B., Habullah S., Hollenbach, P. and Klem, B. (2010). The gift of disaster: the commodification of good intentions in post-tsunami Sri Lanka. *Disasters*, 34, Suppl 1, 60–77.

Kothari, U. (2005). Authority and expertise: The professionalisation of international development and the ordering of dissent. *Antipode*, 37, 425–446.

Lenneberg, C. (2010). To respect or not to respect . . . ethical dilemmas of INGO development practitioners. In K. Horton and C. Roche (eds), *Ethical Questions and International NGOs: An Exchange between Philosophers and NGOs*. Springer Science and Business Media, 193–206.

Lindstrom, J. and Henson, S. (2011). *What Does the Public Think, Know and Do about Aid and Development? Results and Analysis from the UK Public Opinion Monitor*. Brighton: Institute of Development Studies.

Lough, B. and McBride, A. (2014). Navigating the boundaries of active global citizenship. *Transactions*, 39(3), 457–469.

McCloskey, S. (2011). Rising to the challenge: Development education, NGOs and the urgent need for social change. *Policy & Practice: A Development Education Review*, 12, 32–46.

Mendel, S. and Brudney, J. (2014). Doing good, public good and public value: Why the differences matter. *Non-profit Management and Leadership*, 251(1), 23–40.

Meynhardt, T. (2009). Public value inside: What is public value creation? *International Journal of Public Administration*, 32, 192–219.

Meynhardt, T., Gomez, P. and Schweizer, M. (2014). The Public value scorecard: what makes an organisation valuable to society? *Performance*, 6(1), 2–9, available online at www.alexandria.unisg.ch/229529/1/EY-Performance-Organization-valuable-to-society1.pdf (accessed 24 May 2016).

Moore, M. (1995). *Creating Public Value – Strategic Management in Government*. Cambridge: Harvard University Press.

Morfit, S. (2011). "AIDS is money": How donor preferences reconfigure local realities. *World Development*, 39(1), 64–76.

Munk, N. (2014). *The Idealist: Jeffery Sachs and the End of Poverty*. New York: Anchor Books.

National Trust (2006). *The Public Value of Heritage*, National Trust, available online at www.thetalkingwalls.co.uk/PDF/nationalTrust_valueOfHeritage.pdf (accessed 12 September 2016).

Nixon, M. (2014). *Creating Public Value: Transforming Australia's Social Services*, Ernst and Young, Australia (accessed 14 June 2016).

O'Dwyer, B. and Unerman, J. (2007). From functional to social accountability: Transforming the accountability relationship between funders and non-governmental development organisations. *Accounting, Auditing and Accountability Journal*, 20(3), 46–471.

Offenheiser, R. and Holcombe, S. (2003). Challenges and opportunities in implementing a rights-based approach to development: An Oxfam America perspective. *Nonprofit and Voluntary Sector Quarterly*, 32(2), 268–301.

Orgad, S. (2013). Visualizers of solidarity: organizational politics in humanitarian and international development NGOs. *Visual Communication*, 12(3), 295–314.

Osserwaarde, R., Nijhof, A. and Heyse, L. (2008). Dynamics of NGO legitimacy: How organising betrays core missions of INGOs. *Public Administration and Development*, 28(1), 42–53.

Oxfam (2015) *Annual Report 2014–2015*.

Oxford English Dictionary (2016), available online at www.oxforddictionary.com/definition/English/public (accessed 22 July 2016).

Plewes, B. and Stuart, R. (2007). The pornography of poverty: A cautionary fundraising tale. In D. Bell and J. Coicaud (eds), *Ethics in Action*. Cambridge: Cambridge University Press, 23–37.

Rawlence, B. (2016). *City of Thorns: Nine Lives in the World's Largest Refugee Camp.* London: Portobello Books.

Smirl, L. (2015). *Spaces of Aid: How Cars, Compounds and Hotels Shape Humanitarianism.* Chicago: University of Chicago Press.

Srinivas, N. (2009). Against NGOs?: A critical perspective on nongovernmental action. *Nonprofit and Voluntary Sector Quarterly*, 38(4), 614–626.

Stoddard, A. (2003). *Humanitarian NGOS: Challenges and Trends.* Humanitarian Policy Group (HPG) Briefing, 12, Overseas Development Institute.

Stoker, G. (2006). Public value management: A new narrative for networked governance? *American Review of Public Administration*, 36(1), 41–57.

Tallon, R. and McGregor, A. (2014). Pitying the third world: towards more progressive emotional responses to development education in schools. *Third World Quarterly*, 35(8), 1406–1422.

Tembo, F. (2003). The multi-image development NGO: an agent of the new imperialism? *Development in Practice*, 13(5), 527–532.

United Nations (1945). *Charter of the United Nations,* available online at www.un.org/en/sections/un-charter/un-charter-full-text/index.html (accessed 12 September 2016).

United Nations Human Rights Declaration (1948). *The Universal Declaration of Human Rights,* available online at www.ohchr.org/EN/UDHR/Documents/UDHR_Translations/eng.pdf (accessed 22 July 2016).

Vestergaard, A. (2013). Humanitarian appeal and the paradox of power. *Journal of Critical Discourse Analysis*, 10(4), 444–467.

Weidenbaum, M. (2009). Who will guard the guardians? The social responsibility of NGOs. *Journal of Business Ethics*, 87, 147–155.

Wood, G. (1997). States without citizens: the problem of the franchise state. In D. Hulme and M. Edwards, (eds.), *NGOs, States and Donors: Too Close for Comfort?* Houndmills, UK: Macmillan, 79–92.

15 The public value of the sociology of religion[1]

John D. Brewer

Introduction

This chapter is a contribution to the theorisation of public value social science by the application of this approach to a long established field, the sociology of religion, which can be intellectually renewed by adopting a public value perspective. In my definition of public value social science (Brewer, 2013; 2014), it undertakes research that is undergirded with an explicit ethical responsibility to our shared humanitarian future by addresses issues that enable social science to respond to twenty-first century global challenges and threats. While this approach is explained further and expanded on later in the chapter, the chapter's principal argument is that the sociology of religion has weakened and marginalised itself by its obsession with secularisation to the point where it became the sociology of secularisation, and can be renewed and revitalised by the application of a public value approach. The re-entry of religion into the public sphere opens up the opportunity for sociologists of religion to practice public value social science. The chapter argues that a public value approach in the sociology of religion enables it to engage with some of the global challenges that threaten the future of humankind and for this subfield to move from the margins of sociology to the centre of public value social science.

Many branches of social science have dialogued with the term 'public' and have come to realise the need to occupy the public sphere in new forms of intellectual engagement and ethical commitment. The term public (and *publics*) has become the zeitgeist of reflexive modernity (Brewer, 2013, 2) because it raises fundamental questions of accountability but also moderates them with questions about responsibility. 'Public' not only defines sets of issues in which social scientists should be interested, it asks whose perspective on these issues they should consider the most important, causing us to reflect on to whom we feel answerable and responsible. This has encouraged many social science disciplines to shift from deploying a narrow professional discourse to engagement with publics in the civil sphere using vocabulary these publics can understand. Many branches of social science have responded in their own way to these issues by the formulation of approaches like 'public sociology', 'public anthropology' and 'public international relations' (see, for example, Burawoy, 2005; Lawson, 2008). This chapter is intended as a challenge to sociologists of religion to reflect on them also.

The argument is premised on the idea of the return of religion to the public sphere. This re-entry into the public sphere, or what US academics term as the return 'the public square' (see Audi and Wolterstorff, 1997) – terms that are indistinguishable

– has occurred irrespective of the real decline in religious practice in many parts of the world. In this respect, the sociology of religion has benefited from the emergence of what social scientists outside the sub-field call individualisation (see Beck, 2010). Individualisation results in people in late modernity being able to construct the meaning of their own lives as a reflexive project within loosened structural constraints, giving them a new sense of 'self'. Individualisation has impacted on religion in two ways that once marked the distinctiveness of the sociology of secularisation: a decline in religious observance and identification; and the importance of choice for those remaining believers when determining their preferred form of religiosity. Religiosity gets turned into a preference not a duty. But late modernity has paradoxically undermined the sociology of secularisation (this is a theme articulated well in Beck, 2010; Habermas, 2006; 2008; Micklethwaite and Wooldridge, 2009; Sievernich, 2003), giving us the terms 'post-secularity' and 'de-secularisation'. In now constructing the meaning of their own lives reflexively free from the constraints of tradition, institutions and structures, some individuals, groups and communities have brought religion back into the public square.

Most sociologists of religion therefore now give witness both to the growth of secularisation *and* to a growing public role for religion. It is with the re-emergence of public religion that sociologists of religion can gain a publicly recognised voice in the civil sphere and begin to articulate the public value of the sociology of religion by establishing the sets of issues it engages with and the publics to which it is answerable and responsible.

This chapter therefore proceeds in the following stages. First it specifies the growing significance of religion to the sets of issues that affect society's humanitarian future in the twenty-first century. Secondly it identifies the challenges this throws out to how sociologists of religion envision their role within the public sphere. Thirdly, it discusses various opportunities for public engagement by sociologists of religion, before describing some of the ways sociologists of religion are already entering the public square and impacting on public debate.

From the sociology of secularisation to the return of public religion

Social scientists have begun to take religion seriously again. Whilst sociologists of secularisation concentrated on the decline of the social significance of religion, many inter-disciplinary social scientists from outside the sociology of religion saw religion as an important process in explaining key aspects of late modern social life (for example, Beck, 2010, Habermas 2006, 2008; Calhoun et al., 2013). They benefit from *not* being sociologists of religion because they see beyond the limited range of concerns of this sub-discipline and envisage a potential for the study of religion that sociologists of secularisation cannot. While these figures are sometimes quarrelsomely dismissed (the idea of post-secularity, for example, has provoked a hostile reception from, amongst others, Gorski and Ates, 2008; Martin, 2011), other sociologists of religion have moved the boundaries of the sub-field and join in the celebration of the public role of religion. This in part goes to make up what Linda Woodhead (2014a), refers to as the 'new sociology of religion'. The return of public religion occurs, however, at the same time as which there is real decline in religious practice in many parts of the world. The return of public religion does not imply a return by the majority to the pews. The paradox of public religion in late modernity is that the pews remain empty. It is no longer the numbers of devotees that endow religion with social significance.

What are the reasons why 'god is back' (a term taken from Micklethwaite and Wooldridge, 2009)? The individualisation thesis within contemporary social theory is important to this. There are two lines of argument that explain the re-emergence of religion in the public sphere. One sees religion as a key social process embedded in the very social condition in late modernity; the other argues religious practice is wrapped up with the range of complex social problems that threaten the future of humankind in late modernity. These lines of argument are closely related but are distinguished for the sake of clarity here.

Individualisation theory is chief amongst those analytical accounts of the late modern social condition that argue for the revival of religion as a social process. Individualisation results in people in late modernity being able to construct the meaning of their own lives as a reflexive project within loosened structural constraints, giving them new opportunities, freedoms and choices. In arguing thus, Ulrich Beck is dealing with issues that have defined the social sciences from their inception with the emergence of modernity in the eighteenth and nineteenth centuries, but which he sees thrown into particularly high relief in what he calls the second stage of modernity. Late or second stage modernity is better characterised, he says, as reflexive modernity (also see Beck et al., 1994), in which the individual becomes the central unit of social life as a result of the loosened ties of tradition, institutions and structures, enabling people to self-steer or reflexively manage their own lives. Individuals thus come to live a life of their own choosing, and in so doing radically re-orientate and re-order society with the throwing off of constraints embedded in the collectivity and through the emphasis on personal choice and decision making. This means the collapse of the public-private distinction (Brewer, 2005), the domestication of the public sphere with a whole series of behaviours formerly reserved for the private sphere (Kumar and Makarova, 2008), and the deconstruction and fragmentation of the social structure.

It is a matter of intense theoretical debate just how loosened are the structural constraints in late modernity, and adherents from within the sociology of religion to the analytical ideas of Pierre Bourdieu (such as Wood and Altglas, 2010), for example, see structures as retaining more solidity than Beck implies. Nonetheless, even Altglas is forced to accept that individualisation has impacted on religion in two ways that once marked the distinctiveness of the sociology of secularisation: a decline in religious observance and identification as participation in institutional religion declines once people are free of traditional constraints; and the importance of choice for those remaining believers when determining their preferred form of religiosity. Religiosity gets turned into consumption not obligation as Davie (2015, 133) puts it. God isn't so much dead as turned into shopping or 'exoticism' (Altglass, 2014), 'floating forms of religiosity' like kabbalah classes, yoga and tree hugging.

But late modernity has paradoxically also undermined the sociology of secularisation. In now constructing the meaning of their own lives reflexively, people are making gods of their own choosing. Beck (2010) argues that religion as a social process is both empowered and disempowered by secularisation. Driven from its place at the centre of society, religion has passed its responsibilities to science or the state, enabling it to be religion and nothing else, reducing it to the indestructible human need for spirituality and belief in the transcendent free from institutional trappings (25).

By decoupling institutional religion from subjective faith, there has been a decline in institutional religion simultaneous with a rise of individual religiosity (40), because religion is now called on to be nothing more or less than belief in the transcendent. This results in the return of gods, but, as Beck's book title says, gods of our own choosing. There is a 'massive dissemination of religiosity' (29) but voluntarily so on the basis of the reflexive individual's need for spirituality; and in a de-institutionalised form that dissolves the territorial unity between religion, nation and society in favour of personal, individualised, do-it-yourself religion (43).

This is, of course, an essentially European denouement, for Beck is attuned to the widespread and popular arguments in the sociology of religion about the growth of Christianity in the Global South (on which see Brunn, 2015; Hunt, 2015) and to the emergence of religious pluralism in Europe as the decline in institutionalised Christianity co-exists with both the growth of Islam and do-it-yourself religion. It is for reasons like this that some have argued that religion has returned to the public square in the West on the back of the rise of Islam (Malik, 2007). This hints towards the second line of argument that explains the return of public religion.

Beck goes on to address the second line of argument into which the return of religion is embedded – that it addresses and is wrapped up in key issues fundamental to our humanitarian future. He emphasises one in particular. Global religious conflicts between the monotheistic world religions have generated a new type of tolerance whose goal is no longer 'religious truth' but peace (2010, 45). Reflexive modernity finds itself suspended between tolerance and violence. Institutionalised *in*tolerance of religious others comes up against cosmopolitan respect for what Boltanski (1999) calls the distant, marginalised other, the dissonance between which creates a public discourse that is no longer about religious truth but about the religious foundations and practice of peace, justice and tolerance. The expanding literature on religious peacebuilding proves this point, as key representatives of this literature deploy religious principles in debates about just and unjust peace (Philpott, 2012), the moral imagination needed by peace builders (Lederach, 2005), and the understanding of justice (Wolterstorff, 2008, 2013). Brewer and Hayes (2011, 10–12) make the point that transitional justice studies is now a place where theologians and sociologists of religion meet criminologists, lawyers and social scientists, and that some of the best work done on political forgiveness is from a religious perspective (for example, Amstutz, 2004; Shriver, 1995, Torrance, 2006; Volf, 2006).

However, the growth of religiously motivated organised violence in late modernity and the attendant rise in interest in peace is not the only global challenge that has promoted a focus on the return of religion to the public sphere. In her account of the role of religion in public life in Britain today, Davie (2015, 197–218) records the penetration of religion into law, particularly around balancing the conflicting legal demands between religious freedom and freedom of speech, as well as the relationship between religion and politics, ranging from the political engagements of religious practitioners to involvement in political campaigns and policy issues, and the role of religion in welfare and health care. This point will be returned to later, suffice here is to say that there is now widespread recognition in the sociology of religion of the public resurgence of religion (see Beckford, 2012, 6–8 for a review). Late modernity has created new risks and fears, new issues and citizenship engagements and demands, which are in turn, Sievernich (2003, 26) writes, 'productive of "religiosity"'. Bosetti and Eder also write that 'today religion is returning to the public sphere' (2006, 1);

hence, the now almost ubiquitous citation in the sub-field to Casanova's (1994) idea of the de-privatisation of religion.

This has enabled a small number of sociologists of religion to also see that in some very limited and special cases religion never really left the public domain (see for example Arweck and Beckford, 2012; Beckford, 2012, 6–8; Davie, 2015, 197–218; Harrington, 2007). These are instances like Northern Ireland, where religion was wrapped up in conflict (see Brewer, 2015), or for specific ethnic groups, who in migrating took their religion with them, or in resurgent world religions, like Islam, or enduring forms of religiosity, like the many fundamentalisms (for reviews of these religious developments globally see Brunn, 2015; Hunt, 2015; in Britain see Woodhead and Catto, 2012). This is also the reason why the idea of 'collectivistic religion' (Jakelic, 2010) still has currency in the sociology of religion in restricted spaces and can co-exists happily as a concept alongside that of the 'deconstructed church' (Marti and Ganiel, 2014).

From public religion to public value

I wish to take this shift toward revitalised public religion for granted and will not argue with sociologists of secularisation about justifying the public role of religion. I want instead to offer an invitation to those sociologists of religion that accept religion's public face concerning one implication that follows from religion's re-entry into the public domain: namely, for sociologists of religion to intellectually renew their sub-field by locating it at the centre of public value social science. This can be done by gaining a publicly recognised voice in the civil sphere and beginning to articulate the sets of issues to which the sociology of religion is relevant. I have taken some time to document the return of religion to the public square because this needs to shadow another revival: re-occupancy of the public sphere by sociologists of religion. In short, there is a need for more public voices in the field of the sociology of religion based on issues of inequality, injustice, democratic deficiencies, violence and discrimination about which sociologists of religion can speak out loudly. I suggest that by adopting the approach of public value social science, sociologists of religion can intellectually renew their sub-discipline so that it becomes more than the sociology of secularisation, and thereby shift it towards more mainstream currents in social science and away from the backwater which the sociology of secularisation places it in.

To do this I must first explain how I characterise the public value of social science (see Brewer, 2013; 2014). I argue that social science is a public good in its own right because it cultivates through its subject matter, teaching, research and its civic engagements a moral sentiment and sympathetic imagination toward each other, including toward the distant and 'strange' other. This moral sentiment enables us to see each other as social beings, capable of living only in groups as social animals, with a shared responsibility for the future of humankind. In the past, some forms of social science – in particular the sociology of secularisation – approached human nature in ways that distanced, destabilised, or disabled people as voluntaristic agents. Literally, it enervated and 'dehumanised' them. This is ironic in the case of the sociology of secularisation given that human dignity is such a central emotion and one directly relevant to the 'emotional regimes' or 'feeling rules' garnered by religious practice. Secularisation theory, however, dissipates the idea of the religious agent, by rendering their emotional performances and discourses as socially insignificant and of no interest as a topic for the sub-field in face of the declining number of believers, although the idea of religious emotions is vastly under-developed in social science generally. Some work is emerging nonetheless by anthropologists of religion (Davies, 2011) and sociologists of religion (Riis and Woodhead, 2010; Soulen and Woodhead, 2006). However, practising the kind of public value social science I envisage here is itself a moral commitment which 'rehumanises' social science. In particular it helps in recognising human dignity as one of the key religious emotions (on god and human dignity see Soulen and Woodhead, 2006).

The humanising role of social science is further enhanced because another aspect of its public value is that it makes people aware of themselves as comprising a society, helping in the development and dissemination of key social values that make society possible – social sensibilities like trust, empathy, altruism, tolerance, compromise, compassion, and senses of belonging – as well as by assisting in society's ongoing betterment and improvement (see Brewer, 2013, 151–158). The social sciences help us understand the conditions which promote and undermine these sensibilities and identify the sorts of structural conditions, public policies, behaviours and relationships that are needed in culture, the market and the state to ameliorate their absence and restore and repair them. Public social science therefore not only generates information about society, it is the medium for society's future reproduction and sustainability. Put another way, it is the way in which society can find out about itself and in so doing regenerate the idea of society itself for the twenty-first century.

It is my contention here that the sociology of religion is a key sub-discipline in public value social science. This is because when no longer neutered by the obsession with secularisation, we can see the growing significance of religion to the 'big issues' that affect our humanitarian future in the twenty-first century. Let me give just five examples of 'big issues' in which religion, religious belief or religious practice is centrally implicated, some of which have been referred to above:

- the link between religion, conflict and organised violence;
- the role of religion in transitional justice, statecraft, diplomacy and international affairs, and with it the growth of religious peacebuilding;
- the implications of religious freedom as a human right, resulting in two tensions: a) between freedom of religion and freedom of expression in the context of multi-cultural diversity and religious plurality, and b) between equality and the tendency to be intolerant to religious others;
- the centrality of religion to the ethical issues surrounding various medical practices and advances, concerning birth, life and death, and with it religion's incursion into intimate decisions around marriage, gender, sexuality and the body; and finally
- the role of religion in responding to the global democratic deficit.

My intention here is not to document how religion is positioned in relation to these big issues but to show that by their centrality as global concerns, religion has been drawn back into the public square. The return of public religion is not therefore solely premised on analytical assumptions in individualisation theory about the nature of the late modern social condition, which can be challenged theoretically, but as an empirical argument based on observation of current affairs. Perhaps only the last issue requires further explanation.

What I mean by the global democratic deficit is the involvement of faith-based NGOs in filling the void left by the withdrawal, unwillingness or inability of governments to provide state services, such as welfare, education, medical care, emergency and disaster aid, ethical trading, legal and social justice and the like. This democratic deficit ought to be expected in non-democratic states in the Global South with weak economies, but could hardly have been anticipated now also in some democratic ones in the richer Global North. Under the impulse of neo-liberal ideas about rolling back the state, small government, the narrowing of the welfare state, and the deregulation and privatisation of public services, notionally democratic societies evidence a democratic deficit in which religion has almost returned to its medieval form as hospitality for the poor and sick (on the role religion and religious-based NGOs play in Britain in service provision of welfare and medical care see Davie, 2015, 206–214; Dinham and Jackson, 2012; Johnsen, 2012).

In drawing attention to these sets of issues my point is that in dealing with them, public religion has returned with a vengeance. The 'big issues' that have provoked its return are 'public' mostly because they are controversial, contested, unpredictable, and problematic. Ironically, they are often referred to as 'wicked problems', meaning not that they involve moral judgements, but that they are profound and threatening to our humanitarian future (on the origins of the term 'wicked problem', see Head and Alford, 2013).

There is another dimension to the controversial nature of twenty-first century public religion that is relevant to my contention about the need for a resurgent public value sociology of religion. The paradox of late modernity's post-secularity is that when religion does penetrate into these issues, the public reaction is contradictory. Some people object to the involvement of faith communities, the comments of religious leaders and to the public presence of religion on the grounds, as Habermas (2006, 15) says, 'from their viewpoint, religion no longer has any intrinsic justification to exist'. Nye and Weller (2012) document a series of conflicts and controversies over religion in Britain, using them as a lens into charting the extent of religious change in post-war Britain, pointing to the end of religious monopoly and dominance, and the shift in what is controversial about religion from Catholicism, to new religious movements and now to Islam (2012, 49–50). The ending of Christianity's religious monopoly is shown in two ways: a decline in respect and tolerance for the interventions of Christian leaders; and the rise of religious pluralism in which commentary by Christian leaders in the public square now competes with leaders of other faiths and of none. Comments from church leaders on current affairs, for example, especially when critical of government policies, are often ridiculed. Successive Archbishops of Canterbury have clashed with Conservative Party governments in Britain and despite the Church of England being the established church and regardless of the common observation that the Conservative Party is the Anglican Church at prayer (which in terms of congregants is the case, but not so for Anglican leaders according to research undertaken by Woodhead, 2014b), several Conservative prime ministers attacked them for their policy pronouncements, which were thought to be anti-government (in the case of Mrs Thatcher see Woodhead, 2012, 10–11). Religious spokespeople are therefore in a bind: the public voice of religious practitioners is silenced while the public presence of religion is amplified. Individualisation, with its impetus toward rejection of institutional religion, is undermining the bearers or carriers of faith at the very time when faith is becoming more publicly significant.

We are thus at a paradoxical moment in public religion. Secularisation is proceeding apace while religion is becoming ever more socially significant, but this public role provokes ambivalence or controversy. This is a huge problem for faith communities in knowing what to say publicly about which sets of issues, when to say it, and how, without heaping abuse on their own heads from a public that has in the main rejected institutional religion. But we are also at a paradoxical moment in the sociology of religion.

The public value of the sociology of religion

I argue in this section that the current moment offers a huge opportunity for sociologists of religion, for sociologists of religion are not subject to the same constraints on exercising a public voice as faith practitioners. This moment throws out a challenge to how sociologists of religion see their role within public value social science, and proffers the prospect of a re-invigorated sociology of religion. Let me list the various opportunities which make-up what I contend is the public value of the sociology of religion:

- to engage in teaching and research that results in better understanding of the social significance of religion, its opportunities and constraints, and its strengths and weaknesses;
- to engage in teaching and research that deals with the 'big' global issues threatening our humanitarian future in the twenty-first century as they involve religion and faith;
- to disseminate research findings to the public as much as to academic audiences;
- to develop a public voice that places sociologists of religion in the public sphere, speaking about the key global issues to which religion and faith pertain;
- to engage in and help to shape public debate about these 'big issues';
- to develop strategies of civic engagement, locally, nationally and globally, in which sociologists of religion, collaborate with all the stakeholders in their research, in developing co-produced knowledge that speaks into real life situations of ordinary people;
- to engage in teaching and research that seeks to improve the lives of ordinary people regardless of whether they are faith carriers or not.
- to continue to articulate the public relevance of religion and faith, and thus also the sociology of religion, to the inter-personal and public policy problems of the twenty-first century world.

Three observations are necessary here. First, engagement in the public square in the above manner will help in the reversal of the marginalisation of the sociology of religion within mainstream social science. This marginalisation is deeply felt by sociologists of religion themselves, for while in numerical terms there are very many who describe themselves as such – in the British Sociological Association, the religion study group is second only to medical sociology in its size – the perception in mainstream social science that the sub-field is a one-point discipline (namely, secularisation) downgraded the sociology of religion (see Davie, 2014, 446). This marginalisation is out of kilter with the founders of social science in the eighteenth and nineteenth centuries, when religion was made into one of the premier social processes. However, on the basis of my arguments, the revival of the sociology of religion can occur in tandem with that of public religion through the practice of public value.

Second, these engagements do not impugn the secular nature of the sociology of religion, which long ago shifted from being faith-based and, in effect, a form of 'religious sociology' (on religious sociology and its clashes with the sociology of religion in early Britain and the USA see Brewer, 2007). One of the reasons why Bourdieu (2010) criticises sociologists for their entry into the realms of religion and politics is because their claims, he argues, are not based on sociological research but on their religious, ethical or political 'social positioning'. I disagree fundamentally if by this Bourdieu means social scientists have no ethical responsibilities, a view in support of which one can cite Max Weber, who criticised value-based articulation at the same time as which emphasising the importance of social scientists having ethical responsibilities (see Brewer, 2014, 128–130). But I agree with Bourdieu when he says sociologists of religion do not have to have religious beliefs to be publicly engaged. My precepts of public value are ethical but not religious, although the ethical pluralism that undergirds them can include religious frameworks. In this respect, interestingly, it seems anecdotally that many of the most publicly vocal sociologists of religion are also people with personal faith despite Bourdieu's views (for example, Peter Berger, Andrew Greeley, Linda Woodhead and Gladys Ganiel). These precepts, however, do not require faith for them to be implemented. They are imbued with scientific and professional rigour. What they permit, however, is for sociologists of religion *as social scientists* to think ethically and act politically in the twenty-first century when analysing the public face of religion and its impact on our humanitarian future.

A third observation is that there are several sociologists of religion who are already seizing these opportunities, resulting in a number of important initiatives in which sociologists of religion are involved that reflect on aspects of public debate. I am not suggesting there is no such thing as public sociology of religion; I am inviting more of it. While there are many social sciences – feminism, political sociology, inequality studies, to name a few – that have a public voice, I wish to mention briefly three examples from within the sociology of religion, covering one case each from Great Britain, Northern Ireland and the United States. Examples like this can be found aplenty; and my choice is highly selective. I believe, however, that with the return of religion to the public sphere, public value social science can become the default position in the sociology of religion. In outlining them my purpose is largely descriptive to illustrate the potential.

The British example is Linda Woodhead, professor of the sociology of religion at Lancaster University and head of the Religion and Society research programme and recipient of a Queen's honour (MBE) for public service in 2013. She is a prolific writer but it is her work with the Westminster Faith Debates series that I wish to cite. Woodhead co-founded the Westminster Faith Debates in 2011 with the Rt. Hon. Charles Clarke, former Home Secretary. They were originally created to publicise findings from the Religion and Society programme, but have since become an annual series.

Three features distinguish the Westminster Faith Debates that serve them well as an example of the public value of the sociology of religion. First, they address some of the key challenges facing our humanitarian future today but do so from a religious perspective. Annual themes have been, in order, religion and public life, religion and personal life, global religious trends, and religion, violence and cohesion. Second, they involve interaction between academics, practitioners, politicians and policy-makers, ensuring that the debates work at the interface of theory and practice. They have brought researchers into conversation with prominent figures in public life like Tony Blair, Richard Dawkins, Rowan Williams, Polly Toynbee, Trevor Phillips and Shirley Williams, amongst others. Third, the debates are disseminated publicly in order to provoke and encourage civic discourse. Podcasts are made and distributed online, and remain accessible on the website of the Westminster Faith Debate series (see http:// faithdebates.org.uk/). The debates have been picked up and covered by BBC radio, *The Guardian, The Independent, The Times,* the *Evening Standard* and other UK and international media. The series has its own blog in order to make use of new forms of social media.

This has given Woodhead an unusually high public profile for a sociologist of religion. She is a regular commentator and writer in the public sphere, writing for *The Tablet* magazine, *The Guardian* and *The Observer* newspapers. She has appeared on BBC 1's The 'Big Questions' and BBC Radio 4, including news programmes like 'PM', the popular 'Thought for the Day' series, as well as on 'Analysis', 'Thinking Allowed' and Women's Hour. She has written a major report for the Equality and Human Rights Commission and was invited to the World Economic Forum summit in Davos in 2013.

I can illustrate my point about public value by referencing as my second example, the work of Gladys Ganiel in Northern Ireland. Admittedly this is on a smaller scale than Great Britain, which befits the size of the place, but while part of the United Kingdom, Northern Ireland has conflicts all of its own which raises its profile. Ganiel is also a prolific writer but I cite only her engagement with the Hope and History campaign (see www.hopeandhistory.com/) in dealing with the legacy of the conflict and in informing public debate about how Northern Ireland might become reconciled to its past. A small group of churchmen and women from all the main Christian denominations in Northern Ireland developed a policy statement featuring a wonderful alliteration – history, humility and hope – in which Ganiel was closely involved, both in scripting it and disseminating it. The statement was formulated at the start of the Haass-O'Sullivan talks that took place in late 2013, and was designed deliberately to have a public effect. The Haass-O'Sullivan talks were established by the Irish, British and US governments to assist local political parties in Northern Ireland to negotiate an agreement over how to deal with the past. The Hope and History campaign was a consciously religious contribution to this debate, linking history (the past) to hope (the future) but in an attitude of humility given the many victims who suffered in the violence and in the light of everyone's responsibility for the past. The statement was quite short and featured a brief elaboration of the alliteration – what humility, history and hope mean in Northern Ireland.

The statement had a deliberately religious hue, calling for prayer, and encouraging all people of faith to commit to it. The statement was endorsed by all four main denominations and undertook a campaign to garner signatories in support. At the last count in June 2015, they had 1540 signatories. They have a webpage and a Facebook account to popularise the statement. They have 878 likes of Facebook. They have since developed an advent liturgy as a focus on humility, history and hope for use by ordinary people in local neighbourhoods in the period leading up to Christmas. It is called 'Into the Neighbourhood' to reinforce the ambition of engagement in the public square (see www.hopeandhistory.com/wp-content/uploads/2013/09/HOPE-AND-HISTORY-ADVENT-LITURGY-final.pdf).

Ganiel herself has a public profile in Northern Irish political debate. She runs her own website 'Building a Church Without Walls' (see www.gladysganiel.com/), intended for people interested in the contribution of Christian debate to current affairs in Northern Ireland and other post-conflict societies. Ganiel is also a regular blogger about current affairs on popular social media sites dealing with Northern Irish current affairs, like SluggerO'Toole (see http://sluggerotoole.com/), and she is a regular commentator on BBC Northern Ireland radio and television programmes and in the press, including *The Church of Ireland Gazette, Time Magazine*, and the *Irish Times*. She has also appeared on BBC Radio 1's 'Faith Diary Report'. This represents another excellent example of a sociologist of religion using their public voice in a variety of media in the public square based on expertise developed from within the sociology of religion.

My last example is from the United States. David Little, a research fellow at Georgetown University's Berkley Center, is a leading authority on the history of religious freedom, ethics and human rights, and in the area of religion and conflict resolution. Until retirement in 2009, he was TJ Dermot Dunphy Professor of the Practice in Religion, Ethnicity and International Conflict at Harvard Divinity School and as an Associate at the Weatherhead Center for International Affairs at Harvard University. The work of his I wish to cite as demonstrating public value, however, comes from his time as senior scholar in religion, ethics and human rights at the United States Institute of Peace (USIP). USIP was at the forefront of interest in the US in religious peacebuilding and received a multi-million dollar grant to explore the role of religion in conflict resolution and peacemaking. Little directed the programme and was lead author on very many reports, policy briefings and consultative papers for successive US Administrations. The USIP now offers skills-training to religious actors and leaders so that they can serve effectively as peacebuilders in local, national, and international arenas. The emphasis in on fostering peaceful inter and intra-faith coexistence, respect for religious difference, and collaboration on shared problems across religious identity divides. It offers research, analysis, and toolkits to explore the role of religion in conflict and peacebuilding and to counter and prevent violent extremism that has a religious dimension. Little is a prolific writer, on topics like political Islam, Ukraine, and Sri Lanka, and from 1996 to 1998 he was member of the Advisory Committee to the US State Department on Religious Freedom Abroad.

Conclusion

Public value social science is motivated by an ethical responsibility to engage with the major global challenges that threaten the future of humanity and to show the relevance of social science to the promotion of the social good. The sociology of religion can be part of this agenda by changing its focus away from the sociology of secularisation toward the significant role public religion plays in many of the twenty-first century's global challenges. This chapter has tried to illustrate the public value of the sociology of religion and demonstrate how sociologists of religion can reposition themselves and their sub-discipline by practising public value social science. In the three examples cited above for example, David Little demonstrates how it is possible to engage upwards to work with governments, foreign policy advisors and policy makers, people who are normally kept at arm's length by social scientists in preference for engaging downwards to organic grassroots groups. Ganiel shows how sociologists of religion can engage downwards and speak into local circumstances, affecting issues that are vitally important locally but which penetrate little outside. Woodhead exemplifies the national and international engagements that sociologists of religion can develop on the basis of their research and interests. They disseminated their research outside the ivory tower, engaged different sorts of publics, locally, nationally and globally, and dealt with the 'big issues' in a way that utilised their expertise as sociologists of religion but for the purposes of engaging a public audience. They articulated the public relevance of religion and faith, and thus also the sociology of religion, to the interpersonal and public policy problems of the twenty-first century world. That is, they represent the opportunity to develop public value sociology of religion.

Note

1 A shorter version was delivered as the Plenary Address to the European Sociological Association's Sociology of Religion Network Conference 'Religion in the Public Domain', Belfast City Hall, 3 September 2014.

References

Altglas, Veronique (2014) *From Yoga to Kabbalah*. Oxford: Oxford University Press.
Amstutz, Mark (2004) *The Healing of Nations*. Lanham MD: Rowman and Littlefield.
Arweck, Elisabeth and Beckford, James (2012) Social Perspectives. In Linda Woodhead and Rebecca Catto (eds), *Religion and Change in Modern Britain*. London: Routledge, 352–372.
Audi, Robert, and Wolterstorff, Nicholas (1997) *Religion in the Public Square*. Lanham MD: Rowman and Littlefield.
Beck, Ulrich (2010) *A God of Our Own*. Cambridge: Polity.
Beck, Ulrich, Giddens, Anthony and Lash, Scott (1994) *Reflexive Modernisation*. Stanford: Stanford University Press.
Beckford, James (2012) Public Religions and the Postsecular: Critical Reflections. *Journal for the Scientific Study of Religion* 51(1), 1–19.
Boltanski, L. (1999) *Distant Suffering*. Cambridge: Cambridge University Press.
Bosetti, G. and Elder, K. (2006) Post-Secularism: A Return to the Public Sphere. *Eurozine* 17 August.
Bourdieu, Pierre (2010) Sociologists of Belief and Beliefs of Sociologists. *Nordic Journal of Religion and Society* 23(1), 1–7.
Brewer, John (2005) The Public and the Private in C Wright Mills's Life and Works. *Sociology* 39, 661–677.
Brewer, John (2007) Sociology and Theology Reconsidered: Religious Sociology and the Sociology of Religion in Britain. *History of the Human Sciences* 20, 7–28.
Brewer, John (2013) *The Public Value of the Social Sciences*. London: Bloomsbury.
Brewer, John (2014) Society as a Vocation: Renewing Social Science for Social Renewal. *Irish Journal of Sociology* 22(2), 127–137.
Brewer, John (2015) Northern Ireland: Religion, Religiosity and Politics in a Changing Society. In Stephen Hunt (ed.), *Global Handbook of Contemporary Christianity*. Leiden: Brill, 208–227.
Brewer, John and Hayes, Bernadette (2011) Post-Conflict Societies and the Social Sciences: A Review. *Contemporary Social Science* 6(1), 5–18.
Brunn, Stan (2015) *The Changing World Religion Map*. New York: Springer

Burawoy, Michael (2005) For Public Sociology. *American Sociological Review* 70, 4–28.

Calhoun, Craig, Mendieta, Eduardo and van Antwerpen, Jonathan (2013) *Habermas on Religion.* Cambridge: Polity.

Casanova, Jose (1994) *Public Religions in the Modern World.* Chicago: University of Chicago Press.

Davie, Grace (2007) Vicarious Religion: A Methodological Challenge. In Nancy Ammerman (ed.), *Everyday Religion.* Oxford: Oxford University Press, 21–36.

Davie, Grace (2010) Vicarious Religion: A Response. *Journal of Contemporary Religion* 25(2), 262–266.

Davie, Grace (2014) The Sociological Study of Religion: Arrival, Survival, Revival. In John Holmwood and John Scott (eds), *The Palgrave Handbook of Sociology in Britain.* London: Palgrave, 437–458

Davie, Grace (2015) *Religion in Britain.* Chichester: Wiley Blackwell.

Davies, Douglas (2011) *Emotion, Identity and Religion.* Oxford: Oxford University Press.

Dinham, Ada, and Jackson, Robert (2012) Religion, Welfare and Education. In Linda Woodhead and Rebecca Catto (eds), *Religion and Change in Modern Britain.* London: Routledge, 272–294.

Gorski, Philip and Ates, A. (2008) After secularisation? *Annual Review of Sociology* 34(1), 55–85.

Habermas, Jurgen (2006) Religion in the Public Sphere. *European Journal of Philosophy* 14(1), 1–25.

Habermas, Jurgen (2008) *Between Nationalism and Religion,* Cambridge: Polity.

Harrington, Austin (2007) Habermas and the 'Post-Secular' Society. *European Journal of Social Theory* 10(4), 543–560.

Head, B. and Alford J. (2013) Wicked Problems: Implications for Public Policy and Management. *Administration and Society* 45(3), 1–29.

Hunt, Stephen (2015) *Global Handbook of Contemporary Christianity.* Leiden: Brill

Jakelic, Slavica (2010) *Collectivistic Religions.* Farnham: Ashgate.

Johnsen, Sarah (2012) The Role of Faith-Based Organisations in Service Provision for Homeless People. In Linda Woodhead and Rebecca Catto (eds), *Religion and Change in Modern Britain.* London: Routledge, 295–298.

Kumar, K. and Makarova, A. (2008) The Portable Home: The Domestication of Public Space. *Sociological Theory* 26, 324–343.

Lawson, G. (2008) For a Public International Relations. *International Political Sociology* 2, 17–35.

Lederach, John Paul (2005) *The Moral Imagination.* Oxford: Oxford University Press.

Malik, A.B. (2007) Take Me to Your Leader: Post-Secular Society and the Islam Industry. *Eurozine* 23 April.

Marti, G. and Ganiel, G. (2014) *The Deconstructed Church.* Oxford: Oxford University Press.

Martin, David (2011) *The Future of Christianity.* Farnham: Ashgate.

Micklethwaite, John and Woodridge, Adrian (2009) *God is Back.* London: Penguin.

Nye, Malory and Weller, Paul (2012) Controversies as a Lens on Change. In Linda Woodhead and Rebecca Catto (eds), *Religion and Change in Modern Britain.* London: Routledge, 34–54.

Philpott, Daniel (2012) *Just and Unjust Peace.* Oxford: Oxford University Press.

Riis, Ole and Woodhead, Linda (2010) *A Sociology of Religious Emotion.* Oxford: Oxford University Press.

Shriver, D. (1995) *An Ethic for Enemies.* Oxford: Oxford University Press.

Sievernich, Michael (2003) Pastoral Care for the Sick in a Post-Secular Age. *Christian Bioethics* 9(1): 23–37.

Soulen, Kendall R. and Woodhead, Linda (2006) *God and Human Dignity.* Grand Rapids MI: Eerdmans

Torrance, A. (2006) *The Theological Grounds for Advocating Forgiveness in the Socio-Political Realm*. Belfast: Centre for Contemporary Christianity.

Volf, M. (2006) *The End of Memory*. Grand Rapids, MI: Eerdmans.

Wolterstorff, N. (2008) *Justice*. Princeton, NJ: Princeton University Press.

Wolterstorff, N. (2013) *Journey Towards Justice*. Grand Rapids, MI: Baker Academic.

Wood, Mathew and Altglas, Veronique (2010) Reflexivity, Scientificity and the Sciology of Religion: Pierre Bourdieu in Debate. *Nordic Journal of Religion and Society* 23(1), 9–26.

Woodhead, Linda (2012) Introduction. In Linda Woodhead and Rebecca Catto (eds), *Religion and Change in Modern Britain*. London: Routledge, 1–33.

Woodhead, Linda (2014a) Linda Woodhead on the New Sociology of Religion. Social Science Bites, Sage, available online at www.socialsciencespace.com/2014/11/linda-woodhead-on-the-new-sociology-of-religion/ (accessed 3 June 2015).

Woodhead, Linda (2014b) 'What British People Really Believe About Society, Politics and Religious Institutions. *Modern Believing* 55(1), 59–67

Woodhead, Linda and Catto, Rebecca (eds) (2012) *Religion and Change in Modern Britain*. London: Routledge.

16 Employers' organisations and public value[1]

Leon Gooberman and Marco Hauptmeier

Introduction

Employers in the UK often engage in collective action to coordinate economic activities and employment relations with the aim of gaining advantages for their businesses. They can do this through membership of employers' organisations. Research by the authors identified 447 employers' organisations active throughout the UK (Gooberman et al., 2017c). Employers' organisations are not monolithic and the variety of organisational types reflects the many different reasons behind association. They range from more traditional organisations bargaining collectively over pay and conditions, through those that seek to influence government policy through lobbying, to those that focus on providing a range of business-related services to their membership. Of particular interest are new types of employers' organisations, such as employer forums that focus on individual topics such as disability, inclusivity or corporate social responsibility.

The concept of public value has been applied to various forms of organisations (e.g. Moore, 1995; 2013; Bozeman, 2002; Meynhardt, 2009; 2015) but these have often been within the public sector. Limited research has been carried out on public value within private sector or non-profit bodies. Our chapter contributes to the discussion on public value by exploring the extent to which the concept can be extended to employers' organisations, bodies formed from public and/or private sector employers.

Our research question is: to what extent do employers' organisations contribute towards public value creation across workplaces and society? We identified two groups of organisations that contribute, drawing on definitions (e.g. Benington, 2011; Bozeman, 2007; Budd, 2014) that go beyond Moore's (1995) conception of such value as a summary equivalent of private value in corporate management. These broader conceptions provide theoretical approaches that enable us to assess the public value contribution of EOs; hybrid organisations that organise democratically, depend on membership subscriptions and commercial income, and draw their members from either public or private sector employers (or both).

The first group was comprised of employer forums (Bowkett et al., 2017; Demougin et al., 2018). These promoted equality, diversity and corporate social responsibility within their employer members through voluntary self-regulation, creating public value in the workplace. Employer forums also influenced governments to adapt policy, creating public value for society. The other group of employers' organisations was those involved in collective bargaining with unions (Gooberman et al., 2018 forthcoming). These organisations delivered public value within the workplace through their joint creation of regulated and equally available pay and employment conditions. The mechanisms by which employers' organisations contributed towards public value creation varied. Employer forums independently created value through promoting voluntary self-regulation, while forums and bargaining employer organisations produced value through interactions with, respectively, governments and unions.

However, we also find that many employers' organisations did not contribute towards the creation of public value. For example, it is difficult to identify public value creation within the lobbying carried out by many employers' organisations, which often focused on advancing the narrow particularistic interests of their membership. Despite these variations, we find that some employers' organisations, as collective organisations across the public and private sectors, contributed towards public value creation across workplaces and society.

Following this introduction, we begin by discussing the theoretical and empirical challenges surrounding public value, before outlining our approach to sourcing empirical data. We then discuss how our data can be interrogated to expose employers' organisation activity within the broad sphere of public value. The subsequent sections outline our empirical findings and use two employers' organisations as examples that illustrate our overall findings in more detail. We then assess how employers' organisations contribute towards the creation of public value, before concluding.

Applying public value to employers' organisations

Public value is part of a public management approach that stresses how networked and collaborative governance can address public challenges to deliver values beyond efficiency and effectiveness. However, public value is a debated concept, and any attempt to apply it to employers' organisations highlights three questions, namely: what is public value; can public value be measured; and, can public value be applied to employers' organisations?

What is public value?

There is a 'marked lack of consensus in the academic community about what constitutes public value' (Welch et al., 2015: 132), with literature generally being formed around three accounts. The first (Bozeman, 2002) features a normative perspective equating society's identification of agreed rights, duties and privileges to public value. This account proposes that while such rights, duties and privileges are contested within democratic debate, a relative consensus can be identified from constitutions, legislative mandates, policies, literature reviews, opinion polls, and other formal and informal sources (Beck Jorgensen and Bozeman, 2007). The second account (Moore, 1995; 2013; 2014) defines public value as a summary equivalent of private (economic) value in corporate management, measured against the extent to which a set of public (social) values are realised at reasonable economic, political and social costs. Such public values are defined as desirable outcomes relating to the quality of individual and collective life for citizens (Moore, 2013). While the former account proposes that societal consensus drives the formation of public value, the latter argues that such value emerges from public managers' orchestration of policy development through a 'strategic triangle'; comprising outcomes that are administratively feasible and can win support from government and the public.

The third account (Meynhardt, 2009; 2015) is very different from the first and the second. It is non-prescriptive and psychologically based, proposing that public value emerges from the values characterising the relationship between an individual and society. This definition of public value operates across four dimensions, namely; moral-ethical, political-social, utilitarian-instrumental and hedonistic-aesthetical. The public value that an individual attaches to an experience is based on the extent to which the experience satisfies his or her basic needs. This satisfaction is assessed against each of the four dimensions through a 'public value scorecard' that identifies and assesses public value creation in different situations across the public, private and non-profit sectors to 'better understand their role in a given social context' by 'acting as a dialogue tool about mutual interdependencies in pluralist societies' (Meynhardt, 2015, 168). Bryson et. al. (2015) noted linkages between these theoretical strands. For example, if public managers create public value through producing that which is valued by the public as per Moore's approach, such value can be assessed against more specific public values including those produced by Bozeman's societal criteria or those linked to Meynhardt's more psychological approach. Overall, public value enables managers and society to explore how values can be delivered by organizations acting within the public space, defined as the web of institutions, rules and knowledge held in common by citizens and held in trust through government and public institutions (Benington, 2011).

How is public value measured?

The lack of consensus on public value is reflected by differing approaches to its measurement. First, public value mapping (Welch et al., 2015) identifies public value as that which exists at a policy or societal level. It then assesses whether public value failures have occurred; maps relationships between values before linking public value to market failure or success. Second, Moore's focus on public managers is reflected by his public value account that uses a public value scorecard to assess the implementation of government policy. This scorecard incorporates cost-side accounts such as financial and social costs, as well as benefit side accounts such as the achievement of collectively valued social outcomes. Finally, other approaches exist that are non-prescriptive and based on individuals' views, as opposed to assessing institutional outcomes. These include Meynhardt's (2015) public value scorecard, drawn from individuals' ranking the value of an experience along each of the four dimensions identified as being linked to public value. Despite the existence of these approaches, detailed assessments of public value creation are few in number (Williams and Shearer, 2011), while the nature of employers' organisations present a challenge to the application of public value.

Can public value be applied to employers' organisations?

Employers' organisations are in many senses hybrid organisations in that they can draw their members from either public or private sector employers (or both). They are organised along democratic principles but are dependent on membership subscriptions and commercial income, not government funding. Employers' organisations are concerned with issues that matter to their membership, including those linked to work and employment. Activities can include collective bargaining, lobbying governments and aspects of private voluntary regulation.

Limited research has been carried out on public value within private sector or non-profit bodies. These have often been regarded by the literature as being little more than 'alternative providers' in efforts to diminish the state, or 'service agents' for the delivery of government policy (Osborne and McLaughlin, 2004). Despite the lack of research, public value can encompass the private sector, with Beck Jorgensen and Bozeman (2007) arguing that 'public values and public value are not the exclusive province of government, nor is government the only set of institutions having public value obligations' (373–374).

The applicability of the three approaches to public value outlined earlier to different types of organisations is varied. Moore's public value scorecard is aimed at measuring value created by the public sector and has limited relevance to hybrid bodies such as employers' organisations, while the application of Bozeman's approaches has been largely restricted to governments' activities such as science policies (Welch et al., 2015). However, Meynhardt's public value scorecard has been applied within private sector or hybrid organisations but its application requires data gathering across either; workshops and surveys; workshops and online assessments; large-scale surveys, or; in-depth interviews within each organisation or social media analysis (Meynhardt, 2015, 160). While this approach could be used for assessing individual organisations' public value contribution, there are practical difficulties in collating data sufficient to assess the collective contribution made by the 447 organisations in our database.

Given these difficulties, do any approaches exist within the literature that could be tested against our data to enable our research question to be answered? The only other organisational type with a primary focus on the employment relationship, unions, has been considered by the public value literature (Budd, 2014). Given the shared foci of both organisational types, albeit from different perspectives, Budd's (2014) approach is useful starting point for laying out a framework of the type of public value that could be created by employers' organisations. Importantly, Budd identified how work, and therefore its regulation, goes beyond purely economic significance and is also important for 'our individual and collective material and psychological health and for the quality of democracy and other social relations' (2014, 513). This finding enabled the activity of institutions linked to work to be included within the broad parameters of public value.

Against this background, Budd (2014) identified two types of public value created by trade unions. Importantly, both types were linked to public value definitions (e.g. Bozeman, 2007) that move beyond economic value, as well as Benington's definitions of social/cultural value ('adding value to the public realm by contributing to social capital, social cohesion, social relationships, social meaning and cultural identity, individual and community wellbeing') and political value ('adding value to the public realm by stimulating and supporting democratic dialogue') (2011, 45).

The first type of public value created by trade unions was the creation of publicly valuable outcomes in the workplace, most notably through collective bargaining structures. These structures standardised employment terms and conditions within or across workplaces through agreements between unions and employers. Agreements often led to positive outcomes such as wage premiums and the ability of employees to seek redress through formalised grievance procedures. The second type of public value was defined as publicly valuable outcomes in democratic societies. These outcomes emerged from unions' role outside the workplace such as their pursuit of common interests in the social and political arenas through techniques such as lobbying governments.

Our research question is: to what extent do employers' organisations contribute towards public value creation across workplaces and society? Martin and Swank (2008) argued that collective employer bodies are generally business organisations providing commercial services for individual members. If this is always the case, then the large number of employers' organisations identified by our empirical research means little. However, the literature (e.g. Budd, 2014; Meynhardt, 2015) suggests that public value can be created by private and semi-private organizations, as well as by collective organisations (unions) linked to the employment relationship. Our task is therefore to interrogate our data to identify activities carried out by employers' organisations before assessing if these activities contribute towards public value creation.

Data and methodology

Our data are drawn from two sources. The first is our database of employers' organisations (Gooberman et al., 2017b, 2017c). While previous definitions of employers' organisations focus on those active within collective bargaining (Traxler, 2004), we used a broader approach that takes account of the shifting patterns of collective organisation. For an organisation to be included in our database, it had to fulfil three criteria, namely: a membership base comprised predominantly of employers, or of individuals acting as employers; its members must pay subscription charges; and, it must be active within collective employment relations and/or human resource management (Gooberman et al., 2017b). Collective employment relations activity includes participation within collective bargaining structures or the provision of linked advisory services, while human resource management activity might include advising members on health and safety, employment law, equality or recruitment. We used these criteria to identify 447 employers' organisations.

We then developed a proforma comprising 60 questions to be answered for each employers' organisation across: membership composition and type; internal governance structures; the services and activities provided to, and on behalf of, their members and; the extent and type of relationships with government, agencies and unions. The database was mainly populated from employers' organisation websites although some other sites were used. These were: the government's Certification Office, which holds data on employers' organisations active in collective bargaining; the Financial Analysis Made Easy database containing information on turnover and dates of origin for some employers' organisations; and, the parliamentary website identifying employers' organisations that had appeared before select committees.

The second data source comprises 98 interviews with representatives of employers' organisations and experts that have working relationships with employers' organisations. Initial interviewees were selected to represent a cross section of organisational types, such as peak, sectoral and regional bodies. Subsequent interviewee selection was also based on snowball sampling, where initial interviews were randomly selected and subsequent interviewees were those suggested in earlier interviews. Interviews were semi-structured and pursued similar themes to those in the proforma, while they were recorded and transcribed. Although data was not generated for all of the employers' organisations in our database, these were used to provide a deeper understanding of key activities identified by our database and to assist with the compilation of the two organisational examples.

Our method featured a three-stage approach. First, we interrogated our database as to the type of activities carried out by employers' organisations across employment relations and human resource management to identify those that are most common. We then examined the extent to which such activities can be considered as delivering public value, drawing on approaches and concepts outlined by Budd (2014), Bozeman (2007) and Benington (2011). Second, we examined two examples of employers' organisations; the Business Disability Forum (BDF) and the Engineers Employers' Federation (EEF). These were chosen as there is little detailed research on how employers' organisations provide collective services and these bodies are suitable for illuminating the constructs within public value theory. They provide an interesting contrast, with the EEF representing the more traditional type of organisation that pivoted away from collective bargaining towards a greater range of member services, while the BDF is one of a new type of employers' organisations, a cross-sectoral employer forum that focuses on a single social issue such as disability or corporate social responsibility. Finally, we discuss our findings to aid future empirical research and theoretical development.

However, our methodology has some limitations. The first limitation arises from our use of data drawn from the internet. As the 'public face' of organisations, websites serve three audiences: they provide information to existing members; attract new members by highlighting services, and; represent EOs to the public. While the risk of reputational damage implies that EOs are unlikely to systematically present inaccurate information on their websites, there can be no guarantee that such data provide a full overview of all their activities. We have addressed this limitation by triangulating data with interviews, but practical considerations meant that it was not possible to interview representatives of all the EOs listed in our database. The other limitation is our focus on EOs, as opposed to their members (e.g. individual employers). Such a research focus, either in the form of a member survey or interviews with employers, would provide further insight into employer organisations' contribution toward public value creation.

Findings

What is the scale, structure and sectoral composition of employers' organisations?

Data on membership numbers were available for 357 employers' organisations (80 per cent of those in the database). These organisations had a combined membership of over 750,000 employers. However, the scale of membership varied widely from just 6 to some 195,000, with a median of 170. Only 14 had more than 5,001 members, with seven having more than 10,000. Examples of large employers' organisations included the Federation of Small Businesses (c. 195,000) and the Confederation of British Industry (c. 190,000) (Gooberman, Hauptmeier and Heery, 2017d). Employers' organisations generally had a chair, a governing body to guide and oversee activity, an annual general meeting and a document that set out their governance. Democratic governance was common, with evidence that a governing body is in place existing for 384 bodies (86 per cent of those surveyed). There was evidence of membership elections to governing bodies for 267 organisations (70 per cent of those with a governing body evidenced).

The database also allocated each employers' organisation to a Standard Industrial Classification code, based on an identification of the sector in which its members were most likely to operate. All but three per cent of employers' organisations focused on one sector, although the small number of cross sectoral employers' organisations often had very large memberships, with examples including the Federation of Small Businesses and the Confederation of British Industry. Employers' organisations were most likely to be active in manufacturing (some 13 per cent), construction (some 11 per cent) and wholesale and retail trades (some 11 per cent). They were least likely to be active within accommodation and food service (some 2 per cent), agriculture, forestry and fishing (some 2 per cent), financial and insurance services (some 4 per cent) and information and communications (4 per cent). Most employers' organisations represented private sector employers, with 371 (83 per cent) of all organisations surveyed generally drawing their membership from such employers. However, while organisations representing the public sector are fewer in number and in membership, their reach was likely to be greater given the size of their members' employment bases in areas such as the National Health Service and local government.

What are their activities?

The most common activity was lobbying with the aim of influencing government policy, with 327 employers' organisations (73 per cent of those surveyed) stating that they had some relationship with government, whether responding to consultations, issuing policy statements or other types of lobbying activity (Gooberman et al., 2017b). However, developing and sustaining political relationships was often dependent on informal and private communication. Despite this, some quantitative data were available, as the House of Commons' committees depended on a steady flow of expert witnesses to be examined by MPs carrying out subject specific inquiries. Our analysis of parliament's website showed that 140 employers' organisations (31 per cent of those surveyed) were questioned by MPs' committees over the past decade (ibid.). The topics on which they were questioned covered a very wide range with, as examples, the Consumer Credit Trade Association being questioned on payday loans and the Association of Labour Providers being queried on modern slavery.

The second most common activity was the provision of training, with 309 organisations (69 per cent of those surveyed) reporting such activity (ibid.). However, provision ranged from the delivery of a small number of seminars to larger training schemes with external accreditation. Schemes with some external accreditation, often from bodies such as City and Guilds, was provided by 163 employers' organisations, although the number of people receiving training was usually relatively small given that employers' organisations rarely have a prominent role within the UK's fragmented systems of vocational training.

The third most common service was the provision of member codes of conduct/best practice benchmarking (ibid). Codes were used by 232 employers' organisations (52 per cent of those surveyed), often with disciplinary provisions if the code was not followed. However, codes were generally restricted to narrow customer relationship issues, as opposed to any broader conceptualisation of public good. For example, the British Vehicle Renting and Leasing Association's code set out customer service standards which all members must follow as a condition of membership, with serious breaches potentially resulting in expulsion (British Vehicle Renting and Leasing Association, 2011, 5). However, 11 employers' organisations were employer forums with a focus on single issues across diversity, equality and corporate social responsibility (Gooberman et al., 2017c). These focused on raising employment standards within their employer members, often through using a voluntary standards-based approach based around best practice benchmarking.

The fourth most common service was the provision of advice on employment law, provided by 208 employers' organisations (47 per cent of those surveyed) (Gooberman et al., 2017b). In general, employers' organisations tended to offer their subscribing employer members a helpline operated by an outsourced commercial provider. For example, the Federation of Small Businesses offered a legal helpline in cooperation with law firms while its Legal Protection Insurance Policy also covered legal representation within Criminal Prosecutions, Employment Tribunals and Personal Injury (Interview with Federation of Small Businesses representatives, Belfast, 3.6.2015; Interview Federation of Small Businesses representative, London, 2.3.1015). The fifth most common type of activity was support within recruitment and selection, with 146 employers' organisations (33 per cent of those surveyed) being active within recruitment and selection, generally through providing a vacancy advertising service.

While participation in some type of collective workplace bargaining was once a primary activity for collective employer organisations, the declining coverage of collective bargaining over recent decades means that this was no longer the case. As a result, the provision of services related to collective employment issues was restricted to 59 employers' organisations, 13 per cent of the total. At the same time, the extent of their involvement varied widely, with 43 being signatories to some type of joint agreement regulating pay and working conditions (Gooberman et al., 2017c).

Overall, most employers' organisations generally provided a relatively narrow range of human resource management and employment relations services, with relatively few providing support across all, or most, of the activities listed above.

Employers' organisations and public value

We use two criteria (Budd, 2014) to explore whether activities carried out by employers' organisations can be considered as creating public value. The first is the extent to which such activities contributed to public value in the workplace, defined as 'levelling the [. . .] playing field between organizations and employees and thereby providing working conditions that respect human dignity' (510). The second is how workplace issues can have 'spillover effects into the broader socio-political realm' (511), often through workers and unions from multiple workplaces pursuing common interests in the political and social arenas. Table 16.1 applies both criteria to the activities described in the previous section to identify those that might involve contributions to public value creation by the organisations in our database.

The activities that have least potential for public value creation are those that focus on creating economic value within individual employer members. For example, employment law services aim to reduce the risks associated with individual

Table 16.1 Employers' organisation activities and public value

Type of activity	Potential for contribution to public value creation?	
	Workplace	Democratic society
Lobbying	In part	In part
Training	Yes	Yes
Code of conduct/best practice benchmarking	In part	No
Employment law	No	No
Recruitment and selection	No	No
Collective bargaining	Yes	Yes

employment relationships, such as the financial implications of staff grievances. Conversely, those activities that have greater potential for contributing to public value creation are those that produce outcomes that go beyond narrow conceptions of economic value (e.g. Gooberman et al., 2017b). These findings relate to how the public value approach proposes that organisations seeking to create such value should move beyond implementation of policy and institutional norms, instead seeking out opportunities to make significant improvements to the lives of the public.

Can the four activities identified as having potential for contributing to public value creation (lobbying, training, private voluntary regulation and collective bargaining) be considered as doing so?

First, lobbying inevitably reflected the vast variety of collective interests represented by employers' organisations. For example, we analysed the representation of 20 major employers' organisations to one House of Commons Select Committee (the Innovation, Universities, Science and Skills Committee) between 1997 and 2009. We found that these employers' organisations collectively made 42 appearances before the committee across twenty subjects, ranging from: engineering and physical sciences based innovation; the work of the Engineering and Physical Sciences Research Council; and, putting science and engineering at the heart of government policy. Identifying public value within large volumes of lobbying activity depends on an assessment of the extent to which the employers' organisation is seeking to influence government policy so as to make improvements to the lives of the public. In some cases, this will overlap with the collective interests represented by the employers' organisation, with examples including the desire of manufacturing employers' organisations to see greater levels of investment in education or the Business Disability Forum pressurising governments to improve legislative protection for disabled workers. However, this is not always the case. Lobbying carried out by employers' organisations often refers to egoistic particularistic interests (Olson, 1982) and has little relevance to public value either in the workplace or more broadly in democratic society.

Second, while training can often be considered valuable by the public, such activity carried out by employers' organisations should not be considered as creating significant levels of public value. Importantly, employers' organisations are not providers of large-scale training and did not generally take part in government-led training initiatives. Examples such as the EEF with its focus on apprenticeships are rare, and most employers' organisations confined themselves to training activities that are small in scale and limited in breadth. While some employers' organisations did produce public value through their provision of training, the overall volume of value produced was unlikely to be significant.

Third, while codes of conduct were common, they generally related to purely commercial manners. However, the best practice benchmarking carried out by the 11 employer forums identified within our database presented a more nuanced picture, with such regulation acting both to adjust the working conditions of employees within employer members as well as being used as examples of best practice to influence government policies (Gooberman et al., 2017a, 2017c). Such activity often constituted a type of voluntary regulation of the labour market. They were often new organisations, with their rise reflecting the increasingly hybrid nature of employment relations in the UK, in that they simultaneously sought to influence employment policy and practice of both governments and their employer members within their specific topic. Their promotion of best practice within employment relations qualified them as being active in promoting public value.

At the same time, while employer forums were few in number, their reach was wide given the profile of their membership base. For example, we examined the membership composition of five organisations (Opportunity Now; the Business Disability Forum; Race for Opportunity; Employers for Carers; and, the Employers Network for Equality and Inclusion), finding that they had a collective membership of 499 employers, 73 per cent of whom had more than 1,000 employees. A small number of these were defined as 'champion members' or equivalent and were often very large companies (see Table 16.2).

Fourth, collective bargaining enables negotiations over wages and employment conditions to be conducted between representatives of employers and employees. While coverage has fallen over recent decades, 23 per cent of the workforce is still covered by collective bargaining agreements, equating to 16 per cent of those in the private sector and 44 per cent in the public sectors in the United Kingdom (Van Wanrooy et al., 2013). The remaining systems of collective bargaining display great diversity. In some activities such as parts of the construction industry, traditional joint agreements between employers' organisations and unions remain in place that control pay and conditions (Interview with Electrical Contractors' Association representative, 2.3.15). However, other industries have seen a structural shift with the level of bargaining changing from industry to workplace, while public sector bargaining is often conducted by Pay Review Bodies, a collective method within which employers' organisations play a largely procedural role (Bach et al., 2009). Despite such changes, the participation of 59 employers' organisations

Table 16.2 Employer forums' champion members (or equivalent)

Opportunity Now	Race for Opportunity	Business Disability Forum	Employers Network for Equality and Inclusion	Employers for Carers
Barclays	Army	Allianz	B & Q	Sainsbury's
BT	Deloitte	BBC	Ernst & Young	Centrica
GlaxoSmithKline	Google	Ernst & Young	NHS Employers	Metropolitan Police
Home Office	Mitie	HSBC	RBS	
PwC	Santander	NHS Scotland		
Royal Air Force	Shell	Santander		

within collective structures represented public value generation, given that the system acted to ensure some degree of equality in relation to employment terms and conditions, while providing arbitration mechanisms to resolve collective workplace disputes.

Individual employers' organisations and public value – examples

We now examine two employers' organisations in more detail as examples to illustrate our database findings. After outlining an organisational profile for each, we consider their activities across lobbying, codes of conduct and collective bargaining to consider whether these can be considered as creating public value.

Business Disability Forum

The Employers' Forum on Disability was founded in 1986 and obtained independent charitable status in 1991. Known as the Business Disability Forum since 2012, its aim is to 'make it easier and more rewarding to do business with and employ disabled people' and had some 300 members employing some 20 per cent of the UK's workforce (Business Disability Forum, 2016). The Business Disability Forum's relationship with its employer members had three characteristics. The first was voluntary, reflecting how it provided services that seek to raise employment standards, but participation was voluntary and there are no non-compliance sanctions. The second was value-adding; while the services had a social element, they were justified to the employer members using a business case argument. The final was corporate citizenship; member participation within the Business Disability Forum was promoted by stressing the importance of self-regulation. It had no role within collective bargaining.

Most employers' organisations focused their lobbying and influencing activity upwards on governments and their agencies, but the Business Disability Forum also sought to influence downwards by changing the employment related behaviour of its members. As a result, the organisation's key service offering was its Business Disability Standard, incorporating surveys that measure disability management within participating members. While performances remained confidential, they were used to assess performance on a gold/silver/bronze basis (interview with Business Disability Forum representative, London, 7.7.15). This acted to encourage participating organizations to continually review and improve their working culture and practices in relation to disabled people, thus promoting and publishing self-regulation by business (Gooberman et al., 2017b; 2017c).

When carrying out more traditional lobbying activities such as that focusing on influencing government behaviour, the Business Disability Forum tended not to present itself as representing the interests of its members, but rather as a knowledgeable organisation in its own right. Since its foundation, Business Disability Forum continually campaigned for the strengthening of disability law in the UK. Its key role in influencing the state during its early years was in relation to the Disability Rights Taskforce advising on the development of the Disability Discrimination Act.

More recently, it lobbied the government over the replacement of the Disability Discrimination Act with the 2010 Equality Act to ensure that the principles contained within the earlier act were retained. It also appeared as a witness before a number of House of Commons committee inquiries. For example, it provided written and verbal evidence to the Work and Pensions Committee Inquiry on the government's reform of the Access to Work Scheme that funds adjustments for disabled people. As part of this process, it structured a consultation that gave the Department of Work and Pensions an insight into the practical objections from disabled people and business (interview with Business Disability Forum representative, London, 7.7.15). Finally, the depth of its relationship with government was reflected by its representation as panellists at every regional event of the government's Disability Confident campaign. Overall, the Business Disability Forum was heavily involved in the creation of public value through its activities, given its focus on corporate citizenship and in furthering self-regulation so as to achieve better outcomes for disabled people in the workplace.

EEF – The manufacturer's organisation

The EEF was founded in 1896 as the Engineering Employers' Federation to represent the interests of engineering employers in relation to unions (Wigham, 1973). For most of the twentieth century, its main activity was collective bargaining. By the late 1970s, its national wages and hours agreement with the Confederation of Shipbuilding and Engineering Unions was the largest such agreement in the UK. However, this agreement collapsed in 1989, forcing the EEF to reinvent itself as an organisation focused on lobbying governments and providing services to its membership, which stood at some 2,000 employers in 2014 (Certification Office, 2014). The EEF moved beyond its initial focus on engineering to represent employers across most UK manufacturing sectors, rebranding itself as the Manufacturers' Organisation to reflect the changing focus of its operation. It made no effort to regulate the employment relationship, either on a formal basis through collective bargaining or an informal one such as voluntary codes of conduct.

Membership was no longer based on an assessment of the balance of power between employers and employees and the linked role of the employers' organisation, but instead on the individual advantages that can be gained through lobbying and access to services. Recent activity included pressing for legislation to impose a two year back-stop on back holiday claims and lobbying in favour of the UK remaining within the European Union (Gooberman et al., 2017b). It had a policy and representation team with, for example, specialist employment and skills lobbyists in place, as well as those based in Brussels. It used a range of lobbying methods in recent years. First, it responded to government consultations, reacting to 45 within employment and skills over a two-and-a-half-year period prior to early 2015, as well as submitting to the Low Pay Commission. Second, other documents were produced to influence government, such as skills surveys used to highlight areas of deficiency. Third, staff met regularly with government officials to press their case. Fourth, the EEF hosted round tables where government ministers meet with members and finally, the EEF was a frequent witness for House of Commons inquiries (interview with EEF representative, London, 5.2.2015). Overall, the organisation considered itself to be 'very clearly and deliberately apolitical', taking care to maintain contacts with opposition politicians and their advisors as well as those in government (interview with EEF representative, London, 4.11.2014).

The other key component of the EEF was member-based services. One of its most important services encompassed employment issues such as tribunals and discrimination claims, staffed by some ninety HR and legal advisors (interview with EEF representative, London, 5.2.2015). Other services included consultancy across health and safety, learning and development as well as climate change issues. Within training, it delivered some 10,000 training days annually across a broad range of qualifications, including at its apprenticeship training centre in the West Midlands. Although the EEF advised on employment issues, it did not produce codes of practice that sought to raise standards and did not advise its members on how their businesses should be run. Overall, while the EEF's involvement in training provision and some lobbying activities may have included public value elements, it had only a limited involvement in the production of public value and instead focused on supporting the commercial and regulatory interests of its membership.

Discussion

Our research question is: to what extent do employers' organisations contribute towards public value creation across workplaces and society? We begin by noting the lack of consensus as to what constitutes public value (Welch et al., 2015) and the limited empirical research on public value creation by the private, or semi-private, sector. Some existing approaches to public value mapping (e.g. Moore, 2014) focus on the public sector, while others (e.g. Meynardt, 2015) depend on data yet to be collected on employers' organisations. However, an assessment of public value created by the other organisational type active within the employment relationship, unions, has been carried out (Budd, 2014).

Employers' organisations exist to advance the collective interests of their employer members, providing services across topics linked to the employment relationship. However, in most cases, their conceptualisation of such services was narrow and reactive. Services were designed to generate economic value for their members through reducing the legal and operational risks that can accrue from individual employment relationships. Such services included the provision of legal helplines, advisory services and other forms of support such as assistance with employment tribunals (Gooberman et al., 2017b). Lobbying covered a range of issues over and above employment relations but it is difficult to identify coherent strands of public value being created by such activity, with lobbying often focusing on advancing the narrow particularistic interests of their collective membership. Despite this, there will be occasions where these interests overlap with broader public interests. Examples could include ensuring more state investment in vocational education, with employer organisations assisting public managers to create public value as set out by Moore (1995; 2013; 2014), although further research is needed to identify such trends within the broad mass of lobbying activity.

However, this focus on narrow particularistic interests is not true for all employers' organisations. We identify two groups of organisations that contribute towards public value creation, drawing on definitions of public value (e.g. Benington, 2011; Bozeman, 2007) that go beyond Moore's (1995) conception of such value as a summary equivalent of private value in corporate management. These broader theoretical conceptions enable us to test, for the first time, the extent to which these hybrid organisations contribute toward public value creation. The first group of employers' organisations that contribute towards public value creation is employer forums. While these are few in number, their scope and scale is significant. In terms of scope, they actively sought to promote equality, diversity and corporate social responsibility within their employer members through promoting forms of voluntary self-regulation, creating public value in the workplace. Employer forums also influenced governments to change their policy and practice (Gooberman et al., 2017a), acting to create public value for society as a whole in a way that is often similar to those of unions (Budd, 2007). In terms of scale, a significant proportion of employees in the UK work for organisations that are members of these organisations, with many of the UK's largest firms and public-sector organisation being active.

The other group of employers' organisations active in providing public value comprised those involved in collective bargaining. While the scope of such bargaining is greatly diminished when compared to previous decades, it still has some significance within the public sector and elements of the private sector (Brown et al., 2009). While the extent to which bargaining outcomes constitute a normative consensus as per Bozeman's (2007) definition is contested within democratic debate, it is reasonable to conclude that some employers' organisations are delivering public value within the workplace. They do this through their joint role with unions in creating regulated and equally available pay and employment conditions, as well as arbitration structures to resolve differences between employer and employees. Finally, the governance of most employers' organisations could also generate public value in line with Benington's definition of political value as 'supporting democratic dialogue' (2011, 45), given that the use of democratic structures acts to promote democratic values throughout their employer members.

Conclusion

We find that some employers' organisations, as collective organisations across the public and private sectors, contribute towards the creation of public value across individual workplaces and society. Employer forums independently create value through promoting voluntary self-regulation, while forums and bargaining employer organisations produce value through interactions with, respectively, governments and unions. Our findings demonstrate how the concept of public value creation can be extended to include hybrid organisations active within employment relations.

However, our findings constitute only a first step into the previously unexplored terrain of public value production by employers' organisations. We do not attempt to identify the volume of public value created by employers' organisations either independently or jointly with unions or governments, as their under-researched nature mean that data are limited. Future research could address this gap by carrying out in-depth empirical studies on individual employers' organisations, potentially making use of Meynhardt's (2015) public value scorecard to measure the extent and volume of public value creation.

Note

1 Parts of this chapter, in particular the empirical data, draws on work published by the authors (Gooberman, Hauptmeier and Heery, 2017a, 2017b, 2017c, 2017d, 2018 forthcoming).

250   *L. Gooberman and M. Hauptmeier*

References

Bach, S., Givan, R. and Forth, J. (2009). The Public Sector in Transition. In Brown, W., Bryson, A., Forth, J. and Whitfield, K. (eds), *The Evolution of the Modern Workplace*. Cambridge: Cambridge University Press.

Beck Jorgensen, T. and Bozeman, B. (2007). Public values: an inventory. *Administration & Society*, 39(3): 354–381.

Benington, J. (2011). From private choice to public value? In Benington, J. and Moore, M. (eds), *Public Value: Theory and Practice*. Basingstoke: Palgrave Macmillan, 31–51.

Bowkett, C., Hauptmeier, M. and Heery, E. (2017) Exploring the role of employer forums – the case of Business in the Community Wales. *Employee Relations*, 39(7): 986–1000.

Bozeman, B. (2002). Public value failure: When efficient markets may not do. *Public Administration Review*, 62(2): 145–161.

Bozeman, B. (2007). *Public Values and Public Interest: Counterbalancing Economic Individualism*. Washington, DC: Georgetown University Press.

British Vehicle Leasing and Rental Association (2011). *Code of Conduct*. London.

Budd, J. (2014). Implicit public values and the creation of publicly valuable outcomes: The importance of work and the contested role of labour unions. *Public Administration Review*, 74(4): 506–516.

Brown, W., Bryson, A. and Forth, J. (2009). Competition and the retreat from collective bargaining. In Brown, W., Bryson, A., Forth, J. and Whitfield, K. (eds), *The Evolution of the Modern Workplace*. Cambridge: CUP.

Bryson, J.M, Crosby, B.C. and Bloomberg, L. (2015). Discerning and Assessing Public Value: Major Issues and New Directions. In Bryson J.M., Crosby, B.C. and Bloomberg, L. (eds), *Public Value and Public Administration*. Washington, DC: Georgetown University Press, 1–24.

Business Disability Forum (2016). About us. Available online at www.businessdisabilityforum. org.uk/about-us/ (accessed 12 December 2017).

Certification Office (2014). Annual Return, EEF. Available online at www.gov.uk/government/uploads/system/uploads/attachment_data/file/480564/255E_2014.pdf

Demougin, P., Gooberman, L., Hauptmeier, M. and Heery, E. (2018) A New Form of Voluntarism – Private Regulation through Employer Forums. Manuscript. Cardiff.

Gooberman, L., Hauptmeier, M. and Heery, E. (2017a). Countervailing Power and the Evolution of Employers' Organisations in the United Kingdom. Manuscript. Cardiff.

Gooberman, L., Hauptmeier, M. and Heery, E. (2017b). Employer Interest Representation in the United Kingdom. *Work, Employment and Society*, published online first.

Gooberman, L., Hauptmeier, M. and Heery, E. (2017c). A typology of contemporary employers' organisations in the UK. *Economic and Industrial Democracy*, published online first.

Gooberman, L., Hauptmeier, M. and Heery, E. (2017d). The Unexpected Survival of Employer Collective Action in the UK. Manuscript. Cardiff.

Gooberman, L., Hauptmeier, M. and Heery, E. (2018 forthcoming) The decline of Employers' Associations in the UK, 1976 to 2014. *Journal of Industrial Relations*.

Martin, C-J. and Swank, D. (2008). The political origins of coordinated capitalism: business organizations, party systems, and state structure in the age of innocence. *American Political Science Review*, 102(2): 181–198.

Meynhardt, T. (2009). Public value inside: what is public value creation? *International Journal of Public Administration*, 32(3-): 192–219.

Meynhardt, T. (2015). Public Value: Turning a Conceptual Framework into a Scorecard. In Bryson, J.M., Crosby, B.C. and Bloomberg, L. (eds), *Public Value and Public Administration*. Washington, DC: Georgetown University Press, 147–169.

Moore, M. (1995). *Creating Public Value: Strategic Management in Government*. Cambridge, MA: Harvard University Press.

Moore, M. (2013). *Recognizing Public Value*. Cambridge, MA: Harvard University Press.

Moore, M. (2014). Public value accounting: establishing the philosophical basis. *Public Administration Review*, 74(4): 465–477.

Osborne, S.P. and McLaughlin, K. (2004). The cross-cutting review of the voluntary sector: where next for local government-voluntary sector relationships. *Regional Studies*, 38(5): 573–582.

Olson, M. (1982). *The Rise and Decline of Nations: Economic Growth, Stagnation, and Social Rigidities*. New Haven: Yale University Press.

Traxler, F. (2004). Employer associations, institutions and economic change: a cross-national comparison. *Industrielle Beziehungen*, 11(1/2): 42–60.

Van Wanrooy, B., Bewley, H., Bryson, A., Forth, J., Freeth, S., Stokes, L. and Wood, S. (2013). *The 2011 Workplace Employment Relations Study First Findings*. London.

Wigham, E.L. (1973). *The Power to Manage: A History of the Engineering Employers' Federation*. London: Springer.

Williams, I. and Shearer, H. (2011). Appraising Public Value; Past, Present and Futures. *Public Administration*, 89(4): 1367–1384.

Welch, J., Rimes, H., and Bozeman, B. (2015). Public Value Mapping. In Bryson, J.M., Crosby, B.C. and Bloomberg, L. (eds), *Public Value and Public Administration*. Washington, DC: Georgetown University Press, 131–146.

17 Public value creation through the lens of women's entrepreneurship

Shandana Sheikh and Shumaila Yousafzai

Public value creation beyond public management

Conceptually, the concept of public value (PV) refers to the value that affects the community or people; the benefits that accrue to the people because of an activity, program or initiative. The notion of public value (PV) has been widely discussed in the literature but mostly in the context of public management, policy or politics. While the government has a significant role as the guarantor of public values, it is not the sole contributor towards public value creation (Jørgensen and Bozeman, 2007). As scholars suggest, Public value is deeply rooted in society and culture, in individuals and groups, and not just in government (Melchior and Melchior, 2001 in Jørgensen and Bozeman, 2007, 374). Hence, in a complex and changing environment, policymakers, public managers, and private, voluntary and informal community sectors must interact to create PV that its recipients perceive as valuable (Bryson et al., 2017).

Scholars have defined PV as "an emergent management paradigm that goes beyond the market-oriented view of public management and offers a broad framework to assess the challenges to management caused by network governance" (Stoker 2006: 42), and as a concept that encompasses a strategic framework for public service and reforms (Benington, 2005). While such approaches to studying PV may strengthen the democratic processes, but they do not ensure the authenticity of the value created i.e., they do not ensure that public managers will create value that addresses the needs, challenges and problems of the people for whom it is created. A focus on public policies, implementation of those policies, public outcomes and performance may thus limit the scope of PV creation in the hands of the public alone and present dangers in assessing public value creation.

The Strategic framework (Moore, 1995) views public managers as creators of PV, responsible for articulating, legitimizing and authorizing public value. Moore's framework puts major responsibility for PV creation in the hands of public managers,[1] viewing them as explorers who with others, seek to discover, define and produce public value" (Moore, 1995: 20–21). This view is criticized as it views Public Value creation only through the lens of the Public Managers and thus ignores all other actors who may be involved in the production and the receipt of such value. Moreover, while this perspective on public value holds public managers accountable for striking a balance between what is doable and what is authorized, it may not be achievable, since it ignores other actors who may have a role in PV creation. In line with this criticism, Benington (2009, 233) discusses PV as part of a *public sphere*: "a democratic space which includes, but is not co-terminus with, the state within which citizens address their collective concerns, and where individual liberties have to be protected". Therefore, public value is a concept that extends beyond the public and thus adds value to all the actors who are part of the public sphere. This suggests that public value is not just governmental i.e. relating solely to the public. Instead, it is a complex link between the individual and the society through a varied network of relationships (Jørgensen and Bozeman, 2007, 373). Value creation is thus the value of the networks or the relationships between different actors within the public sphere that co-create/produce value.

In view of the above, in this paper we argue that a holistic understanding of PV is developed when PV is studied from the *creator's* and the *recipient's* perspective. From the creator's perspective, this entails a debate as to whether creation of PV is limited to public management (the government), whose responsibility is to carry out activities that are in the interest of the public managers or whether PV extends to parties who create value that also benefits the people. Alternately, one may discuss the possibility of a third perspective, wherein PV is co-created by both the public and the people in the public sphere. If value relates only to how it is perceived by the people who are affected by it, it must be created with them, keeping in mind their needs and problems and adding value that addresses those needs. Thus, if public creators of value fail to create value that is perceived as valuable in the public sphere, people themselves may take the creators' role and produce PV through other activities. This further initiates a discussion concerning whether the private sector and individuals have any role in creating PV, whether they can be entrepreneurs of public value, considering that they are part of the public sphere and are affected by it.

This argument connects well with Bryson et al. (2017), who highlights the importance of entrepreneurial spirit, strategic action and leadership in producing and promoting PV. With regards to the public sector, middle managers have been viewed as most significant entrepreneurial people and an important source of initiating entrepreneurial ideas (Borins, 2000, 500; Morris and Jones, 1999, 83). However, while public managers may be acknowledged as entrepreneurs of value for initiating activities that benefit the people, entrepreneurial firms and individuals are not well recognized as creators of PV even though they may initiate activities that contribute to value creation at multiple levels and for multiple actors in the public sphere (Edwards et al., 2002). Moreover, value created from activities of public managers may not result in positive value outcomes for the public, i.e. the people at whom value is targeted. Supporting this view, Meynhardt refers to value creation in the context of public entrepreneurship as a mechanism of creating value for the public (Meynhardt, 2009). This entails an efficient management of the activities that create value and an evaluating process to realise the consequences of social problems. Public value management therefore involves entrepreneurial ideas that are co-produced with the citizens, who are directly or indirectly impacted by the value outcomes of these ideas. This involves active engagement and dialogue with all stakeholders in an effort to develop entrepreneurial ideas with multiple actors across institutional boundaries (Meynhardt, 2008, 459 as cited in Meynhardt et al., 2012).

We suggest that being part of the public sphere and affected by it, entrepreneurs can use their entrepreneurial activity to promote a social cause and create multiple forms of value that impact everyone in the public sphere (Benington, 2011). We also argue that the extent of this value is affected by the entrepreneur's *capabilities*, the *task environment* in which the entrepreneur operates, and the value being created. Our position reflects the individual or private arbiters of value who may not be operating primarily for the public interest but may contribute to PV through their activity in ways that promote their own material well-being, others' well-being, moral and legal duties to others and the creation of a just society (Moore, 2013). Hence, when viewed from this perspective, PV becomes an aggregate of the various types of values that result from the activities of an individual or firm, the benefit of which accrues not only to the individual or firm but also to other stakeholders, citizens, society.

Entrepreneurship as an avenue for public value creation

Entrepreneurship has been studied in terms of its effect on establishing new industries (Audretsch et al., 2006; Baumol, 1996; Birch, 1979), improving the quality of life (McMullen and Warnick, 2015), and promoting economic growth in both developed and developing economies. Although entrepreneurial outcomes related to financial performance, wealth creation and firm survival are significant (Haugh, 2006; Ucbasaran et al., 2001), focusing on these outcomes alone results in a one-sided analysis, wherein entrepreneurship is evaluated and appraised solely in monetary terms and without reference to its social (Zahra et al., 2009) or public (Bryson et al., 2017; Moore, 1995) impact. Certainly, this focus excludes social entrepreneurs whose primary motive is to create social value and to fulfil their communities' unmet needs.

Despite the significance of value derived from social entrepreneurship, it does not fully capture the multiple levels and forms of value in entrepreneurship (Korsgaard and Anderson, 2011), particularly the totality of value that accrues from business activity for the creator and the recipient. The reasons for this shortcoming are many. First, value creation in social entrepreneurship requires a deep understanding and awareness of social problems that need solutions (Lautermann, 2013), which complicates the entrepreneurial process of creating value. Second, social entrepreneurship is not the only form of entrepreneurial activity that generates social value; the current focus on social entrepreneurship demonstrates the lack of recognition given to value creation in other types of entrepreneurship. For example, certain commercial enterprises may not exhibit growth only in economic terms, such as expanding profits and increasing sales, but also in a social sense by achieving social outcomes and creating value for themselves and other stakeholders. Private-sector activities may not share the same goals as the public sector, may not fit within a specific context and may not be subject to the same accountability (Rhodes and Wanna, 2007), but these activities should not be excluded as contributors of PV in the public sphere. Private entrepreneurs employ resources to achieve economic outcomes, and public entrepreneurs seek to fulfil social interests and achieve public objectives (Ostrom, 1990). However, the goal for both is to capture value from their individual capabilities, advantages and potential (Pitelis and Teece, 2010). To advance the discussion on public value creation (PVC), value may be studied as an interdependent activity within the public sphere through activities carried out by both the public sector and private organizations, groups and individuals, beyond social enterprises.

Focusing on social entrepreneurs, the evaluation of entrepreneurial outcomes in terms of value creation often ignores the important contribution to PV of other kinds of entrepreneurial activity. Research documents that entrepreneurs are more likely to come from ethnic, religious and other minority groups (Weber, 1958; Kets de Vries,

1970; 1977), yet the contribution of these individuals in terms of value creation goes unrecognized. For instance, women entrepreneurs tend to be under recognized for their economic and social contribution through entrepreneurial activity. This is mainly due to the gender bias in entrepreneurship which primarily associates men as entrepreneurs and women as 'other' (Welter, 2011; Marlow et al., 2008). Especially, in developing and transitioning economies such as Pakistan, women face several challenges from their entrepreneurial environment which prevents them from pursuing entrepreneurial opportunities (Rehman and Roomi, 2012). Specifically, in rural areas where socio-cultural and religious norms guide appropriate behaviour for women, constraints in accessing entrepreneurial opportunities are higher. This in turn ignores the value-related outcomes that accrue through women's entrepreneurial ventures, which may be significant contributors of PV. Therefore, to advance the debate on and challenge the notion of underperformance in women's entrepreneurship, the value created from their entrepreneurial activity, beyond economic value must be evaluated. This would enable a detailed understanding of the dynamic nature of the entrepreneurial process by focusing on public- (social-) value-related outcomes that result from the interplay of the public sphere and the actors within it (Alvarez and Barney, 2010; Calas et al., 2009; Welter and Smallbone 2011).

A framework for public value creation through women's entrepreneurial activity

To contribute to this literature, we present a framework (Figure 17.1) for exploring PVC in the context of entrepreneurship and women's entrepreneurial activity (WEA) in particular. Incorporating Moore's (1995) strategic framework to PVC and building on Bryson et al.'s (2017) advancement of Moore's work that defines PVC as a holistic process that is multi-sector, multi-actor, multi-logic, multi-setting and multi-place, we highlight the role of WEA in creating PV at multiple levels. We argue that women entrepreneurs are '*actors*,' that is, *creators of PV* through their entrepreneurial activities. We suggest that the resulting PV is influenced by *women's capabilities*. Acknowledging the contextual embeddedness of entrepreneurship, implies that women's' capabilities are affected by the *public sphere* in which they operate, that is, the entrepreneurial environment or entrepreneurial ecosystem, which facilitates or constrains the potential of women to create PV. As creators of PV, women entrepreneurs may have important spill-over effects on multiple actors who may co-create PV in the public sphere. Finally, we argue that the PV women entrepreneurs create must be *legitimized and authorized* by key stakeholders, policymakers, business sectors and communities that support, enable and promote WEA and the PV created through it.

To explain the intricacies of PVC through a women's entrepreneurship lens, we analyse our proposed framework by detailing the five key elements involved detailed in Table 17.1.

Actors

Actors are woman entrepreneurs who initiate entrepreneurial activity from their homes or in an outside physical space and create value through their business. Other actors may include the family and household nexus of women who support

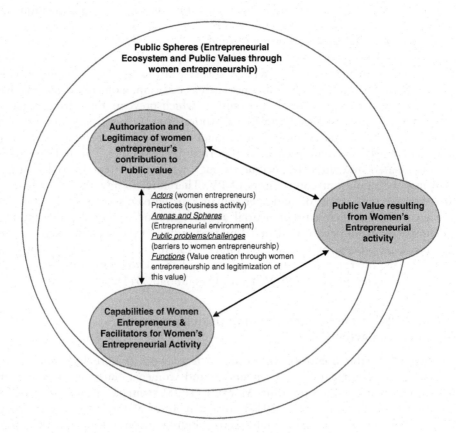

Figure 17.1 The framework for PVC through WEA

Source: adapted from Bryson et al., 2017 and Moore, 1995

Table 17.1 Five key elements of the strategic framework for PVC through WEA

Actors	Women entrepreneurs (those who initiate and manage business activity)
Practices	WEA (high/low growth and profitability, formal/informal, small/large)
Arenas and spheres	Context in which entrepreneurship takes place; The Entrepreneurial Ecosystem / Entrepreneurial environment (culture, finance, institutions, markets, social support, human capital)
Public problems and challenges	Barriers to WEA (problems of recognition, social acceptance as entrepreneurs, cultural barriers, finance constraints, institutional constraints, resource constraints, gender inequality)
Functions	Creation of value through entrepreneurial activity (multiple forms of value that contribute to PV; value accrual for individual woman entrepreneurs, the family and household, the community and society, and public stakeholders; legitimization of this value through appreciating and recognizing the efforts of women entrepreneurs as drivers of social change, designing and implementing policies that support WEA, reduce barriers and facilitate the creation of PV through it.)

Source: adapted from Bryson et al., 2017

or constrain the value-creation process. In addition, the society or community with which women entrepreneurs interact can influence the value process, and governmental and other non-profit agencies may affect WEA and women's ability to generate value.

Practices

Practices relate to the business activity that women entrepreneurs undertake. We argue that women entrepreneurs can create different types of value, regardless of their businesses' size and scope. Thus, it is not only financial performance that drives success and value creation but also the non-financial outcomes of value that affect the creator and the recipient of the value. We re-define success as what the individual woman entrepreneur perceives as success, and which may be financial or non-financial. Therefore, a woman may not earn high profits from her business but may add value to herself as an individual and to her household, thereby seeing herself as a successful entrepreneur.

Public spheres, arenas and problems

PV is not a concept so much as being relative to the environment in which it is created (Rhodes and Wanna, 2009). Therefore, PV is not an absolute standard; it changes based on the conditions of the task environment (Moore, 2008 as cited in Alford and O'Flynn, 2009). PV should be related to the current problems and circumstances of the public sphere and the needs of the recipients in it. The evolving nature of public and private entrepreneurship, wherein each activity has spill-over effects on the other (Klein et al., 2010), also reflects the intertwined nature of PVC. For example, private entrepreneurs may be constrained by their institutional environment, which may affect the extent of value creation. Alternatively, private entrepreneurs may create value that extends to the public sphere, such as when enterprises that aim to alleviate poverty or reduce violence against women are established. Considering that WEA is contextually embedded in the *public sphere* (i.e. the entrepreneurial ecosystem), we acknowledge the impact of the various elements of this sphere/ecosystem and their impact on the creation of PV.

Value creation in the public sphere (i.e., the entrepreneurial ecosystem) encompasses a range of elements, including *finance* (the financial capital required to engage in and promote WEA), *culture* (the value that a given society attributes to WEA), *the support system* (the physical and technological infrastructure and professional and moral support to women entrepreneurs*)*, *human capital* (the knowledge and education levels of women), *markets* (the networks and clientele that are accessible to women) and *policy* (government policies regarding women entrepreneurs*)* (Isenberg, 2011).

Institutional polices (regulatory, normative and cognitive; North, 1990) may support or constrain entrepreneurial activity and the resulting PV value that results from it. For example, developing countries like Pakistan – which are characterised by political instability, weak legal and institutional structures, low economic growth, and strong socio-cultural and religious norms, gender roles and attitudes— present unique *challenges and problems* to women entrepreneurs because of a constrained *policy sphere*, i.e. institutional element of the entrepreneurial ecosystem (Isenberg, 2011).

While institutions play a significant role in influencing entrepreneurial activity in an economy, these institutions' impact on entrepreneurs may be indirectly influenced by other factors, such as the society's prevailing cultural norms, beliefs and values (culture sphere i.e. cultural element of the entrepreneurial ecosystem) (Isenberg, 2011). A country with strong regulatory institutional systems may have weak cultural support that constrains individuals' entrepreneurial efforts.

Alternatively, when both formal and informal institutions are weak, entrepreneurs may reap the benefits of other elements, such as their human capital (human capital sphere i.e. human capital element of the entrepreneurial ecosystem) (Isenberg, 2011) and social capital (social support sphere i.e. social support element of the entrepreneurial ecosystem) (Isenberg, 2011). Socio-cultural norms in developing countries may limit women's mobility by expecting them to stay within the boundaries of their homes and to fulfil family and household responsibilities (Roomi, 2008; Rehman and Roomi, 2012). Such constraints may limit a woman's ability, affecting the value created from it. In the same context, gendered policies that result in unequal distribution of resources may restrict women's ability to succeed in business. In such circumstances, women may rely on social networks that enable them to overcome the weakness of their entrepreneurial environment so they can contribute to the PVC process. In addition, entrepreneurial activity may be affected by the *market sphere* (i.e. Market element of the entrepreneurial ecosystem) (Isenberg, 2011), wherein access to resources and markets (local and international) facilitate women in their businesses and help them to create PV. In summary, a woman's ability to create value from her business is affected by the public sphere and the actors within it.

Functions

As a function of entrepreneurial activity, we also highlight the importance of value created by women entrepreneurs within a context, as well as the relevance of this value to others in the public sphere. Entrepreneurship is a complex phenomenon that involves a range of inputs (multiple actors) and outputs (multiple forms of value). Therefore, we suggest that WEA contributes to PV creation through multiple value outcomes, including value creation at the *individual level* (value accruing to the female entrepreneur herself); *the business level* (value accruing to the entrepreneurial activity being undertaken); *the household level* (value accruing to the family of the female entrepreneur, the household and its members) and; *the community or society level* (value accruing to the other stakeholders and the society). The aggregate of these multiple frontiers of value formulate into PV that women entrepreneurs create through their businesses (Figure 17.2). Examining this universe of PV through entrepreneurship generates rich insights into how women entrepreneurs create and add value in a constrained public sphere.

Collectivity of PV through multiple dimensions of value creation in women's entrepreneurship

Value creation at the individual level

Female entrepreneurs can add value through engagement in entrepreneurial activities. Entrepreneurship improves their personal bargaining power, which can promote their

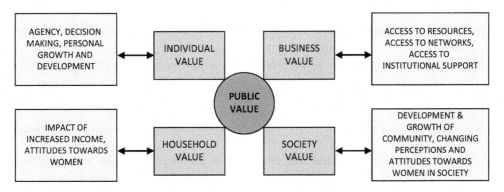

Figure 17.2 Multiplicity of value outcomes in PVC in WEA

personal growth and development and improve their overall well-being and quality of life (Beath et al., 2013; Haneef et al., 2014; Haugh and Talwar, 2016; Kantor, 2003). We propose that the three aspects of value creation at the individual level that are due to a women's engagement in entrepreneurial activity are: *enhanced agency, increased involvement in decision-making, and enriched personal growth and development.* These outcomes are discussed in detail to clarify holistically value creation at the individual level.

Enhanced agency

Agency includes factors like engagement in paid work outside the home, management and control over family assets, mobility outside the home, involvement in household and family decisions, and investment- and property-related decisions (Schuler et al., 2010). Entrepreneurship and business ownership can provide women with increased agency and control over their lives, which can increase empowerment. The empowerment process is a combination of internal and external factors, where internal factors include agency over and access to the productive resources that are necessary to recognize and act on opportunities in the environment. Kantor (2003) discusses how women may not have control over their income, despite having independent earnings from their business, because of the perceived norm that money coming into the household belongs to the man, regardless of who earned it, thereby denying women access to their income. Therefore, even if women have access to entrepreneurial resources in their environment, their ability to translate these resources into business activities depends on the level of agency that enables them to make life choices and act on them (Kabeer, 1999) – that is, the ability to overcome resistance from families and society in general, to pursue one's personal life choices, and to exert control over decisions regarding one's life and possessions.

A woman's agency may be identified in various aspects of her life. In contrast to women in paid employment, a female entrepreneur and businessperson may have control over the income that she generates from her business and a say about how the income is spent in the household (Haneef et al., 2014; Kantor, 2003). Women's access to an independent income may result in intrinsic benefits like increased empowerment, including the opportunity to develop as entrepreneurs with autonomy and independence, enhanced economic status, influence in investment-related decisions, control over family finances and personal savings, freedom to receive/accept invitations to join social groups, participation in committees and other member groups, and reduced social stigmas against working women (Haneef et al., 2014). Independence in earnings may also lead to an overall sense of well-being and improved quality of life and satisfaction among female entrepreneurs, particularly in rural economies, where such independence can help them to move out of poverty. Entrepreneurship may also result in increased agency and control over the investments and assets to which women may not have had access prior to becoming entrepreneurs (Beath et al., 2013).

Hence, entrepreneurship may not only give women independence to follow their career choices but also empower them with control over their wealth, assets and decisions regarding this wealth. Women may create social value because of changing attitudes and perceptions of themselves and other women, including their daughters and young girls in their community, thereby empowering other women. Value accumulated from increased agency at the individual level can contribute to elevating women's status in their entrepreneurial environment and to building positive self-perceptions among them.

Increased involvement in decision-making

Women's engagement in entrepreneurial activities and contributions toward household income can lead to positive individual-level outcomes, such as increased involvement in decision-making regarding family, income and household matters (Haugh and Talwar, 2016). Engagement in entrepreneurial activity may increase women's say in issues related to reproductive health, such as child spacing and fertility (Kabeer, 2001; Mayoux and Mackie, 2007), and their involvement in decisions related to their children's education and marriage, particularly for female children. They may also have greater control in decisions regarding what is spent on food, housing, clothing, medicine and leisure activities (Beath et al., 2013). In developing economies, discrimination against education among girls results in low levels of skill and knowledge in the female population (Jones et al., 2011), so with a say in decision-making regarding their children, female entrepreneurs can promote equal distribution of resources between male and female children.

An enhanced role in family decision-making can also be seen in a woman's choices regarding political participation in terms of making decisions related to their political choices, voting in elections, and standing for positions in political parties. Women may also be able to make decisions regarding their social interactions in their communities, whether those interactions be business-related or not. For example, female entrepreneurs may see their mobility restrictions reduced because of their independent income and agency over their decisions, particularly in patriarchal cultures where gendered social norms and traditions restrict women and prevent them from accessing key opportunities in employment and entrepreneurship. In developing and under-developed nations, women are marginalised by their gender and face challenges from their entrepreneurial environment. For example, women in certain countries, may require permission to leave their homes or must be accompanied by a male member of the household, even when they visit a doctor or a family member or attend social events (Kantor, 2003). The stereotypical attitudes and gender bias in the society view men as sole income earners and women as caretakers of their homes and family, which restricts women from accessing opportunities that may benefit their businesses, such as recruiting new customers and accessing new markets. Midst such constraints and barriers, entrepreneurship may be a means to empowerment and an increased role in decisions that affect their lives directly and indirectly, thereby contributing to value creation for the individual woman entrepreneur.

Personal growth and development

Despite the barriers faced by women and the constraints on their performance and growth in business, female entrepreneurs can to add value to their lives by enhancing their personal growth and knowledge base through experience in business activity. Business ownership may encourage women to fight for their rights and against injustices perpetrated against them. By owning and managing a business, women may gain in confidence and self-esteem, which positively influences their psychological and emotional well-being (Haugh and Talwar, 2016). Moreover, despite being limited in their opportunities and resource bases, women entrepreneurs may enhance their knowledge by learning to run the business and to deal with clients and suppliers and by equipping themselves with skills like marketing, financial, leadership, management and social skills. Improvement in all these aspects of life tends to elevate their status, leading to overall development and growth for women in general (Sahab et al., 2013).

Beyond knowledge and skills, entrepreneurship may also result in growth in terms of the self-perception and confidence that may motivate women to develop their businesses despite the hostile entrepreneurial environment (Haugh and Talwar, 2016). In addition, through their entrepreneurial activity, women's perceptions of gender roles in the society, attitudes about and tolerance of discrimination against women in society, and decisions regarding personal life and family may be transformed. Through such individual transformations, women entrepreneurs create value that transcends beyond economic value to contribute to significant social change at the individual and societal levels.

Value creation at the business level

Beyond the value for the individual entrepreneur, entrepreneurial activity can also add value to the entrepreneur's business domain, mainly through access to the institutional support, resources and social networks that women accrue by being in business and gaining knowledge and experience with it.

Access to resources

Female entrepreneurs in some societies are constrained by social and cultural norms that restrict their access to resources, including the education and training, networks, and social support that are essential in fostering WEA, particularly in developing economies where barriers to female entrepreneurship are high (Subramaniam, 2011). One of the major impediments female entrepreneurs face is access to financing, as financial institutions often deny women access to business loans because of their poor formal education, lack of technical skill and knowledge to start and develop competitive businesses, the small-scale nature of their businesses and lack of access to collateral to secure loans or credit (Dzisi and Obeng, 2013). Moreover, socio-cultural barriers restrict women from accessing social networks to build the social capital that would enable them to access key resources for business, which restricts their growth potential and performance.

Female entrepreneurs gain access to resources mainly by using their social networks to help identify opportunities in terms of new markets, customers, suppliers and processes that enhance value creation in business. By developing relationships with business and personal contacts, female entrepreneurs can build strong networks that can help them to serve new markets and customers. Networks can also be an integral source of financial capital for entrepreneurial women (Bruderl and Preisendörfer, 1998; Waldinger et al., 1990). Beyond social networks, human capital – the combination of education, experience and learning – can help female entrepreneurs to access resources like financing and markets. In economies where women have low levels of education and negligible experience in employment, the vicarious learning that is acquired when women gain information and knowledge from observing others, including other entrepreneurs (Santarelli and Tran, 2013; Shane, 2000), helps women sustain and develop their businesses. Learning by doing plays a significant role in enhancing entrepreneurs' intellectual development, adds to their human capital throughout the entrepreneurial process and helps them make sound decisions and take wise action in times of uncertainty (Malerba, 2007; Minniti and Bygrave, 2001; Schumpeter, 1934; Shane and Venkataraman, 2000). Therefore, even when women have limited access to resources, their human capital, knowledge base and social networks help them to obtain access to key resources for their businesses and so add value to their enterprises. Consequently, while an adequate resource base is a pre-requisite for entrepreneurship, the opposite may be true in the context of WEA, as women initiate an entrepreneurial idea from their homes and build and use their networks and knowledge bases to the access resources that help their businesses to grow and develop.

Access to networks

Participation in entrepreneurship can be a way for women to access the networks that enable them to exploit opportunities and create more value. Networks present entrepreneurs with opportunities for access to financing (Shane and Cable, 2002), knowledge and technology (Owen et al., 2004) and help to hone entrepreneurial skills (De Carolis and Saparito, 2006). Entrepreneurs who are embedded in many networks increase their exposure to opportunities and ideas (Cooper and Yin, 2005), which enables them to create value for their businesses. One significant source of opportunities in an entrepreneur's network is other entrepreneurs. Female entrepreneurs whose networks consist of successful women can benefit from their experience and learn from how they overcame challenges in business. Family is also an important source of contacts for female entrepreneurs, as family members can help them to solve business-related problems, arrange resources for business activities and direct them to people who may help to solve complex problems (Kao, 1993). Beyond family, access to mentors in the entrepreneurial environment can inculcate positive entrepreneurial attitudes into them, increase access to key resources through the mentor's contacts, and encourage them toward entrepreneurship (Latu et al., 2013; Timmons and Spinelli, 2009). Access to a network base builds female entrepreneurs' social capital and supports them in the process of value creation.

Access to institutional support

The institutional context of entrepreneurship consists of the formal and informal institutions that influence women's ability to succeed in business and to create value from it. Formal institutions include the political and economic laws and regulations (e.g. market entry and exit regulations, private property rights), that either support or limit opportunities for entrepreneurship and either restrict or broaden the entrepreneurial outcomes of value creation. Formal regulatory institutions relate to the governmental process of creating and enforcing rules and regulations that increase or decrease the difficulty in starting a business. For example, difficult procedural requirements could slow new entrepreneurial activity and affect the growth of existing ventures by increasing bureaucratic costs (Autio, 2011; Estrin et al, 2013). Informal institutions, including the socio-cultural environment, shape the female entrepreneurs' behaviour and influence their potential to create value. Economies with weak institutions tend to have a negative perception toward women in business, to have fewer women entrepreneurs and less value creation than do economies with strong institutions. Institutions can also contribute to female entrepreneurs' human capital by promoting education and experience, equal access to opportunities in the labour market for women and the dissemination of information for women who are seeking to start a business. In addition, effective and efficient institutional arrangements help to provide women with access to financing.

Women may gain institutional support because of their entrepreneurial efforts, particularly their economic contributions through their business activities. Moreover, experience and reputation in business may help female entrepreneurs build contacts and gain access to institutional support. Differences in the context of entrepreneurial activity determine the extent of institutional access and support that women may be able to secure for their businesses. For example, women in developing countries may face strict barriers against accessing institutional support because of gendered institutions and bias in the distribution of resources among entrepreneurial actors. Moreover, the socio-cultural norms that prevail in the society may cause difficulties for women who operate within institutional voids by restricting entrepreneurial activity and, thus, the value-creation process.

Value creation at the household level

WEA can lead to significant changes in household dynamics, which may affect the value-creation process in female-owned businesses. Value creation at the household level is a critical factor in explaining women's entrepreneurial development and social change. The positive impact of increased income from WEA on the household members can improve overall well-being and quality of life, and improve their attitudes toward women so they are viewed as independent and entrepreneurial.

Impact of increased income

With WEA comes increased income, which may have a positive impact on the household members in terms of an improved standard of living and an increase in the family's overall happiness and well-being (Dsizi and Obeng, 2013; Haugh and Talwar, 2016; Kabeer, 2001). Higher income may support increased spending on nutritious food for the family, especially for children, and may improve living conditions by enabling better sanitation, sewage and water facilities, particularly in rural economies where housing conditions are poor. Increased income may also have significant effects on the children in the household, particularly female children, by giving them access to education. In patriarchal societies, the preference for education is given to the male child while the female child is involved in housework and trained to fulfil domestic responsibilities. Increased income through entrepreneurial activity, may encourage households to invest in females, resulting in an overall higher number of females being educated[2]. Furthermore, increase in income may enable families to have access to health care (Dsizi and Obeng, 2013), bringing with it increased life expectancy. Hence, the impact of increased income from WEA may bring positive value creation to households by improving their well-being and happiness in life (Kabeer, 2001).

Attitudes toward women

WEA may also have a positive influence on attitudes and gender roles in the household. Scholars have discussed the spill-over effects of work on family (Greenhaus and Powell, 2006), including the respect for participation in paid work (Hammer et al., 2002), improvement in women's status, sharing of domestic responsibilities, and reduced instances of genital mutilation, domestic violence and abuse, polygamy and early marriages. According to resource theory (Blood and Wolfe, 1960), access to resources like education and employment tend to be good predictors of women's participation in decision-making. Women in business have an increased role in decision-making in the house and may earn respect and recognition for their entrepreneurial efforts and contributions to the household's income. Following the same line of thought, bargaining models of households suggest that the resources that are available to each partner determines his or her bargaining position in the relationship (McElroy, 1990). Resources such as employment opportunities, education, family support, and networks increases the woman's bargaining power of women and shifts the household's power dynamics (Kantor, 2003).

WEA can also influence the attitude about gender roles and the power relationships in the household, thereby contributing to value in the household. Particularly in patriarchal societies, women are expected to bear the responsibilities of the house, the children and the elderly, while men are expected to be employed outside the home and bear the responsibilities of supporting the family financially (Mayoux, 2001). These responsibilities restrict the time and energy that women can devotee to business, thereby lowering their prospects for growth. By embarking on entrepreneurial activity, women may change the gender roles in the household, including sharing domestic responsibilities and child care. WEA may help women to challenge patriarchal norms and change the traditional ideas of the woman as sole caretaker of the house and family. If men and women share the household workload, women will have the opportunity and time to focus on business responsibilities (Haneef et al., 2014; Malhotra et al., 2002).

Another area in which WEA can add value is in women's decision-making role in the household (which we also discussed at the individual level of value creation). Value at the household level may be reflected by increased involvement in decisions that affect both men and women but for which the decisions have traditionally been made by the male. Such decisions include the number of children to have, child spacing, and the use of contraception, including abortion. Thus, entrepreneurship may provide women with increased control over decisions that affect their personal lives (Kabeer, 1999; Malhotra et al., 2002). Women's opinion in decisions about their families, particularly children, may also increase. Such decisions include those related to the children's education, choice of school and selection and timing of children's marriages (Haneef et al., 2014; Haugh and Talwar, 2016).

Value creation at the societal level

The impact of WEA at the societal level has been discussed in several domains, including those of economic vitality, stability and the availability of goods and services. In terms of social impact, the society's security, values, attitudes, lifestyles and norms may be influenced by WEA. Addition of value in terms of contributing to the community's overall development and growth includes increasing well-being, raising the quality of life, creating employment, promoting gender equality and improving satisfaction with life (Haugh and Talwar, 2016; Nicholls, 2009; Welter and Xheneti, 2015; Zahra and Wright, 2016). WEA can also change the perceptions of and attitudes toward women in a society, resulting in greater support for female entrepreneurs. These changes include influencing gender norms and traditions, enhancing the status of and respect for women in the society, and inculcating positive motivation to become entrepreneurs and increase their independence in others through role models (Haugh and Talwar, 2016; Mayoux and Mackie, 2007).

Development and growth of the community

Female entrepreneurs can become agents of social change by promoting the society's overall development and growth through entrepreneurship. Social outcomes in this regard pertain to local community development through increased employment for the local population (Birch, 1979; Haugh, 2006) and providing and increasing the choice of goods and services that meet the community's needs. In societies with strict religious and traditional norms that restrict a woman's mobility outside the home, a female-based enterprise like a health service may be a significant source of services to other women in the community, thus contributing to value creation at the community level.

Women may also add value in the form of increased knowledge and awareness among the members of the community about various aspects of business and its impact on their lives, the community's involvement in services, enhanced trust and strengthening of social relationships, empowerment of people and improved quality of life (Gibb and Adhikary, 2000; Haugh, 2006). Beyond society's development and growth, female entrepreneurs can add social value by being role models and setting an example for others, especially other women, to become entrepreneurial and contribute to the community in a similar way (Haugh and Talwar, 2016; Hockerts et al., 2006). In addition, women may play an active role in resolving conflicts between members of the society because of their increased respect and status in the society. They may assist other women in setting up their businesses by improving their confidence and skill sets (Haneef et al., 2014; Korsgaard and Anderson, 2011). Occasionally, WEA may even break down gendered norms and barriers to the progression of women in the society by changing attitudes toward women (Haugh and Talwar, 2016). Thus, female entrepreneurs may act as agents of social change in their society by promoting society members' overall quality of life and improving their satisfaction with life (Haugh and Talwar, 2016; Nicholls, 2009; Welter and Xheneti, 2015; Zahra and Wright, 2016).

Changing perceptions of and attitudes toward women in the society

WEA is influenced by external elements in the entrepreneurial environment, including attitudes toward, perceptions of and behaviour toward women in the society, specifically males' attitudes, the social and cultural constraints that constrain women's opportunities and institutional policies that limit women's participation in economic and political activity (Schuler et al., 2010).

Social norms are felt at all stages of a woman's life in traditional societies. For example, the preference for boys leads to early abortions of female foetuses as well as in poor nutrition and health among girls. Discrimination in access to education limits girls' ability to develop skills and acquire knowledge (Jones et al., 2011). Moreover, the risk of violence, early marriage (before adolescence), and early child-bearing result in restricted mobility and control over decision-making (Watson et al., 2014). With regards to institutional barriers, the regulatory laws, policies and rules established in a society limit women's participation in several spheres of life. For example, laws on property inheritance, buying and selling disempower women and make them vulnerable to males. Female entrepreneurs are also discriminated against in terms of access to key resources like financing, which prevents them from realizing their full potential in their entrepreneurship efforts.

In the presence of social constraints on women in a society, entrepreneurship can bring about social change by empowering women to fight for their rights and to change gendered assumptions about women. Through entrepreneurial efforts, women can show that they can be agents for social change and justify their increased freedom and mobility. They may exercise agency, have control over their life decisions and overcome societal resistance to pursue their goals in their personal and professional lives. Moreover, women in business can increase society's respect and recognition of women (Haugh and Talwar, 2016). Similarly, women may influence gendered institutions in their entrepreneurial environments because of their entrepreneurial efforts and contributions to value in their societies. In this regard, women may gain access to entrepreneurial resources from institutions that were once available only to male entrepreneurs. Being in business can also help women gain knowledge about the ways of doing business, the rules and regulations regarding business activity in various markets and strategies with which to overcome institutional voids. Entrepreneurship empowers women and enables them to overcome injustices that may hamper business performance and affect their personal lives (Kabeer, 2001; Mayoux and Mackie, 2007; Tankard and Paluck, 2016; Zahra and Wright, 2016).

We define Public Value as the aggregate of the four levels of value, i.e. Individual, Business, Household and Society. One possible way to gauge an empirical measure of public value creation may be determined through the following three steps. First, notice that Individual Value is a sum of three indices including Agency, Involvement in Decision making and Personal Growth and Development. If all these were found among the women entrepreneurs, they would each be assigned a value of 1. In this case, the Individual Value will contribute to PV in maximum amount, which would equal 1, which is simply the average of the three sub-indicators of individual value. In the second step, this methodology is repeated for other value levels i.e., business, household, and society. In the final step, each of these value levels are averaged to obtain a measure of aggregate public value creation through women entrepreneurship. Table 17.2 presents an example of how this indicator may be aggregated for public value through women entrepreneurship.

Once an aggregate measure of PV is obtained, we will use simple statistical techniques, such as Ordinary Least Squares (OLS) to infer the significance and magnitude of the various elements of the entrepreneurial eco-system vis-à-vis PV. This will not only enable us to extract the important elements of the eco-system vis-à-vis their contribution to public value, but also identify those that do not.

Moving forward: a collective approach to PVC

As argued in this chapter, PVC is a multi-faceted phenomenon that involves multiple actors that interact and co-create PV in the public sphere. Arguing that PV is relevant only to public management and policy-makers limits the scope of value creation from several other activities. This chapter outlines one such case, the contribution of women entrepreneurs in creating PV through their entrepreneurial activity. In doing so, we: a) highlighted the multiple dimensions of value (Individual value, business value, household/family value and community value), which aggregate to PVC through WEA, to document the role of women as change agents in the society and to evaluate

Table 17.2 An empirical example of measure of PV through individual and business value

Value type and sub indicators	Assigned value (Case 1)	Assigned value (Case 2)	Assigned value (Case 3)
Individual value			
-i- Agency	1	1	1
-ii- Involvement in decision making	1	1	0
-iii- Personal growth and development	1	0	0
Cumulative PV through individual value	1	0.66	0.33
Business value			
Increase in networking	1	1	0
Access to institutional support	1	0	0
Cumulative PV through business value	1	0.5	0

the entrepreneurial outcomes from a public lens; b) suggested that WEA's creation of PV is influenced by the public sphere (i.e., entrepreneurial ecosystem) in which it takes place in terms of its ability to facilitate PV creation; c) highlighted the important role of legitimizing women as entrepreneurs and as PV creators for their contribution to the public sphere.

We present these ideas in Figure 17.3 and propose recommendations for future researchers and implications for policy-making to advance the debate on advancing PV by facilitating and legitimizing WEA as an avenue for PVC.

Facilitating women entrepreneurs in the public sphere and promoting PVC

The process of creating PV depends on the environment in which it is created (Zahra et al., 2009). Hence, we suggest that facilitating the creation of PV in the public sphere requires supporting WEA, regardless of their businesses' size and sector. While some policies support women in business, most are targeted at high-growth and profit-oriented businesses (Aslund and Backstrom, 2015) and ignore the micro-women entrepreneurs who may not be high-profit-oriented but may be important contributors of social value. We argue that the contexts in which entrepreneurs operate present them with unique challenges, so an entrepreneur's performance should be judged from a broad environmental perspective. Knowledge of the context helps to define a need or entrepreneurial idea that can result in an outcome of value and, hence, PVC. We recommend that future researchers evaluate entrepreneurs, specifically women, in a variety of contexts and business sectors and explore the value-related outcomes that originate from WEA. Focusing on the context also highlights the role of public managers in providing support to women entrepreneurs, particularly those who are in the informal economy. Such support may be achieved by strengthening elements of the entrepreneurial ecosystem. For example, the government could improve finance opportunities for women entrepreneurs and provide them with access to education on business skills and knowledge. In addition, regulatory and normative institutions must be conducive to WEA and, thus, the PVC that can emerge from it. Policies should be redesigned to cater to women and new ones that promote WEA should be formulated.

Legitimizing PVC through WEA

The literature establishes that the legitimization of PV is a key aspect in it being validated across the public sphere, for all concerned agents. Thus, we suggest the authorization of PV through WEA as a key to its creation and facilitation. Such authorization entails a double responsibility: to legitimize women entrepreneurs, such as those in the informal economy and micro businesses, and to legitimize the multiple aspects of value that results from such activity. Efforts are required across a variety of frontiers to achieve this goal. For example, governments can play an active role in validating, recognizing and appreciating the value outcomes of women entrepreneurs in creating public value. As for the business sector, it can support women by providing support services, including business skills, training and financing. The non-profit sector may also enable women by means of initiatives that may facilitate WEA and PVC by women entrepreneurs. Finally, the community can play an active role in legitimizing the PV of women entrepreneurs. Through their businesses, women meet the needs of their communities and add value to it, so appreciation of women's entrepreneurial efforts

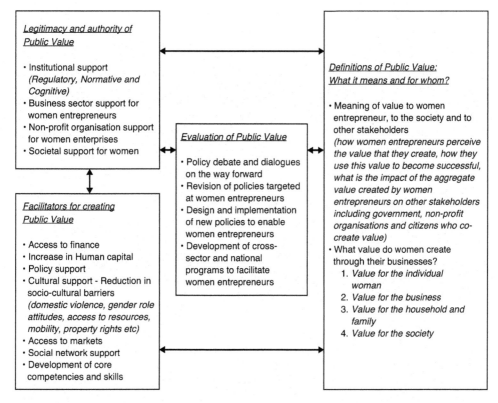

Figure 17.3 Public value governance in WEA

Source: adapted from Public Value Governance Triangle: Bryson, Crosby and Bloomberg, 2015, 15

by fellow community members, citizens, and household and family members can encourage women to become more entrepreneurial and contribute to PVC. As part of the public sphere, the community can also co-create value with women entrepreneurs by providing emotional and social support to women who initiate entrepreneurship.

Notes

1 Entrepreneurs of value who have "a restless and value seeking imagination" and operate within a framework of democratic practices (Benington and Moore, 2011, 3).
2 This may, of course, depend on the gendered traditions and socio-cultural norms of the society, which may view female education and independence as negative and thus may not allocate any income to the girl child.

References

Alford, J. and O'Flynn, J. (2009). Making sense of public value: Concepts, critiques and emergent meanings. *Intl Journal of Public Administration*, 32(3–4), 171–191.

Alvarez, S.A. and Barney, J.B. (2010). Entrepreneurship and epistemology: The philosophical underpinnings of the study of entrepreneurial opportunities. *The Academy of Management Annals*, 4(1), 557–583.

Aslund, A. and Backstrom, I. (2015). Creation of value to society – a process map of the societal entrepreneurship area. *Total Quality Management and Business Excellence*, 26(3–4), 385–399.

Audretsch, D.B., Keilbach, M.C. and Lehmann, E.E. (2006). *Entrepreneurship and Economic Growth*. New York: Oxford University Press.

Autio, E. (2011). High-Aspiration Entrepreneurship. In Minniti, M. (Ed.), *The Dynamics of Entrepreneurship*. Oxford University Press, Oxford. 181–208.

Baumol, W.J. (1996). Entrepreneurship: Productive, unproductive, and destructive. *Journal of Business Venturing*, 11(1), 3–22.

Beath, A., Christia, F. and Enikolopov, R. (2013). Empowering Women through Development Aid: Evidence from a Field Experiment in Afghanistan. *American Political Science Review*, 107(3), 540–557.

Benington, J. (2005). *From Private Choice to Public Value*. Paper presented to the Public Management and Policy Association. London: PMPA.

Benington, J. (2009). Creating the public in order to create public value? *Intl Journal of Public Administration*, 32(3–4), 232–249.

Benington, J. (2011). From private choice to public value. *Public Value: Theory and Practice*, 31–49.

Benington, J. and Moore, M.H. (2011). Public Value in Complex and Changing Times. In J. Benington and M.H. Moore (Eds), *Public Value: Theory and Practice*. Basingstoke: Palgrave Macmillan. 1–20.

Birch, D.G. (1979). *The Job Generation Process*. Cambridge, MA: MIT Program on Neighborhood and Regional Change.

Blood, R.O. and Wolfe, D.M. (1960) *Husbands and Wives*. New York: Free Press.

Borins, Sandford (2000). Loose cannons and rule breakers, or enterprising leaders? Some evidence about innovative public managers. *Public Administration Review*, 60, 498–507.

Brüderl, J. and Preisendörfer, P. (1998). Network support and the success of newly founded business. *Small Business Economics*, 10(3), 213–225.

Bryson, J., Sancino, A., Benington, J. and Sorenson, E. (2017). Towards a multi-actor theory of public value co-creation. *Public Management Review*, 19(5), 640–654.

Calás, M., Smircich, L. and Bourne, K. (2009). Extending the boundaries: Reframing 'entrepreneurship as social change' through feminist perspectives. *Academy of Management Review*, 34(3), 552–569.

Cooper, A.C. and Yin, X. (2005). Entrepreneurial networks. In Hitt, M.A. and Ireland, R.D. (Eds) *The Blackwell Encyclopedia of Management-Entrepreneurship*. Malden, MA: Blackwell. 98–100.

De Carolis, D.M. and Saparito, P. (2006). Social capital, cognition, and entrepreneurial opportunities: A theoretical framework. *Entrepreneurship Theory and Practice*, 30(1), 41–56.

Dsizi, S. and Obeng, F. (2013). Microfinance and the Socio-economic Wellbeing of Women Entrepreneurs in Ghana. *International Journal of Business and Social Research*, 3(11), 45–62.

Edwards, C., Jones, G., Lawton, A. and Llewellyn, N. (2002) Public Entrepreneurship: Rhetoric, Reality, and Context. *International Journal of Public Administration*, 25(12), 1539–1554.

Estrin, S. Korosteleva, J. and Mickiewicz,T. (2013). Which institutions encourage entrepreneurial growth aspirations? *Journal of Business Venturing*, 28(4), 564–580.

Gibb, A. and Adhikary, D. (2000). Strategies for local and regional NGO development: combining sustainable outcomes with sustainable organizations. *Entrepreneurship & Regional Development*, 12(2), 137–161.

Greenhaus, J.H. and Powell, G.N. (2006). When work and family are allies: A theory of work-family enrichment. *Academy of Management Review*, 31(1), 72–92.

Hammer, L.B., Cullen, J.C., Caubet, S., Johnson, J., Neal, M.B. and Sinclair, R.R. (2002). *The effects of work-family fit on depression: A longitudinal study*. Paper presented at the 17th Annual Meeting of SIOP, Toronto.

Haneef, C., Pritchard, M., Hannan, M., Kenward, S., Rahman, M. and Alam, Z. (2014). *Women as Entrepreneurs: The impact of having an independent income on women's empowerment*. Available online at www.enterprise-development.org/wp-content/uploads/Women-as-Entrepreneurs_The-impact-of-having-an-independent-income-on-womens-empowerment_August-2014.pdf (accessed 20-04-2016).

Haugh, H. (2006). Social enterprise. Beyond economic outcomes and individual returns. In Mair, J., Robinson, J. and Hockerts, K. (Eds), *Social Entrepreneurship*. New York: Palgrave MacMillan.

Haugh, H.M. and Talwar, A. (2016). Linking social entrepreneurship and social change: The mediating role of empowerment. *Journal of Business Ethics*, 133(4), 643–658.

Hockerts, K., Mair, J. and Robinson, J. (2006). *Impact at the "Bottom of the Pyramid": The Role of Social Capital in Capability Development and Community Empowerment*. New York: Palgrave MacMillan.

Isenberg, D. (2011). The entrepreneurship ecosystem strategy as a new paradigm for economic policy: Principles for cultivating entrepreneurship. *Presentation at the Institute of International and European Affairs*.

Jones, N., Harper, C. and Watson, C. (2011). *Stemming Girls' Chronic Poverty: Catalysing Development Change by Building Just Institutions*. Chronic Poverty Research Centre Working Paper.

Jørgensen, T.B. and Bozeman, B. (2007). Public values: An inventory. *Administration & Society*, 39(3), 354–381.

Kabeer, N. (1999). *The Conditions and Consequences of Choice: Reflections on the Measurement of Women's Empowerment*. Geneva: UNRISD.

Kabeer, N. (2001). Resources, Agency and Achievements: Reflections on the measurement of women's empowerment. *Development and Change*, 30(3), 435–464

Kantor, P. (2003). Women's empowerment through home-based work: Evidence from India. *Development and change*, 34(3), 425–445

Kao, J. (1993). The worldwide web of Chinese business. *Harvard Business Review*, 71, 24–36.

Kets de Vries, M.F.R. (1970). *The Entrepreneur as Catalyst of Economic and Cultural Change*. Unpublished Doctoral Dissertation, Harvard University, Graduate School of Business Administration.

Kets de Vries, M.F.R. (1977). The Entrepreneurial Personality: A Person at the Crossroads. *The Journal of Management Studies*, 14, 34–58.

Klein, P.G., Mahoney, J.T., McGahan, A.M. and Pitelis, C.N. (2010). Toward a theory of public entrepreneurship. *European Management Review*, 7(1), 1–15.

Korsgaard, S. and Anderson, A.R. (2011). Enacting entrepreneurship as social value creation. *International Small Business Journal*, 20(10), 1–17

Latu, I.M., Schmid-Mast, M., Lammers, J. and Bombari, D. (2013). Successful Female Leaders Empower Women's Behaviour in Leadership Tasks. *Journal of Experimental Social Psychology*, 49, 444–448.

Lautermann, C. (2013). The ambiguities of (social) value creation: towards an extended understanding of entrepreneurial value creation for society. *Social Enterprise Journal*, 9(2), 184–202.

Malerba, F. (2007). Innovation and the dynamics and evolution of industries: Progress and challenges. *International Journal of Industrial Organization*, 25(4), 675–699

Malhotra, A. Schuler, S.R. and Boender, C. (2002). Measuring Women's Empowerment as a Variable in International Development. Available online at http://siteresources.worldbank.org/INTEMPOWERMENT/Resources/486312-1095970750368/529763-1095970803335/malhotra.pdf (accessed on 16-08-16).

Marlow, S., Shaw, E. and Carter, S. (2008). Constructing female entrepreneurship policy in the UK: Is the USA a relevant role model? *Environmental Planning C*, 26(1), 335–351.

Mayoux, L. (2001). *Jobs, Gender and Small Enterprises: Getting the Policy Environment Right*. SEED Working Paper, No. 15. Series on Women's Entrepreneurship Development and Gender in Enterprises. Geneva: International Labour Organization.

Mayoux, L. and Mackie, G. (2007). Guide to Gender Integration in Value Chain Development, "Making the Strongest Links". *International Labour Organization*. Available online at www.ilo.org/wcmsp5/groups/public/@ed_emp/@emp_ent/documents/instructionalmaterial/wcms_106538.pdf (accessed on 19-08-16).

McElroy, M. (1990) The Empirical Content of Nash-bargained Household Behavior. *Journal of Human Resources*, 24(4), 559–583.

McMullen, J.S. and Warnick, B.J. (2015). The downside of blended value and hybrid organizing. *Academy of Management Proceedings*, 2015(1), 10130.

Melchior, M. and Melchior, A. (2001). A case for particularism in public administration. *Administration & Society*, 33, 251–275.

Meynhardt, T. and Diefenbach, F.E. (2012). What drives entrepreneurial orientation in the public sector? Evidence from Germany's federal labor agency. *Journal of Public Administration Research and Theory*, 22(4), 761–792.

Meynhardt, T. (2009). Public value inside: What is public value creation? *International Journal of Public Administration*, 32(3–4), 192–219.

Minniti, M. and Bygrave, W. (2001). A dynamic model of entrepreneurial learning. *Entrepreneurship: Theory and Practice*, 23 (4), 41–52.

Moore, M.H. (1995). *Creating Public Value*. Cambridge, MA: Harvard University Press.

Moore, Mark H. (2013). *Recognizing Public Value*. Cambridge, MA: Harvard University Press.

Morris, Michael H. and Jones, Foard F. (1993). Human resource management practices and corporate entrepreneurship: An empirical assessment from the USA. *International Journal of Human Resource Management*, 4(4), 873–896.

Nicholls, A. (2009). We do good things, don't we? Blended value accounting in social entrepreneurship. *Accounting, Organizations and Society*, 34(6), 755–769.

Ostrom, E. (1990). *Governing the Commons: The Evolution of Institutional Forms of Collective Action*. Cambridge, UK: Cambridge University Press.

Owen-Smith, J. and Powell, W. (2004). The effects of spill overs in the Boston biotechnology community. *Organization Science*, 15(1), 5–21.

Pitelis, C.N. and Teece, D.J. (2010). Cross border market co-creation dynamic capabilities and the entrepreneurial theory of the multinational enterprise. *Industrial and Corporate Change*, 19(4), 1247–1270.

Rehman, S. and Azam Roomi, M. (2012). Gender and work-life balance: a phenomenological study of women entrepreneurs in Pakistan. *Journal of Small Business and Enterprise Development*, 19(2), 209–228.

Rhodes, R. and Wanna, J. (2007). The Limits to Public Value, or Rescuing Responsible Government from the Platonic Gardens. *Australian Journal of Public Administration*, 66(4), 406–421.

Roomi, M.A. and Parrott, G. (2008). Barriers to development and progression of women entrepreneurs in Pakistan. *The Journal of Entrepreneurship*, 17(1), 59–72.

Sahab, S., Thakur, G. and Gupta, P.C. (2013). A Case Study on Empowerment of Rural Women through Micro *Entrepreneurship Development. Journal of Business Management*, 9(6), 123–126

Santarelli, E. and Tran, H.T. (2012). Growth of incumbent firms and entrepreneurship in Vietnam. *Growth and Change*, 43(4), 638–666.

Schuler, S.R., Islam, F. and Rottach, E. (2010). Women's empowerment revisited: a case study from Bangladesh. *Development in Practice*, 20(7), 840–854.

Schumpeter, J.A. (1934). *The Theory of Economic Development: An Inquiry into Profits, Capital Credit, Interest and the Business Cycle*. Cambridge, MA: Harvard University Press.

Shane, S. (2000). Prior knowledge and the discovery of entrepreneurial opportunities. *Organization Science*, 11(4), 448–469.

Shane, S. and Venkataraman, S. (2000). The promise of entrepreneurship as a field of research. *Academy of Management Review*, 25(1), 217–226.

Shane, S. and Cable, D. (2002). Network ties, reputation, and the financing of new ventures. *Management Science*, 48(3), 364–381

Stoker, G. (2006). Public Value Management: A New Narrative for Networked Governance? *American Review of Public Administration*, 36(1), 41–57.

Subramaniam, M. (2011). Grass roots and poor women's empowerment in rural India. *International Sociology*, 27(1), 72–95.

Tankard, M.E. and Paluck, E.L. (2016). Norm Perception as a Vehicle for Social Change. *Social Issues and Policy Review*, 10(1), 181–211

Timmons, J.A. and Spinelli, S. (2009). *New Venture Creation: Entrepreneurship for the 21st Century*, 8th ed. New York, NY: McGraw-Hill.

Ucbasaran, D., Westhead, P. and Wright, M. (2001). The focus of entrepreneurial research: contextual and process issues. *Entrepreneurship Theory and Practice*, 25(4), 57–80.

Waldinger, R., Aldrich, H.E. and Ward, R. (Eds) (1990), *Ethnic Entrepreneurs*. Newbury Park, CA: Sage.

Watson, J., Gatewood, E. and Lewis, K. (2014). A framework for assessing entrepreneurial outcomes: an international perspective. *International Journal of Gender and Entrepreneurship*, 6(1), 2–14.

Weber, M. (1958). *The Protestant Ethic and the Spirit of Capitalism*. Trans T. Parsons. New York: Charles Scribners & Sons.

Welter, F. (2011). Contextualizing Entrepreneurship – Conceptual Challenges and Ways Forward. *Entrepreneurship Theory and Practice*, 35(1), 165–184

Welter, F. and Smallbone, D. (2011). Institutional perspectives on entrepreneurial behavior in challenging environments. *Journal of Small Business Management*, 49(1), 107–125.

Welter, F. and Xheneti, M. (2015). Value for Whom? Exploring the Value of Informal Entrepreneurial Activities in Post-Socialist Contexts. *Exploring Criminal and Illegal Enterprise: New Perspectives on Research, Policy and Practice*, 5, 253–275.

Zahra, S.A. and Wright, M. (2016). Understanding the social role of entrepreneurship. *Journal of Management Studies*, 53(4), 610–629.

Zahra, S.A., Gedajlovic, E., Neubaum, D.O. and Shulman, J.M. (2009). A typology of social entrepreneurs: Motives, search processes and ethical challenges. *Journal of Business Venturing*, 24(5), 219–532.

18 Museums and public value[1]

Taking the pulse

Carol Ann Scott

Introduction

Mark Moore's theory of public value (1995) emerged at a time when the New Public Management (NPM) was enjoying prominence. Associated with a top-down and directive form of government administration, NPM made the public sector directly accountable to government through performance contracts, funding agreements and the provision of evidence that inputs and outputs were being managed effectively (Kelly et al., 2002).

NPM was firmly in place when New Labour first took office in 1997. It usefully served the needs of a new administration seeking a whole-of-government approach to policy implementation. Government funded agencies would deliver New Labour's economic and social policies in return for grant-in aid. Funding agreements reflected this. The Rt. Hon Chris Smith, then Secretary of State and Minister for Culture, Media and Sport described the 'new relationship' between government and the recipients of public funding as part of the modernisation and reform agenda which sought returns on public investment in line with government policy.

> Three year funding will be accompanied by three year funding agreements and all recipients of funding from DCMS will have a clear responsibility to deliver against demanding output and outcome based targets. . . . The advent of resource accounting across Government will ensure that DCMS ties its expenditure to its objectives, and we will need to be assured that public money is being used appropriately to meet public objectives.
>
> (DCMS, 1998, 3)

Museums were particularly identified with the delivery of social inclusion, one of the cornerstones of New Labour policy (DCMS, 2000). Social exclusion (DCMS, 1999) would be counteracted by proactively seeking to diversify visitorship and by encouraging participation from hitherto unrepresented sectors of the population.

In practice, New Labour's social policy agenda and its implementation through the New Public Management received a mixed reception from museums. On the one hand, many of the principles underlying policies of social inclusion, social cohesion, diversity and access found a responsive audience in a sector transitioning to the 'new museology' where a major shift was underway from a focus on collections to a greater emphasis on audiences and a corresponding interest in telling the stories of marginalised and under-represented groups.

While many of the issues underlying the government's social agenda resonated with the museum sector, its model of implementation received a mixed response. The overwhelming emphasis on delivering the instrumental outcomes of social policy was viewed as a narrow perception of what constituted the full range of museums' impact and value. The emphasis on 'instrumental values' was seen to over-ride other values, in particular that of intrinsic value, the personal experience of individuals that encompassed

> all those wonderful, beautiful, uplifting, challenging, stimulating, thought-provoking, terrifying, disturbing, spiritual, witty, transcendental experiences that shape and reflect their sense of self and their place in the world [and] the rootedness that culture provides.
>
> (Holden, 2006, 22)

Harder to capture than the statistical data and numerical evidence associated with the performance accountability of instrumentalism, intrinsic value went largely under-reported. As a result, acknowledging the full range of values arising from museums, measured through a holistic model that would accommodate qualitative as well as quantitative data became something of a mantra for the sector.

In theory and in practice, Mark Moore's concept of Public Value captured the imagination of the cultural sector in the early 2000s. It was developed with the publicly funded sector in mind, aimed at fulfilling public institutions' mission to make a positive difference in the individual and collective lives of citizens and offered a refreshing alternative to the top-down and directive model of public sector management in place at the time.

Mark Moore's theory of public value

Mark Moore's model of public value proposed an alliance of authorisers (government, bureaucrats and funders) and operational agencies (publicly funded institutions) that would work together in a combined effort to create value for the public. It held out hope for a new, consensual accord between authorisers and providers based on the common ethos of public service. It envisaged a role for public managers as proactive stewards of public assets, a role for policy makers and bureaucrats as visionaries and a role for the public in their role as active citizens- co-producing and legitimating 'public value'.

Moore went further. Public value was not only a management concept- it required practical principles for implementation. Moore stressed strategic, intentional, results-based planning and measurable outcomes. Measurement, in particular, was central to the practice of public value, a point on which Moore was unequivocal.

> performance measures are so important in developing and executing a value-creating strategy that it would be fair to say that one does not really have a strategy until one has developed the performance measures that go along with it. Developing and using performance measures is essential in managing each point of the strategic triangle. The measures are also essential in integrating the three parts of the triangle into a coherent whole. They allow ... managers to move from the realm of strategic potential to concrete, value-creating performance.
>
> (Moore and Moore, 2005, 81)

Moore situated the creation of public value firmly in the civic domain where it would address issues of common concern for present and future generations. For Moore, these issues of common interest were synonymous with meeting 'unmet and unresolved social needs' (Moore, 2007), a wide remit which could encompass building social capital, increasing social cohesion, contributing to cultural identity, encouraging individual well-being, fostering democratic dialogue and supporting sustainable development (Benington in Moore and Benington, 2011).

It was Moore's proactive approach to addressing social issues that appealed to New Labour during its term of office when, although Public Value was never substituted for the New Public Management, it did enjoy prominence in the discourses around social policy and public engagement. It stimulated a flurry of interest within government[2] as well as from policy research bodies such as the Work Foundation.[3] When the BBC sought to renewal its license in 2004,[4] it argued its case on the basis of the public value that it produced. In 2005, the Heritage Lottery Fund (HLF) commissioned DEMOS[5] to report on at the impact of HLF funding from the point of view of the public value resulting from HLF investment. From 2006, Arts Council England instituted a major research programme examining the public value of the arts (Bunting 2007) and in 2006, the Heritage Lottery Fund, the Department of Culture, Media and Sport, English Heritage and the National Trust made public value the subject of its conference on *Capturing the Public Value of Heritage*. The purpose of the conference captures the spirit of the time in which both the government and the cultural sector were actively engaging with the concept.

> In her essay *Better Places to Live*, Tessa Jowell [then Secretary for State and Minister for Culture, Media and Sport] challenges us all to find a new language for capturing the value and benefits of heritage. Public Value is potentially providing that framework. Public Value is about the contribution that public services can make to economic, social and environmental well-being that goes beyond what is normally measured through performance targets. It is about capturing the wider impact and outcomes of services.
>
> (HLF, DCMS, EH, NT,[6] 2006, 1)

However, as O'Brien notes, the concept of public value has had an uneven trajectory in the UK. It is O'Brien's view that theoretical uncertainly surrounding the meaning of public value has not helped it to weather changing political conditions. He argues (in Scott, 2013, 146) that a lack of clarity around the concept has contributed to its diffusion, 'making it possible for the concept to be taken up in a range of contexts (often in surprisingly contradictory ways)'. Additionally, he suggests that public value has failed as a measurement framework, rendering it unable to provide an evidence base commensurate with the 'forms of economic valuation useful for the cost-benefit analysis associated with UK central government' (in Scott, 2013, 149).

While there is evidence to support both these claims, they form only part of the story. The loss of currency around the term 'public value' and its decline in the public discourse of museums is attributable to several factors. Moreover, while the *term* 'public value' is used less, the public value approach is evident to some degree in the increasing trend among museums to consciously consider the work that they do in terms of the positive social difference it can make. However, as the mantra of the 'social work of museums' is increasingly adopted by the sector, its implementation is revealing the complexities and the challenges related to the language used, how the impact of activity directed at the public realm is measured and whether the public actually wants museums to move in these directions. These issues are explored through the following three case studies.

Public value and cultural values

Definitional uncertainty surrounding the term 'public value' appears to be one of the factors contributing to its waning usage. It has been described as an advocacy strategy to make the case for the value of arts and cultural heritage in a time of rapid political change and declining resources, as a management model, as a framework for measuring the performance of public organisations and as an ethos for public sector provision based on its reciprocal and normative dimensions.

> Public value can be seen in two ways: First what the public values and second what adds value to the public sphere.
>
> (Benington in Moore and Benington, 2011, 42)

O'Brien argues that this definitional uncertainty worked against the survival of public value as a concept when the social agenda of New Labour gave way to economic policy in the wake of the global financial crisis (in Scott, 2013, 146). While O'Brien's argument goes some way to explaining its weakening in the political sphere, its waning in the cultural sector is also due to its becoming subsumed within the larger 'value' debates that dominated cultural discourse during the late 1990s and into the first decade of this century.

The widely-held perception that New Labour's instrumentalist agenda had been imposed from above, diverting cultural activity from core purposes and effectively relegating the importance of intrinsic value to the side-lines, became increasingly contentious. A circuit breaker occurred in 2003 when *AEA* consulting[7] and the think-tank, DEMOS, joined forces to organise the *Valuing Culture* forum. Invited guests from the then government and bureaucracy were challenged to recognise the wider universe of values generated by culture and experienced by cultural users. The focus at the forum was on giving intrinsic value a seat at the table.

At the forum, Adrian Ellis of AEA forcefully argued that intrinsic value was 'underarticulated and, given an environment where there is a strong bias towards the quantifiable, undervalued' (2003, 3). The impact of this and other impassioned presentations became evident when the Hon. Tessa Jowell (then Secretary for State and Minister for Culture, Media and Sport) drafted a personal monograph following the forum titled *Government and the Value of Culture* (Jowell, 2004) in which she acknowledged that the 'intrinsic' value of culture was as important as its instrumental impact. This effectively opened the discourse to a wider conversation about the range of values associated with cultural activity and its outcomes.

In 2006, John Holden sought to bring further clarity to the values debates by repurposing Moore's strategic triangle and aligning each of the authorising, operational and public nodes to one of three types of value. He aligned instrumental value with the authorising sector of funders and policy makers, institutional value with the operational public sector agencies and intrinsic value with the individual experience of users arising from cultural engagement. This approach brought clarity to the discussion around cultural value. The perspectives of all major stakeholders were admitted and the fact that culture produced different types of value of importance to each stakeholder group was acknowledged. Public value was reconstituted as 'institutional value', a designation which may have further served to diffuse its meaning within the cultural sector. There were also attempts to subsume all 'forms' of value (intrinsic, instrumental, institutional and use value) within an overarching rubric. Ellis used the term 'cultural value' at the *Valuing Culture* forum, a phrase that was subsequently adopted by both John Holden in his two monographs[8] (2004; 2006) and by Sara Selwood in her 2010 study of the cultural impact of the UK's national museums.

On the one hand, a legacy from this period of value debate is a more nuanced awareness that cultural value is multivariate. On the other hand, building a case for culture based on values' identification, measurement and articulation continued to present challenges. Holden argued, that the cultural sector needed an overarching and

> convincing narrative to validate its activities – a narrative that must convince the world at large. A new language is needed to develop both a cast-iron case for public funding of culture and the systemic and organisational forms and practices needed to deliver continuing public support. This will only come about if we can find ways to recognise why people value culture, and if we can find ways to articulate how public institutions – funders and funded cultural organisations-create value.
>
> (Holden, 2004, 47–48)

At one point, it seemed that the overarching concept of public value might provide that convincing narrative, energising the sector, resolving the impasse between authorisers and service providers and focusing on creating public good in the civic domain. Over a decade has passed since Holden's challenge. In ensuing period, the convincing narrative is yet to be defined and other factors have intervened to influence and deflect focus away from public value as an overarching concept. Although the term 'public value' has not travelled well, elements of its practice have travelled better.

Changing political conditions

In an ideal world, Moore's theory and practice of public value involves a proactive process in which authorisers and operational managers jointly decide how public assets can be used to address issues of common concern to citizens. In the face of massive decreases in public spending over the last six years, the focus for public sector managers has been necessarily diverted to the struggle for institutional survival.

A change in government from 2010 coinciding with the world financial crisis, witnessed a shift from a social to an economic policy focus. Since then, year-on-year cuts to public funding have been the norm. The Museums Associations' 2015 survey of the impact of these cuts on museums found that, among the respondents to the survey, 'total income had decreased for 47% of respondents in 2015, 52% in 2014, 49% in 2013, 32% in 2012 and 58% in 2011' (MA, 2015, 5), forcing the attention of both national and local museums to secure and maintain sustainable subsidies.

The funding dilemma has impacted how museums define themselves to funders and bureaucrats. Increasingly, the case for funding is based on evidence of 'contributory value' to a social agenda established by external stakeholders. This is evident in the Association of Independent Museums' (AIM)[9] Social Impact Toolkit, '*Evidencing Environmental and Social Impacts of Museums*' (2014) where museums are advised to examine their existing activity for evidence of direct, indirect or longer term contributions to 'outcomes that are valued by specific audiences' (AIM 2014: 4).

'Contribution' is the approach underlying the 2015 report prepared by the National Museum Directors Council (NMDC) in anticipation of the Comprehensive Spending Review of November that year. Titled *Museums Matter*, it provides a combination of statistical and case study evidence to demonstrate that the UK's national and major regional museums add to the achievement of nine public priority areas.[10] Though the term 'public value' is not used in the report, NMDC nevertheless identifies museums as 'civic institutions' with a role in 'maintaining a healthy and prosperous civil society' (NMDC, 2015, 4). A similar approach was adopted by Arts Council England (ACE) for their 2014 Advocacy Toolkit. ACE have built on the outcomes of their 2014 evidence review, *The Value of Art and Culture to People and Society*, abstracting highlights from the review and combining them with statistical data to show how art and culture impacts the economy, health and wellbeing, education and society.

Is contributing to public policy priorities creating public value? Yes, to some degree. But one of the factors that differentiates this situation from what Mark Moore envisaged is whether the operational sector is engaged in the identification and setting of those priorities. In practice, the public agenda continues to be defined by those authorising policy and funding, leaving museums to argue their public value in terms set by others. A more proactive approach is evident when the priorities are set by museums themselves and directed intentionally towards social impact and social change. This, however, uncovers another set of challenges.

Social change, the public and public value

The stated purposes of the Federation of International Human Rights Museums (FIHRM) appear to be aligned with Moore's vision of the role of public value in addressing unmet needs and unresolved social issues. FIHRM began as an initiative of the International Slavery Museum at National Museums Liverpool (NML), a consortium of museums with an acknowledged history in addressing one of Britain's more controversial social issues. In 1996, under the directorship of the late Sir Richard Foster, NML was the first museum in the UK to curate an exhibition on the international slave trade and to discuss the enabling role that the Port of Liverpool played in transporting slaves during the eighteenth and nineteenth centuries. A decade after this first exhibition, NML opened their International Slavery Museum[11] and in 2010 the Slavery Museum coordinated the establishment of the Federation of International Human Rights Museums (FIHRM).

The Federation of International Human Rights Museums (FIHRM) is now a world-wide coalition that locates its practice firmly within the framework of social activism, arguing that

> to be socially responsible, ethical and engaged in current social discourses museums have to be more active in trying to reconsider their social value so that they can fulfil their duty of social responsibility.[12]

FIHRM aims to support museums dealing with 'difficult, politically-loaded, and controversial subjects'. Its stated purpose is to address human rights issues by 'challenging contemporary racism, discrimination and other human rights abuses' through subjects such as the transatlantic slave trade, genocide and the plight of many indigenous peoples (www.fihrm.org/about/).

The current president of the FIHRM is also both Director of National Museums Liverpool and President of the UK Museums Association. Some common threads are discernible across the stated purposes of the FIHRM and the Museum Association's vision for the sector.

In the UK Museums Association's strategic direction for museums (*Museums Change Lives*), references to the term 'public value' are absent but underlying principles such as the public as co-producers ('Audiences are creators as well as consumers of knowledge' (MA, 2013, 4)) and the public service ethos at the heart of public value ('Good museums offer excellent experiences that meet public needs' (MA, 2013, 4)) resonate with Moore's guiding principles.

Museums Change Lives also shares with FIHRM the view that museums can and should engage in social change and social justice ('Effective museums engage with contemporary issues; Social justice is at the heart of the impact of museums; Museums are not neutral spaces' (MA, 2013: 4). *Museums Change Lives* states that

> museums can be ambitious about their role in society. All museums, however they are funded and whatever their subject matter, can support positive social change.
>
> (MA, 2013, 3).

Within these documents, the use of 'social', in the definitional sense of 'society', is the preferred term. There is also an undercurrent of the 'transformational' in the language used, something which can be detected in other literature emerging around the theme of the social work of museums. This is, in fact, the title of the book by Lois Silverman (2010) who states in the Preface her belief that 'the most important and essential work museums do is to use their unique resources to benefit human relationships and, ultimately, repair the world'.

Repairing the world is a tall order and an approach which has its critics. Bennett (1989) and Holden (2006) dispute claims that museums can compensate for structural inequalities in society, a view shared by Appleton (2002) who questions the suitability of museums as agents of social change, and their capacity to assume responsibility for solving deep-seated socio-economic problems. In their critique of the public value concept, Rhodes and Wanna (2007) further argue that public value poses a threat to public managers by expecting them to act in overtly political ways and by encouraging them to become self-appointed interpreters and guardians of the public interest.

Social activism also sits uncomfortably with the strongly held view of museums as neutral, unbiased and, therefore, trustworthy institutions.

> Museums hold a unique position of being trusted, which is particularly important given the perceived lack of trusted organisations in society such as the government and the media. Both of these are seen as biased and operating under agendas. Members of the public who took part [in this study], see museums as the guardians of factual information and as presenting all sides of the story.
>
> (Britain Thinks, 2013, 3)

Most importantly (and though it may be stating the obvious), the public need to be consulted about social interventions that are likely to affect them. Moore is adamant that understanding citizens' preferences and involving them in value creation is essential and that failure to do so may result in services not delivering value that the public view as legitimate.

In this spirit of consultation, the Museum Association commissioned Britain Thinks to conduct research with the public 'to understand perceptions of and attitudes to the roles and purposes of museums in society' (Britain Thinks, 2013, 3). It was the Museums Associations' intention to use the outcomes of the study to inform the development of its strategic plan. At the time, the Association had adopted 'public benefit' (Heal in Scott, 2013, 169) as its framework and was seeking to test public perceptions and responses to several areas of proposed social intervention. This is all in line with the co-production ethos that Moore espouses but what it revealed is a salutary lesson. Co-production admits other values and others' values may not be aligned with those of the institution or the organisation.

Although the Britain Thinks study found that museums are highly valued by the British public, it also found that the public had equally strong views about what should be the limits of museums' social intervention. In the opinion of the respondents, museum work in caring, preserving and exhibiting the collection, building knowledge and providing information were the highest priorities. Fostering community development, helping the vulnerable and protecting the environment were rated as low priorities. Providing a forum for debate and promoting social justice and human rights were challenged outright.

> This is not to say that people felt museums cannot broach controversial subjects, but that they should remain neutral in the displaying of information, rather than act as a leader in telling people what to think. The role of museums is very much seen as having a moral standpoint, as opposed to a political standpoint. . . . The public (negatively) interpreted these purposes as promoting a political/subjective viewpoint.
>
> (Britain Thinks, 2013, 5)

Involving the public in interventions which may affect them is essential, a principle which Moore emphasises and which UK museums are embracing. However, when the public are involved, as the results of the Britain Thinks study demonstrates, the results may not be aligned with the social activist agenda of either the institution or its management.

Proving public value

Joanne Orr (in Scott, 2013, 173–184) describes what might be one of the rare examples where an authorising sector and the operational sector have joined forces to deliver a programme.

In 2010, the Scottish Government requested Museums and Galleries Scotland (MGS) to accept the role as the National Development Body to deliver the Scottish Government's National Strategy for museums. The strategy has been developed through a wide consultative process with the Scottish museums' sector discussing and debating the national themes outlined by government. From the time of adopting this new role, MGS has defined its work through the lens of public value and is one of the few museum organisations that consistently uses the term.

> Scotland's museums and galleries will be ambitious, dynamic and sustainable enterprises: connecting people, places and collections; inspiring, delighting and creating public value.
>
> (MGS, 2012, 14)

While the term 'public value' is liberally used throughout the strategic plan *Going Further: the National Strategy for Scotland's Museums and Galleries* (2015–19) and its companion document, *Realising the Vision; Delivering public value through Scotland's museums and galleries* (2015–19) it is nowhere specifically defined, leaving it, as O'Brien foreshadowed (in Scott, 2013, 149), open to being reconstituted and adapted to new purposes. Within the MGS strategy and delivery documents, the overriding inference is that public value will be achieved as a *logical outcome* if the combined aims[13] of the National Strategy are realised.

> Ultimately the Strategy Delivery Cycle offers the means to achieve the vision for the sector, driving up the public value that can be delivered by museums and galleries.
>
> (MGS, 2015, 42)

The objectives of the National Strategy are laudable and some, such as 'strengthen connections between museums, people and places to inspire greater public participation, learning and well-being', focus directly on beneficial outcomes for the wider public. But while Moore stressed the need for intentional, results-based planning linked to clear measures of achievement, the MGS approach is indicative of a generally held view that museum activity automatically accrues to the public realm. This tendency is noted in the critical review undertaken by Scott et al. (2014) for the Cultural Value Project, which found a widely held but largely untested assumption that the aggregation of museum activity and participation by users will make a positive difference in the public domain. In fact,

> we have surprising little evidence that positive encounters in the museum accrue to the public realm and what kind of social difference and change might result.
>
> (Scott et al., 2014, 29).

Ruiz (2004) points out that this lack of social impact evidence is directly attribut-able to the absence of clear, measurable objectives. She concludes that '[e]valuation, particularly of social inclusion initiatives, requires clear formulation of project aims and should look for sustained changes in the community' (2004, 29). While monitor-ing and evaluation are embedded in the MGS Strategy, there is a tendency to assess the 'outcomes' against the objectives of the strategy rather than its 'impact' on the Scottish population as a whole. One of the reasons cited for the diminution of public value in the general discourse is its failure to prove itself in ways commensurate with the 'forms of economic valuation useful for the cost-benefit analysis associated with UK central government' (O'Brien in Scott, 2013, 145). Development of a robust evidence base demonstrating that museum activity creates measurable public value puts the sector on notice that its approaches to both planning and evaluation require a more systematic approach.

Conclusion

Public value has not become the overarching framework within which museum activity can be directed, planned, measured and substantiated. While it has been the casualty of changing policies that have deflected attention from its social message to one where economic survival is increasingly paramount, it has also suffered from an incomplete understanding of the essential principles underlying its successful implementation.

What does survive is its focus on the public and creating impact in the civic domain evident in the emerging emphasis on the social role and responsibility of museums. Implementing the social responsibility agenda is also revealing some of the inherent tensions and contradictions for museums which is part of an iterative process in which museums are redefining their role and their relationships with the public. As O'Brien (in Scott, 2013, 154) states

> Frameworks take on a life of their own, morphing and transforming as they move from context to context. Whilst the prospects for the language of public value may be pessimistic, its adaptation in the UK to concerns with immeasurable forms of value, rhetorical strategies of defending cultural funding as well as offering frameworks that have tried to engage with narrowly economic versions of tech-nocratic policy making, suggest the lessons of public value may have embedded themselves within the UK's cultural sector.

Notes

1 Several references in this chapter have been published in *Museums and Public Value: Creating Sustainable Futures* (Scott, 2013).
2 Kelly, G., Mulgan, G. and Muers, S. wrote *Creating Public Value: An Analytical Framework for Public Service Reform* for the Strategy Unit of the Cabinet Office in 2002.
3 Blaug, 2006.
4 Collins, 2007; Davies, 2004.
5 DEMOS describes itself as Britain's 'leading cross-party think-tank'. It produces original research, publishes innovative thinkers and hosts thought-provoking events. See www.demos.co.uk/about/
6 Heritage Lottery Fund (HLF), Department of Culture, Media and Sport (DCMS), English Heritage (EH) and the National Trust (NT).

 7 AEA Consulting has been operating since 1991 and describes itself as one of the world's leading cultural consulting firms. See http://aeaconsulting.com/about
 8 *Capturing Cultural Value: How Culture Has Become a Tool of Government Policy* (2004) and *Cultural Value and the Crisis of Legitimacy: Why Culture Needs a Democratic Mandate* (2006).
 9 A museums association dedicated to supporting independently funded museums in the UK.
10 The priority areas are: creating a thriving, vibrant and diverse cultural life for the nation; contributing to regional prosperity; developing tourism – museums are the country's most popular visitor attractions; strengthening the UK's soft power; developing peaceful and prosperous communities by creating safe and welcoming community spaces; promoting health and well-being; education, life-long learning, skills development and apprenticeships; being world leaders in scientific, technological an creative innovation.
11 23 August 2007 is the date of the annual International Day for the Remembrance of the Slave Trade and its Abolition marking the beginning of the slave uprising in Santo Domingo and the bicentennial year of the United Kingdom's Slave Trade Act of 1807, which abolished the slave trade in the UK.
12 FIHRM and INTERCOM 2014 conference *Museums and Social Impact*, 1–4 May, Taipei, Taiwan.
13 Maximise the potential of our collections and culture; strengthen connections between museums, people and places to inspire greater public participation, learning and well-being; empower a diverse workforce to increase their potential for the benefit of the sector and beyond; forge a sustainable future for sector organisations and encourage a culture of enterprise; foster a culture of collaboration innovation and ambition; and develop a global perspective using Scotland's collections and culture.

References

Appleton, J., 2002, 'Distorted priorities are destroying museums'. *The Independent*, 29 May, 16.

ACE (Arts Council England), 2014, *The Value of Arts and Culture to People and Society – An Evidence Review*. London: Arts Council England.

AIM (Association of Independent Museums), 2014, *Evidencing Social and Environmental Impacts of Museums: AIM Advocacy Toolkit*. Available online at www.aim-museums.co.uk/content/evidencing_social_and_environmental_impacts_of_museums/

Benington, J., 2011, From Private Choice to Public Value? In Moore, M. and Benington, J. (eds), *Public Value: Theory and Practice*. London: Palgrave Macmillan, 31–51.

Bennett, T., 1989, 'Museums and the public good: economic rationalism and cultural policy'. *Culture and Policy*, 1(1), 37–51.

Britain Thinks, 2013, *Public Perceptions of – and Attitudes to – the Purposes of Museums in Society. A Report Prepared by Britain Thinks for the Museums Association*. Museum Association, Arts Council England (ACE), Welsh Government and Museums Galleries Scotland.

Bunting, C., 2007, *Public Value and the Arts in England: Discussion and Conclusions of the Arts Debate*. Available online at www.artscouncil.org.uk/publication_archive/public-value-and-the-arts-in-england-discussion-and-conclusions-of-the-arts-debate/

Blaug, R., Horner, L. and Lekhi, R., 2006, *Public Value, Politics and Public Management: A Literature Review*. London: The Work Foundation.

Collins, R., 2007, *Public Value and the BBC*. The Work Foundation: London.

Davies, G., 2004, *The BBC and Public Value*. Social Market Foundation: London.

DCMS (Department for Culture, Media and Sport), 1998, *A New Cultural Framework*. London: DCMS.

DCMS (Department for Culture, Media and Sport), 1999, *Policy Action Team 10: Report on Social Exclusion, Social Exclusion Unit*. London: DCMS.

DCMS (Department of Culture, Media and Sport), 2000, *Centers for Social Change:*

Museums, Galleries and Libraries for all: Policy Guidance on Social Inclusion for DCMS Funded and Local Authority Museums, Galleries and Archives in England. London: DCMS.

Ellis, A., 2003, 'Valuing culture', paper presented at the *Valuing Culture* event held at the National Theatre Studio on 17th June 2003, organised by DEMOS in partnership with the National Gallery, the National Theatre and AEA Consulting.

HLF (Heritage Lottery Fund), DCMS (Department of Culture, Media and Sport), EH (English Heritage) and NT (National Trust), 2006, *Capturing the Public Value of Heritage*, 25–26 January 2006. Royal Geographical Society: London.

Holden, J., 2004, *Capturing Cultural Value: How Culture Has Become a Tool of Government Policy*. London: Demos.

Holden, J., 2006, *Cultural value and the crisis of legitimacy: why culture needs a democratic mandate*. London: Demos.

Horner L., Lekhi R. and Blaug, R., 2006, *Deliberative democracy and the role of public managers: Final report of The Work Foundation's public value consortium*. London: The Work Foundation.

Jowell, T., 2004, *Government and the Value of Culture*. London: DCMS.

Kelly, G., Mulgan, G. and Muers, S., 2002, *Creating Public Value: An Analytical Framework for Public Service Reform*. London: Strategy Unit, Cabinet Office.

Moore, M., 1995. *Creating Public Value: Strategic Management in Government*. Cambridge, MA: Harvard University Press.

Moore M., 2007, *Creating Public Value: Strategic Management in Government*. Presentation at CIPFA Conference, 12–14 June, 2007: Scotland.

Moore M. and Moore G., 2005, *Creating Public Value Through State Arts Agencies*. Minneapolis: Arts Midwest.

Moore M. and Benington J. (eds), 2011, *Public Value: Theory and Practice*. London: Palgrave and Macmillan.

MA (Museums Association), 2013, *Museums Change Lives*. London: Museums Association.

MA (Museums Association), 2015, *Cuts Survey 2015*. London: Museums Association.

MGS (Museums and Galleries Scotland), 2015, *Going Further: The National Strategy for Scotland's Museums and Galleries*. Edinburgh: Museums and Galleries Scotland.

MGS (Museums and Galleries Scotland), 2015. *Realising the Vision: Delivering Public Value Through Scotland's Museums and Galleries 2015–2019*. Edinburgh: Museums and Galleries Scotland.

NMDC (National Museums' Directors Council), 2015, *Museums Matter*. London: NMDC.

O'Brien, D., 2013, Public Value and Public Policy in Britain: Prospects and Perspectives. In Scott, C.A. (ed.), *Museums and Public Value: Creating Sustainable Futures*. Farnham: Ashgate, 145–157.

Orr, J., 2013. Going Further: Public Value in Scotland. In Scott, C.A. (ed.), *Museums and Public Value: Creating Sustainable Futures*. Farnham: Ashgate, 173–184.

Research Centre for Museums and Galleries (RCMG), 2000. *Museums and Social Inclusion: The GLLAM Report*. Research Centre for Museums and Galleries (RCMG) and Group for Large Local Authority Museums.

Rhodes, R. and Wanna, J., 2007, The limits to public value, or rescuing responsible government from the platonic guardians. *The Australian Journal of Public Administration*, 66(4), 406–421.

Ruiz, J., 2004, *A Literature Review of The Evidence Base For Culture, the Arts And Sport Policy*. Edinburgh: Research and Economic Unit of the Scottish Executive Education Department.

Scott, C.A. (ed.), 2013, *Museums and Public Value: Creating Sustainable Futures*. Farnham: Ashgate.

Scott, C., Dodd, J. and Sandell, R., 2014, *User Value of Museums and Galleries: A Critical*

View Of The Literature. Arts and Humanities Research Council. Available online at www2. le.ac.uk/.../rcmg/publications/cultural-value-of-museums

Selwood, S., 2010, Making a difference: the cultural impact of museums. *National Museums Directors Conference* website. Available online at www.nationalmuseums.org.uk/media/ documents/publications/cultural_impact_final.pdf

Silverman, L., 2010, *The Social Work of Museums*. Abingdon: Routledge.

Weil, S., 2003, *When the Public Comes First, What Follows: Ten Consequences of Decentralising the Collection and Shifting the Focus to the Public*, public lecture at the Powerhouse Museum, Sydney, Australia 27 August, 2003.

19 Public value and cultural heritage

Kate Clark and Rob Lennox[1]

Introduction

> The strategic problem for public managers came to be: imagine and articulate a vision of public value that can command legitimacy and support, and is operationally doable in the domain for which you have responsibility.
>
> (Moore and Khagram, 2004, 9)

In the past 20 years concepts of public value have made their way into widespread use within cultural heritage. Many professionals and academics (e.g. Clark, 2004; 2014) have explored the relationship of heritage and the public and this work has affected the theories and management of heritage in a substantial way. One particularly influential catalyst for the use of public value in cultural heritage was an event in 2006, which brought together representatives from citizens' juries, as well as academics, community groups, heritage practitioners, politicians and think-tanks to debate the value of heritage (Clark, 2006). The event was inspired by a study undertaken by John Holden and Robert Hewison for the Heritage Lottery Fund (2006) which drew on Mark Moore's 1995 work *Creating Public Value*. They used Moore's public value thesis to argue that heritage needed to develop an effective framework for defining why heritage was valued and relevant to society, which focused on outcomes, measured performance, and effectively communicate this to stakeholders including politicians and the public.

Despite the decline in the prominence, use and discussion of public value theory in heritage in the 2010s, public value thinking is still relevant to heritage (Lennox, 2016). In particular, Moore's 'authorising environment' still provides an effective basis to guide the strategic engagement of heritage sector organisations with their political, professional and public stakeholders in a way that resonates with museum practice on audience development.

This chapter provides an overview of how ideas of value have been used in heritage, and how concepts of public value have added to that debate. It also provides a brief summary of that work, considers how research into the way citizens (or non-specialists) value heritage projects is vital to the process of heritage management, and sets out how the framework for public value operation could work in a way which might have broader application and thus contribute to thinking about public value in other contexts.

Public value and heritage

Over the past two decades, there has been a growing discourse within cultural heritage which reflects a shift from thinking of heritage primarily in terms of national patrimony and material importance to one which emphasises the connections between people and their environments (Ashworth et al., 2007; English Heritage, 2000). These 'public' concerns define a heritage which is dynamic, plural, and experienced, rather than static, objectively assessed, and materialistic. People care about their heritage, visiting historic sites and museums, campaigning to save much-loved local assets, volunteering for, or visiting historic places, and there is a thriving third sector supporting it. At a wider policy level, cultural heritage plays a role in culture and the arts, the natural and built environment, the economy, and society more generally; it shapes identity and distinctiveness, helps create social inclusion and jobs, and contributes to environmental performance and the quality of public spaces.

Yet, for organisations which seek to claim a share of public funding, any argument of heritage for heritage's sake is likely to be insufficient. Rather, organisations must continually reflect upon value in order to retain a connection with people, remain in touch with their desires, as well as generate income and justify investment, in order to compete with wider claims on resources. The question of what is worth protecting and why has always been central to managing cultural heritage, so there is a considerable literature around heritage values and how they are defined. Over time a distinction has emerged between two different kinds of value for heritage - the significance of heritage items that is the reason for protecting them, and the benefits that flow from investing in heritage. The distinction between these two different ways in which investing in heritage creates value has been explored in more detail through the GCI (Getty Conservation Institute) values project (GCI, 1998–2005; Avrami et al., 2000), and is reflected in policies such as the English Heritage Conservation Principles (English Heritage, 2008) and the Council of Europe Faro document (CoE, 2005).

The first kind of value - of special interest or 'significance' underpins decisions about what to protect and justifies the resources put into its long-term care, especially when its original use or function no longer exists. Statements about value or significance underpin the formal system of protecting archaeological monuments such as Stonehenge from the late nineteenth century onwards, and historic buildings and places as part of the land-use planning system that emerged in the UK primarily after World War II. Sites normally need to have a level of importance that justifies that protection, intervention and sometimes funding. But ideas about significance or meaning go beyond protected sites – there are lots of different ways in which people value places, or collections or things and understanding those values is a core part of managing any kind of heritage (e.g. ICOMOS, 2013; English Heritage, 2008; Historic England, 2015; Russell and Winkworth, 2010).

In addition to ascribed values (i.e. attachments or feelings), value can also be assessed in terms of the benefits – which may *arise naturally* as a consequence of the interaction of people and place (e.g. feelings of happiness, wellbeing, identity, or pride) or may be *created* directly as a result of investment in or management of heritage (Lennox, 2016). These benefits take a range of forms and can be economic, social, or environmental.[2]

In terms of economic benefits, there may be jobs created through repairing historic buildings, through operating heritage sites to attract visitors, and indirectly through the contribution that heritage makes to the wider liveability of places. There may be direct or indirect investments in local businesses, and benefits to individuals through the increased financial value of protected heritage assets and delivered through tourism (Throsby, 2010; Rypkema, 2005; Oxford Economics, 2016; Mason, 2010).

In terms of social benefits, museums, sites and other heritage attractions provide opportunities for enjoyment, and learning. People who take an active part in heritage projects as volunteers report greater confidence, friendship and such projects can be routes into employment. Revitalised heritage places such as public parks can contribute to amenity and the local quality of life, and provide health benefits in terms of outdoor recreation and exercise (e.g. Historic England, 2016).

There are also environmental benefits to caring for cultural heritage – retaining older buildings reduces waste, there is embodied energy in the materials used to construct them, and older buildings can often perform better than newer buildings in energy efficiency tests, and in overall greenhouse gas reduction, especially if the energy embodied in construction is taken into account.

But in all of this, there has been less focus on how heritage organisations themselves create value through what they do or the services they provide. In his work on public value, Mark Moore has looked at how public sector organisations create value in the absence of a clear mandate to generate a profit or create financial value for shareholders (Moore, 1995). His work on the police goes beyond traditional models of value measurement such as crime reduction statistics, to look at how the police create value through the service they provide, and measures such as trust and accountability. With Gaylen Williams Moore, he also applied public value to arts organisations, which have traditionally measured value through targets such as audience numbers, arguing that such narrow measures fail to capture the many other ways in which engagement with the arts can create value for individuals or communities (see Moore and Williams Moore, 2005). In that work he also recognized the need to understand different audiences for that value.

Public value in the heritage sector

The inspiration for applying public value to a cultural heritage organisation came through a project undertaken by John Holden and Robert Hewison for the Heritage Lottery Fund (HLF) (see Holden and Hewison, 2004). Set up in 1994, the HLF had by 2004 given over £3bn to heritage projects, covering the full range of heritage including tangible and intangible heritage, objects, sites, buildings, collections and places including historic areas. The HLF has an explicit philosophy of involving communities in heritage, and is not restricted to funding heritage that is protected by statute.

The fund already had an active policy of evaluating the impact and benefits of its funding including evaluations of targeted programmes for public parks, large museum projects and local heritage, as well as studies focussing on economic, social and neighbourhood outcomes from funded projects (Clark, 2004). The result was a mass of economic and social data which could be used for many different purposes.[3] However, taken together these studies did not create a compelling narrative around the value of investing in cultural heritage – nor did they provide a framework for critically evaluating the wider effectiveness of that funding.

In order to address this challenge, Demos, a prominent centre-left think tank who had close connections with Tony Blair's New Labour government, commissioned

Holden and Hewison to explore new ways of capturing the value of investment in heritage and on why culture needed a 'democratic mandate' to overcome a crisis of legitimacy (Holden, 2005; 2006). They reviewed different models for value for heritage including economic models, anthropological and environmental models. Crucially, they drew attention to Moore's work on public value in organisations (Holden and Hewison, 2004; Moore, 1995). They identified nine measures that together covered the various different ways in which the public and cultural value of HLFs processes, practice and outputs might be captured. These were:

- Stewardship
- Enhanced trust in public institutions
- Equity and fairness
- Resilience in the organisation and systems they are funding
- Value for money
- Well being
- Prosperity
- Learning
- Strengthened local communities.

In effect, this work broadened out the concept of the value of heritage to include organisational values (trust, equity and fairness, and resilience); as well as more traditional indicators relating to the benefits of funding to heritage (stewardship) and the benefits that flowed from investing in it (wellbeing, prosperity, learning).

For example, Hewison and Holden (2004) brought together existing concepts of value in heritage with Moore's thinking about public value to create a powerfully simple model for conceptualising the different ways in which heritage organisations can create value. These organisations, the model explains, can create value for the public by caring for, protecting or providing access to what is significant to people, by delivering wider economic, social and environmental benefits through doing so, and finally by ensuring that the way in which is accountable, trustworthy, fair and delivers good value for money.

The three kinds of value were labelled 'intrinsic', 'instrumental' and 'institutional' values (or perhaps more memorably, 'significance, sustainability and service'). Together they can be used in advocacy to articulate the different ways in which heritage creates value or in evaluation and research to present data around different kinds of outcomes and impacts. This model (see Figure 19.1) enabled researchers to draw on other impact frameworks such as sustainability or wellbeing outcomes, whilst also recognising that the special nature of heritage lies in its meaning for people.

In their more recent work, Meynhardt and Bartholomes (2011) note that concepts of public value are grounded in individual perceptions of value. This issue was also addressed as part of that original HLF project through a series of individual citizens juries which sought to work in a detailed process with non-specialists. In terms of what was significant to them, Jurors identified the most important values for heritage projects as:

- knowledge value,
- identity value,

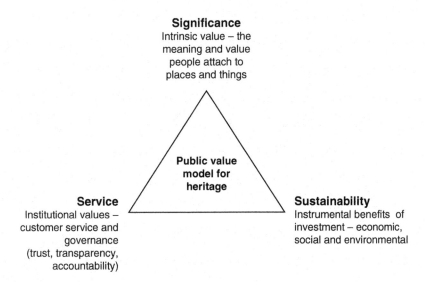

Significance
Intrinsic value – the
meaning and value
people attach to
places and things

**Public value
model for
heritage**

Service
Institutional values –
customer service and
governance
(trust, transparency,
accountability)

Sustainability
Instrumental benefits of
investment – economic,
social and environmental

Figure 19.1 Public value model of heritage
Source: adapted from Holden, 2006

- bequest value and
- distinctiveness value.

The most important longer-term benefits for them were economic benefits in terms of regeneration and growth for the area in which projects were located, but they also identified broad, place-based benefits, such as the reputation of the area and reductions in antisocial behaviour as important. They highlighted the benefits to the community of projects including greater public spirit and mutual understanding, and also benefits to individuals such as skills and confidence (Mattinson, 2006).

Although the HLF itself was not the focus of the study, there were positive responses from the jurors to its approach to heritage. There was feedback on the types of projects funded, the importance of inclusivity, worries about the sustainability of projects and support for the enthusiasm of project representatives themselves.

Representatives from the citizen's juries were participants in the 2006 'Capturing Public Value of Heritage' conference where the aim was to open up a dialogue between as many different groups as possible about why heritage mattered and to whom, rather than necessarily to put forward any one single way of valuing heritage (Clark, 2006). As well as structuring information from the citizens' juries, the tripartite model for the public value of heritage was also used as a framework with which to interrogate the mass of data collected by HLF through its many evaluations and surveys including economic and social impact surveys, programme evaluations, customer service data and other data in order to explore the extent to which HLF could be shown to demonstrate value in each area (Clark and Maeer, 2008).

This was in contrast to some other heritage sector forays into public value, which have been seen as less about providing an evidence base (or exploring existing data) and more about generating platitudes about the public value and benefit of heritage (Lee et al., 2011). Yet, Meynhardt and Bartholomes (2011) remind us that public value is created through relationships between public sector organisations and the public, and that organisations can both add public value by increasing that perception of value, but also reduce it through poor institutional practice. The creation of public value is thus more akin to a process of engagement rather than a simple rhetorical narrative.

In more recent years, the literature around the value of heritage has continued to grow, particularly around contested values for heritage sites. For example, a major Arts & Humanities Research Council (AHRC) initiative includes seventy pieces of original work covering the cultural value of arts and heritage including museums and the historic environment (Holden and Balta, 2012; AHRC, 2015; Crossick and Kaszynska, 2015), and the value of heritage has continued to be a key topic for AHRC.

However, in the UK at least, since the economic recession in 2008, there has been a greater focus on evidencing economic sustainability in a new age of austerity. As a result, public value thinking has lost ground more widely and in the heritage sector where some came to doubt the validity of the framework. This led to the risk of the sector continuing to present a narrow protectionist base which does not connect with wider agendas and is of limited value to contemporary society. The very narrow approach to defining heritage and its value ultimately limits the potential for the sector to develop its relevance and engage in the way that Meynhardt and Bartholomes suggest (Lennox, 2016).

The authorising environment for heritage

In the context of pressures on the current sector, reinforcement of the public-centred, value-led understanding of the historic environment could be one way to enable the sector to respond better to political and social influences which act to shape the reputation, relevance, and political sustainability of the sector in practice. To do that, thinking about public value creates an opportunity for the sector to build stronger relationships within its 'authorising environment' – the key stakeholders or audiences on whom the sector relies for legitimacy and relevance.

The idea of the authorising environment was originally defined by Moore (1995), and for arts and culture organisations at least, characterised as falling into two main groups – 'up the line' funders and politicians, and 'down the line' visitors and customers. But, in reality, there are also a range of other organisations and groups who enable heritage bodies to function. Therefore, for cultural heritage organisations, the 'authorising environment' can be seen as made up of four broad groups:

- Politicians – elected members who, through state bodies, may be responsible for a significant proportion of the funding for heritage organisations and who in effect 'authorise' such organisations;
- Peers – professional groups in the museum or heritage sectors who often set ethical standards and have expectations around best practice (for example curatorial ethics, conservation standards);

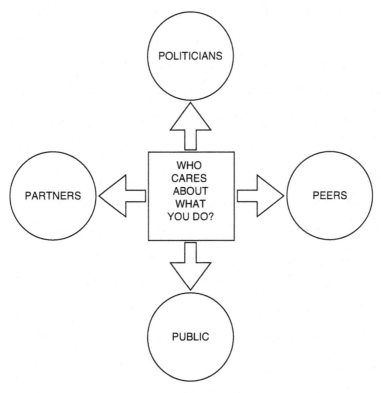

Figure 19.2 The authorising environment
Source: Clark, 2015

- Partners – the wide range of people and organisations in relevant positions outside the professional sector who actively work with heritage organisations such as businesses, non-heritage NGOs, supporters or benefactors;[4]
- Public – consumers who visit, live near or make use of heritage assets or places, including families, tourists, local people, individuals, as well as groups such as schools, education and special interest groups.

The basic model above (see Figure 19.2) shows the relationship between a heritage organisation and its authorising environment. This has been further developed by Lennox (2016, 238–242) who explores how organisations who adopt a public value framework for operation and seek strategic engagement with these audiences can pursue positive outcomes, such as enhanced democratic legitimacy and wider relevance.

However, in order to pursue better relationships with public, professional and political stakeholders and thus operate more effectively within this authorising environment, it is also important for heritage organisations to recognise that each of these different audiences might value heritage institutions in different ways. Therefore, having identified different audience segments, the next step is to establish what matters to them in terms of public value. This is akin to the museum and arts practice of audience development.

Table 19.1 Institutional values and audience priorities

	Politicians and public servants	Peers – professional colleagues	Partners – donors, volunteers, businesses	Public – visitors and service users
Internal procedures – audit, procurement	✗		✗	
Accountability	✗		✗	✗
Value for money	✗		✗	✗
Meeting budget targets	✗			
Health & safety	✗		✗	✗
Physical access to sites and collections		✗		✗
Customer service	✗			✗
Professional conservation standards		✗		
Ethical standards	✗	✗	✗	✗
Programmes, events and activities			✗	✗
Economic benefits/job creation	✗		✗	
Social benefits			✗	✗
Conservation of heritage assets		✗		✗

Table 19.1 provides examples of some of the different priorities that these groups might have. The table draws on the example of the typical reporting requirements of a medium-sized cultural heritage organisation, including a range of formal reporting requirements, such as targets, budget cycles, annual reports, audit and risk functions, customer surveys, visitor surveys, focus groups, as well as the informal requirements of working with different groups.

There are no hard and fast lines between types of value and audience – the key point is to explore and recognise Moore's argument, that different audiences might have different perceptions of value, and to take that into account when developing strategies to measure and account for the different ways in which heritage organisations create value.

Conclusions

In the mid-2000 public value theory offered a framework to justify heritage investment based on outcomes which produced public benefits. It took the truism that heritage mattered because people value it (in itself a fairly recent concern when justifying heritage practice) and provided a way to conceive of heritage as a tool to public benefit and to hold organisations to account for their institutional performance.

This chapter has set out to raise awareness of that earlier work on the public value of heritage and at the same time, to note some of the ways in which heritage practitioners have used ideas about value, including audience development. The overall aim has been to suggest that such thinking might have the potential to contribute to wider debates about public value in the business community.

Notes

1 Note that the views expressed in this article do not necessarily represent those of our employers.
2 Maeer, Robinson and Hobson compile annual survey of literature in the field of the value of heritage across museums, the natural and historic environment (Heritage Lottery Fund 2016). The annual Heritage Counts survey includes updates on recent research in the field as well as themed pieces.
3 Examples of evaluation reports are available at www.hlf.org.uk/about-us/research-eva luation/programme-evaluation
4 The model does not explicitly include staff – within an organization there is also effectively an internal authorizing environment which for any individual manager might include their line manager, their staff, their peers in their own department, and partners in other areas.

References

AHRC (Arts and Humanities Research Council) (2015). Cultural Value Project research activities. Available online at www.ahrc.ac.uk/research/fundedthemesandprogrammes/culturalvalueproject/research-activities/

Ashworth, G., Graham, J. and Tunbridge, J. (2007) *Pluralising Pasts: Heritage, Identity, and Place in Multicultural Societies*. London: Pluto Press.

Avrami, E., Mason, R. and de la Torre, M. (2000). *Values and Heritage Conservation*. Los Angeles: The Getty Conservation Institute, Available online at www.getty.edu/conservation/publications_resources/pdf_publications/values_heritage_research_report.html

Bakhshi, H., Freeman, A. and Hitchen, G. (2009) Measuring intrinsic value – how to stop worrying and love economics. Mission Money Models. Available online at https://mpra.ub.uni-muenchen.de/14902/ (accessed 7 January 2018).

Bakhshi, H., Fujiwara, D., Lawton, R., Mourato, S. and Dolan, P. (2016). *Measuring Economic Value in Cultural Institutions*. A report commissioned by the Arts and Humanities Research Council's Cultural Value Project. Available online at www.ahrc.ac.uk/documents/project-reports-and-reviews/measuringeconomicvalue/ (accessed 7 January 2018).

Belfiore, E. (2009). On bullshit in cultural policy practice and research: notes from the British case. *International Journal of Cultural Policy*, 15(3), 343–359.

Clark, K. (2004). Why fund heritage? The role of research in the Heritage Lottery Fund. *Cultural Trends*, 13(4), 65–85.

Clark, K. (ed.) (2006). *Capturing the public value of heritage: proceedings of the London conference*. London: English Heritage. Available online at www.academia.edu/3639888/Capturing_the_Public_Value_of_Heritage

Clark, K. (2010). Values in cultural resource management. In G. Smith, P. Messenger and H. Soderland (eds) *Heritage Values in Contemporary Society*. Walnut Creek, CA: Left Coast Books.

Clark, K. (2014). Values-based heritage management and the Heritage Lottery Fund in the UK. *APT Bulletin: Journal of Preservation Technology*, 45(2–3), 65–71.

Clark, K. (2015). *York Seminar Series*. [Lecture] York, University of York Department of Archaeology, 23 January 2015.

Clark, K. and Maeer, G. (2008). The Cultural Value of Heritage: evidence from the Heritage Lottery Fund. *Cultural Trends*, 17(1), 23–56.

Crossick, G. and Kaszynska, P. (2015). Understanding the value of arts & culture – the AHRC Cultural Value Project.

English Heritage (2000). *Power of Place*. London: English Heritage.

English Heritage (2008). *Conservation Principles, Policies and Guidance for the Sustainable Management of the Historic Environment*. Available online at www.english-heritage.org.uk/professional/advice/conservation-principles/

English Heritage (2011). National Heritage Protection Plan Framework Document. Available online at www.english-heritage.org.uk/publications/nhpp-plan-framework/nhpp-plan-framework.pdf

CoE (Council of Europe) (2005). *Faro Convention. Council of Europe Framework Convention on the Value of Cultural Heritage for Society.* Available online at http://conventions.coe.int/Treaty/EN/Treaties/Html/199.htm

Fujiwara, D., Cornwall, T. and Dolan, P. (2014) *Heritage and Well-Being.* Available online at http://media.wix.com/ugd/9ccf1d_8b7b5a4cf12641b5be13acf728a8c150.pdf (accessed 7 January 2018).

GCI (Getty Conservation Institute) (1998–2005). Research on the Values of Heritage. Available online at www.getty.edu/conservation/our_projects/field_projects/values/values_publications.html

Gillespie, M., Bell, S., Wilding, C., Webb, A., Fisher, A., Voss, A., Smith, A.W.M., Macfarlane, J., Martin, N., Foster, T. and Lvov, I. (2014). *Understanding the Changing Cultural Value of the BBC World Service and the British Council.* Arts and Humanities Research Council. Available online at http://oro.open.ac.uk/42254/

Heritage Lottery Fund (nd). *Trustee and Members Handbook, Section 2: Organisational Context.* Available online at www.hlf.org.uk/aboutus/decisionmakers/Newhandbook/Documents/02_Organisational_Context_%20History_Legislation%20_Governance_Documents.pdf

Heritage Lottery Fund (2013). *A lasting difference for heritage and people - HLF strategic framework 2013–18.* London: Heritage Lottery Fund. Downloaded at: www.hlf.org.uk/lasting-difference-heritage-and-people-our-strategy-2013–2018

Heritage Lottery Fund (2016). *Values and Benefits of Heritage – A Research Review.* Available online at www.hlf.org.uk/values-and-benefits-heritage (accessed 7 January 2018).

Historic England (2016) *Heritage and Society.* London: Historic England. Available online at https://historicengland.org.uk/research/heritage-counts/2016-heritage-and-place-branding/heritage-and-society/

Historic England (2015). *Managing Significance in Decision-taking in the Historic Environment.* Historic Environment Good Practice in Planning Advice Note 2. London: Historic England. Available online at https://content.historicengland.org.uk/images-books/publications/gpa2-managing-significance-in-decision-taking/gpa2.pdf/

Holden, J. (2005). *Capturing Cultural Value: How Culture has Become a Tool of Government Policy.* London: Demos. Available online at www.demos.co.uk/files/CapturingCulturalValue.pdf

Holden, J. (2006). *Cultural Value and the Crisis of Legitimacy.* London: Demos. Available online at www.demos.co.uk/files/Culturalvalueweb.pdf

Holden, J. and Hewison, R. (2004). *Challenge and Change: HLF and Cultural Value.* London: Heritage Lottery Fund. Available online at www.hlf.org.uk/aboutus/howwework/Documents/ChallengeandChange_CulturalValue.pdf

Holden, J. and Hewison, R. (2006). Public value as a framework for analysing the value of heritage: the ideas. In K. Clark (ed.), *Capturing the Public Value of Heritage: The proceedings of the London conference 25–26 January 2006.* London: English Heritage, 14–18.

Holden, J. and Balta, J. (2012). *The Public Value of Culture: A Literature Review.* European Expert network on Culture. Available online at www.eenc.info/wp-content/uploads/2012/11/JHolden-JBalta-public-value-literature-review-final.pdf

ICOMOS. (2013). The Burra Charter. *The Australia ICOMOS Charter for Places of Cultural Significance.* Available online at http://australia.icomos.org/wp-content/uploads/BURRA_CHARTER.pdf

Lee, D.J., Oakley, K. and Naylor, R. (2011) 'The public gets what the public wants'? The uses and abuses of 'public value' in contemporary British cultural policy. *International Journal of Cultural Policy,* 17(3), 289–300.

Lennox, R. (2016). *Heritage and Politics in the Public Value Era: an analysis of the historic environment sector, the public, and the state in England since 1997* (Doctoral dissertation, University of York). Available online at http://etheses.whiterose.ac.uk/13646/

Little, B. (2002). *The Public Benefits of Archaeology*. University of Florida Press.

Mason, R. (2010). Assessing values in conservation planning: methodological issues and choices. In G. Fairclough, R. Harrison, J.H. Jameson Jnr. and J. Schofield (eds), *The Heritage Reader*. London and New York: Routledge, 99–124.

Mattinson, D. (2006). The Value of Heritage: What does the Public Think? In K. Clark (ed.) *Capturing the Public Value of Heritage: The Proceedings of the London Conference 25–26 January 2006*. London: English Heritage, 86–91.

Meynhardt, T. and Bartholomes, S. (2011). (De) Composing Public Value: in search of Basic Dimensions and Common Ground. *International Public Management Journal*, 14(3), 284–308.

Moore, M.H. (1995). *Creating Public Value: Strategic Management in Government*. Cambridge: Harvard University Press.

Moore, M.H. (2013). *Recognizing Public Value*. Boston: Harvard University Press.

Moore, M.H. (2014). Public value accounting: Establishing the philosophical basis. *Public Administration Review*, 74(4), 465–477.

Moore, M.H. and Khagram, S. (2004). *On Creating Public Value – What Businesses might Learn from Government about Strategic Management*. 2004. Working paper of the Corporate Social Responsibility Initiative. Available online at www.maine.gov/dhhs/btc/PDF/On-Creating-Public-Value.pdf

Moore, M.H. and Williams Moore, G. (2005). *Creating Public Value through State Arts Agencies*. Arts Midwest/The Wallace Foundation: Minneapolis. Available online at www.wallacefoundation.org/knowledge-center/Documents/Creating-Public-Value-Through-State-Arts-Agencies.pdf

Morris, W. (1877). *The SPAB Manifesto*. Available online at www.spab.org.uk/what-is-spab-/the-manifesto/

Oxford Economics (2016). The impact of Heritage Tourism for the UK Economy. Report for the Heritage Lottery Fund. Available at www.hlf.org.uk/economic-impact-uk-heritage-tourism-economy (accessed 7 January 2018).

Rypkema, D. (2005). *The Economics of Historic Preservation: A Community Leaders Guide*. Washington: National Trust for Historic Preservation.

Russell, R. and Winkworth, K. (2010). *Significance 2.0. A Guide to Assessing the Significance of Collections*. Commonwealth of Australia 2010. Available online at www.environment.gov.au/heritage/publications/significance2-0/

Throsby, D. (2010). *The Economics of Cultural Policy*. Cambridge: Cambridge University Press.

Part 3

The challenge and the opportunity that the concept of public value poses to social science and universities

20 The public value of social science
From manifesto to organizational strategy

Martin Kitchener

Introduction

John Brewer (2013) argues that mounting challenges to social science present both a need, and an opportunity, for a new public social science that is based upon: consideration of the *value* of social scientific scholarship, post-disciplinary approaches to producing knowledge of relevance in addressing society's problems, and strong engagement with the civic and policy spheres. While Brewer's manifesto lays a firm conceptual foundation for a new public social science, he gives little consideration to how it will be created, organized and delivered within university schools. Meanwhile, although Mark Moore's (1995) implementation triangle framework has led many organisations to consider the outputs, environment and capacity of their public value strategies, there are no reports of its application within university schools of social science.

Adopting a post-disciplinary approach of the type advocated by Brewer (2013), this chapter combines inspiration from the, hitherto unconnected, sociological and management streams of public value scholarship to outline an organisational strategy for the delivery of new public social science within university social science schools. Section one introduces the contemporary context of social science as comprising growing external and internal challenges that require strategic responses. The second part introduces Brewer's (2013) public social science manifesto and Moore's (1995) implementation framework. After using Brewer's conception of the new public social science to specify the output element of the implementation triangle, the chapter draws from the higher education management literature to outline environmental and capacity elements that will influence the development of public social science within higher education. The chapter concludes with an appraisal of the prospects for the development of public value strategies within university schools of social science.

Social science under threat

Despite mounting evidence of its positive social and policy impacts, and estimates that it contributes £5billion to the United Kingdom (UK) economy alone, social scientific scholarship in public universities faces an uncertain future within the new global political economy of higher education (Bastow et al., 2014). Although there is some national variation in experience, five common themes have emerged: university markets have been opened to private providers; there is increased private investment in public universities; academic knowledge is being commodification into products/serves to be bought and sold; capitalist enterprises, such as the five major academic publishers, increasingly extract private value (revenue) from the 'scholarly gift economy' of unremunerated writing and reviewing work; and quasi-markets are being created for fee-paying students (Ginsberg, 2011; Holmwood, 2011; Crow and Dabars, 2015).

Against this backdrop, social science disciplines (including law, economics, human geography, management, and sociology) share a number of important features including: a subject matter (the social nature of culture, the market and the state), a public value that derives from that subject matter, and a mounting set of external and internal threats (Brewer, 2013). First, the new political economy of higher education disadvantages schools of social science in public universities doubly because: (a) they are typically required to cross subsidize, to a greater extent than their counterparts within private providers, both research, and the teaching of schools of science, technology, engineering and medicine (STEM), and (b) the new private financiers of public universities tend to prioritise investment in the value propositions of STEM schools, over claims of the normative value of their social science counterparts (Brewer, 2013).

A second external threat to university social science arises from the emergent, multi-layered system of performance accountability which sees: research and teaching 'excellence' assessed, league tables abounding, work allocation models attempting to count the 'contribution' of staff, and an 'impact agenda' which stresses instrumental and shifting *effects* of research activity over its "inbuilt and unchanging worth" (Brewer, 2013, 6). In some ways, the performance expectations of social scientists appear to enlarge within the new political economy of higher education (e.g., generating increasing grant revenue). In other ways, however, they simultaneously appear to contract: as the 'value' of academic labour becomes more closely aligned with notions of efficiency, as displays of 'citizenship' are relegated to peripheral, and as traditional, broad, academic roles are dissected into more specialist research, teaching and administrative posts. It has been argued that such conditions threaten the capacity of social scientists to combine teaching, research and engagement activity to advance the public good (Watermeyer, 2015). More specifically, some social scientists have decried the emergence of an academic-publishing complex (Gabriel, 2017) in which social science has fallen into "bloated obscurity", its only purpose being to provide forms of private value such as "career tokens to academics, ranking tokens to institutions and vast profits to publishers" (Marinetto, 2017). Some analysts believe that, under this new 'institutionalized hierarchical order of academic capital production', it is no longer possible for universities to pursue strategies to advance the public good, and that the only viable response is for individual social scientists to attempt countervailing 'tactics' through their own work (Marinetto and Dallyn, 2017).

A third challenge to social science emanates from those, inside and outside the Academy, who argue that it does not engage effectively with wider society. This claim has, of course, been levelled at universities more generally and it has intensified post-Brexit. It was re-iterated recently by Dame Minouche, Director of the London School of Economics and Political Science (LSE), who argues that because universities too often "neglect to emphasise the public goods that we produce", they appear part of a "distant and malevolent elite" (reported in Havergal, 2017, 1). In a similar vein, Sir Anton Muscatealli (2017, 14), chair of the Russell Group, argues that UK universities must "speak up" to provide evidence of their impact on the economy, and their social impact at the individual level as "engines of social mobility", and at aggregate levels as "generators of social cohesion".

A second internal threat to social science arises from the fact that much of its current practice is (single) disciplinary, conducted from bunkers and silos. Within these contexts, practitioners tend to remain preoccupied with issues that have long defined the intellectual arena of the separate disciplines as they professionalized, rather than with, the inherently post-disciplinary, contemporary grand challenges such as innovation and sustainability. In one outcome of that traditional model of social science, it tends to be written only to the like-minded and is (almost) impenetrable to the public, policy-makers, and media.

Crucially, despite the advocacy of the Academy of Social Sciences (2017) and its Campaign for Social Science (http://campaignforsocialscience.org.uk), and, in part, because social science has not yet successfully matched the value claims offered to society by STEM, academic social science is now struggling to maintain material and social support from universities, government, and other stakeholders.

Brewer's (2013) public value of the social sciences

Brewer's (2013) response to the challenges facing social science is to offer a manifesto for a new public social science that is based upon: consideration of the *value* of social scientific scholarship, post-disciplinary approaches to producing knowledge of relevance in addressing society's problems, and strong engagement with the public and policy spheres. Brewer's underpinning idea is that, just as when social science emerged out of moral philosophy in the eighteenth century, a new public social science is now *needed*. The specific need is for the nurturing of a moral sentiment towards each other as social beings, and to recognize we have a shared responsibility for the future of humankind through understanding, explaining, analysing and ameliorating grand challenges, with the hope of economic and social improvement. Social science is, in this formulation, a public good for its own sake for cultivating this sympathetic imagination through its subject matter, teaching, and civic engagements. Whilst recognizing the need to also demonstrate the use and price values of social science (e.g. financial contribution to parent universities, and the wider economy), Brewer emphasises its normative public value which arises from three features: (1) the distinctive *value* of its scholarship; (2) the potential of the post-disciplinary production of knowledge for use in addressing society's problems; and (3) wide engagement with civic society.

(1) The value of social science scholarship

Brewer (2013: 165) is clear that social science contributes to all forms of value (use, price and normative), but his interest is in prioritizing, protecting and promoting its normative public value. With *public value* defined broadly in terms of humanitarian futures and societal good, Brewer lists a range of contributions which social science can make towards realizing public value, which includes:

(a) both generating information about society, the market, and the state, and acting as a medium for their reproduction;
(b) promoting moral sentiments that realize a body of citizens appreciative of the distant and marginalized other; and
(c) contributing to economic and social improvements that extend well beyond short-term policy 'impact'.

These are both an accurate summary of social science's *character*, and a desirable set of *contributions* within which the aspirations of university schools of social science can be accommodated. Moreover, these goals reaffirm those aspirations, for example, in the promotion of moral sentiments that sustain the social awareness of society and encourages social scientists to *actively* make public issues of private problems, and to undertake social science to improve the lives of people by addressing those problems.

(2) Post-disciplinarity

The second element of Brewer's manifesto is his commitment to post-disciplinarity, which has three features: (1) it is problem, not discipline, oriented, (2) a concern for grand challenges, and (3) collaboration across all branches of knowledge, not just across the social sciences. Specifically, he argues that the identification of academics (including, but not restricted to, social scientists) with specific disciplines (among the social sciences, and beyond) can stifle scholarship and innovation. In contrast, he argues, post-disciplinarity is a better foundation for addressing complex societal problems which require a variety of expertises and methodologies. Sustainability, and decent work, for example, require post disciplinarity because they demand complex treatment that go well beyond redistributive justice. They invoke moral and philosophical ideas about human dignity but also have technical dimensions that that are best understood by breaking down barriers between medicine, the natural sciences, and the social sciences. It is problem focused and encourages collaboration across all branches of knowledge not just across the social sciences because: problems are no longer defined in terms of the received wisdom of individual disciplines, by the technical features required to understand, analyse, explain and ameliorate them.

(3) Engagement

The third main component of the new public social science is wider engagement with the policy makers, practitioners and publics with whom the nature of problems will be determined, and knowledge will be created. As Brewer (2013, 200) notes, this may cause discomfort for some 'critical' social scientists and this will mean moving beyond dissemination towards working with governments, big business and other elites as well as marginalized groups, Non-Governmental Organisations (NGOs), charities and local community groups. Under this model:

> Research becomes participative, in which research questions are not defined solely as the preserve of the professionals; it is a form of co-produced knowledge. Public social science needs to be co-produced with the publics that name it as such.
> (Brewer, 2013, 186)

In contrast to narrower conceptions of impact (e.g. those involved with the UK Research Excellent Framework [REF]), the humanitarian impact of the new public social science will be achieved through local, national and global activities, including research, teaching and civic engagement in order to create, persuade and prompt publics to civic action.

While Brewer's manifesto lays a firm conceptual foundation for a new public social science, it gives little consideration to how it will be organized and delivered within university schools and departments. To address this gap, the next section introduces Moore's (1995) implementation triangle framework which has been used by many public organisations, outside the university sector, to consider the outputs, environment and capacity of their public value strategies.

Moore's public value implementation triangle

In a line of scholarship that began before, and has developed independently from Brewer's, Mark Moore's (1995) main proposition is that managers of public organizations facing growing demands and reducing budgets (e.g. heads of university social science schools) should apply resources to increase value in a way that is 'analogous' to value creation within private enterprise. Whilst the resulting public value must include financial benefits, it should also involve that which benefits society more generally. For Moore and Khargram (2004, 9), the key strategic challenge for managers attempting to deliver public value is: "to imagine and articulate a vision of public value that can command legitimacy and support". As a practical aid to this task, Moore's implementation framework prescribes that managers focus on three complex issues represented as the 'strategic triangle' (see Figure 20.1).

The central message contained within the triangle is that organizational strategies to deliver public value must satisfy three tests. First, they must create publicly valuable outcomes. Second, they must mobilize sufficient legitimacy and sustain support from key stakeholders within the organizations' 'authorising environment'. Third, strategies must be operationally feasible; that is, be supported by requisite finance, technology, staff skills and organizational capabilities (Moore, 1995, 71). It is fully recognised that, in practice, these factors are rarely in alignment, and addressing this issue may challenge managers seeking to implement public value strategies.

Moore's (1995) work has stimulated considerable interest internationally amongst policy practitioners, scholars, and consultants (Williams and Shearer, 2011;

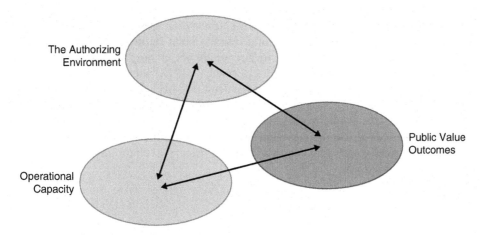

Figure 20.1 Strategic triangle for public value social science
Source: Developed from Moore 1995, 71

Bryson et al., 2016; Centre for Public Impact, 2016). However, there are still very few empirical investigations of efficacy, and much of the literature continues to be 'exhortatory' and/or prescriptive (Williams and Shearer, 2011). Perhaps the most famous empirical case in the UK is that of the British Broadcasting Corporation (BBC) whose 2016 charter renewal bid was based explicitly on Moore's ideas. Whilst there are few reports of public value forming the basis of strategies in universities, Vogel (2016, 3) argues that they should draw inspiration from the BBC, and use the delivery of public value as a means of addressing the gulf that has emerged between universities and society:

> public value thinking could help them [universities] get closer to their communities and articulate purposes that the public would get behind. This in turn could help diffuse tension between academics and managers, if managerialism were mobilised in the service of a project that academics might find more inspiring. Clarity of purpose would allow for greater differentiation between universities – research intensives, balanced, teaching-focussed – and more importantly, provide a more robust foundation for dealing with government and the new regulator, the OfS [Office of Students].

Whilst Vogel (2016) makes no mention of the published criticisms of the BBC case (Oakley et al., 2007), he does argue that it might be "much harder" to argue the public interest of higher education (than public broadcasting). Building on Brewer's (2013) articulation of the public value of social science, the next section elaborates an implementation triangle for university social science schools.

A public value implementation triangle for social science schools

The preceding section introduced Moore's work and explained why it may offer a promising basis for the creation of organizational strategies for university social science schools facing mounting economic and social challenges. However, as noted by Moore and Khargram (2004, 9), the imagining and articulating of any public value strategy requires "tough substantive and analytical work." As a first step in that direction for social science schools, this section employs Vaughan's (1992) method of 'elaborating' (refining, specifying, updating) 'sensitizing' general theory (in this case, Moore's implementation triangle). Using insights from multiple disciplines, each of the three elements of the implementation triangle are elaborated for the context of university schools of social science. First, Brewer's (2013) sociological conception of the public social science is used to offer an articulation of their public value outcomes. Second, key actors and relationships within schools' authoring environment are highlighted following the public management scholarship of Bryson et al. (2017). Third, from the higher education management literature, an outline of schools' 'operational capacity' is drawn from Losada et al.'s (2011) notion of a 'chain' of value delivery in higher education schools.

1. The public value of social science schools

As agreed by Moore (1995), and his critics (Rhodes and Wanna, 2009) within the public management field, local understandings of public value and its outcomes will need to be developed for different task environments. Given the economic and social challenges to social science that were identified earlier, Brewer's manifesto appears to have great potential as a conceptual foundation and moral compass for the development of public value outcomes in university schools of social science. With *public value* defined broadly in terms of humanitarian futures and societal good, the primary goal of social science schools would be to sustain social awareness of the grand challenges facing their discipline(s), and undertake social science to improve the lives of people by addressing those problems. From this perspective, the purpose of (public value) university would be to promote economic and social improvement from outcomes including:

- Teaching and learning that develops moral sentiments to promoting economic and social improvement.
- Research that generates information about society, the market, and the state that informs society, the market and the state about themselves.
- Engagement activity directed towards social amelioration and improvement in society, the market, and the state.
- Strong and progressive models of self-governance.

2. The authorising environment of social science schools

The second element of Moore's public management strategic triangle recognises the importance of legitimacy for the survival and success of all organisations. The basic idea here is that all public organizations need authorization from societal stakeholders to continue operating:

> The idea of legitimacy and support goes beyond the idea of material and financial support; it is also concerned with a kind of social and political "legitimacy" about how a particular organization maintains its right to operate in a particular social and political environment as well as economic viability of financial sustainability.
> (Moore and Khargram, 2004, 12)

This view recognises that public organizations, including social science schools, build their legitimacy and support by offering to produce something of public value that may not generate an immediate revenue stream from customers willing and able to pay for the service offered. This approach rests on a set of three main assumptions, which appear to hold for university schools: (1) organizations have more or less legitimacy, as indicated by school/discipline rankings (e.g., REF) and accreditations, (2) their legitimacy is based on multiple aspects of conduct and performance (teaching, research and engagement), and (3) relative legitimacy influences competitive position (reported associations between league table ranking and student recruitment). These features are suggested to be influenced by mechanisms including: the operation of internal morale, the attraction of economic actors with social reputation, and the avoidance of costly regulation.

An organization's social licence to operate is granted by what Moore terms the 'authorizing environment' which comprises stakeholders who have claims on/interests in the organization, and some capacity to press them in ways that influence the organization's activity. Whilst Moore's focus is principally on a (singular) strategic decision-making public manager, Bryson and colleagues' (2017, 642) development of his triangle recognises that public value 'entrepreneurship' typically occurs in complex, multi-actor, multi-level settings and often takes the form of co-production and inter-organisational collaboration within or across sectors. This elaboration of activity at the centre of the implementation triangle directs attention towards different kinds of actors and their practices interacting during attempts to create public value. In doing so, it is recognised that actors will likely refer to multiple (and possibility conflicting) authorising logics, practices, and environments to inform their view of publics, value, and public value (Reay and Hinings, 2009; Jacobs, 2014; Dahl and Soss, 2014). Following Moore (2013, 90–91), management of these differences requires combinations of four types of labour: (1) *philosophical* work, 'naming and justifying' the nature of public value to various stakeholders, (2) *political* work, 'building a broad, stable agreement' amongst stakeholders around the outcomes of the philosophical work, (3) *managerial* work, linking derived performance measurement and management systems, and (4) *technical* work, finding or developing empirical measures that can reliably capture public value strategy enactment.

For social science schools looking to adopt a public value strategy within their complex contexts, Bryson et al.'s (2017) conception of the centre of the implementation triangle suggests that each of Moore's (2013) areas of implementation work will need to be tailored and targeted towards legitimising activities in at least three directions: (a) inwards, to faculty, students and staff, (b) upwards, through institutional and political structures e.g. colleges/faculties, advisory boards, and university leadership, and (c) outwards, to all societal stakeholders including government, employers, professional bodies.

3. Operational capacities of social science schools

The third element of Moore's (1995) implementation triangle emphasises that, for university social science schools looking to implement public value strategy, it is imperative that consistency is demonstrated between their 'espoused' mission, and their 'enacted' capacity and operation. Failure to achieve this would likely strengthen both: (a) criticisms of ethics in higher education governance, and (b) the scepticism of those who question the motives and/or capacity of public value strategies (Rhodes and Wanna, 2007). Beyond this injunction, however, Moore has remained "fairly silent" on the kinds of practices necessary to enact public value strategies (Bryson et al., 2017, 642). Building on Losada and colleagues' (2011) representation of the 'chain' through which value is created a higher education, the following sections elaborate the four 'subsystems' of a social science school's operations that would require attention for the successful enactment of a public value strategy: education, research, engagement, and governance.

Education

While there have been various programmatic statements about challenge-led and post-disciplinary social science within and beyond discussions of public value, less attention has been given to the teaching agenda of the new public social science. From the earlier discussion, key features of that agenda would include: (a) promoting moral sentiments in students that help realize a body of citizens appreciative of the distant and marginalized other, and (b) enabling and encouraging students to contribute to economic and social improvements. Whilst there is some evidence that the ambitions of students of sociology-based social sciences (including criminology and social policy) are not solely about individual enhancement (McLean et al., 2012, 8), there is little to suggest that the transformative goals of new public social science education are being achieved in disciplines such as law and business. Brewer (2013, 179) argues that this would require students to perform the life-changing and life-enhancing knowledge they are learning, such as through assisting them to see how this knowledge helps them understand and make sense of their own lives and the lives of others locally, and globally.

A first step in ensuring that a school's education activities deliver public value of the type outlined above would require a comprehensive review of the content, delivery, assessment, feedback and marketing of all programs (undergraduate, postgraduate and post-experience), and other services provided to students (e.g., careers advice). An emphasis would be placed on developing post-disciplinary teaching of grand challenges, such as equality, sustainability, and innovation. An excellent example of this is provided by the 'Sociology of Peace Processes' course at Aberdeen University (Brewer, 2013, 182). Beyond the mapping of curricula content against the public value strategy, a key element of the education review would assess the coherence between education policies/practices and the school's espoused public value commitments. In one example, the feedback students/participants receive on their work is a critical moment during which the 'real value' given to learning is 'declared', thereby manifesting what the school feels regarding the participant and what he/she values in their business education. Within a public value school this understanding would lead to assessment procedures that considered students' appetite to challenge the status quo, and the development of a sympathetic imagination towards the pursuit of economic and social improvement through post-disciplinary, challenge-led, project work with a variety of organizations. At HHL in Leipzig, public value is integrated within a leadership model and module which is mandatory for all courses throughout curriculum (HHL, 2017).

Given the mounting competition for students among social science schools, it is likely that candidate selection would pose two significant challenges for the public value school. The first arises from potential tensions between a public value strategy, and parent universities' demands for increasing student revenue. The second involves the need to assess prospective students' (and faculty's) capacity and motivation for public value (inter-disciplinary, challenge-led) teaching and learning. In placing an emphasis on characteristics such as service motivation, for example, it would be consistent for public value schools to include some assessment of this within selection procedures.

Research

Following Brewer (2013, 169), a social science school with a public value strategy would concentrate its research capabilities on promoting economic and social improvement by conducting post-disciplinary research designed to generate information about society, the market, and the state that informs society, the market and the state about themselves. This may, or may not, involve individual academics collaborating with others across disciplinary boundaries, as inter, or multidisciplinarity usually infers; it may involve instead, researchers moving outside their intellectual orthodoxies to themselves approach the issue from perspectives outside their own discipline. Behavioural economists' application of standard social-psychological approaches within studies of market behaviour present a good example of this. Whichever approach to post-disciplinarity is taken, public social science research would prioritise theoretically-informed, engaged, and empirically driven investigations of grand challenges.

It is to be expected that the new public social science research agenda may be resisted by those who argue it is not new, by those who claim it undermines (uni) disciplinary research, and by those who fear collaborative and engaged research. Post-disciplinarity will also clearly have significant implications for the organizational structuring of social science schools within universities. It is not well suited to the single subject schools/departments that produced so much of traditional social science scholarship and use local languages as barriers to integration. Instead, more receptive contexts would seem to be provided by organizational settings such as some of the larger, social-science based and multi-disciplinary business schools (e.g., Cardiff), and Brewer's (2013: 176) vignette of University College London's (UCL's) organization around four grand challenge themes: global health, sustainable cities, intercultural interaction, and human well-being.

Whilst this post-disciplinary research agenda often requires no choices to be made between public good and private career interests, a key issue will involve the extent to which faculty are permitted to continue with complete freedom to research all that they consider interesting, from their disciplinary silos. At the other extreme, a school could specify a selection of grand challenges to be explored in post-disciplinary ways (as at UCL). Between these two poles, there are many options which preserve academic autonomy while establishing and incentivising some grand challenge lines of research.

In addition to the significance of schools' choice among these approaches, the criteria used to sanction lines of research would signal how public value is understood locally. It is important to note that some of the major funders of social science research, including Research Councils United Kingdom (RCUK), are increasingly advocating collaborations on global challenges such as the Global Challenges Research Fund (www.rcuk.ac.uk/funding/gcrf/). Brewer's (2013, 13) illustration of his own research on peace studies provides a great illustration of this.

Engagement

Brewer's (2013) manifesto for public value social science contains a clear injunction for social science schools to more deeply and productively engaging with the social nature of culture, the market, and the state. Enacting this, to move beyond mere dissemination, will require considerable effort for many schools to encourage social scientists to work with governments, big business and other elites as well as marginalized groups, NGOs, charities and local community groups. Under such an approach, relevance and impact would be achieved through local, national and global activities, including research, teaching and civic engagement to create, persuade and prompt various publics to civic action directed towards social and economic improvement.

This agenda would begin with the formulation of research projects and teaching curricula when different publics can be involved as co-producers; long before any data are collected or lessons delivered. Such civic engagement within new public social science schools will require writing and discussing plainly, clearly and well. It will require the identification of civic partners and the development of capacity to manage these new relations. Care must be taken, however, to mitigate the risk of what Watermeyer (2015) reports as academics with an appetite for public engagement, becoming 'lost in the third space' where their public interactions are not directly linked, or attributable to, research. For such a group, who unlike senior colleagues engaging with high profile stakeholders, tend to be early in their careers and lacking the kinds of intellectual and institutional capital that would give their public displays clout, their engagement may be treated by their departments as of limited value. Put crudely, they can be perceived not so much as academics, but what Macfarlane (2010) calls 'para-academics'. Furthermore, they can be prone to "receiving the negative press of their peers, many whom, ostensibly with either jealously, superciliousness or inflated ego, allege the profligacy amongst 'do-gooders'" (Watermeyer and Olssen, this volume). Whilst inadequate institutional incentives and support may compromise the fruition of social science departments' public engagement, they may motivate some academics to interface with publics in more creative, open, varied, democratic and less pre-determined ways (Brewer, 2013). Because the rise of international research collaborations, such as those funded under the RCUK global challenges initiative, afford the opportunity for engagement at a global level that universities want to promote and idealise, there may not necessarily be a Hobson's choice between public good and personal career interests. However, in this regard, different local contexts will likely require different balances being struck between agency and structure.

Governance

For any social science school that adopts a public value strategy, there is a clear obligation for it to operate a strong and progressive model of governance to its own operations. Whilst many variants are possible and will need to reflect local contingencies, the conception of public value offered earlier suggests two foundations. The first follows the commitment to promoting economic improvement and requires a school to make a financial contribution to its parent university, and the wider economy. This could be pursued through commitments to distributed leadership approaches, sustainability (potentially indicated by carbon targets), and equality and diversity (potentially indicated by Athena SWAN accreditation). Crucial to all of this will be policies affecting faculty and staff and specifically, the capacity to embed public value commitments within processes such as hiring, appraisal, mentoring and promotion. Equally important will be the external partners that the School choses to collaborate with. In addition to links with discipline relevant professional bodies, a public value strategy would encourage a broader set of relationships across the public, private and third sectors including NGOs, charities, social enterprises, and local community groups.

Discussion and conclusions

Adopting a post-disciplinary approach of the type advocated by Brewer (2013), this chapter combines inspiration from the sociological and management streams of public value scholarship to outline an organisational strategy for the delivery of new public social science within university social science schools. While Brewer's manifesto lays a firm conceptual foundation for a new public social science, it gives little consideration to how it will be created, organized and delivered. In contrast, while Moore's (1995) implementation triangle framework has led many organisations to consider the outputs, environment and capacity of their public value strategies, it provides no basis for articulating the public value outputs of university social science schools.

The first outcome of this chapter elaborates Moore's implementation triangle with Brewer's (2013) sociological conception of the public value of university social science schools. From this perspective, their purpose is to promote economic and social improvement from outcomes including:

- Teaching and learning that develops moral sentiments to promoting economic and social improvement.
- Research that generates information about society, the market, and the state that informs society, the market and the state about themselves.
- Engagement activity directed towards social amelioration and improvement in society, the market, and the state.
- Strong and progressive models of self-governance.

The second contribution of this chapter draws from the public management scholarship of Bryson et al. (2017) to emphasise that the 'authoring environment' of social science schools are comprised of multiple and overlapping layers of agents and relations. This would direct the architects (or 'entrepreneurs') of any public value strategy to seek authorisation: (a) inwards, from faculty, students and staff, (b) upwards, through university and political structures, and (c) outwards, to external stakeholders. The third contribution of this elaboration drew from the higher education management literature (Losada et al., 2011) to portray the 'operational capacity' of schools to enact a public value strategy in terms of its education, research, engagement and governance 'subsystems'. From this exercise it is clear that, while Brewer's (2013) new public social science implicates some new practices in these areas, it reinforces the importance of many existing ones, and offers a serious challenge to other modes of practice.

In essence, this chapter presents a blueprint for an alternative, public value, model of university social science schools that is designed to address their shared contemporary challenges through an explicit commitment to, and prioritisation of, delivering economic and social value. This approach will require social scientists to join in post-disciplinary research teams and work with partners (from local community representatives to the senior executives of major corporations and policy makers at all levels) to address grand challenges such as innovation and sustainability. In doing so, faculty in their teaching and research will be well placed to help act as the conscience of social science within the new political economy of higher education. Ironically, the notion of 'impact' as currently cast (by REF) may be highly problematic, but it might just help promote the sort of post-disciplinary, challenge-led and engaged public value research that Brewer might have hoped for in regard to social science.

Even though Brewer's (2013) manifesto is motivated by a critique of the pervasive audit culture and marketization processes of the contemporary political economy of higher education, some analysts believe that he underestimates the extent to which such conditions will countervail against organizational strategies designed to deliver public value. Marinetto and Dallyn (2017) argue, for example, that public value cannot be orchestrated at the organizational level while simultaneously conforming to the new 'institutionalized hierarchical order of academic capital production' that supports the over-production of research papers, and the spiralling profits of a capitalist publishing oligopoly. This chapter has been neither blind to, nor silent about, the growing extraction of private value from university social science departments. It has recognised that these conditions increasingly influence the work of social scientists and will present a major hurdle to enacting espoused public value missions, in addition to the other hurdles discussed earlier including parent university income demands, and the problems of developing post-disciplinary teaching and research.

In contrast to Marinetto and Dallyn (2017), however, this chapter suggests that the only viable response to these challenges is not just for individual social scientists to adopt 'tactics' to deliver public value through their own work, whilst complying minimally with (possibly conflicting) institutional demands. Instead, this chapter presents a more optimistic view of the potential for social science schools to develop organizational strategies to deliver public value through the promotion of both economic and social improvement. The burgeoning debates over the value of public universities are creating a challenging context for academics across the disciplines. But they are also producing an environment where leaders of social science must now act. Like Brewer (2013, 161), this chapter is not arguing that social science needs to change purely in order to appease our critics, or appeal to our paymasters among students, universities, research councils and government. While the contemporary political economy of public management has provoked discussions of value by Brewer, Moore and many others, the primary driver of change for the new public social science is the essential worth of our subject area, which requires us to be relevant in diagnosing, analysing, understanding and ameliorating the conditions of culture, the market and the state in the twenty-first century.

This chapter has presented an outline of a post-disciplinary, challenge-led, and impactful model for the delivery of new public social science with university social science schools. While it recognises the countervailing powers within the current political economy, it is clearly no panacea for all of social science's ills, and it will certainly not be applicable to all schools operating globally. However, for university social science schools with some combination of a strong multi-disciplinary base, commitments to social and economic improvement and progressive governance, it might prove a productive basis from which to motivate, co-ordinate and support the tactics of individual social scientists as they seek to re-engage with society, and deliver new public social science.

References

Academy of Social Sciences (2017). *Making the Case for the Social Sciences: No. 6 Management*. London: Academy of Social Sciences.

Bastow, S., P. Dunleavy and J. Tinkler (2014). *The Impact of the Social Sciences: how Academics and their Research Make a Difference*. London: Sage.

Brewer, J.D. (2013). *The Public Value of the Social Sciences*. London: Bloomsbury.

Bryson, J., A. Sancino, J. Benington and E. Sorensen (2017). "Towards a Multi-Actor Theory of Public Value Co-creation". *Public Management Review*, 19(5): 640–654.

Centre for Public Impact (2016). *The Public Impact Fundamentals: Helping Governments Progress from Idea to Impact*. Boston: Centre for Public Impact.

Crow, M. and W. Dabars (2015). *Designing the New American University*. Baltimore: Johns Hopkins University Press.

Dahl, A. and J. Soss (2014). "Neoliberalism for the Common Good? Public Value Governance and the Downsizing of Democracy". *Public Administration Review*, 74(4): 496–504.

Gabriel, Y. (2017). "We Must Rescue Social Science from Obscurity". *Times Higher Education* Opinion, August 10.

Ginsberg, B. (2011). *The Fall of the Faculty*. Oxford: Oxford University Press.

Havergal, C. (2017). "New LSE Director's Four Point Plan to Restore Trust in Academy," *Times Higher Education*, August 31. Available online at www.timeshighereducation.com/news/new-lse-directors-four-point-plan-to-restore-trust-in-academy (accessed 5 September 2017).

HHL. (2017). *The Leipzig Leadership Model*. Leipzig: HHL Academic Press.

Holmwood, J. (2011). *A Manifesto for the Public University*. London: Bloomsbury.

Jacobs, L.R. (2014). "The Contested Politics of Public Value". *Public Administration Review*, 74(4): 480–494.

Losada, C., J. Martell and J. Lozano (2011). "Responsible Business Education: Not a Question of Curriculum but a Raison D'etre for Business Schools". In M. Morsing and A.S. Rovira, *Business Schools and Their Contribution to Society*, pp. 163–174. London: Sage.

Macfarlane, B. (2010). "The Morphing of Academic Practice: Unbundling and the Rise of the Para-academic". *Higher Education Quarterly* 65(1): 59–73.

Marinetto, M. (2017). "Rage Against the Academic Publishing Machine Does Not Need to Be Futile". *Times Higher Education* Opinion, 21 December.

Marinetto, M. and S. Dallyn (2017). "The Public Value of Academic Research: A Critique of John Brewer's Public Value Social Science". Working paper, Cardiff Business School.

McLean, M., A. Abbas, and P. Ashwin (2012). "Pedagogic Quality and Inequality in Undergraduate Social Science", paper presented to the Research Symposium at the University of Nottingham, 27 January.

Moore, M.H. (1995). *Creating Public Value: Strategic Management in Government*. Cambridge, MA: Harvard University Press.

Moore, M.H. (2013). *Recognizing Public Value*. Cambridge, MA: Harvard University Press.

Moore, M. and S. Khagram. (2004). *On Creating Public Value: What Business Might Learn from Government about Strategic Management*. Corporate Social Responsibility Initiative Working Paper No. 3. Cambridge, MA: John F. Kennedy School of Government, Harvard University.

Muscatelli, A. (2017). "Ignore the Cacophony, but Speak Up". *Times Higher Education*, September 21. Available online at www.timeshighereducation.com/opinion/ignore-the-cacophony-but-speak-up (accessed 29 September 2017).

Oakley, K., R. Naylor and D. Lee (2006). *Giving Them What They Want: The Construction of the Public in "Public Value"*. London: Burns Owen Partnership.

O'Flynn, J. (2007). "From New Public Management to Public Value: Paradigmatic Change and Managerial Implications". *Australian Journal of Public Administration*, 66(3): 353–366.

Porter, M. and M.R. Kramer (2011). "Creating Shared Value". *Harvard Business Review* January 50–73.

Reay, T. and C.R. Hinings (2009). "Managing the Rivalry of Competing Institutional Logics". *Organization Studies*, 30(6): 629–652.

Rhodes, R.A.W. and J. Wanna (2007). "The Limits to Public Value, or Rescuing Responsible Government from the Platonic Guardians". *Australian Journal of Public Administration*, 66(4): 406–421.

Vaughan, D. (1992) "Theory Elaboration: The Heuristics of Case Analysis". In C.C. Ragin and H.S. Becker (eds), *What is a Case? Exploring the Foundations of Social Inquiry*, pp. 173–202. New York: Cambridge.

Vogel, M. (2016). "Universities Can Rediscover Public Value by Learning from the BBC. Available online at http://wonke.com/staff/martin-vogel/ (accessed 23 April 2017).

Watermeyer, R. (2015). "Lost in the 'Third Space': The Impact of Public Engagement in Higher Education on Academic Identity, Research Practice and Career Progressio". *European Journal of Higher Education*, 5(3): 331–347.

Watermeyer, R. and M. Olssen. "The Dissipating Value of Public Service in UK Higher Education." This volume.

Williams, I. and H. Shearer (2011). "Appraising Public Value: Past, Present and Futures". *Public Administration*, 89(4): 1367–1384.

21 Knowledge exchange seminar series

An effective partnership to increase the public value of academic research findings

Sally Shortall, Eileen Regan and Claire Dewhirst

Introduction

This case study presents an example of the public value of social science as developed by Brewer (2013a). Brewer underlines the importance of applying skills to the analysis of the fundamental problems of culture, the market and the state. Public value research contributes to the common good in society through various impacts. Impacting on government policy and law is one such impact; one that is significantly enabled by the number and quality of the relationships between key players in the policy and law-making contexts, including departmental ministers, legislators, departmental and parliamentary officials, third and private sectors and academia. An essential component in that facilitation process is the establishment of forums to nurture and develop those relationships so that understanding and trust can flourish.

Since 2012 the "Knowledge Exchange Seminar Series" (KESS) has created such a space in Northern Ireland (NI).[1] Formally partnering NI's legislative arm of government – the Assembly – with the three local universities – Queen's University of Belfast (QUB – since 2011), Ulster University (Ulster – 2012) and The Open University (OU-2013), KESS provides a non-partisan space for all sectors, including public, third and private, along with academia, to consider research findings of relevance to governance in NI. This is especially important in NI. As Benington (2007) notes, the public sphere is contested territory, with competing interests and ideologies at play. In NI, the public sphere is particularly contested and fraught. KESS provides a space for multiple actors to engage in the public sphere. It fosters relationships between various sectors and academics; ultimately seeking to promote evidence-led policy and law-making in NI.

This chapter first explains the origins and design of the KESS model. Thereafter it sets out its central components, describing how over the last five years it provided space to facilitate relationships between key players in the policy and law-making contexts in NI, resulting in a number of impacts.

Model origins

In 2008 and 2009 Professor Sally Shortall worked as a "Knowledge Exchange Research Fellow" in a NI Executive department, supported by the Economic and Social Research Council (ESRC). The Fellowship highlighted complex issues when using evidence in this arena, which largely arose from officials' apparent reliance on what was perceived as "useful evidence" or no evidence. Shortall's observations led her to believe that there needed to be more effective engagement between policy-makers and academics.

After returning to QUB, Shortall contacted the Assembly to gauge interest in whether a regular seminar series could facilitate such engagement. In 2011 she was directed to Eileen Regan, a Senior Researcher in the Research and Information Service (RaISe). Drawing on their individual experience and insight, as well as their discussion with various interested stakeholders, they concluded an annual series should be established.

Model design

Working closely together, they designed the KESS model; one that would provide a non-partisan forum in which relevant, objective, robust, evidence-based academic research findings could be presented in an accessible manner, in order to facilitate subsequent discussion among key players, ultimately aiming to promote evidence-led policy and law-making. It exemplifies the emphasis placed by Brewer (2013a; 2013b) on communication and language. When engaging in public value science, communication and language style changes. Less professional vocabulary is used. Now we write to make ourselves understood, rather than for professional acclaim. With this in mind, the defined KESS aim and objectives are set out in Box 1.

Four key components they identified to enable the implementation and delivery of KESS were: the Annual Programme; the Seminar Format; the Policy Briefings and Presentations; and Committed Resources, as explained below.

BOX 1: KESS AIM AND OBJECTIVES

Aim:

To provide an annual seminar series where the public sector joins with academics to consider research findings for the purpose of promoting evidence-led policy and law-making in NI.

Objectives:

- To impact on the development of policy and law in NI, the seminars will seek to develop understanding and awareness of issues that relate to the Programme of Government of the NI Executive.
- To encourage engagement and debate among a spectrum of attendees, the seminars will aim to encourage attendance from MLAs and their staff, Assembly staff, public and private sector employees, academics and representatives from voluntary and community groups.

Annual Programme

The Annual Programme is formulated following an open KESS bid at all three university partners for academic research finding presentations. The applications are reviewed by the KESS Panel (see sub-section below), which – amongst other things – determines whether the proposed presentation/s form/s part of the Programme. The Panel considers whether the proposal/s is/are:

- Relevant to governance in NI, as guided by the annually compiled "Hot Topics List" generated by Assembly Secretariat in light of ongoing and future departmental and Assembly business relating to policy, legislation and the budget; and,
- Objective, evidence-based and robust.

Each Programme is launched, usually by the Assembly Speaker; and then delivered from October through June, in Parliament Buildings. The 'hot topics' is an example of Brewer's (2013a) description of collaboration between government and academics, where the focus is on the problem rather than a specific discipline. The 'hot topics' go out to the universities and people from multiple disciplines to any one problem. The process is participative. While academics can propose seminars that are not on the 'hot topics' list, the research questions or topics are compiled in partnership with government. They are not solely the preserve of academics, rather it is an example of co-produced knowledge.

Seminar format

Each seminar follows a set format:

- Welcome provided by a RaISe researcher, who facilitates the seminar.
- Opening Remarks made by the Chair, the Deputy Chair or a Member of the given Assembly statutory committee, in his/her committee capacity (non-party political): they highlight the relevance of the academics' policy briefings and power point presentations to the committee's portfolio.
- 20-minute Presentations of research findings given by academics from the university partners.
- Discussion/Question & Answer follows the academic presentations, when a broad spectrum of attendees is welcome to participate. Attendees include, e.g., Assembly Members and their staff, political party staff, Assembly and departmental officials, those from the voluntary and community sectors and the private sector, and members of the public. Such discussion allows for robust engagement from a wide range of perspectives.
- Networking occurs following the discussion, when participants and attendees are encouraged to engage further, to enable relationships between them.
- Posting of seminar publications (Policy Briefings and Power Point Presentations) and presentation video clips follows each seminar *via* the KESS webpages and social media.

For each series, Table 21.1 sets out the number of registered attendees, excluding those for launch:

Table 21.1 KESS registered attendees – Series 1–5

Series	Total seminars	Registered attendees
1: March 2012 – July 2012	11	179
2: October 2012 – May 2013	16	375
3: October 2013 – May 2014	14	422
4: October 2014 – May 2015	16	587
5: October 2015 – June 2016*	16	484

* During Series 5 two political events took place – the May 2016 Assembly election and the June 2016 Referendum on the European Union – which potentially adversely impacted, to a lesser or greater extent, on the delivery of that KESS Programme.

Policy Briefings and Presentations

Academics participating in KESS are expected to provide a written Policy Briefing (5–6 pages) and a 20-minute oral presentation of their research findings, using a power point. Each is to be "fit" for KESS purposes, meaning it is to comply with academic standards, i.e. objective, evidence-based and robust, drawing on databases such as Northern Ireland Longitudinal Study Research Support Unit (NILS-RSU) and those made available by the ESRC and the Arts and Humanities Research Council (AHRC). In addition, each is to be accessible to non-specialists, meaning it is to be in plain English, explaining the relevance of their findings to policy and law in NI and identifying potential issues and recommendations arising from their findings. This again exemplifies Brewer's notion of public value (2013a; 2013b). Science has to be different in order to collaborate with different publics. We see here a process where scientists are self-consciously changing their method of communication in order to make themselves accessible to different groups of people. Academic knowledge must not be the preserve of professionals.

Academics' Policy Briefings, PowerPoint presentations and video clips of their oral presentations are posted on the KESS webpages following each seminar. Table 21.2 provides an overview of page views and video plays for each series:

Table 21.2 Landing page views and video clip plays – Series 1–5*

Location	Landing page views (all time)	Video clip plays
Main KESS landing page	30920	N/A
Series 1	495	864
Series 2	3859	1401
Series 3	1215	6448
Series 4	1008	7535
Series 5**	670	3797

* The KESS landing page archives content to an individual series page only after the given series has completed. This means each series page goes "live" only after that series finishes.

** During Series 5, at the end of the Assembly mandate in 2016, restructuring of the Assembly website and related changes to video clip packaging both decreased access to content on KESS webpages.

Academic workshops

To support academics who participate or wish to participate in KESS, RaISe provides them with workshops. The workshops are designed to demystify devolved government in NI and encourage academics to make their research more relevant and accessible in policy and law-making. The workshops identify key stages in the policy and law-making contexts, which present unique information and research needs for departmental ministers and legislators, as well as the officials supporting them. To follow those stages, the workshops highlight key departmental and legislative information and data, and how to track them. This enables academics when compiling Policy Briefings and presentations, enhancing their ability to outline implications arising from their recommendations, including social, financial and environmental, and to sharpen potential lines of questioning arising from their research.

Academics regularly comment that the workshops have increased their understanding of how the departments and the Assembly work relative to one another, serving to better equip them when presenting their research at KESS.

The workshops also encourage academics to join with colleagues from other disciplines, when applying to KESS. Year on year there is an increased number of joint applications to participate in KESS; and such collaborative working has helped to advance inter-disciplinary KESS Programmes of greater relevance and import in both the policy and law-making contexts, as well as academia.[2]

Good practice example at conferences/workshops

KESS has featured as a good practice example at conferences and workshops where legislative staff, academics and students have been in attendance. For example, at the Inter-Parliamentary Research and Information Network (IPRIN) in 2014 and 2016, the Assembly's RaISe presented KESS as a unique legislative-academic engagement model; and subsequently has shared the KESS experience with the Scottish Parliament's Information Centre (SPICe), to enable that Parliament's adaptation of the KESS model for its context.

In 2013 KESS was invited by the Library Association of Ireland to make a presentation about KESS at its annual Government Libraries Seminar; attendees included government librarians, other public servants and academics. In 2015 KESS was invited by the Northern Bridge, a doctoral training partnership programme involving Newcastle University, Durham University and QUB, to present on KESS at the programme's annual public policy engagement workshop. In 2017, Newcastle University invited KESS to advise their Policy Academy on how they might develop a KESS for the North East of England. Part of this engagement was the delivery of workshops for academics on how to engage diverse audiences. KESS is currently being developed between the Policy Academy and local councils in the North East.

Committed resources

Central to KESS are its committed resources, i.e. the "KESS Panel" and the "Administrative Team". Both include representatives from the Assembly's

RaISe and the university partners, and are essential to the planning and delivery of KESS.

KESS Panel

Since its creation, the Panel proactively establishes and agrees policies, practices and procedures to govern the formulation and delivery of the Programme. Its aim is to maximise each seminar's engagement potential, bringing together an array of departmental and parliamentary officials, third and private sectors, academia, and legislators (in their individual or committee capacities).

The Panel acts as the "gatekeeper" of the series. During its annual cycle, it formulates the Programme from spring through the summer, which includes: the dissemination of an open bid for applications at the university partners in the spring;[3] and, the Panel's selection of successful applications in accordance with KESS standards in the summer (as noted above). In addition, from autumn to the summer the Panel delivers the Programme, starting with the annual launch, which is hosted by the Assembly Speaker and is widely attended.

Over the years the Panel rejected applications to participate in KESS for various reasons, such as partisanship, poor evidence or lack of relevance to Assembly business, and provided written explanation for its reasons.

The Panel also managed oversubscription by decreasing individual presentation timeframes (to 20-minute intervals), and increasing the number of presentations per seminar. As a result, there has been an increase in the total number of presentations in the Annual Programme, as highlighted in Table 21.3.

The Panel also received criticism that it did not include a broader spectrum of opinion on certain topics; and that it did not allow non-academic research to be presented. On each occasion it explained the nature of KESS to the complainants, and actively encouraged them to participate in the seminar's discussion period, making their findings/views known, and enabling more robust engagement, albeit "challenging".

The Panel utilises various mechanisms to facilitate monitoring and review of KESS, e.g. evaluation of feedback questionnaires completed by attendees and academics participating in KESS, as well as *ad hoc* feedback sessions with, e.g. Assembly committee chairs, Members and officials. Extracts from the main findings of KESS feedback questionnaire evaluations are highlighted in Table 21.4. More recently the Panel has formed a Sub-Panel to develop an impact evaluation strategy and implementation plan.

Table 21.3 KESS Programmes – Series 1–5

Series	Individual seminars with: 1 academic presentation	2 academic presentations	3 academic presentations	4 academic presentations	5 academic presentations
1: 2012	11	0	0	0	0
2: 2012–13	14	2	0	0	0
3: 2013–14	5	3	5	1	0
4: 2014–15	1	10	5	0	0
5: 2015–16	2	8	6	0	0

Table 21.4 Extracts from KESS Feedback Questionnaire Evaluations – Series 1–5

Series	Extract
1: 2011–12	*'Great opportunity to hear about research findings (as opposed to hearing about practice only).'*
2: 2012–13	Seminar subject matters were *'relevant and timely'*. *'This is an excellent opportunity for invaluable networking.'*
3: 2013–14	Seminars gave a *'good understanding of the practical implementation of the legislation'* and were *'directly relevant to recently announced initiative by the Department for Finance and Personnel in respect of public services reform and innovation'.*
4: 2014–15	*'The Knowledge Exchange Seminar Series is important to translating research and policy and disseminating research findings.'* *'Listening to three parallel topics together and being able to integrate common threads across them.'* *'Great series! I am enjoying many of them.'*
5: 2015–16	*'All very useful and a lot of information provided in the pack to accompany the presentations.'*

Administrative Team

The Administrative Team provides essential support enabling both the organisation and delivery of the Annual Programme. It plays a pivotal role in disseminating relevant papers, publicising the Programme through electronic mailings, social media and the internet, and organising the launch.

Conclusion

As this chapter highlights, KESS is an effective partnership that increases the public value of academic research findings. During each annual series, KESS seminars create a space in NI for a variety of key players to come together and discuss academic research findings to promote evidence-based policy and law-making, fostering relationships between those players in terms of their number and quality.

Similarly, KESS academic workshops serve to facilitate those relationships by better equipping academics to participate in KESS, e.g. when compiling their Policy Briefings and power point presentations, helping them to meet Assembly committee's unique information and research needs.

Finally, for the last few years KESS's annual programmes highlight how they have promoted inter-disciplinary work, both intra and inter-institutionally, featuring seminars that cover a wider breadth of disciplines, with academics from both the KESS partner universities and other universities. This too helps to nurture and develop relationships. This breadth of disciplines reflects Brewer's (2013a: 2013b) call for disciplines to cooperate to address complex social problems. It has happened organically through KESS as scientists realise they need to collaborate in order to analyse fundamental social problems.

Notes

1 KESS website: www.niassembly.gov.uk/assembly-business/research-and-information-service-raise/knowledge-exchange/
2 Examples of KESS Programmes can be found on its website: www.niassembly.gov.uk/assembly-business/research-and-information-service-raise/knowledge-exchange/
3 A single or joint application may be made to the Panel by a university partner academic only. Where a joint application is made, academics from other institutions may be included.

References

Benington, J. 2007. From private choice to public value? In Benington, J. and M. Moore (eds), *In Search of Public Value – Beyond Private Choice*. London: Palgrave.

Brewer, J.D. 2013a. *The Public Value of the Social Sciences: An Interpretive Essay*. London: Bloomsbury Publishing.

Brewer, J.D. 2013b. Public Social Science. Plenary Lecture to the Inaugural Ka Awatea Conference Massey University, Auckland, New Zealand. 14 November.

22 The dissipating value of public service in UK Higher Education

Richard Watermeyer and Mark Olssen

Introduction

In the UK, as across many parts of the world, the 'spectacle' (Debord, 1995) of higher education's (HE) marketization (Bok, 2003) has brought about not only seismic change in the organizational practice of universities but complaint and resistance from many of its constituents, who perceive the abandonment and dissolution of the university as a protected habitus of critical, democratic and free thought (cf. Docherty, 2014; Giroux, 2014; Holmwood, 2011). What some describe as a state of 'crisis' (Burawoy, 2011) for the university is attributed to and/or seen to have been accentuated by the global economic downturn of 2008 and, in the particular case of the United Kingdom (UK), the perseverance of its national Government with a politics of austerity and extreme scrutiny in the distribution of public funds.

The funding of universities, as one part of the UK Government's overall science budget, has neither escaped nor been insulated from significant cuts that have resulted not only in the 'tightening of belts' across the HE sector but an insistence that universities commit to fiscal rationalization. While new public management (NPM) technologies have come to dominate the sector, the thinking of many institutional managers has been monopolized – potentially obscured and/or corrupted – by blind faith in the certainty of continuous performance evaluation as a lever for high performativity, maximum output and, in the context of human resourcing, a justified cost benefit. Accordingly, the conditions of academic labour and concomitantly the production and presentation of the academic self have been radicalized by seemingly unrelenting pressures to effectively perform within a highly competitive and unforgiving market economy.

The rise of managerialist governmentality (Zipin and Brennan, 2004) is inversely correlated, for many, to the despoiling of the traditional liberal academic code. Cherished, 'traditional' tenets of impartiality, self-governance, objectivity, autonomy, criticality and the kinds of freedom associated with what has been called the 'collegial-democratic' model of university governance (Raapper and Olssen, 2015), as exercised in 'flat' structures through bodies like 'senates', and premised upon the sovereignty of the professoriate, are said to have been subjugated to, or replaced by, systems based upon hierarchical line-management, performance targets, and appraisals and audits, which have elevated new norms of individualism, competition, managerialism, entrepreneurialism, careerism and game-playing. Others, however, caution that the latter characteristics of academia are nothing new nor unique to HE's marketization. These commentators dispute accounts of a 'golden' age of academia and claim instead that where neoliberal behaviours appear more prolific it is only because a spotlight, by which the academic profession is observed, has intensified. Notwithstanding this, the purpose of academia and what it means to be an academic are challenged where models of knowledge production are contested and reconstituted and an emphasis on academics' economic performativity and accountability, or as we have elsewhere argued, 'auditability', raised (Watermeyer and Olssen, 2016, see also Collini, 2012; Sayer, 2014).

However, while performance expectations of academics appear to enlarge in the context for instance of demands for generating greater sums of research income, they also in rather oxymoronic fashion appear to contract, where the value of excellence in academic performance is singularly attributed to capitalistic proficiency. The academic role, therefore, appears to be simplifying, unbundling and atomizing. Critics talk of the deprofessionalization and segmentation of academic labour into specialist functions (cf. Olssen and Peters, 2005). We might think, for instance of a dissection of roles into those who specialize only in research or only in teaching or only in academic administration. This kind of professional segregation would seem to remove academics further from a sense of their holistic and 'true' identity, yet also further divorce them from a sense of the aspiration and intention of the scholar as an individual committed to the advancement of knowledge for the public good.

Despite a myriad of policy level 'interventions' designed to reintegrate more of a public consciousness among academic cohorts (cf. Watermeyer, 2011; 2012; 2015), the prevailing managerial diktat within universities has continued to relegate displays of citizenship to peripheral, invisible and disincentivized aspects of academic life. Even in the context of peer-review systems established to determine the contribution of the academic community to the public sphere, the more abstract and less easily evidenced 'impacts' of academics on public communities fall a long way short in the pecking order to researchers able to demonstrate concrete economic benefits from their research. The deterioration of the academic public role has been, furthermore, compounded by the ascent of a culture of complicity, critical lethargy, ennui and professional fear among academics (cf. Docherty, 2016). Regrettably, for many acquiescence and an avoidance of 'speaking-truth-to-power' is an intentional, survivalist strategy intended to militate against the potential censure from and vituperation of managerial elites, whose sensitivities towards and bias against those less willing to 'play the game' are particularly acute.

In this chapter we seek to trace the attempted conversion of the university from what can be called a public good model to one serving private interests. We seek to delineate these two models in theoretical terms in order to document the way and the extent to which quasi-market processes have been introduced and have transformed the practices of academic life. We consider also what prospects exist today for resistance and challenge by both students and academics themselves to the current neoliberal higher education agenda. Our conclusion is that while certain supply-side techniques of governance may in certain senses assist in ensuring both efficiency and accountability, a reinstatement of the ideal of the public good is both possible and necessary to permit a re-professionalization of academics as custodians of an autonomous independent tradition of knowledge production, necessary in an ultimate sense to underwrite the democratic integrity of the university, in Montesquieu's sense, as a "*corps intermediaires* whose necessary function it is to loosen the giant unity of the state by . . . professional separatism" (Röpke, 1971, 143).

In the aftermath of the neoliberalization of higher education

The proliferation and normalization of a mindset that equates academic achievement and success with market competitiveness has caused to fracture and/or distance academics from a sense of professional identity; at least an identity evocative of an Enlightenment ideal of scholarliness and Mertonian norms of scientific endeavour. Many academics appear to slide passively towards unproblematic collusion with or deference to repressive modes of institutional governance, which with consummate efficiency and stealth manage to unpick their rights of autonomy and freedom as critical agents, seemingly in large part without their even knowing. Indeed, we might moot that the entrenchment of the neoliberal Academy is predicated upon the success of its repressive desublimation (Marcuse, 1969) of academics and the easy perpetuation of a myth of academic freedom and autonomy in a milieu of intensifying regulation. Concurrently, among the academic tribes there are market players and entrepreneurial opportunists who relish in a kind of rampant individualism and breed of success defined by their sole-owned achievements and singular focus on career-advancement. Such a tribe of self-interested careerists are those criticized for operating like 'city-traders' detached from and uninterested in little else bar the 'bottom-line'. These are a tribe who have relinquished their affiliation to an ideology other than the corporate and are consequently unrestricted by appeals to an academic sensibility of moral purpose and scholarly integrity (cf. Macfarlane, 2005).

And so, aside from a 'subversive', and often as happens, zealous few who dare directly challenge the 'law' of what is valued in the neoliberal Academy and, therefore, the dominance of a paradigm of fiscal rationalization, whose protests and defiance we should add tend to be met with brutal recrimination, there lies a majority of compliant knowledge workers. Whilst their compliance may in part sit uneasy and seem to conflict with what are albeit increasingly lampooned quaint romanticizations of a past 'golden age' of academia, the precarity of their occupational situation manifest most tellingly in the casualization, deprofessionalization and hyper intensification of academic labour, ensures their institutional obedience. As does, we may speculate, an urge to compete and to benefit from the affirmation from belonging to and participating within what Lucas (2006) refers to as 'the game' of academic life; which itself intimates a kind of pleasure compensation. Consequently, the neoliberalization (Peck and Tickell, 2002) of academia appears to have spread largely without interference or interruption and now infests its first generation progeny who have known no other than a career assembled and oriented by the pursuit of money as the ultimate indicator of excellence and esteem. Though we fashion, in part, an intentionally bloated caricature of the state of the academic profession, it is a caricature that many working as researchers and teachers and of course support staff within UK universities recognize and are sensitive to.

There is in fact an overwhelming sense of the higher education sector in the UK and also more globally being at a point of profound change, some say crisis, in terms not only of its organization but membership. This is of course partially explained by major societal trends not least among which, globalization, has altered the nature of knowledge production and the role of knowledge producers (cf. Gibbons et al., 1994; Leydesdorff and Etzkowitz, 1996), among whom we count academics as a major constituent. Higher Education has also, in the UK context especially, undergone rapid massification with significantly more members of the general populace attending universities. With changes in the funding formula for universities and students, a new global market of higher education has emerged in the UK with universities jostling to attract the brightest minds not only for confirmation of their excellence but so as to feather their financial nests. They appear thus increasingly to run like businesses and major corporations applying market logic to their operational strategy. Yet, for the most part, universities in the UK are 'public' institutions – public in so much as they receive significant patronage from the public purse but also public because they are imbued with a public mission or rather a mission in furthering and protecting the public good. Of course, as global events from 2008 onwards have manifest, what constitutes the public good is notoriously difficult to define or reach consensus on. Indeed, the public good much like a definition of the public itself is an altogether nebulous and contested term.

The blurriness of a concept of the public good especially in the context of universities as one such catalyst and custodian has arguably been further exaggerated where the forces of global recession and the sudden collapse of financial markets in 2008 made it even less clear how this was to be achieved, indeed, if it was even possible. For universities, as public institutions, their contribution to the public good would have to be understood and moreover scrutinized on the basis of their footprint on public life or in other words, a measurable economic and societal contribution. In the context of universities as educational providers this might be easily justified. Perhaps less so, however, where a major part, if not, controversially the most important or value-laden part of what universities do – at least as they perceive it – is research and the production of new knowledge funded by Government. What followed in the UK were policy led innovations for the evaluation of research that would help determine the contribution of research to public users. Simply put, researchers would find themselves having to articulate the ways with which their research achieved impact.

This was formalized in two ways. First, in the form of pathways to impact statements, newly mandated aspects of competitively sourced research funding proposals, administered by the UK's research councils, which demanded researchers articulate what the prospective impacts of their proposed research would be and how they would mobilize these. Second, the impact of research would be assessed as a part of the UK's performance-based research funding system, the Research Excellence Framework (REF) 2014 successor to the Research Assessment Exercise which began in 1980s Thatcherite Britain and the onset of neoliberal economics. Through an impact statement/template and narrative based impact case study, researchers submitted claims of the impact of their research to evaluation by disciplinary sub-panels of academic peer-reviewers and user-assessors.

The significance of impact case studies to academics and their institutions has been widely acknowledged and comparisons made between their worth and that attributed to outputs in the context of what is ultimately awarded in the form of approximately £1.6billion of Quality Research (QR) monies. Various calculations have posited an excellent impact submission to be the equivalent of seven of the very best journal articles or, in pure financial terms, anything up to the value of £350k over the REF period; tending to be five to six years. The value, therefore, of academics achieving impact and consequently, one would assume the value of their public interface, was felt to rapidly escalate. However, the precise terms of the REF, particularly as they related to what counted or more saliently in this instance, didn't count and caused many to speculate that case studies submitted to the REF would bias forms of public interactions that generated 'hard' or easily evidenced impacts. These were generally acknowledged as being financial impacts such as, for instance, the patenting of a newly discovered drug. At the very least, such impacts would be quantitatively characterized and thus presumably more authoritative declarations of economic and societal contribution. Furthermore, institutions in making their best, or rather most conservative judgements about how to engineer impact and thereafter sourcing the kinds of evidence most likely to convince and invoke the generosity of REF evaluators in their scoring, conceived of 'user-beneficiaries' in more narrow terms.

Subsequent review of the six thousand plus impact case studies submitted to the REF reveal a huge bias towards impacts reported on policy and specifically the UK Parliament (cf. Watermeyer and Lewis, 2016). In our own disciplinary field of educational research, user beneficiaries tend to mirror this kind of trend and bifurcate into policy-makers and practitioners. In simple terms, the REF (and RCUK) has had an effect in at once both formalizing a requirement for academics to be publicly involved yet also essentially, delimiting and homogenizing the kinds of engagement and publics that might be pursued.

Where academics' public interface, or what in the higher education vernacular is designated 'public engagement', has been, for want of a better word, 'institutionalized', concerns have been raised apropos the extent to which engagement is meaningful in terms of anything other than as a lever for 'positional goods' (Hirsch, 1977): as a means to attract grant income; high evaluative scores; or in fashioning an image – or chimera – of the university despite its private interest and motivation, as a public institution. New inventions of governance in the research funding landscape have seemingly caused something of a deviation away from the idea of academics engaged in a variety of creative, imaginative, experimental and risk-laden public relations to a confinement with predetermined and typically elite stakeholders. And why? Well, what impresses more in the context of claim-making? The testimony of the CEO of a major international corporation or the gratitude of a local community support group? The answer is depressingly self-evident. Furthermore, the framing of a 'public engagement' agenda in higher education has led to many academic researchers perceiving it as an 'activity' unrelated to research or as an add-on that mainly corresponds to matters of scientific literacy, public understanding and trust and therefore how science accrues legitimacy in the public sphere and concomitantly how scientists attain a 'licence to operate' within the agora. As an activity, however, and though one clearly with significant benefits in operational and evaluative terms to academics, public engagement is not without cost. Indeed, the cost of engaging the public is understood in terms not only of time and money but professional identity. In purely institutional terms the cost of public engagement requires rationalizing, and very much, we suggest, on the terms of cost-benefit or more explicitly, what the institution receives as a return on its investment of having its academics engage the public; which results in the shrinkage of the public interface where only forms of public engagement that may be finally justified are sanctioned.

The institutionalization of public engagement in universities, where it is co-opted and rationalized exclusively as a vehicle for impact generation, not only suggests a diminishing academic-public interface but a conspicuous paradox. Where academics engage public groups for the purpose of public accountability, their intention is in satisfying systems of evaluation more perhaps than addressing public needs. More bizarrely, also, is the central if not pivotal role of the public in justifying the contribution of academics. The existing system of impact evaluation as it occurs in the UK's REF stimulates, therefore, almost an inversion of the academic-public contract, where instead of academics operating in the interest of the public good, the public or publics are recruited into an academic designed system of governance where they operate as defenders of academic labour. For academic impact see the public, it seems.

An impact agenda for higher education as it occurs in the REF is all the more problematic for rendering the public interface as something that occurs safely and in the terms of that which is measurable. Dealing with each in turn, there is to begin, ostensibly no motivation for an academic to engage the public in any which way other than that, which returns a positive performance-related outcome. Yet such outcomes may be extremely hard if not impossible to engineer. Indeed, the very notion of engineered outcomes suggests something altogether mechanistic and pre-ordained about the impact generation process. Such a characterization flies in the face of the arguments put forward by many who object to the determinism and reductionism inherent in prospective impact claiming, which, as has been noted, feature as a core component of competitive funding processes (cf. Watermeyer, 2016a; 2016b). Such objectors reasonably argue that impact is a consequence of serendipity and is something that occurs on its own terms and crucially at its own pace. Furthermore, they argue that in planning for impact, especially in such terms as a pathway, a linearity is imposed upon research which neglects the consideration of a myriad of other potential albeit unanticipated impacts that stem from a public interface. Ultimately, an impact agenda, whilst predicated on a notion of boosting the extent of academic researchers as agents of the public good, may cause the narrowing of the definitional parameters and possibilities of their public impact. Concurrently, rationalizations for public engagement, particularly those promulgated by institutional managers and senior administrators, may become increasingly prescribed and curtailed to forms of interaction that lever not public but positional goods that favour the institution. Overall, therefore, we see a collapsing of a notion of academics' public responsibility into a responsibility for being high performers for their institution. The rhetoric may be of satisfying public needs but the underlying intention is of satisfying institutional expectations.

Where a public interface is rationalized on the basis of academic performance, there lies also an implicit danger that public engagement becomes something dominated and sequestered by academics with an aptitude for generating impacts that achieve high evaluations. In other words, the emergence of a value hierarchy of engagement types – that sees, for instance, a prioritizing by institutions on policy or corporate stakeholder engagement – means that forms of engagement that are institutionally endorsed and encouraged, will likely be undertaken only by more established (and networked) senior academics. There is also a potential risk that public engagement will become increasingly disciplinary specific or concentrated and marginalized in subject and knowledge domains where the link to public beneficiaries, and, therefore, those able to testify to the impact of academic research, is strongest. The formation of an, albeit tacit, hierarchy of public engagement in universities may cause a distancing effect on academics from undertaking certain forms, which they may perceive beneath them. In a most cynical assessment we might speculate that the majority of academics, certainly those for whom public engagement remains a 'third-stream' activity, will be inclined to engage the public only where the reward from doing so is explicit and realistic and features as formal demand of performance evaluation.

Fundamentally, we perceive a risk that the institutionalization in universities of public engagement will turn the public from being an opportunity with which academic researchers might respond, for example, to issues of social justice and inequality, to an opportunity for self-aggrandizement and narcissism, where the 'public interface' is reconfigured as a performance indicator and mark of esteem. Of course, potentially a greater danger still is that where public engagement cannot be justified on the basis of its contribution to a university's positional goods, such as for instance through the REF, that it will not only become potentially a more marginal activity but may even be actively discouraged by senior management. Watermeyer (2015) reports on the dangers of academics with an appetite for public engagement becoming 'lost in the third space', where their public interactions are not directly linked or attributable to research. For such a group, who unlike those engaged with high profile stakeholders tend to be early in their careers and lacking the kinds of intellectual and institutional capital that would give their public displays clout, their engagement is either treated by their institutions as valueless or alternatively of limited value, but even this not in an academic sense. Indeed, the majority of these kind of engagement enthusiasts are those who exist very much outwith (or beneath) the research enclave and tend to be understood as pursuing a different kind of labour that has less to do with the role of being an academic and more that of professional service staff, particularly those stationed in university marketing and student recruitment offices. Put crudely, they are perceived not so much as academics but what Macfarlane (2010) calls 'para-academics'. Furthermore, they are prone to receiving the negative press of their peers, many whom, ostensibly with either jealously, superciliousness or inflated ego, allege the profligacy amongst 'do-gooders'.

We find, therefore, a conflicting state for academics' relationship with the public. There are many who engage as a matter of duty and on the basis of a conviction that their role as academics is intrinsically bound to servicing the public good and that public engagement is inherently a good thing. There are equally many who engage as a matter of professional expectation and in fulfilment of their contractual obligations. Where the role of the academic is becoming increasingly confused yet simultaneously appears to be hollowing out in conjunction with a pressure to perform and the growing bureaucratization of higher education, the ascendance of one ontology of public engagement gains precedence over another. Specifically, we opine that where the legitimacy of academic personhood and the sustainability of an academic career is now in the neoliberal epoch, contingent upon compliance with a paradigm of performativity, then the viability of the concept of the 'public intellectual' erodes. This has led some like Frank Furedi (2006) to ask 'where have all the intellectuals gone' and others like Richard Sennett (1998) observe the 'corrosion of character' within academia. Theorists like Samuel Bowles (2016) meanwhile lament the problem of 'homo economicus' and appeal for a refocusing by the scholarly community on a moral economy.

Academics' ambition to be publicly connected and perhaps relevant would appear thus antagonistic to and demotivated by a corporate orientation in higher education, which despite a policy discourse of 'science and society' forecloses opportunities for academics to be 'authentically' publicly involved and accountable. Moreover, it would seem that academics are losing their right and/or appetite to expose themselves to forms of risk that are so much the condition of scientific endeavour and scientists operating within the *agora*. We refer here especially to what is consistently reported as the enervation of academics as free, autonomous and critical agents (Schrecker, 2010; Williams, 2016). We intimate also what other authors have described as the 'ruination' (Readings, 1998) of the idea of the university not least the despoiling of its symbolization as a paragon of democratic principle. We link the capitulation of the university to neoliberal ideology not only to the denouement of public intellectualism – or its debasement to intellectual celebrity – but the drawing-in of the university as a space of free and open thought. We also, however, suggest alternative and liminal spaces for academics' public interface.

The death and rebirth of criticality: into the agora

The closing or dumbing down of criticality and critical community on campus, exemplified by the collapsing of staff and student unions – as historically speaking, bastions of collective independent action – into the formal organizational governance of institutions; the privileging of the campus as a 'safe space' exercised with trigger warnings pre-empting and/or cauterizing the 'threat' of 'subversive' behaviour, words, even thoughts; the emergence of covert online discussion forums such as the UK *Guardian* newspaper's 'Academics Anonymous'; the scarcity of non-conformist academic 'role-models' in the public arena; and in large part the homogenization of student activism as a protest motivated by an increasingly manicured consumerist experience (cf. Bok, 2003; McGettigan, 2013) raises profound questions about the role of the university as a public institution and where its protagonists are heading (Collini, 2017, Newfield, 2008).

The role of the academic surely is to ask difficult questions. The role of science is to contest established 'truths' in the search for new and improved 'realities'. Yet asking difficult questions and contesting the norm intimates a kind of proactive approach to being critical that is increasingly at odds with and uncharacteristic of the neoliberalized – critically averse – intellectual and institution. Moreover, such a vision of science and scientists is surely antithetical to the perpetuation of the 'safe university' and disruptive to the idea of the university as a 'knowledge factory' (Röbken, 2004). In such a way then, the public intellectual who seeks to engage with powerful knowledge in the transformation of the public sphere and thereby talk meaningfully to power is a spanner in the works of new managerialism where s/he represents (perhaps inadvertently) an escapologist to the panopticon of performativity. The agora therefore almost represents the binary opposite of the university. Where the public is openness, the university is closed. An engagement with the agora thus represents a breach from academics' containment in the 'black box' of science. The motif of the ivory tower is one arguably got wrong. It is perhaps not so much that academics are architects of their isolation and seclusion rather that the conditions and conventions of their employ have cut them adrift – which is not to give immunity to those who defy and resist public integration. In fact, we might posit that there has been an overall unfair characterization of academics as disinterested and disconnected from their public communities.

Whilst this kind of diagnosis has provided essential fodder for the rationalization of a range of initiatives focused on embedding 'culture change', a 'coercive realism' (Evans 2010), and a more publicly engaged academy and crucially, furthermore, the transition of the Academy into an 'audit culture' (Shore and Wright, 2000), it has overlooked what many academics already commit to as a part of their public mission.

Indeed, much has been (mis)assumed in the context of a 'deficit' Academy one not too dissimilar to the kind of deficit *public* often critiqued in the social studies of science literature. In this way, we argue that it is unhelpful and disadvantageous to propose culture change, when much of the culture already pre-exists albeit in ways that are less obvious or obviously aligned to the criteria of performance evaluation. And this trope is to our mind key. Indeed, we propose that a culture change discourse has further accentuated the kinds of bureaucratization all too familiar to the neoliberal Academy, which suffocate the kinds of experimentality, ingenuity and risk that characterize intellectual life as it operates in the agora. A culture change trope also oversimplifies what we have already referred to as a normative depiction of public engagement as an inherently good thing when there is, we would argue, greater complexity and nuance in terms of conceptualizing academics 'being' in the agora.

Inculcation of a public engagement culture and a battering ram approach marketing the benefits of public engagement have we would argue served to infantilize academics much in the way forms of micro-management and super-surveillance currently do. Moreover, there is a patent disjuncture observable between a top-down 'policy' discourse that sermonizes the necessity of achieving a publicly engaged Academy and the 'bottom-up' lived experience of what counts as important within and by universities that in the various ways already discussed compromises the ability of academics to meet such an aim. There is a chasm between the aspiration of public engagement as imagined and demanded by those outwith the institution yet looking in, and the dominant organizational model of academic labour – which is increasingly structured by workload allocation models that unitize academics' time – in which public engagement features unevenly, faintly and/or as peripheral concern.

Conclusion

Ultimately, we perceive a significant cleft between a model of 'public engagement' institutionalized and quasi-mandated and a 'public interface' enacted by academics that circumvents higher education incentivization, regulation and organizational restrictions. Our supposition is, therefore, that academics' public interface is one that should not be governed or form a part of what the university, as a neoliberal institution, does or is. In fact, the 'authenticity' and sustainability of academics' public interface demands, to our mind, an intentional avoidance of the university as a relational gatekeeper or broker. Indeed, the university becomes almost an irrelevancy and hindrance in the pursuit of more meaningful, expansive and productive expressions of academics in the agora. Furthermore, it is perhaps more profitable to move beyond a focus on incentivizing academics' public interface or complaining of when incentivization and forms of recognition and reward, that are inherently economic or economically-related, are not present. Whilst an absence of institutional incentives may, as we have reported elsewhere (cf. Watermeyer, 2015), compromise the fruition of an institutional and sector defined culture of public engagement, it may also motivate academics to interface with the public in more open, varied, democratic and less predetermined ways (see also Brewer, 2013). Crucially also, in the absence of the institution, academics and their public co-conspirators may be afforded greater agency, freedom and independence from which to shape, own and maximize the benefits of their relationship. In such a way, academics may find themselves emancipated from the ties of incentives applied, albeit unequally, by institutions and across the wider higher education system for the purpose of inculcating desirable behaviour (of which there is a similar dearth of consensus), which Bowles (2016), as one among others (cf. Sandel, 2012; Satz, 2010), attributes to the demotivation of the individual as an agent of 'public action' (Arendt, 1958).

Embracing a 'moral economy', however, demands bravery, selflessness and conviction by academics in transcending and even perhaps transgressing the borderlines of institutional governance. Entering the agora demands an acceptance that they may need to relinquish and even sever an institutional umbilicus; accept that their identity or contested identities play out beyond the walls of their institutional affiliation (cf. Whitchurch and Gordon, 2010); and accept a challenge of participating within an oppositional politics that resists and actively disputes the dogma of performativity. As a consequence, some may find themselves ostracized or removed to the margins of institutional life. For others, an academic life of 'one foot in and one foot out' and a balance between satisfying the (shallower) demands of the institution with the (more substantive) demands of being a 'public intellectual' may be attempted.

Fundamentally, the responsibility for an academic-public interface should, we would argue, be placed back in the hands of academics and supplanted from managerial or regulatory classes who dictate, with autocratic panache, what is and what isn't important. This ostensibly, requires a 'positive' disenchantment with the idea of the university as a public institution and suspension of belief in its sanctity as a site of critical endeavour for the public good. Certainly, where to be public is to be critical and 'other than', academics might consider themselves amidst a moratorium on the university as an engine of the public good, where criticality has become a form of contraband and performativity – and for that matter, chicanery – are ascribed not only legitimacy but priority.

A reinvestment with the public might then occur, but crucially as one which is not institutionally (or even systemically) governed and instrumentalized but individually inspired and curated, yet which also has the potential of engendering critical solidarity and community, and translation into a more efficacious form of accountability. Academics must go beyond the institution; they must succeed it. After all is the bulldozing of institutional boundaries not the very catalyst and aspiration of their public interface? In going beyond, their 'diaspora' might reveal a more democratically prosperous, meaningful and dare we say, *impactful* public interface that escapes the shackles of performativity, new managerialism and other such egregious inventions of neoliberalism.

References

Arendt, H. (1958). *The Human Condition*. Chicago: University of Chicago Press.

Bok, D. (2003). *Universities in the Marketplace*. Princeton, NJ: Princeton University Press.

Bowles, S. (2016). *The Moral Economy: Why Good Incentives are no Substitute for Good Citizens*. New Haven and London: Yale University Press.

Brewer, J. (2013). *The Public Value of the Social Sciences*. London: Bloomsbury.

Burawoy, M. (2011). Redefining the public university: Global and national contexts. In J. Holmwood (ed.), *A Manifesto for the Public University*. London: Bloomsbury Academic.

Collini, S. (2012). *What are Universities For?* London: Penguin.

Collini, S. (2017). *Speaking of Universities*. London: Verso.

Debord, G. (1995). *The Society of the Spectacle*. New York: Zone Books.

Docherty, T. (2014). *Universities at War*. London: Sage Swifts.

Docherty, T. (2016). *Complicity: Criticism between Collaboration and Commitment*. London and New York: Rowman and Littlefield.

Evans, M. (2010). The universities and the challenge of realism. *Arts and Humanities in Higher Education*, 9, 13–21.

Furedi, F. (2006). *Where Have All the Intellectuals Gone?* London: Continuum.

Gibbons, M., Limoges, C., Nowotny, H., Schwartzman, S., Scott, P. and Trow, M. (1994). *The New Production of Knowledge: The Dynamics of Science and Research in Contemporary Societies*. London: Sage.

Giroux, H. (2014). *Neoliberalism's War on Higher Education*. Chicago: Haymarket Books.

Hirsch, F. (1977). *The Social Limits to Growth*. London: Routledge and Kegan Paul.

Holmwood, J. (2011). The idea of a public university. In J. Holmwood (ed.), *A Manifesto for the Public University*. London: Bloomsbury Academic.

Leydesdorff, L. and Etzkowitz, H. (1996). Emergence of a triple-helix of university-industry-government relations. *Science and Public Policy*, 23(5), 279–286.

Lucas, L. (2006). *The Research Game in Academic Life*. London: Routledge/Society for Research into Higher Education.

Macfarlane, B. (2005). The disengaged academic: The retreat from citizenship. *Higher Education Quarterly*, 59(4), 296–312.

Macfarlane, B. (2010). The morphing of academic practice: Unbundling and the rise of the para-academic. *Higher Education Quarterly*, 65(1), 59–73.

Marcuse, H. (1969). *An Essay on Liberation*. Boston, MA: Beacon Press.

McGettigan, A. (2013). *The Great University Gamble: Money, Markets and the Future of Higher Education*. London: Pluto.

Newfield, C. (2008). *Unmaking the Public University: The Forty Year Assault on the Middle Classes*. Cambridge, MA: Harvard University Press.

Olssen, M. and Peters, M.A. (2005). Neoliberalism, higher education and the knowledge economy: From the free market to knowledge capitalism. *Journal of Education Policy*, 20, 313–345.

Peck, J. and Tickell, A. (2002). The urbanization of neoliberalism: Theoretical debates on neoliberalizing space. *Antipode*, 34(3), 380–404.

Raaper, R. and Olssen, M. (2015). Mark Olssen on the neoliberalisation of higher education and academic lives: An interview. *Policy Futures in Education*, 14(2), 147–163.

Readings, B. (1996). *The University in Ruins*. Cambridge, MA: Harvard University Press.

Röbken, H. (2004). *Inside the Knowledge Factory: Organizational Change in Business Schools in Germany, Sweden and the USA*. Wiesbaden: DUV.

Röpke, W. (1971). *Economics of the Free Society*. Chicago: H. Regnery Co.

Sandel, M. (2012). *What Money Can't Buy: The Moral Limits of Markets*. New York: Farrer, Straus and Giroux.

Satz, D. (2010). *Why Some Things Should Not Be for Sale: The Limits of the Markets*. Oxford: Oxford University Press.

Sayer, D. (2014). *Rank Hypocrises: The Insult of the REF*. London: Sage Swifts.

Sennett, R. (1998). *The Corrosion of Character: The Personal Consequences of Work in the New Capitalism*. New York and London: W.W. Norton.

Shore, C. and Wright, S. (2000). Coercive Accountability: The rise of audit culture in higher education. In M. Strathern (ed.), *Audit Cultures: Anthropological Studies in Accountability, Ethics and the Academy* (pp. 57–89). London: Routledge.

Shrecker, N. (2010). *The Lost Soul of Higher Education: Corporatization, the Assault on Academic Freedom, and the End of the American University*. New York: New Press.

Watermeyer, R. (2011). Challenges for engagement: Toward a public academe? *Higher Education Quarterly*, 65(4), 386–410.

Watermeyer, R. (2012). From engagement to impact? Articulating the public value of academic research. *Tertiary Education and Management*, 18(2), 115–130.

Watermeyer, R. (2014). Issues in the articulation of 'impact': The responses of UK academics to 'impact' as a new measure of research assessment. *Studies in Higher Education*, 39(2), 359–377.

Watermeyer, R. (2015). Lost in the 'third space': The impact of public engagement in higher education on academic identity, research practice and career progression. *European Journal of Higher Education*, 5(3), 331–347.

Watermeyer, R. (2016a). Impact in the REF: Issues and obstacles. *Studies in Higher Education*, 41(2), 199–214.

Watermeyer, R. (2016b). Public intellectuals vs. new public management: The defeat of public engagement in higher education. *Studies in Higher Education*, 41(12), 2271–2285.

Watermeyer, R. and Lewis, J. (2017). Institutionalizing public engagement in UK universities: Current perceptions and future predictions of the state of the art. *Studies in Higher Education*. doi: 10.1080/03075079.2016.1272566

Watermeyer, R. and Olssen, M. (2016). Excellence and exclusion: The individual costs of institutional competitiveness. *Minerva*, 54(2), 201–218.

Whitchurch, C. and Gordon, G. (eds) (2010). *Academic and Professional Identities in Higher Education: The Challenges of a Diversifying Workforce*. New York and London: Routledge.

Williams, J. (2016). *Academic Freedom in Age of Conformity*. London: Palgrave Macmillan.

Zipin, L. and Brennan, M. (2004). Managerial governmentality and the suppression of ethics. In M. Walker and J. Nixon (eds), *Reclaiming Universities from a Runaway World*. Maidenhead: Society for Research into Higher Education and Open University.

23 How far would you go?

Assessing the carbon footprint of business travel in the context of academic research activity

Dominic Medway, Gary Warnaby, John Byrom, Martin Grimmer and Rebecca Abushena

Introduction and research context

A growing focus on the topic of climate change, carbon footprints and other associated environmental issues has pervaded society, and has *inter alia* generated extensive comment (Kotler, 2011; Polonsky, 2011), albeit with varying periodic emphasis, depending on current events and the vagaries of news agendas. Madeleine Bunting (2009), in a column in the UK newspaper *The Guardian* drawing on the ideas of Amitai Etzoni, argues that the environment has become one of the great 'moral megalogues' of our age – namely, a subject on which millions of members of society hold opinions and freely exchange their views in a variety of settings and contexts. Whilst such megalogues have no clear beginning or end, over time they can lead to changes in culture and people's behaviour.

'Sustainability' is a term that has become intimately connected with this environmental megalogue. Barlett and Chase (2004, 6) conceptualise sustainability as 'an intersection of three domains': (1) the *economic*, relating to the production of goods and services to support the livelihood of populations; (2) the *social*, relating to issues such as social justice and political participation, and (3) the *environmental*, relating to the maintenance of biodiversity and the health of biological systems. Arguably, all three of these domains have direct implications for public value (O'Flynn, 2007) and the sustainable use of resources. Indeed, Swilling (2011) explicitly links sustainability and public value and goes as far as to state that this 'is rapidly becoming the unifying challenge of our generation' (94).

Hamdouch and Depret (2010, 474) suggest that "green economy' markets are now reaching a critical mass'. As is the case with virtually all other economic sectors, the issue of sustainability in the environmental domain has obvious relevance to demonstrating public value in higher education (HE). In this context, the *environmental* domain tends to assume the greatest initial importance in engendering sustainability within a given university or institution, with the assumption that social and economic benefits relating to this sustainability will consequently follow (Barlett and Chase, 2004). US case studies of sustainability projects in HE appear to support this view, with much of their focus being on reducing carbon footprints and reducing the waste (through recycling and reusing) which emanates from university campuses and facilities. The US also witnessed the creation in 2007 of the American College and University Presidents' Climate Commitment (ACUPCC), a pledge signed by approximately 660 college and university presidents to 'lead their institutions towards carbon neutrality' (Breen, 2010, 686). According to the ACUPCC, the HE sector:

must exercise leadership in their communities and throughout society by modeling ways to minimize global warming emissions, and by providing the knowledge and the educated graduates to achieve climate neutrality. Campuses that address the climate challenge by reducing global warming emissions and by integrating sustainability into their curriculum will better serve their students and meet their social mandate to help create a thriving, ethical and civil society.

(Second Nature, n.d.).

In the UK too, evidence suggests a similar 'environmental' orientation in the sustainability initiatives of many universities. Examples include: carbon reducing travel-to-work plans (incorporating payment for university parking, and cycle-to-work schemes); educating staff and students on environmentally-conscious practices (such as turning off equipment and lights when not in use), and a facilities management approach to carbon neutrality and wider sustainability in terms of activities such as recycling and energy efficiency. Many of these initiatives generate obvious 'quick wins' in terms of immediate reductions in energy usage and carbon emissions (Breen, 2010).

Of course, such concerns are not limited to HE institutions, as most businesses will arguably see the value of operating in an environmentally sustainable manner. To illustrate some of the issues relating to how businesses – and the individuals that comprise them – may potentially accommodate some of these concerns in the course of their activities, this chapter specifically examines the challenges facing academics in calculating the carbon footprint of their research activities. It goes on to address some of the potential public policy issues that consequently arise at the macro-, meso- and micro-levels, which themselves have practical management implications. The chapter applies a number of official carbon calculators to the travel involved in a small-scale research project in the marketing subject area. Rather than reporting the substantive research findings generated by the research project itself, the focus of the chapter is on the methodology employed in assessing the specific carbon footprint of our research activities. This is calculated using three carbon calculator models, proposed by three different types of organisations from the public and private sector. Attempts are made to establish the potential offset costs of the CO_2 emissions from this research project and to highlight the implications of our findings for considerations of public value more generally.

Fostering sustainability in higher education

Moving to consider a conceptual framework by which sustainability may be fostered, Velazquez et al. (2006) propose a model which emphasises the need for an overall *vision* in the co-ordination of sustainability initiatives, and also identifies four key strategies for fostering sustainability (see Figure 23.1). These include: (1) *Education* (as a way to promote sustainability in institutions); (2) *Research*; (3) *Outreach and Partnership* (for example, with governmental and non-governmental agencies, the private sector and the wider community to develop, promote and implement sustainability initiatives); and (4) *Sustainability on Campus* (to which most of the examples of sustainability projects in HE mentioned briefly above refer). It is this second area of research *practice* with which this chapter is concerned.

Velazquez et al.'s (2006) model, while focussing on the strategic level, appears to overlook how the *process* rather than the outcomes of research can contribute to

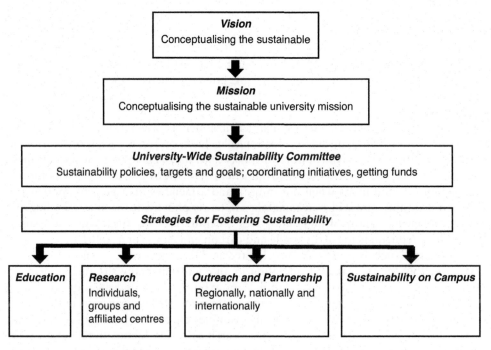

Figure 23.1 The sustainable university model
Source: adapted from Velazquez et al., 2006

sustainability in the social domain. In short, if those who are doing research at the behest of their universities do not change their behaviour when going about the task (e.g. by gathering data and disseminating outcomes in a sustainable manner), then any resultant findings and recommendations regarding sustainability may start to look rather hollow – more a case of 'Do as we say, not as we do' (see Corbyn, 2009). Such situations potentially undermine the good work relating to sustainability being planned and implemented in other parts of the HE sector, which demonstrate to stakeholders how public value is being maximised. A carbon-reducing policy emphasis in relation to facilities management on campus, for example, makes little sense when coupled with a strategic drive for the higher visibility of academics at international conferences that can only be reached by air travel.

Hamdouch and Depret (2010) emphasise the importance of what they term a 'policy integration strategy' in providing a wider framework for sustainable development and its regulation. Such a strategy may relate to numerous areas (e.g. industry, energy, transport, housing etc.), be deployed at different spatial levels (from local to global), and incorporate various actors at the *micro-* (i.e. individuals, civil society), *meso-* (i.e. companies, industries), and *macro-* (i.e. public administrations, government agencies) levels. Factors influencing sustainability in terms of the micro-level processes by which individual academics conduct and disseminate their research will also emanate from the meso-level (i.e. policies set by the university at which they work) and the macro-level (e.g. in the UK, policies and agendas of the various research funding organisations, some of which relate to issues of public value).

At these higher levels, there is arguably lesser emphasis on issues relating to sustainability. Thus, at the meso-level there seems to be less evidence of UK universities thinking about how to make research activity more sustainable. Various authors have identified barriers which deter such sustainable practices in HE institutions, such as financial pressures (Barlett and Chase, 2004), lack of time, ambiguity about what actually constitutes a 'sustainable practice' (Breen, 2010), and lack of administrative support (Velazquez et al., 2005). At the macro-level, whilst consideration of ethics and risk assessment are now an integral part of research grant applications to a number of funding bodies, environmental impact forecasts of the research process itself (in terms of data collection, dissemination and so forth), appear, in comparison, largely overlooked

Sustainability considerations have clear linkages to public value. In their inventory of what constitutes public values, Beck Jørgenson and Bozeman (2007, 360) identify sustainability under the value category of the 'public sector's contribution to society', pointing to the fact that the public sector should work towards the common good and not unnecessarily deplete resources. Indeed, Rutgers (2014, 39, emphasis added) notes that '[p]ublic values are specific values that concern "the good of society" or the "general interest," that is, the *sustainability of society* and the well-being of its members, irrespective of immediate personal preferences or interests.' Despite these parallels, issues of public value in relation to sustainable research practice remain underexplored: a shortcoming that this chapter seeks to address.

Empirical research

Within the context of an absence of guidance from external sources, and in the spirit of reflective practice, we decided to question what the carbon footprint of our own research activities was, in an effort to ascertain the sustainability of our personal research practice. Kenny and Gray (2009, 1) define a carbon footprint as 'a measure of an individual's contribution to global warming in terms of the amount of greenhouse gases produced by an individual [which] is measured in units of carbon dioxide equivalent'. In recent years, there has been much media comment about the size of individuals' carbon footprints and the factors impacting upon this, as well as the existence of a variety of means by which carbon footprints can be calculated. The importance of this increased awareness is further highlighted by Kenny and Gray (2009, 1–2):

> The calculation of individual and household carbon footprints is a powerful tool enabling individuals to quantify their own carbon dioxide emissions and link these to activities and behaviour. Such models play an important role in educating the public in the management and reduction of CO_2 emissions through self-assessment and determination.

In attempting to work out our own research-oriented carbon footprint, we focus on a small-scale qualitative research study, typical of much collaborative research activity that goes on today in higher education. The research itself focused on the management and marketing of the historic Roman frontier system of Hadrian's Wall in the UK, which incorporates a number of archaeological sites and related tourist attractions – the specific methodology and main findings of the project are outlined in Warnaby et al. (2010; 2011; 2013). This research involved several visits to interview participants, and to collect observational data, at various locations in northern England, as well as trips between the co-researchers' universities to write up findings. Outcomes from the research have been disseminated at academic conferences in London, Berlin, and Boston, USA (Bennison et al., 2008a; 2008b; Medway et al., 2008).

Methodological considerations

Kenny and Gray (2009) distinguish between direct (or primary) and indirect (or secondary) carbon footprints. The direct/primary footprint is a measure of an individual's direct emissions of CO_2 from the burning of fossil fuels including domestic energy consumption and transportation. The indirect/secondary footprint is a measure of the indirect CO_2 emissions from the whole lifecycle of products or services we use, including those associated with their manufacture and eventual breakdown (Grimmer et al., 2015). In order to assess the carbon footprint of the above research project we decided to focus solely on travel, as this was the one thing that could be directly and easily connected with the research activity. Thus, we focused on the *primary* carbon footprint of the research project.

The data collection and dissemination trips described above were undertaken by authors Medway and Warnaby (along with our colleague David Bennison, late of the Manchester Metropolitan University Business School). The travel was undertaken either individually, or in pairs, but never by all three researchers together. Each of the three researchers kept a log of their journeys related to the research project. This included details of the mileage or distance covered for each trip (calculated in all instances using Google Maps), the mode of transport used (namely, taxi, car, aeroplane, bus, tram and train), and whether a journey was shared with a co-researcher.

We considered trying to work out the carbon footprint of more indirect/secondary aspects of the research activity, such as a half-day meeting in a university office, or a couple of nights' stay in a conference hotel. However, from an early stage it became apparent that this was simply too complicated, not least because there are issues regarding apportionment – that is, whether the carbon footprint of heating and lighting a university office or hotel room would be much different if the research activity was not taking place within it. This resonates with the notion of indirect carbon emissions embedded within goods and services, namely:

> the way in which the carbon footprint of a product, as measured by a full lifecycle assessment from 'cradle to grave', can be represented in terms of kg of CO_2 per kg of product.
>
> (Institute of Grocery Distribution, 2009)

Working out the carbon footprint of a service product such as a hotel room, for example, poses the same kinds of difficulties as the Carbon Trust encountered when trying to determine the full carbon footprint of a packet of Walkers Crisps in 2007. This process took several months and required a comprehensive audit of energy use in the products and processes involved in every stage of the Walkers Crisps supply chain, from potato farm to end consumer (Carbon Trust, 2008a). Such ambiguities and complexities surrounding the more indirect carbon emissions were one of the reasons we kept the focus solely on travel activity.

Further, we did not include in our assessment what could be termed 'linked-opportunity travel'. An example of this occurred relating to a conference in Boston, when one of the researchers took the opportunity to travel further to Toronto to meet with an academic colleague based there. Such a journey would never have happened without the visit to Boston, but a boundary had to be drawn between travel purely related to the research project, and that linked loosely to the project by opportunity and chance. This side-trip example conforms to what is termed a 'shadow' carbon footprint, that is, the footprint that is not embedded in the activity itself but rather results from the activity. Typically, such shadow footprints can only be found (or seen) by those with knowledge that the activity causing them (or 'casting' them) has occurred. They remain imperceptible to anyone else. Thus, the trip to Toronto from Boston to see a colleague was part of the shadow carbon footprint of this research project, and was not something we took into account.

The data from the journey logs were entered for each of the three travel-active researchers into a combined spreadsheet. The kilograms of carbon dioxide (not carbon itself) emitted for each journey, and subsequently each researcher, and then the project as a whole, were determined using three carbon calculators. Kenny and Gray (2009) state that the criteria for the choice of calculator models in this type of context include: 1) *complexity and relevance* (i.e. inclusion of as many sources of CO_2 as possible within the calculator); 2) *reliability* (i.e. a model/calculator developed by an expert team or organisation), and 3) *recommendation* (i.e. a model/calculator recommended by either a government department or state energy or environment agency). These criteria informed our choice of the following carbon calculators:

- The Defra/Carbon Trust calculation method (Carbon Trust, 2008b) was chosen because it is recognised by the UK Government.
- The GHG Protocol Initiative calculator for 'CO_2 Emissions for Business Travel. Version 2.0.1' (www.ghgprotocol.org/calculation-tools) was also chosen because of its pan-national and official recognition; it being a product of a multi-stakeholder partnership of businesses, non-governmental organisations (NGOs), and others, convened by the World Resources Institute (WRI) – a US-based environmental NGO – and the World Business Council for Sustainable Development (WBCSD) – a Geneva-based coalition of 170 international companies (World Resources Institute and World Business Council for Sustainable Development, 2004).
- The native energy calculator (www.nativeenergy.com) was chosen as it represents one of a range of commercially focused calculators, which are attempting to capture carbon offset business. It appears to use its own unique calculation method but this involves combining carbon emissions data and guidelines from a number of sources, including the GHG Protocol Initiative calculator.

Such footprint models and calculators are widely available and according to Kenny and Gray (2009, 2):

> calculate the individual or household primary footprint by converting the amount of electricity, oil, gas or coal used per year into CO_2 emissions. They also convert the number of kilometres driven in a car, kilometres on various types of public transport and air kilometres to CO_2 emissions.

We adopted the processes involved in each of the calculators as described in their respective guidance documentation. Considering one mode of transport – car travel – in more detail, and indicative of the issues involved, a number of factors required further consideration. For example, the fuel consumption of cars was recognised differently by the individual calculators. Thus, the suggested figure for CO_2 output by small car travel varied from 0.26 kilograms per mile for the GHG Protocol Initiative carbon calculator to 0.29 kilograms per mile for the Defra/Carbon Trust calculator. Even greater disparities were evident with regard to large vehicles, with 0.35 kilograms per mile and 0.48 kilograms per mile respectively. There were also variations between calculators in what constituted a small and large car in terms of engine capacity. Such differences explain the notable divergence in overall CO_2 output figures between Defra/Carbon Trust and the other two calculators used. Similar variance in categorisation occurred with other transport modes such as air travel, where there were different understandings of what distances constituted long- and short-haul flights and the levels of emissions these flight lengths produced.

We exercised judgement as to how the guidance for using the calculators was applied with regard to the specific context of the research project. The goal here was to introduce some level of consistency and comparability between the calculators, and this required certain assumptions to be made. For example, shared journeys were a problem when trying to determine the carbon produced for each researcher and the project as a whole. In the end, for shared journeys by all modes of transport other than car (including taxis), we entered the full journey footprint into each researcher's total and for the project as a whole. This makes sense, as carbon footprints for a train are worked out in the three carbon calculators we used on the basis of individual passengers. To enter shared journeys on a train as one single journey, or two half journeys, would therefore be inaccurate in that context. For journeys by private car, however, we decided to allocate the whole associated carbon footprint for the car journey to the car driver. Any researcher sharing a car with this driver would therefore receive no carbon footprint for the same journey. Of course, the carbon footprint for a car with a passenger in a shared journey, as opposed to one without, will be slightly higher due to added weight. However, we felt this was a distinction not worth pursuing, especially as an end goal of this exercise was to produce an approach to measuring the carbon footprint of research activity that was simple enough to be easily replicated by others. Similar levels of assumption were applied regarding other modes of transport. For example, for the sake of consistency, taxis were categorised as average/medium sized cars in terms of their fuel consumption and consequent CO_2 output across all three calculators.

In terms of analysing the resulting data, we looked at a number of factors including miles travelled by researchers, both individually and collectively, via different transport modes, and the CO_2 emissions from this in kilograms, as determined by the different carbon calculator models outlined above. Another avenue of exploration included distinguishing between the miles and CO_2 emissions related to data collection, and those relating to the subsequent research dissemination. The outcomes of this analysis are detailed in the findings.

Following the above, an attempt was also made to establish the potential offset costs of the CO_2 emissions from this research. We took three different carbon offset online buyers/traders and applied their charges to the CO_2 kilogram totals established for our research using the three different carbon calculator models. These offset buyers were www.carbonbalanced.org, Royal Bank of Scotland (RBS) and JP Morgan ClimateCare. The Carbon Balanced website charged the most for purchasing carbon offset at approximately 1.5 pence per kilogram of CO_2. The JP Morgan ClimateCare website charged the least at approximately 0.86 pence per kilogram of CO_2. The RBS charge was around 1.26 pence per kilogram of CO_2.

Findings

CO_2 emission calculations

The number of miles travelled for all researchers combined, broken down by each of the key modes of transport, is given in Table 23.1. Using our three chosen carbon calculators we then show the estimated kilograms of CO_2 produced for each mode of transport. A key point to note is that air travel constitutes the bulk (78.2%) of the 14,305 miles travelled for this relatively small research project. Train and car are the next most popular forms of travel, covering around 10.6% and 8.7% of the total miles covered for the project respectively.

What is also clear from Table 23.1 is that the amount of CO_2 produced by a particular mode of transport does not always precisely reflect the contribution of that mode of transport to the research project's mileage total. For example, as noted above, air travel accounts for 78.2% of the project's mileage but between 77.4% and 85.6% of the CO_2 produced by the project depending on which calculator is used. Equally, train travel accounts for 10.6% of the project's total mileage, but produced between 5.1% and 5.8% of the CO_2 output. As well as emphasising which are the less polluting forms of transport, and specifically here that train travel is 'greener' than air travel, such observations also illustrate how much CO_2 kilogram totals produced by these different forms of travel vary according to which of the three carbon calculators is used. This is due to the different ways in which the three calculators estimate carbon output from various modes of transport. For example, the same train journey

Table 23.1 Basic CO_2 calculation totals

Mode of travel	Distance/ miles	CO_2 emission kgs (Native Energy)	CO_2 emission kgs (Defra/Carbon Trust)	CO_2 emission kgs (GHG Protocol)
Car	1238.9 (8.7%)	340 (6.1%)	435 (15.1%)	359 (13.4%)
Taxi	111.4 (0.8%)	75 (1.4%)	37 (1.3%)	29 (1.1%)
Train	1521 (10.6%)	319 (5.8%)	147 (5.1%)	147 (5.5%)
Tram/tube	234.8 (1.6%)	49 (0.9%)	30 (1.0%)	40 (1.5%)
Air	11,183 (78.2%)	4742 (85.6%)	2226 (77.4%)	2097 (78.4%)
Bus/coach	15.9 (0.1%)	5 (0.1%)	2 (0.1%)	4 (0.1%)
Totals	14,305	5530	2877	2676

can be slightly different in terms of its carbon output depending on which calculator is used. Variation also occurs because of categorisation and classification differences within individual transport modes between the different calculators, as noted above. Air flights, in particular, are generally divided into short-, long- and medium-haul categories, with associated variations in carbon output per mile travelled (with shorter-haul flights typically being more polluting). However, the boundaries between these categories, in terms of what mileage constitutes long-, medium- or short-haul, varies between calculators.

Offset costs

Taking into account our three different carbon calculators and our three different CO_2 offset buyers outlined above, we ended up with nine possible permutations of offset cost for our whole project. These can be seen in Table 23.2. It is worth noting that offset costs vary from £82.95 to £23.08. In short, the most expensive possible CO_2 offset cost was almost four times the cost of the cheapest. Nevertheless, even the most expensive offset figure was minor when taken as a percentage of our total project budget, including travel, which we calculated at approximately £6000.

Kenny and Gray (2009) emphasise that these models and calculators are provided by a range of organisations – including government agencies, non-governmental organisations and private companies – and that there are no standards or codes of practice associated with them. In their comparative analysis of six different carbon footprint models for household contexts these authors identified significant differences in both inputs and outputs based on the same base-level consumption data. The existence of potentially significant differences and inconsistencies between models was also evident in this research, as demonstrated above.

Discussion

This chapter has outlined attempts to calculate the carbon footprint of a small-scale research project, which is arguably typical of much of the academic research activity in marketing and business practiced in UK universities. It raises a number of issues

Table 23.2 Offset costs

Carbon totals	Carbon buyers	Offset purchase costs (£)	Offset cost as % of £6000 project budget (%)
Native Energy 5530 kgs CO_2	www.carbonbalanced.org	82.95	1.38
	www.rbs.co.uk	69.58	1.16
	www.jpmorganclimatecare.com	47.70	0.80
Defra/Carbon Trust 2877 kgs CO_2	www.carbonbalanced.org	43.16	0.72
	www.rbs.co.uk	36.69	0.61
	www.jpmorganclimatecare.com	24.81	0.41
GHG Protocol 2676 kgs CO_2	www.carbonbalanced.org	41.04	0.67
	www.rbs.co.uk	34.16	0.57
	www.jpmorganclimatecare.com	23.08	0.38

relating to what can (and cannot) be realistically included in such calculations. For the purposes of ease and simplicity we focussed on the primary footprint aspect of travel in isolation, although this should not negate the impact of other – more indirect – sources of CO_2 emissions. Despite the fact that the approach described above inevitably minimises the full implications of this research project in terms of its carbon footprint, the cost of accurately calculating secondary aspects of the carbon footprint would be prohibitive with regard to both time and cost.

In their discussion of policy integration strategy relating to environmental/ sustainability issues, Hamdouch and Depret (2010, 483) highlight the need to redefine 'the space and modes of interaction of the institutions . . . that are in charge of the environment', and recognise the inter-linkage between different spatial levels in determining and developing the institutional contexts within which environmental policies are now located. They emphasise that the co-integration of sustainable development policies 'calls for governance that is multi-level (spatially), pluri-sectoral (even trans-sectoral) and multi-actor' (ibid.). The following discussion considers some of the wider implications for the conduct and governance of business and marketing research (or indeed, academic research more generally) undertaken within HE institutions. It is structured using Hamdouch and Depret's (2010) classification of micro-, meso- and macro-levels (in relation to the nature of the actors involved).

Micro-level issues

In this specific context, micro-level issues can be considered as being related to the actions of individual researchers, and the factors motivating those actions. A key aspect of analysing the carbon footprint of this particular project was the proportion that arose from dissemination activities (85%) rather than data collection (15%). This ratio may of course vary from subject to subject, and indeed, from research project to research project. For example, where travel to, and data collection from, specific – and often remote – locations (such as measuring the melting of ice caps in the polar regions) is an integral element of the research, the consequent carbon footprint of such data collection activity will inevitably be higher. However, for many research projects in the marketing discipline, such as the one described above, even where data collection may be undertaken across a disparate geographical area, there is greater scope for data gathering through virtual means, such as online surveys for quantitative research, or via mechanisms such as Skype, Google Hangout etc. for those projects where qualitative data are sought (although the specific methods of data collection used will inevitably be guided by the research objectives of the project in question).

However, it is not unusual for the travel associated with research dissemination to be significantly greater than that for data collection. Whilst the freedom of action of researchers relating to the location(s) of data collection activities may be heavily constrained (dependent on the specifics of individual research projects), the same may not be said of dissemination activities, where individual researchers may have far greater scope to make decisions that directly impact on the carbon footprint of their research activities. Thus, for those academics for whom the environmental impact of their research activities is an important consideration, the implications of this raises questions as to the role of conferences, where much dissemination usually occurs. At some point in their careers, many academics will have flown perhaps half way around the world to present their research to a handful of people in a small parallel session at an international conference. Can such activity continue to be justified in the future? Are we, as researchers, going to have to much more overtly and explicitly *justify* our attendance at conferences, if not to our institutions, then perhaps to our own consciences?

This is not to suggest that the days of academic conferences are numbered. There will – arguably – always be a role for such gatherings in terms of networking and related activities; and the serendipity arising from the connections made at conferences should not be ignored. Indeed, in relation to the specific project outlined in this chapter, two book chapter outputs (Warnaby et al., 2011; 2013) arose from attending conferences. However, given the increasing scope for virtual interaction to occur (and in the current economic climate of austerity, where travel budgets may be curtailed, such virtual interaction may be ever more important), perhaps we need to ask ourselves whether traditional face-to-face conference attendance is always necessary.

Even when academics decide that they do have to travel in person to an international conference to present their work and/or network with like-minded colleagues, they can consider ameliorating the environmental impact, notably via *offsetting* their carbon emissions. This project has shown that, depending on the carbon calculator and/or offset provider chosen, there can be a significant cost differential here, and that whatever calculation is used, the cost is not severe. There is, of course, also a wider question as to whether offsetting is effective. In an op-ed column, scientist James Hansen (2009) argues that the practice of carbon offsetting is analogous to the notion of indulgences in the Middle Ages, whereby sinners paid the Church for forgiveness. It could be argued that as individuals we have to decide whether our consciences (if not our souls) are salved by offset payments. Hansen (2009, 30) goes on to state that, 'most purchased 'offsets' to fossil fuel carbon dioxide emissions are hokey'. Given the variation in offsetting costs for this small project, there does clearly need to be much greater awareness and transparency, so that an informed decision can be made as to what an appropriate and realistic offsetting expense really is.

Meso- and macro-level issues

The actions of individuals inevitably occur within the context of – and influenced by – wider meso- and macro-level forces. Hamdouch and Depret (2010) state that meso-level factors relate to companies and industries, and macro-level factors to public administrations, government agencies, and so forth, thereby encompassing wider issues of research policy and governance at university and (inter)national levels. These factors contextualise the activities of individual researchers. The boundaries between the levels can be somewhat porous, as influence is exerted between them in the pursuit of effective, dynamic, policy integration strategies.

Thus, returning to the issue of dissemination of research at conferences, individual subject-specific departments/schools/faculties may have a 'pecking order' of conferences based on their perceived 'quality', and funding may be skewed towards those deemed more worthy. This will inevitably influence the decisions made by individual researchers. With regard to the cost of offsetting the impact of travel to such conferences, the policy of different universities may vary (if indeed a policy exists at all), and the associated expense is something that some universities may not sanction.

If the level of individual HE institutions is regarded as the meso-level, then in this particular context, the policies and actions of funding agencies could be considered as constituting the macro-level. For example, it is conceivable that at some point in the future an expense relating to ensuring the environmental sustainability of a research project (for example, via offsetting) becomes a mandatory budget line in research grant applications to funding bodies. Given the variations in both calculation methods (see also Kenny and Gray, 2009) and offset costs shown above, it seems obvious that in the increasingly cut-throat competition for research funding there must be some commonality of approach to such calculations in order for appropriate judgements on the environmental impact of research to be formed in an equitable and fair manner. As noted above, we focused only on calculating the direct carbon footprint of the travel relating to this specific project and ignored more indirect costs because of the impracticality of their accurate calculation with the limited resources available. However, more extensive research, on behalf of (or sponsored by) funding regimes, could potentially produce estimates of such indirect costs. Researchers could then use this information to calculate the environmental costs inherent in their research activities in a more holistic way.

This would have implications at the meso-level in that it would serve to focus attention on the environmental accounting practices of higher education institutions for the purposes of research (and possibly for other areas of their activities) – both in terms of the methodologies used and the personnel who have to operationalise them. Indeed, it is conceivable that at some point in the future, at the micro-level, we as individual academics may be given a carbon budget to manage, just as many institutions now provide individual faculty staff members with a yearly allocation for research expenses. Taken to its logical conclusion, this could result in cap-and-trade schemes for carbon offsetting in academia right down to the level of the individual. In such instances, the possibility of even greater levels of university bureaucracy in administering such systems is very real. Undertaking a cost-benefit analysis of such activity would be an obvious priority.

Conclusion: implications for public value

Ultimately, it could be argued that the onset of the sustainability megatrend means that, within the university sector (and indeed other economic sectors), it is crucial that individuals take responsibility for their own actions. In the HE context there are numerous examples of such institutional changes being driven by individuals (e.g. Asquith, 2007; Barlett, 2004; Button, 2009; Jahiel and Harper, 2004; Uhl, 2004), arguably motivated by perceptions of public value – with Meynhardt and Bartholomes (2011) articulating the need to account for such perceptions, whilst also recognising their inherent subjectivities. Indeed, it could be argued that in academia the freedom of action of individuals (for example, in terms of whether or not to attend events such as conferences) is greater than in other sectors, where individuals may be compelled through business necessity to travel far and wide (with consequent implications for their own individual carbon footprints). However, this does not preclude the need for all those who have to travel long distances for the purposes of their work – for example, to attend or exhibit at trade shows etc. (which in many ways can be seen as analogous to academic conferences) – to ask questions regarding the environmental sustainability of their practices (specifically in this context, in relation to business travel to and from these events).

What this chapter has indicated, however, is the need for individuals at the micro-level to operate within a clear framework of understanding at the meso- and macro-levels, as progress on matters such as carbon neutrality within the sector in which they operate is only likely to come about with management vision and commitment. This will hopefully provide a context within which individual action and a degree of all-important, yet responsible, individual freedom can still occur.

At the meso-level, in the specific HE context of this chapter, any university (or faculties/schools/departments therein) would benefit from having a transparent policy for academic conference attendance, based not only on standard rationales such as the academic reputation of the conference, but also on measures of sustainability. Key questions come to mind here. What is the environmental (and economic) cost of travel to the conference, and does its academic standing truly justify this? What is the likelihood of the proposed conference paper being converted into a high-level journal output; and if the chances of this are low, then is attendance worthwhile? How many people from a given institution are visiting the conference? (There are sometimes opportunities for synergy if one person can attend and present two or three related papers). Comparable questions could be asked in the context of other sectors to consider the relative merits of attending events such as trade shows and practitioner conferences.

At the macro-level, all universities operate on a competitive basis when it comes to matters of obtaining research monies from national and international funding agencies. If the sustainability of individual research projects is to become a significant issue in the HE sector, which it arguably should, then there is a need for consistency and simplicity in how environmental metrics such as carbon footprints should be calculated. This approach would allow fairer comparison and assessment of research proposals on sustainability grounds. It could also help towards a more general move for universal standards in sustainable research practice within higher education, which would ideally trickle back down from macro-level through meso- and micro-, in the same way that views on matters such as journal quality have. This reinforces the porosity between the macro-, meso- and micro-levels of sustainability management in the HE sector, and the fact that action and willingness to change is a function of both individual academics as well as university management and the country-relevant governance regime of the sector.

Arguably, the meso- and macro-level considerations outlined above could apply equally to other economic sectors (albeit with modification, to reflect potentially different sector-specific norms). Indeed, if these sustainability considerations are part of a wider 'moral megalogue', then there is no reason why good practice in this regard may not transfer between different sectors so that sustainability considerations (in this case, specifically relating to carbon footprints arising from business travel) permeate more widely. Furthermore, in this specific context, consideration should be given to the interactions between universities and industry. With knowledge exchange and industry impact becoming increasingly prevalent in the HE sector (Ankrah and Al-Tabbaa, 2015), acknowledgement of how sustainability and broader corporate social responsibility concerns influence university-industry relationships should also be explored to the benefit of both parties, and consequently for society as a whole.

References

Ankrah, S. and Al-Tabbaa, O. (2015). Universities-industry collaboration: A systematic review. *Scandinavian Journal of Management*, 31(3), 387–408.

Asquith, C. (2007). Going green equals good business. *Diverse Issues in Higher Education*, 24(6), 14–15.

Barlett, P.F. (2004). No longer waiting for someone else to do it: A tale of reluctant leadership. In P.F. Barlett and G.W. Chase (eds), *Sustainability on Campus: Stories and Strategies for Change*. Cambridge, MA: The MIT Press, pp. 67–87.

Barlett, P.F. and Chase, G.W. (eds) (2004). *Sustainability on Campus: Stories and Strategies for Change*. Cambridge, MA: The MIT Press.

Beck Jørgensen, T. and Bozeman, B. (2007). Public values: An inventory. *Administration and Society*, 39(3), 354–381.

Bennison, D., Medway, D. and Warnaby, G. (2008a). Fissures in the place product: The challenges for marketing management. Paper presented at the 1st Institute of Place Management Conference, London, 26–27 February.

Bennison, D., Medway, D. and Warnaby, G. (2008b). The city and the wall: Fragmentation and coalescence of the place product. Paper presented at the Marketing Cities: Place Branding in Perspective Conference, Berlin, 4–6 December.

Breen, S.D. (2010). The mixed political blessing of campus sustainability. *PS: Political Science and Politics*, 43(4), 685–690.

Bunting, M. (2009). My battle to cut carbon: A baffling, frustrating path to a more honest life. *The Guardian*, 7 September, 29.

Button, C.E. (2009). Towards carbon neutrality and environmental sustainability at CCSU. *International Journal of Sustainability in Higher Education*, 10(3), 279–286.

Carbon Trust (2008a). Working with PepsiCo and Walkers: Product Carbon Footprinting in Practice. Case Study CTS058. London: Carbon Trust.

Carbon Trust (2008b). Energy and Carbon Conversions: 2008 Update. Fact Sheet CTL018. London: Carbon Trust.

Corbyn, Z. (2009). When it comes to saving the environment, academics don't practise what they preach. *Times Higher Education*, 2 July, 16.

Grimmer, M., Miles, M., Polonsky, M. and Vocino, A. (2015). The effectiveness of life-cycle pricing for consumer durables. *Journal of Business Research*, 68(7), 1602–1606.

Hamdouch, A. and Depret, M.-H. (2010). Policy integration strategy and the development of the "green economy": Foundations and implementation patterns. *Journal of Environmental Planning and Management*, 53(4), 473–490.

Hansen, J. (2009). After Copenhagen's failure, we can at last tackle climate change honestly. *The Observer*, 27 December, 30.

Institute of Grocery Distribution (2009). Carbon footprinting and labelling. Available online at www.igd.com/Research/Sustainability/Carbon-footprinting-and-labelling/ (accessed 26 April 2017).

Jahiel, A.R. and Harper, R.G. (2004). The green task force: Facing the challenges to environmental stewardship at a small liberal arts college. In P.F. Barlett and G.W. Chase (eds), *Sustainability on Campus: Stories and Strategies for Change*. Cambridge, MA: The MIT Press, pp. 49–66.

Kenny, T. and Gray, N.F. (2009). Comparative performance of six carbon footprint models for use in Ireland. *Environmental Impact Assessment Review*, 29(1), 1–6.

Kotler, P. (2011). Reinventing marketing to manage the environmental imperative. *Journal of Marketing*, 75(4), 132–135.

Medway, D., Bennison, D. and Warnaby, G. (2008). Branding a Roman frontier in the 21st century. Paper presented at the Association of American Geographers Annual Conference, Boston, MA, 15–19 April.

Meynhardt, T. and Bartholomes, S. (2011). (De)composing public value: In search of basic dimensions and common ground. *International Public Management Journal*, 14(3), 284–308.

O'Flynn, J. (2007). From new public management to public value: Paradigmatic change and managerial implications. *Australian Journal of Public Administration*, 66(3), 353–366.

Polonsky, M.J. (2011). Transformative green marketing: Impediments and opportunities. *Journal of Business Research*, 64(12), 1311–1319.

Rutgers, M.R. (2014). As good as it gets? On the meaning of public value in the study of policy and management. *American Review of Public Administration*, 45(1), 29–45.

Second Nature (n.d.). The presidents' climate leadership commitments: Climate leadership statements. Available online at http://secondnature.org/climate-guidance/the-commitments/ (accessed 26 April 2017).

Swilling, M. (2011). Greening public value: The sustainability challenge. In J. Benington and M.H. Moore (eds), *Public Value: Theory and Practice*. Basingstoke: Palgrave Macmillan, pp. 89–111.

Uhl, C. (2004). Process and practice: Creating the sustainable university. In P.F. Barlett and G.W. Chase (eds), *Sustainability on Campus: Stories and Strategies for Change*. Cambridge, MA: The MIT Press, pp. 29–47.

Velazquez, L., Munguia, N. and Sanchez, M. (2005). Deterring sustainability in higher education institutions: An appraisal of the factors which influence sustainability in higher education institutions. *International Journal of Sustainability in Higher Education*, 6(4), 383–391.

Velazquez, L., Munguia, N., Platt, A. and Taddei, J. (2006) Sustainable university: What can be the matter? *Journal of Cleaner Production*, 14(9–11), 810–819.

Warnaby, G., Bennison, D. and Medway, D. (2010). Notions of materiality and linearity: The challenges of marketing the Hadrian's Wall place product. *Environment and Planning A*, 42(6), 1365–1382.

Warnaby, G., Bennison, D. and Medway, D. (2011). Branding a Roman frontier in the 21st century. In A. Pike (ed.), *Brands and Branding Geographies*. Cheltenham: Edward Elgar, pp. 248–263.

Warnaby, G., Bennison, D. and Medway, D. (2013). The management and marketing of archaeological sites: The case of Hadrian's Wall. In C. Walker and N. Carr (eds), *Tourism and Archaeology: Sustainable Meeting Grounds*. Walnut Creek, CA: Left Coast Press, pp. 111–126.

World Resources Institute and World Business Council for Sustainable Development (2004). *The Greenhouse Gas Protocol: A Corporate Accounting and Reporting Standard*, revised edition. Geneva: World Business Council for Sustainable Development.

Epilogue
24 Reflections on the public value project

Mark H. Moore

It is thrilling to see how the theory and practice of creating public value has been taken up and developed – both in the *academy* as a subject of inquiry, research, and teaching; and in the world of *practice* as a useful guide for improving the quality of individual and social life from particular positions in particular contexts. Particularly important, perhaps, is John Brewer's idea that it has challenged social science and academics to "create global citizens with a responsibility to our shared humanitarian future." This is a vision of public value that reaches well beyond my initial aspiration to support those granted discretionary control over the collectively owned assets of states in their efforts to create more prosperous, sociable, and just societies.

I am grateful to have been given a chance to offer a personal commentary on how the "public value project" has developed over time. I call it the public value *project* because the work has escaped the authorship (even the sponsorship!) of any particular individual. As this and other recent publications have shown, the concept of public value is "out there"; It is being actively developed and used by many creative, resourceful, and committed scholars to increase our shared understanding about the particular conditions in our world that might reasonably be called "public" and how collective institutions (led by individuals in particular institutional positions) might use those positions to improve those conditions.

The commentary begins with my particular aims and purposes in framing the challenge facing public managers as one of "creating pubic value." It then traces the development of the ideas through the processes of both *simultaneous invention* and *diverse development* as it has been grasped by scholars with both broader and deeper perspectives than my own. The ultimate aim is to show how the various tributaries might now be contributing to a potentially powerful intellectual tide that is wider and stronger than at least what I imagined at the outset, and why that might be important to scholarship and to the world at large.

Public value and the neo-liberal tide

In framing the concept of "creating public value" as the important goal of public management, I sought to find some kind of intellectual and practical purchase on a political discourse that seemed to be not just drifting, but enthusiastically galloping towards a view of individual and collective life that seemed wrong – wrong in both in the empirical sense that these ideas were inconsistent with the conditions in which we lived, and wrong in a more philosophical sense that they did not fully capture the values that could (and *should*!) guide individual and collective life.

Privileging individualism; ignoring interdependence

On one hand, the global elite had marched right through the values of liberal democracy and was increasingly embracing a radical kind of individualism that emphasized the wants and rights of individuals over the duties and obligations that each of us might have towards others as a result of our evident and growing material and social interdependence.

Promoting materialism over living in right relationships

On the other hand, the world seemed to be embracing an equally radical commitment to material conditions as the measure of individual and social welfare over the idea that a good individual and collective life might be defined in terms of the quality of individual and social relations and the ability of individuals to live dignified, autonomous lives free of economic exploitation, social bigotry, or political oppression.

Ignoring the value of the state as a contributor to valued social conditions

In the rush to protect individual liberty, and expand material prosperity, we lost sight of the vision of a liberal state – a state that could simultaneously; 1) protect the economic, social, and political rights that enabled individuals to live with dignity and autonomy; 2)collectively impose duties on private individuals and associations to refrain from actions harmful to individual rights, or the welfare and justice of the society as a whole. We also lost sight of the fact that the legitimacy of that state depended crucially on a cultural willingness and capacity for free individuals to ban together not only in celebrating their individual freedom, but also to become the architects of their own restraint through laws and social norms that embodied a widely shared and philosophically tested idea of justice – or, less grandiosely, perhaps to a more contingent idea of *right relationships* among individuals and between individuals and the state and other powerful social institutions.

Favoring commerce and markets over civil societies, polities, and ideals of justice

This pell-mell rush to individualism and materialism as the ultimate purposes of a society was reflected in the growing dominance of markets over states. Increasingly, the state was viewed as the "unproductive sector" – the social institution that was not only failing to produce anything of value, but also undermining the value-producing capacities of societies held by private corporations seeking to satisfy the material desires of consumers and the profit-maximizing desires of investors. The use of state authority to advance social welfare and justice by creating rules that protected consumers, workers, investors, and those living in natural and man-made physical environments was recast as a regulatory burden that prevented economic development. The idea that social welfare and justice might depend on the use of tax dollars to pay for research and development, subsidies to support infrastructure programs, educational efforts that could build human capital, and so on – all efforts that could be expected to support economic prosperity in the future without burdening the private sector – was dismissed as unnecessary for enhancing the prosperity of the society, let alone its civility or justice.

Treating citizens as customers

The rush was also reflected in the practices of both politics and public administration. In the realm of politics, the idea of marketing candidates to a gullible public gained standing over the idea that elections should engage individual citizens in self-government. The idea that there was no such thing as society, and that voting was simply a device to advance one's own interests, reduced what could be a collective discussion about the kind of society in which we all might want to live to a tally of simple up and down votes on ideological issues. In the realm of public administration, public managers were encouraged to think of the citizens they encountered on the other side of the counter when they were delivering benefits or obligations as "customers" to be "satisfied."

But this metaphor obscured the real nature of these transactions. Some of these transactions involved the delivery of benefits and services, and insofar as the services were supposed to improve the quality of an individual beneficiary's life, one might liken the beneficiary to a customer. But the beneficiaries usually did not pay the costs of the benefits they received. Partly as a consequence, many of these benefits and services were rationed, and granted only to eligible populations. They were also often limited in terms of the scope, amount, or quality of the services provided. And many had "strings attached" to the provision of the benefit designed to encourage beneficiaries to take actions that would reduce their future dependence on public largesse. In short, the client beneficiaries often had to take quite a bit less than what they thought they wanted, needed, or deserved as individuals, and accept what they were given as the result of a collective decision by citizens and taxpayers rather than a reflection of their own views of entitlement.

The difficulty with the metaphor was even more obvious in the frequent cases in which the individuals on the other side of bureaucratic encounters had obligations imposed on them to pay their taxes, stop polluting the environment, refrain from physically attacking their spouse, or drive more soberly or slowly to protect themselves and others from serious injury. In these cases, the most satisfaction government could expect to produce for such customers is grudging compliance. Explaining why the rules existed, how to come into compliance with the rules, and reassuring "obligatees" that the rules were being enforced equitably and fairly was important *intrinsically* as a matter of the just enforcement, but also useful instrumentally insofar as doing so increased compliance with the rules. Whether or not a particular individual felt "satisfied" with this kind of encounter was somewhat beside the point.

Obscuring the importance and value of public duties and the use of state authority

At the core of the confusion that overtook public administration when we began talking about individuals and customers was the obfuscation of the core fact of public administration: those engaged in public administration, by definition, used assets that were different from those used by private-sector – or even voluntary sector – managers. They made regular use of the authority of the state to accomplish their purposes. This is obvious in the case of regulatory and enforcement agencies, which use the authority of the state to draft an army of private individuals and associations to achieve a particular social good. It is less obvious in the case of service agencies, but even here we have noted the use of state authority both in rationing access to benefits, and in turning the benefits into incentives for good behavior by attaching conditions to the acceptance of the benefits. And, one must keep in mind that the money used to fund government provided services come primarily from the use of state taxing authority.

The origins of public value

At the time of this pell-mell rush to individualism, materialism, and a sharply limited state, I had begun my career working at Harvard's Kennedy School of Government. As an undergraduate at Yale, I had been tutored in two special programs. The first, a program for freshman and sophomores, was called the Directed Studies Program – an odd appellation because the program was anything but "directed." It took students through a broad sweep of disciplines including philosophy, politics, economics, sociology, psychology, history, literature, and the history of art.

The second, for juniors and seniors, was a special major called "Politics and Economics" modeled after Oxford's famous Politics, Philosophy, and Economics major. That program required participants to take several courses in economics, but focused most intently on getting through a reading list of 164 books or articles that had been selected by an interdisciplinary faculty. Both programs required not just copious reading but also reams of written responses, weekly seminars, and general intellectual toil under the guidance of particularly demanding professors. As Professor Charles Lindblom, who directed the Politics and Economics program, wryly explained to me when I applied: "This is not a program for everyone."

The combination of these programs prepared me for multi-disciplinary "big think." I loved the ambition and the challenge of "thinking big" about social issues. But it was the late sixties, and I was eager to be more than a thinker. I wanted to learn to think in a cross-disciplinary, rigorous way about particular practical problems so I could solve them – not just intellectually, but for real.

The year I graduated from Yale, the Kennedy School launched the Public Policy Program at Harvard. I was headed to Yale Law School, but Professor Lindblom drew my attention to this new program, and suggested it might be right up my alley. "You were always more interested in practical problems," he said, "maybe this is the place for you." I applied, got in, and found myself in an environment that seemed ideally suited to my particular interests and capabilities.

In retrospect, the ambitions of the Public Policy Program and the Kennedy School seem both a bit too grandiose and a bit off target. The challenge of developing (1) the methods of analytical, empirical inquiry that could accurately frame important public policy choices, (2) the leadership skills that could mobilize legitimacy and support for the right decisions, and (3) the managerial techniques that could deploy assets to achieve the desired results was several steps beyond what a faculty recruited from different academic disciplines could expect to achieve – even in the long run, let alone the short run.

The difficulties were compounded by the fact that we placed a bit more confidence than we should have in the analytic frameworks and empirical methods of academic social sciences, particularly economics. In doing so, we left out the appropriate consideration of what a colleague of mine described once as CHILE – an acronym that stood for Culture, History, Institutions, Law, and Ethics. This initial mistake was rectified to some degree by the later inclusion of history and ethics; and those economists who were drawn into the world of developmental economics were gradually drawn into the world of institutions; but, in the way of human institutions, the original bias turned out to be hard to re-balance.

It also gradually became clear from both reflection and social science research that the school's emphasis on policy analysis (using formal analytic frameworks to support rational decision-making and social science methods to understand the causes of particular social problems and the likely effectiveness of particular policy interventions) was distorting. It was one thing to imagine a policy intervention that was both logically sound and empirically likely to solve the problem; it was quite another thing to have a real, dynamic policy-making process actually choose that option and a real, functioning organization actually implement it. In neglecting the problems inherent in designing, managing, or participating in processes of policy development on one hand, and deploying assets in large-scale efforts to produce real changes in the world on the other, the big investment in getting a good idea could easily be wasted.

I had not come to the Kennedy School to learn about public leadership and management as practices that affected how governments made and implemented policy choices. I had come, like many others, to whisper in the ears of those talented and brave individuals who were prepared to run for office or take on executive positions in government and to face the hard work of organizing good policy-making processes and managing complex organizations and projects. I was trying to learn how to be a good policy analyst and designer, not a leader or manager.

But, for whatever reason, I was given a special assignment at the Kennedy School: to work with my colleagues there, as well as some colleagues from the Business and Law Schools, to develop concepts of public management that were more like those used in business management – more *strategic* in the sense that they were more focused on achieving valued results, better able to measure those results, more experimental and innovative in seeking improved performance, more responsive to changing conditions, and more capable of mobilizing capacities outside of government to help achieve publicly desired social outcomes. That became the assignment of a lifetime. I have been at it ever since.

Big (academic) think and little (practical) think

I go through this personal history for a particular reason – namely, to explore one important aspect of the public value project: the relationship between the "vocational" idea of creating public value on one hand, and the much broader academic and philosophical idea of public value on the other. I noted above that as an undergraduate I had been specially prepared for "big think" – the kind of thought that is carried on by social philosophers and great social observers and commentators. As a graduate student, my training had shifted to "practical think": how to imagine and test particular ideas to deal with particular problems in particular settings.

I was pretty sure there had to be some connection between the two worlds, but I decided that my principal commitment had to be towards "practical think." And it is for that reason, that I developed and presented the work on public value as a method for addressing the practical tasks facing individuals in specific positions in government agencies. But I knew that in framing the problem in that way, I was asking those in the positions I sought to help to take on much more intellectual, moral, and practical responsibility than they might have imagined was their lot in life.

Indeed, the first essay I wrote that set out some of the basic ideas of creating public value was entitled "Small Scale Statesmen." The title was meant to emphasize the fact that in taking on the responsibility for leading public action from positions that held some degree of policy discretion and executive authority, it was hard to escape from performing all the functions that we associated with statesmen – at least in the relatively small, particular domains in which they operated.

More recently, I have begun to refer to the intellectual qualifications for public leaders and managers as those required of "micro-political economists." In doing so, I am definitely *not* suggesting that they differentiate themselves from macro-economists by abandoning an empirical approach to describing real economies in favor of highly abstract, theoretical models that leave out the politics and hide the philosophy. Instead, I am suggesting that an empirical focus on the solution of relatively small problems requires deployment of a wide set of intellectual tools drawn from philosophy, politics, and economics. As my colleague Thomas Schelling once observed, "just because a problem is small, doesn't necessarily mean that it is simple."

From my perspective, then, the challenge was to go from big thinking within single disciplines, to small, more applied thinking that was focused on particular questions about how the assets of the state should be deployed to create a good and just society – or at least one that was better and more just than it was before. To give this challenge a simple, practical thrust, I described the challenge as "creating public value." I hoped that we could find the methods that would allow us to leave as little intellectual quality behind, and introduce as few distortions as possible as we moved from big, philosophical think to the little practical think. Just as a physician has to carry both scientific knowledge about illness, its causes, and current treatments, and a capacity for human connection and motivation into the diagnosis and treatment of a given patient to maximize the chance of healing, so a public leader has to carry both scientific knowledge about the characteristics of a problem and its possible solutions, and insight into human values and behavior into the process of organizing collective thought and action to improve social conditions.

Table 24.1 Different objects of intellectual inquiry and different levels of care in thinking

How one thinks \ What one thinks about	General causal hypotheses (social science research)	Actionable solutions (practical problem solving)
Thoroughly and carefully	Quadrant I: Excellent social science	Quadrant II: Thinking carefully and rigorously about practical problems
Shallow and sloppy	Quadrant III: Mediocre social science	Quadrant IV: Muddling through

One useful way to think about this dilemma is captured in a diagram that I have used to orient incoming faculty at the Kennedy School to what I believe is the unique challenge facing "public policy" schools. The matrix presented above (Table 24.1) cavalierly divides the world into two different objects of thought: general causal hypotheses about how the part of the world that is under investigation actually works (social science research); and ideas about how to plausibly make that part of the world better (practical problem-solving). In principle, one can approach either of these intellectual tasks with varying degrees of analytic clarity, empirical accuracy, and rigorous logic. Thus, the matrix distinguishes bluntly between intellectual work that is "thorough and careful," on one hand, and work that is "shallow and sloppy" on the other.

What is important to note, I think, is that we academics tend to think that only two of the cells of this matrix can be occupied: work that is focused on causal explanation that is thorough and careful (Quadrant I), and work on practical problems that is shallow and sloppy (Quadrant IV).

The reason for this assumption, I suspect, is that as one moves from the work of science (generating and testing general hypotheses about how the world works) to the world of practical problem solving (imagining, implementing, and evaluating policy interventions to solve particular problems), many issues pop up that are hard for science to resolve. For example, as one moves from the abstract and general to the concrete and particular, the array of variables and their potentially important relationship to one another tends to increase. One also moves from the use of the concepts and methods of a single discipline to the use of concepts and methods from many disciplines. Even more importantly, one moves from a purely *descriptive* effort to one that is *prescriptive*, and requires the introduction and discussion of important human values at stake in the action as well as accurate predictions of what might occur. Finally, one moves from a stance that is objective and above the fray, to a position where action is required, and real consequences ensue for the thinker and those who are affected by the thought that guides social action.

Each of these moves represents a departure from what academics think is a prerequisite for high quality intellectual, academic, and scientific work. The work on the right hand side of this matrix is by nature applied, multi-disciplinary, prescriptive, and finds its ultimate social justification in action that improves social conditions rather than in the accumulation of scientific knowledge. Each departure from the established norms of scientific research can be seen to diminish the (academic, or scientific) quality of the work, even as each departure may increase the practical value.

What I think is important for us public value scholars to realize, however, is that our special challenge is to occupy Quadrant II. That is the quadrant that focuses on thinking deeply and carefully about the practical problem of how best to use a particular position one occupies in society to improve the quality of individual and social life – to apply intellectual rigor even when the pressure is on to act in the concrete now, rather than in some distant future when all might be known and possible.

The strategic triangle

To guide those particular, concrete efforts to improve individual and social life, I embedded the concept of public value in a second, closely related concept called the *strategic triangle*. The strategic triangle was constructed to provide the basis for challenging students to take an active, agentic stance and commit themselves to "creating public value" in their professional roles. I did this in part because I did not want the concept of public value to get lost entirely in the philosophical abstractions of what was value, who was the public, and what did they want. I did not think there was a useful general answer to that question. Instead, I thought that those questions would have to be worked out over and over again in particular concrete cases. But I wanted to provide our students with a framework that would improve their ability to assess their environments and to imagine and test what might be both valuable and possible to do. Central to that effort was the normative idea of public value, but also the important practical (and normative!) question of how a public could be called into existence, give legitimacy and support to a particular conception of public value, and help produce (and evaluate!) the impact of particular governmental actions.

This is "applied" work in the sense that it focuses on diagnosing and acting on particular social problems. Such may be informed by existing knowledge and established methods of social science. But to anyone who has actually done this work in a serious way, calling this work "applied" fails to do it justice. The reason is that working out plausibly useful answers to practical problems always means going beyond what social science currently knows about the likely effects of particular interventions. There are always new facts to be gathered and always new methods to be deployed in gathering those facts. There are also new methods for organizing the facts in a way that can logically and empirically support arguments for doing A rather than B or C in the given situation. And there are always important philosophical and normative judgements that suggest the consequences of A are better than B or C and important questions about how to engage those who will feel the effects of the choices, who are in a position to authorize them, and who will actually implement them.

Public value inquiry as a sustained dialogue between academics and social change agents

In sum, the idea of public value was coined and developed as a kind of provocation to the prevailing ethos in economics, politics, and public management, and (as Timo Meynhardt reminds us) in psychology and business management as well. Once coined in this particular way, the concept opened up avenues for other academic disciplines to join the practical, normative discourse about how those interested in improving society might make a contribution. The lessons of psychology and anthropology about the best and worst of human nature as we seek to act rationally, altruistically, and dutifully in collaboration with others; the important lessons from sociology and biology about the power of hierarchy and status as both motivational and organizational features of social life; the lessons that history holds for our understanding of the possibilities, limits, and dangerousness of human societies; and the wisdom of philosophy and law that forces attention on the just and the fair as not just a procedural constraint, but as a quality of the society in which we live that can help us feel just, secure, and connected; all become relevant to public policy making and collective life. The challenge in all this remains to sustain the intellectual commitment to quality thought, logic, and evidence even as practical necessities require us to depart from the existing knowledge and methods of social science. The commitment of public value scholars has to be to the more general principles of the Enlightenment with its emphasis on reason and the aspirations of humanity, not to the narrower ideas of science, or the particular social science disciplines we have developed as useful instruments for describing pieces of individual and social life.

It is in this spirit that I offer a general perspective on how the work of many scholars, and particularly those writing for this volume, has widened and clarified the concept of public value and raised even deeper intellectual questions about human societies, what they value, how they decide to act, and (most importantly, perhaps) how they learn and improve.

Widening and clarifying the concept of public value

From my perspective, the most important development in the public value project has been to carry the idea of public value well beyond its initial application as a challenge to public managers to articulate and measure the value that they were producing for citizens to include:

- a much wider definition of what constitutes public value,
- a much wider appreciation of how the concept might be used across different organizational platforms and sectors to create public value, and
- a deeper understanding that the sources of energy for these wider social efforts lie in the social values and aspirations of individuals who attach significant value not only to their own immediate material welfare, but to the welfare of others, their duties towards others, and their ideas of a good and just society.

Public value as the purposes of a properly constituted and democratically guided government

Starting off with a sharp focus on government and the electoral, legislative, and policy politics that surround the decisions and actions of democratic governments made sense since it made the important substantive claim that government was *not* the unproductive sector to be minimized, but instead a sector that was creating value for citizens that was important for citizens to learn how to use for their own well-being. Moreover, it claimed that government produces value not only through publicly financed services of various kinds, but also in its juridical role as the enforcer of the "rules of the game," establishing and protecting rights that endow individuals with both dignity and agency and ensuring that we respect one another's rights and live up to the duties that impose on ourselves as democratic citizens.

The phrase "public value" also took advantage of the fact that the word value had two quite different connotations, with quite different political meanings. On one hand, the idea of value had a nice conservative ring. Value meant money, cash on the barrel head, objective evidence that something tangible and useful had been produced. This aligned with the idea that government, like business, should have a clear "bottom line."

On the other hand, the word value evoked the possibility that important moral values were at stake in what government chose to do and the effects it produced. It reminded us all that making public policy and managing government's operations was not merely a technical enterprise, but one that was shot through with philosophical values – not just utilitarian ideas defining the "good," but also deontological principles defining the "just and fair." Connected to the idea of fairness and justice were important democratic principles that specified the conditions under which a polity could legitimately make decisions about how best and most justly to use the collectively owned powers of the state.

The idea that values, and particularly democratic values, might be an important part of public policy making made the use of the word "public" along with the idea of "value" particularly important. The liberal tradition insisted on the intrinsic value of individuals, and their right to have and pursue their own values in their individual lives. We knew that individuals valued their own sense of satisfaction with their lives. And we knew that individuals might value conditions beyond their own material welfare, and take voluntary action (or agree to required actions) to support public purposes.

But what could it possibly mean to attach the word *public* to the idea of value – particularly in the context of liberal democratic theory which insisted that the only reliable arbiter of value was individuals, not collectives? How could a "public" that consists of individuals with many different interests of their own, and many different ideas about how the society in which they live should be organized for the common good possibly speak articulately and coherently about the particular conditions in society that they as a pubic valued?

The answer to this question lies at the core of democratic theory, and constitutes an enduring paradox. On one hand, liberal societies insist that the important arbiters of value are individuals making choices not only about their own lives, but also about the kinds of society in which each would like to live. On the other hand, liberal societies believe that they cannot legitimately deploy the collectively owned assets of a democratic society unless some kind of "public" is formed that explicitly authorizes and legitimates the action.

The reason is that a democratic society assumes that the assets that can be deployed by a state –both tax dollars and regulatory authority – are collectively owned. Consequently, when publicly owned assets are deployed, the public as a whole becomes the appropriate arbiter of value – not particular, discrete individuals.

Of course, democratic societies have created institutions and processes designed to create a more or less satisfactory *unum* from a highly heterogeneous and fractious *pluribus*. These structures and processes include three branches of government, elections of representatives, legislative hearings, administrative rule-making, citizen consultation, ombudsmen, and so on.

Yet, we know that these processes are inevitably quite imperfect. We have mathematical theorems that show that it is impossible for individuals with different views about valuable states in which they would like to live to come to a stable, consistent view that can satisfy them all. But what is impossible in theory, we seem to do every day in practice.

Every day democratic governments make choices about how best to use collectively owned assets to advance the common good. And while we can hardly expect perfection in these choices, we can have ideas about what constitutes a better or worse collective choice, and seek to realize those ideas in actual practice. We can't pretend that the process of deciding collectively about how we will use the collectively owned assets of the state to improve social conditions will ever be as simple as the process of individuals making consumer decisions in markets. It will always and inevitably involve arguing with one another not only about what we want for ourselves, but also what we might want for others, or think we owe to others, or what we might reasonably demand from others, or what aggregate features of the society we share might constitute a good and just society. But neither can we avoid the challenge of making that messy process as good as it could possibly be.

Indeed, given the declining legitimacy of government, a key question in the theory and practice of creating public value has become the key issue that John Dewey identified a century ago: namely, what methods can best be used to "call a public into existence that can understand and act on its own interests." Without a competent public, how can we know what social conditions are publicly valued?

Public value as purposes that leverage private capacities

As the public value project moved forward led by public value scholars like John Benington, Jean Hartley, John Alford, John Bryson, Barbara Crosby, Timo Meynhardt, and others, this relatively narrow focus on public value as synonymous with collective action taken by governments, guided by citizens, and produced with the use of the money and authority of the state widened significantly.

The first shift was an understanding that the government does not produce public value acting purely on its own, relying solely on government money and government agencies. The government uses its *money* not only to pay for public employees to produce publicly valued results directly, but also to contract with commercial and nonprofit service delivery organizations to achieve public purposes, spelled out in more or less exacting detail in the terms of the contract.

Similarly, the government uses its *authority* to require private actors – corporations and individuals – to contribute to public purposes. It uses taxing authority to raise the money it uses in various activities (services, programs, benefits, contracts, etc.). It uses regulatory authority to control crime and violence; protect the natural environment; reduce discrimination in economic domains such as housing and employment; and protect the rights of citizens to assemble, petition the government, and vote.

The government also uses its *moral authority* through the "bully pulpit" – a lighter form of normative regulation than laws, sanctions, and enforcement – to mobilize private actors to contribute to public purposes out of a sense of civic duty or public spirit. Government's efforts to foster and encourage a sense of public duty can act as a kind of "force multiplier" that augments the money and law enforcement authority that citizens expect government to use sparingly.

When a public purpose aligns closely with widely recognized public norms of patriotism, civic duty, or social beneficence, for example, that alignment can affect the attitudes of those on the receiving end of both public services and public obligations. Those receiving job training might work a bit harder to transition out of public assistance if they trust that it is good and just that they do so. Those asked to give up the convenience of driving themselves home after a night of drinking might be more inclined to make alternative arrangements if they believe such a claim is good and just.

The effect of using the "bully pulpit" to preach civic virtues can have important effects on those who are not directly clients of government activities, but have close relations with those who are. John Alford has observed the potentially powerful impact that spouses, children, parents, friends – sometimes even nosy strangers – can have on the behavior and condition of those who are on the receiving end of government services and obligations.

The power of the "bully pulpit" can also reach individuals in their roles as citizens, taxpayers, and voters, and engage them in the process of deciding together as citizens how the collectively owned powers of the state might best be used to create prosperous, sociable, and just social conditions.

Public value as voluntary private efforts to improve individual and social conditions

The focus on the government's use of the bully pulpit to create, sustain, or energize a particular public purpose reminds us that it is not only the state, using public assets, acting on behalf of a political collective, that has and seeks to advance public value. We can also see that *private* actors – both individuals and collectives, voluntary and commercial – might be active in producing what they view as public value *on their own*. Indeed, the idea that the voluntary sector and the commercial sector might both embrace their own particular ideas of public value, and pursue them using their own privately held assets has been one of the most important extensions of public value theory advanced through the work of John Bryson, Barbara Crosby, Timo Meynhardt, and Martin Kitchener. Consider the idea of public value in the context of both voluntary sector organizations, and commercial organizations.

Public value and the voluntary sector

In principle and in practice, one might expect significant overlap between the conditions that become the focus of government's efforts to create public value and those that become the focus of philanthropists, volunteers, non-profit organizations, and civic associations. The moral concerns of individuals and voluntary associations cover a front that is as wide as government, and sometimes wider.

Two key features, however, differentiate the voluntary sector from the government. First, the voluntary sector is not able to use the authority of the state – at least not directly. Second, as long as those acting in the voluntary sector do not rely on public authority and public money, they, rather than the state, act as the arbiters of the value they create: they are entitled to embrace and act to improve any part of individual and collective life as long as it is within legal limits defined by the state.

This establishes an important point that is easily missed in the discussion of public value. Individuals and voluntary associations of individuals can hold and act on views of public value that are individually held and voluntarily pursued without the aid of the state. The existence of the voluntary sector creates a domain within which the definition and pursuit of public value is at least partially distinguished from the activities of politics and government.

Public value and commercial enterprises

It is only a small step further to wonder whether private commercial firms could also be engaged in creating public value. To some, the answer to that question is "no." Indeed, the whole idea of public value was to point to a realm of value that was distinct from the value pursued and produced through commercial enterprise. But Timo Meynhardt and other public value scholars who have been advancing both the "stakeholder view" of corporate governance and the concept of "corporate social responsibility" have argued persuasively that the commercial sector, too, can produce public value.

This argument begins with the idea that while economic welfare may not be the *only* condition that individuals and societies value, it is certainly an individually and publicly valued condition. The activities of commercial enterprises and markets have obvious social benefits. Consumers benefit from a flow of relatively low-cost, high-quality products and services to choose from. Employees benefit from the disposable income they earn. Investors benefit from making good bets on companies with good ideas, and in doing so, finance the development of new products and services and perhaps "give back" to the public realm. This is at least in part why government not only grants for-profit enterprises license to operate, but also often provides incentives and subsidies of various kinds to support economic prosperity – locally, nationally, or internationally.

The problem, of course, is that these benefits often come with significant costs that register not only in the realm of material wellbeing, but also in the realm of social and political relationships. Commercial enterprises have produced and distributed products that were unsafe and harmful as well as beneficial. They have cheated investors and customers, and exploited workers. They have polluted the air and water, despoiled beautiful natural environments, and upset delicate ecological balances with uncertain but potentially negative – even disastrous – consequences. They have systematically discriminated against women and racial minorities in employment, housing markets, financial services, and other consumer domains. They have devised and used methods for influencing social and political movements to advance their own commercial interests, often by downplaying or concealing bad consequences of their actions.

To counter the negative consequences of otherwise valuable efforts, societies decided to use the authority of the state to discourage firms from inflicting harm and injustice and to demand compensating actions or payments if harms were inflicted. Opponents of these measures decried them as unjust appropriations of property and complained about the inefficiency they created in the pursuit of economic value, and they have had some success in rolling back governmental regulation. Of course, while it is sensible to question and debate whether the impact of given regulations harm economic prosperity more than they help reduce potentially negative effects of commercial activity, to imagine that regulation *per se* is destructive to economic welfare or is unjust is willful ignorance.

More recently, as regulations have been rolled back in pursuit of economic prosperity (without worrying too much about the loss of public value in other realms of human life and aspiration), voluntary associations and businesses themselves have tried to replace state regulation with voluntary commitments to increased social responsibility. In many respects, the movement for corporate social responsibility (CSR) is an effort to replace the regulatory efforts of the state with softer efforts to take advantage of whatever public spirit might exist among commercial enterprises to cause the firms to reduce the negative economic, social, and political consequences of their actions. If such norms exist and prove effective in reducing negative externalities without relying on the authority of the state, one could reasonably say that the reduced use of regulatory authority and the money required for enforcement has increased (net) public value.

Success in animating an effective commitment to CSR would also suggest that both individual and public desires to force commercial firms to reduce their harmful effects were alive and well – and strong enough to change boardroom behavior. It is important to see that this can happen without actually changing the hearts and minds of the commercial executives. When individuals use their market positions as customers, investors, and employees to express their social and political values, *economic* as well as social and political pressures mount on the commercial executives. In effect, they would feel the effect of a form of regulation that moved out of the realm of politics and the state, and into the realm of voluntary individual and social action taken within commercial markets!

Assuming for a moment that we can deal with the potentially negative externalities of commercial enterprises through regulation or economic and social pressures, the question remains as to whether the purely positive economic value produced by firms is publicly valuable as well. I think the simple answer to that question is yes. All other things being equal, a prosperous economy producing significant advances in material wellbeing in the provision of water, food, shelter, medical care, education, jobs and entrepreneurial opportunities must be seen as socially and publicly as well as economically valuable.

This conclusion can create ideological problems for those who think the idea of public value should remain apart from the idea of commercial or economic value. It can also create significant practical difficulties when civic and governmental actors seek to enter into different kinds of public-private partnerships. They might not be clear enough in their mind what the public – *not including direct economic beneficiaries* – might want and expect from the deal. They may also find themselves politically handicapped in the negotiations if the commercial enterprises have already intervened in the political process in a way that gives their economic contributions to the society more importance than they might have in some more perfect democratic process.

These are everyday questions for public officials – those who work with private developers to create new projects in distressed cities, for example, or procurement officers seeking to contract with commercial enterprises to produce some kind of public value and wondering whether to prioritize getting the most public value at the least public expense versus, say, helping to stimulate a local economy or promoting minority-owned ventures.

Despite these problems, it might be important for society and government to recognize when business is contributing to public value through its impact in *social* and *political* realms, as well as in *economic* realms. The development of multiple "bottom lines" designed to reveal the full spectrum of valued effects of firms and partnerships certainly helps public officials and citizens exercise due diligence when entering public-private partnerships, but before leaving the subject of how commercial firms contribute to public value it is important to investigate the economic effects of these partnerships in one additional respect.

Both private firms and public-private partnerships represent methods for not only *producing* economic value, but also *dividing up* the economic value they generate. A firm can decide how to distribute its profits among its various economic stakeholders. It can give more of the overall value it creates to consumers by lowering prices or increasing the generosity of its warranties and guarantees. It can give more of the overall value it creates to workers by increasing wages, improving the safety and quality of the workplace, or providing health and retirement benefits. It can give more of the overall financial value it generates to investors by increasing dividends.

A private/public partnership can give more or less of the economic value to be created and the risks to be absorbed to the commercial firm or to the public purposes that justified the use of public as well as private assets.

Economic theory tells us that competitive market pressures will push the allocation of economic rewards towards customers. We might imagine that strong public oversight of the use of public assets in private public partnerships would push towards the allocation of economic value towards the public purposes that justified the use of public assets in public private partnerships. But, since one cannot assume this will always be the case, it is wise to keep a close eye on the *size of the profits being earned by commercial firms in competitive markets, and on the financial value that is being taken out of private public partnership by the private, commercial partner.*

At the core of these cautions is the simple idea that one cannot rely on social actors whose fiduciary responsibility is to generate revenues to return to their shareholders rather than the other stakeholders in their environment to fully realize the publicly valued social, political, and economic aspirations of the society in which they operate. Indeed, it is for this reason that one might define the public value of a firm very narrowly in terms of the valuable economic, social, and political effects that it has on the society *that earn no excess profits for the firm*, or even more narrowly, as the valuable social and political effects that produce *no revenues at all*! That condition would put them in the same social position as nonprofit enterprises which are not allowed to keep and distribute any profits, and also in the position of a profit-maximizing firm in a perfect market in which all the profits above the market cost of capital are gradually taxed away by the rigors of competing for customers.

Different arbiters of value

The discussion above focuses on how the concept of public value can be used to assess the contributions made to public value by producing organizations from three different realms: politics and government, the voluntary sector, and commercial markets. These sectors can be distinguished from one another to some degree by the different purposes they claim to serve and the different effects they have on individual and social conditions. But because their purposes often overlap, it is often easier to distinguish among these sectors on two other grounds.

Different assets being deployed

One key difference lies in the particular assets that producing enterprises within these sectors use. Government agencies and public-sector enterprises that make use of voluntary and commercial enterprises to achieve their goals rely primarily on tax dollars and state regulatory authority. Voluntary-sector organizations (not only those that produce and deliver services, but also those that engage in politics and policy advocacy and provide arenas within which individuals can protect and anchor their cultural and religious identities) depend on a flow of money and labor from those who share a collective interest or a social cause. Commercial organizations depend primarily on private investors seeking financial returns generated by a flow of revenues from consumer purchases.

Different arbiters of value associated with different assets

The different kinds of assets being used lead directly to the second key difference: which particular social actors are – at both the philosophical and practical level – the recognized arbiters of the value being produced.

- When state money and authority are being used, the appropriate arbiter of value is the society or the public as a whole acting through the more or less imperfect processes of (ideally democratic) politics and governance. And the effects produced by the effort have to be evaluated in terms of whether they contributed to the common good and to the overall justice and fairness of the society.
- When the essential assets are money and labor contributed voluntarily without any expectation of a material reward delivered to the donor in exchange, the arbiter of value is the individual or the voluntary association of individuals making the contributions. The effects of such efforts are presumably evaluated in terms of their particular individual or collective idea of a good and just society.
- When money and labor are provided to commercial firms to begin, sustain, or grow their enterprises, the key arbiters of value are, in the first instance, the investors who think they will be able to make money from an idea about a product or service that would be valued by consumers, but ultimately the consumers who decide whether or not they want to use their hard-earned money to buy the particular product or service on offer. The effects of such efforts are valued primarily in terms of customer satisfaction, but the impact on the economic welfare of investors and of employees might also be noted as important effects.

This quick review of the different sources and kinds of assets that are used to start, sustain, and grow organizations in the public, private, and voluntary sectors exposes a critical issue in the definition and pursuit of public value: who is the proper arbiter of the public value of a given enterprise and what do – or should – they value? Are individuals the appropriate arbiters of value or are collectives? If it is collectives, does it matter how they form themselves into a collective, and what particular assets they rely on? And do these voluntary associations form primarily to protect the material welfare of their members such as business lobbying groups or trade unions, or to advance more or less idiosyncratic visions of public policy such as the National Rifle Association or the Children's Defense Fund?

Much of the discourse about public value begins (and ends!) at the *aggregate social level* and focuses on both overall levels and distributions of material welfare. Many see public value in economic development, and particularly in making such development "sustainable" by carrying all individuals (particularly those at the bottom) along with the tide, and ensuring the continued health and safety of our natural and man-made physical environments.

But the idea of public value also often extends beyond levels and distributions of *material well-being* to include concerns about the *dignity and autonomy of individuals* and the *quality of social relationships* they can enjoy in their economic, social, and civic life. This depends on the capacity of a society to defend its individual members from bigotry, discrimination, and oppression, which may, in turn, depend on the creation, enforcement, and utilization of rights to combine voluntarily in collective

enterprises. And to some, the idea of public value extends all the way into the political realm to ensure that individual citizens in states are not only protected from state
oppression, but also empowered to criticize social conditions and the performance of
governments and participate in the choices that are made about how to use the collectively owned assets of the state.

What often gets overlooked when we are looking at the giants of our economic,
social, and political life pushing one another around is the real status and character
of the *individuals* who are the key constituent elements of our economic, social and
political life. We make individuals prominent – indeed sovereign! – in commercial
markets, and we give them significant standing as voters in periodic elections. But
where are the individual citizens in more continuous daily life – in their continuing
efforts to monitor and evaluate what government is doing in their name, and to give
advice about how government could be more responsive not only to their economic
interests, but also their civic and political aspirations? What is it that individuals in
their role as citizens want? What is it that they are prepared to support with their
labor, their money, or their voice?

It is an important question for a simple and somewhat paradoxical reason: the
pursuit of public value may not endure unless there are individuals who have public
aspirations and desires as well as concerns for their own material welfare. Unless
individuals hold, and are motivated by, some concerns about the social and public
conditions in which they live, we cannot meet the challenge of creating a society in
which social and public conditions become the focus of both individual and collective action.

One way to formulate this problem is to follow the lead of Timo Meynhardt and
distinguish between individuals and collectives as arbiters of value in society, and to
concentrate first on what it is that individuals might desire for themselves and others
as features of the society in which they live.

There are, of course, many different ways of describing the different values and
motivations that individuals might have in making choices about how they will act in
their own intimate spheres and as they step out into the wider society and participate
in different kinds of collective enterprises. One framing I have found useful is based
on the work of James Q. Wilson in *Political Organizations* and Jenny Mansbridge in
Beyond Self Interest and is presented below (Table 24.2).

In this scheme we start with the idea that individuals will naturally and inevitably be concerned about their own material well-being. This familiar image of an
individual who is "rational" in the pursuit of their own material well-being has
become all too familiar in social science – at least in part because the actions of
such individuals are easy to model and predict. We will call this individual *homo
economicus.*

Table 24.2 What individuals value

Valuer \ Valued object	Individual material well-being	Welfare of others	Responsibilities and duties towards others	An idea of a good and just society
Individual	Homo Economicus	Homo Altruisticus	Homo Civicus	Homo Politicus

We then turn to the possibility that individuals might value the welfare of others – that their spirits might go up when others are happy and down when they are unhappy. Of course, this feeling might not be very strong, and might not spread evenly across all members of the society. In fact, it is likely that individuals' concern for the welfare of others starts with those we hold near and dear, and diminishes as the other people under consideration become increasingly remote and abstract. Indeed, in some cases, one person's satisfaction might increase as the satisfaction of others (those viewed as adversaries) declined. But however strong, and however widespread, sinews of "fellow feeling" connect us to one another's plight. We can call a person motivated by these feelings *homo altruisticus*.

Moreover, socialization has instilled in most of us, to some degree, a sense of duty and honor that is fulfilled by living up to social standards and norms that define good or virtuous behavior towards others. Kindness to others might be one of those virtues, and in that respect, this motivation might overlap with the altruistic values described immediately above. But unlike behavior towards others generated by a sense of love or altruism, the satisfaction that comes from doing one's duty depends at least in part on a shared social understanding of what one is supposed to do without regard to how one feels about it or the particular beneficiary. We can call this particular class of motivations those associated with *homo civicus*.

The last category of motivations is those associated with the social or political aspirations that individuals use both to evaluate the aggregate states of the society within which they live and to guide their efforts to do what they can to change aggregate social conditions using the various platforms on which they stand. This differs from the two categories described above in that the object being valued is not the status of particular individuals to be helped through individual action, but social conditions to be helped not just through small-scale individual action, but through collective action in larger economic, social, and political realms. We will call the person with this class of motivations *homo politicus*.

This scheme provides a typology of the values, interests, and motivations that might guide individuals in choices they make about how to deploy their own personal resources, but also how they might choose to participate in collective life through the institutions and processes we associate with the various sectors of society: the market economy, the voluntary sector, and politics and government. In some important respects, one can think of this as a representation of the potential demand side of society's efforts to produce public value beyond merely economic value. It is from these individual wellsprings that the effective demand for producing public value will or will not arise and provide the opportunity for producing organizations across all sectors to respond to this demand.

Table 24.3 shows how these different individual motivations get bundled together and aggregated up into various kinds of collective efforts to advance those more or less social and public aspirations. In doing so, it suggests that public value can be defined partly in terms of what is valued (economic welfare, meeting the needs of those less advantaged, living up to our duties to one another as well as insisting on our rights, and helping to create and enjoy inhabiting a good and just society); and partly in terms of who is doing the valuing (individuals, voluntary associations of individuals, and polities bound together in a sovereign state.)

It also points to how limited the conventional ideas of the private and the public are in describing both what individuals in a society might value, and the arenas in which

Table 24.3 How individuals with more or less commitment to public values combine to express and advance their individual and collectively held views of public value

Valued object / Valuer	Individual material well-being	Welfare of others	Responsibilities and duties towards others	An idea of a good and just society
Individual	Homo Economicus	Homo Altruisticus	Homo Civicus	Homo Politicus
Voluntary Associations	Unions	Churches, temples, mosques	Civic associations	Political parties
	Trade associations	Public charities	Social movements	Policy advocacy groups
	Professional associations	Philanthropists	Media	Issue campaigns
Polity	Economic policy	Social policy / Health policy	Laws and regulations / Civil rights	Democratic governance

they could operate to develop and act on ideas of social and public value. The pure versions of the private and public sectors exist in this table only in the upper left and lower right cells of the table. All the rest of the table points to the fluid ways in which individuals, acting not only for their own material welfare, but for the good of others, in accordance with what they understand their duties to others to be, and in pursuit of public value might combine to produce local and larger versions of prosperous, sociable, and just societies.

I don't mean to suggest here that everything will be fine as we jostle up against one another in trying to define and pursue public value in different domains, using different platforms for advancing our individually and collectively held ideas. It manifestly will not be fine. There will be conflict and struggle over the question of what constitutes public value – over what people would like (and deserve) to have materially for themselves, and how they would like to live in association with other individuals to whom they are linked through bonds of beneficence, duty, and shared citizenship/humanity.

But one important path forward for public value scholarship is to explore the various structures, processes, and individual actions launched from particular institutional platforms that can help call into existence a public that can become wiser and more articulate about public value and find the means for pursuing it. To accomplish that goal, we will have to work not only within the existing structures and processes and conceptions of social and public value, but also reach down and under these institutions to recover the individually held views of public value and carry them into larger and smaller public spheres where they can be effectively challenged, deliberated upon, and resolved in ways that will not only guide but also motivate action across the three sectors. We have to reclaim our sense of interdependence and recover the idea of a public embodied not only in the state, or in voluntary sector organizations, or even in commercial organizations, but most importantly in our own private lives.

Moving forward: the public value of public value

The public value project has clearly moved a great distance. Starting as a narrow, vocational project, it has blossomed into a larger humanitarian project focused on building the capacities of democratic governance, and the pursuit of the good and the just. Given current political conditions, the future of any such project looks a bit rocky. Surely the challenges of global interdependence and mass migration will strain not only the institutional limitations of our existing governments. It is possible that they may strain even the capacities of human nature. But in such times, it is crucial that we understand and stay sharply focused on what is valuable – both philosophically and practically – about the idea of public value and how that idea can be more widely embraced and used in governing our increasingly interdependent lives at local, national, and international levels.

To me, the great value of the concept of public value – particularly as it has been developed by others – has been the stark challenge the concept poses to the pervasive view that only individuals can be the arbiters of value, and that the only things that individuals do or should value is their own material welfare.

- By using the word *value* rather than efficiency or effectiveness, we can hold open a space for the values of altruism, duty, and justice to survive in our social life and influence the choices and actions of our social and public institutions.
- By using the word *public*, we can not only reclaim the critical role of government in creating good and just societies, but also focus attention on the processes through which publics can be formed in which our interdependence is recognized and successfully managed not only through government, but through individual and cultural commitments to values that elevate the conditions of the least advantaged and most oppressed in the society as part of our shared concerns.

Valuable as the abstract concept might be in pushing against the neo-liberal tide, it is only when the idea is brought to bear in concrete, practical circumstances that real important work can be accomplished. And it is this fact that reveals a second key feature of the public value project: namely, that the success of the project depends critically on sustaining the intense, on-going dialogue among academics and practitioners that has brought it this far. As the papers in this volume show, it is the connection between the academy and the world of practice has given the project both intellectual vitality and practical significance.

Solving social problems, improving social conditions, or exploiting social opportunities will always require policy designs based on the intellectual contributions from many different academic disciplines.

The resources and actions needed to enact the designs will often depend critically on organizations drawn from all three sectors of society – more or less temporarily united in a complex network that can achieve the public value that more or less perfectly united them.

The prospect of academics and practitioners working together to

build a collective capacity to define and pursue a particular conception of public value in a particular place and time,

informed by values that include civility and justice as well as prosperity,

and to help cultivate individual citizens and voluntary associations that love and support these values

is, I think, part of the humanitarian project to which John Brewer calls us as academics. It is also the project one might take on as an active citizen who hopes that the experiment in democratic self-government might not "perish from the earth."

Index

Page numbers in *italics* refer to figures. Page numbers in **bold** refer to tables.